Meyerhold, 1936

KONSTANTIN RUDNITSKY

MEYERHOLD
THE DIRECTOR

Translated by George Petrov

Edited by Sydney Schultze

Introduction by Ellendea Proffer

Ardis   **Ann Arbor**

Konstantin Rudnitsky

MEYERHOLD THE DIRECTOR

English translation by George Petrov,
Edited by Sydney Schultze

Published by Ardis, 2901 Heatherway, Ann Arbor,
Michigan 48104. First edition limited to 1000 copies.

LIBRARY OF CONGRESS CATALOGING IN PUBLICATION DATA

Rudnitskii, K. (Konstantin)
    Meyerhold, the director.

    Translation of : Rezhisser Meĭerkhol'd.
    Includes bibliographical references and index.
    1. Meĭerkhol'd, Vsevolod Émil'evich, 1874-1940.
2. Theatrical producers and directors—Soviet Union—
Biography. I. Title.
PN2728.M4R813   792'.0233'0924 [B]   81-7982
ISBN 0-88233-313-5   AACR2

CONTENTS

PREFACE

For decades the accomplishments of the director Meyerhold were legendary, like the cities of Kublai Khan; the West periodically received reports from dazzled travellers, viewed poor sketches of a few of the temples, but was unable to form a clear idea of the place as a whole. How can one bring alive the theatrical discoveries of a director dead for forty years, a non-person in his own country for twenty years? One cannot preserve a theater performance; even if filmed, the essence is lost. In Meyerhold's case, the years of official silence defeated all efforts to recapture the past. But then, during the years of the Thaw, after Meyerhold's "rehabilitation," articles and memoirs began to appear, testifying to the power of theatrical memory to outlast imposed amnesia.

However, it was the appearance of Konstantin Rudnitsky's landmark study which finally allowed the world to get a sense of Meyerhold himself, as well as his theatrical innovations and the era in which he lived. The author had broad and unprecedented access to previously locked archives, collections of ephemeral newspapers and journals, and unpublished memoirs. As a leading historian of the theater he was able to interview the lucky survivors, those who had worked with Meyerhold but not shared his fate. The result is a work of scholarly and historical value, and in the Soviet context it is a sensational book as well. Indeed, given re-newed severity of censorship (some plays can no longer even be mentioned), it is unlikely that this book could be published today. It is not only a book about Meyerhold the director. Its scope is so large that purely by the way many other important questions about the Russian theater in our century are answered. For example, one may learn more about Stanislavsky's influence on the Russian stage here than in many of the books devoted to Stanislavsky. The quotes from the contemporary theater critics are especially enlightening; they show the theatrical milieu that Meyerhold had to contend with, and how he could actually thrive on controversy. What interests Rudnitsky here is Meyerhold's development, how the director who could stage the anemic plays of Maeterlinck could move directly to Mayakovsky—and end his career with Dumas. Directors cannot be understood in isolation; they must be seen in the context of their time, in the context of their colleagues—and this is what Rudnitsky provides, with rich documentation.

Rudnitsky does not discuss Meyerhold's private life or his theories unless they specifically influence a given production. Thus, Meyerhold's exercise for the actor—Biomechanics—is given little treatment in this book. The effect of Rudnitsky's work is to demonstrate that evaluating Meyerhold only by his "tricks," or even by his theoretical writings, is to receive a false picture. Meyerhold's approach changed with almost every production, every scene; he was not, after all, a philosopher or a mathe-matician—he was a director, and a special kind of director, a man of endless and productive imagination. His writings on theater are much less representative of him than, say, Stanislavsky's are of Stanislavsky. As Eisenstein wrote, Meyerhold could only teach by actually rehearsing—his official lectures were relatively unenlightening.

The present volume excluding the introduction, is an unabridged translation of *Rezhisser Meierkhol'd*, published by the Academy of Sciences in Moscow in 1969. Learning of this project, the author sent various corrections; in some cases these are deletions, in others—additions. This will explain why the translation sometimes differs from the published Russian text. For the most part, these changes are minor, and do not alter the sense of any important points. Many of the photographs and other illustrations in this volume did not appear in the original Russian edition.

Several people deserve gratitude for their labors to produce this volume. Marjorie Hoover did a draft translation of the first three chapters; Francey Oscherwitz compiled the index of names and plays; Fred Moody, Christine Rydel, Greg Churchill and Marysia Ostafin provided invaluable editorial assistance.

Selected Bibliography

In Russian:

N. Volkov, *Meierkhol'd* (M.-L. 1929), 2 volumes.
A. V. Fevral'skii, *Desiat' let teatra Meierkhol'da* (M. 1931).
Vstrechi s Meierkhol'dom (Sbornik vospominanii), (M. 1967).
V. E. Meierkhol'd: Stat'i, pis'ma, rechi, besedy (M. 1968), 2 volumes.
V. E. Meierkhol'd, *Perepiska 1896-1939* (M. 1969).

In English:

Edward Braun, *Meyerhold on Theater* (New York, 1969).
Edward Braun, *The Theater of Meyerhold* (New York, 1979).
Marjorie Hoover, *Meyerhold. The Art of Conscious Theater* (Amherst, Mass., 1974).
Paul Schmidt (ed.), *Meyerhold at Work* (Austin, 1980).

INTRODUCTION

The man who would become one of the main figures of the Moscow stage was no Muscovite, nor even a Russian. This most cosmopolitan director was born in the provinces, in the city of Penza, some 350 miles southeast of Moscow geographically, and light years away culturally. Penza was the kind of place Chekhov's characters dream of escaping, and when Meyerhold was working on the production of *The Inspector General* he told Ehrenburg that he used his memories of Penza for the stagnant atmosphere. But Penza nevertheless had something to offer him in the way of training, since the touring theater and opera companies visited regularly, and were often entertained at the Meyerhold home.

The family was fairly well-to-do at first; they had money for cultural events, including a box in the theater. Meyerhold's father was a German Lutheran, come to make his fortune in Russia as a vodka distiller. Meyerhold's mother, a German from the Baltic city of Riga, had a love of the arts herself, and encouraged her youngest son's interest in theater and opera.

Karl Theodor Kasimir Meyerhold was born on January 28, 1874 in Penza, the youngest of eight children. His passion for amateur theatricals appeared early, but on graduation from high school he enrolled in the Law Faculty of Moscow University, perhaps fearing that he might not manage a career in the theater. By this time the Meyerhold family had suffered financial reverses, and the young actor had begun professional performing for money in Penza. In preparation for his future career—whether as a lawyer or actor—in 1895 Meyerhold became a Russian citizen, converting to the Orthodox faith, and taking a Russian name: Vsevolod (after the prose writer Vsevolod Garshin—a choice indicating a passionate temperament, given Garshin's qualities) Emilievich (from his father). He had no wish to serve in the German army; he felt himself Russian, and wished to have an Orthodox wedding when he married his fiancee, Olga Mikhailovna Munt. Olga and her sister Evgenia were both fascinated by the theater, and Meyerhold's letters to them show that he had a high regard for their knowledge and understanding. Meyerhold and Olga Mikhailovna married in 1896, and had one child, Maria.

One senses that the marriage could not compete with his entrance into the Philharmonia, and his appearance before Stanislavsky in class productions. From this moment on Meyerhold's rise was remarkable. His *approach* to the theater was often questioned—by his teachers Nemirovich-Danchenko and Stanislavsky among others—but never his originality. His was the sort of prickly, palpable genius that others could actually sense, and certainly Stanislavsky did.

Nothing could have been more dissimilar than teacher and student. Stanislavsky, suave, even-tempered, handsome, was the all-knowing, all-forgiving father. Meyerhold, impossibly temperamental, awkward and angular, was the son. But for the course of their lives, the two men were almost preternaturally aware of each other's plans and accomplishments: in a sense they were the only two competitors in a race. Stanislavsky was charmingly remote, and one could seldom get close to him as a person, which was precisely what Meyerhold wanted and needed to do. However, these two strong personalities appeared to be taking different paths to theatrical truth, and their break was violent and dramatic. No matter what Meyerhold said and wrote about Stanislavsky's system as outdated, nothing affected his real feeling for Stanislavsky himself. As Eisenstein wrote: "His love and admiration for Stanislavsky were amazing, even during the fiercest years of his battle against the Moscow Art Theater."[1]

The inevitable break was painful: who, if not Stanislavsky, could understand and evaluate what Meyerhold was trying to do? In the mid-1930s Stanislavsky realized that what linked them was more vital than what separated them, and there was a rapprochement, as each seemed to move closer to the other's ideas.

Superficially, the Meyerhold who wrote to Chekhov, staged plays for Komissarzhevskaya and was mad for the Symbolists seems almost unconnected to the man who propagandized "Theatrical October"; but he was the same restless, thoroughly modern man. Meyerhold was sincere in his enthusiasm for the Revolution, I think. Influenced by the socialist tutor who infected his charges before their irate father threw him out, Meyerhold was sensitive to political problems. He was shaken by the 1905 Revolution, and never ignored what was happening on the street. During the Civil War he was arrested by the Whites in the South, for being a known Bolshevik sympathizer. He joined the Party in 1918, a move which was seen as rash by those who did not expect the Bolsheviks to hold power long; but Meyerhold's art, as well as his personality, required that he understand and be a part of the main currents of contemporary experience. In more ways than he could foresee, he would share the fate of his contemporaries.

In 1921, after working in various official theater organizations, Meyerhold began his first courses in directing. This workshop attracted some of the best minds of the younger generation: Eisenstein, Okhlopkov, Ilinsky, and Babanova, two major directors and two major actors, respectively. There was another student who attracted Meyerhold's special notice: Zinaida Nikolaevna Raikh, the beautiful wife of the famous poet Sergei Esenin. Raikh and Meyerhold fell in love, and as usual Meyerhold took no half-way measures: she became his wife, the main actress of his theater, his muse, and his best friend. Naturally this change was not without repercussions in his theater, where there were accomplished performers who felt that Raikh was not up to the standards of the theater. Critics, too, were happy to carp at Meyerhold's wife. The critics who had been reviled by Meyerhold at open disputes no doubt realized that Meyerhold took criticism of his star actress more seriously than that directed at himself. There are differing opinions even now as to her abilities as an actress, but by the late 1920s there is little doubt that she matured into an accomplished performer. But it would not really matter if she had not; her importance to Meyerhold, and his importance to her can be seen in every letter he wrote— it was a love affair that never dimmed. Even if Raikh was a mixed blessing for Meyerhold, a love that made him vulnerable in new areas, one can only be happy, as Pasternak said, that Meyerhold could work with the one he loved.

In terms of influence and acclaim, the twenties were Meyerhold's golden years. His productions may have been financially unrewarding, but in the context of avant-garde theater he was without competition. His extraordinary productions were debated and praised, damned and banned, extolled and applauded—but seldom ignored. He was born to outrage and excite, and he was ready to go to any lengths to involve his audience in a play.

Meyerhold the man was full of contradictions. He was ugly in an attractive way, a bit of Ichabod Crane in his physique; and we may see in his body the ultimate explanation of those rather jerky biomechanical movements (the smooth Stanislavsky could never have thought them up). As is natural, Meyerhold constructed a type of theater which made the best of his own particular gifts, a theater which turned his flaws into requirements to a degree.

Meyerhold's charm was overwhelming, when he wished it to be, but his love (except for his family) was volatile and unreliable. He could bring all the power of his passionate intelligence and warmth to an encounter, and the next day the bewildered friend would be treated like an enemy. Meyerhold was constantly imagining intrigues and plots, and seeing slights where there were none. He was quick to punish the imagined guilty parties, by silence or scenes. Eisenstein has left us a description which distills the essence of this side of the Master:

> Meyerhold!
> A creative genius and a perfidious man.
> The untold torments of those who loved him devotedly as I did.
> The untold moments of triumph, watching the magic creativity of this inimitable theatrical wizard.
> How many times his actor Ilyinsky left him!
> How his actress Babanova suffered!
> What torments—thank God they were short-lived!—did I go through, before I was thrown outside the gates of Paradise, out of the ranks of his theater, because I had "dared" acquire a collective of my own on the side—in the Proletkult.[2]

Eisenstein saw his own traumatic break with Meyerhold as a repetition of Meyerhold's with Stanislavsky, as if Meyerhold were doomed to reenact the relationship with those closest to him. Like Meyerhold, Eisenstein retained love for his teacher and later reconciled with him. After Meyerhold's death it was Eisenstein who hid the director's archive at his dacha—a very brave act in those years.

Meyerhold had some of the negative traits of a 1930s Hollywood producer, and he could seem a poseur. (For example, enamoured of the military and military accoutrements, he appeared at a rehearsal after the Revolution wearing puttees, a military overcoat, and a soldier's cap with a picture of Lenin on the brim.) But the actors mistreated by him tended to return, just as the artists and musicians did, and I think the reason for this is the key to Meyerhold's continuing appeal to the imaginations of Russian theater people: Meyerhold would not take a safe path if there was a dangerous, interesting one available. The people who worked with and for him did not do so for money (there was precious little) or even fame (the reviews could be very hard on the actors). No, it appears that they believed that precisely this director, and only this director, could show them something new. In this they were right. While Stanislavsky and the other directors seemed to be anchored firmly in the nineteenth century, Meyerhold combined the young actors with a radically new concept of the theater. He was the director who could show his actors possibilities during one rehearsal that would have sufficed another director for a hundred rehearsals. The phrase "fertile imagination" is a cliché, but it explains Meyerhold. He was always thinking, always searching for a new way of looking at not just a scene, but a gesture, a musical score, a stage decoration. He allied himself with some of the best musicians and painters of his time, and brought his originality to this aspect of the productions as well. For these actors, artists, and composers, working for Meyerhold was exhilarating.

Despite the controversies his productions occasioned, Meyerhold seemed to be the right director in the right time. His was political theater, he was a convinced Communist, and even if such officials as Lunacharsky were sometimes shocked by his approach, they had no doubt that his essential position was correct. The theater was never a solid success, but periodic hit plays kept it going. Mayakovsky, considered a theatrical genius by Meyerhold, gave the theater some of its most successful contemporary plays, and some of the redone classics were also popular with the public. The theater gained further prestige by its tours abroad, which were met with great interest by the European critics and audiences.

In the late twenties, however, ominous signs began to appear. A number of political events had a serious and negative effect on the world of arts. Into the power vacuum left by a weak Writers' Union (headed by the "bourgeois" Zamyatin and Pilnyak) stepped the group which called itself RAPP (Russian Association of Proletarian Writers), which included the pure-minded fanatic Averbakh, and the young Fadeev. According to their dogma, which soon had Party support, realism was desirable; fantasy, genuine satire, and experimentation were suspect, if not down right un-Russian. The criticism they wrote in newspapers and journals was shrill and frightening; carrers could be destroyed by their attacks.

When Meyerhold staged Mayakovsky's *The Bathhouse*, RAPP's reaction was especially vitriolic. Mayakovsky, seeing that this group had Party support, felt he had to bow to its demands. He joined the group, anxious to follow whatever line the Party deemed correct. When Mayakovsky committed suicide in 1930, many considered that this last vain attempt to make himself over in the image approved by RAPP was one of the causes. Mayakovsky's death was a great shock to Meyerhold, who was having increasing problems himself. He could not get two contemporary works—*The Suicide*, and *I Want a Child*—past the censor, one for its suspicious satire, the other for its sexual content. He put a good deal of work and hope into these productions, and their eventual ban was a bitter disappointment.

RAPP did not hold power for many years. It went too far in its attacks on the many famous writers who were not Communists, and the Party withdrew its support. Later many of the RAPP leaders died in the purges, as did many of their targets. Now in the early 1930s, a new dogma, which did not seem so new at all, was introduced under Gorky's aegis: Socialist Realism, a "realism" which must include "Idea-ness, Party-ness and People-ness," to use its own terminology.

Meyerhold understood now what all of this emphasis on "fact" and "idea-ness" meant: he would have to change his style, and be very cautious about contemporary works. The Soviet playwrights also understood, and in the early thirties began producing such untalented and terrifyingly false works that the twenties seemed a golden age. There was only one choice: produce the wretched plays or do only classics. In 1933 Meyerhold staged his only Soviet play of the thirties, the rather mediocre *Prelude*. His other two contemporary projects never saw final production.

Instead of contemporary plays, Meyerhold's admirers saw what he could do with Russian and foreign classics: Griboedov, Chekhov, Dumas. He revealed unexpected aspects of these works, just as he had with *The Inspector General* in 1926. But his move to realism, whether natural or willed, was not a complete success politically; originality and a feeling for form still showed through. His work here, as Rudnitsky demonstrates, was just as important to him as his earlier work; but Meyerhold was a director meant for contemporary drama, and in this sense the times did not allow him to demonstrate his full range.

In 1932 Meyerhold moved his troupe to a temporary theater while a new theater was being built to his specifications. This was to be his dream theater, but he would never see a play on its stage. It would become the Tchaikovsky Concert Hall instead.

In 1936 the campaign against "formalism" intensified. Shostakovich's music was attacked in two editorials in *Pravda*. Stalin himself was reported to be the real author of "Muddle Instead of Music," and Shostakovich's works were immediately removed from repertory. A month later the Second Moscow Art Theater (which had once been Mikhail Chekhov's) was closed. The theater world had been delivered its warning, but Meyerhold refused to indulge in the required self-criticism. In a Leningrad lecture ("Meyerhold Against Meyerholdism") he criticized the imitators who stole only his theatrical innovations, distorting them, using them out of the context of his motivation and theory. He took this opportunity to defend his friend Shostakovich as well. In March he answered other critics, and with amazing bravery announced his independence.

His enemies found his weak spot: Meyerhold's was the only theater which had no Soviet play in its repertory! This was not a charge to be taken lightly, so Meyerhold began looking for a suitable vehicle. He thought he found it in Nikolai Ostrovsky's incredible melodramatic novel, *How the Steel was Tempered*. In the autumn of 1937 he began to work on this adaptation, now called *One Life*, and observers were fascinated by what he was doing with such seemingly unpromising material. However, the censorship demanded many changes, and the theater was engaged in this work when new hostilities began.

On December 17, 1937 *Pravda* published the article "An Alien Theater," by the president of the Committee for the Control of the Arts, Kerzhentsev. This was a "history" of Meyerhold and his theater, listing every sin real and imagined, ranging from Meyerhold's anti-realistic stance, to the fact that he tried to stage the play *I Want a Child*, written by the "enemy of the people, Tretyakov" (who had since been arrested). The lack of Soviet plays in the repertory was mentioned, but the entire history of the theater was condemned.

> The systematic deviation from Soviet reality, the political distortion of that reality, and hostile slanders against our way of life have brought the theater to total ideological and artistic ruin, to shameful bankruptcy. . . . Do Soviet art and the Soviet public really need such a theater?[3]

The optimists thought that changes could be made; the pessimists knew better. During the January 7 performance of *Camille*, the actor Sadovsky recalls, Raikh was hysterical, the actors were discussing the rumors—and Meyerhold seemed calm. The audience, however, knew what was ahead, and a great number of them forced their way backstage. The decision to close the theater had been made that afternoon, but Meyerhold had not told his troupe. The next day, January 8, they played *The Inspector General*, the last matinee at the Meyerhold Theater, and everyone from the prop man to the last member of the audience, knew it was the last performance. The end of the play, with dummies replacing the actors, took on a new significance:

> The dummies were put in place in darkness. The sound of a gong. The lights went up. And those dead dolls, which Meyerhold had conceived of as a final image of deadness and petrification , were especially terrifying that night, in that last performance of *The Inspector General*.
> The song of the gong again. Darkness.
> End of scene. End of theater.[4]

The same day's *Literary Gazette* announced the decision to "liquidate" the theater, resettle the actors—and to "discuss separately" the question of Meyerhold's future participation in "any further" theatrical activities. The danger was very great. Already many visible people had disappeared; the Great Terror was moving through the Army, the arts, every walk of life. Ehrenburg saw Meyerhold at this perilous time:

> Meyerhold's wife had a nervous breakdown. He himself bore it manfully, spoke about painting and poetry, recalled Paris. He went on working, planning the production of *Hamlet*, even though he did not believe that he would be allowed to produce the play.[5]

This last was certainly true. The leaders of the nation had no liking for either *Hamlet* or *Macbeth*. Ehrenburg makes the point that Meyerhold, like many others, could not believe that Stalin himself was behind it all. There was a strong desire to see Yezhov, the head of the secret police, as the only instigator, deceiving the trusting Stalin. In Meyerhold's case, it was personal animosity on the part of the leader himself which is the most convincing explanation of what happened. Attacks in *Pravda* were not published without Stalin's knowledge, especially where the arts were concerned. Just as Stalin personally disliked Shostakovich's modernist music, he also disliked what he heard of Meyerhold's theater (there is no evidence I know of that he ever attended a performance). Another liability for Meyerhold was that he had been a Party member since 1918, he remembered and possibly sympathized with other leaders of the Revolution, leaders who were now dead or disgraced. When one is rewriting history, the fewer influential eye-witnesses left to contradict the new version, the better. In addition, as Ehrenburg testifies, Meyerhold, who had always admired the military, had friends in the very army now being purged. Meyerhold, understandably, did not wish to see what was happening, although he had enough evidence:

> I recall a terrible day at Meyerhold's. We were sitting peacefully looking through an illustrated monograph on Renoir, when a friend of Meyerhold, the Corps Commander I. P. Belov, arrived. He was very worked up and, without paying any attention to our presence, began to describe the trial of Tukhachevsky and other high ranking officers. Belov was a

member of the Military Collegium of the Supreme Court. "They are sitting like that—facing us. Uborevich looked me in the eyes . . ." I remember another phrase of Belov's: "And tomorrow I'll be put in the same place." Then he suddenly turned to me: "Do you know Uspensky? Not Gleb, Nikolai. There's a man who wrote the truth." And he gave us rather incoherently the gist of a story by Uspensky, I do not recall which, but a very cruel one. Belov left soon after. I glanced at Meyerhold: he sat with his eyes shut looking like a wounded bird. (Belov was arrested soon after.)[6]

At this point, possibly close to arrest, Meyerhold was saved—by Stanislavsky. On January 18, in the middle of his worst period, Meyerhold had sent Stanislavsky a warm and grateful birthday greeting. Now Stanislavsky accomplished a miracle, and rescued the talented prodigal son, giving him a job as his assistant at the Opera Studio; all Moscow was stunned by this development. In this way, Meyerhold was able to work, and to a degree recover from the many blows he had received in a short time.

Stanislavsky, who had a much less open character than Meyerhold, had taken a great risk in doing this: Stanislavsky himself had no idea of just how much credit he had at court. Shortly before his death on August 7, 1938, he told one of his associates: "Take care of Meyerhold; he is my sole heir in the theater—here or anywhere else."[7]

With the death of Stanislavsky, Meyerhold was once again defenseless. He became Director of the Opera Studio, which unfortunately meant that he had certain official duties. He finished Stanislavsky's production of *Rigoletto*, and then intended to do his own production of *Don Giovanni*.

In June of 1939 at a conference of stage directors in Leningrad, Meyerhold made a speech. We still do not know what precisely was contained in this speech, whether it was requisitely self-abasing or openly defiant. The best scholars suspect that Meyerhold did indeed finally perform his act of contrition. But it was not enough—the machine was already in motion, and no one could stop it.

On June 20, 1939, immediately after this conference, Meyerhold was arrested on charges of being a "Japanese spy," among other things. His wife Zinaida Raikh was interrogated in July. One week after her interrogation, on July 17, she was found in her apartment, her throat cut, eleven knife wounds in her body, and her eyes put out. The only thing missing, according to friends, was a file of papers.

The official explanation was that "hooligans" had committed this crime. Interested parties wondered what sort of burglars took nothing of value, and why the vigilant police organs had so little success in finding witnesses or evidence. The barbaric and meaningful manner of Raikh's death, I think, points to the degree of Stalin's hatred for Meyerhold.

On February 1, 1940, Meyerhold was sentenced to ten years solitary confinement. According to Ehrenburg's information he was tried by a secret military tribunal. He would not sign a confession. His final declaration before this court read: "I am sixty-six. I want my daughter and my friends to know some day that I remained an honest Communist until the end."[8]

According to the death certificate he died the day after the sentencing, February 2, 1940, in prison. His friends have no doubt that he was shot.

NOTES TO THE INTRODUCTION

[1] *Meyerhold at Work,* ed. Paul Schmidt (Austin, 1980), p. 9. [2] *Meyerhold at Work,* p. 8. [3] Edward Braun, *Meyerhold on Theater* (New York, 1969), p. 250. [4] *Meyerhold at Work,* p. 215. [5] Ilya Ehrenburg, *Memoirs: 1921-1941* (Cleveland & New York, 1964), p. 425. [6] Ehrenburg, p. 427. [7] *Vstrechi s Meierkhol'- dom, Sbornik vospominanii* (Moskva, 1967), p. 589. [8] *Meyerhold at Work,* p. 67.

Ellendea Proffer
Ann Arbor
April 23, 1981

MEYERHOLD
THE DIRECTOR

IN THE ART THEATER

In the fall of 1896 a strange young man appeared at the Moscow Philharmonia school. Tall, thin, angular, long-nosed, he expressed a desire to take the entrance examination in theater—despite his unprepossessing exterior, he intended to become a professional actor. It seemed that in his home town of Penza the young man had already done some acting—and not just in amateur private productions, but even in public performances at the People's Theater. He played comic roles: Kochkarev in Gogol's *The Marriage*, Schastlivtsev in *The Forest*, Rispolozhensky in *It's All in the Family* by Ostrovsky.

The young man wisely withheld the fact that the Penza theater critics called him "the darling of the audiences" and predicted he would become a famous actor.

He auditioned with Othello's monologue before the Senate. Vladimir Nemirovich-Danchenko, already well-known as a playwright and experienced dramatic coach, immediately realized that the young man had seen *Othello* at the Hunt Club and was imitating Stanislavsky. Usually young people from the country just copied provincial tragedians, roaring and working themselves into towering rages.

The decision was made to admit Meyerhold, Vsevolod Emilevich, to the class in dramatic art. And since he had studied law for a year at Moscow University, he was at once classified as a second-year student.

It was a good class. Many of the men and women in it showed talent. But even with this competition Meyerhold quickly distinguished himself. Many years later Nemirovich-Danchenko took pains to stress the special part Meyerhold had played at the school. Twenty-two-year-old Meyerhold was older than the other men and women in his class, more mature, more experienced.

Nemirovich recalled:

> The subsequently famous director showed great energy in the school's plays, especially in directing group activities with friends. There was one thing unprecedented in the school: after my students had staged and performed five plays they asked permission to stage *The Last Wish* too, practically on their own. And by the end of the month they actually put on the full-length play. . . . The prime mover in this was Meyerhold. I remember another play, *In the Land of Ennui,* a French comedy by Edouard Pailleron. Meyerhold and his friends even did the set on the small school stage; he managed this with great technical skill and directing originality.[1]

At the time Meyerhold was certainly not thinking of becoming a director. The Moscow Art Theater had not yet opened, and the profession of director held little attraction. The very word "director" evoked associations with some kind of behind-the-scenes activity, probably useful but extremely prosaic and subordinate. According to the notions of the day, the director busied himself with back-stage stuff which had nothing to do with theater art. The first thing a young man aspiring to the high calling of artist had to do was determine the particular parts he should play, and also find his "symbol of faith"—that is, set himself moral and esthetic goals worthy of a high-minded devotee of the arts.

Familiarity with the theatrical life of Moscow quickly tarnished the splendor of the young Meyerhold's earlier provincial idols. The acting of the famous tragedian Ivanov-Kozelsky, or Nikolai Rossov, famous as the "Hamlet of Penza," did not bear comparison with the noble simplicity of Maria Ermolova and the subtle artistry of Alexander Lensky. Lensky captured the imagination of Meyerhold for years to come. Many years later he was still imitating Lensky's manner of dress, ordering the same style of collars Lensky wore. Still, Meyerhold disliked many things in the Maly Theater where Ermolova and Lensky were all-powerful. He found ridiculous the grandiloquent and imposing tone of A. I. Yuzhin, of whose characterization of Chatsky *(Woe from Wit)* Meyerhold remarked acidly: "Very little feeling, but a lot of shouting." Meyerhold just as categorically condemned Osip Pravdin as "a bad Repetilov."[2]

By contrast, the shows at the Hunt Club, where the Society for Art and Literature was playing, excited and delighted Meyerhold. He wrote to Olga M. Munt, at that time still his fiancée: " . . . enjoyed myself immensely. Stanislavsky is a great talent. I have never seen such an Othello before and am not likely to see such a one in Russia again. I have seen Vekhter and Rossov in the part. When you think of how they played it, you blush for them. The whole troupe—a dream. Really, everyone in the crowd is alive on stage. The backgrounds—a dream."[3]

These and other comments by the young Meyerhold about the Moscow theater of the time show that he quickly sensed the spirit of opposition to the Maly Theater, which was especially strong at the Philharmonia, where Nemirovich-Danchenko conducted classes.

Nemirovich-Danchenko had taught classes in theater since 1891 and was very enthusiastic about teaching. His classes at the school were paralleled by intensive literary work. He wrote plays, short stories, novellas, critical articles. He was, in addition, a member of the theatrical literature committee responsible for the choice of plays at the Maly. The situation which had arisen at the oldest Russian theater very much distressed Nemirovich-Danchenko, and in 1894 he had presented to P. M. Pchelnikov, manager of the Moscow administration of the Imperial Theaters, a project for the reform of the Maly.

Even Alexander Ostrovsky had written such projects; they all received no attention from the administration. Meanwhile, the leading theater of Russia was gradually buried in a rut of routine.

Having gotten nowhere in his efforts to at least partially reform the Maly, Nemirovich-Danchenko had long dreamed of organizing his own company on a completely new basis. His dreams, as it soon became clear, coincided in many ways with the dreams of Stanislavsky.

In Russia a great theatrical revolution was in the making, the task of which would be to change the whole development of the art of the stage. Without himself suspecting it, young Meyerhold was soon at the very center of the approaching explosion.

On June 22, 1897, the famous meeting of Stanislavsky and Nemirovich-Danchenko took place at the Slavyansky Bazaar Restaurant. It is difficult to know whether the name of Meyerhold was mentioned along with other names in that historic conversation. But in February 1898 Nemirovich showed Stanislavsky his pupils' production of Goldoni's *The Mistress of the Inn*, in which Olga Knipper played Mirandolina and Meyerhold Marquis Forlipopoli.

Beginning in June 1897, as Stanislavsky later remarked, "not a single school production at the Philharmonia was given without my seeing it."[4] Stanislavsky saw young Meyerhold play Ivan the Terrible in Ostrovsky's *Vasilisa Melenteva*, and in other plays as well. The plays ran for a month and Stanislavsky conscientiously attended them all.

Although both Nemirovich-Danchenko and Stanislavsky kept their plans strictly secret, the students of Nemirovich-Danchenko heard about the founding of a new, unprecedented theater. Understandably they were very excited by these rumors. Unlike graduates of the Imperial Drama School, who often stayed on at the Maly Theater (though in walk-on parts), for the Philharmonia students of Nemirovich-Danchenko there was only one way—into the provinces. The very year Meyerhold entered the Philharmonia, Ivan Moskvin had set off upon graduation for Yaroslavl. "He's playing light comedy," his teacher thought bitterly. "After one or two rehearsals he hacks out a stereotype; he's acquiring the vulgar taste of a provincial actor."[5] No one looked forward to such a prospect: Olga Knipper, who studied in the same class with Meyerhold, recalled:

> Vague exciting rumors were already circulating about the founding of a small theater in Moscow, a quite "special" theater; the handsome figure of Stanislavsky with his gray hair and black eyebrows was already seen at the school and in his company the characteristic silhouette of Sanin; they were attending the rehearsals of *The Mistress of the Inn*, making our hearts stop from excitement; by the middle of winter our teacher Vladimir Ivanovich Nemirovich-Danchenko had already told Margarita Savitskaya, Meyerhold, and me that we would stay on in the new theater if the dream of its launching was successfully realized, and we carefully kept that secret.[6]

Again it is Knipper who testifies to "the excitement with which the same class read Chekhov's *The Sea Gull*. Vladimir Ivanovich had already infected us with his vibrant love for the play and we went about with the yellow volume by Chekhov, and read it and reread it and couldn't imagine how one could act such a play. Still, it gained an ever stronger, deeper hold on our spirits, for we were by now subtly in love with it, as if with a presentiment of what was soon to become part of our life, an inalienable, essential part of ourselves."[7]

When Stanislavsky and Nemirovich-Danchenko talked at the Slavyansky Bazaar, Chekhov's name was not mentioned. "Neither Chekhov's name nor his literary image came up in our conversation," Nemirovich-Danchenko remembered later with astonishment. But his own pupils, jumping ahead of events, connected the idea of a new theater with both Chekhov's name and concretely with *The Sea Gull*.

Nemirovich-Danchenko declared many years later that "Meyerhold had a better sense of Chekhov the poet than the others did . . . he was truly cultured."[8]

By graduation Meyerhold clearly stood out among the school's other young actors and actresses. He and Olga Knipper were singled out for the grade of A+. The recommendation which Nemirovich-Danchenko gave him began: "Meyerhold is an exceptional phenomenon among the pupils of the Philharmonia. Suffice it to say that this is the first instance of a student's having the highest grade in all three areas: the history of drama, literature, and art." He further remarked on Meyer-hold's rare conscientiousness, his serious relationship to his work. True, Nemirovich-Danchenko soberly admitted that Meyerhold lacked the charm which would have enabled him "quickly to win the liking of the audience," yet he was convinced that his pupil "had every chance of gaining a very important place in any troupe. The best quality of his stage personality is his broad capacity for varied character parts. He has absorbed more than fifteen big parts—from the strong, obstinate old man to the comic simpleton, and it is hard to say which is best. He works hard, holds the tone of a part well, makes up well, shows flair, and is as experienced as a finished actor."[9]

"The finished actor" Meyerhold was recommended with conviction by Nemirovich-Danchenko for membership in the troupe of the Art Theater then being launched. Together with Meyerhold, other graduates of the Philharmonia were chosen: Olga Knipper, Margarita Savitskaya, Ekaterina Munt [The sister of Olga Munt (Meyerhold's fiancee) — trans.]. Former students of Nemirovich-Danchenko were also called back from the provinces: Ivan Moskvin, Maria Roxanova, A. S. Kosheverov.

The founders of the theater pinned high hopes on Meyerhold. Konstantin Stanislavsky, in his plan for the assignment of parts in Alexei K. Tolstoi's tragedy, *Tsar Fyodor Ioannovich*, with which the theater was to open, gave the title role to Meyerhold. "Who will play Fyodor?" he wrote to Nemirovich-Danchenko on June 12, 1893. "This is the important question. I have begun to think that one person can do it—Meyerhold. All the rest are too stupid for the part."[10] The question of who should play Fyodor was resolved by a competition: six actors auditioned for the part.

Nemirovich-Danchenko, however, was sure from the beginning that Fyodor should be played by Moskvin. *"Moskvin,"* he wrote to Stanislavsky, "is Fyodor and *no one* is better than he. He is an intelligent person *with heart* as well. . . . Moskvin, Moskvin. Take him aside, read a while with him and you will hear new and touching accents. Meyerhold is too dry for Fyodor. . . ."[11] Nemirovich-Danchenko assigned Meyerhold the part of Kuryukov. But Stanislavsky wanted Artem to play Kuryukov and complained to Nemirovich: "I am really afraid of Meyerhold as an old man."[12] The casting was difficult; every possibility was conscientiously and repeatedly analyzed. On June 21 Stanislavsky told Meyerhold: "It is almost certain that you will play Fyodor." But only a few days later Nemirovich-Danchenko wrote, after listening to Meyerhold, that his readings of "the kind-hearted passages" of the part were "poor, stereotyped, without imagination. The strong moments were very good." Stanislavsky still thought that Meyerhold "must play Fyodor," but now cautiously added, "even if only in alternation with someone else."[13]

Of course, Meyerhold could not have known about this correspondence. Carried away with enthusiasm for his new work, under the pressure of which new outlines never before seen in the history of the theater were taking shape, Meyerhold experienced a wave of passionate admiration for Stanislavsky during the days of rehearsal at Pushkino. "Now that I've graduated from school," he wrote his wife [Olga Munt], "I've landed in The Academy of Dramatic Art. Alexeev (Stanislavsky) is not talented, no. He is a director and teacher of *genius*. What a wealth of erudition, what imagination."

Meanwhile, other pretenders to the part of Fyodor passed through Stanislavsky's hands. Moskvin's chances constantly increased. "All at once they'll dismiss me," Meyerhold feared. "There are five candidates, three will play the part. Shall I be one of the unlucky two? I'll go mad."

Nemirovich-Danchenko was to decide the question so crucial to Meyerhold. On August 1, 1898, Meyerhold read through the entire part for him. "I wasn't a bit in the mood, I read badly," he concluded. "I have as much chance of seeing that part as seeing my ears without a mirror."

That summer, Meyerhold apparently experienced sharp jealousy of Moskvin, whom Nemirovich-Danchenko so favored that Meyerhold doubted his teacher for the first time. Stanislavsky immediately won and fascinated Meyerhold; the charm and authority of Nemirovich-Danchenko waned. Besides, Meyerhold learned that Stanislavsky wanted to give Fyodor to him, while Nemirovich-Danchenko insisted on Moskvin.

On August 9, 1898, he wrote in his diary: "I don't mind that by giving up Fyodor I played into Nemirovich's hands—at least I feel calmer: they won't manipulate me like a pawn."[14]

In these words one senses Nemirovich-Danchenko in direct opposition to Stanislavsky. Meyerhold's hostility to Nemirovich-Danchenko, as we shall see further, would grow gradually and later would become one of the reasons causing Meyerhold to leave the Art Theater.

Having failed to win the part of Fyodor, Meyerhold lost hope from the start of achieving an outstanding position at the Art Theater. Of course he had had such a hope—he had graduated from school with the highest honors, he was undoubtedly aware of his intellectual superiority over many of his comrades in the troupe, and he sensed that Stanislavsky thought highly of him. The summer in Pushkino was coming to a close, and the day on which the theater was to open was drawing near. Meyerhold had a part in almost all the plays being prepared, but contrary to his ambitions, he approached that day—the historical beginning of the Art Theater—in secondary roles.

In *Tsar Fyodor* he was to play Vasily Shuisky, in *The Merchant of Venice* the Prince of Arragon, and in *Antigone* Tiresias.

Only in Chekhov's *The Sea Gull* did he have an unquestionably important role: Nemirovich-Danchenko unhesitatingly gave him Treplyov, and soon after the beginning of rehearsals wrote Stanislavsky (to whom the role of Dorn had been assigned from the start): "Everyone is gradually falling in love with the play. Vishnevsky as Shamraev is reading exceptionally well. Meyerhold is very good as Treplyov." Stanislavsky answered:

> I read with great interest what you wrote about *The Sea Gull*. I'm glad for Meyerhold. I'm beginning to read Dorn, but for the moment I do not wholly understand him and am very sorry I wasn't at the *Sea Gull* talks. Unready for Chekhov as I am, or rather, not permeated with Chekhov, I am not able to work in the direction I should. I shall be reading the part. . . . You have no time, but couldn't someone, even Meyerhold, who, as you say, is permeated with Chekhov, give me a hint of what was said at the talks about Dorn and how Meyerhold himself imagines the part, and what Dorn looks like. I should be very much obliged, and then I would come prepared for the tone you have established.[15]

Nemirovich-Danchenko preferred to do without intermediaries and went over his conception of the role of Dorn with Stanislavsky. But it is clear from Stanislavsky's letter that he singled out Meyerhold among the whole troupe, esteemed him, and was prepared to accept his opinion. And even Nemirovich-Danchenko apparently was delighted that Meyerhold was "altogether permeated with Chekhov."[16]

Rehearsals were moved from Pushkino to the Hermitage Building in Karetny Ryad, Moscow. Chekhov came here to the rehearsals of *The Sea Gull*. Ten years later, Meyerhold wrote: "The fact that the Art Theater succeeded in bringing under one roof both naturalistic and mood theater is due, I am deeply convinced, to Chekhov himself and indeed to the circumstance that he himself attended the rehearsals of his plays. By the charm of his personality and his frequent talks with the actors he influenced their taste and their relationship to the requirements of art."[17]

Meyerhold's polemic with the Moscow Art Theater and his effort to distinguish two basic currents ("naturalistic theater" and "mood theater") in its early art will receive special attention later. For the moment we shall note only Meyerhold's reverence for Chekhov, his wish to put all the best in the Art Theater in direct line of descent from Chekhov and attribute it to his influence. In 1907, Meyerhold published one of his diary notes of the year 1898:

> Anton Pavlovich Chekhov, who has come for the second time to a *Sea Gull* rehearsal (September 11, 1898) at the Moscow Art Theater, hears from one of the actors that backstage in *The Sea Gull* frogs will croak, crickets sing and dogs bark.
>
> "And why, may I ask?" Anton Pavlovich inquires in a voice of displeasure.
>
> "It will be real," the actor answers.
>
> "Real," Chekhov repeats, beginning to laugh, and after a slight pause adds, "The stage is art. Kramskoi has painted a genre picture in which he has splendidly caught the faces. Suppose you cut out the nose drawn on one of the faces and inserted a real one. The nose would be 'real,' but the picture would be spoiled. The stage," Anton Pavlovich continues, "presupposes an *accepted convention*. You have no fourth wall. Besides, the stage is art, the stage reflects the quintessence of life. You must not introduce anything on stage that is not essential."[18]

Chekhov's *The Sea Gull* became one of the greatest events in the history of the Russian theater and one of the greatest new developments in the history of world drama. Staging it in 1898 after the resounding failure it had suffered two years before at the Alexandrinsky Theater was for Stanislavsky and Nemirovich-Danchenko an enormously complicated task. In their memoirs both directors later described the help which the author gave them during rehearsals of *The Sea Gull*. But neither Stanislavsky nor Nemirovich-Danchenko remembered Chekhov's notion of the convention essential to the stage—an idea which long remained imprinted on Meyerhold's consciousness.

The first production of the Art Theater, *Tsar Fyodor Ioannovich*, began a new era in the history of the Russian stage. At the Art Theater, for the first time in Russia, the director became the all-powerful master of the theater and the author of the production, the creator of a unified work of theater art which integrated the efforts of the dramatist, the actors, the designer and the composer, and related their creation to contemporary life and the modern audience.

It is common knowledge that the creative experience of the director's theater goes back further in the West than in Russia. Stanislavsky and Nemirovich-Danchenko were influenced both by the style of the Meiningen Theater, with its insistence on the conscientious re-creation of everyday life, costumes, and the whole external semblance of past epochs, and by the work of Antoine, who required that the production be literally "a slice of life"—seized from its midst with all the ruthlessness of naturalism. But the founders of the Art Theater at once gave the art of directing both a deeper meaning and a higher dedication. Both spontaneously and consciously, they linked their theater to the powerful movement of Russian literature in the nineteenth century, giving the stage the aim of enlightenment.

The revolution which the Art Theater brought about in the art of the stage and all of the concrete changes which followed it (the rejection of archaic stage conventions and cliched devices, the insistence on the most exact reflection of everyday life, on verity of "mood" and atmosphere, naturalness of communication, the most subtle psychological nuances) meant, above all, a radical return to authenticity. "A slice of life," honestly given, straightforward, without overtly taking sides—this was the main principle to which the Moscow Art Theater, both modern and historical, adhered.

The fame of this innovative theater very soon spread throughout the entire country. The names of the young Moscow Art Theater actors—Moskvin, Knipper, Savitskaya, Lilina and Kachalov (after 1902)—were soon known everywhere in Russia.

Meyerhold's name was less famous. With the enthusiasm of a pupil, a partisan and proponent of the theater revolution which Stanislavsky and Nemirovich-Danchenko were effecting, Meyerhold accepted without the least hesitation the "symbol of faith" of the Art Theater: the goal of maximum fidelity to life, of complete unconditional truth. To be true to life was accepted as the highest aim of art, the moral duty of the actor.

The creative personality of Meyerhold was born within the walls of the Moscow Art Theater; here it was first shaped and received a powerful impulse toward a further career full of unexpected developments.

Meyerhold's unusual personality brought him to the fore. Among the young actors who experienced with him the laborious self-abnegation of the first productions and the exciting electrified atmosphere of the enormous success which the Art Theater quickly achieved, Meyerhold immediately stood out as unique. In a sense he was the "rara avis" of the Art Theater company. Gradually everyone—directors, authors, fellow actors, and critics—noticed.

Nevertheless, there is no doubt that this exceptionally creative personality was shaped in the Art Theater and was first developed and displayed to the public there. Furthermore, Meyerhold, who began his career by participating in one of the greatest esthetic revolutions, was ever after firm in his belief that innovation is an indisputable condition for genuine art.

Meyerhold's fate within the confines and repertory of the Art Theater turned out to be quite complicated and dramatic.

The role of Treplyov in *The Sea Gull* revealed that Meyerhold was one of the Moscow Art Theater actors who most faithfully sensed the author's intent and most exactly realized the director's demands. True, Meyerhold, as Stanislavsky wrote Nemirovich-Danchenko (after rehearsals in the presence of Chekhov) "at first went off on the tangent of acerbity and hysteria, which did not at all fit Chekhov's intent. Now he has toned down and found the right road. His main problem was that he began in the first act to play the fourth." After the opening of *The Sea Gull*, Nemirovich-Danchenko wrote Chekhov a letter in which he listed Meyerhold among the best players. Meyerhold as Treplyov "was mild, touching and indubitably decadent."[19]

Chekhov received a letter almost simultaneously from Tatyana Shchepkina-Kupernik, who said, among other things, that "Meyerhold as Kostya [Konstantin Treplyov] is full of temperament, young and touching" and one from P. A. Sergeenko, who wrote that "Kostya [Meyerhold] was quite decent and blazed and boiled with just as much sulphur and saltpeter as he was allowed by the author."[20] Sergei Glagol (Sergei Gologushev) remarked in his review that "Meyerhold in the role of Konstantin made a strong and unexpected impression. The player who has been seen before this both as Vasily Shuisky and in the clown part of the Marquis Forlipopoli in *The Mistress of the Inn* suddenly appears before us as a fine dramatic actor, portraying the neurasthenic Konstantin, whose spirit has been broken since childhood. The scene with his mother in the third act was realized by Knipper and him with such sincerity that the audience applauded them in the middle of the act."[21]

However, another opinion was also expressed: that the actor playing Treplyov was too sharp, over-nervous. "Mr. Meyerhold," wrote Alexander Urusov, "projected too many shrieking notes, too quarrelsome an intonation."[22] Nikolai Efros had the same reaction to Treplyov, feeling—not without justification—that sharpness in general characterized Meyerhold's genius as an actor. "Vsevolod Emilevich Meyerhold, then a great admirer of Chekhov and his plays and extremely sensitive to his work, took the difficult and in places dangerous part of Treplyov. But in Meyerhold's stage presence during his years at the Art Theater, there was great sharpness, there was no softness and in his voice the notes of sincerity were weakest of all . . . a Treplyov vexed by his literary failures, a Treplyov worn down by lack of recognition."[23] Such was Meyerhold's rendition of the hero in the opinion of this critic.

When *The Sea Gull* was played for Chekhov in the spring of 1899, he decidedly disliked Roxanova as Zarechnaya and Stanislavsky as Trigorin, but liked Meyerhold as Treplyov. Later, Chekhov more than once singled Meyerhold out among the "cultured people" of the Moscow Art Theater group of actors as the most cultured of all. "This is not an actor who carries you away," Chekhov said, "but you listen to him with pleasure because he understands everything he says."[24]

Meyerhold did not have a part in Chekhov's next play, *Uncle Vanya*, but was given the part of Tuzenbakh in *Three Sisters*. Stanislavsky wrote Chekhov in December 1900 about Meyerhold's work on the role: "Meyerhold hasn't yet found the right tone and is working strenuously."[25] The part came hard, as is clear from the wealth of director's hints which Meyerhold noted down and from the following letter, which Stanislavsky wrote now in January to Chekhov: "Meyerhold is working, but he's stiff, according to reports."[26]

Many years later, Meyerhold described how Stanislavsky tortured him at the rehearsals of *Three Sisters*, for a long time with no result: "The task seemed simple enough: enter, go up to the piano, sit down and begin to speak. But I no sooner began than Stanislavsky sent me back to begin again. At such moments I almost hated him. We did it over ten times, starting from my entrance."[27]

Ten days before the opening, the part had still not taken final form. Nemirovich-Danchenko, who replaced the weary Stanislavsky and finished rehearsing the play, in turn informed Chekhov: "Meyerhold, poor fellow, is wringing himself dry in order to give an impression of *joie de vivre* and to get away from theatrical stereotypes. Work overcomes everything, and in the end he will be good."[28]

The charge of "stereotyping" can hardly have been just: it had been five years since Meyerhold's appearances in Penza and during all those years he had been safely protected from any stereotype behind the walls of the Philharmonia and the Art Theater. The remarks about the "stiffness" of Meyerhold's physical gifts and about his difficulty in projecting *joie de vivre* sound more convincing. The Moscow Art Theater actor, Alexander Vishnevsky, also remarked in a letter to Chekhov that "Meyerhold was awfully *gloomy*, very much recalling Treplyov."[29] However that may be, Nemirovich-Danchenko's prognosis turned out to be correct, and Meyerhold's success in the part of Tuzenbakh was indubitable. M. F. Andreeva (who played Irina) said later, when recalling her partner Meyerhold: "No one could play Baron Tuzenbakh in *Three Sisters* better. Later I played opposite Kachalov, but—pardon me—Meyerhold, despite his impossible physical gifts—his face like an axe, his grating voice—played better than Kachalov."

Andreeva considered Meyerhold an excellent actor in general. "He played the Prince of Arragon in *The Merchant of Venice*. This is not a real part, it is shorter than a sparrow's nose, and what did he make of it? A real Don Quixote, a real Spaniard. He spoke his monologue in such a way that you just sat there and listened with your mouth open. I do not know any part that Meyerhold could have played badly—he was a marvelous actor."[30]

Not all of Meyerhold's roles, which so aroused Andreeva's enthusiasm, delighted the leaders of the Moscow Art Theater to the same degree. His first teacher, Nemirovich-Danchenko, was especially strict and severe in his evaluation of Meyerhold's success as an actor. Everyone was always delighted by Meyerhold's Prince of Arragon; even Stanislavsky, it is known, was delighted. But Nemirovich-Danchenko did not like this work. "My Prince of Arragon," Meyerhold wrote his wife, "does not satisfy him; on the other hand, Alexeev [Stanislavsky] is delighted and has long since stopped criticizing."

The part of Johannes Vockerat in Hauptmann's *Lonely Lives* was very hard for Meyerhold, partly because of the danger of repeating the tone and pattern of the Treplyov role. Meyerhold asked Chekhov's advice about Johannes, and Chekhov sent him a letter cautioning him against superfluous nervousness. "Nervousness should not be stressed," he wrote, "so that the neuropathological nature of the hero will not overshadow or subordinate what is more important, namely the loneliness experienced by only the higher, healthy (in the highest sense) organisms. Depict a lonely man and give as much of the nervousness as the text itself demands."[31] Meyerhold thanked Chekhov for his advice and wrote that he would try to achieve in his characterization "the principal tone of a lonely intellectual, refined, healthy, but at the same time, deeply sad."[32] Nevertheless, judging by the criticisms of the time, he did not avoid excessive nervousness and irritability. Stanislavsky, who conducted the rehearsals, at the start also thought it necessary to avoid "the tone of a sharp, disagreeable, unattractive person," but later, working out the concrete situations of the play, forgot such fears and insistently urged Meyerhold "not to forget the acerbity [of the part]," "to give free rein to his nerves," "not to be afraid of not being liked."[33] These insuperable contradictions led Meyerhold in the final analysis far from the conception of the part which Chekhov had so reasonably suggested. One critic even insisted that Meyerhold played Johannes "as always screaming, an excessively agitated patient in a psychiatric ward."[34] Olga Knipper wrote Chekhov that Meyerhold expended on the preparation of the part "a lot of hard work, a lot of nervous energy, and achieved a great deal, though he is criticized for sharpness, agitation, superfluous display of nerves."[35] On this occasion as well, Nemirovich-Danchenko reacted to Meyerhold's work with completely cold rejection. He drily remarked in one of his letters to Stanislavsky: "This was not Johannes."[36]

Remembering Nemirovich-Danchenko's enthusiasm over his successes at the Philharmonia, Meyerhold now felt that his teacher was disappointed, that his attitude showed a marked lack of confidence and at times hostility to his former pupil. In time, the pupil was converted to a new faith: Stanislavsky became an idol to Meyerhold.

But fate and the repertory dictated that more and more often Meyerhold had to work with Nemirovich-Danchenko.

In the first days of the new twentieth century, the young artist noted in his diary the motto: "Life or death, only not sleep."

Following these proud words came a brief definition of art, its meaning and goal: "Art should put before us a true picture of life. Let the individual himself find in it what he needs without pointers or tendentious emphasis."[37]

This formulation agreed exactly with the early Moscow Art Theater's principles of realism.

Soon, however, disturbed thoughts of agitation, discontent, and protest were expressed in Meyerhold's diary.

This emotional disturbance probably was caused by the fact that Meyerhold had formerly seen his situation at the Art Theater as quite a different one. He had expected more. Like every young actor, he had seen himself in leading roles. This was not, however, the only difficulty; indeed, Meyerhold himself at that time did not understand very clearly what it was. "I am terribly depressed," he wrote Chekhov in January 1900. "I don't understand why my life is so difficult. Probably I have a difficult character, perhaps I'm even neurasthenic."[38]

He was expecting something, some sort of change. In December of that same year (1900), he noted in his diary: "It will soon be time for the Christmas tree. Everyone is glad. But I am waiting for something else. It seems to me as if something were standing outside the door, biding its time to enter and change my whole life."[39]

In 1901 his diary notes became more extensive. As if justifying his future in advance, Meyerhold gave reasons for the necessity of extremes, and protested against "the golden mean." He wrote:

> The most dangerous thing for the theater is to cater to the bourgeois tastes of the masses. One must not listen to their voice, or else one can fall from the "mountain" into the "valley." The theater is only great when it lifts the masses up to itself, or if it does not lift, at least drags them up to the heights. If one listens to the voice of bourgeois taste, it is very easy to fall. One can push upward only when the upward striving is disinterested. One must fight no matter what the cost. Forward, forward, always forward! Even if mistakes happen, even if everything is strange, drastic, terrifying to the point of horror, miserable and shattering to the point of panic, all the same, this is better than the golden mean.[40]

The relationship of the theater to its audience came under Meyerhold's intense and excited scrutiny. The experience of the Art Theater, of course, interested him in this connection above all.

"The bourgeois audience," he wrote, "wants impressionism, moods, words deep to the point of incomprehensibility, not their real meaning. It likes the fact that in these works of literature it is not touched, criticized, or ridiculed. But as soon as something simple but ticklish to the self-love of the bourgeois audience occurs, indignation over the work begins. So you are monotonously, half-heartedly silent."[41]

"Impressionism" and "mood"—the very things on which the Art Theater prided itself in its beginnings. Stanislavsky at this time had maintained categorically: "All art springs from mood." Still more, "stage and drama and art exist for the purpose of awakening a *mood* in the onlooker. Everything should aim for this: the actor, the set, the costumes, the lights and the special effects."[42] It is most important to note that the young Meyerhold experienced as an actor at the Art Theater some vague sense of inadequacy and passivity in this art. In letters to Chekhov, Meyerhold's discontent as an actor ("it is awfully sad, after all, to sit with nothing to do"), his longing for new serious work ("to play Chekhov's characters just as seriously and interestingly as Shakespeare's *Hamlet*") conjoined with anxiety for the theater. Meyerhold was enthusiastic about the production of Ostrovsky's *The Snow Maiden*, staged by Stanislavsky ("The production is amazing. Enough color for ten plays"). But *The Snow Maiden* was a flop—much to Meyerhold's distress.

"Box office receipts are already beginning to decline. Everyone is embarrassed. What is the problem? Obviously, *The Snow Maiden* has outlived its time. Obviously in our 'troubled times,' in the midst of the ruins of our whole way of life—there is little appeal in beauty alone." For the first time Meyerhold criticized Stanislavsky: "Let our chief director take some of the blame; he was too subtle again."[43]

There is every reason to think that in those years Chekhov was the person closest to Meyerhold in spirit. Meyerhold met Chekhov during the rehearsals of *The Sea Gull* in 1898 and "fell in love with him" with all the ardor of youth. Chekhov took a liking to him and more than once mentioned with affection what a cultured man Meyerhold was; he even advised him to write—Chekhov found that his letters showed talent. The dedication on the photograph which Meyerhold gave to Chekhov is indicative: "From pale Meyerhold to his idol." Many years later, Meyerhold recalled: "Chekhov loved me. This is the pride of my life, one of my dearest memories."[44] Or again, "Do you know who first gave me cause to doubt that all the ways of the Art Theater were right? Anton Pavlovich Chekhov. His friendship with Stanislavsky and Nemirovich-Danchenko wasn't at all as idyllic and serene as it is depicted on those tear-off calendars. He did not agree with a great deal at the theater and openly criticized a great deal."[45]

A knowledge of Meyerhold's veneration for Chekhov makes one read his letter to Chekhov on April 18, 1901 with special attention; it is the impetuous and sincere confession of the young actor:

> If I have not written you and given you any real proof of my constant thoughts of you, it is only because I am aware how unfit I am for life and am aware that all my experiences can be of interest to no one.
>
> I am irritable, fault-finding, suspicious; everyone thinks I am an unpleasant person.
>
> And I suffer and think of committing suicide. Let them all despise me. Nietzsche's advice is precious to me: "Werde wer du bist" [Become who you are].
>
> I openly say everything I think. I hate lies, not on the grounds of accepted morality (it is itself built on a lie), but as a person endeavoring to purify his own personality.
>
> I am frankly indignant at the arbitrary actions of the police, such as I witnessed in St. Petersburg on March 4,* and I cannot calmly devote myself to artistic work when my blood boils and everything calls me to join the struggle.
>
> I want to burn with the spirit of my time. I wish that all those who give their lives to theater would become aware of their great mission. I am disturbed by my comrades who don't want to rise above their narrow caste interests, interests foreign to those of society as a whole.
>
> Yes, theater can play an enormous part in the reconstruction of the existing order. . . .
>
> . . . The social movement of these last days has raised my spirits and awakened in me such desires as I had not dreamed of. I again want to study, study, study.
>
> I must know whether to perfect myself or join the fight for equality.
>
> I want to know whether it is truly impossible for everyone to be equal and at the same time be guided by his own concept of morality, which is harmless to others and understandable to all as the manifestation of a kindred spirit.
>
> Then it seems to me that it is impossible to become "master" when the social struggle puts you in the ranks of the "slaves."
>
> I rush about and thirst for knowledge.
>
> And when I look at my skinny hands, I begin to hate myself for being helpless and limp like these hands which have never been clenched in a strong fist.
>
> My life seems to me one long, painful crisis in some terrible extended illness. And I only wait and wait for the crisis to be resolved one way or the other. What is to come does not frighten me, if only the end would come soon, some end. . . .[46]

This letter not only lays wide open before us Meyerhold's inner world, but also gives an explanation of his later actions.

The sharpness with which Meyerhold reacted to the first forebodings of revolution is striking. Striking too is his readiness to participate in one way or another in the fight for freedom. One may be sure that at that time only very few among the intelligentsia took so decided a stand in favor of revolution.

---

*On March 4, 1901, a student demonstration took place at Kazan Cathedral. It was dispersed by police and Cossack cavalry. The students were brutally beaten and several were killed [Rudnitsky's note].

...erhold, 1898, in Pushkino, preparing for *The Sea Gull*

Meyerhold, his first wife, Olga Mikhailovna, and
their daughter Maria, 1897

Meyerhold, 1900

Meyerhold, 1902

Meyerhold, 1906

At the same time, one clearly senses the crisis taking place in Meyerhold's soul, demanding certain decisions.

Meyerhold's letter continues in a strange manner, especially curious because twice in the text very expressive passages from Gorky are quoted.

There is a note in Meyerhold's diary which has already caught the attention of scholars. Alexander Gladkov first published a fragment from it. The phrase, "Everything to which I merely alluded in the letter . . ." and the very content of the diary note, coinciding in many respects with the letter just quoted, lead to the assumption that in the diary Meyerhold simply developed and continued ideas expressed in his letter to Chekhov. In a diary entry, probably from April or May 1901, he writes:

> I often suffer because I have a highly developed self-awareness. I often suffer from the knowledge that I am not what I should be. I am often at odds with my surroundings, at odds with myself. I constantly experience doubts. I love life but run away from it. I despise my own weakness of will and want strength and look for work. I am more often unhappy than happy. But I find happiness as soon as I stop analyzing, as soon as my powers become strong enough so that I can throw myself into the active fighting. In Gorky's new play, someone says: "You have to get into the thick of life." That's true. And the tramp Seryozhka in "Malva" says, "You must always do something so that you are in the midst of people who feel you are alive. You must stir up life more often, so it doesn't curdle." That's true. In the part of Treplyov, Johannes [Vockerat] and Tuzenbakh, there is a great deal of myself, especially Treplyov. When I first played the part in 1898 I had a lot of similar experiences. I played the part of Johannes at the time of my preoccupations with individualistic tendencies. Tuzenbakh's appeals to go to work, to join the active struggle, help me break out of the realm of passive idealism. And here I am, bursting toward vitality, toward trembling, healthy work. I want to boil, to seethe, in order to create, not just destroy, to create in destroying. This is a time of crisis. The most dangerous moment. And a highly developed consciousness, doubts, hesitations, self-analysis, criticism of one's surroundings, preoccupation with doctrines—all this should be not the end, but only the means to an end. All this leads to something else.
>
> I have suffered and I continue to suffer. Everything to which I merely alluded in the letter has of course helped me in my creative work.
>
> My work bears the impress of our troubled times.
>
> New work lies ahead because life begins anew. A new wave has already seized me.[47]

This, then, is the way Meyerhold thinks and writes of himself. These attempts at self-analysis are in striking agreement with what others write and think of Meyerhold. His sharpness, his nervousness, his inclination to extremes, to decisions strained to their limits, are remarked by all his contemporaries. From early on, Meyerhold's conduct shows a certain strangeness, an incapacity to adapt to norms of existence as they arise—even if this means such high, unusually noble and beautiful norms of communal life and cooperative creativity as came into being and were carefully maintained in the Art Theater troupe. But even here in an atmosphere where the usual actors' Bohemianism was considered a disgrace, where cheap farce was ruthlessly rejected, where an extremely cultured spirit predominated, where members of the Moscow intellectual elite, millionaires generously supporting Russian talent, and people connected directly or indirectly with the revolutionary movement (Gorky, Andreev, Kachalov)—even here, Meyerhold was not at ease. His complaints about his own "difficult character," his "neurasthenia" at times brought him to thoughts of suicide, and sometimes to the clear formulation: "My work bears the impress of our troubled times." But he himself still did not understand, of course, what work he was talking and dreaming about.

From the letters to Chekhov and diary notes it is obvious that all Meyerhold's thoughts about the theater were completely determined by excitement over the political situation of the country, and by the ideas of freedom and the struggle for freedom which seized him.

Of course, it is easy to point out the vagueness, even the well-known confusion of his views at that time. He himself was conscious of this as he spoke of his rushing about and thirsting for knowledge, wanting to study. Indeed, he did study: whole pages of his diaries for these years are covered with the titles of books he had read, among which, together with works on esthetics and the plays of Maurice Maeterlinck, Gerhardt Hauptmann, Hermann Bahr, and d'Annunzio, there also appear the works of many contemporary philosophers and sociologists. But with all the inconsistency and vagueness in Meyerhold's program, still his question whether "to perfect himself" or "join the fight for freedom" sounds as if it had already been decided.

In truth, Meyerhold's blood boiled so much that he could not stand aside from the struggle and "calmly devote himself to his work." He wanted by his work to take part in the political struggle. The thirst for action and a sharply propagandistic art gradually and inevitably brought him into conflict with the Art Theater.

Stanislavsky, like Meyerhold, was shaken by the fact that performances of *An Enemy of the People*, which coincided with student unrest in St. Petersburg, with "the clash on Kazan square," occasioned such a decisively political reaction. "While we were standing on the stage playing our roles, we actors were not thinking of politics," Stanislavsky wrote. "On the contrary, the demonstrations occasioned by the performance were for us wholly unexpected." Many years later, while musing on the subject of that unexpected political reaction, Stanislavsky very decisively formulated this idea: "Tendentiousness and art are incompatible; one excludes the other." It seemed to him especially noteworthy about *An Enemy of the People* that the "tendentiousness" came about independently of the intentions of the director and the actors, who "were not thinking of politics." The truth is essential. "Then let the spectator come to his own conclusions and create his own bias from what he has gotten at the theater."[48]

As we recall, Meyerhold, in 1900, had also taken this view of the aims of art: it creates "a picture of life" and "may the individual himself find in it what he needs without pointers or slanted emphasis [in the work]." But a year later, having reached the conviction that the theater must assist social reform in Russia, Meyerhold was probably of the opinion that it was no longer admissible for art to be passive and give only a "picture of life" without commentary or bias.

In Meyerhold's diary there appear notes which show that much in the internal life and in the art of the Art Theater had begun to weigh upon him and irritate him. "Why does a play at the Art Theater get worse with each performance?" he asked. And he answered that question with this formula: "The director is a critic and not a teacher." He compared the acting school of the Moscow Art Theater with that of the MalyTheater: "The visual actor (the Art Theater); wealth of individual strengths (the Maly)."

The result of the comparison was not in favor of the Art Theater actors, whose strength, according to this note, was in their powers of observation alone. This evaluation cannot be considered just in any event, but it does bear witness to Meyerhold's discontent. Also in the diary there appears this note: "A feeling of discontent gives rise to great deeds." And a sharp criticism of the administration of the Art Theater: "The management of the Art Theater represents not the will of the majority, but organized arbitrary rule."[49]

And the management of the Moscow Theater (in any case Nemirovich-Danchenko) began to find Meyerhold a burden. In a letter to Knipper in July 1902, Nemirovich-Danchenko characterized "Meyerhold's turn. of mind" like this: "It is some kind of confused, wild mixture of Nietzsche, Maeterlinck and a narrow liberalism merging into a twilight radicalism. The devil knows what it is. Eggs with onion. It is the chaotic state of mind of a person who discovers a few truths every day, one knocking against the other."[50]

To a certain extent Nemirovich-Danchenko was right of course. Actually, Nietzschean and Tolstoian ideas were "knocking" one against the other in young Meyerhold's consciousness; his thirst for freedom and dreams of revolution were still quite vague and his radicalism had a shade of "twilight." All that is true. But it is also true that the managers of the Art Theater at that time generally viewed radicalism with distrust.

On the other hand, one may assume that the perceptive Nemirovich-Danchenko had an intuition of what Meyerhold himself perhaps did not sense, of the actor's longing to be a director, as can be sensed in his diary notes. The director's vocation was what "stood at the door and bided its time," in order finally to enter on stage and "turn his whole life upside down." He did not waste time dreaming about certain roles and certain plays (in the diaries there are no such expectations); he was dreaming about a theater of an altogether new type and spirit and was already thinking out the repertory of this theater.

Stanislavsky's genius as a director made itself manifest gradually underneath his genius as an actor, and the great director was, at least in part, called into being by the actor's dissatisfaction with the nature of the contemporary theater. Nemirovich-Danchenko's enormous talent as director developed under the pressure of the combined talents of a playwright and a person active in theater who also was unwilling to make his peace with the contemporary state of the Russian stage. However, Meyerhold was the only one of the three who was a director by birth and by vocation. His career as an actor was a prelude, not only brief but also very limited, to his life as a director. In the sharpness, nervousness and angularity characteristic of his acting roles something could already be felt which was not wholly congruent with the harmonious inspiration of the early Moscow Art Theater productions. In these roles not just the strange "sharp" actor came through; the new art also spoke out, of which the director Meyerhold was to become the creator.

The actor Meyerhold expressed himself most fully as Treplyov. The Treplyov theme, and Treplyov's individuality were close to him. Treplyov had proclaimed before Meyerhold: "New forms are needed. New forms are needed." The young actor playing Treplyov in *The Sea Gull* gradually and irrevocably became Treplyov in life. He was prepared in advance to exclaim, "New forms are needed." He had had a presentiment of them.

In one way or another, relations within the Art Theater were growing strained. They became especially so while the theater was rehearsing Nemirovich-Danchenko's play *In Dreams*. Stanislavsky found the play "not at all a silly piece."[51] Meyerhold was of a wholly different opinion. He wrote to Alexander Tikhonov: "There is darkness in the theater. It's wrong to produce Nemirovich-Danchenko's play, a play without talent, petty, falsely animated. All in the style of Boborykin! The author's attitude to the background, and the lines, and the style of writing. It is a shame that our theater stoops to such plays. And Gorky's play is being put off for this. That is what angers me!"[52] Chekhov criticized Nemirovich-Danchenko's play with considerable acerbity; the play was "noisy, high-flown,"[53] he remarked. *In Dreams* had a mediocre opening without any particular success. Meyerhold wrote quite ill-humoredly to Chekhov about this: "Nemirovich-Danchenko's play aroused audience indignation. The author is indifferent about the bourgeoisie, a class so hateful to the audience, especially to the younger generation. The play is varied and colorful, but not significant and not sincere. People saw that the author was a Boborykin disciple and were offended on behalf of their favorites, Chekhov and Hauptmann. They resented the author's trying to squeeze their favorite kind of mood play into a farrago of bad taste. Superficial tricks in close-up. So much work, so much money —for what?!"[54]

Assuredly, hostility toward Nemirovich-Danchenko's play by no means strengthened Meyerhold's position in the troupe.* Meyerhold found himself in direct opposition to the management. This circumstance was clearly of key importance at a moment when it was decided to reorganize the Art Theater as a cooperative of shareholders. Nemirovich-Danchenko carried out the reform at the end of the season of 1901-02. With a status of "comrades with equal rights," together with Stanislavsky and Nemirovich-Danchenko, certain actors became owners of the theater (Andreeva, Artem, Vishnevsky, Kachalov, Knipper, Luzhsky, Moskvin, etc.) and also Savva Morozov, Stakhovich, Chekhov. Not included in the list were Meyerhold, Sanin and several other actors who had worked in the theater from the day of its founding.

Chekhov at once saw the injustice of this: "I wrote Nemirovich that a theater cooperative was a good idea, but the members of it had been badly chosen. Why were Stakhovich and I members, but not Meyerhold, Sanin and Raevskaya? Not names were needed in this, but rules. There should be a rule that anyone who had served at least three or five years, anyone receiving a salary not less than this or that amount should be a shareholder. I repeat, not names are needed but rules, otherwise the whole thing will break up."[55]

---

*Later, Meyerhold told how Stanislavsky became really angry with him in connection with the first night of *In Dreams*. "Someone hissed at the first night of *In Dreams* by Nemirovich-Danchenko. And I at that time had written a letter to Chekhov criticizing the play. They heard about it at the theater (I don't know how), connected my letter with the hissing and told Stanislavsky I had organized the protest. Silly, but Stanislavsky for some reason believed it. He stopped speaking to me" (Alexander Gladkov, "Meierkhol'd govorit," *Neva* No. 2 (1966), 206).

A few days later on February 12, 1902, Knipper wrote: "Sanin and Meyerhold have officially notified the management of their resignation. We all decided to ask them to stay, as they are essential to our enterprise."[56] But it was already too late to repair the damage.

Soon the following note appeared in the newspaper *The Courier*: "Something wrong is going on at the Art Theater. Ferment and schism are rife in the troupe. A whole group of actors is resigning."[57] A few days passed and two of the departing members, Meyerhold and Kosheverov, published a letter in the same paper: "Though we do not wish to make public the reasons which compel us to leave the Art Theater, we do think it our duty to declare that our resignation from the company is in no way connected with considerations of a material nature."[58]

This was the truth. Indeed, it was not at all material, but only moral and esthetic considerations that caused Meyerhold to leave the Art Theater. We have set forth the outline of events and explained the specific conflicts preceding the break. But besides these outward facts there were more serious circumstances which must be kept in mind. The 1901-02 season marked a crisis for the Art Theater. Productions of Ibsen's *The Wild Duck* and Hauptmann's *Michael Kramer* were not particularly successful. The production of Nemirovich-Danchenko's play *In Dreams* was still less a cause for rejoicing.

Only Gorky's *The Petty Bourgeois*, performed in St. Petersburg just before the very end of the season, somewhat improved the situation, but by this time the conflict with the group of actors about to leave the Moscow Art Theater had already taken place, and Meyerhold played Peter in *The Petty Bourgeois* after he had officially announced his resignation. During the whole season morale in the company was low. This is obvious if only from Knipper's letters to Chekhov. Such phrases continually appear: "In general, it is difficult at the theater."[59] "The mood at the theater is bad, unpleasant." "Little joy at the theater. The repertoire is terribly limited: we are preparing at most a third play, and no one knows when that will open. Everything is at sixes and sevens."[60]

In July 1902, after this difficult season, Nemirovich-Danchenko, who was extremely worried about the position of the theater, wrote Stanislavsky about "two trends," which in his opinion were causing the Art Theater enormous harm. "The first trend," he wrote, "is the more sincere, though no less harmful—I call it the Gorkian. It has infected almost everyone, including you. 'The Gorkian trend' is not Gorky. It is quite natural that we must attract to our theater such a prominent artist as Gorky. But 'the Gorkian trend' is a fuss around the name of a man thrown into the limelight by the political life in Russia." Nemirovich-Danchenko went on to assert that political slogan makers followed in the wake of Gorky, and their goal was "Down with Culture!"

The other trend, Nemirovich-Danchenko continued, was "quite unreservedly harmful and even stronger—this was the effort to make our theater 'fashionable.' " Nemirovich was convinced that this "will bring us to a bad end with *form altogether smothering content* in our theater. Instead of our becoming a great art theater with a broad enlightening influence, we shall turn into a little art theater where splendid statuettes are created for nice, likeable, idle Muscovites."[61]

Clearly Nemirovich-Danchenko exaggerated Stanislavsky's interest in "the

Gorkian trend," in "student demonstrations," etc.—at the same time Stanislavsky wrote to Maria Andreeva: "Let's not talk about this student business. You must get used to my simply not understanding it."[62] But many in the theater company were excited by revolutionary ideas. Besides, an extremely acute question arose which was not even touched upon in Nemirovich-Danchenko's letter. This was the question of the actual relationship between, on the one hand, the art of the Art Theater and on the other, the Russian society of that time. In this a conflict was implicit, infinitely more important than any conflicts and "trends" within the troupe itself.

This became apparent during the troupe's guest appearance in St. Petersburg, which so strikingly coincided with the student demonstration at Kazan Cathedral, with its police action and beatings. In the performance of *An Enemy of the People* there was no topical political reference to be found, as everyone agreed (Stanislavsky and Meyerhold and Veresaev and others wrote about that). But the audience ("the audience at this performance was composed of a select intelligentsia; there were many professors and scholars"), the typical pet audience of the Art Theater, demanded a topical reference: "The auditorium was aroused to a high pitch and caught the least allusion to freedom . . . eruptions of applause with political intent kept occurring." And Stanislavsky summed it up: "This was a political performance." It became political not by the will of the company, but by force of circumstances and the will of the audience. The theater did not desire this: "For me," Stanislavsky insisted, "*An Enemy of the People* was one of those plays and productions growing out of intuition and feeling."[63] Tatyana Bachelis wrote that "the political coloration came about on its own in this case—as the result and consequence of psychological truth."[64] With its productions of the following season (*The Wild Duck, Michael Kramer* and especially *In Dreams*) the Art Theater showed that for the time being it had drawn no conclusions from what amounted to a "demonstration"[65] during the performance of *An Enemy of the People* in St. Petersburg. However, it was not long before the Moscow Art Theater production of *The Lower Depths* achieved a once unthinkably radical political resonance.

What conclusions Meyerhold came to and what impressions he received from the performance we know from his letter to Chekhov.

The presentation of life itself in its course, an accurate presentation avoiding all the previous conventions of the stage, was the nature and aim of the realistic imagery in the early Moscow Art Theater productions.

But times changed rapidly and political events made necessary a straight answer to pressing questions; to the amazement of theater directors, the pressure of events broke into their finished productions and put accents of its own in the director's notebooks.

The audience began to do the directing, actively bringing out and shaping political partisanship such as had not been foreseen either by the author or the theater. The audience discovered new possibilities concealed in the objective realism of the Art Theater. Thus directly and immediately did social agitation affect a subtle and, in its own way, highly tempered art.

What had been only yesterday excitingly new, stimulating and daring now seemed faded, passive, timidly inconclusive. "Give us straight answers to the crucial questions," the audience insisted.

Meanwhile it was not at all easy to give them answers. Time was racing forward with such speed that to arrest it in its course, if only to record and recognize it, proved unthinkable. Artists sensed how completely the destiny of Russia was changing and breaking with the past, but could not grasp either its present or future. The realism of Tolstoi and Chekhov was felt to be the limit, the last word; it seemed impossible to push even a step further in this direction. There was good reason for Gorky, under the influence of *Uncle Vanya* and *The Lady with a Lapdog*, to write to Chekhov: "Do you know what you are doing? You are killing off realism. And you will have dealt the fatal blow soon—finally and for good. This form has seen its day—that is for sure! No one can surpass you." The same letter also contains these programmatic words: "Everyone wants something stimulating, vivid, such as should not resemble life but be higher, better, more beautiful. It is absolutely essential that literature today should begin to make life beautiful, and as soon as it does, life will beautify itself, that is, people will begin to live faster, more vividly."[66]

Gorky's own play *The Lower Depths* was an attempt to find a way out of the difficulty, to discover and try out the principles of a new method. A great distance separates Gorky's *The Lower Depths* from his *Petty Bourgeois*. In the latter, he remained almost completely faithful to the esthetic rules of the early Moscow Art Theater. The propagandistically sharp tirades of Nil cut through the strict consistent realism of the accurate "picture of life." In the play *The Lower Depths*, everything has changed until it is unrecognizable. The ordinary routine of everyday life has been rejected in favor of an exotic environment; characters unfamiliar to anyone in the audience are displayed with complete naturalness—their very existence requires proof; the expedition to the Khitrov market was planned like an expedition to equatorial Africa with all the appearance of a daring adventure fielded with great danger.

It was in the inevitability of such dangers that the crisis of the method was displayed with almost comic distinctness. What fine manner of everyday ordinariness the artist must seek at the risk of his life! The cruel naturalism which Gorky insisted upon brought with it a sharp sense of the exceptional. The search for "the stimulating, the vivid, the extraordinary," led to the depiction of a rare and astonishing way of life almost beyond the limit of generally accessible reality.

Gorky went still further. He constructed a drama of life at the lower depths as a debate about the meaning of life. A philosophical discussion about what man is and how he should live rises as if from the nether regions. Such words as "man— that has a proud ring," or "truth is the god of a free man" are put in the mouth of a hopeless alcoholic, a rascal, a complete failure, cheat and liar. And the whole production was crowned with sermonizing about "the beneficent deception."

Thus, it was Luka who became the true hero of the Moscow Art Theater production, with his "prettifying of life." Gorky's play stimulated the imagination of Stanislavsky: the director introduced into the book of his production seventeen new small roles not provided by the author (the music copyist, the manic depressive, etc.). Moreover, *The Lower Depths* appreciably changed the very acting style of the Moscow Art Theater actors. With Moskvin (Luka), Kachalov (the baron), Stanislavsky (Satin), and others in mind, Gorky wrote with unmistakable astonishment after the opening: "Only at the first performance did I see and understand the startling leap made by all these people used to playing the characters of Chekhov and Ibsen; they had somehow abdicated from their very selves. . . . The audience roars, chuckles."[67]

Echoes of the widespread success of *The Lower Depths* exerted a tremendous influence on Meyerhold too. However, Meyerhold did not wait for that important change in the life of the Art Theater; he had already left the walls which had become oppressive to him. On September 22, 1902, far from Moscow in the south, in Kherson, the "Troupe of Russian Actors under the Direction of A. S. Kosheverov and Vsevolod Meyerhold" began their productions.

Meyerhold had become a director.

Meyerhold, 1910

IN THE PROVINCES

Meyerhold's decision to leave the Art Theater and launch a new enterprise in Kherson on his own caused concern among his sympathizers. Chekhov, who had first aroused in Meyerhold "doubts that all the ways of the Art Theater were necessarily right," did not approve the decision to quit the Moscow Art Theater. Much later, Meyerhold recalled: "He wrote me that I ought to stay and oppose what I did not agree with from within the theater."[1] Chekhov's motives are explained in a letter to Olga Knipper: "I should like to see Meyerhold and talk to him, keep up his spirits; he won't have an easy time in the Kherson theater! There is no audience there for plays, they still need farce there. After all, Kherson is not Russia and it is not Europe."[2]

Meyerhold, however, did not wish to adapt to the demands of the Kherson audience. He began the season with *Three Sisters*, followed by Chekhov's *Uncle Vanya* and *The Sea Gull*, then Hauptmann's *The Sunken Bell*, *Drayman Henschel*, *Lonely Lives* and *Michael Kramer*, Ibsen's *An Enemy of the People*, *The Wild Duck* and *Hedda Gabler*, Gorky's *The Petty Bourgeois*, and Alexei Tolstoi's *Tsar Fyodor Ioannovich* and *The Death of Ivan the Terrible*. The fact that "there was no audience for plays" in Kherson, as Chekhov had accurately put it, made itself felt after all. It was unusual for a play to last three performances; only *The Sunken Bell* continued for five.

After four years with the Art Theater, where rehearsals on stage were preceded by discussions and rehearsals while seated at table, where each production was carefully considered, more than once changed and experimented with, where each play was set and "costumed" afresh, where demands were made upon the ensemble to attain a high standard, where a "common tone," a single mood and maximum verisimilitude were achieved, Meyerhold now had to take into account the hard facts of the box office and put on a show as best he could in two or three days, getting across his requirements to his actors in haste, using a small set of props whose appearance he quickly changed for each new play.

Meyerhold had come to maturity in the intelligentsia milieu surrounding Stanislavsky and Nemirovich-Danchenko, but now the kind of craft absolutely needed on the provincial stage began to intrude. True, his first steps as director were in part easier thanks to the fact that some of the actors in the troupe had been trained as he had been at the Philharmonia and the Art Theater (A. S. Kosheverov, Ekaterina Munt, I. N. Pevtsov, B. M. Snegirev); the others were almost all young and viewed the Art Theater as their ideal. Of course, though, this was by no means the decisive factor in the extremely complicated circumstances of Meyerhold's first season of work as a director. Meyerhold immediately revealed some of his own characteristic traits: his fantastic capacity for work, his inhuman energy, his astonishing inventiveness and, most important, his ability to win over, inspire, transform every actor into a fanatic and enthusiast.

In the first season the Kherson theater went through not only almost the entire repertory of four seasons at the Art Theater, but also a number of plays in addition—more than seventy in all. Such figures were not astonishing for theater in the Russian provinces; many companies opened a hundred or more plays a season. What was astonishing was something else: under the conditions of provincial pressure and haste Meyerhold and Kosheverov (who in equal partnership with Meyerhold was responsible for the artistic direction of the troupe and also directed plays) managed to give the theater a quite definitive character and—for those times—an extremely attractive one.

Many years later Meyerhold himself said that he had "started in slavish imitation of Stanislavsky. In theory I no longer accepted many devices of his directing and regarded them critically, but in practice, starting out, I timidly followed in his footsteps at the beginning. I do not regret it because this period did not last long; I quickly and intensively ran through him and this was an excellent schooling in practical directing."[3]

If one considers in what difficult and unfavorable circumstances Meyerhold went through his "schooling in practical directing," then the imitativeness of his first productions becomes quite understandable. Kherson never was—either before Meyerhold's seasons there or afterwards—a "theater town." It was impossible to compare it not only with such famous centers of theater in the provinces as Odessa, Kiev, Kazan, Tbilisi or Yaroslavl, but even with relatively small cities like Novocherkassk or Kerch, where theater had long since become part of community life, where going to plays, talking and arguing about them, was considered the thing to do.

Gennady Neschastlivtsev (the down-on-his-luck actor hero of Ostrovsky's *The Forest*) would probably never even in the worst of times have set out for Kherson, where, as I. N. Pevtsov attests, out of 35,000 inhabitants "no more than 2,000 attended the theater—only a group of officials and the more or less well off. Of these two thousand only around three hundred were such theater lovers that they felt it essential to see an interesting theater event—the first production of some popular play." Meyerhold achieved the impossible, Pevtsov continued. "He won for our productions such prestige that the theater lovers—only three hundred in all—saw each of them several times."[4]

Because of Meyerhold, Kherson was the first city in Russia to have the productions "after the model of the Moscow Art Theater," which became such a widespread, even an inevitable, phenomenon of Russian theater life in the first two decades of our century. The fame of the Moscow Art Theater spread all over Russia, and its mention on a theater poster exerted a great attraction by promising, even if indirectly, at least a distant and approximate acquaintance with the marvelous theater of Chekhov and Gorky, a theater discussed in the capitals and often written about in the newspapers with a great deal of heat and contradiction.

Thus "offprints" of Moscow Art Theater productions, especially of Chekhov and Gorky, very rapidly became a sign of the times. Productions by Stanislavsky and Nemirovich-Danchenko were conscientiously repeated by many Moscow Art Theater artists setting off for the provinces to direct or, on the contrary, by provincial directors coming to Moscow and earnestly recording in their notebooks all the stage sets of the Art Theater, all the backstage noises, all the details of costumes and properties, etc., in order to reproduce them later on their stages. Meyerhold was the pioneer of such copying.

The first season opened on September 22, 1902, with *Three Sisters*, staged with close attention to the Art Theater production. The Kherson correspondent of the magazine *Theater and Art* reported on it:

> This play, which is so difficult to interpret, was so carefully done in its details that those who had already seen it with another company of actors in Kherson did not recognize it. The local paper put it correctly in saying of this production that the play was done with the sensitivity of a concert. The audience which filled the theater pelted the actors with flowers. All were equally good, including the actress in the non-speaking role of the nurse, as she watched the departure of the artillery regiment from the veranda. The producers want to transplant to this remote little corner of the south the principles of the Moscow Art Theater, where they were nurtured, as far as that is possible.[5]

The critic of Kherson's *The South* reported that in the first act of *Three Sisters* "the fresh breeze in the birches" was audible, that in the second "bad autumn weather whistled at the window, which the nurse echoed in her sad song," and that in the third "a nagging general nervousness" was in the air.

A few days after *Three Sisters, Uncle Vanya* was staged. A feature article by De-Lin , which appeared in the local newspaper, gives some idea of how people in Kherson reacted to this show. The article was entitled "People leaving the theater after *Uncle Vanya*" [a title alluding to an epilogue by Gogol for *The Inspector General*] :

> Two ladies: Did you notice, darling, how the flower pot was overturned?
>> And how the clock ticked?
>> And the curtain?
>> And the cricket?
>> And the thunder!
>> And the rain!
>> And how the doctor's light carriage went over the bridge?
>> And how the harness bells rang?
>> And the suit the professor's wife was wearing?
>> And the sleeves on her long mantle?
>> With lace!
>> With ruching![6]

Despite his intellectual preoccupation with directing, Meyerhold appeared in almost every production in an acting role. Strangely enough, however, he did not play the part of Tsar Fyodor, which he had prepared as far back as Pushkino before the opening of the Art Theater, but entrusted it to a beginner, I. N. Pevtsov. In *The Sea Gull* Meyerhold played Treplyov, in *Uncle Vanya* Astrov, in *Ivanov* the title role. One of Chekhov's constant correspondents, B. A. Lazarevsky, who saw the Kherson troupe on tour in Sevastopol, wrote Anton Pavlovich that the company sometimes had the air of the Art Theater and that Meyerhold played Astrov very successfully. "One could not wish for a better Astrov than Meyerhold: distraught, tormented, unable to forget the patient who died under chloroform, angry at a fate which marries off professors to girls like Elena and Uncle Vanya's mother used to be."[7] This evaluation showed that Meyerhold brought to the role of Astrov his own particular interpretation of Chekhov's characters: extreme nervousness, acuity, sharpness; that is, precisely those traits which the directors of the Moscow Art Theater denied and fought. It is unlikely, though, that such a departure from the requirements of Stanislavsky and Nemirovich-Danchenko was intentional. Rather Meyerhold's individuality as an actor simply made itself felt.

The broadened scope of the repertory, which far exceeded that of the Art Theater, was also by no means always the result of considerations of principle. If Sudermann (*Joy of Living, Honor, The Battle of the Butterflies, The Vale of Content*), Przybyszewski (*The Golden Fleece*), Heijermans (*The Good Hope*), Tolstoi (*The Power of Darkness*), and Schnitzler (*The Last Masks*) appeared on the stage of the Kherson theater, it was only because these authors interested and fascinated Meyerhold. Productions of certain plays by Ostrovsky (*Talents and Admirers, The Marriage of Balzaminov, A Late Love, All in the Family*), S. Naidenov's *Vanyushin's Children*, three plays by Vladimir I. Nemirovich-Danchenko (*Gold, The Price of Life, Last Will*), a play by E. Chirikov (*In Yard and Annex*), two plays by I. Potapenko (*Magic Fairy Tale, Aliens*), and finally home products and translations were all staged simply because they belonged to the repertory of the provincial theater at the time or were "in demand at the box office." I. Pevtsov openly admitted, "We were able to argue thus: our repertory of classic drama will include these three plays this year. Consequently, we can work on them during the whole year and the summer until the beginning of the season. In addition, we shall put on some middling literature requiring less care and preparation. Finally, we will do a certain amount of trash to earn our daily bread. So at the cost of our daily bread we sometimes were able to do something quite out of the ordinary."[8]

Nevertheless, the repertory in Kherson differed sharply from that of other provincial theaters. It was unusual in paying particular attention to Chekhov: all his plays were given in a single season. Inclusion in the repertory of such a wealth of plays by contemporary Western writers was exceptional for the provinces: four plays by Hauptmann, three by Ibsen, four by Sudermann, and also works by Schnitzler, Heijermans, Przybyszewski, Fulda.

News of the original direction of the Kherson theater reached Petersburg, and one magazine in the capital noted the "unfailingly high" level of the repertory, "undiluted by various fashionable and profitable low-grade adaptations and other theater rubbish." The same report told how Kherson audiences "immediately appreciated the remarkable sense of form, the intelligence of interpretation, the ensemble work, the artistry of staging and direction, all new to local theater." Meyerhold and Kosheverov "had distinguished themselves not only as good actors, but also as talented directors. The present theater season has shown that when an enterprise is headed by people who are serious and honest in their love and respect for art, then it is possible even in the provinces to chart 'a new course' for a theater, that is, one without the usual 'benefit' system, which imposes an undesirably haphazard and miscellaneous choice of plays, and without advertising and fashionable adaptations. This first wholly successful example of a provincial theater conducted according to an idea with the banner of art held on high, with educational and cultural significance, without concessions to vulgar tastes, and without yielding to mere entertainment, cannot and must not lack imitators."[9]

Apparently the most distinctly original tendencies and new ideas of Meyerhold first came through in full force in his production of a little known play by Franz von Schönthan, *Acrobats*. Meyerhold himself translated the play from the German in collaboration with N. A. Butkevich, an actress of the Kherson theater, and hectographed it with characteristic categorical directives for staging, modestly giving these out as advice from the translators, including sketches for staging.[10] In addition, Meyerhold's "Director's notes for staging *Acrobats*" (January 1903) have been preserved in the archive of Meyerhold material.

These directives "from the translators" and director's notes are the first documentary evidence of an actually realized Meyerhold production which has come down to us. In his staging of *Acrobats*, Meyerhold has observed the Art Theater's indispensable rule of fidelity to life and maximum authenticity. The place of the action is characterized with exceptional care—unusual in the practice of the theater: the wooden structures to be used as dressing-rooms by the actors in the circus should "have steps: raised floors will make the rooms warmer." "To show a live audience in perspective on stage," it is pointed out, "seems impossible in the small space of provincial theater," but nevertheless "it is desirable to have not an audience painted on flats but adults and mostly children seated on stage." A detailed list is given of the "posters and advertisements of various colors and dimensions" affixed to the walls, and "a big bell" is envisioned fastened to one wall "and beneath it six pushbuttons for electric bells."[11] All kinds of circus properties are enumerated in detail; careful blockings are sketched for all three acts and for the last, the most important, there is a general view of the stage from above.

The attempt to achieve "a complete illusion" of reality is reflected also in the director's notes, which require that there be in the first act "extreme disorder." "Everywhere scarves, galoshes, shoes, dirty clothes, hats, umbrellas." In the second act "things should be more or less picked up." It is obvious that this production was staged with care and that all the compromises, which Meyerhold nevertheless had to make, distressed him. "A real clown's costume" was made for Landovsky, the hero, played by Meyerhold himself, and new costumes were made for almost all the characters (the play had a large cast; besides extras, it required twenty-four actors); only the grooms appeared "in the uniforms of the ushers," and the juggler wore "a Neapolitan costume."[12]

The enormous success of *Acrobats* is attested to in an article in the Kherson newspaper *The South*, in which the production is called "a *chef d'oeuvre* of the director's art." The critic wrote: "Here circus life behind the scenes is revealed to the audience without reservation: all the essential gear in use at the circus is there on stage—all kinds of ladders, trapezes, rods, rings spanned with paper, hurdles for horses, juggler's balls, etc. And through a curtain to be raised, dividing the arena, the circus itself can be seen, lighted and full of spectators."[13]

Undoubtedly Meyerhold was fascinated by this new theme of circus life, its exciting entourage, its splendid spectacle. In a certain sense this theme also suited the predilections of his provincial public, whom Chekhov so venomously said required farces. It is curious, though, that in adopting this new theme, Meyerhold assiduously exhausted the means and methods of the Art Theater and turned most careful attention to the detail of everyday reality, striving for exactitude and faithfulness in every minute point. His production shows him in transition. Unerringly seizing upon this melodrama among the run-of-the-mill plays, attracted, above all, by its unusual theme and milieu, Meyerhold staged it in the imitative manner usual to him at that time. And therefore timidly, yet audibly, new notes could be heard. This was unavoidable, for material wholly foreign and unfamiliar to the Art Theater was "treated" by methods of the early Moscow Art Theater.

Meyerhold played an old clown, one who has lost confidence in himself, whom no one applauds any more. In the first two acts, which can hardly have been especially interesting for Meyerhold, the part typecast him as "the noble-hearted father." The clown, who sincerely loved his daughter Lily (played by E. Munt, leading ingenue of the Kherson company), aroused liking and sympathy as a typical character of banal melodrama. But in the third act, which took place behind the scenes at the circus, everything changed, and of course, only this third act seriously interested and excited Meyerhold. Here Landovsky appeared for the first time not in "street clothes," not in an overcoat and top hat, but in a clown's costume, with white-powdered face, ready to go into the ring.

This was an old Pierrot who had already been through the bitterness of failure, but was still trying to overcome fate, and who therefore exaggerated his worth out of self-importance. True, he admitted "having lost subtlety a bit," was agitated from fear of failure, suffered from his collar being too tight, stopping his breathing, but wanted to believe: "I need only make my entry and they'll laugh. My comic entry! What a laugh there will be! I know there will be four encores!"

It is easy to imagine Meyerhold as Landovsky, tall, supple, melancholy and ridiculous, white face, long thin nose, uneasy eyes, a forced grimace of a smile. In this part Meyerhold acquired a new sense of his own physical "gifts," of the "material" he had to work with as an actor. Everything his great teachers and he were used to considering his defects—insufficient good looks, peculiar timbre of voice, a tendency to sharp, eccentric characterization—everything he had previously had to overcome and struggle to transcend, now came to his aid, "furthered" the role and enhanced it with a nervous, haunting melancholy. Without a doubt this part predisposed Meyerhold for many years in favor of Pierrot, aroused his enthusiasm, so to speak, in advance, for the whole theme of [Blok's] *The Puppet Show*—the clown's and Harlequin's role in his art.

According to the stage direction in Act Three, Pierrot-Meyerhold stood for a long time after his return from the ring, covered with shame, silent, looking from the stage apron straight ahead at the theater.audience, listening with a last bit of hope for at least one heartening bit of applause from the dark silence of that other—the circus's—audience. But when at last applause was heard, it was clearly not for Landovsky, but for the next act—a pair of acrobats.

At that moment a theme was sounded on the stage of a provincial theater in Kherson by the unsure hand of a beginning director, one of the most important themes of great twentieth-century art. It resounded in the circus suite of Picasso, especially strong in his "Absinthe Drinkers," in Blok's *The Puppet Show*, Stravinsky's *Petrushka*, and later in Chaplin's *The Limelight*, in Jean-Louis Barrault's pantomimes, in Carne's films (*The Children of Paradise*), Bergman's (*Sawdust and Tinsel*), and Fellini's (*La Strada*), finally and most recently in Heinrich Böll's novel

The Clowns. What was its meaning? What was the feeling and perhaps understanding, even if not a full understanding, of the producer of this essentially pitiful little play in a provincial town in the south of Russia?

Along with the figure of the clown there appeared on stage and screen and the painter's canvas the theme of a pathological confrontation: art in its simplicity and naivete face to face with the overcomplicated life of our time. By returning again and again to their dying clowns, artists, poets, actors and directors were not declaring the surrender of art; on the contrary, they were affirming its immortality.

Of course, at that time Meyerhold could not have grasped the whole measure of the theme which interested and fascinated him. But his enthusiasm for *Acrobats* showed that the period of his apprenticeship as a director and his slavish imitation of Stanislavsky was drawing to an end.

After the completion of its first season in Kherson the company went to Nikolaev for two weeks, then to Sevastopol for two months. The repertory included still more plays: they performed Ibsen's *The Lady from the Sea* and Gorky's *The Lower Depths* and on "an evening of new art" Maeterlinck's *The Intruder* and Schnitzler's *The Last Masks*.

The following season in Kherson was directed by Meyerhold himself without Kosheverov, and the company began to call itself proudly "The New Drama Association."

The change to the new name was significant. Meyerhold was not just "hanging out a new shingle" for his theater; he was declaring a turn onto a new, untraveled road. From distant Kherson he was throwing down the gauntlet to Moscow and the Art Theater. The renaming of the Kherson company was the first sign that there was in Russia a director who would at least try to depart from the esthetic system of psychological realism and in practice apply the principles of Symbolism to the theater. For Meyerhold soon made it known that "New Drama" was for him not only Ibsen, Hauptmann and Chekhov, but also Maeterlinck, Przybyszewski, and Schnitzler.

In the Russian literature of those years the voices of the Symbolist poets Blok, Bryusov, and Balmont were already very much in evidence.

Many people were writing about "worthless realism" and the enormous, still unexplored possibilities of Symbolism. "Symbols," Merezhkovsky affirmed as early as 1893, "must flow naturally and involuntarily from the depths of reality.... We cannot content ourselves with the rough photographic exactitude of experimental snapshots. From indications by Flaubert, Maupassant, Turgenev and Ibsen we require and predict new, yet undiscovered worlds of sensibility."[14]

"Realists," as K. Balmont easily pronounced, "are always mere observers, while Symbolists are always thinkers.... Symbolists are a powerful force, striving to perceive new combinations of ideas, colors and sounds and often perceiving them with irrefutable persuasiveness."[15]

Translations of Symbolist plays by Maeterlinck, Przybyszewski and Schnitzler had appeared and aroused lively interest. Already attempts were being made to stage them.

Still earlier in the mid-eighties of the preceding century Ibsen's plays had become widely known in Russia, and in the nineties, the Symbolist plays of Hauptmann.

They were staged, however, in the spirit of the usual realism of detail, often even with a nuance of naturalism. Symbolist elements were sometimes interpreted as fairy-tale touches, and in this sense the production of *The Sunken Bell* was in principle no different from productions of *The Snow Maiden*. Chekhov had a presentiment of the characteristic traits of Symbolist drama and in part parodied them in *The Sea Gull* in the scene in which Treplyov's avant-garde play is performed. So a parody of a Symbolist play was presented to Russian audiences before they saw any Symbolist plays.

To an art based on the firm ground of perception and reason and on principles of positivism which governed minds in the nineteenth century, Symbolism opposed the principle of intuitive comprehension of all the secrets of existence. The Symbolists were attracted to the unknowable and the inexpressible. They wanted, in Mallarmé's words, to clothe in the form of feeling "the hidden sense of all aspects of life."

From the viewpoint of the theory and practice of Symbolism, the direction in which theater art was developing, as understood and affirmed by the Art Theater—though it had only just been born and only just achieved enormous success—seemed both conservative and futile. Valery Bryusov declared this for all to hear in his article "Unnecessary Truth," published in 1902 in *The World of Art*. It had the impact of a cannon shot.

For Meyerhold the art which had appeared with the Art Theater and flourished there was inadmissible, and all attempts to place any new esthetic system in opposition to that of Stanislavsky and Nemirovich-Danchenko seemed attractive, if only because such attempts helped Meyerhold to see and understand himself. Symbolism irresistibly attracted him. Therefore, it was Meyerhold who several years later most consistently, widely, and graphically carried out in his productions the theatrical program and theory of Symbolism.

In Kherson he realized only early tendencies in this direction, and staged preliminary experiments. His ally, fellow-traveler, and in part also his theoretician was A. M. Remizov, then in Kherson and at the start of his own literary career, and Meyerhold's friend since his early years in Penza, an enthusiastic translator of Przybyszewski and a passionate propagandist of Symbolist ideas. In "The New Drama Association," Remizov became something like the head of the play-reading department. Chekhov and Gorky, Hauptmann, Ibsen, Maeterlinck, Schnitzler, and Przybyszewski were to determine the profile of the new theater according to the idea of Meyerhold and Remizov.

The season opened September 15, 1903, with Gorky's *The Lower Depths*. It is hard to say with assurance what kind of a production this was, though a meaningful answer to this question could explain a great deal. Remizov wrote a year later that Meyerhold had interpreted the play "in his own way," expressing in it a theme of cold, insurmountable despair.

"A cellar with narrow or boarded-up windows—complete monotony—nothing—icy horror. The production conveys disillusionment with life, the director glorifies desperate behavior in the face of the void."[16]

The review in the Kherson newspaper, however, which appeared the day after the opening, in no way confirms Remizov's characterization. "There was a wealth of that famous 'detail,' " it says, "for which both the director and actors have shown such inventive talent. The background of the flophouse was striking in its truthfulness and completeness; the 'folk' scenes were played with the proper enthusiasm and inspiration."[17]

This description does not echo the "icy horror," and there is reason to think that Remizov has "tacked on" his own (moreover, not even his, but Merezhkovsky's) perception of Gorky's play to Meyerhold's production. Later Meyerhold repeated his staging of *The Lower Depths* in Tbilisi, and again no one noticed the fatal "desperate behavior in the face of the void." Meyerhold's Symbolist interests were for the time being more or less distinctly revealed only in the repertory of The New Drama Association. Following *The Lower Depths*, there came: *Before Dawn, Colleague Crampton, Reconciliation, Conflagration,* by Hauptmann; *A Doll's House, Ghosts, Little Eyolf, The Lady from the Sea,* by Ibsen; *The Destruction of Sodom, The Homeland, St. John's Fires,* by Sudermann; *The Farewell Supper* [from *Anatol*], *Flirtation, A Fairy Tale,* by Schnitzler; *Monna Vanna* by Maeterlinck; *The Snow,* by Przybyszewski.

New ideas of the director made themselves clearly felt—as we shall see in a moment—only in the productions of *The Snow* and *Monna Vanna*. This is understandable: Meyerhold felt that Kherson audiences would not be enthusiastic about them. In general, the interest in Symbolism just then taking fire in him immediately caused him to resent Kherson. He had no sooner launched the season with such an original and radical choice of plays when he wrote a bitterly complaining letter to Chekhov: " . . . there are no plays to act: there are so few good plays, so few. . . . The company is bored because there is nothing to be enthusiastic about. We need you to stir up our stagnant waters. We wait, wait. . . ." He asked Chekhov not only for a new play, but also for protection: Chekhov was to "build a fire" under an influential acquaintance in Rostov-on-the-Don, who determined the rent of the Rostov theater for the coming year. "We would like," he wrote in all frankness, "to get out of this hole—Kherson. We are spinning our wheels! We work hard and what for..." The three dots said a lot. In his next letter Meyerhold again came back to the same theme: "How about Taganrog or Rostov for me? It is about time... However, a thousand plans... If only my future might soon be decided. I have such longing for Moscow. Yes, longing..."[18]

Among the "thousand" plans, Moscow already beckoned. Meanwhile, however, it was necessary to win anew the small Kherson audience.

While oriented chiefly toward contemporary drama, mainly from the West (he even translated Hauptmann's *Before Dawn* himself), Meyerhold paid considerable attention also to the classic repertory. During his second season he staged Gogol's *The Marriage;* Sukhovo-Kobylin's *The Affair; The Forest, The Poor Bride, Easy Money, Poverty Is No Crime, The Snow Maiden,* by Ostrovsky; *Woe from Wit,* by Griboedov, and *The Merchant of Venice* and *Midsummer Night's Dream,* by Shakespeare. According to the review, however, "Our actors were by no means up to Ostrovsky, accustomed as they were to the plays of Chekhov, Hauptmann, Ibsen and others, writers of 'mood.' "[19] In *Woe from Wit* and *The Merchant of Venice* Meyerhold unsuccessfully played the leading roles: he was criticized for making Chatsky "the usual neurasthenic," and his Shylock became "a vulgar little Jew, a monster who retained nothing human with his thirst for blood, sharpening his knife with some sort of Satanic leaps of anger and ecstasy." *A Midsummer Night's Dream* (Meyerhold staged it after the example of A. Lensky's production in the New Theater, Moscow, as "a comedy with music," adding Mendelssohn's score to Shakespeare's text) was criticized by the same reviewer for "turning the comic scenes into vulgar farce with shrieks, screams and roars from the artisans, while the couples in love resembled fishmongers and fishwives."[20] *A Midsummer Night's Dream* was also reviewed, but the tone of this was quite different. Another critic enthusiastically wrote: "Meyerhold proved to the audience that he can give more than 'boiling samovars and calico ceilings.' Only a very talented artist-director can unfold on our pitiful little stage such a captivatingly enchanting picture of a moonlit night in the forest and create such a wonderfully beautiful group of elves."[21]

The phrase about "boiling samovars and calico ceilings" had a history. During the second Kherson season Meyerhold turned to the city government with the request that it take on the cost of heating the theater. A debate about this took place in the town council. Not so much the subsidy requested by the theater was discussed as the repertory and the nature of the productions. One of the speakers insisted that boiling samovars and calico ceilings bored the audience, another that "the cultured and most fashionable public continues to go to the theater."[22]

For Meyerhold, however, boiling samovars and all the other "little bits of everyday life" so carefully reproduced in the first season had now lost their attraction. He had begun to think more and more seriously about new forms of "super-ordinary," "extraordinary" theater. A. Remizov reasoned that the production of Przybyszewski's *Golden Fleece* and Maeterlinck's *The Intruder* marked a new direction. Perhaps it was necessary to have gone through Stanislavsky's iron discipline and been awakened by his enormous artistic sensitivity and mastered his method in order to overcome it and "find one's own way." What actually did one's own way mean? Remizov gave a solemn, though unclear answer: "The theater is not a copy of human mediocrity. Rather it is a cult, a Mass in whose mysteries perhaps Atonement is concealed... The 'New Drama' dreams of such a theater."[23]

Despite all the vagueness of these pronouncements, they still made sense. Meyerhold was attracted by something new. In a November 1903 letter to Chekhov inquiring whether *The Cherry Orchard* was finished, Meyerhold promised among other things to send him "Przybyszewski's new play *The Snow* (translated by my friend Remizov)" and added: "You will like the play very much."[24]

Whether Chekhov liked *The Snow* is not known, though most probably it could not have been to his liking. Besides, it is known with certainty that *The Snow* was a flop in Kherson, though Meyerhold invited the author to rehearsals and the opening, as he was then traveling in the south of Russia, and made sure that the presence of Przybyszewski "in person" impressed the inhabitants of Kherson. " . . . On the first night of his play," Evelina Volk-Lanevskaya wrote in her memoirs, published in Kharkov in 1934, "the theater was jammed and the box reserved for the Przybyszewskis was decorated with flowers. The whole company appeared on stage. The director Meyerhold solemnly conducted Przybyszewski, dressed in evening clothes, to the stage. One of the actors made a speech of welcome, full of flourishes and heartfelt warmth. Przybyszewski answered in Polish, after which the audience

Meyerhold's diagram for Przybyszewski's *The Snow*. Kherson, 1903

Meyerhold's plan for Chekhov's
The Cherry Orchard. Kherson,
1904

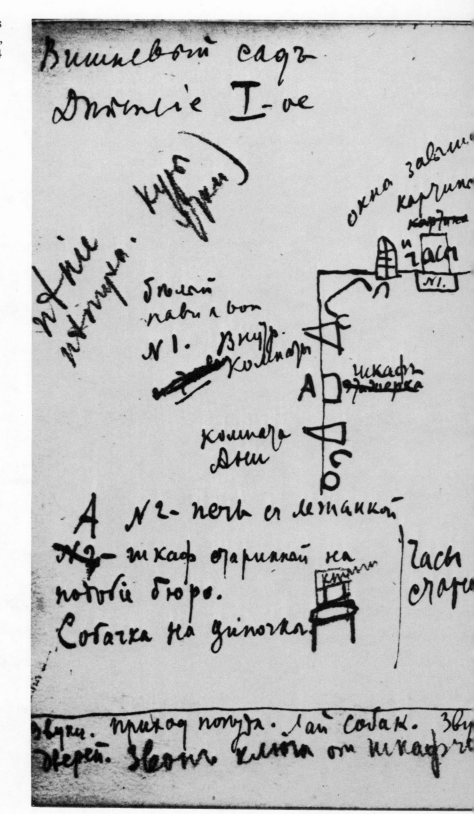

N1 — столъ съ гнутыми ножками (ходилъ въ Кипа)
картина вся задёрнута кисеей.

Желтая мебель изъ "Горе отъ ума".

настоящій русскій графинъ для кваса и квасъ настоящій

шкафъ съ книгами.

мертвой порталъ

буфетъ

Кисейная драпировка

драпри

простой столъ

столъ съ зеленымъ сукномъ

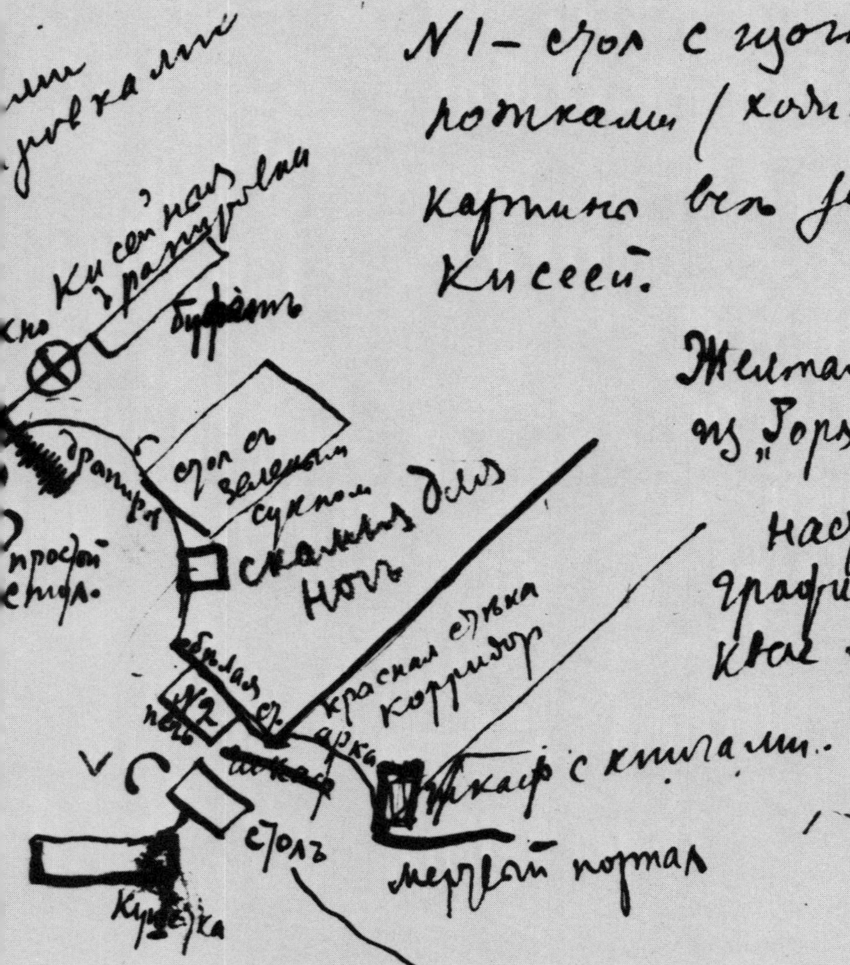

скамья для ногъ

красная ёлка

корридоръ

белая ск

N2

арка

качалка

столъ

Кушетка

(простой Олим...нихъ)

столъ покрытъ бархатной скатертью, высокая лампа съ абажуромъ.

...ществуется экипажей, бубенцы. Хлопанье
...пастухъ на свирели.

Meyerhold and the artist K. K. Kostin, Nikolaev, 1905

E. M. Munt (sister of Meyerhold's wife), actress in the
"Comrades of the New Drama," Nikolaev, 1905

E. Chirikov's *The Jews.* Sketch by the artist K. K. Kostin, Tbilisi, 1906

heartily applauded and presented him with several magnificent baskets of flowers." A. Remizov, who praised Meyerhold's production in *The Scales*, the Moscow Symbolist magazine, was delighted over the way in which the director had been able "to combine in tone, color and plastic image the symbolism of the play and its actual subject"; he solemnly commended E. M. Munt, the actress who played Bronka, "a pure, white snowflake, pressed against the green, fiery, live, merely slumbering winter crop," while he called Pevtsov in the part of Kazimir "an already transparent-blue ice block, carried off into the warm sea away from the polar storms." But the audience obviously did not appreciate this beauty; Remizov bitterly remarked that the audience "nastily wrinkled its narrow brow, and later laughed a lot."[25]

Another Symbolist production of Meyerhold, *Monna Vanna*, was also apparently not a success: "Maeterlinck's brilliant colors," one of the criticisms pointed out, "had lost color, faded, darkened..."[26]

Time and again Meyerhold was compelled to resolve complicated problems of staging by the most primitive means. From the stage properties ledger we know, for example, that for *The Lower Depths* the ladder from the properties for *Ivan the Terrible* was used, that even the modest room for Ibsen's *A Doll's House* was put together thus: "Get the triangular armchair from Munt's apartment. The door in the hall is covered with felt padding—couldn't we use the door from *Three Sisters*?... Ask Olga Mikhailovna [Meyerhold's wife—K. R.] for the Christmas tree decorations."

On the whole, the second Kherson season was less successful than the first, judging by the few press reports. "Having set itself the goal of acquainting the public with innovations in dramatic literature, the company doesn't take such pains any more with their artistic realization,"[27] wrote one correspondent. "The productions are all marked by haste and carelessness; it has become the usual thing for the actors not to know their lines,"[28] remarked another.

The truth was that the few critics in Kherson at the height of that season came into conflict with the director and for that reason their judgments are not altogether trustworthy.*

Still, there is no doubt that this first, and also half-hearted, attempt by Meyerhold to devote himself to "transcendent" Symbolist productions, undertaken under conditions of a provincial theater, would fail to meet with success or recognition. Meyerhold was tentatively feeling out new ways and, for the time being, without any confidence. This was especially noticeable in his production of *The Cherry Orchard*.

The Cherry Orchard was staged in Kherson almost simultaneously with the opening of the same play at the Art Theater, and as Pevtsov bears witness, "without

---

*This magazine *Theater and Art* reported from Kherson: "The regional newspaper *The South* published the following communication from the editor: 'The manager of the municipal theater, V. E. Meyerhold, who has been displeased with the criticism by *The South* of his conduct of the theater enterprise during this season, has allowed himself a completely incorrect and offensive outburst relative to this journal. In consequence, the editor of *The South* considers it unavoidable henceforth to ignore the productions of Mr. Meyerhold's company, that is not to print either announcements or reviews of them.'" The magazine added that in its opinion *The South* blamed Meyerhold for "his tendency to squeeze out a profit," as a result of which "the manager had chased representatives from the editorial board of *The South* out of the theater." [*Theater and Art* 3 (1904), 60]

any sharing of ideas with the Art Theater. Meyerhold did not even see their production, and the play was sent directly to us in Kherson in manuscript form by the author, who was a friend of Meyerhold's."[29] Meyerhold did not know the important changes in the text which Chekhov made at the request of the Art Theater and did not take them into account; the play was acted in its first variant.

Later, in the spring of 1904, Meyerhold saw the Moscow production and remarked in a letter to Chekhov: "I did not quite like the way the play was staged in Moscow. In general." He went on to explain his conception of *The Cherry Orchard* to Chekhov (for whom, as of course he knew, the Moscow Art Theater staging also went against the grain). He wrote:

> Your play is abstract, like a symphony by Tchaikovsky. And the director should apprehend it above all by ear. In the third act, at the dull "thud of feet"—it is just this "thud" one must hear—horror appears, imperceptible to those present.
> "The cherry orchard has been sold." They are dancing. "Sold." They are dancing. And so on till the end. When you read the play, the third act makes the same impression as the ringing in the ears of the sick man in your story "Typhus." Some kind of nagging sound. Merriment in which the sounds of death are heard. There is something of Maeterlinck, something terrifying in this act. I have used the comparison only because I am unable to express it exactly. You are incomparable in the greatness of your work. When one reads foreign writers, one is aware of your unique originality. The West is going to have to learn drama from you.
> At the Art Theater, the third act does not make such an impression. The background has little substance and at the same time, little distance. In the foreground the business with the billiard cue, the magic tricks. Separate. It does not all come together with the continued "thud." And then in the meantime all this "dancing": people are carefree and there is no sense of misfortune. The tempo of this act is slowed down too much at the Art Theater. They tried to create boredom. That is wrong. You have to show a carefree mood. That makes a difference. Carefree gaiety is more active. Then the tragic quality of the act is more concentrated.[30]

This is a very interesting letter. It shows Meyerhold's great perceptiveness in sensing even then the exemplary greatness of Chekhov's work for literature and the theater, from which "the West is going to have to learn." In the solution of just one act—that is, the third act—of the play, a quite unusual solution, in its way, one of genius, as never done anywhere by anyone else, one senses the maturity of an absolutely original talent for directing. On the other hand, of course, it can be seen how much this interpretation depends on Maeterlinck, whose name was incautiously (though also with reservations) mentioned by Meyerhold. Enthusiasm for Maeterlinck, whose *The Intruder* and *Monna Vanna* Meyerhold managed to stage in Kherson, was general at that time; it is perceptible too in Meyerhold's understanding of Chekhov's play.

Though Meyerhold explained to Chekhov his notions of how *The Cherry Orchard* should be staged, he was not guided by them in his own Kherson production, which he had put on three months before. One review which disapprovingly and briefly characterized the production said that Meyerhold made it "some kind of ordinary play with vaudeville lackeys, chambermaid, and governess," and with the nonsensical character of the student Petya, who for some reason pronounced his 'Hail to the new life' with such a nuance of inane comedy that the audience laughed.* Lopakhin was transformed into a stupid peasant's son like a horse without a bridle, which was the last straw in the distortion of the play and made it meaningless. The only interesting figure in it was Firs, played by Mr. Pevtsov."[31] From this review, and also from Pevtsov's account of how he acted Firs, it is clear that the production realized by Meyerhold had in all actuality not even a nuance of Maeterlinck. This is to be explained apparently not by the fact that Meyerhold as an artist who loved and understood Chekhov suppressed his own inclinations (for he had decided without hesitation to propose his own reading of Chekhov's play), but rather that for the time being he imagined and conceived with greater assurance than he carried out.

The relations of the New Drama Association with its Kherson audience worsened. It was a rare play that they were able to bill two or three times. Only *A Midsummer Night's Dream* ran for seven performances, and this was a record in its way.

Meyerhold was aware of the corrupting influence of the small-town milieu on his actors. His gloomy thoughts about this have been preserved in his diary of those years:

> How much and how often actors are accused of living low, decadent, Bohemian, false, dishonest lives, made up of intrigues and mean tricks. Why blame the actors for that? These attacks on actors are unjust. It is true, their milieu is terrible, but actors are not to blame for that.
> There is not a single social institution possessing so many unnecessary elements as the theater. Shady characters who have nothing in common with art are always circulating around the stage. These are people trying to fish in troubled waters. The dregs of life are found around the stage hoping to make some easy money... These shady characters poison the offstage atmosphere of the theaters.[32]

Meyerhold hoped that a different, healthy atmosphere might be found around the theater in a big city and that his new efforts would be more cordially received by a more cultivated audience. The New Drama Association spent the 1904-05 season in Tbilisi, a city with a long and rich theater tradition and many cultured people, where Meyerhold might justifiably count on serious connoisseurs of art and more qualified critics.

He opened the season, as in Kherson, with *The Three Sisters*, thereby alluding again to the kinship of the Association with the Moscow Art Theater. In addition, he produced: *The Sea Gull, Uncle Vanya, The Cherry Orchard*, by Chekhov; *The Lower Depths* and *Summer Folk* by Gorky; Alexei Tolstoi's *The Death of Ivan the Terrible*; Shakespeare's *A Midsummer Night's Dream* and *The Merchant of Venice*; *Ghosts* and *An Enemy of the People*, by Ibsen; *The Sunken Bell, Reconciliation, Schluck and Jau, Rose Bernd* and *Colleague Crampton*, by Hauptmann; Schnitzler's *Director of a Puppet Theater*; Hofmannsthal's *The Woman in the Window*; Strindberg's *Father*; *The Destruction of Sodom, The Homeland* and *St. John's Fires*,

---

*Meyerhold himself played Petya Trofimov; later in Tbilisi he took the part of Gaev.

by Sudermann; *The Good Hope*, by Heijermans; *Vanyushin's Children*, by Naidenov; *The Snow*, by Przybyszewski; *The Torrent of Spring*, by Kosorotov; and Schönthan's *Acrobats*. Thus the Association decided to keep the principles of play selection set up in Kherson. The new troupe at once caught the attention of the Tbilisi audience. The critics remarked right from the start of the season a series of innovations taken from the Art Theater: the abrogation of "benefits" and the request not to enter the auditorium and not to applaud in the middle of an act (Meyerhold had already introduced all these rules in Kherson). In the new building of the Tbilisi artists' club, built only a few years before, the stage was excellently equipped for those times with a revolving circle and a mechanism which permitted separate parts of the stage to be raised and lowered. In addition, Meyerhold arranged for a curtain like that at the Art Theater: dark green in color, it parted in the middle rather than being raised.

The *Three Sisters* was an unquestionable success. The critic of the *Tbilisi Gazette* noted especially the unusual daring of the production: the characters "sat down, took their places on stage not always facing the audience, but with their backs to it, that is, with their backs to that wall which is supposedly removed so as to allow the audience to see what goes on in the room."[33] Another critic also remarked "the kinship with the Moscow Art Theater," which in his opinion made itself felt above all "in the arrangement of the curtain (parted in the middle rather than being raised) and in the striking of a gong rather than a buzzer."[34] The gong, by the way, was Meyerhold's own invention; the Art Theater was satisfied with an electric buzzer.

In Tbilisi Meyerhold completed his schooling in "applied directing." He was able to carry out in practice, as much as was possible in the provinces, the basic innovative principles of the Art Theater. He created a provincial theater at an unheard-of level of culture, and one which possessed a progressive repertory. "The plays are rehearsed and produced under his direction in an exemplary fashion," wrote the correspondent of the journal *Theatrical Russia*. "The troupe too is composed, on the whole, of capable actors. Miss Munt, in ingenue roles, and Messrs. Meyerhold and Zagarov particularly distinguish themselves by their talented acting."[35]

Though the Tbilisi critics also reproached Meyerhold for "unsubtle, insistent realism," for superfluous "Meiningenism,"[36] and pointed out the "slavish imitation" of the Chekhov plays produced by Meyerhold, all the same it was the Chekhov plays and *The Death of Ivan the Terrible*, also staged in the Moscow Art Theater manner, which were the greatest, undoubted successes in Tbilisi. One critic wrote, of *Ivan*: "It would be hard to give a picture of this dark time which is more sustained in style. Tatar cruelty breathed from the stage. The whole background of the tragedy was carried through colorfully in just the right tones. And against this background the figure of Ivan, as acted by Mr. Meyerhold, was delineated down to the smallest details. Of all the parts acted thus far by Mr. Meyerhold, Ivan is indisputably the best."[37] *The Death of Ivan the Terrible* ran for five performances and was sold out the first two times.

The successful production of *The Lower Depths*, in which Meyerhold himself played the part of the baron and Pevtsov played the actor, was also noted.

But Meyerhold was no longer content with success achieved in plays from the repertory of the Moscow Art Theater and with methods borrowed from Moscow Art Theater directors. As he had in Kherson, he now tried some new methods and put surprises he had prepared long ago before the more intelligent and sophisticated Tbilisi audience. One such surprise was a rather luxurious production of Shakespeare's *A Midsummer Night's Dream*; another was to be *The Snow*, by Przybyszewski, which in principle was of greater significance.

A Midsummer Night's Dream was received with approval by the Tbilisi newspapers. The critic of *The Caucasus* remarked that Meyerhold's work "showed great labor, subtle taste and exceptional directorial imagination. A happy idea—that of accompanying the play with the Mendelssohn music written for it—increased the esthetic impression."[38] The newspaper *Tbilisi Gazette* also stated that the play had been staged very well, and with great care.[39]

The production of *The Snow* met with a much stormier reaction. There was an audience protest, the first of many protests Meyerhold was to experience. "*The Snow*, by Przybyszewski, as produced by Meyerhold," *Theater and Art* wrote, "was completely unsuccessful. The audience hissed. At the end of the performance a considerable number of the audience remained seated, expecting something more. Things almost came to the point of an announcement from the stage that it was time to go home, ladies and gentlemen, the play was over!... The management preferred to dispatch ushers, who went from row to row assuring people that this was all, whereupon the audience began to leave."[40]

Almost no information has been preserved on just how *The Snow* was staged in Tbilisi. All that is known is that all three acts began in deep darkness and that the actors rehearsed the play "with loving care," but "they did not put enough into the roles, or rather, they overacted. They all overdid the informality and simplicity of tone and did not project the intent, which remained behind the scenes, lost in the soft rugs of Bronka's house. The failure of the play was ascribed to the noisy, youthful audience."[41]

On re-reading today this forgotten play by Stanisław Przybyszewski, one comes to the conclusion that neither the Kherson nor the Tbilisi audience deserved the reproaches of Meyerhold and his sympathizers among the critics. Thirty years later Meyerhold said, "My Symbolism was born of longing for an art of large generalizations."[42] This judgment, for all its simplification, proves true: it rightly points to the main line of his development without dwelling on particular productions and passing over many divergences. As one of these divergences, *The Snow* stands at the start of the long road of Meyerhold's Symbolist searchings, a play outwardly impressive, deceptively complicated, but actually pretentious and empty. Out of the banal situation of the love triangle, framed in a milieu just as banal, the author has tried to abstract some kind of symbol of fateful predestination, an insuperable passion, to which ordinary earthly love must yield. But Eva, who personifies the fatal passion which destroys the family of Tadeusz and Bronka, is all too close to the familiar figure of the "femme fatale," "the vamp" from a run-of-the-mill melodrama. There is no serious support here for an art of large generalizations, for symbols incorporating significant ideas. The play deceived Meyerhold with its fashionable, slightly mysterious surface and the indistinct somnambulism of its speeches, as it deceived many in those years.

On the other hand, Schönthan's *Acrobats* made a noteworthy impression on the audience in Tbilisi. The correspondent of the magazine *Theater and Art* reported that Meyerhold had found, "if not the big hit of the season, at least a hit. I am talking about *Acrobats,* a play which suits the taste and the level of the Tbilisi audience."[43]

While Meyerhold was thus now depressing, now delighting spectators in Tbilisi, the town council of Kherson was weighing the question of whether to invite him back. Various opinions were aired. Some voices were raised enthusiastically in Meyerhold's favor. It was announced that Kherson townspeople had sent Meyerhold a petition with five hundred signatures urging his return. Other speakers emphatically declared Meyerhold's troupe had "bored the Kherson audience" with its whining and "could please only refined decadents. Town councilor Popov then concluded that sensitive persons could derive the same experience from a psychiatric ward as from the acting of the Meyerhold company..."[44]

Neither his success with the Tbilisi audience nor the debate in the Kherson town council interested Meyerhold any longer. Great changes in destiny lay ahead. A new encounter with Konstantin Stanislavsky predetermined this.

THE STUDIO ON POVARSKAYA STREET

In his book *My Life in Art* Konstantin Stanislavsky himself has told the story of his new encounter with Meyerhold, an encounter destined to make great changes in the art of the Russian stage.

Stanislavsky began to sense, as he himself put it, acute dissatisfaction with his achievement. Vague dreams of a new theater haunted him. His reflections on Vrubel, Maeterlinck, Ibsen and Chalyapin led him to conclude that the time had come when "innovation as such is justified. The new for the sake of the new." He began to think about those forms of art which would make it possible to project "sublime feelings, melancholy at the state of the world [*Weltschmerz*], a sense of the mysteries of existence, the eternal."[1]

In short, Stanislavsky in Moscow, like Meyerhold in Kherson, was thinking about Symbolism. Indeed the other director of the Art Theater, Vladimir Nemirovich-Danchenko, also saw in Symbolism alone at this time the means of salvation for the Moscow Art Theater and the "new tone" essential to the theater.

Nemirovich-Danchenko wrote Stanislavsky in June 1905, no longer about a dead end, but about the "extinction" which threatened the Art Theater. "Extinction threatens our theater, as I see it, not because we lack new talent but because our older members do not want to rise above the level of portraying everyday life... I take this occasion," he went on, "to express to you my conviction, which has grown within me during the last two years, that without bright, truly poetic images the theater is doomed to death. Chekhov's sweet, quietly lyrical people are no longer alive."[2]

In this remarkable letter there is no indication (except the single epithet "poetic") of what is to characterize the "new tone" needed, according to Nemirovich-Danchenko, to save the Moscow Art Theater from its "extinction" and "death." True, even the word "poetic" was strong enough and undoubtedly new to his vocabulary. The repertory, though, which was called upon to express the new tone, shows very clearly that Vladimir Nemirovich-Danchenko meant to turn decisively toward Symbolism: Ibsen's *The Lady from the Sea*, d'Annunzio's *La Gioconda*, Maeterlinck, Przybyszewski.

Let us try to explain what called forth Nemirovich-Danchenko's sudden revulsion against "boring naturalism,"[3] his hostility toward "the most true-to-life actors," his certainty that "Chekhov's people are no longer alive." What was the source of Stanislavsky's anxiety at the theater's constant dependence on "the crudely real," his fear of staying forever among the "Peredvizhniki" [19th-century realists] of stage art?

The crisis apparently first made itself keenly felt in the Moscow Art Theater production of *The Power of Darkness* (November 1902) and still more distinctly in the production of *Julius Caesar* (October 1903). In both instances this amounted to a crisis of Naturalism—not in the odious sense of the term, as it is understood today, but in the best and highest sense, as it was established by Zola in prose and by Antoine in the theater. The word "naturalism" in Russian criticism at the beginning of the 20th century was by no means understood as a term of disparagement.

It meant simply closeness to nature, to truth and to true life. The naturalism of the early Moscow Art Theater was a historically progressive phenomenon. But in *The Power of Darkness* the naturalistic method degenerated into ethnographic historicism.

The same was true also of the production of *Julius Caesar*. The style became repetitious and heavy. It accumulated superfluous accessories, elaborate and unusual justifications. The production was felt to be archaistic and exotic. Stanislavsky said that in *Julius Caesar* the Moscow Art Theater "had started on a downward path and done a production worthy of the Maly Theater."[4] Both these failures (his own and Nemirovich-Danchenko's) Stanislavsky attributed to one and the same cause: the line of "intuition and feeling" had declined in *The Power of Darkness* into a depiction of everyday life, and in *Julius Caesar* into a depiction of everyday life in ancient times. In both cases, he wrote, "the inner intuition of our actors proved weaker than the outer show of production detail," the actors had insufficiently justified from within "the realism of outer production detail."[5] Why, though, had this happened? And why didn't it happen in the production of *The Lower Depths*?

Gorky's play *The Lower Depths* brought the Art Theater as close as possible to the social awakening which preceded the revolution of 1905. "Before *Depths*," wrote Nemirovich-Danchenko in 1903, "the theater was going to the dogs... *Depths* was a tremendous success. The theater at once rose to its deserved heights."[6]

However—and it is important to remember this—with the production of *The Lower Depths* the Art Theater reached the limit of the political radicalism within its grasp. The theater did not go further left than *Depths*, and could not until the October Revolution. Stanislavsky and Nemirovich-Danchenko simultaneously felt a confused and tormenting dissatisfaction. Nemirovich-Danchenko wrote in 1905 that *The Sea Gull* could now have only "the success of familiar melodies, the success of *La Traviata* on the day after *Prince Igor*."[7]

The "unfamiliar melodies" of Symbolism for this reason beckoned attractively. The flimsiness of Symbolist pretensions to bare all "the secrets of existence" had not yet been guessed at. Within the limits of a monograph it will not be possible to show in detail, with the necessary clarification of theory, why Symbolism was so alluring to many of the most creative talents of the Russian stage in those years: Stanislavsky, Nemirovich-Danchenko, Meyerhold, Komissarzhevskaya. Nevertheless, a few—inevitably superficial and approximate—reasons must be given.

Russian writers and artists regarded the future of Russia with alarm and bewilderment. The inexorable course it was taking, analyzed and foretold in Lenin's classic essay, "The Development of Capitalism in Russia," was completely incomprehensible to people unfamiliar with the laws of political economy and acquainted with Marxism only by hearsay. Almost all the Russian artistic intelligentsia was in just this position. Liberal views and scientific dilettantism inspired a belief in the possibility of "normal" European development for Russia, and seemingly promised, in the long run, one form or another of bourgeois democracy as a replacement for obsolete autocracy. Simultaneously, however, there was a presentiment of the impossibility of such a "normal" development for a country situated between two worlds—Europe and Asia. As early as 1866, Tyutchev had made a prophetic pronouncement that Russia was "a special case," that she was "incomprehensible to the mind alone," and "not measurable in standard terms." The whole question was what she was, what was her special case and what one should believe...

"The loss of a sense of the realities, estrangement from the depths of existence—this is the essence of our age; herein lies the crisis of our contemporary consciousness," Nikolai Berdyaev noted in 1906. "This loss is perceived in all the non-physical fields of contemporary life, philosophy, politics and art."[8]

A loss of contact with reality and a feeling of fear in the face of the future pervades almost all Russian poetry at the beginning of the century. Many could have echoed the famous words of Bryusov: "I do not see our reality. I do not know our century."

In the symbol, the image and the idea are related to each other in a complicated kind of tension. The meaning of a symbol cannot be expressed in a rational formula, nor can it be "abstracted" and deciphered from the image. Symbols are capable of several interpretations (unlike allegories, which always have but one rationally comprehensible meaning). And this confused depth of images=symbols inwardly accorded with the vagueness, uncertainty—and sense of crisis—characteristic of the Russian social and political situation at the beginning of the century.

Related to this situation was also the atmosphere of tense expectancy characteristic of Symbolist drama. Any genuinely Symbolist play was permeated with a presentiment of great events—threatening or joyous, but in any case fatefully inevitable. Such a presentiment might be colored with dark pessimism, as in the poetry of Sologub or Gippius, or it might also be luminous and proud, as in Balmont, Bryusov and Blok. The theme of the dawn of fateful but joyous changes to come undoubtedly entered into Russian Symbolist poetry as a reflection of the revolutionary movement.

From the point of view specifically of the theater, it is important to note that the individual opposed to the bourgeois milieu, proudly rejecting bourgeois norms, did not possess in Symbolist drama the freedom and independence essential for action. Partaking of the insoluble and incomprehensible mystery, the individual was a mystery too and tied or subordinated to certain exalted forces high above mankind. Very little was determined by human will and intention. If the individual's conduct was rudely determined in naturalistic drama and predestined by his environment, then Fate ruled man in Symbolist drama. Hence Symbolist drama was unavoidably and consistently characterized by a paradox: negation in a Symbolist play was equivalent to disbelief, protest emotionally close to despair, a longing for wholeness of soul was accompanied by a sense of dichotomy. All his life Blok tried to master and overcome this paradox. And the most consistent Russian producer of Symbolist plays, Meyerhold, grappled with this very paradox and in the end gave in.

Russian artists were unable at this time to comprehend and foretell the fate of Russia and saw only how suddenly that fate was reversed and changed. They perceived, as Boris Pasternak later expressed it, a quite puzzling "rebus in motion." There developed a situation extremely favorable to an art capable of expressing vague presentiments, alarming intuitions, but far removed from concreteness—either in daily life, psychology, social conditions or, above all, in politics. The ambiguity of the images inevitably resulted from this forced renunciation of everyday social reality.

Symbolism was transplanted to Russian soil as an art of expressing generalizations too intangible and immeasurably broad to correspond to the reality of political struggle. Only many years later, after the October Revolution, did Bryusov "sum up": "The Symbolists refused to serve merely practical purposes through literature and wanted to find a broader base and to express ideas equally valuable (as they thought) not just to one class of society, but rather to all mankind."[9] The vagueness of Maeterlinck, to whom the Russian theater was suddenly avidly attracted, quite suited the contradiction between the desire to find meaning in the world, life and fate—and the impossibility of finding the meaning of Russia. Russia was trying to solve such riddles for which the irreality of Symbolism—as the Russian intelligentsia saw it—was associatively suited.

On the other hand, the acuteness of the political struggle in Russia inevitably endowed the images of Symbolist art with a more or less definite ideological coloration and lent meaning to the symbols in the spirit of the social confrontations of the time. In the Russian situation Symbolism was being forcibly cultivated into a political activism alien to it in principle. Russian poets, prose writers, playwrights and directors more than once tried to reduce the ambiguity of Symbolism to this or that unambiguous meaning, to a political allusion or challenge. Such were exactly Meyerhold's original goals, as we shall soon see: he tried to adapt Symbolist drama to the Russian social situation: to activate it, to saturate it with concrete revolutionary content.

The first serious attempt to steer the new course was made not by Meyerhold, but by Konstantin Stanislavsky in 1904 when he staged a production of three little plays by Maeterlinck: *The Sightless, The Intruder* and *Interior*. The hopes he had for this production are evident in a letter he wrote to Nemirovich-Danchenko, in which he said in brief: "Maeterlinck strikes a new note in literature."[10] Work on the production proved unexpectedly difficult for Stanislavsky. "I have not yet found the right tone for Maeterlinck," he wrote his wife, "I cannot calm down and master my thoughts."[11] He tried, in particular, in a completely different Maeterlinckian way, to compose the mass scenes by having people freeze in statuesque poses, because, he wrote Nemirovich-Danchenko, he was "heartily tired" of the "realistic crowd."[12] Nevertheless, his efforts met with failure. As he wrote soon after the production opened, it was received "coldly or with hostility by the audience; nowadays bold phrases, liberal pathos and other such frivolous distractions are needed."[13] This was written on January 3, 1905. The failure, naturally, only increased the worries and doubts of Stanislavsky.

At this point Meyerhold appeared and at once Nemirovich-Danchenko, with disquiet and barely concealed jealousy, saw Stanislavsky "renewed," "as if he had *cast off his chains.*"[14]

Stanislavsky later recalled: "I had found the man I needed so much at that point in my period of searching. I resolved to help Meyerhold in his new projects, which, as I thought, coincided at many points with my own dreams."[15]

We do not have the exact date or concrete details of the talks between Stanislavsky and Meyerhold. Undoubtedly, though, they met in Moscow after the end of the season for the New Drama Association in Tbilisi, probably in March, after February 27, 1905, and before the opening of the Association's productions in Nikolaev in April of the same year. Apparently, many decisions were already made at the time of this first meeting. On April 10, 1905, Meyerhold sent Stanislavsky the text for "the introduction to the project" of a new theater.

On May 1, in the Nikolaev newspaper, a news item appeared that the theater company, the New Drama Association, had left for Moscow and that the "nucleus of the Association" would join the troupe organized by Meyerhold, the "branch of the Art Theater" in Moscow. It was further indicated that the repertory of this troupe would be "somewhat different from that presented until now at the Art Theater."

It should be mentioned that Stanislavsky dreamed at this time of preparing a whole series of companies capable of taking from Moscow to cities in the Russian provinces the principles of handling theatrical matters which had been approved by the Art Theater. As early as February, 1904, Stanislavsky had written "A Project for Organizing a Corporation of Provincial Theaters" which, as he conceived it, would serve to "bring order into the theater business in the provinces" and to "carry out in the provinces the artistic principles of the Moscow Art Theater."[16] As a start, the project envisioned the creation of three companies which would tour Russia, each with a repertoire of fifteen plays.

Apparently it was this idea which led to inviting Meyerhold, whose New Drama Association had already been in fact a kind of Tbilisi branch of the Moscow Art Theater. Though connected with the Art Theater neither formally nor organizationally, it was very close to it in repertory and methods of staging productions. In any case, in Meyerhold's long note entitled "Toward the New Dramatic Company Project at the Moscow Art Theater" we find, further developed and supplemented, the thoughts Stanislavsky had expressed in his plan for a corporation. But Meyerhold went beyond organizational questions. His note begins with an extended criticism of the provincial theater and proposals for renewing the provincial stage, in the course of which he clearly takes into account his own, by no means wholly successful, practical experience:

> Despite the great revitalizing influence the Moscow Art Theater has had on Russian drama in general, the provincial theaters have not given up their fondness for routine and still look askance at new forms of drama.
>
> Some provincial theaters which have only externally accepted the technical devices of the Moscow Art Theater's new directors, imitating them externally, have even done noticeable harm to drama. For by thus pouring new wine into old skins, these imitative theaters have undercut the faith of the naive provincial public in new art. As realized by imitator-artisans, the new art did not live up to the rumors of the beauty of a newborn theater.

Meyerhold went on cautiously to point out the chief task of the new troupe— to renew the art of the Art Theater itself.

"For the Art Theater itself, " he wrote, "the work of the new troupe, young, bubbling with newborn energy, will have the effect that all the mutual encouragement will help the theater return to a tone that will enable it to excite both audience and actors with its constant efforts to improve."

He continued, "The new theater must not be imitative. It must strive at all costs to develop clear individuality, since only individual art is beautiful."

Thus, the program conceived by Stanislavsky in 1904 was changed and extended by Meyerhold, beginning with the latter's initial project: it contained not only the realization of the Moscow Art Theater's principles, but also their renewal, the rejection of imitation and the search for new paths. Meyerhold also suggested the goal of the search: "new means of representation for a new dramaturgy such as the theater has not had until now, a literature which has gone too far ahead, just as contemporary painting has gone far ahead in comparison with the technique of the stage and the actors."

After such preparatory "artillery strafing" there followed the decisive attack upon the Art Theater.

> The Moscow Art Theater's not wholly successful attempt to stage Maeterlinck (an interesting, significant phase in the life of that theater) is attributable not to the fact that the repertoire of Maeterlinck's plays is unsuited to the theater but to the fact that the Moscow Art Theater actors have become too accustomed to acting realistic drama and could not find a means by which to project the new mystic-symbolist plays on stage.
>
> This does not mean, however, that the theater lacks all sense of poetry and mysticism, though it perhaps does not have the vague imprecise impressionistic tones essential for the new drama, nor do the voices of actors trained in the realistic school ring with the mystery and softness of fairy-tale allusiveness.
>
> There have always been two artistic currents in the Moscow Art Theater: a subtle realism and lyricism (but does not the second, after all, really contain the beginnings of mysticism?). But because both realism and lyricism shading into mysticism or simply a great spirituality which engulfs the comedy of realism lie each on a different side on the scales of art, it often happens that the realistic side outweighs the other. Then the Moscow Art Theater, while reaching the highest summit of the subtly realistic representation of Life, nevertheless ceased for a time to be the *avant-garde* theater it alone has a right to be.
>
> The task of the new troupe is to help the Moscow Art Theater all it can not to lose its allure as just such an *avant-garde* theater, destined always to march shoulder to shoulder in the progressive *avant-garde* movement of contemporary "new" drama and painting, and never to allow drama and painting to get so markedly ahead of the technique of the stage and the actors.
>
> If the new company burns with the fanaticism of the quest for the poetry and mysticism of the new drama, emphasizing the subtle realism of the means for projecting realism discovered with the help of the Moscow Art Theater, if the new company works out a very strict discipline, not a boring, academic discipline, not a police discipline, but one such as is necessary for pioneers, such as the Masons had, if the new company can supply capable replacements for those who have left or are leaving the Moscow Art Theater, who can become both actors of the new type and, further, a source of flaming creative energy, if the new company can bring in a new wave of the creative impulse and catch up in it the somewhat hangdog oldsters of the Moscow Art Theater, a new era will set in, and the Moscow Art Theater will again become an *avant-garde* theater.[17]

As we see, Meyerhold was completely frank and sufficiently decisive in his criticism of the Art Theater. But as far as his positive program is concerned, everything remained quite vague.

More often than not, Meyerhold did not succeed in completely realizing even his own discoveries, and he therefore preferred and felt more secure discussing questions of technique and form rather than of the essence and meaning of his innovative experiments, especially in his prerevolutionary work. His intuition had long since outrun his theory. So too in this note an energetic desire for renewal is replaced by listless, indistinct patter as soon as the subject turns to the "embryo of mystic principles."

Meyerhold's appearance at the Art Theater after an interval of three years provoked general excitement. This was not surprising. Though Symbolist poetry since the time of Verlaine and Mallarmé had already won wide recognition, though the plays of Ibsen, Hauptmann and Maeterlinck had entered the repertory of many theaters of Europe, experiments in staging a Symbolist play and the search for its proper form were still just beginning. No one had worked out a complete and logical system for Symbolist theater. The comparatively timid Paris experiments of Paul Faure and the daring, uncompromising creations of Gordon Craig in England were known to almost no one; Meyerhold knew almost nothing of them. The ideas for the theater of Appia and Fuchs existed as yet only in the form of energetic declarations and interesting sketches. Craig in his work was always powerfully attracted to Shakespeare; Appia dreamed of staging Wagner; in his Munich theater Fuchs was preparing to produce Goethe's *Faust*. Innovators in the theater showed little interest in contemporary Symbolist drama and its new works.

In 1905, when the studio on Povarskaya Street was founded, ways of putting Symbolist drama on stage had not yet been defined or tried out. Thus, Meyerhold could not have a clear, positive program. However, he had conceived a broad program of experiments and he was ready to risk failure and scandal, passionately resolved to take chances and to venture unhesitatingly into the unknown, trusting his intuition rather than theoretical conclusions. The things others had only begun to think about he succeeded in doing; he tried now this, now that and swiftly transformed his fantasies into the unexpected reality of a production. So in his presence there always arose an electric atmosphere of danger and great expectations.

In a June 1905 letter to Stanislavsky, Nemirovich-Danchenko gave his version of Meyerhold's return to the fold of the Moscow Art Theater. "At my first meeting with Meyerhold," he wrote, "I spoke of the necessity for a new tone on stage. This gave him the impetus to offer his services." Judging by Nemirovich's letter, he, Nemirovich, opened Meyerhold's eyes, showed him the new way, after which Meyerhold shamelessly " . . . seemed to be suddenly almost an innovator, talked about new tones and new plays, as if no one before him had even thought of such. And you," Nemirovich reproachfully told Stanislavsky, "were so far removed from my artistic efforts (we did not even have the time to discuss them) that all this seemed new to you, and coming from outside, rather than from the crucible of our own theater."

Consequently, Nemirovich-Danchenko declared that the priority in searching for "a new tone and new plays" belonged to him. This declaration, it is true, was strongly contradicted both by Stanislavsky's early experiments with Maeterlinck and Meyerhold's Tbilisi experiments and, most importantly, by Nemirovich-Danchenko's own statement that he had wanted to find the new tone and demonstrate it by the production of a quite banal play by Peter Yartsev, *At the Monastery*, which failed and brought its director only "artistic dissatisfaction."

Disregarding the fruitless question of priority, let us note all the same that even Nemirovich-Danchenko, in his discussion of the need for a new tone on stage, chose not just anyone, but Meyerhold specifically. Later, however, after Meyerhold began to work with Stanislavsky, Nemirovich-Danchenko broke with Meyerhold. Most probably it was Meyerhold he had in mind when he wrote Stanislavsky in June 1905: " . . . there is an example—I do not want to name names—when a person deliberately poisons relationships. I am beginning to think that this person finds it to his advantage that we should not be too close. Whenever there has been closeness and trust between us, he has always been the loser."[18]

Stanislavsky objected drily and firmly that he did not wish to "analyze what kind of person Meyerhold was, whether great or small, sly or straightforward... I need him because he is a tremendous worker."[19]

At this time Stanislavsky and Meyerhold began their new work with enormous enthusiasm. Their ideas, Stanislavsky recalled, "required preparatory laboratory work. There was no place for it in a theater with daily performances, complicated obligations and strictly calculated budget. A special place was needed which Vsevolod Emilevich aptly named 'a theater studio.' This was not a finished theater and not a school for beginners, but a laboratory for the experiments of more or less experienced actors."[20]

The word "studio" had been discovered; it became part of Russian theater art for a long time. Stanislavsky rented for the studio the place of the former Nemchinov theater in the Girsh house on the corner of Povarskaya Street, now Vorovsky Street, and Merzlyakovsky Lane. The auditorium had about 700 seats.

The studio was equipped with taste and elegance, as if competing by the very decoration of its blue and white lobby with the ostentatiously modest gray and swamp-green auditorium of the Art Theater.

The first meeting of members of the "Theater Studio" took place on May 5, 1905. Meyerhold, Stanislavsky, and Savva Mamontov spoke. Characteristically, Meyerhold said almost nothing about the program of the studio; he mentioned only questions of organization in his speech. On the other hand, Stanislavsky's speech presented a "program," in the full sense of the word.

Directly connecting the need to seek new forms in art with the changes in the social life of the country, Stanislavsky said:

At a time of social unrest like the present the theater cannot and does not have the right to serve pure art alone—it must respond to social moods, clarify them for the public, become a teacher of society. Mindful of its high social obligation, this "young" theater must at the same time strive to carry out its chief task, the renewal of dramatic art by means of new forms and methods of stage representation. Just what shape this new art will take and what will be the technique of the new drama it is impossible to say as yet, but to move forward—this is the motto of this "young" theater, to find together with new currents in dramatic literature correspondingly new forms of dramatic art—this is its task.[21]

Later, the opinion was repeated more than once that Meyerhold did not heed Stanislavsky's words about the theater's not having "the right to serve pure art alone," but having to "respond to social moods, clarify them for the public, become a teacher of society." The notes to *My Life in Art* state that this idea of Stanislavsky's was, so to speak, "distorted by Meyerhold and as a result, the Studio on Povarskaya Street was transformed into a laboratory of formalist experiments."[22] Still more often these words of Stanislavsky's are lost sight of in the analysis of Povarskaya Street experiments and are regarded as an empty declaration unrelated to the essence of the undertaking. However, Stanislavsky's thoughts about the high social mission of the new theater were not empty phrases either for him or for Meyerhold.

And not only the external, formal side of the Studio's activity is of interest to the historian.

The credo of the new studio, in Stanislavsky's words,

came to this, that realism, the depiction of everyday life, had outlived its time. The time had come for the unreal on stage... One must show not life as it flows by in reality, but as we dimly perceive it in our dreams, visions, moments of elevated feeling. This is a spiritual state and it must be conveyed in the theater, just as painters of the new school show it in their canvases, musicians of the new trend in their music and the new poets in their verse. The works of these painters, musicians, poets have no clear outlines, definite finished melodies, clearly expressed ideas. The strength of the new art lies in the combination and pairing of colors, lines, musical notes, in the harmony of words. They create overall moods unconsciously affecting their audience. They convey allusions which cause the spectator himself to create through his own imagination.

Stanislavsky specifically emphasized that he was at one with Meyerhold on these important programmatic positions. "Basically, we did not differ and were looking for what had been found by the other arts but thus far had been inapplicable to ours."

The program of Stanislavsky and Meyerhold envisaged the establishment of Symbolism in the theater.

An appropriate repertoire was selected. Plays by Ibsen, Hauptmann, Maeterlinck, Verhaeren, Przybyszewski, Hamsun, Hofmannsthal, Strindberg, Bryusov, and Vyacheslav Ivanov were to be produced. *The Death of Tintagiles*, by Maeterlinck, *Schluck and Jau*, by Hauptmann, and *Love's Comedy*, by Ibsen, were chosen first.

While they were preparing the hall in Moscow, on Povarskaya Street, and Stanislavsky was taking his vacation in Essentuki, Meyerhold began rehearsals with the members of the Studio in the village of Pushkino near Moscow, in the same place where, before its opening, the Moscow Art Theater had rehearsed *Tsar Fyodor*. Stanislavsky felt it necessary "to give the young people full independence."[23] And Meyerhold made full use of this freedom, but he sent Stanislavsky special reports in letters—concerning everything he did and how it was done.

In a report that has been preserved in the papers of the composer Ilya Satz, Meyerhold made the curious remark that the plays of Maeterlinck, particularly *The Death of Tintagiles*, should arouse in the audience "a quivering astonishment at what is, a religious veneration and acceptance."[24] Meyerhold later went on repeating this same thought for some time in slightly different words; it caused him to be reproached for preaching social passivity and the renunciation of the social struggle.

The nucleus of Meyerhold's thinking in these years was different: he wanted to "inject" the abstract imagery of Symbolism by the most energetic means into the reality of the Russian social struggle. To discover, in abstract, "transcendental" images the possibility of direct contact with life and the "explosive" impulses to move it. In plays by Ibsen, Hauptmann, Maeterlinck—above all, by Maeterlinck—he sought the "dynamite" which was "instantaneously" to destroy the old world.

Meyerhold tried to stage Symbolist dramas so as to express the excitement bubbling in his soul. In the director's notebook for *The Death of Tintagiles*, which has been preserved (from the period of the Studio on Povarskaya Street), the text of a speech which Meyerhold intended to give before the opening is noted. This address to the audience fully reveals Meyerhold's intent.

"Just try, when you see the play, gracious ladies and gentlemen, to share Ygraine's indignation not at death, but at its cause, and the plain symbol of the play will develop into one of the problems of socialism."[25]

This first draft is still laconic. But here it takes on greater development:

> The queen who is talked about so much in the play is the symbol of Death. But the symbol may be enlarged in size. Try when you see the play to share Ygraine's indignation not against death, but against its cause, and you will see not just a Symbolist play. Not death but the bearer of death will arouse your indignation. Then the island on which the action takes place becomes our life. The queen's castle represents our prisons and Tintagiles the youth of mankind, trusting, admirable, ideally pure. And someone ruthlessly puts these young people to death... On our island thousands of Tintagileses suffer in prisons.[26]

In this speech, never delivered quite in this form, things are named by name (Meyerhold did make the speech, in a somewhat changed form, at the opening of *The Death of Tintagiles* in Tbilisi). The island is "our life," the queen's castle "our prison," Tintagiles the embodiment of heroism and the pure idealism of champions of freedom, "thousands of Tintagileses suffer in prisons" and die. Our indignation must be directed against those responsible for their death. Quite naturally in the course of such considerations the word "socialism" occurs and Maeterlinck's play is seen as "not just a Symbolist play." At any rate, its "symbol" is realized and takes on the scope of all Russia.

Such were the ideas inspiring the production. Later, discussing in retrospect the "history and technique" of the theater, Meyerhold did not mention these ideas. With the close attention to form that was characteristic of his work at that time, he wrote that the work on *The Death of Tintagiles* had "inspired a method of placing figures on stage in bas-reliefs and frescoes and a means of expressing interior monologue with the help of the music of plastic motion, and provided the possibility of trying out in practice the force of mystical accentuation instead of the former logical accents and the like..."[27] These Meyerholdian experiments with form at the time of the Studio on Povarskaya Street are also extremely interesting, for they determined in many respects the temper of all Russian Symbolist theater.

Meyerhold's plan for Maeterlinck's *The Death of Tantagiles*, 1905

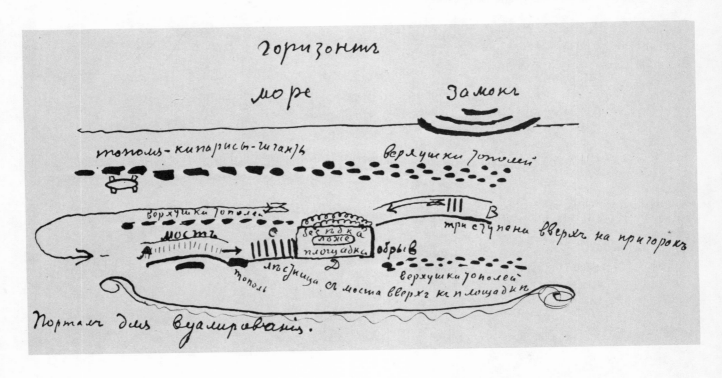

Sapunov and Sudeikin sketch for the costume of
Tantagiles in *The Death of Tantagiles*

Sapunov and Sudeikin sketch for the costume of
Agloval in *The Death of Tantagiles*, 1905

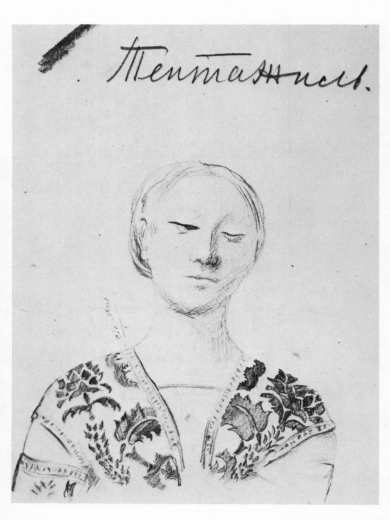

Sapunov and Sudeikin sketch for the servant's
costume in *The Death of Tantagiles*

Hauptmann's *Schluck und Jau*, set sketch by N. Ulyanov

But in analyzing the temper of this production and the new acting techniques invented by Meyerhold, we must not forget what ideas he tried to express, even if unsuccessfully.

The Studio on Povarskaya Street—both Meyerhold and Stanislavsky spoke of this more than once—was a laboratory theater, an experimental theater. The very notion of a studio, then introduced for the first time into theater language, meant that the new undertaking was launched without a finished program (which Stanislavsky and Nemirovich-Danchenko did have when the Moscow Art Theater was founded). Research, testing, and experimentation—this was the intention. A program still had to be sought, developed, discovered. What course and what direction the new enterprise would take no one knew definitely, not even Meyerhold himself.

But the first experiments were staged by Meyerhold. And they at once set him "at odds" with Stanislavsky. Meyerhold's creative consciousness and his work began to show a turn toward new stage forms of Symbolism in the brief period of the Studio on Povarskaya Street.

Essentially, the experiments undertaken by Meyerhold in the Studio on Povarskaya Street were an attempt to represent and embody *the relationship of the artist* to the world and reality rather than show "pictures of life" on stage or the direct representation of the external world.

Instead of objectivity (life itself), the subjective (a relationship to life) was emphasized.

The primacy of the subject over the object and the triumph of the subjective over the objective always ruled in the esthetics of Symbolist theater. Meyerhold set himself the goal of realizing in the material concreteness of figures on stage the logic of the *imaginary and not the observed world.*

In his work on *The Death of Tintagiles* Meyerhold at first gropingly and intuitively ventured into a territory of unknown new forms which harbored numerous surprises. This was a play about the helplessness of a person in the face of fate and death. Maeterlinck removed the person from his social ties and confronted him with a mysterious death. Such abstraction in mystifying symbolic form reproduced, however, the true reality of a time when the individual, the single "little man," found himself incapable of finding his way in the complicated contradictions of a society distorted and disordered by the development of bourgeois relationships. The theme of fate and death appeared as the symbol of the fatal incomprehensibility of social existence.

Meyerhold wanted to give Maeterlinck's Symbolism concrete Russian context. He wanted to use the sad fairy tale of the doomed child Tintagiles and the relentless, repulsive queen signifying Death to get to the heart of contemporary Russian life, its misery, its prisons and deaths. But such an aim by no means freed Meyerhold from the necessity of finding the new means of expression dictated by the Symbolist form of the drama. On the contrary, it obliged him to seek new forms. Meyerhold was inspired by this necessity. For Meyerhold the task consisted in finding stage forms adequate to Maeterlinck's Symbolist poetry and, consequently, forms of Symbolist theater as such.

In this sense Maeterlinck was, so to speak, the most "principled" author of all. If the Symbolist motifs in many plays by Ibsen or Hauptmann were comparatively easily deduced by directors from stage constructions that were realistic in form, derived from everyday indoor life, as it were, then Maeterlinck, subordinating fairy tale subjects to the dictates of internal forces, forcefully demanded the rejection of ordinary life, normal existence, normal conversation.

The last fact proved almost the most essential. All the enormous achievements of the Art Theater were in the sphere of the natural communication of people on stage, communication in which people reached mutual understanding and proximity, or confronted each other in conflict. This system, worked out with great refinement, proved for Maeterlinck on the one hand too rich and full and on the other, insufficiently defined.

The opposition to the monarchy characteristic of the Art Theater since the day of its founding and more or less deeply concealed in the subtext of all Moscow Art Theater productions appeared in *The Death of Tintagiles* in the form of an extended allegory; it came out of the subtext directly into the text but was hidden behind the veil of the fairy tale subject. This fairy tale was told "straight to the audience." It required forms of expression new to the theater, forms which would demonstrate not the community and conflict of people among themselves, but their common doom.

The search for such forms made essential not just ensemble acting, not just harmony, but absolute unison.

Meyerhold, who had very aggressively taken a stand at that time against those practices of the Art Theater which he considered outmoded, nevertheless took from these very same Art Theater practices the most important elements of the new form, the same form which he juxtaposed to the Art Theater's "naturalism."

The Art Theater had brought forth the famous pauses whose silence told the audience more about the characters than did their words.

In the Art Theater, specifically in its productions of Chekhov, the expressive uncompleted utterances, the unfinished or meaningless words—which, however, meant so much—were heard for the first time.

In other words, Chekhov prepared and opened up for Meyerhold the way to Maeterlinck. The Chekhovian form of drama with hidden, internal dynamics peculiar to it, with the "underwater current" of its action (which was given the name of "subtext" in the Art Theater), with its long pauses saturated with important content, with the polyphonic development of its several motifs, was related in many ways to the form of the Maeterlinckian drama. Meyerhold approached Maeterlinck after having been permeated by the musicality of Chekhovian drama, its atmosphere and "mood," its incomplete statements.

Maeterlinck maintained that the words actually spoken have meaning thanks only to the silence surrounding them. The words arise from the silence of the pauses, are born in their quiet.

For this reason, when rehearsing Maeterlinck, Meyerhold made a fetish of the pause, set up the incomplete utterance as a principle and used its intonation as the basis of the whole speech structure of his production.

This was the easiest way to express the Symbolist alienation of the characters, their complete independence of each other, their participation in the general monotony. The internal connections in the dialogue were broken apart and it was turned in essence into a single monologue.

This method is most clearly demonstrated in Meyerhold's director's notebook for the fourth act of *The Death of Tintagiles*. According to the text, three women servants speak at one point. Meyerhold writes with the striking simplicity of genius: "They all speak simultaneously so that each servant's part is the text of the whole act or that part of it where the servants speak. Only from time to time is one of the voices raised above the others. That is, each of the servants speaks the words of *her* part louder."[28]

That is, for the first time in the practice of the theater Meyerhold directly transformed the disjointed dialogue of three characters into a complete single monologue spoken as a chorus ("simultaneously"), differentiating what belongs to each character in this common monologue only by a slight increase in volume. Individual differences were unimportant and almost disappeared. What was shared resounded powerfully, spoken by three voices.

To whom were these voices addressed? With whom, after all, did the characters of this play share? Clearly not with each other. Clearly too, they were not speaking to themselves and not simply "to the audience," as an actor usually does in a monologue. They shared with something standing outside human beings, above them. Cutting themselves off from real life—both on the stage and beyond it—they spoke to fate, to some force which stood above people. The audience, however, did not remain unmoved by these words carried up to heaven from the boards of the stage. According to Meyerhold's intent, the audience was supposed to be caught up in the atmosphere created on stage. The director intended that this atmosphere should flow to the audience throughout the theater, seizing them with its disquieting vibrations, arousing in them unclear hopes and a vague excitement. In this almost prayerful excitement he saw the possibility of moving people, moving their spirits. Such action could not possess the clarity of a concrete challenge; it by no means contained emotional, "infectious" excitement or the spell of political pathos. Meyerhold did not intend this. Interpreting Maeterlinck's fairy tale as direct political allegory, insisting on its closeness to the Russian reality of those years, he clothed this allegory in a primitive, ecstatic form. At that time he viewed the theater as a cathedral of sorts in which actors were the priests and sacristans and the audience the believers. Hence Meyerhold's long discussions of those years about the actor who must "take fire in the ecstasy of creativity in full view of everyone," "show forth the sacred ceremony in creative work,"[29] and so on.

But all these phrases essentially tell us nothing about the concrete form of the production Meyerhold created. Much more illuminating in this sense is a brief note in which Meyerhold formulates as theses the basic principles of his production. On Theater Studio stationery, the director wrote:

> Maeterlinck.
> 1. Experience of the form, and not experience of single psychological emotions.
> 2. A smile for all.
> 3. Never tremolo.
> 4. Read the lines as if there were hidden in every phrase a profound belief in an all-powerful force.

5. Firmness of tone, since blurring will make it sound "moderne."
6. Motionless theater.
7. Do not drag out the ends of words. The sound should fall into a great depth. It should be clearly defined and not tremble in the air.
8. Like a piano. That is the reason for no vibration.
9. No speaking in a rapid patter. Epic calm.
10. Madonna-like movements.[30]

Of these ten points nine are addressed to the actors and only the one mentions "motionless theater," the director's main principle, on which production is based. All the directives to the actors with the exception of the first two and the last one concern the form of speech in the production. The attention paid to word sound predominates here. The sound score of the production was worked out by Meyerhold with extraordinary care.

The director also carefully prescribed such details of sound as "the rustle of the trees," "the howl of the storm," "the sound of the chain," "the screech of hinges," etc. But undoubtedly his chief concern was "the effort to achieve a rhythmic reading."[31] With his declaration of war against the tremolo, blurring, trembling and vibration of the sound and his attempt to achieve firmness of sound, clear definition and epic calm, Meyerhold abrogated the chief goal which the Art Theater had placed before its actors: the goal of psychologically characterizing a given character at a given moment.

The speech of an actor was no longer supposed to render concretely the psychological state of the person one was playing. The private, the personal, the individual, the immediate—the qualities that formed the essence of Art Theater technique —were declared not to merit attention. Meyerhold pushed to the fore the universal element: the tone, the resonance, the intonation for the whole production and all the actors, the rhythm of "reading" obligatory for all. These expressions—"to read," "a reading"—which Meyerhold suddenly used, and which were unthinkable for the Moscow Art Theater, were characteristic in the extreme. Just as characteristic was the example of the piano: the distinct, clear sound of the piano without vibration was to serve as the basic tone for the actors.

These propositions were later developed and supplemented by Meyerhold. Still, it is important to note that he first clearly formulated them at the time of his work on *The Death of Tintagiles*. At that time too the plastic forms of "motionless theater" were first discovered, which were so characteristic for the esthetics of Symbolist theater in general—especially the famous "bas-reliefs."

However, before discussing the plastic form of the acting in this production, let us look at its structure of space.

In the course of his work on *The Death of Tintagiles*, Meyerhold decided not to follow what had become the usual procedure at the Art Theater of building a preliminary model of the set. If we believe his own statement, this decision came about by chance simply because the young artists Nikolai Sapunov and Sergei Sudeikin, who had never worked in the theater before, did not know how to glue one together. Meyerhold always had a capacity for cutting the Gordian knot with one stroke of the sword. He gave instructions not to glue together any of the models and to let sketches of the sets suffice. "When we were turning the model around in our hands," Meyerhold wrote later, "we were turning contemporary theater around. We wanted to burn and stamp the models underfoot; by this we came close to stamping underfoot and burning the outmoded methods of naturalistic theater."[32]

It must be admitted that giving up the model and the long-accepted Moscow Art Theater principle of building the set after real life was unmistakably dictated by the play itself. "The new technique," Meyerhold recalled much later, "was predetermined by the dramatist. There were acts in *The Death of Tintagiles* which last for ten or twelve minutes on stage, the action taking place in a medieval castle. Yet in order to build the set of a castle you need an intermission twice as long as the act, which is absurd. You are forced to think up a 'stylized castle.'"[33]

Meyerhold decided to put on a five-act play with two intermissions; that is, to stage it in three acts. The set of *The Death of Tintagiles* was built by quite ordinary means: a painted backdrop (the horizon), a bridge, a hillock and a summer-house in the main stage area—all this was familiar enough long before the founding of the Moscow Art Theater. Nor was a tulle curtain any novelty; many opera productions had used them before. Giving up the model was a novelty and a challenging act of daring only on the terms of the Moscow Art Theater. The model workshop in that theater was Stanislavsky's pet. The artist Nikolai Ulyanov wrote: "Stanislavsky never looks at the model without a ruler in his hand. He measures everything, figures it all out, junks superfluous features, pulls things together."[34] By giving up models, as Meyerhold himself declared, he gave up "the exact reproduction of nature."[35] The model represented in miniature the future setup on stage. As E. Gunst wrote, "Sapunov and Sudeikin replaced the model by a rough sketch. This meant shifting the emphasis from the topography (that is, the disposition of doors, furniture, etc.) to the purely artistic side of the set... They themselves painted the set; therefore there was no need for especially detailed sketches."[36] Consequently Sapunov and Sudeikin (Sudeikin did Acts I-III, Sapunov Acts IV and V) proposed sets in which *color* was the prime feature, harmoniously organized *coloration*, the color scale. Meyerhold afterwards called this conception "the method of impressionistic plans," especially emphasizing the subtlety of coloration and "tricks of blocking with lighting effects."[37] After the Moscow Art Theater had featured the realistic talent of Viktor Simov, the Studio on Povarskaya Street attracted to the theater the young artists of the new wave, pupils of Konstantin Korovin. Instead of a meticulous presentation of everyday life and a natural, exact reproduction of life, these artists offered the principle of impressionism, mood, emotional effect by means of color, i.e., a purely artistic principle. In so doing, they did not reject reality: there on stage was the shore of the sea, a row of cypress trees, a castle, rooms in the castle, etc. But all the sets for *The Death of Tintagiles* were done in blue-green.

Ilya Satz's music was in harmony with this color system. The main thing was Meyerhold's (unsuccessful) attempt to achieve a rhythmic correspondence of the acting in harmony with the overall spatial and color conception of the production and its music. This was the beginning of "motionless theater," that is, a theater of slow, significant, profound motions, a theater in which the plastic form of the acting was intended to give not a plastic rendering of human motion in real life (as the

Moscow Art Theater tried to do), but the slow "music" of motion in harmony with the hidden spirit of the play. The plastic form was subordinated to the musical rhythm of the motion, not to its real-life logic. Sometimes, at especially significant moments of the action, the actors suddenly froze. At such moments, human faces and bodies became living statues. For the first time a director demanded of the actors sculptural expressiveness. So the living "bas-reliefs" came to be.

The director's notebook for *The Death of Tintagiles* reveals how this principle was realized. Judging by Meyerhold's planning sketch for the first act, the play was done behind a veil: the figures of the actors and the set were visible through a transparent tulle curtain; thus their outlines acquired indistinctness, mystery, unreality. At the back of the stage behind the row of "giant cypresses" a backdrop was visible, representing the sea and a dark castle on a cliff. (Later, however, Meyerhold brought the backdrop forward; a deep stage did not suit his basic directorial conception.) At stage left was a small bridge, in the center a summerhouse, at stage right a hill.

The first entrance of Tintagiles and his sister Ygraine was worked out in great detail by Meyerhold:

> Tintagiles enters downstage on the little hill B and Ygraine upstage. At the top of the hill Tintagiles pauses, kneels, and plucks a flower, a long-stemmed symmetrical lily growing at the top of the hill. Ygraine stands still. Bas-relief. Then they walk on in the direction of the arrow in the sketch. For a time they disappear from view. They are hidden by the little hill D. Then they come into sight again. This time from the left on the little bridge A, Ygraine ahead, Tintagiles behind. They pause. Tintagiles lowers his arms over the railing. (He holds the flower in his hands—and continues to do so the whole time.) Ygraine has stopped and looks at him. Pause. Then they speak.[38]

If we combine this score of action with the general requirement of "Madonna-like movements," which Meyerhold made binding for all the actors, then we have a clear picture of the plastic shape of the production. Stylized gestures, almost ritualistic. The director's indications are unusually exact with regard to the actors' poses. Meyerhold dictates literally every movement in advance.

"Ygraine walks in silence across the little wood C to the little hill D. Turning downstage from the couch with her back to the audience and turning her right shoulder, she sits down on the right edge of the seat. Lowering her head and extending her folded arms over her knees, she begins to speak." Then, he goes on, "the same pose as before. She throws back her head." With her next speech a new movement: "New bas-relief. Pressing her hands to her face (Madonna)," etc. All these exact and strict plastic directives are given for the stretch of only one monologue, Ygraine's first, and are accompanied by schematic but expressive sketches which again fix the *pose* of the actress. Further, to organize the next "bas-relief," Meyerhold remarks, "Now Tintagiles is busy with the flower. The whole following dialogue motionless."

The following notes are curious: "Until the bas-relief has been set up, do not begin to speak"; "bas-relief: nose to nose. The poses change. Cheek to cheek now"; "The whole scene without change of pose," etc.

Meyerhold's whole plastic score is carefully harmonized with the score of sounds, which only at times takes emotion into account. For example, he notes:

"Up to this point, Bellangere has spoken the whole preceding dialogue with a gradual crescendo of excitement. The words 'They will come here' are the high point of this crescendo. She cries out these words tonelessly. These words call forth an echo in the tower. (The echo is spoken by a chorus of serving maids.")[39]

Thus Meyerhold's direction in *The Death of Tintagiles* was primarily direction of "sound" and plastic form.

Vera Verigina, who took the part of Bellangère, recalling rehearsals of *The Death of Tintagiles*, wrote:

> The director banned, above all, the customary naturalistic wave of sound. He compelled us to "trace" straight lines and angles with our speech melodies and did not allow the least roundedness or glissando. Excitement, agitation, fear, grief, joy—all the emotions were projected by means of a cold clear sound—"drops falling to the bottom of a well." No muted or tremolo notes in the voice. Painstakingly, we achieved an inner rhythm and the pauses came as continuations of the dialogue. It was essential to keep that rhythm all the time so as not to be seized by personal emotion.
>
> The rehearsals of *The Death of Tintagiles* took place against a background of simple canvas—this showed to advantage the human figures and movements in the production. The plastic drawing acquired great importance. The movements were the accompaniment to the words and sometimes completed their statement or strengthened the impression they made, foretelling what was to come. Thus Bellangere's musical weeping was preceded by an emphatic gesture of the hands raised with the wrists bent backward. Her weeping was musical and so stylized that it recalled the sound of an instrument.[40]

Stanislavsky came to Pushkino and was shown *The Death of Tintagiles*, as well as scenes from other plays in preparation. "There was a great deal," he wrote later in *My Life in Art*, "which was interesting, new and unexpected. There was great inventiveness and the director's ideas showed talent. I watched a simple rehearsal with great interest and went away with a comfortable feeling."[41]

Verigina told how Nemirovich-Danchenko was also present at the runthrough, and "a lot of people came, actors of the Art Theater, Alexei Maximovich Gorky, Maria Andreeva and others. *The Death of Tintagiles* made a great impression on those present. Stanislavsky beamed. This true artist wholeheartedly rejoiced at the success of the young people. He rejoiced over the opening up of a new field as a scientist rejoices who has unselfishly given his strength and resources to a cause close to his heart." According to Verigina's evidence, Gorky was deeply moved: "The acting on the plane of stylized theater" excited him. "All the others were no less moved. I was told that Vladimir Ivanovich Nemirovich-Danchenko was among them."[42]

The last speculation of Verigina is doubtful: Nemirovich-Danchenko, as we shall see later, spoke very harshly about the productions of the theater studio. Stanislavsky wrote enthusiastically to S. A. Popov:

> I want to share at least on paper my good impressions. Yesterday gave me much joy. It was a great success. Unexpectedly, the whole company of the Art Theater assembled; unexpectedly, Gorky came, and Mamontov. So there was a meeting with the generals. *Schluck* made an excellent impression... *Tintagiles* was sensational. And I was happy for Vsevolod Emilevich... The

—68—

main thing: it became clear yesterday that "there is a troupe," or rather good material for one. This question has been tormenting me all summer, and yesterday my mind was set at rest. Yesterday the pessimists began to believe in the success of the Studio and conceded its first victory.[43]

In Stanislavsky's opinion only one of the three plays prepared under Meyerhold's direction was weak: Ibsen's *Love's Comedy*.

Stanislavsky also shared his impressions of that day with Maria Lilina [his actress-wife]: "They began with *Schluck and Jau*—fresh, young, inexperienced, original and charming... *The Death of Tintagiles*—sensational. It is so beautiful, new, exciting! The whole troupe sees you off at the station; Gorky is in great form and talks enchantingly."[44]

But a few months later, in October 1905, the dress rehearsal took place in the Studio on Povarskaya Street. Stanislavsky was disenchanted.

There were many reasons for this. Some are indicated in the memoirs of this same Verigina:

> *The Death of Tintagiles* production has suffered a misfortune. Rehearsals with the orchestra have not gone well. Satz has not fully caught the rhythm and intonation of the actors, perhaps because there was some uncertainty in them, but more probably because out of inexperience he overlooked them, expressing in the music his own understanding of Maeterlinck's play, as the designers too have done: the sets, so beautiful in themselves and suited to the play, have nevertheless not helped bring out the outline of the motion on stage.
>
> As long as the play was rehearsed against a plain canvas background, it made a strong impression because the outline of the gestures was sharply traced, but when the actors were seen against the background of the sets, the play suffered. The inexperience of the young designers has played a sad part in the production. Sudeikin has not mastered the lighting. Its wonderful green-blue tone changed the color, and drowned and blurred the figures of the characters; their hair and faces took on unexpected shades.[45]

Apparently Stanislavsky saw the same reasons for the failure of *Tintagiles*. S. A. Popov recalled that Stanislavsky told him on that very day:

> "Everything is not as it should be! True, it is a beautiful production, but we do not need it in its present form."
>
> "And how should it be, in your opinion?"
>
> "Simply, a light curtain should be used as a background and dark costumes like silhouettes against it—that is how the actors should play their parts."[46]

The artist Nikolai Ulyanov also recalled that dress rehearsal:

> Half-darkness on stage. Only people's silhouettes are visible. The set is flat, without wings, and hung almost at the front edge of the stage. This is new, and also new is the actors' rhythmic speech, as it is projected from the stage. Slowly the action develops; it seems as if time were standing still. Suddenly a shout from Stanislavsky: "Light!" A tremor is felt in the theater, noise, confusion. Sudeikin and Sapunov jump up from their places, objecting. Stanislavsky's voice: "The audience cannot take darkness on the stage for long, it goes against psychology, they must see the actors' faces!" Sudeikin and Sapunov: "But

the set is made for half-darkness, it loses all artistic meaning in the light!" Again there is silence, with only the beat of the actors' measured speech. But no sooner have they turned on the light than the whole set is ruined. The various elements disintegrate, the set and the figures fall apart. Stanislavsky stands up, the onlookers too. The rehearsal is interrupted, the production not approved.[47]

So Meyerhold apparently did not achieve his main purpose this time: he did not succeed in achieving harmony, combining in the plastic form of "motionless theater" the "impressionist plans" of the sets, the music of the diction and the musical accompaniment of the production into some kind of esthetic unity. At the time of the viewing in Pushkino when the play was given against a background of simple canvas and without music, this harmony was envisioned and expected, but at the time of the dress rehearsal—with sets and music—it did not come together, was not realized—contrary to expectation. It was as if the production separated into its constituent parts, and Meyerhold was not able to put it together again.

He soon realized this himself. In 1908 he wrote about *The Death of Tintagiles*: "This tragedy was rehearsed against a background of simple canvas and made a very strong impression because the outline of the gestures was sharply delineated. When the actors moved to a set in which there was space and air, the play was lost."[48] He recalled that during work on the play "the question of the lack of harmony among the creative artists was troubling. And if it was impossible to harmonize with the designer and the composer—each was naturally inclined in his own direction, each tried instinctively to keep his distance—I wanted to bring together at least author, director, and actor."[49]

We shall talk later about how matters stood with the actors, for here was the chief stumbling block for Meyerhold and especially for Stanislavsky. Meanwhile, let us only mention that misfortune also hit the second play—Hauptmann's *Schluck and Jau*—which Meyerhold showed on the same unhappy day of the dress rehearsal.

Meyerhold's director's notebook for this production has not been preserved. We know only from his own words that he planned to maintain the style of the "powdered wig" age and that the designer Nikolai Ulyanov had represented in the first tableau the grandiose gates of a palace, in the second a luxurious royal bed with a baldachin and in the third bosky summerhouses resembling baskets which stretched across the whole downstage area. In each summerhouse basket sat court ladies, all embroidering in unison a single broad ribbon with ivory needles. Meyerhold wrote:

> The backdrop represented a blue sky with fleecy clouds. The horizon lines were crimson roses the length of the stage. Crinolines, white wigs, the costumes of the actors harmonized with the colors of the set and together with it reflect a single artistic aim: a symphony in mother of pearl, the magic of pictures by Konstantin Somov.
>
> In this decorative tableau everything was supposed to be subordinated to a common rhythm, the movements, the lines, gestures, words, colors, the set and costumes are musically rhythmical.[50]

Meyerhold transposed Hauptmann's play from the middle ages to the rococo age and from a Shakespearean key to that of Marivaux. Such a solution obviously derived from the fact that Hauptmann's intention of creating a variation on a Shakespearean theme proved not entirely satisfactory. Thus the play took on a comparatively light, serene playfulness.

At rehearsals of *Schluck and Jau* Stanislavsky actively participated, "inspiring everyone with enthusiasm," wrote Vera Verigina. "We also received from him very valuable instructions about how to hold ourselves and wear our costumes."

Stanislavsky was especially delighted with Meyerhold's idea for the splendid scene of the embroidering ladies. "When the ladies in the third tableau sit in the latticed summerhouses and embroider the single broad ribbon, a long strip of material lies on our knees. Following Stanislavsky's direction, we embroidered with a stylized movement, raising and moving our wrists to the same side with sentimental grace, each time slightly bending our heads to the same side and glancing at the needle. This was an enchanting sight, expressing that affectation peculiar to ladies in exaggerated crinolines and wigs that recalled fantastic cloud towers."[51]

This scene alone pleased the audience at the dress rehearsal. "Seven princesses are seated in seven latticed summerhouses, through which gleams a sky with fleecy clouds. Off stage Glière's music is heard. Across the whole length of the stage, seven princesses embroider a golden ribbon, which unites them compositionally," the designer Nikolai Ulyanov recalled about his first success. "Loud applause at first from the front rows, then from the whole audience."[52]

Hauptmann's elegant "play of jokes and witticisms" was generously strewn with biting laughs at the ruler's power and at the flattering courtiers and jesters, etc. But apparently in this instance Meyerhold was not able to pursue any particularly serious ideological or political aims. The carnival game which animates the plot of the play was amusing and full of a lot of blunt jokes and puns. The people of the noble court with its princes, pages, banquets, tapestries, hunting horns, jesters, etc., allowed the imagination free rein. To a certain extent, work on *Schluck and Jau* evidently revealed the first possibilities of stylization, to which Meyerhold later devoted a great deal of energy. But for the time being, this was only a careful reconnoitering of new ways, and nothing more. The basic problem for the director remained the same as in *The Death of Tintagiles*: the harmony of movements, lines, gestures, words, music and color. In this case, it was still not resolved.

Valery Bryusov, one of the few onlookers at the Theater Studio dress rehearsal who felt great sympathy with Meyerhold's experiments and in many ways prepared the theoretical way for them, wrote that in this show,

> in many respects, efforts were made to break with the realism of the contemporary stage and to accept stylization boldly as the principle of theater art. In the movements there was more plasticity than imitation of reality: some groups resembled Pompeian frescoes presented as living tableaux. The sets, which were masterfully painted (or rather, created) by Messrs. Sudeikin and Sapunov, did not take reality into account at all: the rooms were without ceilings, the columns of the castle were overgrown with some kind of vines, etc. The dialogue was heard the whole time against a background of music (written by Satz) which drew the souls of the listeners into the world of Maeterlinck's drama. Yet on the other hand one was made strongly aware of the familiarity with stage traditions and of the many years of Art Theater training.

Here Bryusov came very close to the knot of contradictions tightly tied in with the practice of the Studio on Povarskaya Street. He went on: "Actors who had learned the stylized gestures which the Pre-Raphaelites dreamed of kept striving with their intonations to maintain life-like conversation, and continued to try to reflect passion and emotion with their voices as they are expressed in life. The sets were stylized but sharply realistic in their details. The rooms without ceilings were simply rooms in a ruined building; the vines which clothed the columns in the dungeons seemed to be real vines. Where the director's instruction ceased, the usual acting style took over, and it was obvious at once that bad actors were acting without real schooling and without any temperament."

The Theater Studio, Bryusov maintained, "made clear to all who knew it that it was impossible to build the theater anew on its former foundation. Either the building of the Antoine-Stanislavsky theater had to be continued, or everything had to be renewed from the foundation up."

Bryusov's own program was very radical and for those times, too consistently so even for Meyerhold. "Instead of sets with various wings it will be enough," Bryusov proposed, "to use a colored background suitable for the action of the play, but in no way illustrating it. The movements, gestures and speech of the actors should be stylized, should strive not toward an imitation of 'how things really are,' but toward a degree of expressiveness that *never exists* in real life. After all, the word achieves highest expression in verse, whereas people do not communicate with each other in verse even at moments of greatest stress. Give us artistic stylization in the theater..."[53]

It was much easier to make such demands than to realize them in practice. A colored background suitable to the action? Fine, but just what background and how was the degree of its suitability to the play to be determined? Movements and speech are to be stylized, carried to a point of expressiveness which does not exist in life? Fine, but what does that mean when translated into the language of concrete plasticity and living intonation? In principle Meyerhold was completely in agreement with Bryusov. In practice, though, the whole theory of stylized theater resembled a string of question marks. The long road of Meyerhold's experimentation had only just begun.

It is interesting that Stanislavsky's impressions after the dress rehearsal almost coincided with Bryusov's:

It all became clear. The young inexperienced actors were capable of showing the audience their new experiments with the help of a talented director, but only in small excerpts. When it came to developing plays of tremendous inner content with delicate outline and, in addition, stylized form, the young people showed their childish helplessness. The talented director tried to protect actors who in his hands proved to be mere clay with which to mold beautiful groups and tableaux, and with whose help he realized his interesting ideas. But since his actors lacked artistic technique, he could only demonstrate his ideas, principles, searchings, but had nothing or no one to realize them with. For this reason the interesting aims of the Studio turned into abstract theory, scientific formula. I was once again convinced that there is a great distance between a director's dreams and their realization and that theater exists first of all for the actor and cannot exist without him, and that for new art you need new actors with a completely new technique.[54]

—72—

Both Bryusov and Stanislavsky clearly marked off the breach between stylized theater and the concrete forms for realizing this idea proposed and demonstrated by Meyerhold. Stanislavsky was not discouraged by the defeat which he had witnessed and for which he was in part to blame. During the coming years he continued to experiment with producing Symbolist plays and never stopped searching for such acting technique as would permit the actors to project "nuances of feeling," and express from the stage something intangible, eternal, unreal. He was doing such research when he rehearsed Leonid Andreev's *The Life of Man*, Hamsun's *The Drama of Life* and Maeterlinck's *The Blue Bird*. The same search continued in the work with Gordon Craig on *Hamlet*. But, as T. Bachelis aptly noted, Stanislavsky saw the only way to realize these ideas "in the expansion of the possibilities of psychology." Taking this road alone, he did gradually progress from the ambiguity of the experiments at the Studio on Povarskaya Street to the integral "psychic realism" of the First Studio.

Meyerhold saw as the truer road the one suggested by Bryusov, despite all the inevitable complications arising there. Meyerhold declared war on psychology and in his search for purity of form "demanded increased attention to plasticity, rhythm, to the expression of the pose and finally to special reading, the technique of which, like all the other elements of the Symbolist production, he had emphasized in the Studio on Povarskaya Street. Meyerhold proposed a harmonious solution to the whole problem. Virtuosity in the actor's external technique was essential. Also essential was a new, distinct form of projecting the character, which broke simultaneously with both 'the middle-class,' as Stanislavsky expressed it, 'ordinariness of feelings,' and with the calcified stereotypes used in theater for projecting the high and noble. The creation of a new plasticity in the actor, worked out esthetically with special attention to the physical side of the actor's creativity, was essential. A distinct pictorial or bas-relief expressiveness of the stage tableau was essential."[55] Essential finally was a special expressiveness of intonation, as well as a special technique of the word.

"The naturalistic theater," Meyerhold maintained, "does not know the beauties of plasticity, does not compel the actor to train his body, and when it founds a theater school, does not understand that physical sport must be a basic subject if it hopes to produce *Antigone* and *Julius Caesar*—plays which by their music belong to *another* theater."[56]

For Stanislavsky, the main goal remained the expansion of the possibilities of the inner technique of the actor; he was interested above all in the psychic life of the individual, his particularity of character, the nuance of his psychology.

For Meyerhold such a direction was unacceptable and impossible if only because in his *The Death of Tintagiles*, for example, there had been no characters with their own independent life and will, no "individuals" and individual types.

Stanislavsky began to seek the realization of the elevated psychic problems which so engaged him, of "the questions of the spirit" in conflicts between living individualities, in concrete images; they could be realized on stage only by actors in command of all the rich means of psychological expression.

Meyerhold moved toward "the heights of the spirit" by another road—with the help of an integral composition to which the actor had to subordinate himself.

In this composition the actors carried out relatively modest assignments. Such a road inevitably led to the harshest dictatorship of the director.

Meyerhold said later that:

> For me, it was a personal tragedy that Stanislavsky closed the Studio on Povarskaya Street in 1905, but basically he was right. With my usual haste and heedlessness I tried to unite in one whole the most disparate elements: Symbolist theater, stylizing artists and a young generation of actors raised in the school of the early Art Theater. Whatever the problems were, all that just did not go together and, to put it bluntly, recalled the fable of 'The Swan, the Crab and the Pike.' Stanislavsky, with his flair and taste, understood that, and for me when I had recovered from my bitterness at my failure, it was a lesson: one must first educate a new actor and only then put new tasks before him. Stanislavsky, too, came to such a conclusion. Even then features of an early version of his 'method' were forming in Stanislavsky's mind."[57]

Stanislavsky came to the decision to close the Studio during the days when the bitter street fight of the 1905 Revolution was beginning in Moscow.

At first Meyerhold took these events as a good sign for the Studio. He dreamed that *The Death of Tintagiles* would seem a strong and topical comment on the latest happenings, that it would pour oil on the fire of the uprising. Twelve years later he said: "In 1905 a popular revolt was coming to a climax in the streets of Moscow, and *The Death of Tintagiles* was being prepared for the stage in a Moscow studio, the drama of an invisible but terrible queen, whose ghostly figure aroused awe and whose deathly reek caused living things to tremble." [58]

One must conclude, however, that the dress rehearsal for *The Death of Tintagiles* compelled Meyerhold to doubt what had seemed indisputable to him when he began work on the play and when he composed the speech he had wanted to give at the opening. Apparently he realized that in the vague and mysterious form of a Symbolist production the associations which so excited and aroused him ("The queen's castle represents our prisons. Tintagiles is our youthful humanity... Thousands of Tintagileses moan in prisons. . ." etc.) would not reach the audience, would not exert a revolutionizing influence. The basic distance inherent in Symbolism from the reality of the political struggle was an insuperable obstacle to Meyerhold's intention of relating Maeterlinck's fairy tale to the Russian pre-Revolutionary situation, of making the play "relevant" to the threatening atmosphere of 1905.

Does not the draft of his address to the actors of the Studio, preserved in Meyerhold's papers, indirectly attest to this disappointment in the political potential of Symbolist drama? Meyerhold now wrote: "Do not divide into party cells. It is important for an actor to be alone, to be individual in his expression. This is valuable in the actor—that he is original. Every actor must work out an honest world view; the actor must be a Socialist, his heart must be always free, his mind soaring on high, but he must not be a dogmatic believer in revolutionary parties, must not be one of the crowd. His excitement and response to events must ring forth in the characters on stage and not on the streets."[59]

But the characters of the Studio actors were not to "ring forth on stage." The revolution of 1905 conclusively convinced Stanislavsky that the enterprise he had begun had no future. "The revolution broke out," Stanislavsky wrote. "Muscovites were not in the mood for theater. The opening of the new enterprise was far off. The Studio had to be closed in short order."

Stanislavsky no longer believed in its success. "It was dangerous to open the Studio; as it seemed to me, dangerous to the very idea for which it had been founded," he summarized, "for to demonstrate an idea badly is to kill it."[60]

He had not yet given up hope of "demonstrating" this idea well. A few years later, in 1908, he drafted the thesis of a report for the tenth anniversary of the Moscow Art Theater in which he wrote, among other things, the following: "When artistic perspectives became cloudy, the Studio was born. It died, but for all that our theater found its future among its ruins."[61]

And in a more carefully worded "Report of ten years of artistic activity at the Moscow Art Theater," he clearly developed the same idea:

> A group of innovators came together at the ill-starred studio. There was much there that was strange for the level-headed observer—there was perhaps even an element of the ridiculous; but there was also much that was good, sincere and daring. I am the one who suffered from this unsuccessful venture, but I do not have the right to resent it.
>
> The Art Theater is all the more obliged to speak well of its late offspring since it alone has made sensible use of the results of this youthful ferment. With its help, the Art Theater has been rejuvenated, renewed.[62]

Commentators on the collected works of Stanislavsky have tried to interpret all these considerations as unintentional slips of the pen. But it is all said simply and firmly. In speaking of the aid the Moscow Art Theater derived from the Studio, Stanislavsky had in mind, above all, the productions *The Drama of Life, The Life of Man*, and *The Blue Bird*, staged with the help of Leopold Sulerzhitsky. Meyerhold later wrote, "Sulerzhitsky exerted all his efforts in order to transplant carefully the young seedlings of the Theater Studio to the soil of the Art Theater."[63]

The fate of the Studio on Povarskaya Street had been predetermined by the fact that Stanislavsky and Meyerhold had different conceptions and feelings about the "new element" toward which they both were striving. Stanislavsky at that time still believed in the possibility of "peaceful coexistence" for Symbolist abstractions and the live, physical and psychological realization of completely credibly acted characters. Stanislavsky's subsequent Symbolist productions showed his ineradicable striving toward realistic justification and prosaic circumstantiality of Symbolist motifs. (Hamsun's *The Drama of Life* was especially striking.) In his esthetic system the symbol, like any other form of artistic generalization, must arise out of reality, out of its natural stream, out of the truth of mutual relations between people and "the life of the human spirit." The symbol was conceived as the highest expression of that truth, its apogee, its result.

With the radicalism of direction peculiar to him, Meyerhold took a decidedly different tack. This became clear as early as the Studio on Povarskaya Street and disappointed Stanislavsky. The paths of Stanislavsky and Meyerhold diverged for a long time to come.

The Studio productions were not shown to the public; it did not open in this form to audiences. Only some months later did Meyerhold take courage after his terrible defeat and write his wife: "The failure of the Studio is my salvation because it was not right, it just was not right. Only now do I understand how good it was that the Studio failed." It is interesting that the sense of having missed the mark ("it was not right") was for Meyerhold directly connected with the revolution, whose events stirred him so deeply. In December 1905, after the Studio had already closed, he noted in his diary: "I am happy about the revolution. It has turned the theater upside down. And only now is it possible to begin the work on building a new altar."[64]

Meyerhold came unexpectedly soon to this "new altar."

THE THEATER ON OFITSERSKAYA STREET

> In the embrace of a fool and a farce the old
> world will wax beautiful and grow young,
> and its eyes will become clear, fathomless.
> *Alexander Blok*

Had he so desired, Meyerhold probably could have remained in the Art Theater following the closing of the Studio. He had been cast once more as Treplyov in *The Sea Gull* (which commenced another run in 1905) and played the part successfully. Later, Meyerhold would say:

This was something of a bridge to my possible return to the Moscow Art Theater, as K. S. hinted to me. But there were obstacles as well: Vladimir Ivanovich was more than cool to the idea. I myself did not know what I wanted, had lost my sense of direction completely. But in the end there was nothing for me to decide—everything was decided for me by the total absence of friendly contact between myself and my former colleagues [participants in *The Sea Gull*]. When I met them backstage during the play they would irritate me, and I appeared strange to them."[1]

By this time Meyerhold had become, if not a fully self-confident and farsighted director-innovator with a firm knowledge of where and how to travel, then at least a man possessed of a wide program for stage experiments. He was getting a glimmering of a fundamentally new theater, not merely different from the Moscow Art Theater—but its polar opposite. The prospect of slow development within and together with the Moscow Art Theater was unthinkable for Meyerhold, if only because at this time Meyerhold was in the grip of Symbolist art and wished to continue the experiments which he had begun on Povarskaya Street.

At the end of 1905 Meyerhold separated for the second (and final) time from the Art Theater and moved to Petersburg where, not without reason, he expected to find confederates. He appeared at Vyacheslav Ivanov's famous "Wednesdays," became acquainted with Blok, Sologub, Berdyaev, Andrei Bely and many other philosophers, poets and artists.

"Petersburg theatrical life," reminisced G. Chulkov, "was pale and wan at the time... Some kind of new theater was being discussed in Symbolist circles. The time had in fact come to bury naturalism and psychologism. The concept of a Symbolist theater hung in the air. All that was missing was someone from the theater who would dare to undertake the risky enterprise. In those years only one director was dreaming of a revolution in the theater. This was my old acquaintance V. E. Meyerhold."

Together with Chulkov, Meyerhold planned to open the "Torches" ("Fakely") theater. At this time he was thinking a great deal about mysticism. He posited then that mysticism "is the last refuge for those who flee, those who do not wish to bow before the temporary might of the church, but who do not intend to renounce free faith in another world (the other side)." Meyerhold believed that theater was called upon to replace the church, that in theater "a religious enlightenment, a cleansing" must take place. But this did not at all signify, in Meyerhold's mind, a withdrawal from the social struggle. On the contrary, he believed that "mysticism conceals within itself a tireless call to life," and in mystical theater "the riotous soul of man" will hear the call to rebellion, will "find the path to battle." Gorky took part in a discussion of the theater program of the "Torches." With evident agreement, Meyerhold recorded the main theses of his speech: "A. M. Peshkov: Rebellious nature... The broadest principles. Theater must be democratic. Pathos."[2] L. Sulerzhitsky, in Petersburg at the time, was so taken with their plans that he, together with Meyerhold, even traveled to Yasnaya Polyana to ask Lev Tolstoi for a play for the "Torches." However, nothing came of this. "Our attempts to finance the "Torches" theater were futile,"[3] concludes Chulkov.

Like it or not, Meyerhold was forced to return to Tbilisi and renew the activity of the New Drama Association. The Association reappeared, and for slightly over a month, performed in Tbilisi (February 20-March 23, 1906). Then for the summer the group moved to Poltava to work for yet another month and a half (June 4-July 16, 1906). During this time spent in Tbilisi and Poltava, Meyerhold was caught in the difficult bind of having to compromise between his urge to lead the theater in a new direction, following the experience of the Studio on Povarskaya Street, and the needs of the provincial public, which was indifferent to his experiment.

To please the public, the company staged in a traditional manner Trakhtenberg's *Fimka*, Brieux's *Damaged Goods*, Chirikov's *The Jews* and *In Yard and Annex*, Hartleben's *On the Way to Marriage*, A. Svirsky's *Prison*, Sholem Asch's *On the Way to Zion* and others.

None of these plays were subsequently entered by Meyerhold into his list of directed works. Likewise, Chekhov's *Uncle Vanya* and *The Cherry Orchard* did not appear on this list. Nor did Gorky's *Children of the Sun* and other plays produced according to the stage principles of the Moscow Art Theater, with relatively minor changes.

Meyerhold continued his search in only a few productions. Already a mature man of thirty-two, Meyerhold was fatigued by the need to adapt to provincial tastes and working conditions. Meyerhold's letters from Tbilisi and Poltava demonstrate a deep revulsion toward things provincial.

"Here," he wrote to his wife in late February 1906, "there is no satisfaction... In order to work in the provinces I must debase my taste... In a word, awful, awful, awful. I dream of a theater school and of many things which cannot possibly be accomplished in the provinces. Why, why am I destroying myself? And destroy myself I shall, if I remain in the provinces."

Such acute distaste for the provinces on the part of Meyerhold was no doubt fanned by the invitation he had already received from Komissarzhevskaya to begin the new season in her Petersburg theater. Meyerhold had decided to accept this invitation immediately, even before beginning his work in Tbilisi. But Meyerhold had decided to realize his ideas without delay. In this sense, some of his Tbilisi, and especially Poltava, productions are of special interest.

In Tbilisi he immediately advertised two plays from the Studio repertoire: Ibsen's *Love's Comedy* and Maeterlinck's *The Death of Tintagiles*. Each production partly copied Studio stagings. But there was a new element. In *Love's Comedy*

Meyerhold, together with the director Pronin, developed the folkloric aspect of the play, or "Norwegian spots," as he called them: "National flags, tents over balconies, garlands, croquet, hammocks, fiords, starry sky, some sort of special teapot, choral parts all written for Grieg's music..." Evidently this was too much for the public. In any case, the play ran with no particular success.

At first Meyerhold was completely unable to attract the Tbilisi theatergoers to *The Death of Tintagiles*. The play was advertised, but nobody bought advance tickets. Finally, on March 19, the play which Meyerhold had worked on for an entire year was performed. Before the show, Meyerhold gave the speech which he had planned to give at the opening of the Theater Studio, the only additions being some clearly insincere compliments to the Tbilisi public concerning its "sensitivity" and "readiness to accept new art."

The Death of Tintagiles was staged in a dark green frame covered by tulle to the accompaniment of Ilya Satz's music. "The costumes," wrote Meyerhold, "were light colored, as in the Studio. And the entire production, therefore, had to be executed not in the primitive style, but in the colors of a Böcklin painting. Böcklin was so definite that absolutely everyone noticed him. This was not ideal for me, but whatever has unity is valuable." Further along in the same letter, Meyerhold presented a clearer "formula" for the presentation: "Böcklin landscape and Botticelli poses." He was unhappy with the actors: "they were not acting well; pale, uninspired, dry, technical. They irritated me..."

Evidently they also irritated the Tbilisi public, which viewed the production inattentively, even though the shift of the production to "Böcklin colors" was undoubtedly (if accidentally) a concession to provincial taste. Symbolism of the Beklin variety had a certain bourgeois appeal and vulgar effectiveness.

In Tbilisi Meyerhold staged *Miss Julie*, by Strindberg, Hauptmann's *Hannele*, and also a well-known play of the time by Chirikov—*The Jews*. This play was constantly sold out. The pogrom scene, as staged by Meyerhold, was especially popular. "He had the scene take place in absolute darkness and in almost total silence on the stage," recollected V. Podgorny, who had worked for Meyerhold in Tbilisi. "Only some sounds from behind the scenes, a distant din, indicated that there was unrest in the city. And only at the last moment, as the hooligans break in, a loud shot closes the pogrom scene."[4]

In Poltava, important plays staged by Meyerhold were Ibsen's *Ghosts*, Maeterlinck's *The Miracle of St. Anthony*, O. Dymov's *Cain*, Schnitzler's *The Cry of Life* and *The Green Cockatoo*, and Gorky's *The Barbarians*.

Ghosts and *Cain* were staged without a curtain. At the time, this technique was considered to be an incredible innovation for contemporary plays. (In 1898, the Moscow Art Theater had staged *Antigone* without a curtain.) Subsequently, Meyerhold noted: "The realization of this approach was aided by the exceptionally convenient construction of the stage in the Poltava theater where I conducted several experiments in the summer of 1906... In the Poltava theater the ramp is easily disassembled, the area for the orchestra is skillfully covered by a floor at the same level as the stage, and the stage thus constructed becomes a proscenium jutting far into the auditorium."[5]

This modest note relates a very significant and essential event for Meyerhold.

Beginning in 1906, the director's sphere of activity widens decisively. His imagination is no longer bounded by the limits and dimensions of the stage, but envelops the theater auditorium and, furthermore, the entire theater building. From this moment until the close of his creative life, Meyerhold was to demonstrate his aggressive urge to utilize the entire available space in which the production is staged for one specific directing assignment or another; he gradually seized the orchestra pit, the auditorium, the boxes, the entire stage up to the last wall, and spread the production into all corners of the building.

In Poltava the concept of no curtain naturally eliminated changes in staging and setting, and therefore resulted in a unity of space (even disregarding authors' remarks). "Thanks to the elimination of the curtain," wrote the Poltava paper, "the viewer remains at all times before a single stage setting. This reinforces the distinct impression obtained from the drama."[6] Meyerhold subsequently dared to change the scenery before the public's eyes, but in Poltava he had not yet reached this point. Without a curtain—and therefore without changes—was his principle, and this principle was followed.

The Miracle of St. Anthony (presented in Poltava as *The Madman*), thanks to Meyerhold's editing, showed a satirical sharpness. The antithesis to Anthony's truth and Virginia's ingenuousness was the lifelessness of the other characters: "the lifeless people," the bourgeois.

The main theme of Schnitzler's *The Cry of Life* in Meyerhold's production was that of the crushing power of objects over men. This thought was expressed in the roughest, almost naively simple way. The stage was cluttered with objects, and a sofa of exaggerated size dominated the interior where, wrote Meyerhold, "every visitor could appear as if crushed and destroyed by the extreme power of objects." Meyerhold set as his goal "the overcoming of Chekhovian moods in the name of the fatal and tragic"; he experimented with the grotesque and with "mystical depths of tone."[7]

Apparently, in Poltava (or in any case, during that same year—1906), Meyerhold decided to write a book on the theater. At first this work was a large article—"On Theater (History and Technique)"—which was published in a collection by Shipovnik publishers in 1908. The declaration, theoretical basis, and development of concepts for relativistic theater made up the core of the article.

Among Meyerhold's notes for 1906, there is a draft of a letter, undoubtedly intended for K. S. Stanislavsky, in which he tells of his idea for a book. Meyerhold wrote:

In this book (I dedicate it to you) you will find a negative attitude toward that school of dramatic art which you have established in Russia. I underscore the negative aspects of this school intentionally. What you have done is both great and necessary, but it has already passed into the realm of history. This is how rapidly Russian art progresses. You are standing at a new bridge. This is why it might seem that I am writing something that could cause you disappointment while you are still alive.[8]

But in attempting to formulate the fundamental principles of "new" dramatic art intended to relegate Stanislavsky's school "to the realm of history," Meyerhold naturally understood that the new art must at least be demonstrated and fixed in theatrical practice. The Studio on Povarskaya Street had not succeeded in this. Nor had Meyerhold's then little-known Tbilisi and Poltava experiments.

A book would be fine, but what was required was a stage in the capital, and public performances in Moscow or Petersburg—there could be no other way to bring the "new art" to the people.

And so, Meyerhold wrote to his wife: "I cannot not live in the capital. I have undertaken a new affair; it must be concluded. Possibly nothing will come of it, but I must finish what I have begun." He hoped that "perhaps Diaghilev will build a new theater." But Diaghilev's castle in the air was still in the uncertain planning stages, while Komissarzhevskaya already had a theater in Petersburg and was inviting Meyerhold.

As we have already noted, Meyerhold accepted immediately, although he was of the opinion that "this theater is neither here nor there," and in letters to E. Munt he expressed the fear that in Komissarzhevskaya's theater in the Passage "it will be impossible to achieve results."

The artistic side of the plays staged by Komissarzhevskaya's theater in the Passage lagged far behind the high level of the art as directed by K. S. Stanislavsky and V. I. Nemirovich-Danchenko in the Moscow Art Theater. The repertoire of the theater in the Passage, where plays by Gorky, Chekhov, and Ibsen were staged, also included works of a different caliber—for instance, A. Kosorotov's *The Torrent of Spring*, Hermann Bahr's *The Master* and *The Other*. All these compromises were of necessity connected with weak directing. Although A. Petrovsky, N. Popov, I. Tikhomirov and N. Arbatov (all of whom directed at Komissarzhevskaya's) were proponents of Stanislavsky's theatrical "creed," and although they all strove for realism, their understanding of realism was superficial, external, and the better of their works were distinguished only by a general culturedness and superficial plausibility. The unity which was already an essential requirement in the Moscow Art Theater was unknown to Komissarzhevskaya's theater. The weakness of the directors' wills and of the unity of the artistic base was especially discernible in presentations of works by Ibsen and Chekhov.

"Such plays as *The Master Builder, Rosmersholm* or *Ghosts*," said F. Komissarzhevsky, "were stuffed into totally inappropriate settings, and neither style, nor rhythm, nor tone were found for them. Kommissarzhevskaya found her own Nora and her own Hilda, Bravich found his own Rank and Manders, while the others played Ibsen as they did Chirikov or Naidenov." What is said here about Ibsen was equally true for Chekhov, Ostrovsky and Gorky. Inevitably the directing lagged behind the author and leading actress.

Between the 1905-06 and 1906-07 seasons, Komissarzhevskaya's troupe was to move into new quarters—from the Passage on Italyanskaya Street to the specially altered building of the former Nemetti Theater—on Ofitserskaya Street.

Meanwhile, it was clear that the theater as a whole, as a new manifestation of art, had not materialized. Biographers of Komissarzhevskaya tend to regard the Passage theater as the apogee and zenith of her artistic life, and generally do not quote the actress herself, who in 1908 said heatedly:

Yes, my own theater, I am at the goal... What was my program? To say that during the first year in the Passage I decided to stage a certain repertoire and not stage another, I cannot do... Both the first and second seasons were of the naturalistic type... But meanwhile I wanted to tear myself away from the disassociated and definite...

It was increasingly clear to me that the theater must speak only of the *eternal*, and accordingly . . . forms must be sought for its rendition, since the forms of the naturalistic theater are of no use...[9]

In other words, Komissarzhevskaya understood that things had to be done differently, so with her characteristic receptivity and selflessness she turned to the concept of a Symbolist theater.

When Komissarzhevskaya came to the Petersburg circle of Symbolists, she naturally heard Meyerhold's name mentioned at once. Without hesitation she sent him the invitation to head her theater. His experiments, she said, "insofar as I had gathered from hearsay, interested me."[10]

Already in May 1906, Meyerhold had met with Komissarzhevskaya in Moscow. "So far, I will say just one thing," wrote the actress, "that our discussion left me with the most positive impression. For the first time since the creation of my theater I do not feel myself to be a beached fish when thinking of work."[11]

Meyerhold's ability to evoke enthusiasm and Komissarzhevskaya's ability to become enthusiastic joined. They parted excited, happy, and determined.

For the first time Komissarzhevskaya had met a director filled with daring and unexpected plans, searching, innovative and capable (as was already visible then and especially visible subsequently) of transforming actors into fervid followers, students into adherents, and mature actors into students. Meyerhold advocated rejection of naturalistic settings, of all external plausibility in theater and of illusory depiction of life. This could not but attract Komissarzhevskaya, who had for a long time thought, and not without reason, that she and her "theater of the spirit" did not require lifelike settings.

She did not fear the director's "despotism." Meanwhile, Meyerhold already was not concealing his firm belief that the director had to be the only and all-powerful master of the production. It must be said that although the nature of Komissarzhevskaya's talent and the conditions under which her talent had been formed had up to this time always caused her to be a "soloist," she nonetheless—despite the urges of her own artistic nature—sincerely and warmly strove to subordinate herself to the requirements of the whole. Now that she had obtained a director whom she felt to be of the same mind as she, a director capable of realizing her dream of a "theater of a free actor, a theater of the spirit," she was sincerely prepared (although unable!) to give him all her art—like clay into the hands of a sculptor.

Many people warned Komissarzhevskaya against an alliance with Meyerhold. The seeds of conflict were in this union from the start. The actress, fundamentally incapable of complete subordination to the will of the director, was hiring the director least prepared at the moment to give actors even relative freedom. The actress of an essentially lyrical bent was coupling her artistic fate with a director for whom lyricism, as became clear later, was essentially anathema. The high-strung, passionate actress was expressing a readiness to work with a director who demanded the most exact calculation and reproduction of the entire staging...

Many years later, Meyerhold, according to A. Gladkov's notes, would readily and with some frequency recall Komissarzhevskaya. "Komissarzhevskaya," he said, "was an incredible actress, but they wanted her to be Joan of Arc at the same time... Komissarzhevskaya is better remembered for her dramatic roles, but she was a beautiful Mirandolina and was excellent at playing vaudevilles. She possessed a tremendous artistic *joie de vivre*, but at the time no one was interested in that."

Another time he said, "Komissarzhevskaya's beauty was that she could play heroines without being a "heroine" herself."[12] And again he would return to the buoyancy of Komissarzhevskaya: "The time in which she lived did not demand of her all the colors of which she was capable—there was no high romantic comedy in her repertoire, although she had all that was needed: great resources of jocular *joie de vivre* and an internal buoyancy."[13]

During his first years of directing, Meyerhold had dealt with young, quite "green" actors and actresses. Young and inexperienced, he had taught and instructed them and they had hung on his every word. But now it seemed on the surface that the relationship had changed—the director whose productions had been seen only in the provinces had come into contact with the best and most famous actress in Russia. Subsequently, as we have just seen, he spoke about her *joie de vivre*. But in the course of a year's work with Komissarzhevskaya, Meyerhold, as if expressing a trend of the time, did not present her in a single upbeat role. The overall tenor of the theater on Ofitserskaya Street was grim and anxious. Comedies were not performed at all and the audience did not laugh.

Meyerhold worked in the theater on Ofitserskaya Street for exactly one year. This year was a most important one in his life and a significant one in the history of Symbolist experiments in the theater. In the course of this year the world was presented with many of the basic ideas and forms of Russian theatrical Symbolism in "ready" form.

Russian Symbolist poetry already had been a reality for many years, and had brought forth the names of Blok, Bryusov, Balmont and others. As for Symbolist theater, it had been discussed, argued and written about for a long time. Its feasibility and inevitability had been theoretically founded by V. Bryusov, Andrei Bely and Vyacheslav Ivanov, but it had not become a reality in Russia as yet, since neither Meyerhold's first experiments in the provinces nor Stanislavsky's first experiments, nor their joint experiments in the Studio on Povarskaya Street, had received public acceptance.

Komissarzhevskaya's invitation gave Meyerhold the opportunity to continue with his experiments and to test in an open, public fashion—rather than in a studio or laboratory—all the possibilities of Symbolist theater. Or at least those which Meyerhold considered to be feasible and promising.

But at this point we must make several substantial reservations.

After *The Death of Tintagiles* was dress-rehearsed at the Studio and subsequently presented to the general public in Tbilisi, Meyerhold had, evidently, lost hope that he would succeed in giving Symbolist drama—be it Russian or in translation—a clearly political tone capable of revolutionizing the public, and feared that he would not be able to translate indistinct Symbolist drama—be it Russian or in translation—into a clearly political tone capable of revolutionizing the public, and feared that he would not be able to translate the indistinct Symbolist presentiments into the language of concrete social reality. The revolution of 1905 had already been defeated, but this does not mean that Meyerhold's stormy nature had accepted calmly the defeat of the revolution. On the contrary, protest continued to rage within him and was expressed—sometimes in the most unexpected manner—in his compositions on stage. But, in principle, the broad program of revolution in the theater which Meyerhold intended to implement in the theater on Ofitserskaya Street did not suggest or contain a call for revolutionary action. In a letter to Chekhov in 1901, he was hoping for a theater which would cause "all to suffer the same pain, express the same joy, protest against that which outrages all." This was the revolutionary theater which he had attempted to realize in the rehearsals of *The Death of Tintagiles*, but now, in 1907, Meyerhold's temperament changes its course. His goal now becomes the revolutionizing of the theater itself. This is why the presentations on Ofitserskaya Street become a series of startling, outrageous and shocking theatrical experiments that only rarely elicited public admiration.

It is self-evident that in striving to transform contemporary theater Meyerhold expected to establish new relations between the new theater and the public, relations substantially different from those, for instance, which had been formed between the Art Theater and its public. Meyerhold's polemic with the creative method of the Art Theater continued to sharpen, both in Meyerhold's work and in his public utterances.

But the revolution in the theater planned and begun by Meyerhold was not, as people are accustomed to think, merely an application of the theatrical theories of Bryusov, Andrei Bely, Vyacheslav Ivanov or even Maeterlinck.

As we read thoroughly the articles and books by Russian theoreticians of Symbolist theater it is, of course, possible to find more or less comprehensible glimmerings of concepts that were subsequently realized or at least tested by Meyerhold. Some presentations by the theater on Ofitserskaya Street—Maeterlinck's *Sister Beatrice*, first of all—naturally tended to give the false impression that Meyerhold was implementing the great hopes of, for instance, Andrei Bely, who had ascribed to art a religious significance and who was predicting the resurrection of mystery. Andrei Bely stated that "art has no meaning except for the religious; within the limits of esthetics we are dealing only with form; in rejecting the religious significance of art we strip it of all meaning."[14] *Sister Beatrice* is connected with the opinion that, supposedly, Meyerhold's Symbolist theater was also fully in accord with Andrei Bely's view of the theater as a form of worship. Bely had also spoken concretely regarding the desirable and even inevitable form. "The musical nature of modern dramas and their symbolism—do these not point to drama's striving to become a mystery? Drama has arisen from mystery. Its fate is to return. When drama approaches mystery, returns to it, inevitably it will leave the stage-boards and spread through life."[15]

On the other hand, the years-long and varied efforts by Meyerhold to erase the boundary between stage and auditorium, making the public an active participant in the play, cause us to recollect Vyacheslav Ivanov, who asserted that the nature of stage art "is not in the moment of heroic beginning but in the moment of general ecumenism—based not on the individual but on society."[16] It would appear that Meyerhold had rendered the crowning idea and cherished dream of Vyacheslav Ivanov's new theater, whose goal was "that the viewer cease being just a passive audience and himself act on the level of the ideal action on the stage."[17]

Vyacheslav Ivanov's and Andrei Bely's concepts, as we see, are in agreement and indicate a single way: that of "ecumenism,.. the transformation of theater into a shrine, and more—the entrance of theater into the world. In the distance we see the vision of a theater in which the actors and audience combine in a single, life-forming, creative and cleansing action."

Prior to entering Komissarzhevskaya's theater, Meyerhold had become knowledgeable about all the theories of Symbolist theater, both Russian and Western. This is evident from his notebooks, entire pages of which are filled with the names of eagerly read books, articles and tracts by Symbolists of all varieties, Symbolist poets, prose writers and estheticians. Meyerhold was particularly impressed by Georg Fuchs's book, *The Theater of the Future*.

In no way was Meyerhold indifferent to all these ideas. Quite the contrary; his own theoretical statements echo them distinctly.

But theory of theater is one matter, while theater practice is quite another. The actual experience of Meyerhold's theater on Ofitserskaya Street not only scored the first convincing victories for Russian Symbolist stage—such as *Sister Beatrice* and *The Life of Man*. An immensely more important esthetic result of all the experiments in the Ofitserskaya Street theater (at least for Meyerhold personally) was *The Puppet Show*. The daring, persistent experiments by the director were based not so much on concepts previously formulated by the ideologues of Symbolism, as on the unexpressed workings of his own genius, his impulsive perception of the spirit, of the rhythm and emotional structure of modern life. The basic reasons for his failures were, no doubt, Meyerhold's impulsiveness, the theoretical incompleteness of many of his experiments, his stubborn desire to act contrary to the public's wishes, to puzzle and confuse it. But thanks to this same impulsiveness of his genius, Meyerhold, with incredible speed, gave turn-of-the-century Russian art a dominant theme of harlequinade, which was expected by no one—not by Bely, not by Ivanov, not by Bryusov. This renaissance appeared in a new, unexpected form—the renovated tradition of Italian comedy with masques. The great pathos arising from the free interplay of comedians and tragic masquerade is to this day associated with Meyerhold's name in the theater.

If we are to speak of theoreticians of the theater who exerted a real influence on his stagings, if not on his articles and interviews, then among them Bryusov was evidently the closest to Meyerhold. Bryusov's article "Unnecessary Truth" (1902) unquestionably helped Meyerhold to formulate and comprehend his own differences with the Art Theater, and his review of the only show given at the Studio on Povarskaya Street without a doubt expressed his unsatisfied desires in many ways.

In the early years of this century, Bryusov was insisting that "in order to please knowledge and science we must not view art as a mere reflection of life... There is no art that would copy reality. In the external world there is nothing that corresponds to architecture and music. Neither the Cologne cathedral nor

Beethoven's symphonies reproduce that which is around us... Let us leave the copying of reality to photography and to the phonograph—to the cleverness of technicians." And Bryusov cited Grillparzer's elegant aphorism: "Art is to reality as wine is to grapes."[18]

Neither Bryusov's broad statements nor his articles devoted specifically to the theater contained clear answers to concrete questions of theater practice, but proclaimed ideas that stimulated Meyerhold's imagination and which he found most appealing. Bryusov was energetically and lucidly formulating the position which, first of all, completely refuted the validity of the early Moscow Art Theater experience, and second, released the artist from the need to "reflect" modern (i. e., bourgeois) reality, and third, advocated the concept of a beauty independent of and therefore hostile to this reality.

N. Berdyaev formulated this idea with even greater precision and force. The "healthy seed" of Symbolism he perceived

> in the reproduction of the fine, individual tones of the human soul and in the protest against bourgeois coarseness and the total absence of beauty from life. Symbolism finds its vindication in theoretical esthetics, which in no event can consider art to be a reflection of reality. An idealistic world view must recognize the *independent significance of beauty* and artistic creation in the life of mankind. *Beauty is the ideal aim of life*, it raises and ennobles man. We recognize the idea of the independent significance of beauty, by which we mean beauty is an end in itself, and thus we just approach the fullness of human experience. In bourgeois society and its art there is too little beauty, and the opposition to this society must bring into human life as much beauty as possible; beauty into human emotions, into art, into the entire fabric of society. *Esthetic protest has been added to the old forms of protest against bourgeois society.*[19]

There is no doubt that these last words of Berdyaev's contained their own truth. Furthermore, we shall now see that in the first play staged by Meyerhold in the theater on Ofitserskaya Street—*Hedda Gabler*—it was this concept of "esthetic protest" against bourgeois society that was in utter and complete predominance.

All of Meyerhold's work at the theater on Ofitserskaya Street was experimental. Each play was staged as an experiment, the results of which could not be predicted by anyone, Meyerhold included. In each production new forms of staging—some successful, others not—were tested in public. Some of these forms had been in the back of Meyerhold's imagination for some time, others he had just devised. Every guess and every invention immediately became reality in the show. An impossibly rapid tempo was maintained. The speed with which the theater on Ofitserskaya Street changed staging methods before a wide audience is a unique phenomenon. There is no other such example in the history of the theater.

Therefore, there is nothing surprising in the fact that subsequently the entire attention of historians was centered almost exclusively on the stage forms that Meyerhold created with such speed and inspiration, and which neither the contemporary public nor contemporary criticism had time to assimilate or perceive. Meyerhold's year at the theater on Ofitserskaya Street whipped by like a hurricane, leaving behind a broad wake of outraged and delighted, panicked and hostile, approving and incredulous responses: reviews, articles, acid comments and scathing letters to the editor. Nearly all of these responses were in reaction to the unusual nature and startling newness of the staging forms. The ideas remained in the shadows and attracted almost no attention.

Meyerhold himself, in subsequently attempting to sum up the significance of the productions in the theater on Ofitserskaya Street, presented a purely formal analysis. But this does not mean that his analysis was complete. Meyerhold's active form-creation notwithstanding, his formal experiments were not carried out in a vacuum. Time continued to influence them and, inevitably, contributed its own meaning.

The theater on Ofitserskaya Street was inaugurated with the premiere of Ibsen's *Hedda Gabler* on November 10, 1906. Meyerhold suggested to Komissarzhevskaya a controversial interpretation which, however, fully coincided with the overall concept of the play.

Meyerhold saw Hedda as a "heroine of the spirit" thirsting for beauty. Ibsen's play was presented as the tragedy of a strong, exceptional personality perishing in a crass bourgeois environment, in a world totally regulated by "common sense" and inconsistent with true beauty. This is how Komissarzhevskaya played Hedda.

Her acting was a challenge to "quieted time," to bourgeois order and to bourgeois seaminess. Her agitated heroine demanded changes, would not come to terms or calm down. As for the theme of beauty, beauty as the embodiment of anti-bourgeois sentiment and as the form and formula of "esthetic protest" against stagnant living, this theme wholly dominated the production.

The world surrounding Hedda was presented as a product of her imagination. The beauty she dreamed of and for which she was perishing literally flooded the stage. N. Sapunov was autocrat here. Meyerhold had suggested the general lines of the set: a narrow strip of stage, and for the background a large decorative panel. Sapunov understood that here he had incredible potential, and delighted the audience with an exquisite (and subsequently his favorite) composition of blues and oranges.

The externals of the production were praised highly:

> It is romantic. A light-blue northern consonance. The colors do not whirl or run. All is peaceful. All is ghostlike. The stage appeared enveloped in a light blue-green, silvery haze. A blue back curtain. On it, on the right, an enormous window sash as high as the stage. Under it, the leaves of a black rhododendron. Outside the window, greenish-blue sky with glimmering stars (in the last act). On the left of the same curtain, a blue tapestry depicting a silver and golden woman with a deer. Along the sides and top of the stage—silver lace. On the floor—a greenish-blue rug. White furniture. White piano. Green-white vases, white chrysanthemums in them. And white furs on an odd-shaped sofa. And Hedda Gabler's dress like seawater, like the scales of a sea snake.[20]

Yury Belyaev was delighted by the way Hedda (Komissarzhevskaya) blended into this:

> In her red hair, the complex, heavy magnificence of the green dress, in the narrow, extended toes of her shoes and in the tinted fingers one could guess the sorceress capable of transforming herself into a lizard, a snake, a mermaid. This was not Hedda Gabler but her

spirit, her symbol. And everything about her was also symbolic. The stage was muffled in lace which flowed in wide streams along the sides. Vines decorated the veranda. The fairy-tale tapestry, the strange tables and chairs, the edge of the white piano covered by a real snowdrift of white fur into which Hedda would dip her rosy fingers as into snow—all this was not the set for Ibsen's heroine, but rather the dwelling place of her spirit, the manifestation of her habits, tastes and moods.[21]

This praise contained a cautious comment not only on the divergence from Ibsen, but on the fundamental internal contradiction of the production. A. Kugel stated it clearly and without evasions. If Hedda's tragedy is to be perceived as the tragedy of unattainable beauty, then, he wrote, "the background against which the drama transpires must be crass and stifling. But Meyerhold has stylized not the environment in which Hedda resides, but the one which she supposedly already has attained in her dreams. Therefore, the play has become completely incomprehensible, turned inside out. The ideal has become reality. It came out loud and flashy, but the sense has disappeared."[22]

And in fact it was as though the meaning of the role—both Ibsen's and Meyerhold's conceptions—was cancelled by this attempt of Meyerhold's to recreate visually the unattainable beauty yearned for by Hedda. Only by way of the costumes was it possible to see human disharmony through a "harmony of color." The dark-gray suits worn by the solid citizen Tesman and the equally respectable assessor Brack, these gentlemen who know too well how to "live right"; Lovborg's brown suit and Thea's rose dress created some contrast to "cold, regal, autumnal" Hedda's green dress. It appeared as if all these completely real, earthly people had broken into Hedda's world of unreal beauty. But their appearance did not create drama; on the contrary, "when Hedda in her green dress and red wig settles into supernatural yellowish-white fur, and Lovborg in his brown suit, Brack with legs like chiseled balusters, and terra-cotta Thea sit down on light blue poufs," wrote B. Azov, "the combination of these colors creates attractive spots and reliefs that please the eye."[23]

The house Hedda has furnished becomes in the play a house decorated by Meyerhold and Sapunov in accordance with their understanding of beauty. This caused a new dramatic collision, the sense of which was precisely described by the critic N. Yordansky: "Hedda Gabler not only does not accept the bourgeois, but she does not accept the world... This is a most interesting idea for a most interesting drama, the author of which, however, will be Mr. Meyerhold and not Ibsen."[24]

In this precisely harmonized production, Komissarzhevskaya found no opportunity to demonstrate her emotional and lyrical talents. "She was bored by walking and sitting around," O. Mandelstam recollected later. "She would always end up standing; on occasion she would come up to the blue-lit window in Ibsen's professorial living room and stand there for a long, long time, showing the audience her slightly bent, flat back." But he felt that Komissarzhevskaya "attained a high level of virtuosity in this professorial drama of Protestant restraint."[25] But, apparently, this virtuosity was cold and lifeless. In any case, one of Komissarzhevskaya's devoted admirers, Blok's friend Evgeny Ivanov, briefly noted in his diary that the actress plays Hedda poorly, that "she cannot play these." Blok, who had never written about theater before and who, in contrast to Mandelstam, had a serious regard for Ibsen's play, wrote in his review:

> *Hedda Gabler*, staged for the opening, transmitted only unhappy emotions: Ibsen was not understood, or at least not realized—neither by the artist who had painted an exceptionally beautiful set, which, however, in no way was connected with Ibsen, neither by the director who had limited the actors by a wooden wall and narrow stage, nor by the actors themselves, who did not understand that Hedda's only tragedy was the absence of tragedy and the emptiness of a painfully beautiful soul; that her destruction is lawful.[26]

The result was unsuccessful, which evidently prompted Meyerhold to formulate in his notebook "the most fateful question: how to harmonize the evolution of decorative art with that of the actors."[27] The production of *Hedda* had raised this question, but so far Meyerhold had no answer.

N. Sapunov had achieved the direct effect of color and light on the audience—all had felt the beauty of the spectacle. Meyerhold wanted to convey the impression of "a light blue, cold, withering enormity (only this *impression*)" and achieved this aim. He saw the play "in cold light blue tones against the background of a golden autumn,"[28] which is what the audience did see.

Meyerhold had grasped that painting, which until that time had had virtually no impact on the art of the theater, could act directly upon the audience and not be just an "appropriate background." Meyerhold changed the role of painting. But the beauty the art strove for seemed exotic and extravagant and appeared to be mere prettiness; V. Azov sarcastically referred to modern-style statuettes sold in electric lamp shops. The first try was a flop, and depression reigned in the theater on Ofitserskaya Street, where from the start Meyerhold's support had been much less than unanimous, while some of the company were actually intimidated by him.

The next production, S. Yushkevich's *In the City*, directed by Meyerhold and P. Yartsev, likewise did not bring success. In this case, the problem was almost paradoxical. "Bourgeois comfort, cheap 'chintzy' well-being," wrote Komissarzhevskaya's biographer, "this is the atmosphere of the play and its heroes who live under the sign of paltry objects. . . ."[29] In attempting to banish the everyday from the stage, Meyerhold had simply eliminated the entire world of objects, so vital to the impact of the play's characters. He left them surrounded by bare walls. This sort of linear solution did not appear convincing to anyone at the time. Many years would pass before such "bareness" of the stage would cease to irritate the audience. Having destroyed the homely coziness of the play, Meyerhold instead offered the gaping void of a bourgeois existence without ideals. This was a radical departure from *Hedda*'s challenging beauty and a move toward a consciously stressed, pronounced non-beauty. These experiments were connected only by their overly linear sequence.

The transition happened following the premiere of Maeterlinck's *Sister Beatrice*, which took place on November 22, 1906. This production was undoubtedly the best work done together by Meyerhold and Komissarzhevskaya. For the first time in her life, Komissarzhevskaya surely and naturally participated in a play that was directed in the full sense of the word, losing nothing and even gaining some new possibilities.

This happened, first of all, because Meyerhold ideologically and esthetically had adapted the production of *Sister Beatrice* to Komissarzhevskaya, to her theme as an actor and her inevitable sense of leadership on the stage. Here she was the "lead," she was in the center, and the entire production Meyerhold, with characteristic energy, constructed as a "pedestal" for Beatrice (Komissarzhevskaya). Meyerhold had grasped the only possible ensemble for Komissarzhevskaya—one in which the ensemble is but a background for the leading lady. His solution to the show was esthetically advantageous to Komissarzhevskaya. The pale silver and old gold of the tapestries by S. Yu. Sudeikin in the style of Giotto and Botticelli, the figures of the nuns in gray-blue dresses; all this was a glimmering and cool medium in which the living warmth of "the sinful body of the earthly Beatrice" stood out vividly" (M. Voloshin's words).

Sudeikin's art work in *Sister Beatrice*, wrote N. Evreinov, " . . . plays more the role of a musical accompaniment... It strives to be neutral, calm, the soft echo of the dialogue. In *Sister Beatrice* this art work is a low-keyed light blue, monotonously sad but light. . . ."30

The golden-haired figure of Beatrice (Komissarzhevskaya) stood out against this monotonous silvery-blue background. Her ecstatic energy was in sharp contrast to the cold sadness of the stage atmosphere.

Another, more substantial reason for the great and impressive success of *Sister Beatrice* was that the unity of this production, in which both Meyerhold and Komissarzhevskaya expressed themselves fully, was in total harmony with both the spirit and the meaning of Maeterlinck's drama. Meyerhold's direction did not alter the play, did not reinterpret it. It appeared to unfold as if on its own, naturally and simply, freely expressing itself, as if from within. It was this self-induced "openness" that permitted the audience to enter the world of ideas and images, so akin to the attitudes of the post-insurrection Russian intelligentsia. The tragedy of a struggling, aroused spirit was presented—a spirit that had approached the very brink of despair and which had paused, weak and hesitating, in the last hope.

The defeat of the revolution of 1905 was difficult for the Russian intelligentsia to accept. Guilt before the people and differences with them had led many intellectuals to a very difficult emotional crisis. This crisis was expressed on this most approachable stage, obviously and with tragic clarity, in the first esthetically complete and, in its own way, totally Symbolist production by Russian theater—Meyerhold's *Sister Beatrice*. With childlike simplicity and clarity Maeterlinck's play united the themes of an escape from reality and an escape into reality. The image of the play was that of the crossroads at which the Russian intellectual had been deposited by history. The heroine's striving to leave the monastery for the world full of danger, cruelty and terror (and all the more attractive for that), internally corresponded to the schizoid state of the intelligentsia. The play reflected fear of revolution and the hope of being cleansed by fire; the hope for the miracle of the moral transfiguration and resurrection of man.

The grandeur and atmosphere of a religious service, which Meyerhold attempted to attain in this production, were necessary to him also in order to express the theme of awaiting a miracle, changes bringing salvation and capable of returning

A scene from *Sister Beatrice*

Komissarzhevskaya in the title role of Maeterlinck's *Sister Beatrice*, 1906

Scenes from *Sister Beatrice*, 1906

Meyerhold as Pierrot in Blok's *The Puppet Show*,
drawing by N. Ulyanov

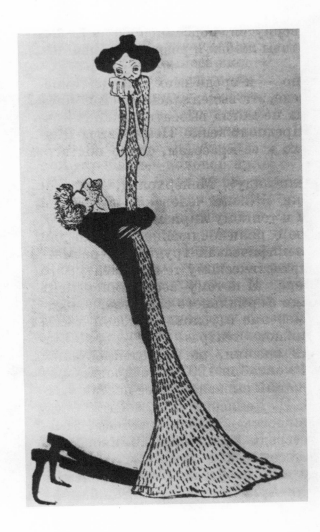

Caricature of Meyerhold and Komissarzhevskaya,
1907. "They didn't understand us."

Sketch for set decoration by N. Sapunov for *The Puppet Show,* 1906

V. Denisov's sketch for set of Maeterlinck's *Pelleas and Melisande*, 1907

V. Denisov's sketch for set of *Pelleas and Melisande*

Scene drawing from the production of Andreev's *The Life of Man*, by A. Lyubimov, 1907
Scene drawing from the same production, by V. Kolenda

Scene from *The Life of Man*, drawing by V. Kolenda

Meyerhold's plan for the ball scene in *The Life of Man*

Caricature from 1907: "Soul" (Dearie)
Meyerhold after "moments of faceless creativity"

„Душка"-Мейерхольдъ
послѣ „моментовъ безликаго творчества".

Жизнь. Сцена 1907. 2.

peace to the soul and harmony to the world. A regret for lost harmony and the prescience of a miracle of release were the main themes of Maeterlinck's drama, Meyerhold's direction and Komissarzhevskaya's acting.

Only out of human sufferings can the miracle capable of altering life arise. This is what the theater asserted in this production and how it interpreted Maeterlinck's "three-act miracle."

Meyerhold, wrote Lunacharsky, "expended considerable talent in order to bring to the foreground the word miracle, which, with a faltering sigh, passes from mouth to mouth in the group of beggars and cripples, and with ecstatic delight between the sisters. A miracle has occurred, be happy and gay, a miracle is possible, the Godhead manifests itself... If not in life, then at least on the stage." Komissarzhevskaya, continued Lunacharsky, "seized one by the heart with tones of revolt and deep grief."[31]

If, while rehearsing *The Death of Tintagiles* on Povarskaya Street, Meyerhold had wished to direct the production in such a way that the play became a sort of allegory, a metaphorical recreation of the tragic Russian political situation, then in his work on *Sister Beatrice* such intentions are not to be felt. This time he did not attempt to see Russia through Maeterlinck. He understood that in Maeterlinck's plays the motif of everyday life appears, in B. Zingerman's words, "symbolically transformed." We can add that this theme of everyday tragedy is encoded in and is expressed through the conventions of symbols. "Words are signalling us more than just their meanings,"[32] Andrei Bely explained. Everything has been altered to the point of unrecognizability, everything has a multitude of meanings and is therefore fatal. As Zingerman writes later in his work, *Ibsen, Maeterlinck, Pirandello*: "Man does not act, but man is acted upon."* The principle of fatality, when "man is acted upon," opened unlimited possibilities for the director. The director obtained an internal, esthetically founded right to "act with the actor."

For Komissarzhevskaya, the lyrical actress who always and in every role opened herself up to the world, the role of Beatrice, simultaneously sinner and saint, martyr and victor, was in some measure a confession. The duality in Beatrice coincided with the painful duality of her own life. The role developed as did her own fate. In those days Komissarzhevskaya would sign her name as "Beatrice" in letters to Bryusov.

The strictly plastic concept of the role suggested by Meyerhold, the musical rhythm of speech which he strove to achieve—these not only did not hinder Komissarzhevskaya, but fully coincided with her capabilities. V. Verigina observed that "she was all trembling inside, but without externally interrupting the strict rhythm of her movements."[33] The other actors, recalled A. Mgebrov, "did not act in this production—they conducted a religious service."[34]

In constructing the entire production on the centripetal principle, concentrating all attention on the figure of Beatrice, Meyerhold appeared to reverse his just attempted "centrifugality," the dispersed action in *Hedda Gabler*. The declarative and challenging art and the flattening out of *Hedda Gabler* into two dimensions he now

---

*See B. Zingerman, *Problemy razvitiia sovremennoi dramy. Ibsen. Meterlink. Pirandello. Voprosy teatra* (Moscow: VTO, 1967), pp. 167-96 [K. R.].

abandoned for the principle of sculpture. Each scene was constructed like a monumental composition, often multi-figured. It is true that this time, too, "the decorations were placed almost on the ramp itself,"[35] and Meyerhold was striving to move the action as close as possible to the audience, but the stage was not extended in width, the scenes were set primarily in the center, the characters were "very tightly grouped together."

Such fundamental changes (in contrast to *Hedda Gabler*, staged ten days previously) bespoke the multifacetedness of the director's previously conceived experiments.

In the surviving director's copy of *Sister Beatrice*, the basic principles to be tested are indicated: "Rhythms of plasticity, rhythms of dialogue. Singsong speech and slow movements. Musical unity. Musical basis in dialogues and the actors' movements. Bas-reliefs, sculpture groups... Mystery... The advantage of the proximity to the ramp."[36]

Comparing Meyerhold's direction with Maeterlinck's text, we see at once the new elements introduced by Meyerhold. Maeterlinck's crowd is silent, while Meyerhold's beggars are asking for bread, pleading for the monastery gates to be opened, begging for alms. The words of the Old Beggar, "Sister, we have seen two phantoms this night" (reminding us that in the night Beatrice together with her lover, Prince Belidor, has escaped from the monastery), seem to be conveyed to the whole crowd of beggars. The crowd is amazed, stilled; wondering "is it she," they "look and wait." Compared to the author, the director strongly stresses the themes of hunger and disaster, and thus activates the crowd. Meyerhold sees the crowd as a "swarm"; he directs the crowd to act "more energetically," saying that the Madonna's (Beatrice's) dialogue must begin "against" the background of the swarm," etc.[37]

Substantial differences are to be observed between the interpretation of the theme of a rebelling, agitated *people* in the early Moscow Art Theater productions (for instance in *The Death of Ivan the Terrible*) in which the director strove for the concrete individuality and independence of action of each character, on the one hand, and the consciously estheticized handling of the *crowd* theme in *Sister Beatrice*, on the other hand. In this latter, Symbolist, spectacle, the audience was presented for the first time with a crowd that was uniform, acted in unison as a single man, did not rebel or protest, but which pleaded at the feet of a heroine-savior; a crowd composed of beggars and cripples. Subsequently, this particular image of the crowd was presented by V. I. Nemirovich-Danchenko in *Anathema* by L. Andreev, and was repeated more strongly in Vakhtangov's production of *The Dybbuk*.

Meyerhold's attention was especially directed at the group of nuns who were at Beatrice's side throughout virtually the entire play. All their gestures were synchronized: together they would "interweave, move apart, spread themselves out on the flagstones of the chapel." Meyerhold consistently grouped the caped and hooded nuns in such a way that together, with their synchronized gestures they would create a sort of plastic accompaniment to the heroine's poses. "The sisters were all in one line," indicates P. Yartsev, "they kneeled and turned their heads in the direction of the chapel. The Madonna descended from the chapel door. . . ."[38] This almost ballet-like movement of the nuns is expressively recorded in P. Troyanovsky's amusing sketch.

The great response of society to *Sister Beatrice* surprised even such aware contemporaries as A. Blok. "What is this, Maeterlinck having success with the public?" asked the poet. "Has something frightful happened? It is as though this random audience has felt the spirit of a miracle that was flowering on the stage... We," continued Blok, "sensed the strong agitation; agitation about love, wings and future happiness. There was the sense of deep gratitude for the sparks of the miraculous that had flown through the auditorium."[39]

Przybyszewski's *The Eternal Fairy-Tale* also brought success to the theater on Ofitserskaya Street. The direction of the play was similar to *Sister Beatrice*: V. I. Denisov's decorations modestly created a soft background: "a canvas painted with the colors of semi-precious stones, which also appeared to glimmer on the costumes."[40] The symmetrical stagings were constructed for the most part in the center stage. The artists' gestures tended toward sculptural expressiveness. It is true that the thought behind the play was somewhat banal and thin. Sonka, the king's consort, indifferent to royal power and honors, even in Komissarzhevskaya's interpretation, was "lifeless and rhetorical." An almost slothful indifference to power was juxtaposed to the concept of strong power. Curiously enough, Meyerhold had planned to show the court hierarchy in a naive fashion, like children playing at theater: "A pile of different-sized blocks, steps, round and square columns is emptied onto the table. With these materials a fairy castle must be built."

Denisov followed these instructions, consciously maintaining naive symmetry in his decorations. The stagings were constructed in accordance with the same intentionally infantile principle. The officials, for instance, "were symmetrically deployed on the stairs—they all looked alike." At the end of the third act their heads, one above the next, appeared in the narrow window slots. "Nearly everything subjective had been inked over in the coloring of their roles." This was the idea. All these officials, Yu. Belyaev joked, were reminiscent of "card jacks."

Meyerhold quickly understood that the brief success of *The Eternal Fairy-Tale* was ephemeral, and came to the conclusion that Przybyszewski was completely at fault, due to "the exceptionally unrewarding material" of the play. "The desired simplicity (of aspirations)," he wrote, "in the name of which the new art has tried to break its lance, this text has transformed into undesirable, cheap 'modernism.'"[41]

Of course, this is true, but it is equally true that striving to achieve the clarity of the primitive, which Meyerhold demonstrated here, required clear thoughts and simple parables. *Sister Beatrice*, despite the complex symbolism, did possess such simplicity. On the other hand, *The Eternal Fairy-Tale*, pretentious, exaggeratedly fatalistic, with an artificial and coquettish plot, tied the actors to a grandiloquent tone and pretentious posturings.

If, after *Sister Beatrice*, Lyubov Gurevich, a loyal admirer of Komissarzhevskaya and the Art Theater, found it "clear that a certain type of play can and even must be played in conditional style, and that thereupon the silent language of colors on the stage and the participation of painters become of significant importance to the viewer,"[42] then S. Przybyszewski's *The Eternal Fairy-Tale*, written as it was by one of the most fashionable Symbolist authors, appeared to raise a large question mark over such assertions.

Neither the play nor the production were in tune with the dominating moods of the time. The crisis caused by the defeat of the 1905 insurrection was a painful disappointment to many, brought others to a state of panicked fear, and caused still others to seek relief through mysticism and religion. The Establishment had shown its fear of the revolutionary movement and of the risen masses. The fundamental emotional basis for all the intellectual and artistic efforts of the time was dissatisfaction. Although chased off the streets, dissatisfaction continued to dominate minds, and appeared, agitated and heated, in each play whose governing idea was the non-acceptance of life as it is "given," as it is. Here is the source for many literary and theatrical variations on the theme of escape from a reality that is unreasonable and unesthetic. Here is the cause of the deep pessimism in literature and on the stage, that "will to death" which, as Blok noted, increasingly "permeated the intelligentsia."[43]

But here we have also the cause of the curious phenomenon that some of Meyerhold's Ofitserskaya Street productions, although highly original in form, although in principle following the esthetic norms of Symbolism, would either attract attention for but a brief while (as did *The Eternal Fairy-Tale*), or were considered dull and weak (G. Heiberg's *Tragedy of Love*, H. Hofmannstahl's *Marriage of Sobeide*). In these plays Symbolism had an imported, overly pacified, estheticized and calming, although pretentious form. The dramas in no way corresponded to the Russian reality and did not touch the soul. Meanwhile, the audience was not at all well disposed toward peaceful contemplation.

On December 30, 1906, two plays were presented in one evening in the theater on Ofitserskaya Street: *The Miracle of St. Anthony* [the censor had renamed it *The Miracle of Anthony the Wanderer*—trans.], by Maeterlinck, and A. Blok's *The Puppet Show*. Each play in its own way was in close touch with the spiritual life of the Russia of those years. The staging of Maeterlinck's drama was basically a repetition of Meyerhold's production in Poltava. In describing his plan for *The Miracle*, Meyerhold often and energetically stressed his wish to "condense" an ironic attitude toward reality. The bourgeois lifestyle became the object of this irony. The director strove for "directness and cartoonness." He tried to stress (with make-up and voice) the repulsive animality of Gústave, Achille, the Curé and the Doctor. He was only partially successful: the artists would slip into vaudeville attitudes. Meanwhile, the director wanted the characters to be not only amusing, but "frightful and even nightmarish."[44] Here Meyerhold noted that such an aim could be easily attained using marionettes. At this point he contradicted himself a dozen times: "A puppet theater is needed, but not only that," but on the contrary, "if a live actor could transmit the deep irony of the author . . . this would be no less significant." He warned that an imitation of a puppet theater "is not a method for creating an actor-doll," he did not wish to "replace a living actor" with a marionette, but was only searching in the esthetics of puppet theater for a key to this play, no more and no less. Such a key had been suggested by Maeterlinck. A marionette-type approach, in accordance with the playwright's will, appeared to be the image of this production.

But the word had been uttered—in the theater, at rehearsals, and soon Meyerhold was saddled with it. The word had been written in "Notes to directing work" in the book *On Theater*, published in 1913. And from then on until his death,

Meyerhold had to deal with the ridiculous charge that he, Meyerhold, supposedly wished to chase live actors from the theater and replace them with puppets.

While discussing marionettes, the historians of the theater had forgotten that the grotesque images in *The Miracle of St. Anthony* had a completely earthly, distinct social address and exposed the soulless, puppet world of bourgeois hypocrites, businessmen and "inheritors." This was a production in which Meyerhold, for the first time in the history of the theater, had mapped out a merciless approach for exposing and illustrating the *mechanical nature* ("puppet theater") of bourgeois existence and psychology. The depths of Symbolism had given birth to a form of anti-bourgeois grotesquerie that attacked the soulless and frightful "Bedlam of the unpeople" (M. Tsvetaeva's expression).

"It is characteristic," notes T. Bachelis, "that E. B. Vakhtangov, who subsequently directed *The Miracle of St. Anthony* twice, in 1917 had polemicized with Meyerhold's approach by lighting the play with a warm, all-forgiving, beatific smile, and then in 1921 developed and asserted with new force Meyerhold's satirical and grotesque solution."[45]

The Miracle of St. Anthony played with great success, but this success was eclipsed almost totally by the public scandal that took place following the showing of Blok's *The Puppet Show*, which was performed later on that same evening.

The Puppet Show was Meyerhold's first step in the subsequent thrust of his artistic development. In *The Puppet Show*, Meyerhold found application for the completely transformed but, for him, ever-seductive themes of masquerade and carnival.

As we recall, Meyerhold had first come into contact with the theme of clowning in Kherson, when he directed von Schönthan's *Acrobats*. Blok's short play presented Meyerhold for the first time with the philosophical and concrete life-related contents of this theme. It gave Meyerhold the opportunity to use a practically declarative form to express himself on a matter of utmost importance for himself: the interrelations between art and reality, Russian stage and Russian life.

Meyerhold himself subsequently believed that *The Puppet Show* was the *true beginning* of his biography as a director. "The first move toward the determination of the direction of my art," he maintained, " . . . [was the] fortunate invention of plans for Blok's wonderful *The Puppet Show.*"[46] Thus, Meyerhold relegated to the prehistory of his development and to the category of fruitless endeavors everything that had preceded *The Puppet Show*. But *The Puppet Show* led the director to new discoveries.

In order to understand the nature of these discoveries it is necessary first to evaluate the great, in a sense critical, significance of *The Puppet Show* to Blok's own art. Later, in his autobiography, Blok wrote that the romantic theme of his poetry was inevitably accompanied by "attacks of despair and irony that found their outcome in my first experiment in drama (*The Puppet Show*, the lyrical scenes)."[47] In 1917 he characterized *The Puppet Show* as "a work that emerged from the depths of my soul's police department."[48] What does this mean and how is it to be understood? What is the significance of the comments made by E. Ivanov, the poet's closest friend, when he wrote that *Beautiful Lady* was partially a preface to *The Puppet Show*?[49]

We find the answer to these questions in all of Blok's lyric poetry preceding *The Puppet Show*. In this material, either in parallel with the exalted symbols of the Beautiful Lady, the White Steed, That Star and others, either intertwined with them, or in apparent contradiction to them, we find that "little swamp-devils" and "swamp-spirits" had been appearing for some time. Blok saw laughing Harlequin in the Beautiful Lady's doorway and in the driveway to a townhouse. In much of his poetry the elevated lyrical theme either alternates with or is displaced by the introduction of glowering irony, notes of bitter tragedy or the gloomy "swamp" theme. The characteristic motif of the inevitably plebeian and poor, but somehow great, theater goes hand in hand with the essential themes of Blok's lyrical motif. For Blok, the idea of a theatrical farce represented the surmounting of lifeless, stagnant and hostile reality.

In a letter to Meyerhold following the dress rehearsal of *The Puppet Show*, these thoughts are forcefully expressed:

> *Any* farce, mine included, strives to be a *battering ram*, to break through the lifeless. The farce embraces and comes forward to meet, discloses the frightful and perverted caresses of matter, as if sacrificing itself to it, and now this stupid, dull matter gives in, begins to trust it, and climbs into its arms. This is when "the hour of the mystery must strike": matter has been fooled, rendered weak and defeated. In this sense do I "accept the world"—the entire world, with its stupidity, stagnation, dead and dry colors—only to trick this bony old bitch and make her young. In the embraces of a fool and a farce the old world will wax beautiful and grow young, and its eyes will become clear, fathomless.

Here, Blok was planning an entire program for overcoming lifeless reality with the force of art. The farce is used not to depict reality or repeat it, but to trick, confuse, and to create anew. The whole world with all its dirt is acceptable insofar as art is capable of altering, cleansing and making it youthful, of making it different.

In essence, Blok's line of thought is in full agreement with the fundamental principle of romantic irony, according to which the artist does not take his subject seriously. The artist is also a free agent with regard to reality and his attitude toward his own work. But romantic irony that makes a fetish of artistic freedom and of the artist's subjective will presupposed an illusory deliverance from reality, a supposed independence from reality. But Blok, permeated as he was by the romantic spirit like all Symbolists, was not so naive. His lyricism is combined with the theme of brave and even aggressive acceptance of reality: "I recognize you, world, accept and welcome you with the clang of my shield." Accordingly, the romantic idea of the "removal" and setting aside of reality, in Blok's interpretation, has a characteristic aggressiveness. Farce is viewed as a weapon of war against hateful, base reality.

Thus, within Symbolist theater we see the appearance of one of the crowning ideas of the entire program of conditional theater—not a reflection but an expression and re-creation of life.

Naturally, while considering these new aims of art, Blok pondered the transcendence of his own lyricism, his "lyrical" soul "tuned to a single song and therefore limited." He hoped to break through these limitations by the theme and mood of farce. "This, for me," he said "is the *cleansing* moment, the exit from lyrical isolation."[50]

Blok's significant letter no doubt suggested much to Meyerhold. The director drew his own conclusions from the poet's program. Blok was overcoming from within the crisis of Symbolist lyricism by way of letting loose the irony from his soul, giving the farce an ironic and destructive sense, which at the same time brought youth and life to the "dead matter" of reality. Meyerhold found here the possibility to leave the esthetic system of Symbolist theater for new endeavors in a wider sphere of activity. The forced other-worldliness of Symbolist theater approached life, opening up to farce, comedy and theatricality, sometimes "frightful and debauched," in Blok's words, at other times uninhibitedly and spontaneously joyous. A new form for his art—that of the conditional theater—was becoming defined, and this form was to become central in Meyerhold's life. The Symbolist productions in the Ofitserskaya Street theater were only a prologue to this development.

For Meyerhold, Symbolist theater was a path for transition to conditional theater.

In many ways, despite its external originality and novelty, Symbolist theater was tied in the closest fashion to psychological theater, the theater of "mood," and developed its stage forms, making them more delicate and soft. Symbolist theater retained the "fourth wall" that invisibly separated actors from audience. The principle of the "staged painting" was retained, with the sole change that this "painting" depicted not the common, everyday course of life, but the world of the fantastic and the unreal. The spectator was not invited "to visit the Prozorov sisters," but was to accept a fairy-tale castle or underwater kingdom as reality.* The arts of pause and subtext which had come from "mood" theater were perfected and elaborated in Symbolist theater. But these were retained, as were the containment of the action in a stage frame and its separation from the audience.

On the other hand, as soon as unreality had become the depicted subject, there was no more need for realistic staging, plasticity and intonation; "life-like" speech, poses and placement of characters on the stage became unnecessary. It was at this point, in the search for sculptural stagings, for special signficance of intonations and in the compression of stage depth, that the possibility opened up for a transition to the esthetics of conditional theater which sought no imitation or illusion in the spheres of reality or of unreal poetry.

The sequence of staging forms is clearly visible in the development of Meyerhold's art.

Chronologically, the production of Blok's *The Puppet Show* coincided exactly with a most significant turn in the graphic arts. Cubism—specifically Picasso's "Les Demoiselles d'Avignon"—first appeared in 1907. There is an unquestionable internal connection between these two events.

Having stepped onto the path of conditional theater, Meyerhold was substantially rethinking the fundamental, generally accepted principles of stage art which had been formulated toward the end of the nineteenth century and which had reached their fullest and most complete expression in the work of the Moscow Art

---

*J. Gassner writes that Symbolists in theater strove to "create illusion" (but illusions of another type than those striven for by realists), that is, *the illusions of unreality*—the expression of the idea that we live in a mysterious "poetic" world and not in the world of concrete facts. Their aim was "with equal ease to cause the unreal to appear real and the real—unreal" (J. Gassner, *Forma i ideia v sovremennom teatre* [Moscow, 1959], p. 125).

Theater. His polemic with the Art Theater grew increasingly conscious and deep.

The decisive rejection of the very principle of the reproduction of reality clashed with the most scrupulous realism of the Moscow Art Theater, its concern for the reality of every mood and feeling, and its striving to achieve the most precise picture possible of the movement of life. This new tendency becomes increasingly visible in Meyerhold's work.

Changes began with the production of *The Puppet Show*.

In the *Puppet Show* production, Meyerhold, who had accustomed the audience in the Ofitserskaya Street theater to a shallow stage and a sculptural expressiveness on the part of the actors, suddenly abandoned these tried and virtually established forms. The full depth of the stage was suddenly exposed. The wings were covered by blue canvas and a blue horizon was hung at the back in such a way that the result was a solid blue background. The light, white, small theater constructed on the stage stood out in sharp contrast.

The "mini-theater," as Meyerhold explained, has its own stage boards, its own curtain, its own prompter's box, its own portal and arch. The upper part of the "mini-theater" is not covered by the traditional Harlequin—the gridirons with all the ropes and wires are in full view. When the decorations are raised in the "mini-theater" into the real gridirons, the audience sees their whole motion.

In front of the "mini-theater" on the stage along the entire length of the ramp a free space was left for the author, who serves as a sort of mediator between the audience and the small stage.

"The action," continued the director, "commences upon a signal from the large drum. First, music plays and we see the prompter climb into his box and light the candles. The 'mini-theater' curtain rises to reveal a three-walled 'pavilion' with one wall to the left of the audience, one in the center and window to the right. On the stage parallel with the ramp is a long table at which the 'mystics' are sitting . . . . below the window is a small round table with a potted geranium and a golden chair on which Pierrot is sitting."[51]

Meyerhold staged the scene with the "mystics" with astounding simplicity. The long table at which the mystics were sitting was covered with black cloth. The cloth hung from the table to the floor, so the audience saw "just the upper part of their figures. Frightened by some reply, the mystics lower their heads in such a way that they become headless and armless. It turns out that these are *cardboard cutouts* of figures on which the suits and cuffs had been drawn with ash and chalk. The actors' hands had been pushed through the round holes cut in the cardboard busts and their heads had been leaning against cardboard collars."[52]

The director's solution is surprisingly bold, original and unusually precise: the mystics who, according to Blok, are gravely awaiting events, become transformed into a species of *moulage*. These painted cardboard mannequins are lifeless and empty, coming alive only when the actors put their arms and heads through the cut-out openings. This is the image of lifeless mannequins that Meyerhold realizes with such direct genius.

"Harlequin," continued Meyerhold, "first appears out from under the 'mystics' table." When the author runs out onto the proscenium he is not permitted to finish his tirade; someone invisible pulls him back behind the curtains by his coattails—it turns out he is tied to a rope that keeps him from interrupting the solemn action on the stage. 'Sad Pierrot (in the second scene is sitting on a bench in the center of the stage,' behind him is a cupid on a pedestal. When Pierrot completes his long monologue the bench and the cupid with the pedestal together with the decorations are raised upward before the eyes of the audience, and a traditional colonnaded hall (by N. N. Sapunov) is lowered. In the scene where masks appear from behind the wings with a cry of 'torches!' prop-men hold two irons blazing with Bengal light, and not only the flame but the two hands holding the irons are visible."[53]

The fact that these two arms of the prop-men were visible to the audience was a point of special—and understandable—pride for Meyerhold. Up until his production of *The Puppet Show* nobody anywhere at any time had dared to reveal to the audience the secrets of stage effects. Theater had not even dreamed of such frankness. In the old folk theater such effects could have been noticeable, but never had been *specially* demonstrated to the public. Until this moment the idea of boldly exposing illusion and revealing the secrets of the "theatrical kitchen" had been utterly foreign to early twentieth-century Russian theater. This theater had aspired to render a picture of life, the atmosphere of life, its mood and spirit. Meyerhold rejected these aspirations.

For the first time, theater plainly told the audience that it was not ashamed of being theater. In Blok's remarks there was a note that "a hand from behind the curtain grabs the Author by the scruff of the neck." Of course, it was this remark that gave such a sharp jolt to Meyerhold's imagination and caused him to construct a theater within the theater, to let the Author out on a leash, to pull him back behind the stage with a rope, and to show the public how decorations are changed in the theater, whose upper curtain Meyerhold had removed without hesitation.

Meyerhold himself played Pierrot—an amusing ne'er-do-well, a solitary dreamer and poet, alienated from life. "Harlequin's bell makes a victorious sound," recalled S. Auslender, "frightful, beckoning masks flicker past, and he, white Pierrot... all sharp-angled, whispering words of unearthly sorrow with constrained voice; he is sort of prickly, soul-piercing, tender but bold at the same time...."[54] Flexible, brittle, tender, sardonically biting Pierrot-Meyerhold was a fantastic but most insistent objection to the cheap farce of life. He was not compatible with this life, was clearly alienated from it, but at the same time he would come in contact with life, only to be roughly pushed away by it each time. Pierrot's spirituality was interpreted as his weakness, his Achilles' heel. His spirituality was equated with his vulnerability. But it was in this vulnerability of Pierrot that Meyerhold, for the second time in his life (Treplyov had been the first time), expressed himself as an actor lyrically developed in a stage image, saw and maintained the higher meaning of the artist's calling. The theme of Pierrot appeared as the theme of the bitter and beautiful loneliness of poetry, and of art doomed to being misunderstood.

It is possible that even more significant and relevant to the time was the sudden and decisive onslaught of Symbolism in *The Puppet Show*. The leader of Symbolism in poetry, Blok, and the creator of Symbolist theater, Meyerhold, had unexpectedly joined forces in this production and, with a sarcastic chuckle, had ripped the solemn covering of secrecy from Symbolist theater. The mystical aspirations of the Symbolists, their expectation of "the maiden from faraway lands" (easily recognizable as Blok's Beautiful Lady), their sighs about "eternal fear and eternal darkness," their phrases about "evanescent" voices (willingly or not, recalling Meyerhold's techniques), all this was rendered and ridiculed in the characters of the mystics. Behind the ponderous weight of their words and the visionary bombast of their predictions a sorry farce was suddenly revealed.

This outraged many Symbolists. Andrei Bely was especially injured, interpreting *The Puppet Show* as treason to Symbolism and discerning "bitter ridicule of his own past"[55] in Blok's play. Bely maintained that Blok was "cursing" with *The Puppet Show*: "mysticism is criticized so strangely by the poet that the question arises whether he has any conception of it."[56] In August of 1907 Bely wrote to Blok: "In your *Dramas* I see constant blasphemy."[57] In an article entitled "World Fragments," dedicated to the publication of Blok's plays, Bely stated that Blok had lost the total sense of reality, that his dramas poeticize the void, that in them there is "the joining of the fragments of a once-whole reality . . . the beauty of confusion but not the beauty of contemplation of the valuable."[58]

Truth is truth: *The Puppet Show* destroyed the abstracted-from-reality and highly conditional unity of that model of existence which the Symbolists had attempted to construct.

The Symbolists' beloved, and one might say crowning, theme of hoping for "the quiet redeemer"—death—was presented with undisguised irony. Before the eyes of the audience Death with the scythe became transformed into the smiling Columbine.

In *The Puppet Show*, Blok and Meyerhold abruptly and with irony "removed" all the coverings and illusions of Symbolism, all its "wonders," mystical aspirations, sweet dreams and dark predictions.

The author and the director of the play, although each in fact headed the artistic movement in his proper sphere, were undisguisedly poking fun both at Symbolism and at themselves. The production ironically underscored the excessive self-importance of Symbolist esthetics and the dystrophy of humor that Blok and Meyerhold sensed in Symbolism.

When *The Puppet Show* was presented, the public was perplexed. According to the testimony of a contemporary, the audience lost its "usual criteria for evaluation" and "divided into two camps: one group was enraged, and hissed and whistled, the other applauded with equal vigor. If after the first presentations of the theater the public had argued politely and relatively peacefully, this time they were cursing each other. Passions flared, and this would happen at each show. The protesters would even arm themselves with keys..."[59] [to whistle through—K. R.]. E. Ivanov, Blok's friend, wrote in his diary: "December 30. The first presentation of *The Puppet Show*. Whistles and applause. The author was presented with a laurel wreath and people were throwing flowers."[60]

Georgy Chulkov had this to say about the premiere:

Everyone who attended this first presentation of *The Puppet Show* remembers the passionate excitement that overcame the auditorium, the stir that took place in the stalls after the last sounds of Kuzmin's sharp, heady, troubled and voluptuous music and when the curtain was lowered, dividing the audience from the mysterious and magical world in which the poet Pierrot lived and sang. Neither before nor since have I ever observed such uncompromising opposition and such delight in a theater audience. The frenzied whistling of the enemies and the thunderous applause of the friends were mixed with shouts and yells. This was fame. It was a true celebration.[61]

Sergei Auslender, the critic, also wrote about the atmosphere at the premiere:

The tumult in the audience resembled an actual battle; reputable people were ready to come to blows; whistles and roars of hate were interrupted by reverberating shouts of mirth, challenge, anger and despair: "Blok, Sapunov, Kuzmin, M-e-y-e-r-h-o-l-d, b-r-a-v-o-o-o...." Facing the smitten crowd, radiant, like a fine monument, in his severe black suit and with white lilies in his hands . . . stood Alexander Alexandrovich Blok. Sadness and amusement could be seen in his blue eyes, while next to him coiled white Pierrot, seemingly boneless, bodiless; a phantom waving the long sleeves of his dress.[62]

A. Dyakonov, when saying that Blok considered the production to be "ideal" (the poet had dedicated *The Puppet Show* to V. E. Meyerhold), states that during intermission " . . . the audience went wild. Young people and Blok's admirers were ecstatic, called him out and gave him an ovation, while the rest of the audience greeted him with whistles and hisses. Much was written about the author, the play and the production... The vast majority of reviews were vituperative and sometimes jeering at the author and his 'Bedlamchik' " [the Russian title of *The Puppet Show* is *Balaganchik*—G. P.].[63]

This is true. Kugel's review, for example, demonstrated the evident confusion on the part of the critics. "Mr. Blok's *The Puppet Show*," he wrote, "is a very strange production that is intended to be slightly weird. The 'farce' is evidently supposed to represent the world; the figure of Pierrot—the role of man as fool. This should be understood, but is not understood because the symbols, similes, allegories and hints by the author are so indefinite, so vague, that the image obtained is of some sort of dance of snowflakes."

And this "dance of snowflakes" caused Kugel to suspect that "Blok and those with him wanted to amuse themselves with a Symbolist allegory at the expense of the public." The public, accordingly, "had full right to be angry...."[64]

When *The Puppet Show* played in Moscow, the audience, according to V. I. Strazhev,

was sharply divided into passionate "friends" and bitter "foes." During the play I could hear around me the snake hisses and derisive "ha-has" from the latter and angry cries of "Quiet!" (loudly) and "Foolishness" (quietly) from the former. After the last words of the sad dreamer Pierrot: "I am very sad. And you are amused?"—and the curtain lowered to the sounds of his mournful pipe, the audience was boiling—people argued and swore, even strangers were practically ready to lay into one another. The "enemies" hurried out to calm down at the buffet and in the smoking-room, while the "friends" pressed toward the ramp and without mercy to hands or throat, called out in a frenzy for the actors....[65]

A. I. Yuzhin, who saw the production in Moscow, wrote to his wife: "Blok's *The Puppet Show* is an indescribable ugliness, but does hit the nerves. Whistles and furious applause."[66]

Meyerhold was always pleased and excited by scandal in the theater. The urges to surprise, astound, baffle and shock were for him characteristic, and there were times when he would sacrifice more serious aims in order to achieve such an effect. His inexhaustible imagination would frequently suggest daring and fantastic solutions. Especially in his youth, Meyerhold would unhesitatingly follow all the caprices of his imagination, if he was certain of being able to arouse amazement at least. He was occasionally capable of jeopardizing the unity and sense of a production for strong effect. But in *The Puppet Show*, a whole series of highly effective Meyerholdian illuminations and director's discoveries flawlessly followed both the spirit and the meaning of the play and production.

The public had become disoriented, excited by the ideological and esthetic newness of Blok's and Meyerhold's creation.

Meyerhold himself understood this perfectly. Five years later, he wrote: "Even though part of the audience did hiss at Blok and his actors, the theater was theater. And, possibly, this very circumstance—that is, that the public dared to whistle so hysterically, best proves that this marked the establishment of an attitude toward the production as to a presentation of the theater."[67] The confirmation of the principle of theatricality, executed so methodically here, put an end to the era of services in a "theater-temple." The idea of the "theater-temple" itself, which had been so dear to Meyerhold just a short while before, was renounced, and the public "emancipated," freed from serious contemplation. For the first time the public was invited to be active, was given free rein.

Meyerhold's harlequinade, which began with *The Puppet Show* and was to remain for a long time one of the basic themes of the director's art, had a deep and important meaning. "The turn to technique and the tradition of mask comedy," said Eisenstein many years later, "was a jerk toward the direction of tangible and exposed counterpoint, tangible in the 'rough' play of the dramaturgical lines and threads of the actions of individual characters, as opposed to the unified polyphony of the nuances of Chekhov's heroes."[68] Meyerhold brought the tradition of *Commedia dell'arte* out of the past, in order to tear the web of "mood" and open the field to action, to reject nervous refinement and develop the full energy of the struggle.

The Puppet Show, as presented in the theater on Ofitserskaya Street, confounded the strict and haughty auditorium. The production seemed cramped in the hall; it seemed to call into the street, promising the boldness and the sassiness of street productions.

But at this moment of significant transition for Meyerhold, the Russian stage, both in Petersburg and Moscow, passed into the hands of Leonid Andreev, one of whose major characteristics was his ability to spell everything out. As opposed to Maeterlinck's mysterious inconclusiveness, his indistinct hints and vague prophecies, Leonid Andreev provided dark predictions, both definite and distinct, and a cry in contrast to the Maeterlinckian mumble.

Andreev's plays caused Symbolist theater to catch up rapidly with the times.

The Russian anger of the day broke through, and was expressed in these plays. This was their attraction. Furthermore, they caused shifts in the esthetics of Symbolism; one could already hear the anguished notes of Expressionism.

This anguish was, in part, the result of a tragic interpretation of Russian life, and in part was generated by the internal contradictions in the development of Andreev's talent. The two poles of Russian art of that time attracted him equally: on the one hand, the social concreteness and relatively precise political program of the Znanie school; on the other, the high-flown otherworldliness of the Symbolism. Andreev attempted to reconcile the Cosmic and eternal ideas of Symbolism with the grim Russian reality. Hence, we see simultaneously the screaming nightmares of his interpretation of reality, along with the crudity, concreteness and civic tendencies of his "cosmism."

Leonid Andreev's strictly logical stage compositions, their rational firmness, together with the exaltedness characteristic of this writer, stripped the Symbolist themes of significance and enigma. In place of symbols Andreev advanced frightening allegories. This was a substitution that almost no one noticed at the time.

A good fifteen years later, O. Mandelstam ironically recollected Andreev's plays as "strong and elemental, understandable to all, thanks to their clearly outlined action." And further, how "He, She, It and other significant characters brought panic to the impressionable Russian intellectual."[69] In 1907, Blok alone, objecting to the criticism of Andreev as an imitator of Maeterlinck, clearly stated the essential difference between them. "There is nothing of Maeterlinck in *The Life of Man*," he wrote, "there is only the presence of Maeterlinck. That is, perhaps Andreev has read Maeterlinck, and that is all. But Maeterlinck never reached such cruelty, such crudity, naivete or lack of subtlety in his statements. It is for this naivete and lack of subtlety," continued Blok, "that I love *The Life of Man* and believe that for a long time there has been no play of equal importance and relevance."

Relevant and important, according to the author of *The Puppet Show*, was the "unsubtle" and "naive," darkly fatalistic representation of "Man's entire life, together with its dark beginning and dark end."[70] Blok was struck by the loud and even hysterical theme of despair voiced by Andreev. "His every phrase," wrote Blok to Verigina, "is a disagreeable squeal, as if from a saw, when he is a weak person, and an animal roar when he is a creator and artist. These cries and screams penetrate me completely, cause me to freeze... I am too close to final despair...."[71]

Andreev's *The Life of Man* was received as the new word in Symbolist Theater. And a new word had in fact been pronounced in this play, since the theme of fate, before which Man is powerless, was clearly tied to the theme and allegorical images of contemporary society. Man was set against a fate (Someone in Gray) equivalent to social law.

It is possible to reverse this thought: contemporary social structure was interpreted as tragic inevitability. The Someone in Gray was its highest manifestation, its stage reality. He spoke in the name of eternity, but this very eternity was interpreted as a hyperbolic image of contemporary times. Correspondingly, the powerlessness of Man, his inability to resist fate, appeared as socially conditioned fatalism. Despair was established as the sole possibility of existence—even with some measure of ecstatic self-annihilation. Both Stanislavksy and Meyerhold were immediately taken with the play. It was accepted for production both by the Moscow Art Theater and V. F. Komissarzhevskaya's Drama Theater.

Meyerhold, who never allowed himself to be outdone, began rehearsals in February 1907, and conducted them at a frenzied pace. Rehearsals took place in the daytime and at night, following evening performances. In Moscow, Stanislavsky was worried. He feared that Meyerhold would guess and use his plan of direction.[72]

These fears proved to be groundless. There was little in common between the Petersburg and the Moscow production of ten months later. Meyerhold presented the concept of the play, as delineated by Andreev, with greater consistency than had the author. In every case when Andreev, according to young Kornei Chukovsky's apt observation, displayed an impulse "to hide in a corner," to downplay the philosophical problem of the piece, Meyerhold would object firmly and consistently, and avoided depicting everyday detail, "showing not 'the life of *one* man,' but 'the life of man in general.' "[73] For exactly this reason, the author's note that "everything is as in a dream" became Meyerhold's guide. Meyerhold hung the stage, which had been opened to its full depth, with gray canvas. The result was a smoky, monochromatic gray space which appeared to billow about the figure of K. Bravich (Someone in Gray) reading the prologue, candle in hand. The stage grew fully dark. Then a lamp gradually illuminated one corner of the stage where Andreev's old women were sitting on the sofa and chairs.

Meyerhold explained:

> Likewise, in all the other scenes, a single source of light would lay a spot of light on some part of the stage, sufficient only to illuminate the furniture placed about it and the actor who is near the light source. By covering the entire stage with gray darkness and by illuminating only separate places, by using only a single source of light . . . it became possible to give the audience the impression that the room walls have been constructed on the stage, but that the audience does not see them because the light does not reach the walls. The role of furniture and accessories becomes greater on the stage empty of the usual decorations.... A single characteristic object replaces many that are less characteristic. The viewer must remember some unusual contour of the sofa, a grandiose column, some sort of gilded armchair, a bookcase the size of the stage, a cumbersome buffet, and, using these separate parts of the whole, imagine the rest. Naturally, human figures have to be molded precisely, like sculpture, and the make-up must be sharply delineated....[74]

"This production," stressed Meyerhold, "showed that not everything in New Theater results in the presentation of the stage as a plane. The aspirations of New Theater are not at all limited, as many people think, to bringing the entire system of decorations to a landscape panel and to melding the actors' figures with this panel, making them flat, arbitrary bas-reliefs."[75]

It was unusual for Meyerhold and the Ofitserskaya Street theater that the play was staged, for the first time, without a decorator. "The decorations and props are according to my plans and directions," noted Meyerhold in listing his tasks as director.[76] In these "directions" of his he was frequently quite radical. Thus, for instance, in the third scene (Ball at the Man's House) where Andreev wanted a "very tall, large, right-angled room with completely smooth white walls," and where the playwright had indicated "incongruity in the correspondence of the parts, their sizes—thus, the doors are disproportionately small in relation to the windows." Meyerhold ignored the notes, in no way striving for a "strange, somewhat irritating" and "disharmonious" effect, and simply set down eight white columns, and in the center hung a large lamp with a shade.

Blok, who watched *The Life of Man* several times from the stage, from the left wing, noted in this context that Andreev's remarks are "dubious in the *stage* sense" and that "Meyerhold did much better in constructing the thick gray-white colonnade in a half-circle and by seating the intentionally idiotic ladies and senile old men at the base of each column."

Blok was of the opinion that *The Life of Man* "is Meyerhold's best production," that Meyerhold and his troupe captured Andreev's " . . . atmosphere, that air which surrounded him and which they were able to transmit to the stage in such a way as even the Art Theater could not do. There was something akin to Andreev in some of the actors and in the director of Komissarzhevskaya's troupe. Even relatively weak actors were able to awaken within themselves that chaos which followed them so closely."[77]

The productions staged by Meyerhold in the interval between the plays by Blok and Andreev (Heiberg's *The Tragedy of Love*, von Hofmannsthal's *The Marriage of Sobeide*, Ibsen's *A Doll's House*) had no great significance. In these productions there were variations of the previously-tested forms.

The ideas that had come to Meyerhold during his work on *The Puppet Show* were not developed in the further presentations of the theater on Ofitserskaya Street. Despite the extraordinary speed with which he worked, Meyerhold, while rushing from play to play, had not had the time to clothe these ideas in specific stage compositions. Furthermore, the plays that he was staging did not permit such an opportunity—they were locked into Symbolist imagery, were inclined toward ponderous immobility and tended toward two-dimensionality along the ramp. Meyerhold had already had enough of these techniques.

The theater, which Meyerhold had just recently forced into the two-dimensionality of decorative panels, wanted to return to its natural three-dimensionality and natural dynamics. Plays like *The Tragedy of Love* and *The Marriage of Sobeide* appeared to resist this desire.

Reviewers wrote about *The Tragedy of Love* and *The Marriage of Sobeide* with liberal irony. A. Kugel wrote regarding Heiberg's play: "Mrs. Komissarzhevskaya was running about in a red raincoat, Mr. Bravich was juggling two suitcases. They spoke of love in the tones of an excellent comedy, then as coarse physiology, then in other ways... But most marvelous of all in this production was Mr. Meyerhold in the role of Poet. We have never seen acting that was duller, less talented or less supportable..."[78] In *The Marriage of Sobeide* the reviewers were puzzled by the juxtaposition of "monotonous delivery" with "pointless, apelike leaps," which, they maintained, "are the latest invention of Mr. Meyerhold. For Sobeide, Mrs. Komissarzhevskaya lacks, first of all, youth... And for Sobeide this is as necessary as for Juliet."[79]

It would appear that this was the first time the press indelicately pointed out to Komissarzhevskaya that she was no longer young. Komissarzhevskaya played in

The Tragedy of Love, The Marriage of Sobeide and *A Doll's House*, but only in playing Nora did she successfully show her old power. For Meyerhold, however, *A Doll's House* was simply a concession to the leading lady and owner of the theater, who was becoming irritated by his experiments. Komissarzhevskaya bluntly wrote to Meyerhold about *The Marriage of Sobeide*: "I would like to believe that fate will give me the pleasure of not playing her in Moscow." She reproachfully reminded the director that already in *Hedda Gabler* she had asked for a precise implementation of Ibsen's remarks. Then Komissarzhevskaya recalled the production of *A Doll's House*, staged in the Passage prior to Meyerhold's arrival: "It is essential to change the atmosphere of the room to make it warmer, and nothing more... The impression must be that of a cozy, soft nest isolated from the *real* world. We will, of course, retain all the *mises en scene*."[80]

It is unlikely that all these wishes pleased Meyerhold. Nonetheless, he retained director Petrovsky's staging. But he did not create the "soft nest." On the contrary, the newspapers reported that "instead of the usual room inhabited by people, we see a fantasy of the director: the wall has been replaced by curtains that reach far upward. This is neither truthful nor attractive."[81] Komissarzhevskaya, who had changed nothing in her interpretation of one of her most popular roles, again performed with great success.

Komissarzhevskaya's triumphs in this old, "pre-Meyerholdian" role, wedged as they were between *The Puppet Show* and *The Life of Man*, visibly demonstrated the contradictions that were ripening at the Ofitserskaya Street theater.

Nearly all the Petersburg critics reacted to Meyerhold's experiments with disdain and sarcasm. The most popular Russian theater magazine of the day, *Theater and Art*, was openly conservative. The magazine was headed by A. Kugel, a talented, clever and acidulous critic, an objector in principle to directors' theater. Kugel's esthetic views had been formed under the influence of the great constellation of talent at the Alexandrinsky Theater—M. Savina, V. Davidov, K. Varlamov and others. Kugel neither understood nor accepted the renovation of the Russian stage through the efforts of Stanislavsky and Nemirovich-Danchenko in Moscow, and Komissarzhevskaya in Petersburg. Even when the Moscow Art Theater and Komissarzhevskaya had received nationwide renown, Kugel continued to oppose them. It is natural that Meyerhold's experiments would irritate and confuse Kugel. He wrote:

I fail to see the substantive difference between the carpentry and paperhanging of Mr. Stanislavsky and the carpentry and paperhanging of Mr. Meyerhold. And this is the crux: the substitution of carpentry and paperhanging for the actor's talent. Does it matter what direction this carpentry and paperhanging take—either toward making everything "as in life" or toward the end that nothing be "as in life"? . . . The point is that the center of gravity in theater has shifted from the acting to the production and mechanics. The mechanics, instead of remaining in an appropriate position, have taken a commanding position and have become transformed into a self-contained art in which the actors have become mere decorations: makeup is not to enhance the face, but the face is to enhance the makeup, the costume is not an addition to the figure, but the figure is an addition to the costume, the gesture is not an addition to the intonation, but the intonation is an addition to a plotted gesture.[82]

In this period, when the fame of the Art Theater was at its zenith, Stanislavsky could casually refer to Kugel as "talented, but of no use."[83]

Meyerhold and Komissarzhevskaya were in a different situation. Not infrequently, Kugel's criticism of their theater was direct and to the point. But even when Meyerhold's success was wholly apparent, Kugel would manage to offer a totally unexpected explanation for such success. Thus, for instance, regarding *The Life of Man*, he wrote: "If the direction of Mr. Meyerhold, who is known for his absurdities, was sufficiently good this time, then it is because the author himself acted as director; that is, the proper person inspired the production, not 'Someone in Gray,' and the grayest of the gray, like Mr. Meyerhold." But Kugel's coarse statement was too far from the truth—we already know that Meyerhold had ignored Andreev's remarks. Meyerhold, continued the critic, "somehow managed to alter the harmonious and unified decorations, the result of which was complete nonsense."[84] It turned out that the production was "adequately good," but still "nonsense." But this lack of logic disturbed no one. On the contrary, for the most part the Petersburg reviewers tended to follow Kugel's lead.

Komissarzhevskaya, who knew perfectly well that Kugel "could not calmly hear"[85] her name, held her position firmly under the fire of criticism and maintained that "only one thing is necessary: firmly and undeviatingly to follow the predetermined path, making allowances for no one and nothing. Each attempt to finish with old forms usually meets with a host of opposition, and one must be prepared for this."[86]

But such heroic readiness to forge forward to new forms no longer meant a full alliance with Meyerhold. Differences emerged immediately following the close of the first season of the theater on Ofitserskaya Street.

Komissarzhevskaya and her troupe went on tour. The repertoire consisted almost exclusively of her old plays: *The Poor Bride, The Battle of Butterflies, The Wild-Woman, A Doll's House* and *St. John's Fires.* Of the plays directed by Meyerhold only *Hedda Gabler, The Life of Man* and *The Tragedy of Love* had been selected. But Komissarzhevskaya played these only infrequently, preferring to play Nora, Rosie, Marikka and Larisa—her basic roles. She played without special success.

Meyerhold's main opponent in the troupe was the actress' brother, the director F. F. Komissarzhevsky, who undoubtedly received full support from K. V. Bravich, a partner of many years, a faithful friend and advisor to Komissarzhevskaya. The constant attacks of the critics, the unquestionable failure of a number of Meyerhold's productions, the fatigue of K. V. Bravich and some other actors from Meyerhold's experiments, and finally F. Komissarzhevsky's dream to head his own theater and indicate a different, more reliable path to "new art"—all these factors inevitably led to conflict within the theater. A strong coalition began to organize against Meyerhold. It became stronger during the tour of Komissarzhevskaya's theater in Moscow. The Moscow public was shown *Sister Beatrice* and *The Miracle of St. Anthony; The Puppet Show* and *The Eternal Fairy-Tale* (two plays were shown on each night). Both Komissarzhevskaya and Meyerhold had wanted badly to play *The Life of Man* in Moscow, but Leonid Andreev, constrained by his arrangements with the Moscow Art Theater, which was rehearsing his play, was obliged to forbid the presentation of the Petersburg production in Moscow.

Komissarzhevskaya ascribed "very great significance" to the performances of the theater in Moscow, awaited them with "mad anxiety," and wished *to show Moscow the face of theater clearly and distinctly.*[87] But, contrary to her expectations, Moscow reviewers responded negatively to the productions of her theater. Even the relatively friendly reviews had hidden poison. The critic in the magazine *Russian Artist (Russkii artist)* wrote of *Sister Beatrice*: "In front of a large, dirty canvas, between two gray strips, a girl appeared—Beatrice, who is already enduring everything that she prays to be shown. The marvelous diction, the pleasant voice of the actress (now, unfortunately, strongly altered by time), the plastic, well-planned, but overlearned and nearly standardized technique, frequently caused one to think of the great school, the excellent details, to compare one intonation with another, one pose with the next, but not to think of Beatrice."[88]

Naturally, the theme of the fall of Komissarzhevskaya's talent, which now was reflected in numerous articles, pained the actress.

Unexpectedly, the circles close to the Art Theater proved to be more supportive. For instance, N. E. Efros responded with great attention to the productions of V. F. Komissarzhevskaya's theater. "In some of the ideas that rule the activity of these revolutionaries of the stage," he wrote, "I either see or sense, through all the multi-colored trash, a great and important truth." Although considering the principles of stage realism to have no substitutes and to be solely correct, N. Efros was predicting their long-range renovation and development:

> The truth of life, the truth of human feeling, always remain the first and unchanging law of stage art. And when this law is violated, stage art ceases to be itself, ceases to be art and soon will collapse under the weight of great uselessness. But the ways to discover and materialize this truth are many and various. And many of the old ways are becoming overgrown. While those who in the devil-may-care urge to innovate will not accept this truth as being the soul of the theater, all their meanderings open up other as yet unclear ways, and these ways, perhaps unexpectedly to the perpetrators, or possibly to their discredit, will lead to the same goal from the opposite direction—to the deep and truthful revelation of the secrets of the soul.

This was a brave and, for those times, unexpected thought, but the future demonstrated that N. Efros had perceptively gauged the prospects for the development of conditional theater.

He continued: "And in the fashion that the Chekhovian 'mood,' which not so long ago had countered realism, not only did not destroy realism, but generously enriched it with new content and widened its framework, so the new material that enters the stage under the banner of Symbolism, after losing much of its window-dressing, will enrich this same realism with beautiful, valuable content."

Finally, N. Efros indicated directly that the Art Theater, too, intended to move in the same direction. "The argument raised by the productions of the Petersburg innovators will see long continuity in Moscow, since the Art Theater is dedicating two of its productions—*The Blue Bird* and *The Life of Man*—to new forms and to the founding of new stage rules. And, of course, Stanislavsky's enormous talent, likewise great in its error, will manage to make its efforts significant."[89]

Of extreme interest was Stanislavsky's opinion of Meyerhold's productions.

Stanislavsky saw *The Miracle of St. Anthony* and *Sister Beatrice*.

But his utterances about that night were lost in old newspaper files and up until the present day had been unknown to biographers of Stanislavsky, as well as to researchers into the work of Komissarzhevskaya and Meyerhold. A reporter of a Moscow newspaper had a discussion with Stanislavsky:

> The conversation first touched upon Komissarzhevskaya's theater.
>
> "It is difficult for me to say," said K. S., "anything definite about this theater. On the one hand, Komissarzhevskaya's points of origin are the same as those of our late Studio, on the other hand she has gone so far in their development... no, come so far, that I... No, I will not say: a rival theater..."
>
> "What sort of competition is there in art?"
>
> "Yes, of course..."
>
> He thought and added:
>
> "Stage realism is essential. You cannot just break with the past. Only infants have their umbilical cut..."
>
> K. S. accepts stylization only as a means to simplify production difficulties, and nothing more.
>
> "Do you remember our *The Drama of Life*? But at the same time this is a most dangerous path. A minor, unsuccessful stroke is enough to destroy a thoroughly planned picture with all the details drawn in. When the curtain was raised on *The Miracle of St. Anthony*, I said to myself: good, very good! Sudeikin's decorations, harmony of life. But 'Mister Joseph, Mister Francis...' and the servant-girl jumping along in time, scrubbing the floor. This is good for a comedy of daily life, but it destroyed the effect of *The Miracle*. And to have a dead woman resurrected before the eyes of the public—this is in very poor taste. This should have been done in some other way."
>
> "That means you do not totally reject the conditional in theater, on the stage boards?"
>
> "I dislike it, only dislike it. The same Komissarzhevskaya in *Sister Beatrice* plays ideally, consistently, without a single incorrect gesture. But Bravich breaks in and it all collapses.
>
> "They say that there were a couple of successful moments in *The Puppet Show*. I have not seen *The Puppet Show*... Although I do not understand what use she has for all this gloom. The urge to remake everything anew, to remove the old, respected axes from the world and replace them with new, flimsy but fashionable ones. A risky venture: if the world does not collapse from these childish attempts then in any case she will bruise her fingers. To break with the past like this—I do not understand it. This is a protest. But what is there to protest? If Komissarzhevskaya returns to daily reality, I would be very happy."[90]

Specific criticisms directed at Meyerhold, along with unquestionably high praise of Komissarzhevskaya in the role of Beatrice, are contained in Stanislavsky's comments. But the main thought, sounding most significant on the lips of the director who was preparing *The Life of Man* and *The Blue Bird*, was that the search for the new cannot be carried out while breaking completely with the old. Stanislavsky defended the concept of continuity in the development process of art. Following the first bitter experience of the Studio, he had come to the conclusion that new forms could be integrated only in an evolutionary, and in no wise revolutionary, manner. "For Stanislavsky," Yu. Kalashnikov justly observes, "the unsuccessful experiment with the production of *The Drama of Life* was a turning point in his method of working with image, which not accidentally coincided with his first attempt to present a unified system. The creator of the system himself understood this completely: "In the period of my activity preceding Hamsun's *The Drama of Life*, I was moving artistically from the external (the periphery) to the internal (the center). Following *The Drama of Life* (now a system), it was the opposite, from center to periphery."[91]

The interview regarding Meyerhold's and Komissarzhevskaya's productions, given shortly after *The Drama of Life*, already contains the definite, firm criterion that everything external be verified by the internal, that all formal (peripheral) solutions are to be rejected if they do not correspond to the living spiritual essence (center).

It is probable that Meyerhold and Komissarzhevskaya attentively studied and variously interpreted Stanislavsky's response.

At precisely the same time the first rumor of a split between Meyerhold and Komissarzhevskaya had appeared and even surfaced in the press.

Back in September of 1907, one month before the event, the Moscow newspaper *Theater* published the "sensational news about the possible departure from V. F. Komissarzhevskaya's theater of the director V. E. Meyerhold." In commenting on this rumor, the newspaper stated: "Having taken the correct and fundamentally and unquestionably artistic principles of stylized and simplified productions, Mr. Meyerhold's revolutionary fervor has driven him so far to the left that this so-called 'simplification' in fact has become such a 'complication' that our brain, which senses the concrete, refuses to interpret what transpires on stage." The absence of the "vital oxygen of artistic truth" was perceived by the newspaper as the main cause for the conflict between Komissarzhevskaya and Meyerhold, and welcomed the decision by the actress to reject "the contrived and laborious state into which her fine talent had been placed by Mr. Meyerhold."[92]

Following the performances in Moscow, the theater returned to Ofitserskaya Street in Petersburg, where Meyerhold continued to work for a while longer. His last three productions in V. F. Komissarzhevskaya's theater bore the stamp of his distraction and internal turmoil.

There were several reasons for this, the chief of which was immediately apparent. Relationships within the theater had become increasingly tense and complex, and the Moscow critics had undermined Meyerhold's authority in the company. A second, less obvious and more fundamental cause for Meyerhold's distraction of this time was that he had already found himself in *The Puppet Show*, and that he knew and felt that *The Puppet Show* had marked the beginning of a totally new sphere of investigation, which in turn would require a series of new experiments. Meanwhile, the Ofitserskaya Street company was tired of experiments. Like any company, this one thirsted for success. And, finally, the most important and most secret cause was that for the leading lady of the company the *Puppet Show* path was impossible. Anyone but Komissarzhevskaya could have followed this path.

In the meantime, the new season had begun. Blok had not given Meyerhold his just-completed *Song of Fate*, since he cherished the naive hope that its production by the Moscow Art Theater was a possibility. The need to find and present to the public something attractive and significant caused Meyerhold to turn to Frank

Wedekind's *The Awakening of Spring*, a fashionable drama dedicated to the "problem" of sexual maturity. This was a questionable solution, and it was not without reason that Blok wrote: "While preparing to watch Wedekind's play I was afraid of refined erotomania." The poet, with unconcealed distaste, spoke of Wedekind as of Maeterlinck's "satiated last-born." "In the center of the play," he noted, "stands the question which he lisps about in his German way. We, in Russia, have never had this matter in *this* way; if it is so today, then it is only in closed circles which are fated to rot slowly, in the classes that emit the odor of a corpse."[93]

In addition to the erotic theme that was capable of generating excitement and creating an atmosphere of scandal about the theater, Meyerhold was evidently intrigued by the complex formal problem of the direction of the work, which was divided into some twenty separate episodes. (It is true that some of the episodes, such as the hayloft scene where the gymnasium student Wendla gives herself to the gymnasium student Melchior, had been eliminated by the censor.) The problem was further complicated by the lack of a revolving floor at the Ofitserskaya Street theater.

Contemporary reviews give us an indication of the manner in which Meyerhold solved this problem. "The stage was in three stories, the lowest of which was divided into three parts and separated from the back plane by some sort of angles."[94] "In the interests of stylization the actors playing the boys and the actresses playing the girls grimaced unnaturally, squealed absurdly and, in all probability, praised the god Eros with most unlovely and amusing body movements."[95]

Even those critics who were inclined to take the play seriously and spoke of the "tragedy of the child's soul" that stemmed from upbringing that repressed the "natural development of healthy, mutual attraction between two sexes" and transformed it into forms of "unhealthy sensuality," even these critics stated that already "by the third performance the hall was, to put it mildly, far from full."[96] The play was a failure.

The production of Maeterlinck's *Pelleas and Melisande* was an even more painful failure, although the reasons for this one were quite different. At the time, this play was of lively interest to many people. Stanislavsky and Nemirovich-Danchenko, for instance, were "measuring" it for the Art Theater repertoire. Stanislavsky, explaining his interest, wrote that *Pelleas and Melisande* "is the only more or less positive play" by Maeterlinck, that "his gloomy plays will not be accepted yet."[97] Nemirovich-Danchenko objected, with reason, that this play appeared to be "the property of the most peaceful currents of society," that it lacked "the notes of battle" with which "our social life is ringing." "Society," he predicted, "will remain deaf" to the beauties of *Pelleas and Melisande.*[98]

Probably, this play intrigued Meyerhold precisely because of this soft, elegiac tone, this theme of the invincible and incomprehensible, the meek and simultaneously all-conquering nature of love. The classic love triangle—the severe and willful Golo, his frail, palpitating wife Melisande and his brother, the tender and pure Pelleas—inevitably resulted in the perishing of all three. Their movement toward destruction was illustrated with Maeterlinck's characteristically shifting contours, the significant mysteriousness of various typically Symbolist details: the wedding band falls into the stream and disappears, the pigeons fly from the tower and do not return, the underground lake gives off the reek of corpses and poisons the castle, and so forth. The themes of love and jealousy merged in a grim and sorrowful medley.

Of all Maeterlinck's plays, and possibly of all Symbolist plays staged in Russia, this one was exceptional in its total divorce from social problems. The play was unable to evoke any contemporary associations, any allusions. Nemirovich-Danchenko's supposition that Russian society would remain deaf to its beauties was soon proven to be true.

In any case, in deciding to stage *Pelleas and Melisande,* Meyerhold apprently expected that, following the exaggerated pathos of *The Life of Man,* such a turn to quiet significance and fine lyricism was inevitable. Furthermore, Komissarzhevskaya badly wanted to play Melisande. But Meyerhold personally encountered one specific difficulty—mild, lyrical drama was foreign to his artistic temperament. This sphere was, for him, the most unnatural, and therefore all his effort was directed to the resolution of problems of a strictly formal nature. But the quest was not for anything new, but simply the application of already tested methods of "static theater" to a new play.

The production was hurried, the distribution of roles a compromise. The play premiered on October 10, 1907, to the laughter and catcalls of the public. Meyerhold's overall direction and V. I. Denisov's execution were criticized the most. The reviewers were puzzled by the decorations, "their distinct cardboardness and cut-out look," noted that the actors looked ridiculous "among gingerbread houses, trees unrecognizably stylized, bows and ribbons...."[99]

The odd word "cardboardness" was on everyone's lips. But this is not surprising: Meyerhold wore a cardboard beard when playing old King Arkel.

Many reviews of *Pelleas and Melisande* were humorous. The reviewers had been entertained. *New Time (Novoe vremia)* acidly related that "the decorations of Komissarzhevskaya's theater can be recommended to provincial theaters—cheap and simple. Against the background of a chintzy curtain covered with flowers there are constantly changing forests, castles and cliffs cut out from cardboard and painted with decadent scrawls."[100]

"What is there to say about *Pelleas and Melisande*?" wrote Kugel in the newspaper *Russia:*

> There were eighteen scenes, variously lighted and decoratively furnished, sometimes with quite beautiful hints. The actors moved like marionettes and both with their acting and sculptural quality reminded us of mosquitoes. Mrs. Komissarzhevskaya is, of course, a talented actress, although not so young as to play girls, and I will wager that if a provincial who had never seen Mrs. Komissarzhevskaya were to be brought in, he would ask "who is this Mrs. Tyushkina who isn't so young and who's playing a fairy-tale princess?" She spoke the entire time in an unnatural voice, imitating a sparrow or robin, or some sort of bird, swallowing the ends of her words. Having ironed herself out, if I may say so, and straightening out, she attained (I must be fair) a sort of unique style, but the style of a toy—a most boring thing."[101]

As we see, Komissarzhevskaya received the worst of the criticism, and was, of course, especially stung by these all-too-frequent references to her age. The actress, wrote N. Tamarin, " . . . moved and gesticulated like a doll, her voice, fine and unusually rich in tone and timbre, was replaced either by birdlike twittering or child-ish squeaks... It was neither touching nor dramatic. Not only did this not give the illusion of childish purity and poetic imagery, but, on the contrary, underscored the jarring nature of the actress' 'youthful' makeup."[102] Again, the same point was delicately made: the actress is 43 years old and Melisande is a girl.

Only Bryusov, who was close to Komissarzhevskaya at the time, supported her. Under the pseudonym "Latnik" he wrote in a newspaper review that "all the un-fortunate errors on the part of the director and the horrible errors of the decorator, all these insulting and ridiculous externals were not able to prevent V. F. Komis-sarzhevskaya from creating a true, fine and bewitching image of Melisande. From the moment that Melisande appears on the stage everything disappears...you see only these childlike, innocent, beautiful eyes, hear only this childlike, melodious voice that expresses so much with its sound."[103]

Blok wrote the severest criticism of the production. He ridiculed V. I. Deni-sov's decorations and noted ironically that Meyerhold, "who no one will deny has talent and inventiveness as a director (which was especially observable in his produc-tion of *The Life of Man*, with some exceptions, and my small fantasy *The Puppet Show*) did not only fail to throw Mr. Denisov's tasteless daubings into the oven, but instead took to account all his cubes, cylinders and 'style moderne'."

Blok summarized:

The production's utter lack of substance seems unarguable; neither is it saved by its several more or less successful touches. Everything that tried to be beautiful and truthful immediate-ly came into conflict with the modernized cube and, alas!, was subjugated by it, since the combat was unequal. The colors of the words, voices, intonations and human gestures were all lost in a sea of modernized black sunflowers.

The conclusion is clear. Theater must turn onto a new path if it does not want to com-mit suicide. I find this unpleasant to say, but I cannot do otherwise—it is all too clear. It is also clear that if there is no new path *yet*, then it is better, a hundred times better, to use the old way. No one living work is helping us out of this dead end. And this last production leaves the impression of a *bad dream*... The production of *Pelleas* has demonstrated that these techniques are endlessly bad. In despairing of these techniques we do not despair of the live people who have made a bad error, but who genuinely love art. Let them prove that they have the strength to break with the bad in their past, in the name of a better future which is wholly in their young and powerful hands.[104]

If Blok's article had been published when it was written (October 1907), it would have created an undoubted sensation. But this did not happen. The magazine for which it was written changed hands, and the article saw the light of day only in 1923, following the death of the poet, by which time the Ofitserskaya Street theater was in the distant past. But the crisis of this theater following *Pelleas and Melisande* was seen by all the contemporary critics, if not with Blok's clarity.

At the time, Blok felt compelled to "use all force to drag Meyerhold from the swamps of bad modernism." With characteristic directness he read his article to Meyerhold as soon as it was written and "saw that he was almost in complete agreement with it."[105] This is very important evidence. It signifies that Meyerhold himself saw, or at least sensed, the bankruptcy and internal insignificance of "static theater."

For Komissarzhevskaya, the failure of *Pelleas and Melisande* was extremely painful. She had placed many hopes on Melisande. Two years later, she said: "I gave all my palpitating love for Maeterlinck and all the fire of my soul to Melisande. But with every rehearsal I noticed the fruitlessness of my work and that of my comrades. Meyerhold stubbornly strove to bring everything into an immobile 'plane,' and we deservedly failed."[106]

The failure of *Pelleas and Melisande* signified not only the crisis of "flat" and "static" theater; in no place, manner or form did the theatrical production interface with the time. It attempted to exist separately, within its own closed limits. Meyerhold's Symbolism prior to *Pelleas and Melisande* had been substantive. Even in *The Awakening of Spring* he had still searched for some sort of contacts—however coarse and false—with the time. But the production of *Pelleas and Melisande* was internally dead.

Immediately after the presentation, Komissarzhevskaya called in K. Bravich and F. Komissarzhevsky. "The theater," she said firmly, "must admit that the entire route it has traveled is an error, and the director must renounce his method of directing the play or quit the theater." F. Komissarzhevsky noted in the theater diary: "The decorative aspect in our theater dominates the actor, constrains him, limits his creativity. Gestures are confined, gestures are not experienced; the monotonously strict rhythm is turning theater into puppet theater, and there lies its doom."[107]

Two days later the artists' committee assembled. Meyerhold understood, of course, that an attack was to be mounted against him, but it is doubtful that he was prepared to hear Komissarzhevskaya announce that the theater's course was disastrous. Nonetheless, she did say so quite firmly. Meyerhold, who had prepared an in-depth and rather self-critical report (the summary of which appears in N. Volkov's book, *Meyerhold* [Vol. 1, pp. 337-41]), was forced to change tactics on the spot. He attempted to counter Komissarzhevskaya's pessimistic prognosis with his certainty that there was no reason to fear for the future of the theater. He said that *Pelleas and Melisande* was the last lap of a finished race. "Further work by the theater in this narrow direction," Meyerhold conceded, "truly would lead to its death." He proclaimed a new program: the rejection of two-dimensional solutions and decorative panels, and a movement toward three-dimensional, sculptural staging. The movement in the direction of puppet theater, which had so frightened everyone, he called an "artistic curiosity."

But these promises to replace two-dimensionality with three-dimensionality did not satisfy the actors. Bravich and Komissarzhevskaya asked bluntly whether "the director would continue to apply the same pressure on the actors as he does with the panel method." Meyerhold, outraged, stated that "regardless of the future method of staging he would continue to apply pressure on actors who failed to understand completely his plan for bringing it to life." At the same time, Meyerhold announced his readiness to leave the theater.

This is what the assembly had been awaiting, but for the moment the actors made no move. Meyerhold was permitted one more try although, according to F.

Komissarzhevsky, Vera Fyodorovna herself had no faith in the attempt.

Meyerhold prepared a new production in a month: F. Sologub's *The Victory of Death*. Sologub's three-act tragedy began with a highly original, boldly conceived prologue: it was as if straight from modern Nevsky Prospect the Poet and the Lady suddenly enter a medieval castle in the far, legendary past. Their conversation about horse-drawn cabs and automobiles, electricity and restaurants, about mystery and intimate theater (!) was in sharp and startling contrast to the words of the medieval characters who spoke of living and dead water, of incantations and amulets, sooth-saying and magic. This prologue with its jarring contrasts reminiscent of Blok's theater was probably the reason Meyerhold had selected Sologub's work. But the prologue was followed by three fairly ordinary acts on the subject of the antagonism between Algista the beautiful and Bertha the ugly. Using her cleverness and attractiveness, Algista had managed to replace Bertha on the King's wedding bed and had reigned as Queen for ten years. Beauty ruled for ten years, but then the cruel Bertha disclosed the trick and moved into the royal palace. The attempt of beauty to triumph over the power of ugliness was unsuccessful, even with the use of lies. The moral is that the almighty ugliness of power inevitably wins. Death is the victor. Death cannot be fooled by beauty...

It would be difficult to agree with N. Volkov that in this case Meyerhold succeeded in staging one of the best productions of the time. But, in any case, this time the press responded rather positively. "In the production of *The Victory of Death* we have seen a distinct break in 'style,'" wrote N. Tamarin in the magazine *Theater and Art*. " . . . The mass scenes were brightly realistic, reminiscent of Sanin's crowd in *Electra*. The noise, shouts, the many nervous gestures and the realism of the groupings were surprising in their contrast to the relief-like quality of the preceding productions. The decorations were also artistically realistic; Mr. Denisov provided real columns for the old castle, not just schematic hints."[108]

Meyerhold himself indicated later that in *The Victory of Death* "the figure of the actor, moved forward onto the proscenium, was placed in a sculptural plane. . . . This high relief permitted the freedom for a realistic treatment of the basic situation of the tragedy. . . . The entire width of the stage was covered with steps parallel to the line of the ramp. They had only to be continued down to the stalls. The theater became afraid of this and stopped midway in its striving to step over the line of the ramp."[109]

In no way did this production appease Komissarzhevskaya. A day after the premiere she wrote to Bryusov:

Meyerhold has staged *The Victory of Death* much like a completely disoriented man. Here there was everything—an unsuccessful attempt to give the actors the plastic poses of ancient tragedy, Meiningen's crowd, Moscow Art Theater laughter, a rhythmic rendition such as we hear when Fyodor Kuzmich [Sologub—K. R.] recites monologues from his plays, and the inevitable picturesque gestures and mimicry of all but a very few of the participants. All this partially pleased the public and completely satisfied the Petersburg newspaper reviewers, who practically with one voice announced that Meyerhold had finally "come to his senses" since he had returned to old forms. I was present at the dress rehearsal and had said that everything from start to finish was bad. I did not have the strength to go to the performance, my soul was so oppressed.[110]

This was the end which had been in the works for so long. It is worth noting that as evidence of treason Komissarzhevskaya pointed to the opinion that Meyerhold had finally "come to his senses" and "returned to old forms." She herself was not at all ready to retreat, and for another entire year, together with F. Komissarzhevsky and N. Evreinov, led the theater along the Symbolist course, but without Meyerhold.

On November 9, 1907, exactly one year after the opening of the Ofitserskaya Street theater, Komissarzhevskaya called the entire company together and read them the letter which had been delivered to Meyerhold that same morning and which became famous in the history of the Russian stage:

> Over the past days, Vsevolod Emilevich, I have done much thinking, and have arrived at the deep certainty that you and I view theater in different ways, and that what you seek I do not. The course leading to puppet theater is the course you have followed the entire time, not counting those productions in which you combined the principles of "old" theater with the principles of the puppet theater, such as, for instance, *Love's Comedy* and *The Victory of Death*. To my great regret, I have realized this fully only over the past days, after much thought. I am looking the future directly in the face and say that we cannot follow this course together. This way is yours but not mine, and in answer to your statement at the last session of our artistic union—"perhaps I ought to leave the theater"—I say now: "Yes, you must leave." Therefore, I no longer can consider you to be my associate, and I have asked K. V. Bravich to inform the company and to explain the entire situation to it, because I do not wish for the people who work with me to work with eyes closed.[111]

For many actors, this decision was totally unexpected. "None of us suspected anything," says V. Verigina. "Those of us who sided with Meyerhold were thunderstruck. And not only we, but many others."[112]

In Meyerhold's notebooks there remain drafts of the letter which he sent to the newspaper *Russia*, in which he challenged Komissarzhevskaya to a court of arbitration. These drafts are more sincere and blunter than the published text:

> An owner rejects—this is one form. A person heading a cultural affair rejects a co-worker—this ought to be a different form. Here V. F. has become an owner and has acted indecently. This stains her and relieves her of the aura of culture... The motives for the rejection are false. But they had to be devised in order to create the rift, which was *inevitable*, and its cause, as you see, is not puppets but something else.[113]

Although many, Bryusov included, considered Komissarzhevskaya's action "impolitic," general sympathy was on her side, and the court of arbitration judged her conduct to be correct.

"Vera Fyodorovna came to the court unhappy, armed with all her charm, and who could convict her? She was acquitted."[114]

So ended Meyerhold's career at the Ofitserskaya Street theater. In a year's work in this theater, Meyerhold had gained significant national recognition. Literally on the day before the rift between Meyerhold and Komissarzhevskaya the observer in the magazine *Russian Artist* stated:

Each new play staged in V. F. Komissarzhevskaya's theater becomes an entire event for Petersburg theater-goers, an event to be discussed for many days. Critical attention is, of course, focused on the staging, since it is expected that Mr. Meyerhold's direction will provide something supernatural, extravagant or different. A fortunate director—his name will not die, it is recorded on the pages of the history of the Russian stage immediately below that of Mr. Stanislavsky. A wide-ranging literature has already been compiled on the subject of Mr. Meyerhold's productions.[115]

When Komissarzhevskaya fired Meyerhold, almost all this "literature," analyzing the conflict between the actress-theater owner and the director, spoke of the complete defeat of the "new theater" with unconcealed glee.

The Petersburg *Theater Review (Obozrenie teatrov)* wrote that "not one of Mr. Meyerhold's productions has been a success. His strivings were of exclusive interest to the first-run public: journalists, artists and theater fans, and their interest was confined exclusively to total deprecation." Fully supporting V. F. Komissarzhevskaya's decision, the newspaper observed that "now Mr. Meyerhold has only to defend his views in the papers. This will be much cheaper for and less harmful to the theater."[116] E. Stark, the critic, summarized: "Between the art of the past and Meyerhold's theater a chasm has been created; between Meyerhold's theater and the art of the future there is no connection, because this art itself does not exist, and it is impossible to predict its nature."[117]

The Moscow newspaper *Theater* published an interview with A. P. Lensky, who said of Meyerhold's experiments: "Why force people to look like puppets? And this striving to create flat theater is an imitation of ancient paintings which we have long ago left far behind."[118]

Only a very few critics, for instance G. Chulkov in the newspaper *Comrade*, pointed out that Meyerhold's year of work in the Ofitserskaya Street theater was not completely fruitless:

V. E. Meyerhold's main service is that in his productions he firmly and consistently carried out the principles of "conditional" theater... Elements of artistic creativity were always present in the dangerous experiments which V. E. Meyerhold dared... Prior to V. E. Meyerhold's entry into V. F. Komissarzhevskaya's theater in Petersburg there had not been a single theater—there were only separate actors and actresses, occasionally of significant talent like, for instance, V. F. Komissarzhevskaya herself. The productions of *Sister Beatrice, The Puppet Show, The Life of Man* and *The Victory of Death* are a stage in the history of Russian Theater.[119]

When passion had cooled, V. F. Komissarzhevskaya clearly and objectively summarized the events that had transpired. In an interview given to the newspaper *Odessa News* in the fall of 1909, she stated that Meyerhold had led the theater "into a dead end." With some amazement, she recalled that the stage of her theater had become a "laboratory for a director's experiments." The public had become disenchanted with her theater. "As soon as I saw this, I decided to break with Meyerhold, but not with conditional theater or with new methods of staging. And even now I value Meyerhold as a great and talented innovator whose search is completely sincere. And his works like *The Puppet Show, The Life of Man* and *Sister Beatrice* I consider to be masterpieces of direction."[120]

Komissarzhevskaya was doubtless right when she criticized Meyerhold for turning her theater into a "director's laboratory," into a sort of public studio. Meyerhold, too, admitted this fault. A year previous to Komissarzhevskaya's interview, he told a reporter of the *Petersburg Gazette*:

> Experience has shown that "large theater" (as we shall call theater aimed at the general public) cannot become a "theater of experiment," and the attempt to place under one roof the finished theater for a general audience together with a studio theater must become a fiasco... "Theaters of experiment" must stand apart. Their task is this: everything is in an embryonic state—playwright, director, decorator, prop-man and the other people who comprise the theater collective. Everything is given impetus, and the hand of the leader (studio director, director, leading actor) leads to the full flowering of the creativity of all the elements of the theater... Hence, finally, the new theater with a new playwright, new actor, new director and new designer... "[121]

But problems of this sort should be resolved in the privacy of the studio and not in public. Meyerhold's subsequent experimental work was carried out separately from the productions destined for a wide audience.

In commenting on Komissarzhevskaya's Odessa interview, N. D. Volkov wrote that it discloses the "principal nature of the Meyerhold-Komissarzhevskaya conflict." Meyerhold's biographer thought that the basis for the conflict "was the rebellion of a significant actress unable to become what she desired—to become the 'new theater.'"[122] N. Volkov's judgment is but partially correct. The contradiction did exist, of course, between the "soloist" actress, which Komissarzhevskaya had always been, and the director-dictator, as Meyerhold proved himself to be in the Ofitserskaya Street theater. As Komissarzhevskaya's first biographer, N. Turkin, observed, "the chief characteristic of Vera Fyodorovna's talent was the power of internal emotional experience, while the chief characteristic of Mr. Meyerhold's productions was external style."[123] This is all true. But we ought to recollect that for the course of this year Komissarzhevskaya selflessly and fully subordinated herself to the director, overcoming and limiting her artistic nature. She wished for but was unable to become "new theater"—N. Volkov is correct here. Furthermore, having parted with Meyerhold, she expressed the fairly distinct opinion that a director's theater is in essence insubstantial. "In theater, in my present opinion, there cannot be a single director... In future theater, when all actors will be living by artistic experience exclusively," predicted Komissarzhevskaya, " . . . there will be no directors, i.e., a unified origin."[124] Such comments demonstrated the full pain and depth of the actress' disillusionment.

But the truth is that Meyerhold, too, was unable to become "new theater." In the final analysis, Komissarzhevskaya and Meyerhold had separated because together they had been unable to reach their intended goal.

Under all conditions and in various authors' worlds, Stanislavsky had determined for his goal the most precise rendition of reality based on most painstaking observation. The descriptive realistic esthetics of the "picture of life" required maximum immersion into the daily life, temper and atmosphere of concrete existence, into the emotional experience and psychology of the individual. This idea and tendency issued from a truthful depiction of life as if by its own strength, occasionally to the artist's surprise.

Meyerhold had upset this whole system. The external objective world with all its detail and nuance, with all its endless wealth, was interpreted as "raw" reality, and therefore was of less interest. The disorganized, multi-hued, uncomprehended reality was felt to be a hindrance. It only prevented expression on matters of substance. Its fragmentedness and busyness opposed the artist's striving to reveal the "truth of existence" which was supposedly hidden beneath the cover of moving, shifting, contradictory and often insignificant facts.

Symbolism was an attempt to stop the motion of life, to rise above reality, and with the power of poetic vision to present the eternal images of the universal tragedy of existence.

This was most difficult to achieve in the theater, where the living body, voice, intonations and gestures of the actor would introduce into the Symbolist constructs the capricious wilfulness of reality. Numerous undesirable details of life were brought in by the actors and appeared to dirty, damage and distort that new vision of life that the director strove to present, the image with which he wished to supplant reality. Therefore, the actor became the most difficult and, in the end, insoluble problem for the Symbolist director. This is why Stanislavsky, for whom the actor was more important than Symbolist ideas (these ideas were not at all organic to Stanislavsky) would retreat at once from the Symbolist program in the name of the actor. But Meyerhold stubbornly and fanatically tested the various methods for taming living actors' flesh: the "static theater" of bas-reliefs and high relief, the theater of extraordinary intonations, of words falling "like drops into a well," of statuesque plasticity, unified rhythm. And Meyerhold was the first to present the painter with enormous, previously impossible power in the theater, not only bringing him to the same level as the actor, but raising him above the actor, since in the creation of new worlds "independent of reality" the painter was the truest and most essential assistant to the director, and the decorations, once painted, would no longer be changed every evening.

People on Meyerhold's stage became reminiscent of mediums listening intently to the voice of Fate. Their motions were slowed, their voices tense and anguished. The atmosphere of the presence of life, its pulse, which the stage of the Moscow Art Theater rendered with all its famous sounds—crickets, breezes, mosquitoes, banging of shutters—this Meyerhold's stage replaced with an absence of life and breath of death. Castle gates squeaked grimly, oceans made fearful sounds. When nature appeared in a production, it would threaten people. Real dimensions vanished: morning, day, evening, dusk, dawn all disappeared—everything that had been so freshly and precisely rendered on the Art Theater stage. A somber and solitary "eternity" had arrived. In the Art Theater, life and objects characterized people and served people. In the Ofitserskaya Street theater, separate, selected objects and the tiny elements of daily life appeared separate from daily life and were significantly hostile to mankind. Objects appeared darkly independent and alive, while persons lost their independence and appeared frozen in frightened anticipation.

Along with daily life, the psychology of the individual was also discarded; "separate" signifies "accidental," "not subject to generalization."

It is true that at the time another fairly original opinion was voiced. In his article "Individualism on the Stage," N. Yordansky wrote:

> The same spirit of revolution which had seized all the manifestations of social existence came to the stage. It caused stage directors to reject "daily life" and to proclaim the rights of the individual. Let the participants in new theater think that they are overthrowing daily life and are founding absolute individuality. History will demonstrate that the overthrown daily life is merely the "old order," that the ideal absolute personality is the personality of the citizen of a new Russia... As a new symptom of the development of individualism, new theater can, with far greater right, be called the child of revolution, which caused Russian stage, too, to become a means in the struggle for the rights and freedom of human individuality.[125]

And in fact, the image of man torn from social connections, and thus seemingly freed from them, was manifested in Meyerhold's Symbolist productions. But only in a few of the productions was it possible to sense the notes of protest and outrage. Much more frequently, the "absolute personality" appeared to be flying above the world, moving apart from it but not objecting to it...

It seemed, said one contemporary, that "life itself ceased to be real": "the external world became but a symbol of something unchanging, eternal, immaterial."[126]

Meyerhold was the first to create Symbolist theater in Russia, and was the first to bring Russian stage Symbolism rapidly to the point of self-denial in *Pelleas and Melisande*. Stanislavsky was still rehearsing *The Life of Man* and was considering *The Blue Bird*, Nemirovich-Danchenko was still preparing *Anathema*, the Ofitserskaya Street Theater was just beginning (now without Meyerhold) to prepare L. Andreev's *Black Masks*, but for Meyerhold the cycle of Symbolist productions was already at an end.

Many years later, Mikhail Chekhov noted perceptively that "he could not wait. Something within him was hurrying. His genius, his untamable will to innovate and create, were all in a hurry."

Thus, Meyerhold hastened to part with Symbolist drama. Others were still playing its epilogue, but he had already quit the Symbolist stage.

Meyerhold's lengthy article, "On Theater (History and Technique)," published in 1908, following the end of his experiments on Povarskaya and Ofitserskaya Streets, an article weighed down by a multitude of quotes by Bryusov, Vyacheslav Ivanov and Maeterlinck, was an attempt to substantiate theoretically all the experiments of the preceding years. In many words, it defended the concept of Symbolist "static theater" at the same time that Meyerhold had already given it up.

This article was crushingly attacked from every side. The Marxist critics A. Lunacharsky and Y. Steklov[127] were sarcastic, A. Kugel ridiculed it in his magazine *Theater and Art*,[128] F. Komissarzhevsky, who had replaced Meyerhold in the Ofitserskaya Street theater, seriously asserted that "an actor cannot be made flat because he is by nature three-dimensional."[129]

Let us not pursue this old argument any further. We shall note only that Meyerhold did not retreat or withdraw. With characteristic haste he moved on. In those places where his theory did not find the requisite terms, it became mired in hazy wordiness and was, in essence, silent. Meyerhold was led on by intuition. This intuition was to extract the energy necessary for further progress from the many experiments of the Symbolist period.

MEYERHOLD AND DOCTOR DAPERTUTTO

Anyway, the reckoning arrives:
See there, behind the grainy blizzard
How Meyerhold's little blackamoors
Are bustling about once more?
Anna Akhmatova

Meyerhold's year of work with Komissarzhevskaya brought him notoriety but not popularity. Journalists, critics and writers reviled him continuously, asserting that his work was the labor of a charlatan. The actual significance of the complex Ofitserskaya Street experience was to become clear only some years later, and even then was not recognized universally. In 1913, Alexander Blok stated that the significance of Komissarzhevskaya's former theater was crucially important; in his words, future histories of Russian theater would discuss the eras B. K. and A. K. (before Kommissarzhevskaya's theater and after).[1]

Even in 1913 this opinion seemed highly original, but in the year of the break-up between Komissarzhevskaya and Meyerhold, the general consensus regarded the brief career of the Ofitserskaya Street theater as a series of faddish and hostile directorial experiments perpetrated upon the talent of Russia's favorite actress. Meyerhold's future fate was the subject of intense attention by numerous journalists.

These journalists all expected approximately the same developments: Meyerhold either would leave for the provinces and oblivion, or he and some other irresponsible "dilettantes" like himself would stage more trendy plays.

But, exactly one week after Komissarzhevskaya read the letter banishing Meyerhold from her theater, the director noted in his notebook:

"November, Saturday the 17th. 2 o'clock. Administration of the Imperial Theater."

And, several days later:

"Wednesday, 21st, 1 o'clock—Golovin. 2 o'clock—Telyakovsky."[2]

These brief notes mark an important event: after being fired by Komissarzhevskaya, Meyerhold was being invited into the Imperial Theaters. At that time the Director of the Imperial Theaters was Vladimir Arkadevich Telyakovsky, whose position fated him to sarcastic, or at best ironic, treatment by future historians. Some researchers and composers of memoirs have been particularly shocked by the circumstance that Telyakovsky had been in the Guards cavalry. Naturally, as chief of the Imperial Theaters "bureau" he was far from caring to revolutionize the stage. But Telyakovsky, a man of culture, was an energetic administrator who took his responsibilities seriously and who did undertake several attempts to modernize his theaters. He had succeeded in obtaining Fyodor Chalyapin for the Imperial Theaters, and had invited actors such as Ekaterina Korchagina-Alexandrovskaya and Boris Gorin-Goryainov, and artists such as Alexander Golovin, Konstantin Korovin and Mstislav Dobuzhinsky.

Telyakovsky's invitation to Meyerhold, however, puzzled even the supporters of the former's innovations. On November 18, 1907, Telyakovsky wrote in his diary:

This morning I summoned Meyerhold, the director of Komissarzhevskaya's theater, who was fired there several days ago. Meyerhold has frequently been attacked by the public and in the press, and this strong hostility toward him has convinced me that he must be interesting in some way. Golovin, Vuich and Krupensky were present as well. I explained to him my personal views regarding art, theater, and the aims that a dramatic theater ought to pursue. Meyerhold told me that he, personally, had changed recently, and that presently he was experiencing an attraction toward old theater—the foreign and Russian classics. I decided that for a time I would not advertise my conversations with Meyerhold, but first would have a talk with Gnedich. I suggested that Meyerhold should direct one play as a trial, and then later be taken on as a director. In the course of the conversation I made a point of asking his opinion of Popov, Lensky, Ozarovsky and our other directors. Overall, Meyerhold impressed me favorably."[3]

Even though the negotiations with Meyerhold had not been made public, the press got wind of them at once. Curiously, the magazine *Theater Review*, published by the Administration of Imperial Theaters, rushed to refute this "silly gossip." The article in *Theater Review* stated: "It is out of the question that Mr. Meyerhold suddenly will be invited to the Imperial stage, if only because Mr. Telyakovsky has never seen a production by Mr. Meyerhold and has never been to V. F. Komissarzhevskaya's theater. The Administration of Imperial Theaters, as is known, is not so eccentric an organization as to turn model theater into puppet theater."[4]

Three months passed, and in March 1908 *Theater Review* returned to this "truly sensational" question. Telyakovsky, in an interview, began to show his hand. This rumor, he said, "is true to a degree... Insofar as I have understood Mr. Meyerhold in a personal interview, he has retreated substantially from his initial excess and understands his errors in Komissarzhevskaya's theater. The matter of his being appointed as a director has not been decided, but it is quite possible that we will call on him for an experiment, but not, of course, to transform the Alexandrinsky Theater into stylized theater. It is possible that, if invited, he would not be a director in the usual sense, i.e., in a specific theater; he could work in both opera and drama. In any event it must be remembered that no excesses can be permitted on the model stage...."[5]

In this diplomatic fashion, Telyakovsky prepared and calmed public opinion. The repentant Meyerhold would not be a director "in the usual sense," nor would he be given any authority; only his advice "might be useful." Furthermore, the matter is not settled, the contract is not signed, the Administration considers the might and grandeur of the Imperial Theaters and reflects...

Meanwhile, everything had been decided. Meyerhold's contract had been signed, and he was to begin work as a director of both drama and opera and as a dramatic actor on September 1, 1908. For Telyakovsky, he prepared grandiose repertory plans. Meyerhold's list included Sophocles's *Oedipus Rex,* Shakespeare's *Henry IV*, Gogol's *The Inspector General*, Lermontov's *Masquerade*, A. Tolstoi's *Tsar Fyodor Ioannovich*, Chekhov's *The Cherry Orchard*, L. Andreev's *The Life of Man*, Ibsen's *Peer Gynt, Hedda Gabler* and *Ghosts*, and Maeterlinck's *The Death of Tintagiles*. Turgenev, Molière and Calderon were also included in the plans.[6] Subsequently, Meyerhold was able to realize only some of these intentions. But it is important to note that the director's overall repertorial orientation had in fact altered in a basic way. The Ofitserskaya Street theater had presented only contemporary works, while the projected program for the Alexandrinsky was composed primarily of classical plays.

The primary reason for this was the need to work with the Alexandrinsky troupe of actors, which was in no way prepared for a contemporary repertoire. In one of his first interviews, Meyerhold mentioned that he felt it essential "to allow for the character of the artistic powers" of the troupe, their fidelity to the so-called "classical repertoire." He promised to make his central task "the tireless resurrection of the ancient repertoire."[7]

This promise would eventually be fulfilled with tremendous artistic effect.

It is interesting that as early as 1908 Meyerhold had prepared a program for stylizing the classics. He stated that *"The Inspector General, Woe from Wit, Masquerade, Hamlet, The Storm* have never been staged so as to be illuminated by the rays of the era. We have never witnessed these plays in the 'aroma' of those reflections that shine at the mere utterance of the title. What a field this is for great theater." He went on to say that "the interests of past actors are united easily here with the problems of new artists."[8]

In the time preceding his employment at the Alexandrinsky Theater, Meyerhold traveled with a group of devoted actors through the provinces—to Minsk, Kherson, Nikolaev, Kiev and other towns. This journey was a kind of epilogue for the New Drama Cooperative. During the tour Meyerhold staged new variations on Blok's *The Puppet Show*, Sologub's *The Victory of Death* and Andreev's *The Life of Man*. Hofmannsthal's *Electra* and Hamsun's *At the Imperial Gates* were staged again as well. Meyerhold described the new interpretation of *The Puppet Show* to Ekaterina Munt in a letter dated March 7, 1908:

> The entire play is out in the orchestra. Audience fully illuminated. Instead of decorations—light, Japanese-style partitions and dividers. Before the start, the author enters through a small red curtain with stars on the proscenium and sits down, joining the public, and watches the performance with it. Later, when the curtain closes on the first part, an "assistant" grabs the conversing author by the coattails and pulls him behind the curtain. When Pierrot is lying alone (in front of the curtain), everything disappears before the public's eyes. There remains the empty floor of the orchestra and the proscenium, with lonesome Pierrot on it. The most effective moment is when the clown lowers his hands into the space between the proscenium (the edge of the stage, as it were) and the first row, crying out about cranberry juice.

This letter is remarkable for demonstrating Meyerhold's increased attention to moments of revelation and stressing the relativistic, playful nature of theater. The director is especially concerned with situations in which the boundary between stage and audience is destroyed. The Author watches the play together with the public, the hall is fully illuminated, Pierrot lowers his hands into the space between the ramp and the first row... The urge to perform "on the edge of the footlights," on the proscenium, has become especially attractive to Meyerhold, and it is with great enthusiasm that he describes his experiments in the "border zone" between audience and stage.

Further experimentation was to be postponed, at least for the time being.

Meyerhold had been perfectly sincere in 1908 when he called impractical and impossible further theatrical experiments before a wide audience. In this sense, the Ofitserskaya Street experience had its effect. From this point on and for a long time to come Meyerhold would strictly segregate his public and studio, his "finished" and experimental work.

"Yesterday at the Alexandrinsky Theater," reported the *Petersburg Gazette*, "the director-innovator made a speech to the actors in which he presented his plans. The lecture was of a calming nature, so to speak... Meyerhold said that he considers turning the Alexandrinsky Theater into a studio an impossibility. For experimentation there exist the small, private stages where he had, in fact, pursued his 'searching,' but in a large theater such as the Alexandrinsky he cannot experiment."[9]

Although Meyerhold did see the pacification of the Alexandrinsky troupe as his primary task, at the time when he was just beginning his employment on the Imperial stage he evidently did not fully realize his surroundings or the anxieties and fears his presence had aroused.

The lead actors of the Alexandrinsky Theater, especially Maria Gavrilovna Savina and Vladimir Nikolaevich Davydov—front-line defenders of the strict tradition of the Imperial stage who regarded Telyakovsky's relatively moderate reforms as wild anarchism—viewed Meyerhold's appearance as a wild prank on the part of the Director. As early as 1908 Davydov wrote: "The Director is a fan of Meyerhold and stylization and all that nonsense. I, however, am their enemy and defend our native art and Melpomene's temple, to which I have dedicated my life, from the intrusion of such innovations and innovators." "Lord," he prayed in another letter, "have mercy on theater and on us mortals! Preserve us from disaster and destroy this rot and these locusts! These base, malicious rats that penetrate everywhere! And send us, O Lord, your Holy Spirit! Bring us to our senses!" Savina also wrote of "Meyerhold, the Director's pet," and expressed her firm resolve to defend "our temple," "our monuments" from the likes of Meyerhold, "Caliphs of the hour."[10]

Savina and Davydov's influence in the Alexandrinsky was more than great—they were not merely listened to but obeyed, and often their word had greater weight than that of Telyakovsky. Furthermore, the actors were nervous about Meyerhold: they had heard plenty about this "charlatan" who dreamed of turning actors into soulless puppets.

Meyerhold was resisted even more strongly by Peter Gnedich, the troupe's manager, and director N. Kornev.

In the course of the first days of Meyerhold's employment at the Alexandrinsky Theater, the experienced Telyakovsky noted: "Of course Meyerhold has already run into unpleasantness with Gnedich, Kornev and others... They try to discredit the new director as much as possible."

When Meyerhold, at the first rehearsal, tried to calm the players, they listened, wrote Telyakovsky, "attentively, although their faces expressed mistrust." And the Director predicted: "There is no doubt that Gnedich with his army of directors will try to hinder the director."[11]

Meanwhile, Meyerhold clearly was not inclined to attach any great significance to this influential and powerful opposition within the theater. From the tactical point of view he made several serious errors in the very beginning. Meyerhold did not begin with the promised classics, but rather with Knut Hamsun's contemporary drama, *At the Imperial Gates*. This play was being rehearsed simultaneously by Komissarzhevskaya's theater, which had just fired him, and by the Art Theater in Moscow. It is true that he assured himself and others that "the results of efforts on plays like Hamsun's have been kept in mind,"[12] and that, consequently, this work would be "finished" and not experimental. Finally, despite Telyakovsky's objections, he took for himself the lead role of Kareno. Meyerhold was attracted to the central image of Ivar Kareno—scientist, philosopher, and proud loner who, in the face of Philistine morality and bourgeois science, proposed his own daring and blasphemous ideas. These ideas were explicitly discussed in the play, but in 1908 were no longer anything new, although they did, of course, retain their stunning impact. Kareno defended what were clearly Nietzschean ideas of amorality, and the righteousness of strength, lauded the "born ruler," "natural despot," and "greatest terrorist." He was prepared to bless warfare if it assisted "the proud march of mankind ever forward," etc. It is difficult to suppose that Meyerhold was seriously interested by this voluntarist fragment. Most probably he identified with Kareno's dramatic fate: deserted by all, persecuted, but uncompromisingly alone and firmly following his intended path.

Telyakovsky wrote in his diary:

> I personally think that Meyerhold has erred substantially in taking the lead role for himself. He ought not to have done this, and I mentioned this to him last summer, but Meyerhold was presumptuous and did not do as I suggested. He not only took the lead but took it away from Ozarovsky, for whom it was intended. It began with a conflict with the actor, which has already turned the troupe against him. Furthermore, he gives some sort of lectures: last time at Suvorin's Maly Theater he mentioned the actors of our troupe, calling them oldsters. ("I do not say useless rags," he said.)[13]

Nikolai Khodotov, one of the very few actors in the troupe to be well-disposed toward Meyerhold, subsequently averred that he, Khodotov, and not Ozarovsky, had been intended for the role of Kareno, and that he had "conceded" it to Meyerhold.[14] In any case, Meyerhold did play Kareno, and his performance aroused violent disapproval already during rehearsals. On September 27, following the dress rehearsal and several days before the opening, Telyakovsky wrote: "All told, the rehearsal impressed me favorably, and I do not find any excesses in the production. Savina was greatly upset and asked me over the telephone if I was really permitting the staging of *At the Imperial Gates*, since according to rumor Meyerhold is acting quite impossibly, which is causing a scandal for the Alexandrinsky Theater. The actors are all excited, each tries to say something about Meyerhold, and undoubtedly they will turn the audience against him too."[15]

Alexander Golovin painted the decorations, beginning eleven years of uninterrupted cooperation with Meyerhold, whose first production in the Alexandrinsky Theater was panned by the fraternity of reviewers. The *Petersburg Gazette* critic, for instance, commented on the premiere of *At the Imperial Gates* as follows:

> The crux of the spectacle consisted of Mr. Meyerhold's double debut as actor and director. "What will he show?" was an unspoken question on many faces. And "he" did, in fact,

show. As director, it was the same Mr. Meyerhold as we knew him in V. F. Komissarzhevskaya's theater. The same striving for geometric lines in set design, the poses and groupings of the performers. The same efforts in the name of construction to merge with the decorations, the setting and the costumes into a monochrome gray spot. The same urge to blur and decelerate the naturally increasing tempo of the play by dragging out the lines, with wearisome pauses and monotonous, deathly delivery. All this was evident, especially in the role played by Mr. Meyerhold himself (Kareno). We have not seen such dry, dull, and wooden acting for a long time.

The review concluded with the insult: "a real dummy was walking around the stage, spoiling both play and production."[16]

Yury Belyaev wrote in *New Time (Novoe vremia)*: "Again 'stylization,' again the 'statuary' style, etc.," grumbled the critic. "On the state stage this was uncomfortable and...offensive... Mr. Meyerhold 'himself' played Kareno in flesh-colored pantaloons and azure coat. It was all indescribably dreary."[17]

The sharpest and most irritated criticism came from *Theater Review*. Meyerhold, wrote I. Osipov, "clearly cheated the administration. . . . For an entire evening he turned the Alexandrinsky stage into some kind of dull, tedious and, mainly, stupid studio." The reviewer praised Golovin's "marvelous decorations" and even acknowledged that "in tones and colors this could be the masterpiece of decorative art," maintaining, however, that this masterpiece "has absolutely no relation to the play." The costumes irritated the reviewer even more. "Meyerhold," he continued, "cannot lower His Directorial Holiness to modern daily clothing. With the assistance of Mr. Golovin, who probably was designing fashions for one of the future generations, he dressed the performers in costumes that at the present time are worn on stage exclusively by café-chantant eccentrics—colored vests and brightly colored trousers."

This review likewise ridiculed the rendition of the leading role. "Meyerhold as an actor is a joke. A dull, unpleasant voice, wooden, immobile face, lanky, clumsy, anti-theatrical, purely cartoon figure—this is the exterior of Mr. Meyerhold the actor." But the reviewer of *Theater Review* praised the other actors—Roman Apollonsky, Grigory Ge, Nikolai Khodotov and Maria Pototskaya. This revealed his desire to contrast as sharply as possible the new director "with sprained brains" with the "model troupe." In the end of the review the hope was expressed that the administration would save "our great Alexandrinsky Theater from further vivisection."

A friendly voice was raised unexpectedly and calmly in the Moscow Art Theater camp. Lyubov Gurevich, who was already close to Stanislavsky and the Art Theater, in her article about *At the Imperial Gates*, made a clear attempt to comprehend Meyerhold's design. "In becoming a director on the state stage, Mr. Meyerhold," wrote Gurevich, " . . . is trying to pour new wine into old skins. The faces of the actors of this theater have frozen into immobile masks that correspond to their usual role. The gift of artistic reincarnation, the play of artistic hints that illuminate the play in the light of ideas and poetry, is beyond the means of these actors." In the critic's opinion, Meyerhold " . . . was very sincere, very simple... But perhaps too simple, resembling himself too much in exterior and manner...."[18]

Two days later, after seeing the same play in Komissarzhevskaya's theater with

Bravich in the role of Kareno, Gurevich was even more emphatically in favor of Meyerhold. "In comparison with Bravich," she wrote, "Meyerhold's somewhat pale image of Kareno suddenly shines with its noble, nervous air of culture."[19]

Within the theater, however, the opinion was that Meyerhold had failed doubly —as director and as actor. From all sides, the Director was informed of Savina's opinion that "inviting Meyerhold dishonored the stage of the Alexandrinsky Theter." Meyerhold had but two supporters: Nikolai Khodotov and Yury Yurev. They, wrote Telyakovsky, "attempt to defend him in the troupe, but this is most difficult in view of the prevailing dislike for him."[20]

Even if there is reason to believe that Meyerhold's Kareno was comprehended neither by the public, the theater company nor the critics (Gurevich excepted), there is no doubt that, on the whole, the production was a failure. This was not caused by exceptionally forceful or bold attempts at "stylization" on the part of Meyerhold, but rather by his caution and constraint. He had denounced loudly the rote manner of performance and the general stagnation of the Alexandrinsky Theater, but in this production he was a fairly passive director. The actors were disobedient: "They either do not wish to rehearse or they cannot," he wrote heatedly. Innovation reached only the external appearance of the production and the leading role. Golovin and Meyerhold together appeared to object to everything that was being done on the stage by the other actors, which some reviewers (I. Osipov, for instance) praised, others practically did not notice, and about whom L. Gurevich said plainly—their faces "were frozen into motionless masks that corresponded to their usual roles." So far, Meyerhold was not trying to change the habits of the Alexandrinsky actors—neither their interpretation of the roles, nor the staging. He was guarding his claws.

The result was an odd and dreary spectacle tormented by unresolved internal contradictions.

Depressed by the failure of *At the Imperial Gates*, Meyerhold was diverted briefly by the idea of a small cabaret theater, the "Seacoast" *("Lukomore")*, which had opened in a Petersburg artists' club. Together with the artists M. Dobuzhinsky and I. Bilibin, he staged three one-act plays there: Potemkin's *Petrushka*, Trakhtenberg's *The Fall of the House of Usher* (adapted from Poe), and F. L. Sologub's *Honor and Revenge*. This was an evening of parody elegantly executed and staged, but—poorly written.

As we recall, Meyerhold's contract with the Imperial Theaters required him to direct opera as well as drama, but the pace of his work had diminished significantly since his arrival on the Imperial stage. In a single season on Ofitserskaya Street, Meyerhold had directed over fifteen productions, while at the Alexandrinsky and Mariinsky Theaters he would usually direct only one or two productions per season. These large reserves of spare time enabled Meyerhold, for the first time in his life, to ponder in depth various new theatrical productions and to prepare stagings of opera with enthusiasm.

In the course of Meyerhold's work on the Alexandrinsky and Mariinsky stages and, simultaneously, in his studio experiments, the fundamental principles of the art of relativistic, or conditional *(uslovnyi),* theater became increasingly distinct.

The general opinion that relativistic theater was antithetical to realistic theater does not withstand serious scrutiny. One could just as well assert that the concept of prose is equivalent to that of realism, while stating that poetry is incompatible with realism.

Relativistic theater and the theater of direct conformity to life are in the same relationship to one another as poetry is to prose. In principle, both types of theater can lead to realism, while either can lead away from it. As Brecht said, there are many ways to speak the truth and many ways to conceal it.

Another equally widespread delusion credits Meyerhold, Gordon Craig, Max Reinhardt and several other twentieth century directors and playwrights the honor (or sin) of inventing relativistic theater. But in fact, relativistic theater had existed in antiquity. The "original sin" of the relative *(uslovnost)* has accompanied the art of theater through the centuries. The theater of antiquity was relativistic, as were the classical theater of Corneille and Racine, the theater of Molière, the Italian masked comedies, Chinese traditional theater, the Japanese Kabuki, and so on. Meyerhold in Russia and Craig and Reinhardt in the West were creating new forms for relativistic theater that corresponded to the ideas, rhythms and spiritual requirements of the new time.

The history of the theater of direct conformity to life is also age-old. The concreteness of life has always fed stage art, entering into the most various and, occasionally, highly acute contradictions with its innate relativism.

The dramatic and ingeniously harmonized picture of such contradictions is clearly evident in Shakespeare's theater. In the nineteenth century the art of the actors Shchepkin and Salvini, their essentially different gifts and temperaments notwithstanding, demonstrated a powerful thrust toward reconciling stage images with the natural in life.

In the late nineteenth and early twentieth centuries the theater of direct conformity to life, thanks to the efforts of its directors, took on artistically perfected form that gave the productions unity and esthetic wholeness.

Thus, a substantially new phase in the development of stage realism was inaugurated.

Somewhat later, based on these achievements of the theater of direct conformity to life, the ground was laid for the renewal of realism in relativistic theater as well.

The main difference between relativistic theater and the theater of direct conformity to life is defined by the manner in which the stage action is viewed.

In the theater of direct conformity to life the action must create the illusion of events actually transpiring "today, here and now," before the eyes of the audience. This theater must be identical to life itself and must reproduce precisely a "slice of life." The action imitates "in the forms of life itself" everything that transpires over the time segment selected by the drama. The more exact and plausible the imitation, the better. The task of the actors of such theater is to experience as much as possible in fact what the character experiences in the play.

The theater of direct conformity to life subjects observations which have been culled from the surrounding reality to a definite ideological concept, and organizes them esthetically. The nature of this theater's image stems from the depths of man's personal experience, his individual psychology. The expressiveness, emotional saturation and impact of this art manifest themselves in the actor's image of a specific person and in the total stage composition—the director's choreography for the production.

In relativistic theater the stage action poetically transforms reality, striving to concentrate attention on the most significant and substantial moments of human existence. The stage action takes dynamic concentrations of reality from life and places them on the stage boards, honing or enlarging events, giving them a different scale and extracting from the everyday the essence discovered by the artist. This interpretation of stage action strongly accents the artist's moment of creation. Therefore, in relativistic theater the actor is obliged to demonstrate the abilities of an independent creator. These talents may be quite varied, depending on the genre, form, and style of the production.

Reality is formed in accordance with the aspect selected for its figurative rendition.

In the theater of direct conformity to life the goal of the actor is sincerity of feeling, and the entire predetermined design of the role is a sort of trap for the expected emotion, an emotion-trap. In relativistic theater the picture alters; the actor follows a predetermined score for the role. Reveling in his art, he transmits this delight (the "joy of metamorphosis") to the audience. While fixing and repeating the external forms of demonstrated emotion, he simultaneously experiences it to a greater or lesser extent. We should note that this boundary is quite flexible and conditional in its own way. Hence the characteristic ability of each type of theater to become penetrated by and merge with the other, especially in the later development of stage art in the twentieth century. Neither type of theater exists in chemically pure form, but both principles can be indicated and defined theoretically.

All the structural elements of theater in our time change in accordance with these two principles.

Characteristic selectivity surfaces already in the area of genre. The theater of direct conformity to life usually (but not always) exhibits a preference for the so-called "play" or "drama," avoiding extremist genres such as high tragedy, buffoon comedy, or farce. On the contrary, relativistic theater prefers exactly these extremist genres. When a tragedy is presented, the audience is informed in advance that the conclusion will be harsh. When a comedy is presented, the audience is promised a happy ending. The theater and the audience "arrange" in advance the emotional coloration of the action. The extreme genres that this type of theater prefers operate with variously rearranged and poeticized specifics of life, and play with emotional and dynamic "concentrations of reality."

The theater of direct conformity to life attempts to confront the audience with all the unpredictable complexity of reality and the unexpected development of events, attempting to conceal both the ending and the emotional coloration of the action from the public. Stage action is to catch the audience unprepared, so that its impact is increased. This is why the genre "play" or "drama" exists; the theater of direct conformity to life warns the audience of nothing in advance, and at the same time is the bearer of detailed and accurate minutiae, both of everyday life and psychology, which make the artistic whole believable.

In the theater of direct conformity to life a *painting of life* is reproduced within the stage-box, separated from the audience by an imaginary "fourth wall." An invisible *frame* is created, cutting the picture off from the audience and simultaneously offering the audience total involvement in the life on stage. Concurrently, the theater strives to reproduce the atmosphere and mood of the action, involving the audience in this atmosphere.

Nonetheless, relativity, as the basic and natural property of any art, does appear in the theater of direct conformity to life—if only in the relativity of the portal frame that encloses the "painting of life," in the relativity of the "fourth wall" principle, in the relativity of Stanislavsky's magical "what if" ("what if" being a declaration of relativity, its manifestation point), etc.

In relativistic theater the action takes place not in the "atmosphere of life," but on the territory of the stage which can be and is frequently connected with the auditorium space. The "fourth wall" is destroyed.

In striving for maximum illusion, the theater of direct conformity to life desires the deep silence of concentration from a darkened auditorium. Applause is forbidden during the action due to the fear of destroying the illusion and mood. It creates an environment of maximum concentration on the part of the audience in the course of action that is perceived as reality, arousing audience empathy for events transpiring onstage.

Relativistic theater seeks applause. Public approbation pleases and stimulates its masters in the creative moment. They readily illuminate the auditorium and otherwise strive to demolish the barrier between the place of creation and the place of reception. Relativistic theater feels confined in ordinary theater buildings. Its ideal is street theater.

In our days action in the theater of direct conformity to life usually develops as a constant "flow of life," avoiding frequent subdivisions. Hence the long, undivided acts. In relativistic theater the action is just as naturally broken up into separate episodes, fragments or "numbers." Moments where the action is stopped completely are possible. Abrupt accelerations or decelerations of the pace, as compared to life, are both considered possible and desirable. On occasion, totally unreal rhythms —even plain, anxious or ridiculing arhythmia—are used.

In the theater of direct conformity to life the players' speech imitates conversational, everyday speech with its pauses, slips of the tongue and even its carelessness. Once again, the more true-to-life, the better. Verse drama becomes deformed in theater of this sort; the rhythmic organization of the verse becomes broken in the name of verisimilitude and verse succumbs to the conversational.

In relativistic theater stage speech is organized musically and rhythmically. The specific organizational principles may vary, as do verse measures. Relativistic theater easily accepts drama in verse, and the verse form dictates to the actor his manner of pronunciation.

It can be stated with certainty that any verse drama (tragedy, comedy or vaudeville) is intended for relativistic theater and has intrinsic objections to the theater of direct conformity to life.

The intrinsic bond between the laws of relativistic theater and the laws of poetry is caused by the circumstance that verse is the most intense and concentrated form of speech. Furthermore, it is a specially organized, rhythmically arranged form of speech. Relativistic theater, meanwhile, is an arranged, specially organized and even more intense and condensed form of action. Here we have an unquestionable unity of principle that is manifested completely in theatrical practice. This kinship with poetry is proven in Meyerhold's stagings of Pushkin, Lermontov, Blok and Mayakovsky.

On the other hand, we see an equally substantial kinship between the theater of direct conformity to life and prose. In any case, practice demonstrated with sufficient clarity the attraction and proximity of the Moscow Art Theater to the great works of Russian prose by Dostoevsky and Tolstoi, and the unattractiveness or inaccessibility of these works to Meyerhold's theater. The universal recognition of Stanislavsky's and Nemirovich-Danchenko's masterpieces of direction has been conditioned to a great degree by the organic connection between their work and the traditions of nineteenth-century Russian prose, which has enriched the cultural and spiritual heritage of mankind.

For an actor in the theater of direct conformity to life there is no such thing as the relative. This is the main relative principle of this "nonrelative" theater—a theater that is, however, separated from the audience by a relative "fourth wall." Hence the understandable impossibility of monologues or asides, or at least the need to justify them with great skill and to adapt them carefully to normal, everyday activity. This problem does not exist for relativistic theater.

It is easy to trace the development of these principles in all the other elements of stage action: in the plastic movements of the actors, construction of the stagings, decorations, costumes, lighting, accompanying noise, music, etc.

Meyerhold was to assimilate, test and demonstrate to the public the most varied forms of relativistic theater. The direction in which he chose to work suggested the need to mobilize the experience and hoary traditions of relativistic theater. Thus, the director's interest turned toward the restoration of Molière's theater, Italian masques, etc. Meyerhold's work in the dramatic theater became fused with his work on the opera stage, since opera, from the point of view of dramatic theater, is a relativistic art form.

Meyerhold's debut as opera director was the staging of Wagner's *Tristan and Isolde* (premiere night: October 30, 1909).

Meyerhold had thought a great deal about this production and formulated his thoughts in a special article that was published in the *Imperial Theater Annual (Ezhegodnik imperatorskikh teatrov)*, and subsequently in his book *On Theater.*[21] Among Meyerhold's theoretical works, the article on the production of Wagner's opera is one of the most significant, since it defines and demonstrates expressively the substantial shift in the director's efforts. In this article there is a Meyerhold still presenting theoretical grounds for the practice of the Ofitserskaya Street theater, and the "new" Meyerhold who, with characteristic haste, is assimilating the principles that soon will lead to a resounding theatrical success in *Don Juan*.

In his article, Meyerhold sharply criticized the traditional Renaissance stage "box" with which were associated (or, better, into which were forced) the contemporary conceptions of realism. The Renaissance stage corresponded to the concept of perspective and the world view developed in that era. The proportions and dimensions of this stage expressed the humanistic principle of the great age where man became "the measure of all things." But times changed and such relationships became questionable to artists for whom the outside world was uninteresting, who strove to express man's idea, thought, soul *beyond the everyday*, outside the daily life of man.

Artistic theater, characterizing man with the assistance and concreteness of the daily round, was satisfied fully by the Renaissance stage. It satisfied the requirements of this theater in the sense that it acted as a frame to a *picture*, separated from the audience by the stage portal.

Meyerhold had already begun to demolish the Renaissance stage while in the Ofitserskaya Street theater, decreasing its depth, increasing its width. Many of his statements on this subject in the article on *Tristan and Isolde* were theoretical reasons for what had been done on Ofitserskaya Street. Quoting Ludwig Tieck, Meyerhold asserted that theaters must be "wide and not deep, similar to bas-reliefs," that the stage must be a "pedestal for a sculpture," and so forth. These statements are of less interest, since they only serve to justify past forms of Symbolist productions.

Far more important are the thoughts that disclose Meyerhold's close attention to the stage forms of Shakespearean and antique theaters, as if prophesying a new understanding of theatricality.

Meyerhold is irritated by the closed nature of the Renaissance stage. "Actors in this stage-box with painted rags hanging (from the sides and above) . . . become lost," he writes. The problem of devising the new stage he sees primarily as the problem of bringing actor and audience closer together, the problem of transcending the "frame" as the boundary between stage and auditorium. He is excited by the idea of nearness between player and audience; by the idea of bringing the stage into the auditorium.

The director's attention is arrested by the "front edge" of the stage, the proscenium. His theater lunges at the audience, tries to leap across the orchestra pit and prepares to step into the auditorium. These ideas are already clear in the article on *Tristan*. Meyerhold writes: "If *on the proscenium*, in front of the curtain, we lay down a rug, giving it the significance of a splash of color in harmony with the side draperies, if the *plane adjacent to the proscenium* is turned into a pedestal for groupings, constructing a 'stage-relief'...—then the inadequacies of the Renaissance stage will be lessened adequately."

The picture-like quality that Meyerhold finds disagreeable is also manifest in the flatness of the Renaissance stage. "The greatest unpleasantness," he writes, "is the stage floor, its evenness. As a sculptor sculpts clay, so let the stage floor be sculpted and, from a wide field become a compact collection of planes at various heights."

One goal, which perhaps should have been unexpected in Meyerhold, and actually was new to him, is the promotion of the *actor* to the center of attention. "The actor, whose figure did not dissolve in the decorative draperies which were now removed to the background, becomes the object of attention as a work of art. And each gesture of the actor becomes increasingly extractive; simple, precise, set in relief, rhythmical."[22]

The program of theatricality that we sense here is entirely logical in all its aspects and serves the soul of theater—the actor.

But this is not the entire significance for Meyerhold of his first work with opera. The distinct relativities of opera caused the director to rethink the very nature of the relative, both for art as a whole and for stage art in particular. "Relativity is the foundation of operatic art—people sing; therefore, the natural cannot be introduced into the play, since the relative at once falls into disharmony with the real, demonstrating its apparent insubstantiality, i.e., the foundation of the art collapses." What to do? How, in opera, is one rid of the question "why is the actor singing and not speaking?" And how, accordingly, in drama is one rid of a thousand analogous questions? He refers to Chalyapin: "In Chalyapin's performance there is always *truth*, but theatrical truth, not the truth of life. It is always raised above life, this somewhat decorated truth of art."[23]

Most interestingly, both Stanislavsky and Meyerhold consider Chalyapin's art to be a beckoning ideal. Although at an increasing distance from each other and following diametrically opposed paths, both directors find in Chalyapin the manifestation of what, it would appear, are irreconcilable views. Chalyapin's image was before Stanislavsky not only when he created the Studio on Povarskaya Street with Meyerhold or when he staged *Hamlet* with Craig, but later as well. The day would come when Stanislavsky, too, would say that his entire "system" was "drawn from Chalyapin."

Meyerhold, meanwhile, sees in Chalyapin's art the triumph of the principles of relativistic theater. Grounding himself in Chalyapin's experience in opera staging, he strives to expand the significance of this experience to the level of the universal. In examining Chalyapin's art he seeks out general laws for all types of stage art.

Furthermore, he immediately proposes a fundamentally new approach to operatic art itself. The opera director, thinks Meyerhold, must find support not in the libretto or literary base (plot) of the work; the sole source of his creativity must be the composer's score. In accordance with Ivan Sollertinsky's precise formula, music is viewed as "the substance of the action."[24]

Some entries in Telyakovsky's journal give an impression of how Meyerhold was assimilating operatic art, and of the conflicts that arose.

October 17, 1909. "Today I attended the first dress rehearsal of *Tristan*... Meyerhold's staging is intelligent and attractive. The costumes are stylish, particularly on those who wear them properly. Cherkasskaya was the misery of the day. She is no Isolde. From the very start of the rehearsal she was scandalous and capricious. Every invention of the artist and director was a hindrance to her." (The artist for the production was A. K. Shervashidze.)

October 25, 1909. "The second rehearsal of *Tristan* was also not without incident. Cherkasskaya was not present this time, but there was an incident with Meyerhold. During the rehearsal Napravnik stopped the orchestra to tell Meyerhold that the brass section was placed too far away and that they were difficult to hear. Meyerhold answered that they are in the second coulisse and that they cannot be moved closer—or if they were to be moved closer they ought to be placed in the orchestra. Napravnik took this suggestion as an insult on the part of Meyerhold, and Walter the orchestra leader stood up and, waving his baton, began to denounce Meyerhold, saying that staging opera his way was completely impossible and ridiculous.

Meyerhold bore himself calmly and with dignity the whole time."

At the premiere Cherkasskaya played Isolde and Ershov played Tristan. On October 30, Telyakovsky wrote with satisfaction: "The opera has gone very well. The orchestra and singers transcended all the difficulties of the staging—the one interfering factor is the staging itself. Meyerhold and Prince Shervashidze are guilty here. All the main scenes of Acts 2 and 3 take place by a rock, and this is very dull. Tristan and Isolde writhe like worms by the rocks and frequently take on unnatural poses."[25]

An extremely characteristic scene appears: Meyerhold is in conflict with the lead performers, the conductor and orchestra leader. Even Telyakovsky, Meyerhold's benefactor, is displeased with the production. Nonetheless, it was Meyerhold's work that the critics praised highly and they accepted his innovations completely: the replacement of the flat plane of the stage by a "stage-relief," the play of a number of planes at different levels, the special attention given to plasticity of movement—in particular, to gestures, "frozen poses," which showed themselves to be "quite acceptable on the operatic stage," etc.

In the production of *Tristan and Isolde*, most attention was attracted by the characteristic theme of the art of that day: the theme of sweet nonexistence, of beautiful death in which, as in Nirvana, inspired lovers find each other and merge forever. I. Sollertinsky subsequently wrote of the "heady Buddhist-erotic atmosphere" of the production, and noted that "this *Tristan* was unusually 'ours' in the surroundings of Russian Symbolism."[26] In support of this assertion he quoted Vyacheslav Ivanov, who had paid special attention to Wagner's *Tristan* in his book *From Star to Star*, interpreting it as a particularly Symbolist work. This is all true, of course, and it is likely that Meyerhold had selected *Tristan* in part because of the long-standing tendency on the part of Russian Symbolists to intertwine the themes of erotica and death. But that is not the significant thing. All the operatic productions directed by Meyerhold on the Mariinsky stage were tragedies. In this period he clearly avoided the popular romantic operas by Verdi, Bizet, Meyerbeer and others. He was attracted by the true tragedians of opera—Wagner, Gluck, Mussorgsky, Richard Strauss, and Dargomyzhsky—just as in drama his sphere becomes almost exclusively *high* comedy and *high* tragedy.

The Wagnerian opera brought Meyerhold his first notable success in the Imperial Theaters. His next work, *Tantris the Fool*, by Ernst Hardt, presented on the Alexandrinsky stage, strengthened this success. *Tantris the Fool* is a modern variation on the same legend of Tristan and Isolde that was on the director's mind at the time. Wearing the mask of the King's fool, Tantris defended his love with the weapons of derisive and mournful humor.

For Meyerhold this work was transitional and, undoubtedly, a compromise. It was somewhere on the line between the new theatricality of *Tristan and Isolde* and the already obsolete system of "motionless theater." Nonetheless, Meyerhold, who felt himself to be well in the saddle after *Tristan*, succeeded this time in obtaining the enthusiasm of the actors—Yu. Yurev, N. Khodotov, M. Vedrinskaya and N. Kovalenskaya.

Following the dress rehearsal of *Tantris the Fool*, Telyakovsky wrote:

The staging is interesting and not trite; I was especially struck by the noble tone of the first act where Vedrinskaya, Kovalenskaya, Esipovich, Yurev and Petrov were most satisfactory. In the second act this nobility was disturbed by the voices of Nikolsky and Osokin. The presence of senators from Vyshny Volochek was felt. The third act with Vedrinskaya and Khodotov was again very beautiful—same with Scenes 4 and 5. Naturally, our regulars did not sympathize with this production, and none of the leads were in the theater. This is understandable. The very word "new" causes them to tremble with indignation.[27]

Like *Tristan* in the opera, *Tantris the Fool* was decorated by Alexander Shervashidze. The premiere was on March 9, 1910. Over two years had passed since Meyerhold's departure from Komissarzhevskaya's theater, and a year and a half since the production of *At the Imperial Gates*. Reviewers had become accustomed to the thought that Meyerhold was in the Alexandrinsky Theater and were relatively objective toward his new work. The tone of the reviews was calm and slightly surprised. With some bewilderment, attempting not to recall their own categorical and dismal prognostications, the Petersburg critics declared a success.

"Mr. Meyerhold's staging," wrote Omega, "is beautiful and rich with successful devices, and this primarily resolved the fate of the play."[28] N. Rossovsky enthusiastically acclaimed the mass scenes: "In an exceptionally true-to-life and interesting fashion Mr. Meyerhold staged the crowd of lepers surrounded by the people, with Queen Isolde and Tristan among the leprous people." He highly praised the entire work by the director, who had "worked hard, very hard, on the bright, beautiful, and truthful staging of the play."[29] Znosko-Borovsky recalled this stage many years later. He was unable to forget the lepers "to whom King Mark sacrificed Isolde the Fair. The impetuosity of their movements, the repetitiveness of their gestures, the increasing, intense rhythm of passion inciting them to possess her, were transmitted with great and terrible pathos."[30]

The magazine *Theater and Art* admitted that the production was "tasteful and competent," but felt that all the interest was concentrated in the three lead performers—Yurev, Vedrinskaya and Khodotov.

Of course, it was natural for Kugel's magazine to attempt to explain the success of the production in such a way as to leave the director (especially Meyerhold) in the shadows. But the fact that Meyerhold had, in fact, staged a production capable of inspiring critics to think about the interpretation of individual roles and about the creative work of individual actors was significant. In Meyerhold's theater the actor was no longer the "stumbling block," but was becoming the center of stage compositions. Such were the first results of Meyerhold's new strivings. Meanwhile, he was preparing for a new, far more bold and important step.

Before taking this step, Meyerhold, true to his decision not to experiment on the large Alexandrinsky stage, undertook two important experiments in studio.

The first experiment was an essentially amateur production—Calderón de la Barca's *The Adoration of the Cross*, staged in Vyacheslav Ivanov's apartment. This apartment was on the top floor of a tall building and was therefore called "the tower." Hence the beautiful but excessively imposing name of the "Tower Theater," where amateurs under Meyerhold's direction staged their single production. The atmosphere of the performance is well reproduced in V. Pyast's memoirs:

V. K. Ivanova-Shvarsalon, Vyacheslav Ivanov's stepdaughter, her girlfriend N. P. Krasnova, and Boris Mosolov together had selected the play. They chose Calderón's *The Adoration of the Cross*, in Balmont's translation, of course. Meyerhold, whom they had attracted to the project, made several abridgements and animated the action, which was too slow for the pace of our life in dramas of those days... The final rehearsals lasted eighteen hours without a break!

The entire background of the stage was draped, hung, covered with endless unfurled, laid out, folded over, bunched up and lushly fluffed rolls of thousands of yards of material of different colors, primarily red and black. Enormous pieces and lengths of old and not-so-old material like this were stored in Vyacheslav Ivanov's apartment. There were woolens, velvets, silks... Sudeikin was captivated by the enormous amount of material; he piled up the material in heaps, creating a true feast for the eyes. He also constructed an especially splendid curtain, or, more precisely, two drapes. At the end of each scene two little blackamoors would draw the curtain from opposite sides; all mechanization, whether in the form of rings on a rod or wire, or in the form of electric light (all light was from candles in heavy candlesticks), was banned from this medieval production.

The blackamoors had to hold the ends of the curtain for the entire duration of the intermissions...

The staged action required a bandit to hand a ladder to the hero and chieftain. But the door from the dining room into the drawing room was too narrow and small to permit the passage of a ladder. This was, however, the door used by the actors. What to do?

Meyerhold did not wish to part with the ladder.

And suddenly he is inspired. The inspiration is truly historic...

"Bring it through here!" cried Meyerhold, pointing left of himself, to the right of the stage—to the door through which the audience entered the dining room from the room adjoining. There were no other doors into the dining room.

"How's that? From the public? Through the audience?"

"But yes, of course. Exactly so. Let everyone step aside."

And so, for the first time in history, at least in contemporary theater, "the actor went out into the audience."[31]

To V. Pyast's account we need add only that the blackamoors were a butler's children, whose faces Meyerhold had blackened with soot, that the costumes were improvised and that this entire project was done half in fun.

This was the first playful impromptu on the subject of the large and serious work that was already begun on *Don Juan*. The second, already more thoroughly thought out, sketch was the production of the pantomime *Columbine's Scarf*, staged in the House of Interludes *(Dom intermedii)*. The House of Interludes was a sort of Studio. In it were united Petersburg actors, actresses, artists, composers, directors—Meyerhold, who, for the time, used the pseudonym "Doctor Dapertutto" —among them.

For a fairly long period this new name indicated a symptomatic "personality split" in Meyerhold. Doctor Dapertutto was a tireless experimenter, organizer and source of inspiration for all manner of artists' studios. The range of his activity encompassed small, impoverished but brightly decorated halls for a selected artistic public. He staged parodies, pantomimes, and presentations in the style of Italian masques and published in a small circulation the magazine *Love for Three Oranges*, refined and intended for only the small circle of his followers. At the same time, the director of the Imperial Theaters, Vsevolod Meyerhold, was staging in the huge, ancient, gilded, many-storied halls of the Mariinsky operatic theater and the Alexandrinsky dramatic theater spectacles that astounded spectators with their scale, opulence, power and energy of form and impressive unity of style.

It soon became clear, however, that there existed an unbreakable bond between Doctor Dapertutto and Vsevolod Meyerhold, that the bold, daring and risky experiments created in little cabaret-type theaters were precursors of the confident and large-scale solutions for the shows on the Imperial stage. Doctor Dapertutto and Vsevolod Meyerhold assisted each other. Doctor Dapertutto, who directed enthusiastic amateurs and shy students, was the author of sudden impromptus and unexpected sketches for the mature, well-thought-out creations of Meyerhold the director, who worked with professional, experienced actors.

The tiny former Story *(Skazka)* Theater was reconstructed according to new requirements: the footlights were dismantled, a wide staircase from the stage into the auditorium was built, the rows of chairs were replaced by small tables in order that the audience (as in a cabaret) "during the performance could ask for food and drink and therefore feel more free and active. The actors entered and left through the auditorium, sat on the staircase, and in one play during a dance in an imaginary tavern, the actor's exclamations of admiration were joined by the same from the hall, which led to a prearranged exchange of angry words with the result that in the auditorium another actress-dancer started to dance on one of the tables to prove her superiority to the one dancing onstage. "32

Among these and similar scenes, Meyerhold's pantomime adaptation of Schnitzler's *Columbine's Scarf* stood out. In Schnitzler's version of the traditional Italian masked comedy—Columbine and Harlequin fooling Pierrot—the tone was tragic. Pierrot drinks poison and dies, Columbine, terrified, runs from the dead man to the wedding ball, dances a quadrille with Harlequin, then returns to Pierrot and drinks a cup of poison in turn. The simple pantomime directed by Doctor Dapertutto in power of impression "equalled the more successful dramatic productions." Especially interesting was the ball scene where "during the old-fashioned quadrille here, there, in windows and doors, Pierrot's white sleeve appears; the dances, first faster, then slower, take on the terrible quality of a nightmare, more so than in life—strange Hoffmann-like creatures grimacing under the direction of a large-headed orchestra leader, who from a chair conducts four improbable musicians... All the fantasy and unreal terror of these short scenes," wrote Znosko-Borovsky, "was transmitted with agonizing passion and intensity, and the duality between truth and the intentional was presented with great force, knocking the audience off balance."33 N. Sapunov was the artist for the production.

In January 1910 Meyerhold undertook—this time in the unexpected role of soloist in a small studio ballet—yet another curious experiment. He played Pierrot in the Studio production of *Carnival*, by the choreographer Mikhail Fokin. Fokin later wrote: "I believe that this was his first contact with the art of rhythmic gesture set to music... He was a man from a different world at the first two rehearsals. His gestures lagged behind the music. Many times he 'showed up' at the wrong time, and 'took off' from the stage without reference to the music. But by the third rehearsal our new mime had matured, and in the performance gave a marvelous image of the melancholy dreamer Pierrot."[34]

In these Studio works—*The Adoration of the Cross, Columbine's Scarf* and Fokin's *Carnival*—the concept of festive theatricality became defined more distinctly. But Molière's *Don Juan*, staged in the Alexandrinsky theater, was to be its true triumph. *Don Juan* was Meyerhold's first full-scale application of the principle of stylization, i.e., the principle of re-creation of the style and atmosphere of a specific era with the assistance of art objects from that era. The period which interests the contemporary artist is largely reproduced with the force of the esthetic system created by that era. (An early effort by Meyerhold in this sphere, as we recall, was the production of *Love's Comedy* in the Povarskaya Street Studio.)

The concept of stylization was proposed by Meyerhold as a counterweight to an idea that had become widespread and had undergone a long period of modifications, with particular consistency and success in such shows by the Moscow Art Theater as, for instance, Shakespeare's *Julius Caesar*, or Gogol's *Inspector General*. This is the idea of museum-like reproduction of the style of the era, down to the last detail. The stylization sought by Meyerhold had as its aim the re-creation of the external traits and details of one style or another, of one manner of life or another which was long past, but it placed before the director and artist the task of presenting a sort of "essence of style," to expose its main themes from the point of view of modern life. In other words, stylization meant a consciously idealized treatment of the past, with a necessary air of admiration. This air of admiring the past, the desire to re-create its generalized, festive and attractive contours, is clearly felt in Meyerhold's work on Molière's *Don Juan*.

Let us note at once that our literature's usual treatment of stylization as something culpable and false is baseless. Naturally, if annoyingly petty stylization is wrought up to the level of a museum-piece, then it may be as empty and false as any artifice in art. This is a matter of taste and measure. Fine, thought out and competent stylization can give—and frequently does give—a superb artistic effect, in a natural manner bringing the audience into the spirit and aroma of a specific period, actively increasing its impact and, most importantly, reconciling the audience to the artistic style of the work and to the theatrical tradition of the production. In *Don Juan*, the stylization was most appropriate, and Meyerhold's production could serve as a standard for the precise resolution of problems of stylization in new contemporary works of truly high style.

Naturally, it was the era of Louis XIV that was reproduced—the age of Molière and Racine. Meyerhold wanted the production to re-create the atmosphere of a Court performance of that period. But Meyerhold did not deem it necessary to subject his production to the "archeological method" or "to worry about the precise reproduction of the architectural details of ancient stages."[35] Rather, he was creating a free, contemporary variation on the theme of a French Court production of the late seventeenth century.

In May of 1909, Meyerhold gave Golovin detailed instructions "for the set" of *Don Juan*. The fundamental principles of the overall staging had already been determined by that time. Furthermore, many specifics of the form were defined firmly and unequivocally:

The stage is divided into two planes:

1) Proscenium, the construction of which is subject to the principles of architectural art: this plane is designed exclusively for "reliefs" and the actors' figures (the latter act only in this plane).

The proscenium very strongly jutting out into the auditorium. No footlights. No prompting booth.

2) The rear part of the stage is exclusively for the artists' canvases; places where the actors do not enter with the exception of the final scene (Juan's downfall, burning), and even then the actors' figures will appear on the line separating the first plane from the second.

Immediately, Meyerhold added: "The line separating the 1st plane from the 2nd is marked by a conditional partition, which is occasionally opened or removed, depending on the decorative composition of the stage."[36]

In these few words a program of blinding innovation and astounding boldness was set forth. Meyerhold eliminated the footlights and moved the proscenium, where *all* the action was to transpire, far out into the auditorium. He stressed particularly that the players would act *only* on the proscenium, and only for the final scene did he indicate a spot at a relative depth, at the border between the proscenium and the rear plane. This rear area was completely handed over to the artist and his canvases. In this fashion were defined the fundamentally new relationships between theatrical decorations and the figures of the living actors in the first place, and between the actors and the audience in the second place.

Somewhat later, and possibly already during work with Golovin, other general principles were established for the staging. Full illumination in the auditorium, diminishing only during the most pathetic moments of the action, the general framing of the stage in accordance with the spirit of a Court production of Molière's time, etc.

Already in this initial explication of 1909, Meyerhold had a tapestry in the foreground. This tapestry concealed the background; behind it were changed, and subsequently presented to the audience's view, paintings corresponding to one or another place of action. "I would like," continued Meyerhold, "in this same Act I to utilize the effect of relativistic candelabras on the proscenium... When the viewer enters, he sees in the semi-darkness the stage where candle flames flicker in high gilded candelabras and the Gobelin design is slightly visible. A soft overture signals the beginning of the act. Little blackamoors (6-8) run in, quickly extinguish the candelabras, the stage is brightly lit, the blackamoors vanish, and the act begins in a major key, joyous tones." Regarding these blackamoors, Meyerhold added: "The little blackamoors are introduced to place and remove accessories and furniture on the stage between the acts. During the intermissions, music is heard from behind the stage; its purpose is to entertain the viewer."

Having received Meyerhold's instructions, Golovin set to work at once and in total secrecy. Golovin and Meyerhold, both excellent inventors, were secretive and suspicious, ever fearful that someone would discover their "inventions." The intensity of Golovin's work may be judged by his 1910 note to Meyerhold: "Whole days and half the nights I am spending with *Don Juan*."[37]

In striving to reproduce the spirit and style of a Louis XIV period presentation,

Meyerhold was more interested in capturing tendency of style, rather than in reproducing all the details. He felt that "it would be an error to try to reproduce an exact copy of a stage from Molière's time." For, in his opinion, Molière dreamed of "expanding the frame of the stage of his time." During the time of Moliere there was no proscenium jutting out into the audience in the manner Meyerhold had conceived. But Meyerhold asserted that Molière had wanted to move the action from the depths of the stage "to the proscenium, its very edge."[38]

The decision to perform the whole comedy on a large proscenium deep in the auditorium arose not from the historical specifics of seventeenth-century theater, but from Meyerhold's interpretation of Molière's theatrical ideas:

How obvious are the benefits for Molière when his work is performed on the proscenium, artificially created under all the unfavorable conditions of the modern stage! With what ease Molière's grotesque images come to life on this forward-jutting platform. The atmosphere that fills this space is not choked by columns, while the light that pours over this dust-free atmosphere plays only on the supple figures of the actors. It appears as though everything around has been created to further the play of bright light from the stage candles and candles from the auditorium, which is never plunged into darkness during the entire production.[39]

In Molière's time there were no productions without a curtain. Nonetheless, Meyerhold eliminated the curtain. Golovin told how Meyerhold was guided by the following considerations: "No matter how well the curtain is decorated, the audience regards it quite coldly. Curtain art is received casually, weakly, since the viewer has come to see what is concealed behind the curtain. After the curtain is raised, some time is required for the viewer to assimilate all the charms of the environment surrounding the players in the play. It is another matter with a stage open from beginning to end: by the time the actor appears on the stage, the viewer has already managed to 'breathe in the air of the period.'"[40] For the same reason, it was decided to use the music of Rameau for the accompaniment to the play.

While Golovin was preparing the decorations and costumes, Meyerhold was working with the actors. He was striving for an almost ballet-like grace of movement, a casual dance rhythm, "melodic walk," plastic lightness and grace. All this was new, and surprised the Alexandrinsky actors. "I witnessed," recalled Yakov Malyutin, an actor regularly present at the rehearsals, "with my own eyes, confusion on the faces of some participants in the production, disagreement and even protest on the faces of others. Only Yurev, rehearsing for the role of Don Juan with youthful high spirits and receptivity, would catch every suggestion of the director's in mid-flight and sincerely try to do everything that was demanded of him... And, finally, he succeeded in making his Don Juan accord completely with all the requirements of the director's plan—he was light, happy, illuminated with fine and gracious humor, and in no way was reminiscent of the former monumental Yurev heroes. This was not at all easy for him to achieve...."[41]

It was not easy for Meyerhold, either. But, having inspired Yurev, he aroused the enthusiasm of the other performers. (Elvira was played by Kovalenskaya, Don Carlos by Vertyshev, Charlotte by Timé, Mathurine by Rachkovskaya, Pierrot by Ozarovsky, Dimanche by Bragin, etc.) Particular problems arose with Varlamov, who was assigned the important role of Sganarelle.

The famed Konstantin Varlamov shunned all innovation and was not at all disposed to heed Meyerhold. He was old and disinterested in directorial experiments. "Varlamov warned in advance," states Timé, "that he knew the play and the role, and came to just one of the final rehearsals. He was allowed to do this. Alas, not only was he unable to flitter about the stage, as all the characters including Don Juan were doing, but Varlamov was no longer able to spend the entire time on his feet. Then, Meyerhold together with Golovin the artist, the true co-author of the production, placed special benches covered with felt not far from the footlights for Varlamov."[42]

But this was not the end or the resolution of all the difficulties. Meyerhold had moved the proscenium into the auditorium and had removed the footlights and the prompting booth. But Varlamov had never learned the lines and could not act without a prompter. Sganarelle's role is important, it contains seven long monologues and, notes Malyutin, "the absence of a prompter in his usual spot could have led to a real catastrophe."[43]

Meyerhold turned to Telyakovsky with a special letter in which he insisted that the Director force the actor to learn his lines. But this did not help. Then Meyerhold found an amusing way out of the situation. Golovin was ordered to construct two elegant screens with little windows which were to be placed on the right and left edges of the stage. Before the beginning of the performance, two prompters dressed in Louis XIV period costumes, with large powdered wigs and manuscripts in hand, sat down behind the screens, drew the curtains over the windows and began to "supply the lines." Since it was unthinkable to drag Varlamov away from the prompters, both of Sganarelle's benches were placed near the screen. Timé recalls:

> And a miracle happened: Varlamov sat on his bench, all the performers fluttered around him according to precisely measured choreography, and the impression was created that Sganarelle was exceptionally mobile and subserviently "gets round" his master!.. Occasionally, Varlamov would get up from his bench. In the graveyard scene, according to Meyerhold's plan, he was to walk the length of the ramp, illuminating with a lantern the important people sitting in the first row. This was fairly risky, but Varlamov played with such sincerity that no one was insulted, and applause followed this one and only walk of the actor across the stage.[44]

Timé was completely accurate here. The role began with Sganarelle's entry from the depths of the stage "in an unusually colorful, artistic and characteristic striped costume decorated with ribbons, directly toward the audience, coming right up to it, to the very edge of the jutting proscenium," says Yurev. "Varlamov walks with an open, good-natured, unusually happy face, having not yet spoken a word, and his appearance alone causes such animation that it seems like the advent of a holiday."[45]

The third difficulty, finally, was to avoid disharmony between Yurev (Don Juan) and Varlamov (Sganarelle). Varlamov was heavy, Yurev's Don Juan was light and dashing; Varlamov's speech was juicy and savory; Yurev's rapid, hasty, "almost without inflection. All attention was concentrated on changes in tempo and the rapid, bold switching from one rhythm to another, precision of diction and variety of typeface—cursive, brevier or nonpareil—and bolder type only in special cases, coloring them with one or another soft, gentle color, thus achieving the limits of craftsmanship."[46]

Meyerhold resolved that in this case the best form for unity would be a forthright contrast between the speech of the master and servant, Don Juan and Sganarelle. He did, of course, keep in mind the limitless capabilities of Varlamov's talent. The task of rhythmic and tonal connection with the partner was assigned to Varlamov; not even assigned, in fact, but simply left to him and his improvisational gifts. "The artistic sensibility of Konstantin Alexandrovich Varlamov," Yurev recalled later, "suggested to him the way to weld our lines together, while in the meantime Varlamov remained the full master of his tone and gave rein to his tempestuous talent, and did so in such a way that there was no disharmony between us."[47]

If, prior to rehearsals with Meyerhold, Varlamov had been hesitant about his "fancies" and complained that he was too old to "dance the French *prisiadka*," by the end of the rehearsals, he was delighted, according to Golovin: "Here's a real director! He doesn't seat me in the fourth room of the suite where no one sees me and where I see no one, but puts me on the proscenium... Everyone said 'Meyerhold, Meyerhold,' but here he sets things up so that everyone sees me and I see everyone."[48]

The dress rehearsal of *Don Juan* was held on November 6, 1910. Telyakovsky wrote in his journal:

> Golovin's staging is incredibly beautiful. The time of Louis XIV is depicted in complete detail, starting with the props and decorations and finishing with the astonishingly beautiful costumes. The naivete of the concepts of Louis XIV's time is reconstructed. Varlamov as Sganarelle, Yurev as Don Juan and Kovalenskaya as Elvira are very good in their roles. Rachkovskaya, Timé and Ozarovsky are not bad, if a bit cartoonish. Overall, the rehearsal made a very good impression, and I believe that the play will be most successful. It is important that plays are successful this season, despite the absence of Savina and Davydov.[49]

The premiere of *Don Juan* was set for November 9. All Russia was in mourning on that day, on account of Lev Tolstoi's funeral. In some theaters the shows had been cancelled altogether. But the Administration of the Imperial Theaters did not venture even to postpone the premiere, and *Don Juan* was performed on the assigned evening. Despite such an unhappy coincidence, the theater, again according to Telyakovsky,

> was completely filled—the auditorium had a smart appearance. From the first act the actors, the director Meyerhold and the artist Golovin were called to the stage. These calls continued for the duration of the performance. The entire audience was pleased, and did not leave for a long time after the end of the performance and called the performers some 20 times. Everyone on stage was pleased, too. The success of a classical play without Savina is, of course, most significant for the Alexandrinsky Theater and demonstrates once more that serious plays can be successful.[50]

The first reviews were almost unanimously delighted. Meyerhold had never known such success. L. Vasilevsky wrote in the newspaper *Speech (Rech')*: "Here the Alexandrinsky Theater has given free rein to esthetic innovation, the creativity of the director's fantasy, and this production will be entered into the history of our—this time not at all trite—stage as a credit for its directors."[51]

Yury Belyaev, in *New Time*, especially stressed the unusual nature of the spectacle created by Meyerhold and Golovin:

> The Alexandrinsky Theater has a different look now. Elegant, stylish, smart. They are showing Molière's *Don Juan* and are asking you to be surprised. This is no "Louis Quatorze the Sixteenth" of the sort that our theaters usually offer us, but a gorgeous artistic production by Golovin that evokes audience applause after the first act.   Meyerhold directs. In the stylistic sense he is far removed from the usual stagings of Molière. If you like, this is his own variation on the theme of *Don Juan*. Variation of stylization, but in any case something original and beautiful. The talented Golovin's "palace of comedy," these stylish "trellises" with a faded rust tapestry that opens in the depths of the stage, transmit the mood of an ancient holiday to the spectacle. The little liveried blackamoors reminiscent of black kittens run and tumble on the soft carpet, burn incense, ring a silver bell. Wax candles gleam. The mysterious tapestry parts and, uncovering scene after scene, tells the fantastic adventure of Don Juan.[52]

Golovin himself later described the spectacle:

> Three chandeliers were over the proscenium. The proscenium itself was lit by two enormous candelabras. There were no footlights at all, while the auditorium was fully illuminated. The walls were framed with cockades against a background of trellises and tapestries. The background curtain's motion would conceal and reveal small paintings that indicated the place of the action. The entire floor of the stage was covered by a solid blue carpet. The proscenium was moved out to the first row; the front curtain was removed. Wax candles burned, glimmering beautifully, in the chandeliers and candelabras. The stage was served by the so-called "liveried little blackamoors" who, bustling like kittens, lit the lights, rang the silver bell before the start, burned perfume, cried out "Intermission," reported events like Il Commandatore's appearance, brought chairs and stools and greatly contributed to the general liveliness with their running about.[53]

In addition, the little blackamoors caught the lace handkerchief as it fell from Don Juan's hand and would return it to the hero, tied his shoelaces while he argued with Sganarelle, handed Sganarelle the lantern, and upon the arrival of Il Commandatore's statue, hid in terror under the table. "All this is not a trick created for the amusement of snobs," Meyerhold asserted, "this is all done in the name of the essential; to show the entire action veiled by a haze of a perfumed, gilded Versailles-type empire."[54]

The skeptical tone with which the Petersburg papers had been accustomed to write about Meyerhold vanished altogether. N. Rossovsky wrote: "Let all the directors who compete with Meyerhold call him a trickster of the stage, but we, in the name of truth, must recognize Mr. Meyerhold's original artistic creativity."[55] Yu. Belyaev stated that "Meyerhold arrived as the true 'master' of the stage, illuminated by fantasy and scientific erudition."[56] However, the owner of *New Time*, A. Suvorin, fairly soon "corrected" his reviewer. Following the second showing of the comedy an anonymous note appeared in *New Time*:

"Yesterday I watched *Don Juan* on the Alexandrinsky stage in the interpretation of Mr. Meyerhold and Mr. Golovin (the decorator). The audience laughed when Varlamov entered. The rest is dull... Were it not for the ever-kind Varlamov, who plays only himself and whom no director can cause to stray from the true path, Molière's comedy would have flopped in Meyerhold's model production."[57]

The well-informed Telyakovsky noted in his diary that this article had been "penned by Suvorin."[58]

Several days after the premiere, another irritated review appeared in Kugel's magazine *Theater and Art*. A week later Kugel printed his own objections. He admitted that the production "is unquestionably successful, it appeals to the public; there is much beauty in the decorations and costumes and in the concept of the staging as well, which is intriguing from the point of view of externals." Kugel thought, however, that in the production "the elements of painting and decorative art," etc., "so overwhelm the elements of theater that one does not even want to think of the latter." In the critic's opinion, the acting was lost "in the auditorium burning with lights, before this carpet-pottery-lace museum production with the scurrying little blackamoors." The critic wrote that everyone acted badly, that "Yurev gives no interpretation, no image of Molière's *Don Juan*, while Mr. Varlamov cheats himself in the role of Sganarelle."[59]

The greatest attention, however, was attracted by Alexander Benois's article, which appeared in *Speech* under the scornful title, "Ballet in the Alexandrinka." The article could not have been completely objective, since at the time of its publication Benois was an active participant in an extremely heated conflict between Telyakovsky and Diaghilev. There is no need to enter into the details of this conflict. We shall note only that in the context of the intensive polemics of the day, the attack on Meyerhold's *Don Juan*, dazzlingly executed by Benois, was conceived and received as another in a series of powerful attacks on the Administration of the Imperial Theaters. At that time, Benois personally was more sympathetic than not toward Meyerhold and his work. He began the article with somewhat equivocal thanks to the director "who treated the Petersburg public to three hours of highly diverting and elegant entertainment. At the same time, I thank him for the delightfully staged pantomime *Columbine's Scarf* in the House of Interludes. With beginning actors, with the poverty of means of a private enterprise, he achieved the impression of great artistic refinement by means of clever combinations and his selection of plastic effects."

The article then turned to *Don Juan* itself. Not without irony, Benois called the director of this production a superlative ballet master, and the show itself a "dressy farce" that transmitted neither the essential content of Molière's work nor the deep thought behind it. "Why," asked Benois, "did Meyerhold assign the role of Sganarelle to Varlamov? This is a tremendous error. For the entire chorus of puppets (I make another exception for Ozarovsky)—*only one actor*. And what a wonderful, divine, yes, by God's grace, actor!.. When this monumental Sganarelle spoke, there remained no doubt before me that he was a true and great artist whose place is not with the others only because the others should not be on the stage at all."

The article concluded with a discussion of the Russian stage which, according to Benois, was ailing because "what is central to theater is forgotten and even held in contempt. There is contempt for the actor's art and for the realization of the dramatic idea. It is wonderful that Meyerhold has taken to working with the plastic. It is to his great credit that Russian actors have learned to walk, move their arms and legs and turn around. But can this be all?"[60]

The major objections to Meyerhold's staging of *Don Juan*, therefore, were on two points:

The staging is too ornate; painting has gained a too-important, self-sufficient position (Kugel).

Molière's play is not understood and is developed shallowly. Molière has been usurped by the "ornate farce" and its human ingredient "forgotten" (Benois).

The near future was to demonstrate, however, that the prospects for painting in dramatic theater were to be considerably wider than they appeared to Kugel, for instance. In this sense, the *Don Juan* of Meyerhold and Golovin was the opening of a new age in theater. Less than a year later, the Moscow Art Theater dispensed with the services of V. Simov, the permanent stage painter. In 1911 Simov had still been the decorator for *The Living Corpse*, but then Nikolai Sapunov was invited to assist Gordon Craig in *Hamlet*, Mstislav Dobuzhinsky for works by Turgenev, Nikolai Roerich for *Peer Gynt*, Alexander Benois for Molière's farces, Dobuzhinsky again for *The Possessed*, Benois for Goldoni and for the staging of Pushkin, Boris Kustodiev for Shchedrin's *The Death of Pazukhin*, and so on. Real painters had come to the best Russian stages. In the Moscow Bolshoi Theater, Korovin was frequently the decorator. In the Alexandrinsky Theater, Golovin had found a firm place. He worked with Meyerhold continuously until the Revolution, after which he worked with Stanislavsky.

The innovation was not only in the radical growth of the painter's participation in the staging, but also in the interrelationship between the delicate, upbeat, colorful *Don Juan* ("rusty" golden tapestry, blue carpet, flaming red portal whose color merged with the red upholstery of the Alexandrinsky Theater, the dark blue sky)—and *the atmosphere of the city where the production was staged*, the atmosphere of Petersburg. Kugel himself wrote many years later: "Petersburg, reflecting in its bureaucratic population the sun-like play of the throne, was saturated through and through with flippance, nihilism, skepticism, and the irony of empty souls. The theater was constructed along the same lines."[61] If, in 1929, when he wrote these words, Kugel had recalled Meyerhold and Golovin's *Don Juan*, he perforce would have conceded that the range of color and the entire atmosphere of the production transmitted both the "sun-like play of the throne" and the associated "flippance, cynicism, skepticism and the irony of empty souls."

The full genius of Meyerhold's rendition of Molière's comedy is especially clear when we compare this criticism with the Meyerholdian conception of the personage of Don Juan. Meyerhold saw Don Juan as a gallant courtier, a decadent aristocrat, a philosopher-skeptic, a jesting tempter, and so on, until in the finale of the play this changeable hero is thrown directly into Hell. Don Juan, said Meyerhold, "is a puppet required by the author for the sole purpose of balancing his accounts with a crowd of countless enemies." Hence the masks of Don Juan. According to Meyerhold, he is "merely a wearer of masks. We see on him either the mask of decadence, faithlessness, cynicism, and the falseness of a courtier of the Sun King, or the mask of the accusing author which he had to wear to court ceremonials and before his crafty wife."[62]

This was intended to be the very heart of the production, whose image was merging directly with the ornate hall of the Russian Imperial Theater. Inside the Alexandrinsky Theater, Don Juan—Yurev—gallantly and acidly played the buffoon, scoffed at himself, at morality, philosophy, and the king.

Nearly a month after the premiere of *Don Juan*, Telyakovsky wrote: "Not one show, I believe, has aroused such interest and so many arguments as *Don Juan*. Every day there is news of various meetings where the production has been discussed by amateurs, artists and professors. Evidently, all Petersburg has become interested in this. The play has been performed to a full house 9 times already."[63]

Meyerhold himself probably reached several conclusions on the basis of such a striking success. He had gone sufficiently far in his efforts to crack the Renaissance box-stage. A new form of staging appeared, one that took the actor outside the "frame" of that painting that the traditional stage presented. The distance between the actor and audience had been transcended. The actor drew as close as possible to the audience.

However, at the same time a highly intensive and fundamentally significant phenomenon was taking place, which the director must have noted. By overstepping the frame of the stage, the actor simultaneously rejected any claim to the unassailable fidelity to life and authenticity of his character. In physically approaching the audience, the actor simultaneously was breaking out of the old system of relating to the viewer, from the system that expected an empathy or a merging between the audience and a live, authentic person there on the stage. There, on the stage, a genuine Astrov or a genuine Othello, Kareno, or Don Juan could be suffering, happy, defeated, or victorious. Here, on the proscenium, in front of the very noses of the audience and capable even of dropping down to the stalls, stood the actor. To approach the audience meant also to withdraw from it and to become elevated above it, and required a new basis and new forms of interaction.

The discoveries in *Don Juan* did not completely resolve the most complex problem that inevitably arose each time "playful theatricality" was stated as a principle and contrasted to "psychological vitality." Naturally, Meyerhold continued to study this problem for several years.

"Here is my essential idea," he remarked in his notebook two years after *Don Juan*, "in the theater of play the viewer is always alive (active); in psychological theater the viewer dies (is passive)."[64]

Don Juan survived for many years in Meyerhold's production. It was revived in 1922 and in 1932.

"The young generation of artists brought fresh motifs to decorative painting. Nonetheless," Meyerhold admitted in 1910, letting the cat out of the bag, "between the directors and the painters there is an argument about who will obtain the conductor's baton." But with his alliance with Golovin in the production of *Don Juan*, Meyerhold proved to "the city and the world" that this argument could be succeeded by complete agreement. The matter of repertory was more complex.

Meyerhold was now objecting strenuously to weak imitation, to "that contemporary Russian drama which constructs its plays in the manner of Hauptmann, Ibsen or Chekhov. The German and Scandinavian theaters and Chekhov's theater of mood—these are the stereotypes that have become worn out by the modern playwright who has filled the entire Russian stage," he wrote. Meyerhold was certain that the public was "aimed in two directions: 1) to gaiety in Cabaret-style small theaters, 2) to unflagging appreciation of Classical repertory—and these will soon crush modern repertory completely."[65]

Everything Meyerhold did at the time was in accordance with these views. He staged the classics on the Imperial stages and experimented in intimate cabaret-type theaters.

Experiments in the realm of "theater of play" were undertaken persistently by Meyerhold whenever one or another group of amateurs or studios was at his disposal. Meyerhold, Znosko-Borovsky wrote later, "strolled his imagination through various theaters of all possible countries and ages: Spain, the Orient, Italy, pantomime, Hoffmann—his inspiration came from everywhere. He would take theatrical elements that appealed to him, never intending to reconstruct them precisely and always remaining the same as he had been from the very start...—a director sensitive to the beauty and expressiveness of self-sufficient theatrical forms, and the enemy of banal copies, sentimental declamations and actors' pathos."

Znosko-Borovsky himself gave Meyerhold the opportunity to "stroll his imagination" to the imaginary "Duchy of Comarille," where Znosko-Borovsky's comedy, *The Transformed Prince*, took place. The comedy was staged by Doctor Dapertutto in the House of Interludes on December 3, 1910, with decorations by Sudeikin and music by Kuzmin.

The Duchy invented by Znosko-Borovsky was reminiscent of Spain, Italy and France. A happy staged suite on romantic themes was offered. Not only did the play not require specifics of daily life, national color, rendition of the spirit of the time, etc., but these were all in fact plainly forbidden. The action took place in a relative world, in a relative country, and although the heroes called themselves Spaniards, this was also clearly a convention, underscored further by the fact that the plot of the play was forthrightly similar to the plot of Fonvizin's *The Minor*. The Spanish prince, like Mitrofanushka, shouts "I don't want to study, I want to get married," and tears to shreds the books brought to him by the "Spanish" scientists Tsyfirkino and Kuteikado... The parody and playfulness of the play permitted Meyerhold to merge completely stage with audience—he had sought this for a long time.

In one episode in *The Transformed Prince*, an actor

dressed as a soldier crawled out from under the decorations (this stresses at once that the theater is only representing a battle and is not trying to convince the audience that a real battle is taking place) and began to speak. It was in his monologue that the entire furious battle scene passed by, with the participation of great imaginary masses of enemy troops. He spoke, shots rang out, cannonballs flew and finally he, terrified, tumbled down the stairs and ducked under the first available table.[66]

Then, with a cry of "every man for himself," he ran out of the hall...

Thus, Meyerhold directed action simultaneously on the stage and in the hall where the audience was seated at tables, as in a cabaret. The dancer in the auditorium competed with the dancer on stage. Actors would crawl onto the stage from under the decorations and then would move freely into the auditorium. Actors were "planted" among the audience, participated in the action and involved viewers in interactions with other actors, as planned in advance by the director.

Theatricality was victorious, it united everyone present in entertaining action. Not only were stage and auditorium united, but viewers were turned into actors and actors into viewers.

However, the next works assigned to Meyerhold in the Imperial Theaters did not provide a vehicle for further experiments along the lines of those in the House of Interludes. On the Mariinsky stage, Meyerhold directed a revival of *Boris Godunov*. The revival was hasty and Meyerhold addressed himself formally to the work as to a duty. His interest was aroused only by the mass scenes of the opera. Once again he opposed the principles of the Moscow Art Theater for mass scenes with his own principles, which had been discovered already in *Sister Beatrice*. Shortly before, in 1908, during the "Russian season" in Paris, the director Alexander A. Sanin, attempting to transfer the Art Theater methods to operatic stage in his staging of *Boris Godunov*, polished each role in the crowd, split the crowd into separate individuals and attempted to grant each extra his own mode of behavior. Meyerhold argued with this approach. "Sanin," he told the correspondent from *Stock Exchange News (Birzhevye vedomosti)*, "has individualized the crowd in his production. His method is analytical. My crowd is not divisible into individuals but into groups. For instance, the blind and the crippled go by—they are all one group and the public must recognize them at once as a whole... Take the crowd of boyars... Must we divide it into separate, dissimilar boyars when they comprised a unit of servile menials?"[67]

Uniform crowd movements were, however, too familiar to the operatic stage, and the choir, mechanically following Meyerhold's instructions, did not achieve that expression which the director attempted to give the mass scenes. What appeared effective and fresh on the dramatic stage, both for Meyerhold and Reinhardt, for instance in *Oedipus Rex*, in opera seemed superimposed on the operatic crowds' familiar routine of monotonous movements and lost expressiveness. Alexander Benois observed with irritation that "such scenes as the coronation, as the *Kromy* . . . were flaccid, and no one understood anything in them. The coronation is all right, an ordinary operatic procession, and the uprising in the *Kromy* is all right, a popular scene, which is inevitable in any Russian opera." In the choir of *Boris Godunov*, wrote Benois, there "was not a single genuine gesture," and the stage was "governed completely by dead things."

True, this article by Benois was another shot fired in his continuing battle for Diaghilev and against Telyakovsky, a war that he was conducting persistently and intently. Accordingly, the Paris production staged by Sanin at Diaghilev's was in every way contrasted to the production directed by Meyerhold at Telyakovsky's. It turned out that in Paris, *Boris* which, as Benois (erroneously) supposed, "will hardly become a popular opera soon," looked enchanting, while in Petersburg it looked bad. "Among the mute paintings and puppets there walks a single living artist—Chalyapin. In Paris everything was living, burning, speaking to mind and heart; therefore, the total impression was tremendous."[68] But, despite his overt partisanship, Benois was correct in this case: Meyerhold's staging was not successful.

In the Alexandrinsky Theater, Meyerhold staged a one-act play by Yury Belyaev, *The Red Tavern*. This fairly elegant bagatelle by Belyaev invited the audience into late eighteenth-century Russia, into the entertaining company of carousing officers and actresses. Their party came to an unexpected end toward morning with the appearance of Baron Munchausen. The ghost of the great prevaricator arose to the light of flaming punch in order to praise the beautiful lie that saves. In essence, the whole idea behind this cozy and pleasant production could be formulated in the well-known words of Beranger, spoken by the Actor in the play *The Lower Depths*: "Honor to the madman who evokes golden dreams in mankind..."

This idea, as well as the impression of the entire play, was undermined by the fact that Munchausen was played by Ge, an affected and cold actor.

Immeasurably greater problems arose in the process of staging Lev Tolstoi's *The Living Corpse*. This was one of the rare times when Meyerhold shared his responsibilities with another director; he directed Tolstoi's drama together with Alexander Leonidovich Zagarov, whom he had known well from the Moscow Art Theater and the New Drama Cooperative. Konstantin Korovin was appointed as the artist for *The Living Corpse*. Here arose a special difficulty for Meyerhold. His relationship with Korovin was complex, since the relations between Korovin and Golovin were complex. Korovin and Golovin had worked for many years in the Imperial Theaters, were rivals and did not acknowledge each other. Telyakovsky's diary contains several highly expressive remarks on this matter. "An amazing thing," he wrote, "is this attitude of Korovin's and Golovin's to each other and to their directors Melnikov and Meyerhold... Both are my friends and colleagues, but they cannot work together, and if Golovin approves of a director Korovin will refuse to acknowledge him."[69]

Golovin was working steadily with Meyerhold, and this signified that the cooperation between Meyerhold and Korovin would be complicated by mutual distrust. Telyakovsky's remark that both Golovin and Korovin were his friends is not quite accurate. The Director of the Imperial Theaters was much more attentive to Korovin, Chalyapin's friend, and therefore some of Korovin's demands during the preparation of *The Living Corpse* were acceded to against the wishes of Meyerhold and Zagarov.

It was also unfortunate that the directors were located in Petersburg, while Korovin was in Moscow. Most importantly—possibly decisively—Meyerhold was not sincerely enthusiastic about *The Living Corpse*.

At this time, Meyerhold was already preparing his production of Lermontov's *Masquerade*, which occupied his mind completely. Meanwhile, in the press, passions were stirring concerning *The Living Corpse*. The text of the play had been found among Tolstoi's manuscripts after his death, and Nemirovich-Danchenko immediately obtained the precious work. He granted the Moscow Art Theater the right to produce this play first, agreeing even to delay its publication until after the premiere. While the Art Theater conducted its rehearsals (there were eighty-three), the text of the play was guarded in strictest secrecy. "In view of fears that *The Living Corpse* might somehow appear in the press before its publication by Tolstoi's survivors," reported *Footlights and Life (Rampa i zhizn')*, "the dress rehearsal of this play at the Art Theater will be closed to the public, since there are fears that speculators may bring their stenographers to the rehearsal and record the play verbatim."[70] All this security only served to increase the excitement surrounding the upcoming premiere of *The Living Corpse*.* But, all sensation aside, the general interest in the unknown play by the writer-genius was completely natural and understandable. Meyerhold, who together with Zagarov was to direct the first staging of this play in the capital, judging by his remarks at the time, did not share in the general excitement.

He and Zagarov had become acquainted with the play comparatively early—in April 1911. Subsequently, Meyerhold gave two interviews and each time said essentially nothing about *The Living Corpse*. In a conversation with a reporter from the *Petersburg Gazette*, he spoke with animation about Lermontov and Gogol, but not about Tolstoi. In a conversation with a correspondent from *Footlights and Life*, he again evaded a discussion of *The Living Corpse*, but did touch upon techniques of theatrical stylization and virtually introduced the concept of the grotesque to the vocabulary of Russian theater:

> We can create stage stylization in all its fullness and power by transforming this method into a *new approach*.
> The new approach of which I speak and which alone, from our point of view, completely reclothes stylization on stage, is defined by the word "grotesque."
> I happen to be writing an extensive work on this approach. The first time I applied this approach on stage was in Blok's *The Puppet Show*, but it was insufficiently expressed. Already in *Columbine's Scarf* and in *Don Juan* I attempted to operate more boldly using this approach. Before us are two productions for this season, *Masquerade* and another play which I am keeping in secret for the time being—in these I shall continue the efforts I have begun in this area....**

Meyerhold continued:

> What is basic to the grotesque is the progress of the viewer from one just-deciphered plane of perception into another, totally unexpected one.
> Then: any gesture, any step, any turn of the head—in a word, any motion is examined as an element of dance, understood as it was understood in old Japanese theater.
> I am most interested in clowns, their quick, rhythmic change from one movement to the next in the most unexpected leaps. You get what you do not expect at any given moment...
> Like the polarity between Hofmannsthal and, say, Hoffman: on the stage there is the polarity between hack writing and theatricality with its grotesque.[71]

---

*"There is a cloud of excitement and publicity around *The Living Corpse*," reported *Theater and Art* 40 (1911), p. 742. It was written that " ... in one of the Moscow theatrical libraries *The Living Corpse* has been secretly published in typescript and widely sold to provincial entrepreneurs. At first the price of a copy reached 300 rubles (!!). Toward the end, a copy would sell for 50 rubles. There is to be an official investigation of this secret sale" (ibid., 718). There were reports, too, that the play was prepared for cinema (p. 720), that it was published in Paris in French, and that the inhabitants of Moscow were becoming acquainted with the French text (ibid, 708), etc., etc.

**The "other play" is evidently Calderon's *The Constant Prince*, staged only in 1915, while work on *Masquerade* continued until 1917.

There is a great deal of substance in this conversation. With greater emphasis than ever, Meyerhold is contrasting theatricality and "literariness." For the first time, he speaks firmly about the possibility of the dramatic theater's using the experience of vaudeville clowns, and immediately he perceives the characteristic expressiveness of *alogism*, which he subsequently will utilize quite energetically. And finally he ventures to pronounce the word "grotesque," immediately evoking an acid comment by the tragedian N. Rossov. "Theater awaits a 'great' future," ironizes Rossov, "with such an approach to stage stylization... Such a theater of the 'grotesque' will have undoubted success in cachectic society, and it is possible to collect an immense number of actors for the grotesque...."[72]

Regardless of how well based Rossov's irony may have been, it is clear that from the point of view of possibilities for the grotesque and stylization, *The Living Corpse* did not allow much room for a director's imagination. But there was an even greater obstacle between the director and the play. In contrast to a multitude of his predecessors, Meyerhold never experienced an attraction toward Tolstoi's philosophy. This distance from Tolstoi, characteristic of Meyerhold's entire long creative path, is one of the most characteristic traits of the director's spiritual identity. The entire intellectual and emotional composition of Meyerhold's personality, his active nature, struggled against Tolstoi's ideals of moral self-improvement, pacifism, and so forth. For Meyerhold, this complex of ideas was too passive.

And although it is known that in November 1905 Meyerhold and L. A. Sulerzhitsky visited L. N. Tolstoi in Yasnaya Polyana, and that Meyerhold often recalled this meeting, he was not enthusiastic about Tolstoi's teachings.

In the early twentieth century, when Meyerhold became formed as an artist, all Russian culture was experiencing the extremely powerful influence of Tolstoi's genius. It was a triple influence: ideological, moral and stylistic. In the realm of stage art, the position closest to Tolstoi was occupied, naturally, by the Art Theater. "The Tolstoian element," Nemirovich-Danchenko wrote later, always "nested in the organism of the Art Theater."[73] In the Art Theater's work with *The Living Corpse*, this seemed to come to the surface, and the Moscow Art Theater's staging of *The Living Corpse* in 1911 sounded like a manifesto, a public announcement of the solidarity between "Chekhov's theater" and Tolstoi, his social positions and his teachings.

The dress rehearsal of *The Living Corpse* in the Art Theater became a sort of demonstration: all of Tolstoi's spiritual and actual descendants were present—his sons and daughters, Chertkov, and others.

The significance ascribed to this production by the Art Theater is shown by the fact that Stanislavsky and Nemirovich-Danchenko, after a lengthy interruption, worked as co-directors of *The Living Corpse*. This production was called forth—after the memorable flop of *The Power of Darkness* in 1902—to prove the closeness between the Moscow Art Theater and Tolstoi's realism, and the task was brilliantly executed.

Meyerhold and Zagarov, working in parallel with the Art Theater, found themselves, whether they wished it or not, in the position of having to compete with the Art Theater under conditions that were totally unfavorable to the Petersburg directors. Evidently they both understood that some organic bond existed between

Tolstoi and the Art Theater. In any case, they undertook—completely in the spirit of the Art Theater—an expedition "into the thick of life" in search of concrete material for the staging. Such expeditions had been undertaken by Moscow Art Theater actors and directors back in the days of working on *The Lower Depths* and *The Power of Darkness*.

In one of the Moscow newspapers in the summer of 1911 there appeared a notice that

> Meyerhold and Zagarov have come to look over the Moscow flophouses and to visit the Gypsies. Both are necessary for the staging of *The Living Corpse*.
>
> "We considered driving to Khitrovka," says Zagarov, "but at the Art Theater we were shown a letter from Tolstoi's former secretary. This letter makes it clear that the pub in *The Living Corpse* is taken not from Khitrovka but from Rzhanov Alley. We drove there, but it was too late, so this first time we limited ourselves to a quick look around. It was 'not recommended' for us to travel further. We have made arrangements with the Gypsies and tomorrow we shall visit their apartments in order to familiarize ourselves with their domestic arrangements."
>
> In Petersburg, as in Moscow, *The Living Corpse* will be staged in purely realistic colors.
>
> Neither director doubts the success of Tolstoi's work in Petersburg.[74]

The announcement that in Petersburg the play would be staged "as in Moscow," i.e., as in the Art Theater, indicated the basic thrust of the directors' efforts. But their optimistic forecasts were to be far from fulfilled.

In his report to Telyakovsky about the form that he expected the production to take, Meyerhold proposed "to divide the play into short scenes (with a rapid development of the events portrayed)," that would succeed each other almost without pause. Only two intermissions were possible, he indicated, "one is even better." Meyerhold wished to cover the edges of the stage with black velvet, "to immerse the frame in total darkness, and to concentrate the light on the actors. This idea, evidently, was not to Korovin's taste.

Two actors in the Alexandrinsky troupe were capable of playing the role of Fyodor Protasov—Roman Apollonsky and Nikolai Khodotov. Both the directors and Telyakovsky were certain that Khodotov would perform better. But Khodotov, a drinker, was unreliable. Furthermore, he refused to play the part unless the part of Masha was awarded to Elizaveta Timé. Korovin opposed this and wanted Masha to be played by the Moscow actress N. Komarovskaya and was able to gain the victory in a power play behind the scenes. Telyakovsky issued the order that surprised many: "The actress of the Moscow Maly Theater, Mrs. Komarovskaya, is assigned to Petersburg for participation in *The Living Corpse*." This also decided the fate of the leading role; Apollonsky performed at the opening. The other parts were assigned as follows: I. Stravinskaya as Liza Protasova, Yu. Yurev as Karenin, M. Savina as Anna Dmitrievna Karenina, V. Dalmatov as Prince Abrezkov, B. Gorin-Goryainov as Alexandrov, and A. Petrovsky as the investigator.

The most various complications afflicted the preparation of the staging. The debate concerning the Gypsy chorus was especially stormy. Meyerhold and Zagarov's idea of introducing a real Gypsy chorus into *The Living Corpse* insulted the

Alexandrinsky "regulars." Savina "spoke against inviting the Gypsy chorus, stating that she would not even walk near the theater if Gypsies were singing." Still, the audition of "real Gypsies" did take place, but was unsuccessful. Then a chorus of actors was created. "About 25 people were willing to sing, and it did not sound bad," noted Telyakovsky.[75]

The first dress rehearsal took place on September 23 without an audience. Telyakovsky was unhappy. "The play," he wrote, "was quite unfinished..." The Director was reassured somewhat by the premiere. "The performance went with great enthusiasm," he observed, " . . . Savina, Dalmatov and Gorin-Goryainov were especially successful in their roles."[76] But the production received bad reviews. Kugel, particularly irritated that the Alexandrinsky Theater "plods behind the already bankrupt ideas of the Art Theater" mentioned "these drawn-out, clumsy rhythms, these 'overpaused' pauses at every step, this larding of the briefest movements of the soul with constant mime play resembling a grimace—this all hails "from there," from the sickly Moscow Nazareth before which Mr. Telyakovsky stands with gaping mouth."[77]

Lyubov Gurevich darkly stated that:

This was an extremely characteristic production by our state theater... The play, to almost the same extent as Chekhov's *The Sea Gull* in its day, reveals all its failings... Our state troupe as a whole is far removed from any ideological interests, from any higher spiritual requirements and artistic penetration into the tragic contradictions of the human soul. The actors clearly tried to perform Tolstoi's play "nobly"; in any case, many of them understood that a special sort of simplicity was required for its performance. What use was that? Their simplicity was internally impoverished and artistically impotent.[78]

Thus the attempt by Meyerhold and Zagarov, the former Moscow Art Theater actors, to introduce some Art Theater techniques to the Alexandrinsky was equally unsatisfactory to Kugel, who opposed the Art Theater in principle, and to Gurevich, who supported Stanislavsky's ideas.

When Khodotov and Timé took over the roles of Fyodor Protasov and Masha, much changed for the better.

Furthermore, there were two powerful stage images in Meyerhold's direction of *The Living Corpse* that the authors of memoirs do not mention and which have been forgotten by subsequent theater historians. In the first scene of Act Five—the scene of Protasov's confession, "in a dirty saloon," according to Tolstoi's remark—Meyerhold suddenly opened the entire depth of the Alexandrinsky stage. All the previous scenes were staged by the footlights, on the proscenium, out front, but this scene suddenly presented a distant and somber perspective. Empty, identical tavern tables went off into the distance and over each table, repetitiously, hung unlit lamps. Protasov, head down, sat with his interlocutor at the first table. In the depth of the stage behind the arch one could see the next room of the tavern which was suddenly illuminated when, according to Tolstoi's remark, "from behind is heard the cry of a woman," who is led away by a policeman. An atmosphere of concentrated nausea hung over this whole scene in somber accompaniment to the words of the drunkard to whom Fyodor was confessing: "Yes, your life is extraordinary."

"The saloon," Kugel commented ironically, "is permeated with some sort of 'diabolism' and resembles no saloon in the world. This is simply half-baked nonsense with pretensions to some sort of Symbolist 'happening.'"[79]

Conceivably, Meyerhold's "diabolism" was in fact "half-baked." Still, the director's intentions are interesting (perhaps influenced by Van Gogh's *Night Cafe*), in the way they were partially revealed in the finale. Here, Meyerhold's main instrument was the quiet, nearly soundless shot of Protasov's suicide. In the corridor of the law court one heard the faint, indistinct, insignificant sound of the termination of a man's life. The director wished to stress the commonness of death, the ordinariness of the destruction of an individual within the grimy walls of an official institution, to show the indifference and silent operation of the bureaucratic machine that seems to trample a person absentmindedly.

Such unexpected directorial illuminations were the first intimations of Expressionist images of human solitude in the deserts and labyrinths of the modern city. In the desert of the tavern and the labyrinth of the court, personality became lost, and it perished.

These illuminations were, apparently, impulsively suggested by the director's imagination upon sudden contact with the dramatic nerve of the play and remained only episodes in a production which lacked overall form.

Parallel with the rehearsals of *The Living Corpse*, Meyerhold—again with Golovin—was staging Gluck's opera *Orpheus and Eurydice* in the Mariinsky Theater. Eduard Napravnik was the opera conductor, Mikhail Fokin the ballet-master, Leonid Sobinov played Orpheus and Maria Kuznetsova played Eurydice.

The principles discovered in working with *Don Juan* were now confidently and consistently transferred to the operatic stage.

First of all, the principle of stylization was retained. "It would be possible," wrote Meyerhold, "to present *Orpheus* in the costumes in which it was performed in Gluck's time. On the other hand, it is possible to give the audience the full illusion of ancient reality. Both interpretations appeared to be incorrect to the painter and director, since Gluck had been able to combine the real with the relative in one plane quite skillfully." Therefore, the opera "was examined as if through a prism of the age in which the author lived and worked."[80] It was in this key that Golovin attempted to paint the decorations and design the costumes.

The division of the stage into two parts, which had been done in *Don Juan*, was new to opera. This is stressed particularly in an unpublished article with corrections in Meyerhold's hand. Meyerhold wrote that it would be an innovation "to divide the stage into two planes: the forward, surrounded by embroidered, not painted decorations, and the back-stage, where all is under the power of the paintings."[81] Thus, the foreground was decorated with embroidered cloth and the back with painted backgrounds. Two curtains were used: the first "main" curtain was crimson with silver embroidery, while the second was sandy gray with lace arabesques, mother-of-pearl incrustations and crimson borders.

This time Meyerhold paid special attention to platforms. In contrast to the flat floor of the *Don Juan* set, the set for *Orpheus* was raised in portions, permitting the dynamic construction of multi-figured compositions. At first only ballet groups were in question; Meyerhold wanted to move the chorus behind the scenes. "Because

E. F. Napravnik is participating most closely in all the enterprises concerning *Orpheus*," the same unpublished article continues, "Golovin and Meyerhold have managed, with his permission, to move the chorus behind the scenes (the author intends it to sing behind the scenes once out of three times). This permits the elimination of the characteristic disharmony in opera between the movements of disparate parts of the scene—chorus and ballet. If the chorus were to remain on stage, it would be noticeable immediately that one part is singing and the other dancing..."[82]

But another, more interesting decision was reached. The chorus remained on stage, mixed with the corps de ballet and was transferred to the complete jurisdiction of the choreographer Fokin. According to Fokin's own testimony, he staged the Hell scene with particular enthusiasm. Fokin explained:

My idea was this—when the curtain rose, the whole stage would be covered with motionless bodies. Groups in the most unnatural poses, as though frozen in spasms, in awful hellish torment clung to high cliffs and hung down into chasms (trap doors opened in the floor). When the chorus sang . . . this entire mass of bodies made a single slow motion, one fearful collective gesture. As if a monster of incredible dimensions had been aroused and was beginning ominously to rise. One gesture for the entire long phrase of the chorus. Then the whole mass, after pausing for a moment in a new configuration, shrivels just as slowly, then begins to crawl. Everything, the depiction of shadows, the whole ballet group, the entire male and female chorus and the whole theater school—all this was crawling, changing places. Some crawled from trap doors onto cliffs, others were crawling down... Naturally, no one in the audience could understand where the ballet began and the chorus ended."[83]

By placing platforms on the stage floor, Meyerhold strove to achieve maximum dynamism for the ballet crowds. "Thus," he wrote, "in the second scene Orpheus's path into Hell leads downward from a great height, while along the path before it there are two large rocky promontories. With such a placement of planes the figure of Orpheus does not merge with the mass of the Furies, but looms over them."[84] Golovin elaborated: "The scene of the antechamber of Hell synthetically expressed two struggling directions: Orpheus's movement downward and the movement of the Furies, who at first meet Orpheus with menace but then quiet down."[85] In this dynamic scene with the Furies, Fokin wanted "a hellish dance around Orpheus."[86]

Neither Meyerhold nor Fokin nor Golovin made reference to the "source" of their efforts at stylization. Meanwhile, it is possible to say with certainty that they were inspired by Dante's *Divine Comedy*, specifically by Doré's illustrations for *The Divine Comedy*.

At several points Meyerhold purposely stressed the relativity of the production and strove for effects that were clearly circus-like. In the finale, he indicated, "when Orpheus, Eurydice and Cupid step out onto the proscenium the panorama behind them is covered by the embroidered (main) curtain, and the final trio of the scene is sung by the actors as a concert number."[87] While they sing, the decorations are changed behind the curtain and then, upon a signal from Cupid, the curtain is raised again and the apotheosis follows.

Judging by everything, work on *Orpheus* began very harmoniously, but differences appeared as the opening night approached. They arose because in several interviews Fokin attempted to ascribe the staging to himself alone.[88]

Fokin, noted Telyakovsky in his diary, "is proving that the staging is his and that Meyerhold's role is very small."[89] The dress rehearsal was held on December 19, 1911. Telyakovsky wrote:

> The theater was filled. Despite some unsuccessful moments, the staging of *Orpheus* is quite exceptional in its beauty and originality. When the curtain was raised for the last scene, the entire audience began to applaud and call for Golovin. Sobinov accomplished his task very well, even though the part is difficult for him. Kuznetsova sang well, but her dances in heaven are poor, ponderous and completely out of place. In fact, this number spoils the entire impression of *Orpheus*: a dancing Eurydice is utter nonsense. I spoke with Fokin about this, but he assures me that she is a wandering soul and therefore must run around like a goat. It is generally difficult to speak with Fokin these days: he has become so conceited that he fails to recognize that if there is anything new or developing in ballet, it is thanks only to Golovin and Korovin."[90]

The conflict between Fokin and Meyerhold was discussed in the press as well. It was even said that the dress rehearsal of the opera "was wrecked,"[91] even though it had gone quite smoothly.

Following the premiere (December 21, 1911), passions cooled and success reconciled the rivals.* "A tremendous sensation was created by the staging in the Mariinsky Theater of Gluck's opera *Orpheus and Eurydice*," wrote the reviewer of the magazine *Footlights and Life*. "One could sense the total unity between the sacred intent of the decorating artist, director and performers... Golovin, Meyerhold and Fokin deserve an ovation!..."[92]

Even Benois approved this time. "The moment when the darkness of the underworld is succeeded by dawn and you see beneath the bleak, brightening sky the endless, beautifully melancholy forests in which the souls of the righteous reside: this moment is among the most magical that I have seen," he wrote.[93] Kuzmin wrote later, echoing Benois's sentiments: "The funereal, otherworldly, half-sleepy atmosphere covers all events with a haze, the blissful drowsiness of the shadows is extended to gentle sounds, and you feel yourself half alive, half dead, grieving and noble."[94]

In the period between the premieres of *The Living Corpse* and *Orpheus*, Meyerhold commenced a new series of extremely interesting experimental works. The first of these, the pantomime *Harlequin the Marriage Broker*, was performed in the hall of the Nobles' Assembly in Petersburg on November 8, 1911. It was repeated twice with variations, first in the home of the writer Fyodor Sologub, and then in the summer of 1912 on the amateur stage in Teryoki.

The pantomime *Columbine's Scarf*, adapted from Schnitzler in 1910, had been subordinated wholly to a dance rhythm and it modernized Italian masked comedy by placing it in the key of Hoffman-like grotesque, "a terrible dance on the boundaries of the amusing and the frightful." In rehearsing *Harlequin the Marriage Broker*, Meyerhold attempted to reach the popular sources of naive comedy, and to resurrect

---

*However, a decade and a half later in emigration, Fokin insisted again: "I staged the entire opera" (M. Fokin, *Against the Current* [Leningrad-Moscow, 1962], p. 503).

the basic traditions of commedia dell'arte in their pure, unsullied form. This harlequinade, he wrote later, "was staged with traditional methods arrived at after a study of commedia dell'arte scenarios."95

Vladimir Solovyov, a young director immersed in the study of ancient theatrical forms, wrote the libretto for the pantomime based on the old Italian comedies. Solovyov was to remain Meyerhold's closest collaborator. The roles were traditional: Harlequin, Smeraldina, Pantalon, Doctor, and two parts introduced by Solovyov— Silvius and Aurelia (the second pair of lovers).

On the stage of the Nobles' Assembly, Meyerhold, together with the painter K. I. Evseev, placed painted partitions on the left and the right. One represented the house of the Doctor, the other the house of Pantalon. ("Behind these partitions," Meyerhold explained, "standing on tables...Pantalon and the Doctor would appear, nodding to each other in a mime of conversation."96) All stagings of the production were obviously and strictly symmetrical, every movement was in upbeat, measured tempo. This naive delicacy was interrupted by moments of purposely coarse buffoonery, by prearranged or improvised *lazzi*.

Lazzi, or "theater jokes," which were the favorite weapon of actors in masked comedy and were performed with virtuosity, became the subject of the director's intense attention. Meyerhold's mimes treated each other to shoves and blows, they fought, cavorted, then suddenly jumped from the stage into the auditorium. Silvius chopped Pantalon's paper nose off with a wooden sword, whereupon the Doctor immediately attached a new nose. Any improvisation on the part of the actors was supported. The director stated subsequently that he had selected the wordless variety of harlequinade—pantomime—precisely because "more than other forms of scenic incarnation it is capable of bringing theater closer to a rebirth of improvisation."97

There was, evidently, a deeper reason for the director's attraction to pantomime. Meyerhold's basic idea at the time, that of the renaissance of theatricality, caused him to make radical juxtapositions of theatricality and literariness. This concept evidently gave rise to an interest in a theater totally free from the power of literature, a theater without a play or predetermined text. The commedia dell'arte was just such a form.

Curiously, after studying in depth the experience and forms of masked comedy, Meyerhold and Solovyov developed this mute, pantomime variant. It was as if Meyerhold was stating his desire to eliminate the word altogether, if only for temporary experimental purposes, to examine the "nucleus" of theater—pure, wordless action. Literature, operating exclusively with words, was eliminated altogether. It was important to make certain that it was expendable, and to prove that theater as such is possible and exists outside of literature and the spoken word. The experiment was a manifest success and was repeated under different stage conditions.

In Sologub's home the mummers played their parts in contemporary tuxedoes, suits and evening dresses, but they wore masks. This was, as early as 1912, the principle for the costuming used in Vakhtangov's famous *Princess Turandot*.

The third staging of *Harlequin the Marriage Broker*, substantially revised, was performed in Teryoki.

In the summer of 1912, a large group of actors, artists, musicians and writers headed by Meyerhold arrived in Teryoki, near Petersburg. Among them were N. Sapunov, N. Kulbin, Yu. Bondi, L. Yakovleva, V. Pyast, V. Solovyov, L. Blok, V. Verigina, A. Mgebrov, V. Chekan and others. For the summer they organized the "Teryoki Cooperative Theater of Actors, Musicians, Writers and Painters," a semi-amateur undertaking that set to work enthusiastically. "The theater," recollected Alexander Mgebrov, "rented the Teryoki kursaal on most reasonable terms, and we immediately set about transforming the stage itself: Meyerhold tore off the wings, curtains—in a word, everything that could be reminiscent of the theatrical box. Large gray canvases were hung on the stripped platform, and the theater seemed to turn into a ship...."[98]

It was on this stage that *Harlequin the Marriage Broker* was performed again, with Kulbin's new decorations. There was another characteristic addition—a new role was added to the pantomime, that of the Author who read the prologue and participated in the action as a whole, the only character with a right to speech. The word was heard in the midst of mute action and changed its character.

The reviewer from the magazine *New Studio (Novaia studiia)* described the production of *Harlequin the Marriage Broker* in Teryoki. He stated that the production as a whole was executed in the manner of Callot, and continued:

The set simplified to the point of naivete, the colorful costumes, predominantly reddish-brown, yellow and green, the decorations painted by Kulbin, all this, according to the general plan of the theater, was intended to create a suitable frame for the naively bright, somewhat buffoon-like nature of Italian comedy. The back curtain—the background for the action—is a sky with a purposely crudely painted portion of roof, along whose narrow peak the flour-covered Harlequin either creeps along or stops in order to throw handfuls of stars. Lower, at the very edge of the roof, could be seen the bent figure of another harlequin, flying head down, while against a background of blue sky, there was a distinct yellow stupid disk of the Moon on the left, a mask on the right.

Such were the externals of the production. The reviewer continued:

The movements of the actors, their mime, gestures, were precise, airy, minted, as it were... the movements of the Author mannered and extreme, his reading (the prologue) with cries and pauses was typical of the Harlequinades. The connection between the viewer and the action on stage was emphasized—by the Author's address to the public at the start and end, and by the joint scene where the Author and Harlequin run into the auditorium...[99]

Thus, *Harlequin the Marriage Broker* was performed three times before an audience.

The first presentation took on a form closest to the ancient tradition of masked comedy, like a creation of learned restorers, fusty scientists desiring to re-create and revive the theater's distant past.

The second staging was in the style of charade, in a completely unreal form boldly renovated, abruptly removed from tradition and placed by means of costume in direct connection with the present.

Finally, there was the third, most bulky and eclectically complicated presentation. The stamp of the overdecorated, the ornamental and annoyingly estheticized lies heavily over the entire third staging. The pretentious appearance of the spectacle, the reduction of attributes of the commedia dell'arte to the level of heraldry (fan, mask and tambourine are exhibited demonstratively on the partitions, like coats of arms), Kulbin's drawings of black harlequins and the yellow moon, all this seems to leave the framework of the production and becomes an object of contemplation, bizarre and exotic.

In these years harlequinade, evoked from faraway places by a wave of the director's hand, enters into direct contact with contemporary Russia, and the times give it new meaning. The happy bustle of the comedians who hide their faces behind masks is played out in an unsteady and untrue light, careless scenes appear to be hinting at some mysterious and symbolic meaning hidden behind the frolic. The crude street theater obtains a bitter, heady aftertaste. Farce threatens with tragedy, the cranberry juice smells of real blood. It is all preposterous and representative, stupid and significant. Intoxication with the moment, the flying instant of play, is suddenly replaced by fear of fate, which plays with people.

Beginning with *The Puppet Show* (1907), masks dominate Meyerhold's imagination. Their functions may vary, and in fact in Meyerhold's work they do vary. In the *Puppet Show* period the mask is interpreted with romantic irony; it covers the suffering human face with a fixed ironic grimace, it conceals pain and, shieldlike, protects the refined and sensitive soul from contact with dirty, crude reality. Furthermore, the man whose face is concealed behind the mask obtains a certain demonic independence from everyday life, becomes elevated above it and derides it fearlessly, bitterly. Even when perishing, he celebrates his victory over dead, soulless matter.

In the period of staging *Don Juan* and the numerous studio variations by Meyerhold on the themes of Italian commedia dell'arte, the use of masks gains new significance in his art. The masked actor in Meyerhold's small stages of this period is a materialized call to return to ancient forms of theater, to its naivete, its playful nature. The mask becomes the battle insignia of retrospection, stylization; the mask calls back to the magnificent past. Its simplicity and immobility (a single, laconic expression on the "face" for the duration of the piece) decisively countered the pretensions of psychology to show refinement and change in the soul, the soul's vibration. The mask invoked simplicity, spiritual health and happiness. It juxtaposed the art of the intelligentsia with simple folk art.

But the three versions of *Harlequin the Marriage Broker* proved that such an interpretation of the mask cannot endure. The play of masks gained new significance; the mask gradually became a sign of life's guile, falseness, and double meanings. Now, the center of attention became the theme of internal duality, the double face of the masked person. The mask theme became the theme of concealing man's true face. Such an interpretation of the mask led inevitably to a sensation of the infernal and unknowable, frightful and threatening dynamics of man's existence. The image of Lermontov's *Masquerade* was forming already.

In *Masquerade*, on which Meyerhold was already working, the theme matured, was completely thought out. In the third version of *Harlequin the Marriage Broker* the theme is not yet clear, there is only a faint sensation of its possibilities; there is only the bizarre confusion of the chaotic and slightly sinister play, there is danger and a sweetness which is occasionally unpleasantly saccharine.

These characteristics were stressed even further in the small pantomime, *The Lovers*, which was set to music by Debussy and which was staged after *Harlequin the Marriage Broker*. This was a triumph of stormy Hispanic flavor, exotica, "demonic" qualities, gloom and "Carmenic" jealousy.

In Teryoki Meyerhold also staged Calderón de la Barca's *The Adoration of the Cross*, which had been performed previously in Vyacheslav Ivanov's home "Tower Theater." There the decorations had been by Sudeikin; here, the new decorations were painted by Yury Bondi. The aim was, according to Meyerhold, "severity, gloom and simplicity," as opposed to the opulence and color of the Tower Theater production. White was the dominant color. Meyerhold refused to change the decorations, and Bondi constructed a large white tent on the stage against the background of an equally white split curtain. The actors entered and left through the vertical slits. Blue was used in addition to white: blue stars on the tent, a line of blue crosses on the back curtain. When the scene shifted to the monastery, two actors dressed as novices carried on two three-sectioned screens on which were blue contours of people dressed as monks. "It should be evident to the audience," commented Meyerhold, "that here decorations depict nothing; it is the actors alone who are playing. The set is just a page on which the text is recorded. Therefore, everything connected with the set has been transmitted 'relatively.'"[100]

In *The Adoration of the Cross*, A. Mgebrov played Eusebio and V. Chekan played Julia. Mgebrov wrote later about Meyerhold's work on this play that the director "was not excited by the Catholic essence of Calderón's poetry, but by its core, the canvas on which any design could be drawn, which Meyerhold proceeded to do, forcing us to materialize with maximum expressiveness the most complicated and difficult plastic moments." In Mgebrov's opinion he would occasionally "overdo it," directing actor's movements to be "too flattened."[101]

Blok attended nearly all the presentations of the theater in Teryoki. At the time, his attitude toward Meyerhold's work was complex and often very critical. The evolution of Blok's views on theater, which deserves separate, close analysis, was proceeding in a direction counter to the evolution of Meyerhold. The poet was attracted increasingly to the Art Theater, and found even the productions of this theater to be lacking in lifelike qualities. Following the Art Theater production of *The Living Corpse*, Blok noted in his diary: "All are actors, unique and gorgeous, but—actors. Stanislavsky alone is both an actor and a man, a marvelous combination of life and art. But the Gypsies—are these Gypsies? No, Gypsies are not like this!"[102]

Blok's impressions of the Teryoki theater productions are all the more interesting. There is evidence that he liked the pantomime *Harlequin the Marriage Broker* ("He praised it," recalled Verigina. "He told me: 'Very good, Valentina Petrovna, very professional'."[103]) and did not like *The Lovers* at all. The performance of *The Adoration of the Cross* elicited a most curious response from Blok. He was interested in the actors Mgebrov and Chekan. He noted some successful and unsuccessful moments of their performances and concluded: "Thus Calderón 1) in Balmont's translation; 2) performed by modernists; 3) with decorations that are 'more than relative.' *And yet* this 'Catholic mysticism' *was* expressed as ordinary actors could hardly express it."[104]

Here is the answer to Mgebrov's naively amusing assurances that Meyerhold was uninterested in the "Catholic essence" of Calderón's drama. Meyerhold himself wrote that he wished to express "Calderón's spirit."[105] This intent is visible throughout the form of the production, and Blok, clearly astonished, describes its "more than relative form" (and in another passage mentions how "shocking" were the blue monks "drawn on the screen"[106]), but does maintain firmly that "Catholic mysticism" was expressed. In this way he also defines the ideological sense of the production.

Blok was particularly excited by the play *Crime and Crime*, which was also staged in Teryoki. Blok himself had recommended this play of Strindberg's to Meyerhold. In general, "he was fascinated with Strindberg then, and in typical Blokian fashion, to excess. He spoke of him all the time."[107]

In Strindberg's drama, the love triangle includes the turbulent artist Maurice, his passive wife Jeanne and his lover Henriette, an energetic, "fateful" woman. The play was set in Paris. Strindberg confidently set the mark of fatal predestination over the plot. Everything that transpired with the characters was inevitable, nothing depended on their will or could be averted. The title of the play in Russian, *Vinovny—nevinovny (The Guilty—the Innocent)*, sounded like a question (and was occasionlly written as a question: *The Guilty—the Innocent?*) and placed in doubt man's capability to resolve his fate. All deeds are predestined, determined by passions which man does not control.

Judging by the recollections of Verigina, who played Henriette (A. Mgebrov played Maurice, L. Blok played Jeanne), Meyerhold attempted to stress further the situation indicated by Strindberg: in the part of Jeanne "the warmth of a suffering passive nature was eliminated. The heroine was depicted in tragic terms." Henriette was depicted as "truly fateful." Meyerhold wanted her first appearance "to predict the outcome to the audience. She entered in a looping path, without looking at Maurice, who was standing by the counter and looking at her. Meyerhold told me at the rehearsal: 'This way, you draw Maurice into the noose immediately.' In my hands I held large red flowers on long stems..." In Meyerhold's interpretation, Maurice's consternation and feeling of impending doom assumed a "catastrophic character."

V. Verigina refutes N. D. Volkov, Meyerhold's biographer, who asserts that in this production the director "returned to the old principle of immobility to which he subordinated the actors." She observes that "immobility became manifest only in the concluding chord, or there where it was essential and flowed out of internal action... In some scenes, in fact in the most important ones, the dynamics of the action were not at all totally contained in the visual moments of lines and colors, but grew through motion. In the scenes between Henriette and Maurice there is constant motion, Henriette slipping away and approaching and, finally, a turbulent move back from the foreground along a tangent to the depth of the stage, to Maurice."

This time too, special attention was paid to the reading of the lines. "Meyerhold," wrote Verigina, "gave intonation a definite direction. He prohibited flexibility, modulation and diversity... The coloring of the sound was of great significance; each role had its own, and there was an overall metallic coloration and external frigidity created by this image of concealed emotion coupled with energetic sound."

This same aim—the creation of a tense atmosphere of hidden passion—was served by active pauses, "exclamations of silence" that Meyerhold used to punctuate key moments of the drama. One of these pauses—Henriette's first wordless appearance with the flowers—has been described above. Here is another: "Maurice was sitting at a small table, a bottle of champagne before him. Henriette was behind Maurice's back: her suddenly extended hand took a glove from the table and with a slow movement of the fingers stuffed the glove into the glass. The result was an intense dialogue between eyes and hand."[108]

Such pauses also helped the director to transmit the Parisian atmosphere. Meyerhold sought out expressive details: "Paris," wrote Mgebrov, "is in a glove, in the way Henriette or Maurice treat it; Paris is in a scarf casually wrapped around Maurice's neck. With all the complexity of psychological drama, Meyerhold did not miss a single one of these details and worked on them with inspiration."[109]

The play was staged some two months after Strindberg's death and, consequently, Yury Bondi, the artist, enclosed the stage in a wide black frame. At the back of the stage were openwork screens, a kind of transparency, depicting in black silhouette against a yellow or dark blue sky, the trees in the park or the restaurant hall. In the restaurant in the background stood a large sofa and over it was an enormous window illuminated by the light of dawn. In the garden was a single semicircular bench over which hung silhouettes of tangled black branches. In order for the actors' figures to be equally silhouetted against the dominating yellow background, virtually all the stagings were constructed in the background, in the depths of the stage. The reviewer from *New Studio* observed that the director had transferred "the entire center of gravity, the whole noise and disturbing line of action from the forward part of the stage to the better illuminated background. (Illumination is from behind the cloth—the figures are silhouetted. The players move to the foreground of the stage only when the play requires a demonstration of their alienation from and non-participation in the general course of the action.)"[110]

The footlights were extinguished, the wide proscenium dim and, therefore, the actors did move to the foreground only when they were seemingly excluded from the action, while their lines during such times sounded like asides, a sort of commentary on the action.

The dimming of the proscenium served still another purpose: a chasm of darkness separated the actors from the auditorium. "The actors," wrote Verigina, "did not see the audience, were wholly engrossed in each other, but, performing for someone in the distance they were propelled by creative instinct far beyond the proscenium." Consequently, the action became "concentrated"; the audience, wrote the actress, "was drawn in toward us beyond the footlights."[111]

The dominating color—yellow—gradually intensified, seemed to increase. The idea of leitmotifs of colors corresponding to the spirit and meaning of a play became of interest to Meyerhold at this time. The production was conceived as a coloristic whole. At the end of the restaurant scene when the window was opened, the stage was drenched in the yellow light of dawn and, simultaneously, a servant entered with a vase with yellow flowers.

On the day after the performance, Blok wrote:

> The production was festive and, despite individual failures, was real... As I heard this language for the first time on stage I was astonished: simplicity has been brought to

frightening dimensions: the life of a soul translated into the language of mathematical formulas, which formulas in turn are written in symbols reminiscent of the zigzag of a lightning bolt against an extremely dark cloud... The director (Meyerhold) and the decorators (with the director's assistance) evidently either understood or felt this, and therefore all eight scenes are on a stage that is dimly illuminated, while the background is a blue-black curtain through which disorderly lights are shining. Occasionally a red spot appears on it, there is a constant flickering of wine bottles (the Paris cafe), the shiny top hat and narrow suit of the hero who is being propelled into the horrible by the mathematics of Destiny, then the mugs of the detective and the commissioner; the red coat of the coquette and the ruby reflection from the cross on her breast; suddenly, in the cafe in a stage situation that is almost absurd, we see aspects of Sophoclean tragedy. The police commissioner unexpectedly and absurdly begins to resemble a messenger from an ancient tragedy.[112]

Blok's description is redolent with what another poet called "the oil of Parisian painting," indefinite impressionistic illumination, Edouard Manet's pubs, Toulouse-Lautrec's coquettes and "mugs," the flaming red spots of Van Gogh. But the director added to this color the excitement of drama and its tension. Here, as in some episodes of *The Living Corpse*, early Expressionist motifs could be discerned.

Specifically Expressionist here was the interpretation of human passions as forces not controllable by man. Emotion was presented as an uncontrollable instrument of fate. Man appeared divided, with his goals, desires and intentions on the one hand, and his passions as something separate, independent of and above him. This is what Blok had in mind when speaking of "the mathematics of Destiny." Everything "fateful" was contained in Strindberg and was presented in the drama, while the "mathematics" were added by Meyerhold. It was Meyerhold who attempted to find the most precise plastic expression for every movement of the soul. He translated emotion into the language of color and movement, strictly defined its every external manifestation, created a strict, mathematically exact score for the augmentation, uplifting, and extinguishing of emotion. He expressed Strindberg's disharmony through the algebra of painstaking production. The author's fatalism—lingering, and indistinct—became dynamic, rapid, and precise in this production.

Meyerhold also was experimenting in another, more upbeat area; in Teryoki he staged Shaw's comedy *You Never Can Tell*. Almost no record remains of this production, staged July 15, 1912. Meyerhold did not enter it into his list of directed works and evidently did not ascribe any great significance to it. There is only Mgebrov's comment that the long final act of the comedy, which "did not come out right" during the rehearsals, Meyerhold

"suddenly, with one stroke of the pen . . . eliminated, but, in order to save the situation, i.e., to preserve the unique Shavian theatricality, Meyerhold invented an astoundingly naive, but at the same time deeply theatrical effect: this picture of extended English reconciliations, the distinctly English psychological contrivances, he transformed into a gala carnival of colorful fantasy. Shaw himself probably did not suspect that such fantasy could be concealed within. Meyerhold and Bondi decorated the entire set with colored lights, all of us were wearing odd masks, and Meyerhold embroidered a unique and highly entertaining carnival on Shaw's canvas. Overall, he won a significant victory: Shaw was very well received.[113]

This was, indeed, a bold conclusion to the characteristic Shavian intellectual word game, a mute pantomime in the spirit of the commedia dell'arte.

So ended the summer season in Teryoki. Following all these engrossing experiments, Meyerhold was to return again to the Alexandrinsky Theater, where he naturally felt far less free. Earlier, in spring, Fyodor Sologub's *Hostages of Life* had been selected for staging.

Following the break with Komissarzhevskaya, over a period of five years, Meyerhold had not staged any new Russian plays (with the exception of the Yury Belyaev one-act bagatelle *The Red Tavern*). Much had changed in his art over this period; most significantly, the overall tone of Meyerhold's composition was raised to a higher key. The weighty slowness, the static solemnity and the torpid statue-like quality had given way to dynamic, expressive intensity, a light and sharp rhythm. The pulse beat faster, the muscles tensed. Now, in comedies, his actors boldly interacted with the audience, strolled along the proscenium edge, jumped down into the hall, fought and tumbled. In dramas, his actors forgot the gloomy majesty and proud, solemn ceremonial. There, where majestic monastery fortresses and looming towers had stood, he now hung white curtains with arbitrarily marked battlements. Disquieting, seemingly mobile pictures of Parisian restaurants and the nervous rhythms of rapidly alternating sets appeared in place of the elaborate interiors of Hedda Gabler's house and motionless actors. There was the aura of happy ancient theater and of the menacing modern city. The leaping clowns, bustling little blackamoors, dancing courtiers and ladies in perfumed skirts, the ecstatic faith of Calderón's monks, the intense passion-conflict of Strindberg's heroes and heroines—all this was expressed precisely, rapidly and succinctly.

There were no parallels to the heightened key of Meyerhold's direction in the Russian stage literature of his time, except for one play that caught his interest. This play, Fyodor Sologub's *Hostages of Life*, he staged in the Alexandrinsky Theater.

Hostages of Life was interesting in that it began in a realistic manner, but toward the finale, by means of an elegant and subtle process in the plot, the play shifted into the symbolic. The young, beautiful and proud Mikhail Chernetsov and Katya Rogacheva worship each other and dream of changing life for the better by uniting their fates. Mikhail will become a great scientist, a brilliant engineer, and then Katya will help him change the whole world. But the prose of life sets up rough obstacles on the way to this bright ideal. The lovers are poor. Consequently, Sologub's young protagonists decide to submit to good sense for the interim, in the name of love and high dreams. Katya will marry the successful businessman Sukhov, while Mikhail will marry Lenochka, the daughter of a wealthy landowner. But Lenochka has been warned that this is a temporary measure, that as soon as Mikhail becomes wealthy and, consequently, becomes able to rebuild life on a wide scale, Katya will leave her husband at once and will return to her beloved, while Lenochka will be obliged to depart. Lenochka Lunagorskaya, also called Lilith, loves Mikhail truly and, ready to help him in all ways, accepts her role in the plan without objection.

Curiously enough, the plan is carried out. Several years later, when Mikhail has become rich and famous, Katya, who has borne her husband two children, leaves husband and children and goes to Mikhail. Tender Lilith leaves the genius who, having gained a comfortable and solid position in life, will now execute his great mission together with his eternally beloved Katya.

In the beginning of the play, Lenochka, or Lilith, was presented as a quite real, if oddly intense, landowner's daughter, but gradually shifted to an unearthly avatar of Dream. It turned out that Mikhail had lived several years not simply with a rich girl and not simply at her expense, but with Dream, exalted and beautiful. After parting with Mikhail, this Dream will go forth and aid other such proud, lonely and needy strugglers.

The unearthly and allegorical figure of Lilith, shifted from its position in reality, gave a duality to the entire structure of the work.

In a sense, Sologub's play had inspected and rejected the long tradition in Russian literature according to which alienated men who did not know how to apply themselves to real life became entangled with beautiful, pure and inaccessible women. The impracticality of these men corresponded to the inaccessibility of the women. Furthermore, the inaccessibility of the woman gave meaning to the life of the man: while Tatyana loves Onegin he does not need her. As soon as she becomes inaccessible, she is all that he wants. Blok's Beautiful Lady, a symbol of female inaccessibility, was a sort of conclusion to this tradition. In Sologub's far less talented play, every woman is accessible and ready to serve the active, energetic and uniquely willful Mikhail Chernetsov; both earthy, healthy, emotional Katya and the ephemeral, unearthly Lenochka-Lilith.

It is possible that this figure of an energetic youth, firmly and decisively heading for his goal, interested Meyerhold especially. The totally bourgeois, entrepreneurial element in this active character remained unnoticed.

Shortly before the opening, Meyerhold stated that his task was to use "the realistic tones of performance and setting to show the 'symbolism' of the play, whose real basis must in no way be understood in the sense of the everyday." Sologub, continued Meyerhold:

> divided the play into four parts of a symphony of color. When, in the first act, dusk approaches behind the glass doors in an old Russian estate, you will remember the orange light that will begin to play along the walls of the glass gallery of the fading estate. In the second act it appears as if strings have been strung along blue walls, and when Katya weeps upon parting with Mikhail it seems as though this room is an Aeolian harp where strings and not people are weeping. When, in the third act, the lunar dances are supplanted by orange light streaming in from the adjoining room where chandeliers and a fireplace are lit, you will know that life-loving Katya will appear in her red dress and here, bathed in these orange rays, will take place a dialogue between two eternally quarreling premises—Dream and Reality. In the fourth act, Katya is as a white seagull beating against the red prairie schooner in which Sukhov is taking Katya over the potholes of his career.[114]

Consequently, from the very start Meyerhold rejected the stylistic duality of Sologub's drama and refused to take seriously the realism of its first acts. He stated directly that he did not wish to interpret "in the sense of the everyday" the "real basis of the play." The images which Sologub had first grounded, then strove to use in gradually leading the audience to the general symbolic conclusion of the drama, now left the ground at once.

It had never occurred to Sologub to divide the play into "four parts of a symphony of colors." This was Meyerhold's decision, and had been tested in Teryoki while directing Strindberg: color expressing emotion. In discovering in the play a conflict between "two eternally quarrelling premises, Dream and Reality," Meyerhold at once, in the first act, removed Lenochka-Lilith from the everyday, made her ephemeral and mysterious. She, in contrast to the earthly and emotional Katya, was unearthly from the very start. This decision caused Meyerhold to transform Lilith's dance in the third act (when the protagonists decide on the compromise) into a separate, significant ballet number. Something like an engagement between Mikhail and Dream was represented. The sober, thought-out, prosaic act—a marriage of calculation—appeared to transpire in a sort of mystical trance.

Substantial changes were introduced into the course of the play, and these perplexed the rational Telyakovsky. Folowing the rehearsal of November 3, 1912, after giving a glowing review of Golovin's decorations ("simply excellent") and noting with approval the performances of many actors and the direction of the first two acts, Telyakovsky wrote: "The second half of the play pleased me less, both in staging and execution. I discussed this with the author Sologub, Meyerhold and Golovin. In the third act, the real is intermixed with the fantastic, conversations with dances on scattered resin, cigarettes, etc. I am certain that this is the Achilles's heel of the play that will be attacked by the press. It will be difficult for the audience to understand and, especially, to draw a conclusion from the play." At the following rehearsal, the dress rehearsal, Telyakovsky observed:

Some things were abbreviated and changed in accordance with my agreement with the author, and the play only gained by this. Only Tkhorzhevskaya's dances remained relatively long. Many actors attended the rehearsal and, characteristically, none of the oldsters. Savina, Davydov, Varlamov and Strelskaya were absent. These conservatives, like all old people afflicted with sclerosis, permit nothing new, particularly the success of young people, and since the play is basically well performed and promises to be successful, they protest. This is all as old as the world. Michurina and Apollonsky were the only older, honored ones present. Several newspaper critics were discussing and arguing about the play during the intermission. Undoubtedly this production will cause much talk.[115]

On November 6, 1912, the opening took place in an electrified atmosphere. "Yesterday," wrote the reviewer from *The Evening Times (Vechernee vremia)*, "was a day of combat in the Alexandrinsky Theater. Our model classical theater, which once rejected Chekhov's *The Sea Gull*, staged a play by Sologub, such an original, such a unique, but talented and great Russian writer... For the entire time the atmosphere felt heavily electrified. It smelled of a thunderstorm."[116] The press reviews are evidence that both the play and the production were objects of great interest. Reviews in newspapers and magazines discussed from every viewpoint Meyerhold's directing techniques, Golovin's decorations and the performance of the lead roles. (P. I. Leshkov played Mikhail, E. I. Timé played Katya, N. K. Tkhorzhevskaya played Lilith, and B. A. Gorin-Goryainov played Sukhov.) In the *Petersburg Gazette* Omega-Troziner reported that "the play had an undoubted, great success,"[117] while in Suvorin's reactionary *New Times*, Yury Belyaev gushed that "everything was beautiful."[118]

Alexander Benois discussed the production from another point of view. He criticized the director for overemphasizing the mystical content of the play while underplaying the realistic motifs. On stage, he regretted, "there is no Sologub with his feeling for life. Everything superficial in Sologub has been retained. Even worse, the superficial has been exalted to a great degree. The real Sologub appears by contrast to be either completely covered over, or filters through accidentally, but only thanks to 'non-Meyerholdian' elements, some sort of remnants of 'natural theater.'"

In truth, that supposed reality that was called on to conceal and engulf Sologub's allegory in realistic everyday details appeared to dissolve and vanish in Meyerhold's production. This tendency of the director's was especially pronounced in the interpretation of the part of Lilith who, as was mentioned above, was drawn immediately outside the bounds of reality and as early as the first act resembled some spirit slipping among living people. Benois wrote that Tkhorzhevskaya's Lilith "as a whole, took on the appearance of a hysterical modernist, a living-room decadent miss, losing completely the enchantment of her wildness, her odor of fields and forest." However, Benois admitted immediately that "the rendition of Lilith on stage" seemed to him "impossible." From the role as a whole, he continued, "there comes the frigid cold of allegory—allegory and not symbol... So there is a sore spot in the play. It cannot be eliminated or corrected, and it must in fact have poisoned the entire attitude of the artists in the production to their problem."[119]

Sologub's Lilith puzzled others as well. This image also perturbed the venerable Merezhkovsky, who was most unhappy with the generous praise given to Sologub and Meyerhold by Belyaev in Suvorin's *New Times*.

"Well, finally," wrote Merezhkovsky in the newspaper *Speech*, "the 'dear boys' from *New Times* had to admit that an 'event' had transpired... For many years all they did was throw garbage at any attempt to alter 'the existing order of things' in art generally and in theater in particular. And now, suddenly, instead of garbage—laurels. Now, really, isn't this a bit hasty?"

In seeking an answer to the question of why applause for Sologub was emanating from this citadel of reaction, Merezhkovsky incisively analyzed the play *Hostages of Life* and revealed the cynical meaning contained within. He wrote:

The good old worldly morality is far less a friend of Philistinism and a greater enemy of banality than a dream such as this, which requires prostitution and nicely obtained capital for its realization. Worldly morality is closer to the true dream-faith which embodies and breaks life in a revolutionary way, than is the fruitless old-maid morality of isolated romantic hermits.

"When Lilith leaves," Merezhkovsky commented on the finale of the play,

it is useless for the reunited lovers to speak of some kind of new life; this is a lie, the rhetoric and romanticism of this same undefeated banality, undefeated Philistinism. No, there will be nothing better, but everything will be the same as before: the new little pair, the new Adam and Eve, will bear new children, and Adam's eternal first wife Lilith will return to them, even more aged and fruitless, and will trick the children with her dream as she tricked the father and, having done so, will depart once more. And the children, the grandchildren and great-grandchildren will all perish in banality. And there will be no end to this.[120]

Sologub's motivations were somewhat incoherently explained in *Speech* by his wife, the writer Anastasia Chebotarevskaya. In her letter to the editor she wrote that first of all, Merezhkovsky incorrectly understood and "did not wish to understand" Lilith and, secondly, this image cannot be "interpreted" and "explained." Lilith, and the play as a whole, "can only be felt by the heart, the soul."[121]

Nonetheless, nearly everyone "felt" in the play and in Sologub's Lilith the same thing that had been sensed by Merezhkovsky. "Dmitry Sergeevich's article has great force," noted Blok in his diary.[122] The magazine *New Studio* stated flatly that the play asserts "the victory of practical sense," that "the dream directed Mikhail to the practical and correct path of waiting, the path of gradual achievement." The magazine went on to state clearly that Katya returns to Mikhail "only when life has supplied Mikhail with material means," that the dubious victory of the dream "is achieved soberly and conveniently."[123]

The comments on Meyerhold's direction and Golovin's decorations frequently repeated the epithet "sweet." A. Kugel wrote that in the play and production "there is, with all the digression and premeditation, what I would call 'sweetness'..."[124] D. Filosofov stated that the chief defect of the production "is that prettiness which harms beauty," "in excessive sweetness."[125] With suspicious frequency, the reviewers noted that "everything was beautiful."

The article in *New Times* was, in fact, entitled "A Beautiful Evening," and the "dear boy" Yury Belyaev exclaimed, "The decorations by Golovin, this magician of decorative art, were beautiful. Meyerhold's legendary staging was beautiful, the performance by the young actors was beautiful..." Of Meyerhold's direction it was even said that it was "harmonious and delicate."[126]

Dubious comments of this sort probably should have disturbed Meyerhold, but he demonstrated no signs of concern.

The concept of *style moderne* had long been established in Russian architecture and Russian applied arts. Although this term is not commonly used in the context of theater, it appears to me that it permits us to define precisely the nature of that crisis which is felt in Meyerhold's art in the period between *Don Juan* and *The Constant Prince*, i.e., between 1910 and 1915, and which was expecially vivid in his stagings of *Electra* and *Pisanella*.

A characteristic of *style moderne* is ornate and luxurious decoration. In architecture, this tendency was particularly visible: the striving to conceal the functional intent of a building or its separate elements was pervasive. An iron fence would pretend to be intertwining branches, a railway station would be built as a cottage from a Russian fairy-tale (the Yaroslavsky station in Moscow by the architect F. Shekhtel), the public baths were framed in Moorish arcades and covered with luxuriant decorations with a plant motif. Among the lilies and orchids, peacocks and swans so beloved by the modern, one would frequently see energetically thrusting busts and heads of long-haired women. The highly tectonic and visually fluid system of architectural design contained a distinct element of mystification, since, in essence, this was decoration applied to a wall, like wallpaper or decorated cloth.

The *moderne* avoided straight lines and clear geometric contours. Curves, breaks, caprice and flowing design reigned supreme. The frontal approach was rejected; the front door of a building would, as a rule, be placed in a corner especially and elegantly trimmed for the purpose. Windows either were stretched along a wall, becoming flattened ovals, or stretched upward, rounded off oddly and narrowed. The flat surface of the wall became mobile—bay windows, sudden juttings and unexpectedly indented loges or balconies decorated with whimsical metal railings and generous mouldings created the impression of the disturbance of the entire surface, simultaneously exuded power and voluptuous languor, energy and affectation. The passion for ornamentation, for colored majolica inserts, tiles and stained glass testified to the desire of *style moderne* architects to make people's lives brighter, multi-colored, rich in sensations. In every movement of the style one sensed an inclination toward a different, removed, even otherworldly beauty.

It is not enough to say that the *style moderne* rejected life's prose. Unthinkable outside the comfort that had appeared at that time, when the affluent lifestyle already was simplified and decorated with electricity, sewage systems, and a water supply, the *style moderne* undisguisedly was proud of these "conveniences," boasted of them and swaggered in their luxury. Architects of the *style moderne* subordinated their buildings to the range and geometry of streets (the days of estates were over; urban land had appreciated), and inscribed new buildings into the established urban landscape. Nonetheless, they strove to stress at every possible occasion the uniqueness of each structure, even if the building was not a railway station, bank or private dwelling, but an ordinary apartment building with rented units. Sometimes such a multi-storied building would resemble a fairyland castle, its roof thrusting out toward the sky, with powerful sculptured figures and groups in niches, and glimmering stained-glass windows in the stairwells.

An aftertaste of theatricality came to architecture. The *style* was exotic. Enormous seashells of a sort unknown in Russian were as attractive to the *style* as were the archetypal Russian gingerbread or the motifs of old Russian wooden church architecture, which now was being reproduced painstakingly in stone and brick. Analogously, the German *Jugendstil* sought to find its decorative themes in the medieval German epos and in Dürer, and the English architects—in Gothic, and Gauguin—in old Breton crucifixes.

In the applied arts the *style moderne* at once manifested its expansionist energy and rapidly became universal. Not only furniture, but electrical fixtures, typefaces, writing implements, writing pads, ashtrays and crockery succumbed to its capricious forms, becoming decorative, Oriental, and immediately stating their pretentions as independent spirits. In the applied arts, the motifs of lilies and orchids, women's busts and torsos and myriads of ornamental fantasies obtained extremely rapid circulation. Japanese screens and Chinese fans became fashionable, as did objects made of ivory and malachite, colored glass, and iron and bronze castings. Ladies at the end of the nineteenth century wore sleeves with disproportionately large puffs and dresses laced tightly at the waist, and in the early twentieth century they wore enormous feathered hats...

It would be unusual for such an aggressive and all-pervading style so filled with fantasy and effectiveness to miss affecting the stage. The *style moderne* first stepped onto the stage-boards with Symbolist drama; for example, in the productions on

Ofitserskaya Street of *The Marriage of Sobeide* and *Pelleas and Melisande*, the decorations had been conceived in the *style*. But, in the period of his Symbolist presentations, Meyerhold used the *style* for decorations exclusively. In *Hostages of Life* there was already a definite stylistic and ideological unity. The play, which added exaltation of bourgeois common sense, represented life's prose as a poetic dream and stated that cynicism is cousin to high dream and that practical adaptability is a sure means to the realization of inspired plans, was staged with all the appropriate energy and capriciousness of the *style moderne*.

As the reigning style of the day, the *moderne* was reflected also in presentations by the Art Theater. A review of the Art Theater's *In Life's Clutches* stated that Hamsun's drama appeared as a "dazzling zoological tragedy, brightly colored, heady, almost stifling"—in the production there was "much music, a mass of red and white flowers, passion, death from snakebite, more death..." No one, apparently, was able to avoid this tide.

When Meyerhold staged Sologub's play as a "symphony of colors," not only was he implementing in drama Scriabin's idea of light and coloring for music, he also was striving to achieve "beauty," which was essentially independent of the play. The dance numbers that he introduced into the show and which were criticized as "long sessions in the taste of barefoot bumpkins" were, at best, a sort of response to Isadora Duncan's tour, which had been received with great enthusiasm by the Russian public shortly before. The ornate, the heady, and the exquisite became goals in themselves and approached the operatic. Regarding the finale of *Hostages of Life*, P. Yartsev wrote:

> The play ends in apotheosis. The light goes out in the front part of the stage and goes on in the rear, behind the curtain. And when Lilith, after crossing the stage slowly in a straight line along the footlights, steps up to the curtain and lifts up its right edge, there where a building wall had been standing is a landscape.
>
> A circle of silver light is aimed at Lilith's face and continues while she utters her last words. At the same time, we see how Katya and Mikhail—who had been embracing in the darkness at the other end of the curtain—hurry to slip away behind the curtain and off the stage.
>
> This comes from really bad theater, from operatic theater.[127]

This elevated operatic apotheosis, however, was a quite logical conclusion to Meyerhold's production. The presentation did possess a definite unity. This play, which pictured prostitution as the sole path to the purity of high thoughts, and the "reasonable egoism" and adaptability of certain individuals as the most direct means for realizing wonderful dreams, was set in the sugary prettiness of Russian *moderne* so suitable to this entire compound of ideas.

It would be naive to think that the lavish forms of the Russian *moderne* penetrated Meyerhold's art from outside. He himself created these forms, intuitively grasping and expressing the new rhythms of reality itself in his stage compositions. His *moderne* expressed the Russian situation of the 1910s, a time of exceptional bourgeois undertakings, energy, force and dynamism. Russian industrialists and merchants were rapidly becoming Europeanized. The figure of the businessman achieved an ever more prominent position in society. The practicality and resourcefulness of the businessman were examined in literature and art as Russia's main hope. We have seen this already in the premiere of *Hostages of Life*. Even in Gorky's works of that time the businessman, merchant, industrialist, transformer of Russia, is frequently viewed with great sympathy. His grasp, sense of scale, his European and American qualities, are seen as an antithesis to Asiaticism and the age-old Russian backwardness. Accordingly, the esthetic requirements of the new master have an effect on Russian culture, too. The powerful, the monumental, the durable, the effective and the imported become attractive. "Make it beautifully for us..." But the fact that much in Russia opposed the bourgeois spirit, and that this energetic activity had no long-term historical prospects, gave to Russian *style moderne* its characteristic sugariness, excessive luxury and kitsch.

It was during this period that Meyerhold's art manifested with special distinctness his love for shocking effects and grandiose spectacles. Meyerhold's critics had reason to call him the *Effektmacher*. He was, in fact, a virtuoso of theatrical effect, which in its own way was unsurpassed in the field of "gala presentations" and "grand spectaculars." Fortunately, this trait of his usually was fully subordinated to other, immeasurably more important and serious esthetic goals. But in the 1910s Meyerhold's stagings do reflect the showy and ornate, the exotic and opulent, of the *style moderne*.

Following *Hostages of Life*, Meyerhold staged Richard Strauss's opera *Electra* on the Mariinsky stage and d'Annunzio's *Pisanella* in Ida Rubinstein's private Paris theater. In these works Meyerhold demonstrated more than the feasibility of developing some of his favorite staging approaches in new situations; at the same time, both productions demonstrated that Meyerhold's crisis was intensifying, that *style moderne* ideas and forms were continuing their development within his art.

Even Telyakovsky noticed this. Following the first dress rehearsal of *Electra* (Richard Strauss's opera with the libretto by von Hofmannsthal) on February 14, 1913, the Director of the Theaters wrote: "Golovin's decorations are superbly executed and very interesting, and are modeled on the latest archeological discoveries in Crete. Meyerhold's staging is interesting, but in places the *style moderne* is mixed in, regarding which I spoke to him after the finish—some gestures of the actors are particularly comical." A day later, after the second dress rehearsal, Telyakovsky added: "The hand movements, especially those of Electra, are frightfully annoying and sometimes—even worse—are comical."[128]

These gestures that so irritated Telyakovsky had been borrowed by Meyerhold from the frescoes uncovered by Arthur Evans in the course of his excavations on Crete between 1903 and 1909. The Russian archeologist B. L. Bogaevsky, who participated in the Cretan digs, acquainted Meyerhold and Golovin with sketches of the monuments from the distant age when the myth of Electra was composed. Golovin had made the greatest use possible of these materials; his decorations were intentionally archaic.

Golovin subsequently wrote:

The main level was raised slightly. Gray stone steps connected it to the footlights. there was no prompter's box. Two pole-axes on blood-red stands stood on the steps, while two black and gold lamps were above. A light blue curtain covered the entire stage. A festive palace facade was erected on the platform and decorated with typical motifs from the Aegean culture. To the left of the audience was a two-story structure with a flat terrace, and further on a red staircase that led from the main level to the interior of the palace, and the throne room was visible, too. An altar decorated with branches was located on the platform of the inner court. The background cloth depicted a dark sky with patches of yellow shining through.

"The decorations," summarized Golovin, "transported the viewer's imagination to historically authentic antiquity."[129]

This was, of course, the aim. But the expressively intense music by Richard Strauss did not correspond so much to the spirit of antiquity as to the spirit of von Hofmannsthal, who had translated the Sophoclean plot into a contemporary key, strongly stressing the theme of the blind power of fate and the invincibility of emotion. The staging of the opera, therefore, was an extremely odd combination of grandeur—in the decorations and poses—and nervousness in the musical and vocal parts. The intonations and the musical score appeared to be in conflict with the exterior of the production.

"Electra," admitted Meyerhold twenty years later, "was a mistake by Golovin and me. We were too involved in the graphics and neglected the music. We became subordinated to archaeology, which became an end in itself."[130] Ivan Sollertinsky gave a correct explanation for Meyerhold's sudden enthusiasm for archaeology: "The little-known pages of history, unaffected by standardized 'costume' dramas, could provide new, unusual color patterns, *exotic sensations,* etc... All these double pole-axes, the blue crinoline frocks with red braid worn by the servant women of the Atreans, the red-skinned slaves holding fire-pots, whose movements later become a menacing torch dance, all these seemed fantastic and strange..."[131]

The audience did not understand *Electra*, and the opera was shown only a few times. However, the fate of the production was decided by yet another circumstance. In 1913 the three hundredth anniversary of the Romanov dynasty was being celebrated festively, and the appearance on the Mariinsky stage of a production in which rulers were murdered caused a scandal. Subsequently, Meyerhold wrote in his reminiscences on his days in the Imperial Theaters:

"In the ten years of my presence on these stages not once (and I am proud of this) was I assigned to direct any festive productions for the Imperial house. On the contrary, we (Golovin and I) were once the target for violent attacks from the yellow press because during the days of celebration marking the three hundred year anniversary of the House of Romanov we dared to put on the Mariinsky stage R. Strauss's opera *Electra*, in which royalty is beheaded."[132]

The exotic element noticed by Sollertinsky in Meyerhold's *Electra* was one of the truest and most indispensable signs of Russian *style moderne*. Exotic plants alien to Russian nature, and various hammered iron vines fenced in the houses of the Ryabushinskys and the Morozovs on Spridonovka and Vozdvizhenka Streets. Exotic foreign flowers were reproduced in landscapes and mosaics. Enormous shells from distant southern seas were imitated by sculptors and decorated the facades of rich houses, tortoise shells served as shades on lamps in professors' living rooms. Distant, otherworldly beauty was mobilized to gracefully decorate the daily life of all-powerful industrialists and all-knowing intellectuals.

Caricature of Meyerhold by N. V. Remizov, 1910. It reads: "Vsevolod Meyerhold, actor, director, reformer, stylizer, and otherwise modernist. This drawing depicts the remains of this talented man who has been eaten down to the bones by the yellow press."

Drawing by A. Rosti-
slavov for a scene from
the production of
Hardt's *Tantris the
Fool*

Yu. Yurev as Prince Mark in *Tantris
the Fool.* Drawing by A. Rostislavov

K. Varlamov as Sganarelle in *Don Juan*

Yu. Yurev in title role, *Don Juan*

Golovin's drawing of the set for Moliere's *Don Juan*, 1910

Cover of "Doctor Dapertutto's" journal
Love of Three Oranges

Left: Yu. Bondi's sketch for a costume for the Studio on Borodinskaya. *Right:* A. Golovin's costume sketch for the Studio on Borodinskaya.

E. Roshchina as Katerina in Ostrovsky's *The Storm*, 1915

A. Golovin's costume design for Katerina, 1915

A. Golovin's set design for *The Storm*

Above: A. Golovin's set design for *The Storm*, 1915
Below: A. Golovin's set design for Pushkin's *The Stone Guest*, 1914

Lermontov's *Masquerade*. E. Volf-Izrael as Nina, E. Studentsov as Zvezdich.
A. Golovin's set for *Masquerade*.

Golovin's costume drawings for *Masquerade*.
Top left: Koviello. *Top right:* The Unknown
Man. *Bottom left:* Nina. *Bottom right:* Blue
Pierrot.

N. Kovalenskaya as Nina in *Masquerade*

Main curtain for *Masquerade*. Drawing by A. Golovin.

Curtain for Scene IX of *Masquerade*. Drawing by A. Golovin.

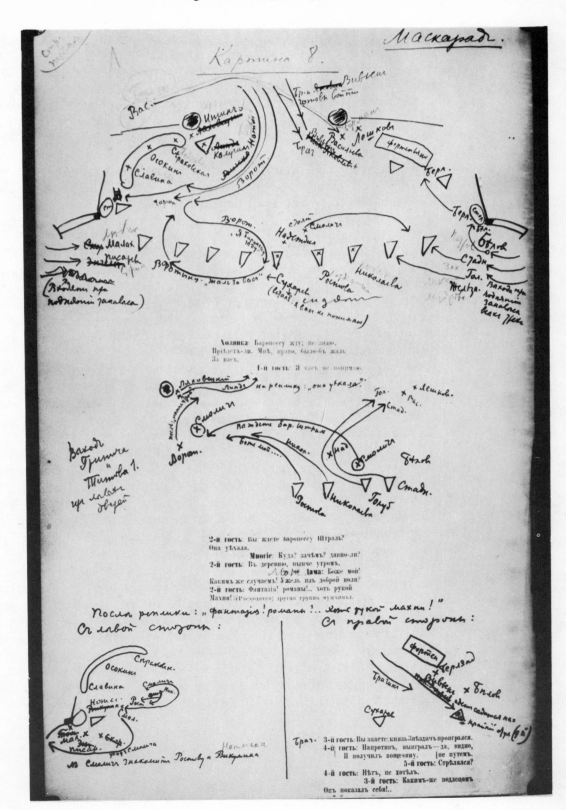

Naturally, the pre-Hellenic Aegean exotica gained preeminence in Meyerhold's and Golovin's *Electra*. Meyerhold's next production rapidly transformed this enthiasm for the exotic to a level of devil-may-care "luxury of colors."

In the same year (1913), Meyerhold staged in Paris, in Ida Rubeinstein's private theater, d'Annunzio's *Pisanella*.

Ida Rubinstein was a wealthy and captious woman, an amateur and dilettante whose tangential course touched many great masters of Russian art. Already at the turn of the century, according to Stanislavsky, she "found the Art Theater antiquated," studied "everything in France and in Germany and in Italy," spent some time in the Imperial Theater troupe, tinkered with a new "Theater on the Neva," "met Duncan, who chased her away,"[133] posed for Serov's famous portrait, tried out for drama and ballet. Since 1908, she had been based in Paris. Fokin worked with her, believing that "something unusual in the Beardsley style could be done with her. Slender, tall, beautiful," wrote Fokin, "she was interesting material from which I hoped to sculpt a special stage image."[134] This image was being created for Wilde's *Salomé*; Fokin and Ida Rubinstein were preparing the subsequently famous Dance of the Seven Veils. Rubinstein first performed this dance in the Olympia Theater. "Her famous name," Stanislavsky wrote from Paris, "stands next to a cast of dogs... I have never seen anyone more naked, and vapidly naked. How shameful! The music and Fokin's staging of the Dance of the Seven Veils are very good. But she is without talent, and naked."[135]

"In the course of the number," Elizaveta Timé epically informs us, "Ida Rubinstein threw off from herself the seven veils one by one and remained in a costume of beads only, which had been ordered especially for this event. In a single day Ida Rubinstein became famous."[136]

Several years later, the bold dilettante had her own theater in Paris and performed in a play written especially for her by the famous d'Annunzio, her dances were choreographed by Fokin again, Bakst painted the decorations and Meyerhold directed. This constellation of talent was not so much the consequence of Ida Rubinstein's dubious gifts, as of her undoubted wealth.

This lavish play about the great Pisan courtesan, written by Gabriel d'Annunzio, offered the "slender, tall and beautiful" Ida Rubinstein many opportunities to demonstrate her charms to the Parisian audience. In the first act, Pisanella was "nearly naked," and she, the slave, was being sold in the Famagusta harbor. In the second act, the spice was that the courtesan turned out to be a saintly pilgrim. She was executed in the third act. But how! A "fragrant death" had been prepared for Pisanella: she was to be smothered in bouquets of roses that had been especially cut for this purpose by "black Nubian women with golden sickles." From the above, it is clear just what sort of spectacle Meyerhold, Fokin and Bakst had determined to present. Judging by the reviews of the show, which was performed on June 11, 1913, there was little true art in this effort of Meyerhold's. "All Paris" was present at the performance. The staging was challengingly lavish, excessively splendid. When two curtains were raised—one, black and gold, the other, purple (there was a total of five curtains in the staging)—the audience saw a black forest of black and gold columns behind which gleamed blue, seemingly enameled walls. The reviewer, feasting on the luxury and beauty, described the unbelievable forms and colors of the archways, portals and arcades, walls, doors, sails, cloaks, even the pillows (lavender with silver) and further "magnificences, excessively spicy, stupefyingly ornate and lavish."[137]

In this stupefyingly lavish production, Meyerhold had at his disposal two hundred extras with whom to compose effective plastic scenes, either by moving the actors forward to the proscenium, or by moving them back into the depths or even into the wings. Beautiful poses were constructed: one figure flattened along the horizontal, another presenting a strict vertical (the messenger and the chaplain at the end of the prologue), etc. The production was pretentious, a daub, even arrogant. It radiated wealth, satiation and was, probably, the quintessence of all the theatrical capabilities of the *style moderne*.

Anatoly Lunacharsky wrote a sarcastic review of *Pisanella* in one of his *Letters from Paris*. The play, he wrote, "is staged in mad luxury. It plays through five stylish curtains in a frame of gilded gothic columns. It might be expected that Bakst's combinations of rhombuses, circles, spirals and so forth, his barbaric diversity of colors, would be a bit annoying, but in the decorations and in the ocean of richest costumes for *Pisanella* our artist created such a kaleidoscope that the audience was dazzled and subjugated." However bedazzled, the audience still discerned, continued Lunacharsky, "the utterly indecent adaptation" of the play and production "to the mistress of the production and the performer of the lead role—Mrs. Ida Rubinstein. This actress, as is known, limps in the area of diction, so the role is rendered almost entirely in mysterious, mute poses. She is a dancer, and so this absurd dance finale has been devised."

This finale, "worthy of *Vampuka*,"* Lunacharsky described as follows: the director suddenly releases from backstage "a swarm of Negroes armed with colossal bouquets of crimson roses. Ida Rubinstein begins to dash about the stage, while the merciless Negroes, dancing, chase her and stick bouquets in her face. In consequence of this operation, Pisanella, not neglecting to make some complex *pas*, breathes her last."

Meyerhold, concluded Lunacharsky, "makes a lot of noise on stage and follows one trick up with another... I left *Pisanella* not just fatigued by the mad dance of colors, but with an unpleasant sensation caused by the unusually expensive spectacle, head-turning, but unnourishing to the mind and poisoning the heart with a feeling of esthetic protest, a spectacle which is somehow akin to various Luna-Parks."[138]

The most vicious was *Russian Word (Russkoe slovo)*. Noting that the production was lavishly set, the reviewer called the performer of the lead part an "ink blot," black amidst this luxury. "Ida Rubinstein," he wrote, "is mincing, simpering and without talent... She has paid generously for her right to participate in this apotheosis, to poison our esthetic pleasure."[139]

A. R. Kugel, commenting on these reviews in his article "The Golden Fly," reasonably asserted that *Pisanella* was a triumph of "female snobbery," that Ida Rubinstein's theater was stuffed with the "shamelessness of luxury, accessible only to 'golden flies.'"[140]

Vampuka: a term for ridiculous operatic stereoptypes, which came into use after the staging of V. G. Ehrenberg's parody opera *Vampuka, the African Bride: A Model Opera in All Respects* (Petersburg, 1909)–(G.P.).

The crisis in Meyerhold's art, clearly visible in *Hostages of Life, Electra*, and *Pisanella*, goes a long way toward explaining the deterioration in the relations between Blok and Meyerhold. Blok's polemic against the artistic path selected by Meyerhold began back in 1907 with his unpublished article on *Pelleas and Melisande*, which the poet had shown to Meyerhold, and continued with ever-increasing vehemence over a period of years. The evolution of Blok's views on theater and other matters was closely connected with the polemic against Meyerhold. Blok did not accept Meyerhold's *Don Juan*, but was delighted with Strindberg's *Crime and Crime*. He was pleased with the pantomime *Harlequin the Marriage Broker* and Calderón's *The Adoration of the Cross*, but the production of *Electra* elicited an angry and irritable response: "*Electra* is, first of all, talentless hubbub."[141] In 1913-14, Blok's comments on Meyerhold are almost uniformly abrupt and intolerant.

The sensitive Blok undoubtedly sensed the changes that had taken place in Meyerhold's art, changes that bespoke the crisis in his art. The poet could only become annoyed at the daubings and banality of the Russian *moderne* that had penetrated Meyerhold's art, especially evident in his productions of *Hostages of Life* and *Electra*. Blok also heard about *Pisanella*, of course.

In December of 1912, Blok and Meyerhold had a major conversation that was fundamentally important for both of them.* Judging by Blok's diary, Meyerhold told him, among other things, that "I like the everyday, but I shall approach it differently than Stanislavsky, I am closer to Stanislavsky than I was in the period of Komissarzhevskaya's theater..." Meyerhold then "developed a long theory that his world view, which contained much from Hoffmann, from *The Puppet Show*, and from Maeterlinck, was being confused with his technical methods as director (puppet theater), arguing that he was closer to Pushkin, i.e., to the humane, than I and many others think. This confusion is caused by the fact that in the period of Komissarzhevskaya's theater he staged many plays in which puppet-like qualities were stressed. Theater, says Meyerhold, is a play of masks; 'a play of faces,' as I said, or 'experience,' as he called the same thing, is essentially the same thing; this is only an argument about semantics."

Thus, Meyerhold said that the puppet-like quality of Komissarzhevskaya's theater was merely a directorial approach, that he was closer to Stanislavsky and Pushkin and the humane than Blok thought. Further, he demonstrated an inclination to equate the concept of "masked play," "play of faces," and "experience," indicating that this was only an argument about words. Meyerhold also stressed that he was "a student of Stanislavsky" and added that the Alexandrinsky Theater must "return to the spirit of the 30s, of Mochalov."

"This I understand," continued Blok, "he is correct about a lot of things. *But*, I think, opinions stand behind words, behind opinions is a cast of mind, an inclination of the heart, and the heart is human. Thus, *for me there remains* unresolvable the question concerning two truths—that of Stanislavsky and that of Meyerhold."[142]

---

*Quite probably this was the day Meyerhold presented Blok with his recent (December) book, *On Theater*. On p. 149, Blok, with understandable irritation, underlined the phrase "Words in theater are merely designs on the canvas of movements" and wrote in the margins: "O my God!" (A. Blok, *Collected Works*, vol. 8, p. 613).

Blok connected the answer to this question directly to the fate of his own theater. He expressed his understanding of life and times in plays that Meyerhold did and Stanislavsky did not wish to stage. In particular, *Song of Fate* was in question. Meyerhold was prepared to stage this piece. "He feels that based on the impression that remains with him, something of his own can grow within him," Blok recorded, "only I must provide him with a great deal of freedom."

Stanislavsky, on the other hand, "sent a long letter about how the play cannot and should not be staged" and Blok "believed this."[143]

However, his next play, *The Rose and the Cross*, Blok gave to Stanislavsky in April 1913, and wrote to his wife: "I am able to trust only him personally (in theater), the rest simply infuriate me—including your Meyerhold."[144] Several days later, it turned out that Stanislavsky again "understood nothing" in Blok's play, "did not respond to it at all, felt nothing,"[145] and in general "told me many frightfully silly things."[146] Nonetheless, Blok's reaction to Meyerhold was even more irritable.

"Again, everything concerning *Meyerholdia* is painful to me," he noted, "I irrepressibly prefer 'healthy realism,' Stanislavsky... Everything that I receive from theater I receive from there, while in Meyerholdia I tire and wilt. Why do they like me? For the past and the present, but, I fear, not for the future, not for what I want."[147]

This note is significant in many respects. It bespeaks Blok's rapid spiritual and creative evolution, his own direction, drawing the poet ever further from Meyerhold. Blok observes precisely and clearly that Meyerhold likes him for "the past and present," that Meyerhold values the author of *The Puppet Show, The Unknown Lady, Song of Fate*, and *The Rose and the Cross*. At the time, however, Blok was seeing his theatrical future in a totally different light.

The juxtaposition of "humanness" *(chelovechnost')* and theatricality gradually becomes personified for Blok in the persons of Stanislavsky and Meyerhold and the poet feels an attraction both toward humanness and to Stanislavsky. Although Blok is irritated by the stagings of the modern Moscow Art Theater and his "impression of the Molière production is the worst possible . . . the Art Theater company has vanished without a trace, the supporting roles are worse than in the Alexandrinka, the young people are Yurevs"[148]—despite this, Blok enthusiastically watches two consecutive performances of *The Good Hope* in Moscow in the Art Theater's First Studio. His reaction:"True delight at the actor's performance. Reminiscent of old times at the Art Theater. Ensemble... Mass scenes, sounds of the ocean and of ships' bells, the decorations are beautifully simple. The audience weeps. All act with muscles drooping, and in a circle, rarely leaving the image."[149] It is this kind of theater that excites Blok. As he plans his new play *The Absurd Person*, he dreams of the "old times at the Art Theater."

The history of this unrealized Blokian idea is another tale. For us it is important only that the planned play was most unusual and, as it turned out, impossible for Blok—a completely realistic drama with a variation on the motif of Chekhov's *The Cherry Orchard*. Blok wanted to become someone else and was unable to do so. In these new directions there was no place for "Meyerholdia"; he saw it as a dead weight of the past which had to be overcome.

The drama in the relationship between Blok and Meyerhold lay in the fact that Blok fought unsuccessfully against the Meyerhold in himself, so to speak, with his own poetic "Meyerholdia." In moving away from Meyerhold he wanted to enter new spheres. In poetry Blok was partially successful; although unfinished, his epic poem, *Vengeance*, on which he was working in those years, testifies to the appearance of a new poetic manner, a new stylistic order. But he utterly failed to do this in the theater.

Furthermore, his love for Stanislavsky turned out to be unrequited. Just as Blok proved unable to express his urge toward humanness in the forms of Art Theater psychological realism or of "spiritual realism" of the First Studio, so Stanislavsky was unable to express his understanding of the "life of the human spirit" in the generalized poetic forms of Blok's dramas. The lengthy period of Blok's attraction to Stanislavsky ultimately yielded up no actual results on the stage. Only Meyerhold's theater then and later realized Blok's theater on the stage.

Consequently, "the matter of the two truths—those of Stanislavsky and Meyerhold," remained an open one, and not only for Blok. An answer can be found only in the art of Meyerhold or of Stanislavsky and could be given only in the form of a production that would fully express the spirit of the time.

Neither Meyerhold nor Stanislavsky staged such a production at that time. The argument between the "two truths" (or two esthetic systems) became prolonged. Both directors moved their research back into the studio. In the fall of 1912, Stanislavsky and L. A. Sulerzhitsky began classes in the "System" in the Art Theater's First Studio. A year later, in the fall of 1913, Meyerhold's Studio on Borodinskaya Street opened.

The juxtaposition of these two studios in Moscow and in Petersburg was a most interesting episode in the history of the twentieth-century Russian stage. The program that Meyerhold intended to implement was worked out in fair detail in his book *On Theater*, published in December of 1912. This was the first book by a director in the history of Russian culture and it contained nearly all of Meyerhold's previously published articles together with a new work,"The Puppet Show." The reader of this volume could easily come to the conclusion that the theoretical foundations of all Meyerhold's reasoning were weak, indistinct and eclectic, and that the rapid evolution of his views occasionally was directed by totally unexpected impulses.

Nonetheless, the general idea of the book, the concept of a struggle against naturalistic theater in favor of relativistic and playful theater, was expressed with sufficient clarity and force.

Among the drafts written by Meyerhold in 1910-11, there is a draft of an article dedicated to Stanislavsky. Evidently Meyerhold wished to dedicate a chapter of *On Theater* to an analysis of Stanislavsky's direction, or perhaps he intended merely to present his views on the subject.

In either case, this work was not completed, but in the outline one senses Meyerhold's great confidence and firmness in criticizing the Art Theater. The outline follows:

Stanislavsky. His path is from characters through characters to characters. Hence his attraction to *The Inspector General*, but his interpretation of it shows most clearly his duality: Naturalist and Modernist. He needs to find a third within himself. This path of his must be without the fellow-travelers Egorov and Simov. These two keep him on the dualistic track. The third element in Stanislavsky must be not the way of rhythmic musical theater, but that of the realist. The theater of characters transformed into the theater of masks, comic and tragicomic. Transitional theater.

About the fellow-travelers. The director and his co-director-artists. How important it is for a director to be an artist. Otherwise, the following heresy—the artist has paints, the director has form. And if the director is not an artist, then at least the director must make it seem that there is only one person.

In *The Inspector General*, its Art Theater version, how was the dualism manifested?

The Drama of Life—painting with sculptural placement of figures.

The Life of Man—graphics.

The Blue Bird—a *carte postale*, absence of plot unity in the acts.

These examples demonstrate that Stanislavsky is relying on the wrong people.

Woe from Wit—verse had to be spoken as prose in order to make the production appear realistic. Stanislavsky as Famusov was the most consistent: either or; he was natural and the verse was unnatural for him. To stress the rhyme, to pronounce the monologues and asides well would be to kill the idea, since the very first thing that strikes one upon reading *Woe from Wit* is its form, i.e., its relativistic nature. Those who in life do not speak in verse begin on stage (not in life) to speak in verse. The first relativistic element allowed by the author obliges those who stage him to follow the relativistic path and no other. One hears people say, how can the relativistic method be used to "stylize" *Tsar Fyodor*? Plays should be staged "realistically" or not at all. Let such a person be consistent and tell Tolstoi to write prose or not at all, since Tsar Fyodor never spoke in verse. But people do not say this to Tolstoi. Since it is permitted for a playwright to step away from the truth, he who interprets it must likewise step away. What is stylized in the text must be stylized in the rendition. It is true that Stelletsky's stylization is more talented than Tolstoi's, but do we not often see on the stage how an actor's interpretation is higher than the images provided by the playwright? Why are the works of talentless playwrights not assigned to third-rate actors? The heights of the actors' and artists' talents must not be limited to the level of inferior works.

It is quite correct that Craig be invited. To each his own. If Stanislavsky gives over the fantastic and mystical element to Craig and leaves for himself the realistic theater, this would be to Stanislavsky's benefit. He can be *masterful* in realistic theater and will not allow himself to be ordered about as it seems to me he was by Egorov in *The Blue Bird*. There, with a well-chosen co-director, he can be most productive creatively. His erudition. His growth in the sense of characters. List the stages.

Stop at the present moment in theater when the merging of director and artist is necessary or God knows what will happen.

Further on, there was a curious discussion of Chalyapin.

Drama theater actors complain that they are being constricted by the forms suggested by the director and artist in the form of a design in harmony with the overall plot, a design to which the movements of his body must be subordinated. The actor is freed. But in the name of what? Chalyapin is not constrained by a design, but is compelled by the requirements of the composer to follow the score strictly. Is this not constraint? But this does not hinder Chalyapin from using his genius to create images. He sets up for himself a new obstacle, the same one that dramatic actors fear: he always has a design. And it is unfortunate that dramatic actors are not subordinated to the author by the precision of rhythm handed to them in the form of a musical score.

In these remarks on Stanislavsky and Chalyapin we see clearly expressed the thoughts to which Meyerhold remained true his entire life: his conviction that the basis of stage art must be a most precise, previously devised and well-learned score for the rhythm, tempo, and staging of the production and roles, the idea that the relativity of the stage should be revealed, not concealed, by a director working closely with an artist. (Ideally, the director should also be the production's artist.) It is interesting, however, that while criticizing appropriately and convincingly the compromises between the lifelike and the theatrical in Art Theater productions such as *Woe from Wit*, Meyerhold expresses certainty that Stanislavsky must follow his realistic path, that in realistic theater Stanislavsky can be the master. In defending his principles he sees distant prospects opening up in the area of characterization.

In 1912, Meyerhold heard of the struggle between "two currents" in the Moscow Art Theater. The essence of the conflict remained unclear for him, but nonetheless together with Golovin he sent Stanislavsky a congratulatory letter. "Here in Petersburg," wrote Meyerhold and Golovin, "there is a rumor that you alone are carrying the full brunt of the awful crisis of the conflict between two currents in the Moscow Art Theater: the old one whose adherents are grouped on the side of naturalistic theater, and the new, which you represent together with the youth, seeking new routes for stage art. With all our souls we wish you victory in your battle!"[151]

Stanislavsky's moderate reply was that he was "sincerely touched" by Meyerhold and Golovin's letter. His reply contained polite objections. "I," he wrote, "cannot complain of my opponents. On the contrary, I respect them. Most of all, 'theater' itself makes me suffer. My God, what a crude institution and art it is! I have lost all faith in everything that serves the eye and ear on stage. I trust only feelings, emotions and, most of all, nature. It is wiser and more refined than all of us, but...!!?"[152]

Stanislavsky's remark on what he had lost faith in was at the same time an objection to Meyerhold: for Meyerhold on the stage there existed only that which "serves the eye and ear." While readily touching upon infernal and mysterious themes which Stanislavsky again began to avoid after working with Craig on *Hamlet*, Meyerhold rejected the idea of any mystery in the creative sphere, preferring the clear, crude and visible. The sphere which Stanislavsky marked with the exclamation points and question marks was of no interest to Meyerhold. Meanwhile, it was this sphere—the sphere of mysterious and creative nature—that was of absorbing interest for Stanislavsky. He spent many years immersed in the study of as-yet-unknown laws of the psychology of creation.

Attempts to fathom the most sacred secrets of creativity and to master them were the objects of stubborn private work by Stanislavsky on his "system" and the experiments he undertook in the First Studio. Consciously avoiding all "that serves the eye and ear on stage," Stanislavsky in the First Studio strove to reach one aim —the maximum and, if possible, the absolute truth of emotion and feeling. Form (any form—of staging, of the plastic, of intonation) did not interest him at all at that time. It was supposed that form would naturally follow truth of feeling. Therefore, the First Studio rejected in principle the idea of a large auditorium and brought to a minimum the distance between actor and viewer. The viewer was to be brought close enough to the actor so as to catch, hear, and feel everything that transpired within the soul of the actor-creator. Such tasks immediately left their imprint on the content of the art of the First Studio.

In concentrating wholly on the soul of man, Stanislavsky's art, wrote T. I. Bachelis,

> for a time seemed to enter the stream of the Tolstoian ethic, was given over to the idea of human self-perfection. In the First Studio created by Stanislavsky and Sulerzhitsky the theater dissolved in the room, merged with life, removed its stage-boards and did not invite an audience of thousands. The great questions of human *spirit* were placed at a remove by agitation of *soul*: the destiny of the age, country, mankind—the fate of the unfortunate "little man." The humanism of tragic conflicts became replaced by the preaching of pity. The object of art shifted to the subjective sincerity of the actor-person, the truth of his personal experiences and his self-expression.[153]

Refined naturalism and attempts to mobilize the actors' subconscious in the First Studio were diametrically opposed to the refined cult of acting, the physical, bodily virtuosity practiced in Meyerhold's Studio. In each case we have one-sidedness carried to an extreme. The extreme polarization of these experiments by Stanislavsky and Meyerhold was a crude and declarative indication of the painful duality in the art of the prewar years.

T. Bachelis observes:

> It would seem that there could be no greater contrast in the history of the Russian stage in the last prewar years than the First Studio of the Art Theater with its *Cricket on the Hearth* and Meyerhold's Studio on Borodinskaya Street with its cult of Gozzi! Soul and body, ethic and esthetic, truth and fiction—everything that always comprises *theatrical unity* in the time of its flowering seemed to become divided and appeared separately in these studios, pushed away from each other. The connection that art receives from a mature artistic method and a unified world view was dissolved.[154]

At the time, Meyerhold no longer denied "emotional experience" as such. He felt only that such an experience inevitably arises on its own, as the result of a well-worked score for the actors' actions in the event that this score is played by a talented artist.

In a 1913 interview, he said:

> Concerning the "problems" of modern theater, I cannot fail to give my view regarding the presently fashionable school of "stage depiction." Such a distinction is a tremendous error.
> It is known that the famous Coquelin in his work on roles began with the externals— but did he not experience them? The difference here is only one of method, in the manner of studying the role. But in essence the talent always experiences a role emotionally, while mediocrity only represents.[155]

Neither Meyerhold nor Stanislavsky ever doubted the need to develop actors' techniques. The contradictions between them concerned the question of *which* technique the actor requires. Then and for a long time after, Meyerhold developed only the *external technique* and neglected internal technique, while in the same years Stanislavsky was working exclusively on *internal technique*, separating it from the external.

The practical work in the Studio Meyerhold supplemented with a theoretical basis in the magazine *Love for Three Oranges*, which he founded. The Studio began work in September 1913, and in January 1914 appeared the first issue of *Doctor Dapertutto's Journal* (Meyerhold was already known under this pseudonym in St. Petersburg as the director of productions in the House of Interludes and in the Teryoki theater).

Both the Studio and the magazine worked toward one mutual goal: the establishment of theatricality in the "purest" forms, those freest from everyday life and psychology. To this end the attention of the magazine focused on the experience of ancient stage art, primarily the Comedy of Masks and Gozzi. In the Studio the main effort was directed toward the development of plastic expressiveness and the improvement of the bodily apparatus. Meyerhold taught a class on stage movements, V. N. Solovyov taught a class on the commedia dell'arte, M. F.Gnesin gave a class on musical recitation in drama. While Stanislavsky in Moscow with his Studio people was trying to penetrate the mysteries of "the very nature" of creativity, Meyerhold was giving his pupils intensive training, to put it in modern terms. His "studists" learned the technique of working on the stage, were trained in full mastery of body, voice, and motion in the assigned tempo. Ideally they were to become virtuosi capable of doing everything required onstage. No secrets. The simplest habits had to be polished to perfection, to automatism. It was important to be a master and, possibly, only this was important. As for theory, its basic postulates as presented in the Studio were sufficiently simple.

In Meyerhold's archives there remain, written in the precise and even hand of some woman "studist" on separate small pages some of these that give us a clear enough idea of the principles Meyerhold instilled in his students.

> The essence of the theatrical business is the complete absence of freedom and full freedom of improvisation. This may sound paradoxical, and it is so.

In Meyerhold's hand is added: *"Freedom in subordination."*

> Each has found his own language: artists, writers, scientists—only actors have not found theirs.
>
> The basic work in the Studio is work on what the modern actor lacks. Externally intense, externally very attractive, internally he remains dead.
>
> Meyerhold *in form* attempted to transmit the entire force of expression without attention to psychology.
>
> If "something" is heard, it does not require comment, does not require special stress in order to affect the heart. Since "something" exists, it will become clear to the audience by itself.
>
> Joy and happiness in movements.

One must admire oneself, the position into which one has been put by the director, which may be neither beautiful nor pretty.

The influence of costume.

The significance of an outcry at a moment of intense action.

There is a connection between architecture and direction but it is not yet clear to Meyerhold.

We are a small reflection of the directorial fire! All give themselves up in favor of the composition without advertising themselves as actors.

Creative lassitude.

Precision, joy, more spark in movement!

It is necessary to be excited, to know that it is a joke—when you go on stage, not seriously, but playfully, like in a nursery.

Clowning and affectation are requisites for an actor. The greatest simplicity must contain an element of affectation.

Art is juggling—actors in Louis XIV's time knew this.[156]

The unknown "studist" recorded another symptomatic quote by Meyerhold directed at the "Ancient theater" of N. Evreinov and N. Drizen: "Ancient theater. Expectation of very substantial reforms in it. The changes turned out to be superficial. Internally, the theater remained as before: actors unable to read verse, ignorant of movement. Such theater resembled an antique shop. Something basic was missing."[157]

Meyerhold sought the "basic" in the area of ultra-refined techniques—to the "juggling" level—of virtuoso acting mastery.

The theses recorded the development and variation of Meyerhold's favorite ideas. It is clear, however, that in no way are these ideas connected with the contemporary life surrounding the theater.

We find an explanation for this in this brief note by Meyerhold:

> Why reflect it, this modern life?
> It must be overcome.
> We must improve the body of man.[158]

This is the most compressed formulation of the program that guided Meyerhold in his own directorial practice and in his Studio work.

It is easy to see the vulnerable link in this fine formula. It is negative, lacks a positive social or humanistic idea. The rejection of modern life and revulsion toward the bourgeois in Meyerhold's case result only in the lack of desire to "reflect" modern life and a desire to improve "the body of man." It is as though the soul has been taken from this body and placed outside the parentheses of Meyerhold's formula. Therefore, his art becomes open to the intrusion of the most various and occasionally contradictory ideas and frequently serves the bourgeois spirit. It is at these times that the *style moderne* appears in Meyerhold's art, marked by an excess of effect and artifice. The student's note about the as-yet-unclear "connection between architecture and direction" is supported in Meyerhold's practice in the most crafty way.

The breath of the *style moderne* was present, too, in Meyerhold's production at the Alexandrinsky Theater of Arthur Pinero's play *Mid-Channel*. Golovin's art brought even the old-timer Kugel to the point of utter distraction. He incoherently and angrily described the white columns, parapets separated "by a hinged gilded wall from further parapets," and quite coherently railed at "the senselessness and self-glorifying pride of this Golovin-Meyerhold fantasy..." Kugel was especially outraged that "Golovin's Meyerholds and Meyerhold's Golovins not only fail to take the play into account, but do not read it either. Let me make a decoration, and then you do what you can... Total lack of understanding for the logical stress of the play, so to speak, for its development, apogee and perigee." There was truth to these rebukes, but it should be added that this salon comedy by the agile Pinero did not deserve serious attention anyhow. Its moral was succinctly presented by the same Kugel: "Woman without children, without work, without social strivings, inevitably must become such a bundle of refined erotica—must become a victim of Eros. And hence, naturally, the nervous disturbance and all that follows."[159]

It is unlikely that Meyerhold would have enjoyed analyzing the cause of the nervous disorder in the pampered lady. The play was staged for E.N. Roshchina-Insarova, who had already played the leading role of Zoe in this drama and who recently had been invited to the Alexandrinsky stage. Meyerhold had his own views regarding this actress—he wanted to cast her in *The Storm*. Meanwhile, a word on the decorations that so outraged Kugel. And not only Kugel: when the actor Apollonsky saw the decorations for Pinero's play, he refused to participate in the production, although he had rehearsed for one of the leading roles. Znosko-Borovsky gave out the secret of the decoration. He wrote that the audiences were amazed "by the decoration, whose half-circle was pierced by frequent passages that left only yellowish cubes with gold baguettes." (Here are Kugel's mysterious parapets.) "But," continued Znosko-Borovsky, "one had only to turn to the auditorium to understand the concept of the director and the artist A. Ya. Golovin: the decoration repeated the lower wall of the auditorium where the boxes had been removed but which still was broken up by many doors... The coloring, baguettes, and placement were all repeated on the stage, which architecturally was merged with the auditorium."[160]

In this way, Golovin and Meyerhold for the first time closed the always-broken ring of the auditorium and surrounded the entire hall, including the stage, with a single golden belt and therefore seemingly pushed Pinero's tinny little play into the stalls—all its salon passions, boudoir problems, and alcove valor. Could it be that there was an intention to expose, to challenge the audience? In any case, the play was not a success and was remembered only for its absurd plushness. Subsequently, neither Meyerhold nor Golovin ever made mention of this work.

Infinitely more important for Meyerhold was another attempt to attract the interest of the general public to the dramas of Alexander Blok. Blok's plays had attracted Meyerhold's strong interest over a period of many years. He wished to stage *Song of Fate* and *The Rose and the Cross* in the Alexandrinsky Theater, but for a number of reasons was unable to succeed in this effort, primarily because Telyakovsky, who generally gave Meyerhold a wide latitude, could not consent to such a bold step and refused to understand Blok's plays. Another no less important reason was that at this time, as we know, Blok had no particular enthusiasm for Meyerhold's ideas.

Nonetheless, in Blok's notebook there is an entry for January 9, 1914, that "Meyerhold has taken two copies of *The Rose and the Cross* to the Director of the Imperial Theaters—for him and for the censor."[161] This means that Blok did consent to Meyerhold's staging the play in the Alexandrinsky Theater.

Meyerhold was unable to get the play passed by the theatrical censor (Blok notes that the censor, "Baron Drizen is obstinate about *The Rose and the Cross*") and was unable to gain Telyakovsky's acquiescence. Nevertheless, he decided to stage Blok's play using his "studists." It was decided to present *The Unknown Lady* and *The Puppet Show* in a single evening. In the Studio, recalled V. Verigina, "the main occupation was pantomime, but notwithstanding, we came to the decision to stage Blok's lyrical dramas in the Tenishevsky Auditorium."[162] It would have been difficult for the young drama students to carry on such a performance, so actors who had previously worked with Meyerhold were invited: A. Mgebrov, A. Golubyov and others. Yury Bondi was the artist for the production.

The seats were removed from the stalls. The audience was seated only in the rows of the semicircular, rising amphitheater, which resulted in something like an ancient stage. On the sides of the stage two small ladders gave the actors access down to the circular area that replaced the front rows. There was, of course, no curtain and the necessary changes of scenery were made in front of the audience.

The premiere of Blok's play was on April 7, 1914, and performances were given for a week in a row. Taking everything into consideration, Blok allowed Meyerhold to work on *The Unknown Lady* and the new revision of *The Puppet Show* with "great freedom,"[163] as the director had requested for *Song of Fate*. In any event, the director's interpretation of *The Unknown Lady* was extremely active and nearly independent of the author's notes.

The Unknown Lady, a play in three "visions," was being staged for the first time. Its first "vision"—a street tavern—was staged in the following fashion. The servants of the proscenium brought out table, stools and counter and then with long bamboo poles they raised a green background behind these objects. The actors walked in carrying glasses and bottles, sat down at the tables and began a drunken bar conversation.

"The players," commented the reviewer for *Theater and Art* ironically, "spoke very indistinctly and softly... The people were simply dressed, some of them in the Russian manner. One wore a green paper wig over a sleeveless Russian blouse, another—a striped one, red and yellow. The women's cheeks were covered with round spots of rouge like dolls... The men wore large red cardboard noses..."[164]

The second "vision" took place on a bridge. This arched bridge was constructed from two halves that again were assembled by the servants of the proscenium, and Meyerhold subsequently ascribed great significance to it. The point is that the "airy and fragile" bridge, which was practically built before the audience, in front of the stage, was already a sort of "construction," a raised platform for the actors and, in any event, a precursor of the as-yet-undiscovered possibilities of construction. In the catalogue of the Meyerhold Theater Museum, published over ten years later (in 1926), there was the following proud assertion: "The first experimental design of a stage under the sign of Constructivism was the erection of a bridge for the second part of Blok's *The Unknown Lady*, in an area free of theatrical elements in the 'Tenishevskaya auditoriya' in Petrograd in 1914....''[165]

"Behind the arched and thin bridge," recalled A. Mgebrov, "two masks (i.e., the proscenium servants)...held up the sky. How incredible it was!.. Along the light-blue airy tulle Bondi had scattered large gold shining stars, and in the blue lights these stars on the fluttering tulle actually did twinkle and shine in a very special way."[166]

When the actors came onto the bridge, each of them was covered by a gauze film by the servants of the proscenium. As Znosko-Borovsky wrote in the magazine *The Contemporary (Sovremennik)*, this was to symbolize "a snowy, starry night. When in the sky a star flared up and fell, all the chandeliers were extinguished and one of the servants lit a simple sparkler, then in total darkness another raised it to the ceiling on a long pole and lowered it; still another servant extinguished it in water and the chandeliers were lit again."[167] At this moment the Unknown Lady arrived "in a black dress with enormously long eyelashes that reached down her cheeks and were drawn on as though by a child. After her came a knight in a great blue cape. Since it was difficult to stand on the ladder in a cape one of the servants assisted him in managing it."

The third "vision" was set in a society drawing-room depicted by Blok with unconcealed sarcasm. "The guests," wrote the hostile reviewer for Kugel's magazine, "also had noses pasted on. They all stood like statues and the footlights were candles held by kneeling women in aprons"[168]—the servants of the proscenium once again.

The servants of the proscenium worked superlatively well:

Dressed in gray, rhythmical, agile, they themselves resembled visions. Furthermore, their worshipful attitude toward Blok's production was transmitted to the audience. The way in which they raised the blue starry sky behind the bridge, covered the group in the tavern with a film of white snow, veiled all those who stepped onto the bridge and especially the way they knelt before the stage holding lighted candles was particularly memorable... They were solemnly carrying on a religious service during the performance.

The play with the Blue Knight's cape, which was ridiculed in the magazine *Theater and Art*, Verigina explained as follows: "one of the proscenium servants reverently spread out the edge of the cape, underscoring its significance and causing the cloth to play, to participate, in the theatrical production..."

The actress noted, however, that Meyerhold and Bondi did not take into account the poor lighting in the Tenishevsky Auditorium, so that many of the effects were lost. Furthermore, Verigina felt that the actress playing the Unknown Lady, Lydia Ilyashenko, was an unfortunate choice. Ilyashenko was beautiful, plastic and musical, but too calm, giving the Unknown Lady the dignity and stateliness of a society lady. Finally, two episodes of the production caused legitimate doubt. When the servants of the proscenium threw oranges into the audience (in order to hint at the connection between the production and the magazine *Love for Three Oranges*), this "did not harmonize with the content of the play." When after the end of *The Unknown Lady*, Chinese children appeared on the stage during the intermission and began to juggle with knives, the public was utterly astonished.

Meyerhold had found real Chinese children "somewhere in the street before the performance and wanted them to appear during the intermission. He was so taken with this idea that nothing could be done, he was quite mad on the idea of these little Chinese children." According to Verigina, the performance by the Chinese in the intermission looked "touchingly clumsy," but "enraged the audience."[169]

The Puppet Show was performed after the intermission in a new and, according to the public, worse directorial version. Meyerhold no longer played Pierrot; the role was taken by K. Kuzmin-Karavaev. One negative aspect, according to Verigina, was that "the performance was taken out into the audience. The action in masks took place in the area from which the first rows had been removed." Consequently, "the actors were in a hostile camp," since "at least half of the audience was deaf to Blok's poetry and hostile toward the director. The actors were compelled to perform while closely surrounded by such an audience... Only the mystics' table remained on the stage."[170]

In some of the reviews of Blok's play (A. Mikhailov in the newspaper *Speech*, L. Vasilevsky in *The Contemporary Word [Sovremennoe slovo]*), there was the thought that Blok's dramas were staged in the forms of the commedia dell'arte. In answer, the editors of the magazine *Love for Three Oranges*, or probably Meyerhold himself, objected: "The proscenium, its servants, movable items, grotesque costuming, etc., can be found not only in Italian improvisational theater but, for instance, in Molière's theater, in seventeenth-century Spain, in wandering English comedy companies, and in Japanese theater. As for the commedia dell'arte, one cannot even talk about it without the four basic masks, improvisation, and traditional acting techniques."[171]

This erudite explanation was simultaneously a tacit admission of a certain eclecticism of methods used in the production. There was much newness and force, some aspects were flat and flaccid, and others were clearly superfluous and alien to the essence of the plot. The rebukes for eclecticism addressed to Meyerhold were at least partially just.

The reviewers almost completely failed to notice the good points of this production.

When reading the old press reviews, angry, bilious, and derogatory for the most part, and the memoirs and diaries of contemporaries describing Meyerhold's production, one becomes amazed not so much at how obstinately—and how alone!—he went against the current, as at the many foreshadowings and glimpses or sketches of the theater of the future. It can only be guessed that Vakhtangov's *Princess Turandot* partially came from *Harlequin the Marriage Broker*, while its connection with Blok's production in the Tenishevsky Auditorium is unarguable. Vakhtangov saw the play and was delighted with it. *The Unknown Lady*, testifies N. Volkov on the basis of Vakhtangov's words, made the "greatest of impressions" on him.[172] Even without this evidence, we would have recognized in Vakhtangov's *tsanni* the servants of the proscenium from Blok's production. Even more significant for Vakhtangov's art was the satirical theme so distinct in the first and third "visions" of *The Unknown Lady*; the ridicule of the Russian petty bourgeois and of Russian uncouthness. This theme was found again in Vakhtangov's *The Wedding*.

Reading *The Unknown Lady* closely, one becomes amazed at Blok's prophetic genius and the exceptional empathy of the director who undertook to work with this theme. For instance, in the "third vision" in the salon the conversation in the beginning is fairly rational although mundane, but suddenly it drops off into complete alogism. Beginning with Chekhovian nonsense, the action appears to jump ahead several decades to Zoshchenko and Ionesco, to the purest theater of the absurd. This odd, shifted, crooked but nonetheless most precise exposure of the automatism and absurdity of Russian life was rendered by Meyerhold on stage on the very eve of the bloody absurdity of world war. There is, of course, a direct connection to the absurdity of the mystics in *The Puppet Show*. And the exposure is placed in painfully acute conflict with the themes of beauty, poetry, and love that pass through both of Blok's plays. Is it so strange that this was not understood?

Blok attended the first performance of this play, then did not come for two or three days, then came again and, writes Verigina, "this time he suddenly liked the performance. Thereafter, Blok did not miss a single performance. He even regretted that he had made a break..."[173] After a long and difficult crisis in their relations, this marked a new closeness between the poet and the director.

In the summer of 1914, Russia entered World War I. Together with the abrupt change in the life of the country the theatrical situation would change, too. Meyerhold expressed his thoughts on this subject in a curious article "War and Theater."

"Who," he asked, "needs everyday nonsense these days? All sorts of psychological motivations, various pan-psychisms and tired people? Who today has need of a camera to photograph today's events? What can they show the public that enters the theater excited by incredible atrocities, the loss of works of art and the destruction of the Rheims Cathedral?"

Meyerhold noted further that "the merging of auditorium and stage is most intense at the moments when people are staggered or strongly excited by something" and presented a program for improvisational theater that required of the playwrights "only a scenario" which the actors would be able to "embroider...with the fine stitch of their art."[174]

These ideas of Meyerhold's, like so many of his others, were premature, first of all, naturally, because the "excitement of the people" that he wrote about was in no way similar to true enthusiasm. Official patriotism was being fanned energetically by the press and took on equally conventional forms.

Meyerhold realized this when he participated in several benefit evenings. On August 15, 1914, in Suvorin's Maly Theater, his staging of Maupassant's *Mademoiselle Fifi*, with Sudeikin's decorations, was performed. "The entire performance," related the magazine *Theater and Art*, "was a non-stop patriotic demonstration. Representatives of all the friendly powers were present in the theater... The hymn of one nation followed the other and the entire audience, as one person, greeted the ambassadors, who bowed low in their boxes."[175] Approximately the same patriotic spectacle took place in other places, and Meyerhold quickly tired of it. He appeared to forget about the war and returned to theatrical occupations.

Two extensive polemical articles that Meyerhold printed in his magazine *Love for Three Oranges* were directed against the programmed production by the Moscow Art Theater's First Studio of *Cricket on the Hearth* ("*Cricket on the Hearth*, or At the Keyhole") and against the Art Theater's production of Pushkin ("Benois the Director"). The second article contained a detailed and, it must be said, very harsh analysis of Alexander Benois's failure. Soon Benois would repay Meyerhold in the same coin.

Since 1911, Meyerhold had been promising and preparing a staging of Lermontov's *Masquerade*. Theatrical humorists already were ridiculing the director's tardiness, but the premiere continued to be postponed. It was to have opened for the hundredth anniversary of Lermontov's birth in 1914, but the war resulted in cancellation of the celebration and the staging did not take place. On January 10, 1915, in the Mariinsky Theater, a Lermontov play was performed. Meyerhold used Golovin's decorations for the first staging ever of Lermontov's drama *Two Brothers*. For Meyerhold, this work was evidently a sort of sketch for *Masquerade*.

L. Gurevich wrote:

> Through all the artistic imperfections of the play and the production, Lermontov's soul regarded us strangely... The role of the young Countess Vera Ligovskaya, a typical Lermontovian woman of vacillating temperament, with humble aspirations to tear herself out from the usual lot of woman, with an involuntary attraction to a powerful, demonically passionate male soul but unable to surrender fully to it... This difficult but noble role was played by the elegant but listless actress Kovalenskaya. Evidently, she comprehended the dramatic significance of her role and, possibly, was even enthusiastic about it, but internally she was unable to grasp its content and she appeared too doll-like in her bright, pretty outfit of the 30s. Evidently, Meyerhold's direction evoked an external acuity of action unusual for this young actress in the more dramatic moments of the play, but this artificially created expressiveness remained internally empty and gave an unpleasant impression of affectation.

However, continued Gurevich,

> . . . the lovely decorations and costumes by Golovin, particularly the semicircular living room in Ligovsky's house and the romantically moonlit, abandoned hall receding into the depths of the stage from some fantastic vestibule with choirs and a spiral staircase, these dressed up and gave a stylistic beauty to the entire production.[176]

In the Mariinsky Theater, *Two Brothers* was performed only once, but for the opening of the subsequent season on September 1, 1916, Meyerhold transferred the production to the Alexandrinsky stage. A. Kugel, who had not reviewed the first performance, compensated for this by writing this time in two publications—in his magazine and in the newspaper *Day (Den')*. In each case he was categorical, as usual. The play, wrote Kugel, "was played really badly, it was pompous and cold." He summarized: "In all, the production of *Two Brothers* is an utterly unnecessary undertaking."[177]

The usefulness of this "undertaking" Meyerhold proved somewhat later: in *Masquerade* some of the ideas used in directing *Two Brothers* were developed and brought to completion.

In the war years, Meyerhold worked almost exclusively on Russian classics. Pushkin, Lermontov, Ostrovsky, and Sukhovo-Kobylin took up most of the director's attention and powers. Also, he was interested in authors like Calderón, Shaw and

Wilde. Meyerhold did undertake to stage a contemporary Russian play: *The Green Ring*, by Zinaida Gippius.

The play was quite original. The well-known writer tried to look at contemporary youth without prejudice. In contrasting the young students' circle, the Green Ring, with adults, Zinaida Gippius appeared to be saying that the new generation was cleaner, wiser, better than the mature generation, which despite its maturity was unable to change the world and transform life. For Gippius, it was important to stress that the children were charitable toward the spiritual capitulation of their fathers. Kind wisdom was attributed to these all-knowing young people. Young people, Gippius hoped, could overcome all the everyday and moral obstacles and build a new life.

However, although she capably depicted the atmosphere of green youth and sketched the portraits of the young men and women and their "spiritual leader" Uncle Mika with life and talent, Gippius clearly was lost before the necessity to delineate in some way the idea that unified the youth. It was impossible to understand what these wonderful and pure young creatures wanted and dreamed of, and where they were being led by the all-seeing Uncle Mika.

Meyerhold understood, probably, that the play lost its way toward the finale, that the acute questions it posed remained unanswered and that the more or less convenient disposition of the fate of one Finochka opened no paths to the correction of the evident disorder in Russian life, the life of both young and old. Even the moral problems that Gippius gingerly touched upon were quickly closed rather than solved. Nonetheless, Meyerhold did accept the play, since the idea of opposing youth—united and friendly—to the older generation—the fathers divided and mired in the everyday—seduced him. There was, after all, a challenge in the play...

The decorations were painted, as usual, by A. Ya. Golovin. The roles were assigned as follows: Uncle Mika—Yu. M. Yurev, Finochka—E. N. Roshchina-Insarova, Elena Ivanovna—M. G. Savina, Vozhzhin—A. P. Petrovsky, Anna Dmitrievna—N. V. Rostova, the Gymnasium student Seryozhka—N. V. Smolich, the student Rusya—M. P. Domasheva.

What was sensational here was the selection of Savina, who had worked once with Meyerhold (in *The Living Corpse*), but who remained one of his chief opponents in the Alexandrinsky Theater. Zinaida Gippius subsequently recalled:

> Meyerhold, the "representative of the new current," sent the play to Maria Gavrilovna Savina, the "representative of the old current." From enemy to enemy. Is that not how Meyerhold and Savina were regarded? Who could expect her to perform under Meyerhold's direction? And in the play of an author whose name since Old Testament times had been coupled with suspicious "decadence"! However, this did happen... "I am first of all an artist," said Maria Gavrilovna. "I consider Meyerhold to be an artist, too. Why should we not be together?"[178]

Telyakovsky's response to the dress rehearsal of *The Green Ring*, held on February 5, 1915, was positive. "The play is well performed. Savina is particularly good in her part. Petrovsky, Domasheva and Smolich are good." But, observed Telyakovsky, "Roshchina is weak and unsuitable."[179]

—212—

By and large, the reviewers ridiculed Gippius' play. The critics were interested only in Savina's appearance in a production by Meyerhold. With some amazement, the reviewers stated that Savina in her declining years (this was her next-to-last role; Savina died half a year after the premiere of *The Green Ring*) presented "an artistic type of empty, shallow woman who does not wish to age, who postures with her 'cross' and loves her daughter with a stupid love. In Elena Ivanovna—Savina—for the entire time, even in her hysteria, you see affectation and bad taste."[180]

Lyubov Gurevich, who watched Meyerhold through these war years "with Stanislavsky's eyes," so to speak, wrote that the staging "in the spirit of highly stressed realism with a well-calculated play of refined color combinations and bright color spots, with stylish new costumes that appeared to come straight from the store" did not make the play convincingly lifelike. "The lively, chattering young people" in the production "seemed...surprisingly without feeling in their mobility and excessive familiarity, surprisingly free of the shyness characteristic for this age that is overcome only by the force of inner surges. The highly unpleasant little old men and women, both prophets and believers, ran around the stage in Gymnasium dresses and shirts."

The same article indicated precisely the most vulnerable point of the play: The fairly well hidden idea of compromise was brought out into the light. L. Gurevich wrote: "Something old, domestically-optimistic, wafts up from this denouement that resolves the drama of a young soul on a plane completely different from that of the development of the plot, an abrupt diminution of it that brings everything down to the question of personal comfort."[181]

The main outcome of the production for Meyerhold was disillusionment. The contemporary play that interested him and was liked by Blok (which meant a great deal to Meyerhold) passed by quietly and unnoticed. Blok's reaction (in a letter to his wife) is curious. "In *The Green Ring* there was no Meyerhold present, but there were Gippius, Savina, Domasheva and some others. The actors played the play to one-fourth of its stature. The play is clumsy with a mass of inadequacies, but nonetheless—it has *stature* and *maturity* even in the hands of actors."[182] In other words, Blok too was intrigued somehow by the problematical nature of this play and he tried to see its "maturity" and "stature" "through the show."

Meanwhile, Meyerhold was excited by the next play on the agenda: Calderón's *The Constant Prince*. In 1915, Meyerhold's openings followed each other in rapid succession: January 10—*Two Brothers*, February 18—*The Green Ring*, April 23—*The Constant Prince* and September 30—*Pygmalion*.

Among the works listed for the year, Calderón's was the essential one. It was to *The Constant Prince* that the magazine *Love for Three Oranges* subsequently dedicated two long articles written by an editor, Zhirmunsky. Another colleague of Meyerhold's, V. Solovyov, later wrote about this production in *Apollo (Apollon)*, indicating that Meyerhold and Golovin this time "offered to the attention of the public a continuation of the staging formula that they had tested first in the staging of Molière"[183]—i.e., *Don Juan*.

With the use of some techniques taken from *Don Juan* (Meyerhold, of course, rejected immediately the tapestries that had set the tone for *Don Juan* and which would have been out of place in *The Constant Prince*), the director firmly delineated the stylistic motifs characteristic of seventeenth-century Spain and in effect ignored the author's indication that the action takes place in the fifteenth century. Meyerhold wished to give the essence of the style of Calderón's day and not of the time in which the events of the play transpire, just as he had stylized Molière's era in *Don Juan*. In fact, this production utilized not only the basic staging principle of *Don Juan* but some of the old Golovin decorations, too.

The permanent decorative frame of the portal was to depict "the chambers of the luxurious ancient castle where the theatrical production takes place." The small blackamoors were replaced by servants of the proscenium made up as Moors. These servants "before the eyes of the audience, change decorations, light candles, shield decoration changes on stage with portable screens and announce the intermission." Meyerhold led them from play to play, in various guises, since these best underscored the moment of open theatricality and reminded the audience that theater was theater.

Zhirmunsky wrote:

> This, although in a somewhat different sense, is the significance of the proscenium, pushed out into the auditorium, where clowns cavort, Fenix and Muley swap lines or the ghost of the Constant Prince walks slowly past holding a lighted candle. Stepping out *onto the proscenium, the actor suddenly steps out of the stage frame, becomes visible not in the two dimensions of a painting but in three—in real life, from every side*, and this contrast only stresses the illusory nature of what takes place on the stage.

Both articles by young Zhirmunsky dedicated to *The Constant Prince* clearly express Meyerhold's ideas. This is evident if only because in his detailed explication of the director's plan the author says not a word of praise. It is all the more interesting to follow the further development of one of Meyerhold's crowning pre-Revolutionary period ideas—the idea to "find *forms and colors, movements and sounds*, that *symbolically* would express the soul and content locked within the dramatic action, which would be an artistic *flesh* until the end of the corresponding *soul* of the poetic work."

This is a presentation of the basic formula of metaphoric theater, which Meyerhold's theater always was. This theater avoids direct correspondences to life, does not reflect life as it is but expresses its essence, its "soul," in its metaphors. The viewer, continued Zhirmunsky, must relate "to the staging as to a painting, to the music of words as to a symphony, to the production as a whole—as to a theatrical spectacle incarnating the internal content of the dramatic production in an appropriate and effective form subordinated to special laws, the laws of theater."[184]

Speaking concretely of *The Constant Prince*, Zhirmunsky observed that this production of Meyerhold's

> creates for the dramatic   work an abstract frame that transmits the basic tone, the basic mood of the action. This artistic scheme does not change through all the acts. Only details change, like harmonic tones indicating the corresponding differences in the various moments of the action. Against this general and generalizing background, which is extremely modest and replaces detail with hints and the clear with the understated, the leading place is given to the actor who is called upon to develop all the refinements of his art.

By so firmly promoting the actor-"soloist" to the front place in the show and asserting that the actor must assume "the full weight of the emotional content of the drama," incarnate "the artistic vision of the playwright-poet in the very sound of his voice, in poses and movements, in gesture and costume,"[185] Meyerhold unexpectedly gave the leading male role, that of the Constant Prince Fernando, to the actress N. G. Kovalenskaya.

The motivation is as follows. Calderón's drama is a play about faith, not the bold and proud faith which is usual for Spanish theater, but passive faith, the faith of love and patience. In this play we meet "the faith of prayers and hope, the faith of non-resistance—*feminine faith*. This is the faith of the Constant Prince."[186] The urge to underscore this femininity and lyric quality and to achieve "some internal force in the fine forms of the apparently weak youth" moved Meyerhold to transvestism.

"The performance by the actress," wrote V. Zhirmunsky, "thoroughly and sensitively depicted the noble image of the prince illuminated by holiness..." Her lines, "full of dignity and humility...created a quiet enchantment." When the role required ecstatic intensity, Kovalenskaya's voice "sounded particularly mysterious and wonderful."[187]

Not everyone shared the delight expressed in Meyerhold's magazine. E. Stark wrote:

> In his search for the realization of that enchanting tenderness of men that we know from Van Dyck's portraits, Meyerhold has had the truly unfortunate thought of giving the role of Fernando to an actress... What is the result of such a trick? Calderón's drama has lost its hero and together with him its ideological interest. This passionate Crusader knight, the bearer of the idea of the deed, of Christian self-renunciation and humility—was there anything like this in the form of the pampered and overly youthful courtier by Van Dyck played by Mrs. Kovalenskaya?"

E. Stark objected, too, to Meyerhold's conscious determination to move the setting of the drama from the fifteenth century to Calderón's period, the seventeenth century. "The Portuguese knights were dressed and made up according to Van Dyck, Calderón's contemporary. There could be no objection to performing *The Constant Prince* set at the time of its writing, had this external condition not caused the decay of the internal." Giving his due to the interesting staging and the entire "very serious, carefully detailed" work by Meyerhold, and seeing there the result of "a specific established conviction" by the artist that needed to be accepted as a whole "or totally rejected," the critic stated that he "selects the second" since he views the play differently. For him, "it is like a bright flame saturated with temperament, while the passions within it collide in a large scale. The people are powerful, as if chiseled from a cliff or cast from steel..."[188]

L. Gurevich wrote in the newspaper *Speech* that Calderón

> remained somewhere far behind the stage and the play turned into an effective decorative performance on themes by Calderón where the eye was caressed by the festively bright sets and costumes by Golovin, the nerves were teased by the extreme deliberateness of the actors' poses and gestures assigned by Meyerhold's directorial instructions. The basic decor

of the stage was borrowed from the staging of Molière's *Don Juan*... Only the changing rear decorations were new, as though placed into a frame. But all this together, the old and the new, the imperially-delicate colors of the front canvases, the sunny springtime colors of the distances, the fantastic props in the light of the chandeliers and two candelabras at the sides of the stage, blacks, original hats and dizzyingly colorful costumes, the movable curtain on poles brought in by two servants and raised on the proscenium during the changing of the set on stage, all this was so bright and so intriguing that without that special "piquant" quality that Meyerhold's direction imparts to actors, they would have appeared, probably, too pale. But Meyerhold's direction made itself felt almost immediately: not one of the actors was spontaneous in Calderón's drama. While reading their monologues they moved forward slowly with cautious, calculated steps as though walking a tightrope; or they froze in place, one leg behind, body leaning back, arm raised tensely...

Gurevich made fun of Leshkov, who in the role of Muley "moved about the stage with nothing less than the leaps of a tiger." Kovalenskaya, in the opinion of Gurevich, "approached her task with evident seriousness and spoke Don Fernando's monologues with pathos, straining her voice, sometimes hurrying, gasping and by the end nearly exhausted. Is there any need to mention that in these theatrical frenzies of the young actress there was not a single note capable of capturing the heart with deep religious ecstasy..."189

Meyerhold could have seen Gurevich's criticisms as compliments. He had achieved what he wanted. As for the "religious ecstasy" and "spontaneity" which Stanislavsky's follower had failed to discover and also the modesty and self-containment that she evidently would have preferred for *The Constant Prince*, none of these entered into Meyerhold's intentions.

The actual content of his festive production unexpectedly coincided with the work of the Moscow First Studio. The theme of human weakness and, furthermore, the theme of the validity of this weakness, the theme of the staunchness of good, entered into and inspired the opulent composition. The poetization of humble faith formed the clear meaning of the entire spectacle. This theme, like the continuous theme of all the First Studio productions, with its "spiritual realism," was intrinsically polemical with respect to the patriotic excitement of the war years. The cult of brute force was clearly and declaratively juxtaposed to the touching femininity of the Prince, his grace and lightness. This was a sort of "deheroization" expressed in naive and direct form. The appointment of Kovalenskaya to the leading male role was explained not by "an instinctive drive toward the piquant" (as Gurevich thought) but by a fully conscious plan that rejected *a priori* any intention to depict "powerful people chiseled from a cliff or cast from steel" (in the words of Stark). Femininity was seen and proclaimed—in the year of the War!—as a virtue greater than masculine boldness. Meekness and steadfastness in the good were idealized.

The principal—and for Meyerhold the most significant—difference from the First Studio was that the theme of the meek and good went hand in hand with the theme of exotic and dreamy beauty. The bright colors in the production stressed the ghostly nature of the expressed hopes and unequivocally stated that these hopes were incompatible with the life surrounding the theater. This is why in the final analysis this was a very sad spectacle.

Naturally, not all the problems that intrigued Meyerhold were resolved in this case. Attention to the style of the author, the drive to stage not only the play but the "whole" playwright, to bring out the special stage aspects of his work in *The Constant Prince,* came second to the even more general task—that of discovering the principles of theatricality of a particular era, that of the seventeenth century. By borrowing from himself the general solution found for the Molière play and by changing very little therein (Golovin's replaceable backgrounds, some aspects of staging, some functions of the proscenium servants), Meyerhold actually was testing and enriching a previously made composition rather than creating new principles, or anything especially Calderonian. What was significant was Meyerhold's proof that it was possible to connect this composition innovatively and *ideologically* with modernity.

In the realm of esthetic problems that arose for the director in all his "major" and "basic" stagings of the classics, the following gradually became the determinant ones: first, the disclosing of the style of the period; second, the style of the author; and third, the establishment of a direct connection between the past and present. Very soon we shall see how all these problems were resolved in *The Storm* and *Masquerade*.

Russia was becoming ever more mired in war and met with one defeat after another on the front. The minds of the people were confused and frantic. They could not understand the defeatist slogans of the Bolsheviks, their patriotic feelings were insulted by the military reverses and the ever-more-evident decay and collapse behind the front. In this difficult period, the stage was unable to adapt to life and all the Russian theater, with the sole exception of the First Studio, which clearly opposed the war, did not know what to stage, how to stage it, or how to act. The sadness that permeated Meyerhold's *The Constant Prince* was fully understandable, as was that estheticizing of the past, which permeated the performance.

Among the many symptoms of the spiritual stagnation which afflicted the Russian intelligentsia at that time was the rapid and unhappy devolution of Kugel's critical talent. His innate conservatism degenerated into peevish grumbling. Kugel devoted long editorials of praise to obvious incompetents like Ryshkov and Trakhtenberg. He praised beyond measure Artsybashev's *Envy* and continued to assert that in 1896 his ridicule of Chekhov's *The Sea Gull* had been completely warranted. To his usual targets—the Art Theater, Stanislavsky, Meyerhold, Leonid Andreev—a new one suddenly was added: Kugel began furiously to criticize Shaw, whose plays were appearing on the Russian stage with increasing frequency.

Meyerhold was staging *Pygmalion* at this time. This production, by the way, has been neglected completely by theater historians. It is true that N. D. Volkov mentions the performance of *Pygmalion* that took place on April 26, 1915, "for charitable purposes" in the Mikhailovsky Theater. But this was a hastily assembled production that was performed a single time, while on September 30, 1915, Meyerhold presented Shaw's comedy in the Alexandrinsky Theater, where it was entered into the repertoire for a long time. Eliza Doolittle was played by E. Roshchina-Insarova, Higgins by B. Gorin-Goryainov, Mrs. Higgins by A. Nemirova-Ralf and old Mr. Doolittle by K. Yakovlev. Kugel used this premiere as a reason for one of his many very long columns attacking Shaw, whom he accused of manifesting the seven deadly sins, like "artistic narrowness," banality, and an urge "to mask dramatic collisions of social inequality."

Kugel briefly mentioned the actors at the end—he had disliked them all. Of Meyerhold he said that the director "staged the play with some sort of incomprehensible apathy. It was all flat, very neat and even in the externals, in the painting of the decorations and the interiors the director did not manifest himself in any way."[190] However, in Meyerhold's staging of *Pygmalion*, which externally was truly modest, there were elements of a sharp attack on satiated snobbery and sleek haughtiness: Gorin-Goryainov played Higgins with an open jeer. Roshchina-Insarova as Eliza Doolittle was fragile and her faltering, quiet weakness and honest straightforwardness at first resisted Higgins's self-satisfaction only modestly and humbly, and then abruptly, unpleasantly, and roughly attacked his culture, which was essentially a sham, and his superiority, which was unjustifiable and false.

For Meyerhold, the conflict here was not in the juxtaposition of poverty and wealth but in the struggle between true talent (Eliza) and the arrogant priest of pseudo-science. His Higgins was a British Serebryakov. Gurevich sensed this and in *Rech'* she even mentioned the organic bond between the talents of Shaw and Meyerhold. Gurevich observed a similarity between the acute, practically paradoxical, treatment of esthetic problems by the British playwright and the Russian director.[191] To a certain extent, Meyerhold's staging of *The Storm*, which whipped up a hurricane of displeasure, substantiated these observations.

The first problem that arose before Meyerhold when he first began to consider *The Storm* was the inevitable problem of the everyday in the play. The director who had always rejected theater of the everyday collided with a playwright who specialized in descriptions of the everyday. Ostrovsky's magnificent language sends its roots deep into the everyday and its details—Meyerhold therefore had to decide how Ostrovsky's text would sound in his production. It almost seems as if Meyerhold turned to Ostrovsky at the behest (and at least in part this was so) of an urge to test his new directorial principles under the least favorable conditions possible, under conditions that were *a priori* disadvantageous.

In a conversation with actors of the Alexandrinsky troupe published later in the magazine *Love for Three Oranges*, Meyerhold concentrated his attention first of all on the manner in which Ostrovsky's text was to be pronounced. He thoroughly studied all the reviews of the first performance of *The Storm* at the Alexandrinsky Theater in 1859. He came to the conclusion that the performers in that distant premiere half a century before his own production were hindered by "peasant jargon" and by a false understanding of populism: when the actor "begins to search out and present (with special emphasis) individual odd expressions and curious words without in any way attempting to master the playwright's speech structure as a whole, without knowing how to gather words synthetically into a unique prosaic melody."

Herein was contained Meyerhold's most characteristic instruction: Ostrovsky was to be interpreted as a poet. In his text one had to capture the melody and find a "rhythmically fine music."

Further, Meyerhold abruptly and with good reason separated Ostrovsky from "genre writers like Potekhin and Grigorovich" and brought him into the circle of such great poets of the Russian stage as Pushkin, Lermontov and Gogol. He pointed out to his audience the fact that in the years of the most intensive stage life of Ostrovsky's plays (i.e., in the second half of the last century), neither Pushkin nor Lermontov were performed on the Russian stage, that *The Inspector General* gave way to the more "accessible" *Krechinsky's Wedding,* while *The Death of Tarelkin* was not performed. In other words, he demonstrated that Ostrovsky was being performed during the time that the Russian stage was taken over by mediocre playwrights and imitators and that the tradition for the performance of Ostrovsky's plays was formed under conditions of the victorious imitative theater of the everyday, during a period of crisis and even total absence of the poetic in theater. "The present-day apologists for the theater of the everyday," Meyerhold observed, "stubbornly pull Ostrovsky back into that circle," i.e., back into superficial genre writing.

Let us leave aside the question of how correct Meyerhold was in his quick analysis of the overall condition of Russian theater in the second half of the nineteenth century. Much more important for us are his concrete intentions. He wished that actors would achieve "true folk character" in that "manner of word pronunciation" associated with "the texts of the theaters of Pushkin, Gogol, Lermontov, Ostrovsky." What is important here is not Meyerhold's characteristic interpretation of the playwrights he named as being complete stage worlds, as special "theaters." More important yet is his overall perception of all these "theaters" as a single, interrupted but renewable, great *poetic* tradition.

It should be noted that Meyerhold, in turning to *The Storm*, attempted to effect the rebirth or even the re-creation of Ostrovsky's *specific* tradition. In the Russian theater of the early twentieth century, Ostrovsky had been until that time uninteresting and of little significance. Only individual theatrical episodes (such as the Moscow Art Theater's 1910 production of *Enough Simplicity in Every Wise Man*) and some important performers (O. Sadovskaya in Moscow, V. Strelskaya in Petersburg and V. Komissarzhevskaya in the capitals and on tour) preserved Ostrovsky's stage life. A. Kugel from year to year would complain in his magazine that there was no one to play Ostrovsky, that people had forgotten how to perform him.

In this situation, Meyerhold's idea to stage—and to stage in a new way—one of Ostrovsky's most important plays obtained a particular significance. In striving to achieve a poetic sound in Ostrovsky's play, Meyerhold instructed: "The least aspects of folk character" presented in the playwright's text do not give the actor the right to deliver the "least aspects of folk character" while performing by stressing "certain words." He declared bitter war on the stressing of certain words, while his aim became to penetrate "the mystery in Ostrovsky's works"[192] that Apollon Grigoriev had pointed out in his day and whose articles Meyerhold cited enthusiastically.

In a newspaper interview, Meyerhold said, however, that in his younger years he "had the great good luck of finding in Moscow an incredible company of Ostrovsky specialists who carefully guarded the traditions of the previous years on how to perform Ostrovsky." He named these "specialists": "I was able to see Mikhail Provych Sadovsky play Tikhon, Rykalova as Kabanova and O. O. Sadovskaya as Feklusha."[193]

Indivisibly connected with the feeling for the poetic nature of Ostrovsky's language, the entire exterior of the production conceived by Meyerhold and Golovin polemicized with the usual and, for the Russian stage, nearly unchanging desire to depict "the Kingdom of Darkness." Golovin recalled later: "While considering the decorations for *The Storm*, I decided to reject an illustrative approach to Ostrovsky's play and strove instead to create a background appropriate to the style of Russian Romantic drama, showing all its national particularities. By including colored ornamentation in the decoration of the walls and set I wished to give the total spectacle a colorfulness and impression of contentment."[194]

In accordance with this plan, the decoration of the first act was clean and smart. In the foreground was a verdant boulevard with precisely trimmed trees, white fencing and low benches. In the background was a pearly-gray vista. V. Solovyov wrote in *Apollo*:

> To the left in the background is a five-domed church the color of red calico where on holidays and holiday eves the most dignified and self-respecting people worship. They walk slowly and with due importance, looking with derision upon those younger than themselves who enjoy strolling along the boulevard, cracking seeds and standing by the white fence and watching the Volga flow by. Birch trees have been planted along the fence and under the birches stand green benches the color of the fence railing. Behind the birches, the fence, and the church flows the Volga, and beyond it an endless distance."[195]

"Such marvelously painted new benches," chuckled the reviewers, "you would not find even on the boulevards in the capital. The population, evidently, was unusually well off, judging by the way they were dressed up even on ordinary days. It was not life in the city of Kalinov, but a continuous carnival, if one is to judge by the costumes."[196]

An "impression of contentment" was given in the home of Tikhon, too. Coffers and caskets banded with wrought iron stood in the corners, a beautiful tile oven presided in the center of the room and a glass gallery shone in the background. "In the house it is quiet and pleasant, a godly delight," observed Solovyov. "The calm quiet of the walls sets off by contrast Katerina's drama." In the third act everything is dominated by the large locked gates behind which the structures of Kabanov's house loom oddly. The consensus was that Golovin's greatest success was the decoration of the ravine. "All these intertwined tree trunks illuminated by a half-moon form a special world very close to the nature of Russian Romantic fantasy. The trees change their sizes. This is the place where lovers meet in the moonlight."[197] One reviewer wrote: "The decoration of the ravine on the shore of the Volga creating a mood of lovers' languor is above praise. There everything is overgrown, tangled."[198]

The next decoration where Ostrovsky's brief note indicates "a narrow gallery with the arches of an ancient, crumbling structure" gave an unexpected and powerful response to the theme of "lovers' languor." Red, crimson and purple colors blazed. A fiery Gehenna was represented. Golovin painted the ruins of a church whose walls retained fragments of a large fresco of the Last Judgment. Against this flaming background, the tragedy was concluded. Despite Ostrovsky's notes, Meyerhold did not return to the decorations of the first act.

The director and the artist firmly led the viewer from the "grandeur" of the first scene to the satiety and contentment of the second and third acts, then to the Romantic languor and sinfulness of the ravine and in the finale gave an unexpected burst of flame. The heroine was to perish in this flame.

The heroine was again Roshchina-Insarova. Meyerhold had no doubts here. He would stage *The Storm* with this actress only—he even dedicated his speech to the actors, demonstratively, to Roshchina-Insarova.

Roshchina-Insarova's talent was considered elegant but nervous. The actress was renowned for sudden transitions from practically ecstatic exaltation to a melancholic, almost emotionally colorless, rapid speech, from sharp and nervous rhythms to weak, extinguished ones. Critics often saw in Roshchina-Insarova the most characteristic sign of the times. Her heroines were seen generally as a series of exaggerated, parodic portraits of the modern woman of the period. She was imitated by society women, her coiffures, dresses and mannerisms passed from the stage into life.

Roshchina had already performed in *The Storm* on the stage of the Moscow Maly Theater in 1911. At that time her Katerina, "a thin, pale woman in a heavy brocade frock and with the same headband pulled down over her forehead,"[199] astounded the critics. A. Kayransky wrote that he could not accept this "excessively nervous, jerky and contemporary image."[200]

Meanwhile, Meyerhold was naturally attracted to such "jerkiness." Roshchina, furthermore, had another important attribute. "In addition to the emotional qualities of her talent," wrote Yu. Yurev, "she always had a great drive to present a bright, precise reproduction of style, which she grasped unusually well."[201] This sense of style and sense of the author made Roshchina-Insarova especially necessary as a performer for Meyerhold and in the compositional and stylistic center of *The Storm* Roshchina ruled by right.

The press was hostile to Meyerhold's *Storm*. Kugel wrote that Meyerhold's production "made an impression that cannot be called anything but depressing." He was, first of all, astounded that instead of the "Kingdom of Darkness" the audience was presented with what one critic called the "Kingdom of Nuts." Kugel recounted:

In this City of Kalinov there is an eternal holiday. All the inhabitants are dressed most ornately, brightly, richly. Dikoi boasts a bright yellow long-waisted coat, poor man Kuligin is in a marvelous gray jacket with a velvet collar, the middle classes wear blue or green or orange coats and so forth. Naturally, Katerina is always in silks, even during her meeting in the ravine. But that's not the worst. Feklusha, supposedly near poverty, is dressed in a high quality dress of exemplary neatness. There is nothing to add about the mad old woman. She walks the streets and boulevards of this unusual City of Kalinov in the same bright golden dress that she has saved from the Hermitage Ball at the time of Catherine the Great and, a marvelous thing possible only in Kalinov, the dress has not a single stain, as though it has just been taken from the trunk.

Such is this masquerade. The color and elegance of the costumes give an impression of illusion, of a fairy-tale life.[202]

Kugel's objections were at least specific. Meyerhold's constant and irreconcilable opponent Benois, in his article on *The Storm*, poured out his displeasure without bothering with argumentation. "This," he wrote, "is something so strange that one is left astonished. These are symptoms of some terrible disease. Here one cannot even level an accusation of carelessness; everything we see has a deliberate and even thorough character. Not just a failure, but monstrous blindness."

In examining the causes of this blindness Benois stated flatly that this was no less than "seeds of German dominance"! Such an accusation in 1916 at the height of the Russo-German war evidently was made quite consciously, since further on Benois in an attack of patriotic excitement affirmed: "In the northern Capital-hothouse, Russian truth ought to be cultivated with particular care, and woe to us if for stupid amusement we distort the exalted and magnificent things produced by our Motherland... The Alexandrinsky Theater must, in addition to various other tasks, be a 'living museum of Russian life,' a magic lantern throwing the 'reflection of all Russia' on the Finnish shores."

Benois did not find this patriotism in Meyerhold's production. He wrote: "Odd buffoons and marionettes walk around among colorless rags, muttering and singing something, all this with no hint at some truth, with no glimmering of life. . . ." Benois was outraged by Roshchina-Insarova. "It is impossible to love this hysterical woman rustling her silks and wrapped in scarves, snarling, dissatisfied with her milieu, a bored and boring lady," he complained. Katerina "only rustles her silks, becomes angry and bored and not one spark from her soul breaks through. This figure is from a glass case in a historical museum and not a living person."

It is interesting that Benois's unappealable sentence was passed not immediately after the premiere but nine months later. The critic explained his belated statement in this way: "It is only recently that I finally saw *The Storm* in the new production at the Alexandrinsky Theater. Its success last season was so great that I was unable to get a seat."[203] This admission is curious. After nearly all the newspapers in a single voice had denounced Meyerhold's *The Storm*, Benois was unable to get a seat for nine months. This indicates that at this time there was no agreement between the reviewers and the public. What interested the viewers and what did they see as the meaning of the show? Telyakovsky's diaries answer this question somewhat.

Following the dress rehearsal of January 8, 1916, he wrote:

The play is performed in the spirit of the 40s and leaves a strong impression. The decorations and costumes that should be the background for the play, in this staging are not only the background but act as a complement to the customs of old Russia that are unfurled before us, thus putting the life of those days into greater relief. Watching Ostrovsky's *The Storm* one sees, first of all, that much in our day has changed only superficially and, second, one understands the reason for the existence and development of many present-day phenomena. In this poetry there is much of the dark force, evil, and ugliness that have sent long roots into Russian life and society, and if Junkerdom is made out of Germans, the true moral and sincere savages of the twentieth century, then these mores laid the ground for the shameless bribe-takers, thieves and lawless legalists of today's Russia. The stress on the insignificance of the poor, and on the power and lawful tyranny of the rich as expressed with full conviction by the characters in the play could not but influence subsequent generations.[204]

Thus Meyerhold's secret motives came to the surface. While avoiding fidelity to life, rejecting the idea of a direct depiction of the "Kingdom of Darkness" and by transforming the prosaic and wild Kalinov into a fairy-city Kitezh, Meyerhold removed the dramatic situation of *The Storm* from the specific historical environment of mid-nineteenth century Russia. This made obvious the relevance of this situation for the early twentieth century. Poeticized, it gained the significance of universality. Instead of the specific merchants' dark kingdom and dark life, there stepped forth the power of dark spiritual forces that even Telyakovsky (by no means the most perceptive viewer) understood. What was essentially Russian stepped forth in a generalized and threatening form, the past merged with the present, and caused one to think anxiously about the future. "In this poetry there is much dark power, evil and ugliness"—this was the emotional conclusion, the sum of the show, as we have just ascertained. What opposed these dark forces? In other words, what was Katerina's theme?

On the day of the premiere Telyakovsky observed that they gave "Roshchina a great deal of applause."[205]

In the reviews, the success of the actress went virtually unnoticed. Only Botsyanovsky wrote in *Stock-Exchange News (Birzhevye vedomosti)*: "Roshchina-Insarova with her large, sad blue eyes and general appearance of a waif, right out of a painting by Nesterov—a better Katerina could not be found... During the menacing prophesying by her emotional voice the hall was deathly quiet... One actually became fearful."[206] Subsequently, the other actors in *The Storm* reacted to Roshchina-Insarova with delight. Khodotov, who played Tikhon, wrote that the actress "was highly successful in the role of Katerina,"[207] while Yurev, who played Boris, remembered her "as though painted by Nesterov" and the music of her speech as "direct from the depths of Old-Believerdom."[208]

The Nesterovian and ikonic beauty of Meyerhold's Katerina, the delicacy and fragility, the martyr-like clasping of her hands, the mournful Old Believer-like singsong delivery all gave the heroine of the show a sad detachment, a practically somnambulistic separation from life. Katerina was by herself and not herself, with an impossible love and inevitable disaster, unable to open herself completely to anyone, misunderstood by all and needed by no one. In complete and frozen solitude she moved through the play. While criticizing Roshchina the critics nonetheless admitted that the best moments of the role were the conversation with Varvara in the first act ("Why do people not fly...") and the meeting with the madwoman in the end of the fourth act, i.e., specifically those moments where Katerina's terror before life, before its prosaic quality and its madness, is most painfully acute. All the reviewers agreed that "the famous scene with the key was feeble."[209] This was inevitable, however. For Roshchina-Katerina, intent and aware of being doomed, this moment of vacillation, doubt and indecision was, naturally, mere convention, while the doubts themselves appeared insubstantial if not contrived.

No, such a Katerina did not hesitate. Out from under the colorful patterned scarf pulled down to the eyebrows, Katerina's anxious, questioning, and unanswering eyes looked distractedly at the key (as if rejecting the key could change anything!), at Kalinov's satiated and pretentious satisfaction, and at the languorous and intoxicating but equally satiated love between Varvara and Kudryash.

It is curious that one of the reviews mentioned that in Meyerhold's production Varvara and not Katerina was "a ray of light. . . ."[210] In any event, Rostova's Varvara performed "energetically" and depicted "a unique girl who could not be intimidated."[211] But for Roshchina-Katerina there was nothing attractive in Varvara's freedom and defiant independence. Varvara was interpreted as the most free and live manifestation of that world of "buffoons" in which all were united—Dikoi, Kabanikha, Kudryash, the madwoman in her bright gold gown dating from the times of Catherine the Great and even Tikhon—a world that distinctly was resisted by Katerina.

Her beauty, cold and severe, was an exterior manifestation of moral purity and a benumbed soul. "When Katerina-Roshchina in Meyerhold's *The Storm* fell on her knees in ecstatic rapture before the images," recalled B. Alpers, "she spread the folds of her heavy silk dress artistically and with a graceful motion raised her thin arms, pausing for a moment as though on the canvas of an exquisite artist."[212]

Here in this most interesting contradiction between Katerina's "ecstasy" and her care for the beauty of the folds of her dress, these "rustling silks" that so annoyed Benois, Meyerhold's heroine was contained complete, as in a drop of water—elegant, refined, and doomed.

Wrapped in her scarves Katerina appeared to know something that no one else knew. She was Nesterovian but also Blokian. The woman who had gone through Blok's poetry and who wore "the patterned scarf down to her eyebrows" stepped onto the Alexandrinsky stage "so calm and light as though she had freely given the Fallen Angel her hand." Her enviable freedom lay in her detachment, her destiny, and her readiness to perish. For Meyerhold this was an inviting image of an essentially Romantic heroine who set against the ornate, satiated and loutish carnival of existence her possibly indistinct and vague but in any case high and prouder predestination.

Such was the first serious large-scale attempt by Meyerhold to stage a Russian classic. It is, however, logical that in the war years, years full of patriotic excitement that served to conceal Russian Imperial ambitions, Meyerhold paid particular attention to classical Russian drama and the Russian past.

It was without his old enthusiasm and spirit that Meyerhold staged the pantomime *Columbine's Scarf* in the spring of 1916 in Actors' Rest, Boris Pronin's small theater whose auditorium walls were painted by S. Sudeikin and the foyer by B. Grigoriev and A. Yakovlev. One of the few reviews read that "the revived pantomime gave the impression of a well-assembled mechanism. And, as everyone knows, a mechanism is a dead thing... The bright and healthy extract of carnival that is preached by Doctor Dapertutto-Meyerhold . . . has blurred and faded."[213]

V. N. Solovyov insisted that the wilting of pantomime had taken place because the artist had been replaced: Sapunov had decorated the 1910 production and Sudeikin did the 1916 version. These two artists who had made their debut together in 1905 in the Studio on Povarskaya Street understood and perceived theater in different ways. Sapunov was perfectly acquainted with theatrical technique. He "had his own colors but always was able to match them to the individuality of the play on which he was working." For Sudeikin theater was "an exhibition gallery of huge proportions." Decoration became his only aim and he would transform the stage into a huge tapestry. Sudeikin, wrote Solovyov, "sometimes does not feel the theater"[214] and he "choked" *Columbine's Scarf* with excessive magnificence.

The coldness of this performance at least partially reflected Meyerhold's cooling toward the idea of pure theatricality. In any event, again (how many times!) while rebuking the Moscow Art Theater for naturalism after its obvious failure in the production of Merezhkovsky's *There Will Be Joy*, Meyerhold unexpectedly came out in defense of "mood" and against "introduced" directorial scenes that were separate from the main idea of the play. He said:

> It is necessary to reject naturalism on the stage and to provide more mood, more vivid, genuine life. Let many theaters err, but it is vexing, painfully vexing, to allow this error in the Moscow Art Theater. In the last play of this season, Merezhkovsky's play *There Will Be Joy*, this naturalistic method of staging is felt quite clearly. I, personally, and a whole circle of Russian theatrical activists adhering to the ideas of a new theater are nauseated by this tiresome naturalism.
>
> I shall tell you that in real theater *it is necessary to perform the play itself and not to present introduced scenes that only take up the time of the actors and the attention of the director.*
>
> . . . The once-burgeoning *enormous* Art Theater gradually lessened, gradually separated from the theater of mood for which it was best prepared and stubbornly, sneering at everything in its path, moved toward antiquated naturalism.
>
> And this is bad.
>
> If the directors of the Art Theater had heeded Chekhov, they never would have left the strictly marked path and never would have reached the dead end where, happy and beaming, they now stand.[215]

Meyerhold's criticism of the production staged by Nemirovich-Danchenko was, evidently, motivated in part by the fact that he himself intended to stage another play by Merezhkovsky, *The Romantics*, at this time. It was set in the 1830s and, consequently, was in line with Meyerhold's particular interest in Russia's past. The hero of the play was Bakunin, played by Yu. Yurev. The premiere of *The Romantics* took place in the Alexandrinsky Theater on October 21, 1916. L. Ya. Gurevich wrote the most thorough and serious discussion of the show. She wrote:

> The name of the central character of the play so exciting to the mind and imagination, the light aroma of an era associated with the images dear to the Russian intelligentsia of Belinsky and Stankevich, the beautiful and tender women's figures in the poetic costumes and hair styles of the 30s; quotations from Romantic poetry and singing to the accompaniment of a harp and the bright-blue moonlight pouring through the windows of the spacious passage of the ancient merchant's house, and in general everything "showy" in the play itself and Golovin's colorful decorations—all this together with the ringing name of the author explains sufficiently well its external success... Merezhkovsky's inevitable "polarity" of images was given this time by life itself: Mikhail Bakunin is the all-destroying flame of thought in the absence of spontaneous feeling, the highest exaltation of a powerful mind, incarnated rebellion and movement; the modest Dyakov is a noble heart uninitiated to consciousness, a man capable of the greatest sacrifice but incapable of catching fire with destructively creative ideas. Merezhkovsky consciously tried to increase this contrast and present images that incarnated the "mind of the brain" on the one hand, and the "mind of the

heart" on the other hand.[216]

In this way, L. Gurevich willy-nilly indicated the purely "intellectual," rational and artificial construction of the play in which emotion (Dyakov) and intellect (Bakunin) were presented in a static antithesis, in a diagram. Meyerhold attempted to destroy this arrangement by offering the actors Stanislavsky's classic prescription: "if you are playing an evil (character)—look for where he is good." Yurev tried to play Bakunin with all the expansiveness and "actor's fire" of which he was capable, recalling even Ferdinand from Schiller's *Intrigue and Love*. The role of the passionate Dyakov was deliberately assigned to the coldly reasonable Leshkov. In this way the plan given by Merezhkovsky was overthrown by the actors. However, with the exception of this plan no idea or thought remained in the play. Even Telyakovsky, who felt that the critics were unnecessarily harsh in their criticism of the play and that "the actors have mastered their tasks and all performed well: Yurev, Kovalenskaya, Yakovlev, Leshkov, Shigorina, Domasheva, etc.", concluded unexpectedly: "There is, of course, little sense in the play and it is difficult to understand the author's aims, but the play is entertaining."[217]

This last comment, with its homey spontaneity, is probably the most correct. Most amusing was the fact that the birth of the idea of Anarchism grew directly out of the banal love intrigue in the Bakunin household... There really was little sense to this play.

The Romantics was followed on the dramatic stage by Dargomyzhsky's *The Stone Guest* in the Mariinsky Opera House. Dargomyzhsky's opera had not been staged since 1872, nearly half a century. Much was resolved for Meyerhold in this work. On the one hand the beloved and proven theme of Don Juan was wrapped up, and on the other hand Meyerhold was confronted with his most important task of those years—the creation of a poetic Russian show. One should not forget that just before the staging of *The Stone Guest*, Meyerhold in his article "Benois the Director" had criticized "to the foundations" the Art Theater's staging of Pushkin, he had accused Benois of completely misunderstanding Pushkin's poetry and style, and he had ridiculed the "rattling of chains, clicking of locks and calls of the night watchmen" and, in general, the heavy naturalism with which Pushkin was performed on the Art Theater stage.

Now Meyerhold had to prove in actual practice that a substantially new approach to Pushkin's Little Tragedies was possible and productive. The fact that this was not a Pushkin play but an opera by Dargomyzhsky both simplified and complicated matters. The inevitable "relativisms" of opera in this case coincided fully with Meyerhold's intentions. At the same time they bound him to an original solution that would completely eliminate the impression of banality and habit. The opera would have to be without the standardized operatic elements. Pushkin was to be heard through and together with Dargomyzhsky.

One of Meyerhold's chief staging ideas this time led to a substantial reduction of the dimensions of the stage.

This idea was suggested by Dargomyzhsky's work itself, which was a recitative chamber opera, and Meyerhold implemented it with his characteristic virtuosity and boldness of spatial solutions. The action was concentrated purposely on a small performing area, a "chamber," in contrast to the usual tendency of opera to spread laterally and seize the entire stage. Golovin built an enormous black-violet and silver portal, decorated it with columns and statues, thereby reducing the mirror of the stage by half. The resulting small stage was covered with a special black curtain. This small stage also was raised up slightly and connected by several steps to the jutting proscenium. In this manner Meyerhold created a most unusual—for opera—combination of a small mirror stage with a great depth that was increased further by the proscenium, and he discovered utterly unexpected possibilities for the construction of scenes receding into the distance.

Speaking of the basic principles for the staging of *The Stone Guest* Meyerhold affirmed that in this work "we have before us a sort of Spain of masquerades from the imagination of the poet whose tastes reflected all the features of the Russian artistic mood of the 1830s."

Thus, the director openly connected his work on *The Stone Guest* with his work on Lermontov's *Masquerade*. He continued: "Consequently, the staging avoids even a hint at the ethnographic in the materialization on stage of Pushkin's Spain."

In other words, an attempt was made to look at the total situation of *The Stone Guest* with the eyes of Pushkin's contemporaries and with the eyes of the poet himself.

The action of three plays staged by Meyerhold from 1910 to 1917—*Don Juan, The Constant Prince* and *The Stone Guest*—takes place in Spain and each time Meyerhold showed Spain from a different point of view; the French, the Spanish and the Russian, retaining the Spanish flavor while stylistically altering the entire presentation of the play in accordance with the spirits of Molière, Calderón or Pushkin.

Therefore, one imagined Pushkin's Spain, the Spain of masquerade. Some specific solutions are interesting. In the first scene, said Meyerhold, "a cemetery is usually shown on stage and they forget completely to show the gates of Madrid (line two of the play: 'we reached the walls of Madrid'). Thanks to the introduction of the proscenium we were able to arrange things so that on stage one feels the nearness of the cemetery and the proximity of the city where Don Juan is going."

Since he felt that in principle Don Juan found all women equally desirable and that each was just a new manifestation of the same passion, that "Laura and Donna Anna are different masks for the identical erotic essence," Meyerhold suggested to Golovin that he make the rooms of the two women identical. This solution brought to the point of acute paradox the thought of fatal error and the soullessness of Don Juan, for whom there is no difference between Laura's open temperament and the secret, smoldering and suppressed sensuality of Donna Anna.

"The third scene," continued Meyerhold, "is the Commander's tomb. The Commander's statue is placed in such a way that the public sees its profile. This causes an exceptional effect in the scene where Leporello invites the Commander's statue to dine with Don Juan."

Finally, Meyerhold described the staging of the finale of the tragedy—here with maximum artistic effect he implemented the capabilities of a narrow and deep stage, presenting "a long corridor leading into the depths along a whole series of steps."

First from the gloomy distance of this corridor "in a design of nervous, trembling zigzags" Don Juan ran out and up to the edge of the proscenium. Behind him in a totally straight line and with slow, inevitable tread the Commander's figure moved toward the public. "This," stressed Meyerhold, "increases the terror."[218]

I. Alchevsky sang the role of Don Juan, M. Cherkasskaya played Donna Anna and V. Pavlinova—Laura. When Laura sang her song she was accompanied by a small orchestra located right on the stage.

This last circumstance perplexed the musical critics, but all in all the reviews of the show, which was first performed on January 27, 1917, were quite favorable.

One of the reviewers wrote that "the character of opera is excellently understood here," that the result of the work by Meyerhold, the painter Golovin, and the orchestra director Malko was "a picture of a show of rare beauty and surprising consistency of mood."[219] Even Kugel's magazine *Theater and Art* commented on the production without its usual irritation. It is true that the reviewer in this magazine wrote that in the production

> . . . the *Guest's* mysticism, hardly noticeable in Pushkin and Dargomyzhsky, was overstressed and gloomy, funereal tones moved to the foreground... In this sense no compromise is made even in the life-filled scene with Laura where intentionally, it appears, the performers' temperament is restrained and the orchestra director is restrained... Mr. Golovin's decorations are bright and beautiful but sufficiently "unreal." The costumes sewn to the drawings of the same painter are also colorful but have a flavor of the masquerade. Ethnographic fidelity is excluded from the staging of *The Stone Guest* on the Mariinsky stage: there is nothing to suggest that the action takes place in Spain.

"However," admitted the reviewer, "there is virtually nothing Spanish in Dargomyzhsky's music with the exception of two of Laura's songs."[220]

It would be naive to suppose that A. Benois would ignore this staging of *The Stone Guest* and miss the opportunity of settling accounts with Meyerhold for his article "Benois the Director." In the next "Art Letter," entitled "Staging *The Stone Guest* on the State Stage," Benois used up an entire arsenal of imprecations to denigrate his old opponent and adversary. He wrote here of the "disgraceful"—none other—"flouting of Pushkin and Dargomyzhsky," the violation of "Russian literature and Russian music," of "vandalism" and "big-city dandyism," "the rape of estheticism," "the caprices of subjectivism"; he said that Meyerhold "murdered a living artist" (i.e., Golovin) and seized the Imperial Theaters ("since now," Benois points out helpfully, "this is no longer Mr. Telyakovsky's theater") and he said that on the stages of these theaters "instead of living actors and living drama appear overdressed puppets dancing some little ballet (always the same one) to the tune of the director."

All this thunder and lightning, the jeering comments on how Meyerhold could become an "irreplaceable arranger of all sorts of holidays" who would invent "allegorical fireworks," make it difficult to discern Benois's positive program. But, in the end, it is mentioned. Benois proclaims that "every line, every word of Pushkin's demands *verisimilitude*." Inquiring "how did Pushkin imagine Don Juan's Spain?", he returns directly to the Moscow Art Theater's recent production:

The mention of El Escorial brought us in the Art Theater to the era of El Escorial's creator, Philip II. Nothing in Pushkin contradicted this and, on the other hand, this obliged the performers to respond with particular thoughtfulness to the manifestation of those emotional experiences that are governed by the demon of lust, the cry of blood and the law of retribution... It was neccessary to begin with the text, to learn it and to become immersed in it, to begin with the creation of characters and the exploration of all the psychological threads. Only after fixing these discoveries in professional rehearsal work would it be possible to give them an external form of expression both in the sense of a plan and the sense of costumes and decoration.[221]

In other words, Benois demanded absolute fidelity to those principles which guided him and Stanislavsky and Nemirovich-Danchenko during their work on the Pushkin play in the Art Theater in 1915. Subsequently, Stanislavsky had praised Benois for "incredible, majestic decorations and excellently styled costumes for this production." But in analyzing his lack of success in the role of Salieri, Stanislavsky, essentially for the first time, placed in doubt those very principles which Benois was defending as absolute. Stanislavsky recalled how he "tried to fathom fully the entire internal essence of the drama," by beginning with the re-creation of the character "from the exploration of all the psychological threads." And he failed. "It is painful," wrote Stanislavsky, "to be unable to reproduce correctly what you feel beautifully within yourself." For these troubles, an answer quite different from Stanislavsky's previous efforts was found. Stanislavsky "understood that we not only on stage but in life speak plainly and ungrammatically, that *our everyday trivial simplicity of speech is unallowable on stage*." This discovery marked a fundamental and extremely important turn in Stanislavsky's approach.

His mind now strove to grasp precisely those spheres of poetry in which Meyerhold had been experimenting for a long time. But Stanislavsky sought out his own, different ways, based on principles of fidelity to organic nature.

"Speech and verse are the same music, the same song," Stanislavsky now averred. "The voice must sing in conversation and in verse, sound *violinlike* and *not hammer out* words like peas against a board. How can we achieve in conversation a sound that is continuous, flowing, merging words and complete phrases, passing through them like a thread through beads and not breaking them up into separate syllables?"[222]

In these thoughts the verbal *form* of the role on which Meyerhold had worked for many years received the focus of Stanislavsky's attention. The staging of Pushkin was a move in this direction.

The problem of reading a verse text remained open and undecided for the Moscow Art Theater. Following the premiere of Pushkin's play, Fyodor Sologub wrote with unconcealed sadness:

Pushkin was staged by a theater that is very good, of course, but one which has moved far from the living movement of Russian poetry. A theater that denies the existence of dramas by Alexander Blok, Valery Bryusov, Vyacheslav Ivanov, Alexei Remizov, and others, decided to return to the source of living Russian poetry, to Pushkin. Most laudable! . . . the verse has spoiled everything. . . . The Art Theater wished to treat Pushkin's created legend as a straightforward depiction of events and experiences. But the forgotten art has had its vengeance by presenting the Art Theater with failure....[223]

This episode with Pushkin's theater caused Stanislavsky to review the entire internal technique he had developed and to ponder again the special means of expression required by drama in verse.

Consequently, Benois attacked Meyerhold from positions that Stanislavsky already had abandoned. The defeat recognized by Stanislavsky was interpreted by Benois as a victory whose lessons were to be learned without question, and thoroughly studied by dissidents. All this together with the irritated, quarrelsome and haughty tone today give Benois's article the significance of one of the most expressive documents testifying to how often the truly new in art is met with an authoritative, important, firm but nonetheless totally powerless, internally anemic and essentially helpless conservatism.

In order to evaluate on merit the significance of Benois's article on Meyerhold's staging of Pushkin, we should add that although Stanislavsky did understand when pondering the role of Salieri the great significance of the error in ignoring the expressive potential of verse, he nonetheless was unable ever to achieve real success in this specific sphere.

Meyerhold radically and thoroughly resolved this problem in *Masquerade*. He had been moving firmly toward this end since the times of *The Death of Tintagiles* and *Sister Beatrice*, but here the difficulties were enormous for him, too, and they partially explain the unusually long time Meyerhold spent working on *Masquerade*.

In February, 1917, this work was finally brought to a close. The dress rehearsal was held on February 23. Telyakovsky observed in his diary: "Golovin's staging is really incredibly beautiful, and in the smallest details. When one sees it it is not surprising that Golovin worked on it for several years. Concerning the acting, I can have no real impression since Studentsov did not speak at all (fearing a sore throat for tomorrow), Yurev rehearsed *sotto voce* and, furthermore, I was continually being distracted...."[224]

The next morning, on February 24, a dress rehearsal with paid attendance was played before a full house. Telyakovsky again watched *Masquerade* and this time his reaction sounded quite disappointed. He wrote:

> The staging of *Masquerade* depressed me. As I had supposed previously and told Golovin, it is not theater's affair to work on detail and minor points of staging to the extent that 5 years are required to do the staging. Of course the decorations, props and costumes are wonderful, separately and together, but these are no longer decorations, costumes, and props but real things as in life, since artists do not become involved in every setting or garment in life.
>
> This so-called excess of taste crushed everything—the play, the actors, and their acting. The result is an exposition in the middle of which the actors were saying something which, despite all their efforts, remained disconnected, so that the show lacked a pivotal point. Not only was there no impression, but it was boring, especially for me, seeing it for a second time. Meyerhold placed and trained the actors with the same floridity and extravagances as Golovin's staging. The fact that there was a single teacher for the actors was apparent, and again it was not at all as in life, since in life not everyone is affected—some simply live. Consequently, both wished to depict life but then depicted a museum with figures from *Coppelia*.[225]

—230—

The situation had become quite acute. The production which had been in preparation for five years, which Meyerhold, in Kugel's acrid words, "built like a Pharaoh building his Pyramid," was being readied during the days when the Russian capital was caught in the flames of the February Revolution.

Kugel's pen recorded the circumstances surrounding the premiere of *Masquerade*.

This show—the first presentation of *Masquerade*—was on Saturday, February 25, when the Revolution already was in full swing. In the streets, distant ones, it is true, there was firing. The trolleys were not running, the streetlamps burned dimly... Scarce cabdrivers asked incredible sums. Cries could be heard and crowds with flags were gathering. There were no people and it was eerie. The theater, however, was full—and at what prices! In the 6th row a seat cost 22 or 23 rubles... At the theater entrance automobiles stood in solid black rows. All the wealth, all the nobility, all of Petrograd's enormous pluto- bureau- and behind-the-lines-ocracy had turned out.

Kugel continued:

On this tragic evening of Russian history there was something that persistently, annoyingly, and continuously confronted the eye. When the first curtain rose, artistically painted by Mr. Golovin, then came a second painted by him with equal artistry, then, for some reason a third and then a fourth of transparent gauze, while in the wings stood portals of undetermined significance with gilded sculptural decorations by Mr. Evseev and the costumes flickered past, one more magnificent, more incredible, more intricate and, I dare say, more stupid than the next, and everyone was exclaiming, "ah, ah, ah, how luxurious, how rich!"—in a word, when this Babylon of mindlessly absurd luxury appeared before me in all its Semiramide artistic lasciviousness I was afraid. I knew—everyone knew—that two or three versts away crowds of people were shouting for bread and that some Protopopovian policemen receiving 70 rubles per diem were pouring machine-gun lead on these hungry people craving bread. And here, practically next door, or in any case so close in the same city, next to the hungering crowds was this artistically debauched, arrogantly wasteful and senselessly decadent luxury for amusement. What is this? Imperial Rome? What next? Shall we go from here to dine on nightingales' tongues at Lucullus's and let the hungry rabble yell, seeking food and freedom?"

The critic continued:

That evening, oh, that evening!—I was outraged violently: the whole decay of the regime in the senseless wastefulness of this so-called artistic staging!.. For the entire time from behind the sculpted portals and absurd curtains that were lowered to the proscenium at the least appropriate moment someone fat and self-satisfied despite all his quasi-artistry would push out insolently and arrogantly and proclaim: "My master has a lot of money! This is not all I can show you!"

Kugel's remarks on the essense of the show were brief and derisive. "The weaknesses of Lermontov's play (and in *Masquerade* there is much that is weak and imitative) are stressed and underscored; the strong sides are shaded and blurred." To perform this play worse than it was performed in the Alexandrinsky Theater "is possible, of course, but to play it more absurdly is impossible, just as it is impossible to stage the play more absurdly... There was not one role performed properly, not one character represented correctly and in the spirit of the author."

The following dark words concluded the article:

> In the last scene a requiem was sung for the dead. Nina, poisoned by Arbenin. The director made an entire spectacle of this requiem. Little old ladies in coats appeared from somewhere, the Arkhangelsky choir sang...
>
> Somewhere in the distance there was shooting and crying for bread...
>
> And in this requiem that concluded the existence of the *Imperial* Theater there was something symbolic.

When Kugel was writing this temperamental, excited and bilious article, he, naturally, could not imagine that the show that seemed monstrous to him would live on the stage in a new, completely transformed world for over two more decades, or that an entire literature would be written discussing this spectacle, that many dozens of articles and many pages of reminiscences would be devoted to it. Or that twelve years later he himself, Kugel, would take a new look at this play (and all of Meyerhold's art). If in 1917 he heard from Arbenin-Yurev only "a cascade of insensitive ups and downs whose name is immoderate declamation,"[226] then in 1927 he saw this Arbenin as "a fatal executioner, irresistible as fate," who kills "with the coldness of a soul impervious to mercy," etc.[227]

Kugel erred often and erred decisively. He was mistaken this time as well. Still, his first review, filled as it is with noble indignation, is far more interesting than the subsequent retrospective and somewhat abashed discussions. In the article written immediately after the premiere of *Masquerade* there is an astonished and angry expression of the essential—that sense of fear, of earth's end, of Empire's end, which in the final accounting dominated Meyerhold's production and which even then, misunderstood as it was, created an enormous impression. The force of this impression breaks through Kugel's review. His whole article appears twisted up. In it are mixed together, piled up, the incredible contrasts of that historic evening: firing in the streets, no trolley cars, crowds gathered with flags to ask for bread. Petrograd is empty and eerie while by the Alexandrinsky Theater automobiles are parked in solid black rows, the theater is filled with all the nobility, all the dazzle and light of the capital and on the stage—a fantastically magnificent spectacle...

It appeared to Kugel that the theatrical performance that he saw was in absurd and ugly contrast with reality, with the grim and catastrophic life surrounding the theater, that Meyerhold's art in this moment demonstrated an extreme alienation from reality, that between the storm of Revolution already roaring through the capital and the production on the stage there were no points in common.

In fact, the situation was different. Meyerhold's spectacle sounded a dark requiem for Empire, a majestic and threatening, tragic and fatal requiem for the world that was perishing during those days.

This is not an inference that Meyerhold over a period of many years consciously had been preparing such a requiem and had guessed exactly the day and hour to place the score on the music stand and conduct. Not at all. In Meyerhold's art much was determined consciously and thoughtfully, but the essence nearly always occurred as if independent of the artist's will or design. Intuition invariably outstripped his reason, suddenly would suggest the most unexpected discoveries and finds which would suit the pulse of the time with uncanny precision and which no one ever could explain adequately. Something totally unexpected would suddenly appear in his stage compositions and subordinate them completely, puzzling contemporaries, surprising or annoying the critics and then presenting the historians with the inconceivable exactitude of coincidence—down to the very day.

So it was with *Masquerade*. The work, which had been slow, progressing in stops and starts, the object of Meyerhold's total enthusiasm or, sometimes, his bored inattention, suddenly matured and was ready precisely at that correct day and hour.*

The unusual circumstances on the days of the dress rehearsal and premiere have been recorded in the memoirs of numerous authors. "The premiere was on the 25th of February, 1917," wrote E. Timé, "and a day later autocracy was overthrown—the February Revolution began. There was shooting in the streets. A bullet killed a student in the vestibule of our theater. Patrols checked documents in the streets. The lights went out."[228]

Ya. Malyutin recalled "the flame of bonfires that had been lit at crossroads," pedestrians at night who, "looking to all sides, hurried home," since "there already was a crossfire in the streets and barricades were being constructed."[229]

In Telyakovsky's diary immediately following the information that the premiere of *Masquerade* was "a great success," "disturbances" in the capital are mentioned. On February 26 he wrote: "This is the second day of disturbances in Petersburg, at first for economic reasons, then shifting to political grounds. Lack of bread and food. There are strikes in factories and plants, even those working for defense. Today there were no newspapers and they say there will be none tomorrow." The next day, February 27, Telyakovsky wrote: "There has been much anxiety in Petrograd since this morning. Various rumors are circulating—including those of uprisings in the army. There is particularly persistent talk of an uprising in the Pavlovsk regiment and of the murder of the commander. The barracks supposedly are surrounded by the Preobrazhensky regiment. Evidently a revolution has begun."[230]

A. Ya. Golovin told how on the way to the premiere of *Masquerade* Meyerhold and he "ran across the Nevsky under fire." He wrote that the "increasing revolutionary movement in the city augured failure for the first show," but nonetheless "the show went magnificently" and in these days attracted "heightened interest."[231]

Of course this interest also could be explained in part by the exceptionally long preparation time of the show and by its fantastic cost. ("Such a volume of objects to be prepared for a show has never been seen in Russian theater, I believe," wrote N. V. Petrov later. "This staging cost three hundred thousand in gold. The scale of the creative undertaking was grandiose. . . ."[232])

---

*N. V. Petrov wrote on this subject: "Of course, work on *Masquerade* was not continuous over five years but went on with interruptions. It would be rehearsed for 2-3 months, then set aside for 1 or 2. Then it would be rehearsed again and again set aside. Sometimes we would rehearse half a year and not touch it for another half year" (Nikolai Petrov, *50 i 500* [M: VTO, 1960], p. 128).

Nonetheless, something else was of far greater importance. The leitmotif of *Masquerade* in the Meyerholdian version became the theme of illusion, sham and ghostliness of that world which in these days was receding irretrievably into the past. The title of Lermontov's drama, *Masquerade*, was decoded by an enormous metaphor that encompassed the entire action from start to finish: the masquerade of an entire era, an entire complex and intricate life, supposedly authentic but in fact a false and lying masquerade of relations that do not express but only conceal, hide and kill real feelings.

A second and no less important leitmotif in the show was that of play. Play replacing life, substituting for its painful but natural and true drama artificial, false and "intentional" dramas designed to excite jaded feelings and unexpectedly ending in real blood and smelling of death. Cards and masks—sham drama and sham people, conditional play instead of life, artificial manners. Thus the phantasmagorical image of the show was created.

In 1911, when he was just beginning to work on *Masquerade*, Meyerhold wrote that the atmosphere of Lermontov's play is saturated with "demonism"; he wrote of "murders through tears" and of "laughter after a murder."[233] The concept of "demonism" gradually coalesced in the figure of Unknown *(Neizvestnyi*="The Unknown" or "The Stranger")*, Meyerhold's special interest. The ominous, enigmatic genius-murderer moved from deep in the last century to the forefront of this show.

The "Unknown," wrote Meyerhold, "is a hired killer. Society hires Unknown to take vengeance on Arbenin for 'his devilish contempt for everything, of which he boasted everywhere...' " "The death of Pushkin and the death of Lermontov, as we recall the evil plots of society in the thirties, these two deaths are the best sources for clarifying the significance and mystery of Unknown. Martynov stands behind Lermontov's back like a shadow and waits for orders from his 'side.'"

This interpretation of the meaning of tragedy also suggested forms for its materialization. Meyerhold was excited by "the conjunction of gloss with *demonism*." Actors, he wrote, must be aware of "beautiful form," even "glossy form," but beneath this sheen passions must rage. Arbenin, continued Meyerhold, " . . . is tossed into the whirlwind of the masquerade so that the web of masked intrigues and accidents envelops him like a fly... When there is no mask and when it is worn by the participants in the masquerade is not to be understood. Thus merge the limits: of masquerade, frightful life, 'society'!"

The search for style led from Lermontov to Byron, from nineteenth-century Petersburg to eighteenth-century Venice. Romanticism was summarized in the formula taken by Meyerhold from P. Muratov's book, *Pictures of Italy*. The formula was: "Mask, candle, mirror—this is the image of eighteenth-century Venice." But the Venetian properties again returned to the specifics of Russian social life of the past century. Meyerhold wrote that the images of Lermontov's *Masquerade* were, for him, "on the boundary of delirium, hallucination."[234]

Ya. Malyutin wrote:

In the interpretation of the director, decorator and composer, Unknown became a symbolic figure in the full sense of the word: his exterior was ferocious, as was the musical theme that accompanied his appearance on the stage, even his very voice was ferocious—

the severe and prophetic voice of a merciless and angry judge. The black mantle and the repulsive mask in which he appeared at Engelhardt's masquerade, the top hat and the tightly buttoned coat that he wore, made Unknown not a man, but a devil in disguise... Unknown's implacable, evil will held in its hands the course of events and predetermine the tragic conclusion of the drama.[235]

This image appears to attain a finality as a specific incarnation of the theme of Fate, which passed through many of Meyerhold's previous spectacles and which only now found its final form in the figure of a single person. Fate no longer floated over the show, permeating the atmosphere and causing all to listen and wait tensely. No, now it entered the crowd, walked through it. He, this fully concrete but enigmatic man enveloped in mystery, carried in himself death for others. Arbenin plays with fate. Unknown plays with Arbenin...

The theme of Fate, of destiny so distinctly personified, gained an all-inclusive significance. By re-creating the atmosphere of Lermontov's time and the style of Nicholas I's Russia, Meyerhold and Golovin in this show presented a wider and more voluminous image—the image of Empire. Taking advantage of the extreme terseness of Lermontov's directions, which allow one only to guess at the place of action, the director and artist majestically erected on the stage the image of palatial, majestic and monumental Russia, and enveloped its festive contours with a sweetly poisonous, bewitching, stiflingly spicy atmosphere. Russia appeared as it no longer was and could not be. In the colorful and dignified movement of the masquerade, in the passion of the game and the intense and risky collision of secret passions, the past arose and gazed menacingly from the stage into the hall.

It should be explained how the production interacted with the time when it was staged. Autocratic Russia was collapsing before everyone's eyes. Its Imperial grandeur became a phantom and everything smelled of decay. The entire solemn ritual of the Court, the magnificent uniforms, the bewitching power of rank, the strict etiquette, the indestructible preeminence of tradition, the arrogance of the nobility, heraldry, orders, epaulettes, reviews, parades—it was as if they had been licked off by a cow's tongue. Everything was disappearing or had disappeared. Everything that had been indubitable, substantial, and weighty reality became mystically ephemeral, dubious; everything was in question. It was all drowning in the Rasputin business, reverses on the front, in corruption, bribery, espionage-mania, in the loud spasmodic patriotism of the newspapers, in drunkenness.

The advertising sections of the Petrograd newspapers were filled with advertisements by jewelers who were buying up gold, silver and precious stones for prices that increased daily. Next to these were addresses of clairvoyants, fortune-tellers and seers: "Learn your fate!" These enterprising visionaries claiming to have come from India or Egypt competed with palmists, fortune-tellers using coffee grounds, and Gypsies who used cards...

At this same moment Meyerhold and Golovin showed worn-out, perishing Imperial Petrograd a splendid and fearful vision, at once opulent and tragic. The words "learn your fate" could have been written on the playbill. The difference between the clairvoyants and Meyerhold was that Meyerhold gave encouragement to no one. The spectacle prophesied disaster and the end of the world. "Sunset of

Empire" the play was called. It was also called "the last spectacle of Tsarist Russia."236

Not for the first time, but in the most consistent and firm manner, Golovin and Meyerhold unified the stage decoration with the decor of the Alexandrinsky Theater hall in *Masquerade*. V. Solovyov wrote in *Apollo*:

> They constructed a proscenium and a sculpted architectural portal that was to be the frame for the show. The alternatingly lowered curtains that permitted the whole play to be performed with two intermissions characterized in a particular way that impression which the audience was to receive from a given scene. Frosted glass mirrors standing on the proscenium reflected the sea of lights in the hall, eliminating the line of the footlights which separated the audience from the stage. The mirrors, an inheritance from the theatrical era in Venice which for many people has recently been the sole source of truth of life, lent to the events on stage a special mysterious air...

The stage " . . . was framed by two staircases with railings. Sofas were placed on the edge of the proscenium and remained unchanged for the duration of the play."237

Golovin's architectural portal with two doors for the entrances of the characters repeated the motif of the auditorium's architecture, and the slender columns of the portal echoed the columns of the side boxes. Rossi had given the architecture of the hall golden ornaments on a white background, while Golovin reflected this motif as in a mirror with white ornaments against a gold background.

The stage was separated from the proscenium by the alternating curtains painted by Golovin. The main one, red and black with cards and masks, was followed by a slit curtain with bells for the masquerade scene, a white-rose-green one for the ball, snow-white lace for Nina's bedroom, funereal black with sewn-on wreaths for the finale.

The system of curtains permitted the director to deal freely with the stage space, either to open up the full depth of the stage (which Meyerhold did twice—in the masquerade and ball scenes) or to contract its dimensions. In addition to the curtains he could use screens for this purpose, framing the proscenium in different ways each time. Consequently, each of the play's ten scenes was differently placed on the stage floor. This changeability of stage space supplemented the overall impression of shifting mystery and ghostliness which Meyerhold strove to achieve.

However, what he required was not the ghostliness of vague visions and not the atmosphere of a mirage. No. He wished to achieve an impression of a shifted and somewhat infernal, totally concrete world, apparently durable and, at first sight, strong and opulent. Therefore "each object was made to Golovin's drawings—there was not a single stock prop or piece of furniture on stage. Even the playing cards, wallets or porcelain knick-knacks in the room of the Baroness—everything had been made in the prop workshop. The furniture and all the accessories were slightly larger than in real life. This made them noticeable and significant."238

Golovin's work on *Masquerade* deserves a separate examination. It is sufficient to say here that the artist had made some 4,000 sketches of costumes, makeup, furniture and props.239

Although we do not have the opportunity to describe in detail Golovin's work, we shall mention his more interesting finds. In the ball scene the artist was able, wrote B. Almedingen, "to create with the light women's dresses an astonishingly ornate background that excellently set off Nina's black train and the Prince's red coat. For Unknown he selected, most appropriately, an eighteenth-century Venetian carnival costume with a half-mask with a hawk's profile and a cape of black Venetian lace—all concealing the 'obscurity' of the character."

Golovin introduced a light-blue Pierrot into the masquerade scene to intrigue Nina and play with her bracelet. Golovin knew perfectly well that the traditional costume for Pierrot was white. But Nina wore a white domino to the masquerade and Meyerhold insisted that Nina have a pantomime scene with Pierrot. Therefore, a white Pierrot was not possible. "I recall," continued B. Almedingen, "how happy Golovin was when he found a picture of a light-blue Pierrot in some ancient volume."240

Meyerhold's work with Golovin, as usual, was in a climate of complete mutual understanding. This is evident, in particular, from the irritated notes in Telyakovsky's diary that Meyerhold had supposedly completely "saddled Golovin," that Telyakovsky and Korovin were devising ways to extract Golovin "from Meyerhold's web," etc. (In this period Telyakovsky's opinion of Meyerhold had deteriorated sharply. The Director felt that "Meyerhold is played out already," and that in general "he is flavoring his lack of talent with Golovin's talented staging."241) But Golovin continued to believe in Meyerhold and did not wish to leave the "web." He captured Meyerhold's ideas in flight and executed them masterfully.

The system of curtains that Golovin devised at Meyerhold's request allowed the director his first opportunity to use an approach which he was to re-use many times: the division of the action into episodes. The curtains often would be lowered in mid-dialogue, Meyerhold would bring the characters out onto the proscenium and then cover the stage with a curtain. This way he gained time for the set changes and achieved either extremely short intermissions or was even able to eliminate intermissions and continue the play without interruptions.

The music for the production—the quadrille, mazurka, polonaise, Nina's romance, the themes of Arbenin and Unknown and the final funeral chorus—was written by A. K. Glazunov.

Complicated problems were resolved by the director during his work with the actors. In the course of the rehearsals some roles changed hands often. For the premiere the roles were assigned as follows: Arbenin—Yu. Yurev; Nina—E. Roshchina-Insarova; Zvezdich—E. Studentsov; Baroness Strahl—E. Timé; Kazarin—B. Gorin-Goryainov; Shprikh—A. Lavrentev; Unknown—N. Barabanov.

Arbenin was the greatest problem for Meyerhold. Evidence of the extreme vacillation in his treatment of this role is contained in two notes written in 1911. In one is written: "Arbenin has a negative, aloof attitude toward 'society.' Lermontov wished to write a comedy in the spirit of *Woe from Wit*. He sounds a satirical note in *Masquerade*. He makes Arbenin into his Chatsky."242 Another note presents a different interpretation of the role: "Pechorinism in Arbenin. Autobiographical traits in Pechorin. Lermontov—Pechorin—Arbenin."243 In the end, the upper hand was had by the second conception of the role, the closest to the truth. Many years later, in 1939, Yu. Yurev, noting particularly the circumstance that the interpretation of the role had not changed with the years, that "Arbenin appeared before me in the first period of my work and became distinctly defined," that "I attempt to render him up to the present day as he appeared in my conception of him," especially stressed the autobiographical features in this Lermontovian figure. "Arbenin," he wrote, "is autobiographical in the main, despite the heavy coloring that Lermontov gave his hero."[244]

By bringing Arbenin closer to Lermontov, Meyerhold supported his interpretation of Unknown, in whom he imagined Martynov, the poet's murderer. Unknown was to be played by V. P. Dalmatov, who had rehearsed excellently for the part. "There was something uncanny in his appearance, and a penetrating cold wafted from his intonations, filling the air with terror that made the flesh crawl." But Dalmatov died long before the premiere and the role was given to the young actor N. Barabanov who, in Yurev's words, "came out of this difficult situation with honor."[245]

When Yurev was preparing his *Notes* for publication—now in print for three editions—Meyerhold had been arrested and his name was not to be mentioned in print. Nonetheless, the actor who had played the lead roles in *Don Juan* and in *Masquerade* and who participated in many other productions by Meyerhold erected in the pages of his *Notes* a veritable monument to the director. They contain, in part, a thorough and loving literary scene-by-scene reconstruction of the production of *Masquerade*.

In *Masquerade* Meyerhold achieved an exceptional coordination of his actors' performances. The unity was constructed in accordance with a complex rhythmic and plastic score based on the rhythm of Lermontov's verse, and the principles for the construction of the ensemble were, in essence, musical principles. "The elegance of the music of speech," wrote Yurev of the sound of Lermontov's dialogues in the show, "coincided with the elegance of their manifest interpretation. The self-contained, the unsaid, hints and half-tones were supplemented by significant pauses and mimicry." This is the manner in which was realized Meyerhold's "assignment for the actors—while observing beauty of form not to forget that passions must rage below this glossy form."

Yurev was given the lead in the ensemble. At first, as Arbenin, he did not make a strong impression and felt uncertain, but gradually he became acquainted with the internal complexities of the part and with Meyerhold's most difficult staging score and, most importantly, "with that intonation of tragic gibe at the equanimity surrounding Arbenin, at the inhuman world in which he lived."[246]

In the show this theme was sounded persistently and in many ways, in the teasing and mocking images of the masquerade, sounding sadly in the dance scenes at the ball, penetrating the intense episodes at the gaming tables, passionately and even demonically and inevitably creating a dark, threatening mood.

Dynamic and turbulent episodes alternated with ones that were quiet and elegiacal. "For instance," wrote a critic, "there is a ball scene—brightly lit hall, slender malachite columns. The guests listening to Nina's romance are grouped artistically by the piano. The 'airiness' of the lace decorations blends with the music of the song, uncovering the nerve of the 'stage situation.' The blindingly golden, shimmering portal, shining and flowing in the mirrors, captivates the spectator bewitched by this unforgettable sight. In everything, in each ornamental curl, in each leaf of the funeral flowers there is a subtle foreshadowing."[247]

Angry, vengeful and mocking irony dictated Meyerhold's famous stagings—the fateful circle of players at the green table, the masks mingling in silent dance, surrounding Arbenin and Unknown...

"Misfortune shall be with you this night," Unknown prophesies to Arbenin while disappearing and reappearing in the silent, colorful mazurka of the masks. In this prophecy spoken with a jeering tone in the eerie, cold and ghostly atmosphere of the show, one could hear the foreshadowing of the fate of all aristocratic Petersburg.

The finale of the spectacle was wreathed with "mystical and infernal terror."[248] The scene of Arbenin's madness was played out against the background of song at the wake. The mirrors, portraits, walls—everything in the large hall was covered with black crepe. At the entrance to the room where the casket was, stood a crowd with lighted wax candles, a nun passed by, the old nurse was helped in, the young cadet busily lighted the candles and passed them around. A. Arkhangelsky's choir sang a prayer behind stage for Nina—but was it just for Nina? The funeral service was based by A. Glazunov on an ancient Church song. This eerie, soul-rending singing was heard as a final prayer for the whole Imperial world that had lived past its time. The black curtain with the funeral wreath in the center was lowered.

Masquerade was, for Meyerhold, in many respects a conclusion, a summation. The many years of work—however interrupted—resulted in a spectacle that manifested most completely several of the director's enduring and best-loved ideas.

The motif of masks and farce which had excited Meyerhold for a number of years obtained a new, profound meaning in this presentation. In *The Puppet Show* the mask had protected a lyric hero from the banality and lifelessness of life and allowed him to cover his suffering visage with an ironic and motionless half-smile. In Meyerhold's studio variations on the themes of the commedia dell'arte the masks called to the rowdiness and the merriment of ordinary people's entertainments, removing the audience from contemporary neurotic reflexes with which Meyerhold juxtaposed the passion and health of stage play. In *Masquerade* these two motifs were synthesized and obtained new meanings. The figure of Neizvestny entered the play as if from the world of Blok's theater, bringing with it the romantic image of unalterable Destiny and the fearful inevitability of the tragic end. In the movement of the masquerade itself, in its marvelous and multicolored play, the masks now denoted the fraudulence and ambiguity of existence, the chameleon-like and inscrutable nature of each and every person. The image of masquerade was read as the image of the illusiveness and ghostliness of life.

In *The Puppet Show* the poet's visions had been illusive. In *Masquerade* reality itself was illusive, but was viewed dryly and soberly by the director-poet. Petersburg was phantasmagoric, reproduced with sparkle and shine in the enormously effective and elaborate backdrops. The world appeared dubious, threateningly mutable and mobile. The monumental stateliness of the era of Nicholas, presented with the maximum opulence of Golovin's decorations and costumes, with its excessive, striking splendor and the intoxicating refrains of Meyerhold's circular stagings, shifted to the edge of catastrophe, collapse, disaster.

This time, the participation by the audience in the action, theoretically and practically so important to relativistic theater, became participation by the audience in history, in the historical act. History, isolated and estheticized, in this way became connected with modernity and was rejected. The past was marked with the sign of death and annihilation, and received a strict sentence not subject to appeal.

Only a few years later Meyerhold would destroy these monumental forms "to their foundations" in *The Dawn*. But, some time later, transformed and sharpened satirically, they would appear again in the contours of *The Inspector General*, thematically connected with the same era and likewise aspiring to discover its style, its essence and illusiveness.

The performances of the actors in *Masquerade* were subordinated to the principle of strictest, down to the nuances, determination of the external plastic picture of the role, to precise observance of the assigned rhythm, tempo, discovered and learned intonations. The form was not only defined in advance, but also polished. The show was a rare example of harmonious creation in which each element—painting, music, acting, staging plan, rhythm, tempo—was firmly tied together by the director's score into a unified whole.

This is the reason for the production's long life. It was reinstated into the theater's repertory in 1923, then revived in 1932 (second edition) and in 1938 (third edition). It was presented with great success even when the creator of the staging was no longer alive and his name had been deleted from the programs and posters. The last performance of *Masquerade* was on July 1, 1941. During the blockade in the fall of that year a bomb struck the theatrical warehouse on Rossi Street, destroying Golovin's decorations almost completely, thus ending the stage life of one of Meyerhold's truly great works.*

The phantasmagoric dying world of play and masks, the world of artificial passions that suppressed true human feelings, continued to excite audiences for an entire quarter century, for so long as *Masquerade* remained on stage.

Much less work was put into the less effective, but nonetheless significant staging by Meyerhold in 1917 of A. V. Sukhovo-Kobylin's trilogy (January 25—*Krechinsky's Wedding*, August 30—*The Affair*, October 23—*The Death of Tarelkin*). This was the first staging of the complete trilogy. However, in *The Affair* and *The Death of Tarelkin* some material that had been removed by the Tsar's censors remained unstaged.

Evidently, Meyerhold was least interested in the first, most popular play, *Krechinsky's Wedding*. He staged it together with A. Lavrentev. The directors consciously constructed the entire staging design around V. N. Davydov, who had been playing Rasplyuev with extraordinary success in *Krechinsky's Wedding* for some thirty-five years and who, naturally, did not wish to alter a single setting or intonation. Yu. Yurev played Krechinsky, replacing V. Dalmatov in the part, L. Viven played Nelkin, K. Yakovlev played Muromsky, N. Kovalenskaya played Lidochka and A. Nemirova-Ralf played Atueva. The decorations for all three plays of the trilogy were painted by B. Almedingen, one of Golovin's students and helpers. The critics' responses to the production were few and uninterested. The play, observed

---

*However, *Masquerade* was performed several times without decorations or costumes in concert performances—first in Novosibirsk in 1942, then in the *Bol'shoi zal* of the Leningrad Philharmonic in 1947.

the reviewer in the paper *Speech,* "drags weakly along."[249]

Meyerhold also staged *The Affair* together with A. Lavrentev. Bozhena Vit-vitskaya wrote to the magazine *Theater and Art*: "Either because of the pacific presence of Mr. Lavrentev or for other connected reasons the production went on without Mr. Meyerhold's fanciful ventures, typical for the 'master of staging.' The decorations and costumes did not scream out, trying to eclipse the content of the play no matter what, and the actors transmitted the author's concept and era not inside-out, but in a manner understandable to the audience."[250]

The reviews noted the success of Sudbinin as Ivan Sidorov, Valois as the Very Important Person, Nemirova-Ralf as Atueva. G. Ge received simply bad reviews as the Important Person. Judging by the very specific and quite believable reminiscences of Ya. Malyutin, the most notable event of the staging of *The Affair* was the performance of Apollonsky as Tarelkin.

The charming, attractive but not particularly energetic "hero-lover" received a character part and "for the first time truly stunned the audience—stunned them with the acuity and force of psychological observation... Apollonsky in this role was able to be merciless with his own gifts: he broke and contorted his walk, made his face unrecognizable... In his Tarelkin everything became mixed, everything inter-twined—the meager aspirations of a half-hungry little official with the most un-bridled greed, cowardice with arrogance, delirious bragging with a bitter and clear understanding of his lot in life."[251]

In 1917, when Meyerhold was staging Sukhovo-Kobylin's trilogy, the turbu-lent political life of the country was pushing theatrical reviews off the pages of newspapers and magazines. There was no time for theater: history was racing from February to October. Consequently, we have only the briefest information regard-ing these three productions. It is clear only that both in the direction and in the decorations for the trilogy "there was a conscious progressive increase in the ele-ments of stage grotesques. In contrast to the graphically quiet decorations (*The Af-fair*, Act 2), showing a government office with a sweep of corridors, in *The Death of Tarelkin*, two designs with deliberately broken contours almost 'relativistically' represented Tarelkin's room and the anteroom of the police station." In *The Affair*, wrote V. N. Solovyov, the directing "utilized the lingering shyness of stage pauses, which inked in slightly the melodramatic style of the play itself," and in *The Death of Tarelkin*—"the manner of exaggerated satire."[252]

The most successful show, peculiarly prophetic and quite memorable, was the third, concluding one—*The Death of Tarelkin (The Happy Days of Rasplyuev)*. This play attracted Meyerhold's intense attention, and it was no accident that he returned to it several years later. In the Alexandrinsky Theater, already renamed the Dramatic State Theater, it was first performed on Monday, October 23, 1917.

A. Kugel wrote: "*The Happy Days of Rasplyuev*, with a nightmare tint, were playing while in the streets the people were noisy and excited, preparing for the second act of the Revolution." Like many of his brothers of the pen, without un-derstanding the historic significance of this "second act of the Revolution," taking October to be a temporary and accidental "turbulence" in the course of history, a quickly passing confusion, Kugel observed sadly: "There was some sort of tragi-comic devilish smile in this, if one may say, an 'inappropriateness' of revelatory satire on the arrogance of the police state and the hypertrophy of power. Where! What! How! All these wilful actions of the police which at another time it would have been easy to laugh at, seemed so far behind... For satire it would be better to seek something nearer."

Kugel, whose article was printed after October (November 12, Old Style), pointed directly at the Bolsheviks, who had seized the reins of government. Considerable time would elapse before people such as Kugel could understand what had happened. The rapid progression of the Revolution frightened them, they began to yearn for the police, the mores of the old regime, and a satire directed against the licence of the police state appeared inappropriate to them. Such moods occasionally led to quite expressive incidents. In the same November of 1917, in *Theater Review*, there appeared a symptomatic column "Nostalgia for the Policeman."

> At the performance of *The Living Corpse* in the Alexandrínsky Theater several days ago there took place an incident characteristic of the times we are experiencing:
>
> In the last scene of Tolstoi's play, as you know, the court is presented. Before the doors of the courtroom stands a policeman. The policeman's role in the structure of the play is most modest and he is played by the simplest extra. But this time the policeman-extra has received a great honor: the audience greeted his appearance with thunderous, prolonged applause.
>
> Chalyapin himself has never seen such an ovation.
>
> What is the matter? The matter is that the Petersburg public misses strong power, power that is "near the population..." The Petersburg audience misses the policeman—a real policeman in "full uniform," with his badge and sword! The audience had suffered long and silently, almost unconsciously. And suddenly here the policeman appeared before it in dazzling form, tangible, real! And the longing broke out in stormy ovation and amusing applause![253]

Kugel's article in more muted form also was expressing the counterrevolutionary atmosphere that caused the audience to applaud the policeman. The production, evidently, did make a powerful impression on the critic, since this determined old foe of Meyerhold did admit this time, however grudgingly, that the staging was impressive and exact. The director, wrote Kugel, found in Sukhovo-Kobylin's play " . . . something from Hoffmann and his fantasy. I would say that Mr. Meyerhold manifested sensitivity and agility—since the overlay of fantasy is able only somewhat to reconcile realistic form with the coarseness of exaggeration and caricature... In the given case this was acceptable—the not quite believable oscillation of worldly and living figures against Almedingen's decorations, which are somewhat fantastic but not totally divorced from life."[254]

The roles for the premiere of *The Death of Tarelkin* were as follows: I. Uralov as Varravin, B. Gorin-Goryainov as Tarelkin, Ya. Malyutin as Okh, K. Yakovlev as Rasplyuev, E. Korchagina-Alexandrovskaya as Mavrusha, N. Shapovalenko as Popugaichikov, A. Chizhevskaya as Brandakhlystova. In his review, Kugel praised Gorin-Goryainov and Yakovlev. Ya. Malyutin recollected:

> Gorin-Goryainov played the protagonist marvelously. This distracted, half-mad, obsessed creature appeared before the audience with Tarelkin's first words... The actor was creating

an image which appeared to embody the decay of Russian law, the internal collapse of officialdom—the sorry bastion of monarchy. There was something frightening in the dead gaze Tarelkin directed into the auditorium; the gaze of a suicide who continued to live after the noose had been tightened to the limit. He was terrifying in his final monologue, too. The tearing off of the wig revealed a bare, lifeless skull, while his face was twisted into some sort of unusually grotesque and lifeless grin.

This frightful and grotesque figure stepped from the grim and bleak environment of the stage—"some kind of nervous smears and spots on the walls underscored the atmosphere of fear and darkness in which Tarelkin's transformations take place."

If those people who were frightened by the October Revolution spoke of the "inappropriateness" of the satire, then the other viewers—the majority—"thought highly of the production that with great passion and depth mocked the damned Tsardom," and anathematized the world where "the living and the dead are no longer distinguishable from each other and the dead celebrate their victory over the living."[255]

Masquerade was performed for the first time on the eve of the February Revolution, *The Death of Tarelkin*—on the eve of October. This was the last premiere in the Alexandrinsky Theater. Its eighty-five-year history was ending with a grotesque satirical show that furiously cursed the past.

Meyerhold's complex prerevolutionary work was also coming to a conclusion.

In the Imperial Theater system this director had worked for ten years to create, essentially, his own special theater, his own stage world, which had almost nothing in common with the traditions and attitudes of the Alexandrinsky and Mariinsky stages. From 1908 to 1917 Meyerhold's productions, operatic and dramatic, were in esthetic contrast to the routine and everyday inertia of the Imperial Theaters where, before Meyerhold's appearance, " . . . boldness, searching, rashness, experiments, even brilliant ones, were impossible. The content of the repertory, the distribution of roles and manner of performance," wrote the experienced Petersburg theater-goer and poet Mikhail Kuzmin, "everything was to move gradually and truly. New trends necessarily had to arrive late, already tested and established."[256] In this kingdom of tradition Meyerhold had succeeded in gaining a place for art that was far ahead of its time.

We are accustomed to believing that an esthetic system is the product of its age and, generally, such a belief is correct. However, any age carries within it a foreshadowing of the future. An artist's intuition may hear such a foreshadowing and express it.

The time during which Meyerhold worked in the Alexandrinsky and Mariinsky Theaters carried the Revolution within itself. Although it was not as yet defined visibly and concretely in everyday life, in essence it was already present and happening. Meyerhold's genius (and Blok's genius) strove to reach this essence, passing by superficial phenomena.

Meyerhold in his youth was anti-bourgeois and hated absolutism. He retained these attitudes while in the honorable but rather difficult position as a director of the Imperial Theaters. We should not forget, however, that Meyerhold's orientation was quite unclear in terms of the specific social and political situation. He did not understand completely the contradictions of class struggle and the strategy, tactics and programs of the Russian political parties. His passionate and radical revolutionary nature—Meyerhold was, by nature, a man of extremes—remained enclosed within the limits of art, in the drive to revolutionize theater and stage forms. After October, looking back, Meyerhold observed that beginning in 1906 his "director-revolutionary face" had become defined, and added at once: "director-inventor."[257]

Meyerhold's inventions and experiments in many of his prerevolutionary productions reflected the catastrophic nature of the times and the tragic contradictions of the age, the approaching (to use Blok's words) "unheard-of changes." Meyerhold's art was created under crisis conditions and therefore was internally dramatic and changeable. Everything striking in the director's experiments, everything that was dictated by a desire to stun the audience or by artistic fashion was forgotten quite rapidly. The legacy to historians was the deflection of Meyerhold's art into estheticism, the fatalistic lassitude of the Symbolist period, the bizarre quality and opulence of his "moderne."

Very frequently, however, the new, as Pasternak said later, "did not arise to replace the old, as it is usual to think, but, quite the opposite, was an admiring reproduction of the model."[258] The new merged with the eternal. What Meyerhold discovered in *The Puppet Show*, in his stagings of Molière, Calderón, Ostrovsky, Lermontov, had both the freshness of the brand new and the fidelity to the eternal nature of theater. In the midst of the refined intelligentsia and aristocracy, on the stage of the state Imperial Theater appeared creations of art with a democratic spirit that stepped across the boundary between the stage boards and the auditorium, eliminating the footlights and the "fourth wall," radically altering all the habitual interactions between actors and partners, actors and audience.

The approaching Revolution exploded the layers of the old culture, placed in doubt the old esthetic values. The time of their reapplication and rethinking were far ahead. Meyerhold had a presentiment of the tragic collapse of the entire old world, the inevitable fall of its opulent magnificence, and the discovery of some as yet unknown, beckoning and frightful horizons. A genius, a revolutionary by nature, he strode swiftly to meet the oncoming storm. Its reflections made unexpected flashes in Meyerhold's art, enriching the theater of the future.

Meyerhold's prerevolutionary work brought the artist directly up to the line beyond which began a new era, a new life that inevitably dictated to art previously unimaginable and impossible demands.

PART II

Meyerhold provided the roots for the theater of the future. So shall the future honor him.

E. Vakhtangov

Golovin's portrait of Meyerhold, 1917

THEATRICAL OCTOBER

Fluffy-haired Molière
Is now replaced by Meyerhold.
He seeks new routes,
His gestures—rough.
Tremble, old theater, be anxious:
He will make you prance!

Eduard Bagritsky

The decisiveness and speed with which Meyerhold at once donated his talent to the Revolution during the first days of October evoked then and continue to evoke consternation. Some are prone to believe (as Meyerhold's opponents believed at the time), that the director of the Imperial Alexandrinsky Theater had quickly and cleverly adapted to power, had understood that the Bolsheviks would become established and victorious and conducted himself in accordance with the circumstances. In 1917-1918, however, the majority of the Russian artistic intelligentsia considered a Bolshevik victory as highly unlikely. The Civil War had begun and many either watched and waited or sided with the Whites who would restore a bourgeois democratic republic or, at worst, the monarchy—in either case a comprehensible form of power. The Bolsheviks, who had dissolved the Constituent Assembly and established the power of the Soviets, were understood by the popular masses but not at all by the "elect" or by many of the representatives of the spiritual elite of the intelligentsia.

The opposite point of view, ascribing Meyerhold's revolutionary leanings to hindsight, is unconvincing, too. The claims that before October Meyerhold had been of a revolutionary cast of mind, although based on several expressive excerpts from the director's diaries and letters that are saturated with revulsion toward absolutism and the bourgeois, prove nothing—in the years preceding the Revolution and during the War virtually every intelligent person in Russia experienced dissatisfaction with the Tsarist regime, while the art of the majority of talented artists was permeated with protest against the bourgeois.

As for Meyerhold, he was a man of art standing apart from specific revolutionary activity, a man of enthusiasms and impetuosity, continuously and totally immersed in theater. He sometimes responded most expansively to the political events in Russia, but never consistently.

Nonetheless, this artist, although lacking in political direction and acumen, was never apolitical. Usually, his art unconsciously, but most sensitively, reacted to the pulse of society. This specific acuity of Meyerhold's perception of the changes of the times became increasingly pronounced from year to year.

Coincidence is not adequate to explain the fact that on the very eve of the February Revolution he staged *Masquerade* and, two days before October, *The Death of Tarelkin*. Meyerhold's art was subordinated to the commands of the time, and in this sense the stormy development of the artist's talent was ahead of his ideological evolution.

Much of this, probably, was the result of the director's great temperament, his incomparable artistic boldness. Meyerhold implemented without hesitation whatever his intuitive genius suggested. Furthermore, he boldly and eagerly—with obvious pleasure—did battle with the audience, the reviewers, and official evaluators of art. The air of scandal that inevitably accompanied his premieres had a direct influence on Meyerhold's art, inflaming in him the sparks of opposition by constantly placing him in a position of conflict with the ruling esthetic and, frequently, with political views. We have already seen that Meyerhold's prerevolutionary work was carried out under conditions of irritated and angry rejection of his art, and attacks by the media that very frequently had an unmistakably political nature.

In 1926 A. V. Lunacharsky wrote: "The connection between Meyerhold's theater and the Revolution is very simple and, I might say, primitive. It is contained partly in the conscious and partly in the unconscious sensitivity of Meyerhold." And, further: "Revolution is bold. It likes innovation, it likes brightness. Tradition does not envelop it the way it does the theatrical Old Believers, and therefore it accepts readily that expansion of realism which, essentially, lies well within its province. It may accept fantastic hyperbole, caricature, all sorts of deformations, if such deformations . . . further the expression of internal real essence by way of artistic transformation."[1]

Meyerhold arrived at Revolution by way of the internal logic of the development of his creativity which in his best productions expressed with sensitivity and dynamics, the rhythm, spirit and intensity of life in Russian society before the Revolution.

Meyerhold's program, from which he never deviated despite all the multifacetedness of his stage productions, postulated the maximum possible use (not the concealment) of the relative nature of theater, the manifestation of its play nature (as opposed to imitating everyday life in actors' art). His program also contained a tendency toward farce. In conflict with the select Petersburg audience a potentially democratic art was ripening, capable of serving the wide masses. The dream appeared of farce, of "New Theater, truly popular theater."[2]

After the Revolution Meyerhold saw the opportunity for the real emergence of such theater. Now his experiments could be staged surrounded by crowds of soldiers, workers and peasants. The theater of Revolution could—and must—speak the language of popular farce. The renaissance of street theater in all its original forms was to take place automatically as the result of bringing theater close to this Revolution which had unleashed the energy of the popular masses. Here, at this point, there is historical law at work, not the biographical accident of the fact that the creator of new theatrical forms—the revolutionary of the theater—Meyerhold, had accepted October immediately.

He staged the first revolutionary show exactly one year after October. He was the first professional director in Russia to do so, but still it had been a year. The year had been an intense and difficult struggle for Meyerhold. The former Imperial theaters responded to the October Revolution by proclaiming sabotage. It is true that as early as the beginning of November performances had resumed in the former Alexandrinsky Theater, but a split had taken place in the troupe. The best-known actors responded with indignation against the new government. On the other hand, the Provisional Committee for the Direction of the Alexandrinsky and Mikhailovsky

Theaters was formed. This Committee supported the Bolsheviks and included the known actors I. I. Sudbinin, I. M. Uralov, the young L. S. Viven and N. V. Smolich, with Meyerhold as the sole director.

The bourgeois papers acidly commented that "the Bolsheviks have gained the ultramodernistic Mr. Meyerhold, who has even been called a Red Guard for some reason,"[3] and observed that of the 83 members of the Alexandrinsky company, 45 had decided to leave the theater, while Meyerhold "definitely moved toward an agreement with Commissar Lunacharsky and remained at his post of director."[4]

Not long thereafter, however, the situation changed radically. After a series of meetings, Lunacharsky won over the actors and nearly all announcements about leaving the company were forgotten. Normal creative life resumed in drama, opera and ballet.

On December 12, 1917, Meyerhold staged at the Alexandrinsky Ibsen's *The Lady from the Sea* (which previously, in the provinces, Meyerhold had staged under the title *The Woman from the Sea*). The lead roles were performed by M. Vedrinskaya and Yu. Yurev. Chronologically, this was the director's first post-revolutionary work, but the spirit of revolution had not penetrated it; the show passed unnoticed and elicited no interest.

In the end of the 1917-1918 season, Meyerhold staged still another show in the former Alexandrinsky Theater—Lev Tolstoi's play-legend *Peter the Baker*. The premiere was on April 8, 1918. The five tiny act-scenes of this unfinished play describe the legendary tale of an evil and miserly rich man who throws a piece of bread at a beggar simply because there is no stone handy. Then miserly Peter becomes ill and in his sleep sees an angel who says that the accidental "good deed" outweighs all the evil deeds of Peter's former life. After regaining his health, Peter intentionally gives all his wealth to the poor, sells himself into slavery and has the proceeds of the sale distributed to beggars. The typically Tolstoian ideas were expressed in this play with the clarity of a sermon. The reworking of the life of St. Peter the Sufferer was subordinated to the ideals of simplification, the brotherly union of rich and poor, and called for mercy.

Actor D. Pashkovsky recollected how the staging of this play was decided:

Those were days of terrible requisitions. It was mattresses for the army. I. M. Uralov comes in and says, "Hey brothers, what a play I've found! I was reading and weeping all night. We must stage it! Everyone's groaning about requisitions, but look how much joy there is here—to give everything possible of oneself! We must prove it to them: carry it ourselves. Let's show this, say, in a religious light." Uralov read us the play. He wept, and all of us with him.[5]

Uralov was a Bolshevik, but was a fervent Tolstoian. Nonetheless, he was not successful in the role. He acted "with whimpers and gasps," his words sounded "dead." Generally, judging by the few reviews, the actors performed poorly.

The unhappiness of the audience and reviewers was caused also by the sketchiness, fragmentedness and, primarily, the didactic tone of the play, which was in distinct disharmony with the intensity of Petrograd in 1918. Furthermore, Meyerhold's direction did not jibe at all with this preaching tone. A. Altshuler observed justly that the production "fractured the religious-mystical basis of the drama."[6] A contemporary reviewer chided Meyerhold and the painter Golovin because in the production "L. N. Tolstoi is forgotten and the picturesque color of the East where Peter the Baker lives is brought to the foreground. The East with its philosophical calm, its voluptuousness, multi-colored garments and bright landscape is, naturally, more arresting than the *starets* of Yasnaya Polyana, barefoot, wearing homespun... Golovin's decorations were a fantastic combination of colors, the groups of 'living goods' buyers and sellers in the market, which Mr. Meyerhold made the focus of his staging, dozed in the sun."[7]

Clearly, Meyerhold was uninterested in the Tolstoian sermon that had moved Uralov to tears. Directing *Peter the Baker*, he and Golovin saw an opportunity to create colorful and exotic pictures of Syria, Damascus, and statuary groups of slaves for sale at the market.

Meyerhold's work had neither a direct   nor a tangential connection with the time or the Revolution, and therefore was not a success.

Different and, in a basic sense, more important was Meyerhold's staging of the opera *The Nightingale*, by Stravinsky, which opened on May 30, 1918, with decorations by Golovin on the former Mariinsky stage. From Golovin's letters to Meyerhold it is evident that they were working on this staging together for at least a year before the premiere, and that Stravinsky himself specifically had wanted Meyerhold to do the staging ("Stravinsky intended to ask you," wrote Golovin in a letter dated July 7, 1918).[8] From Meyerhold's point of view Stravinsky was, at that time, the most important modern composer. *The Nightingale*, based on Andersen's fairy tale, had been first performed in Paris in 1914 and had not yet appeared on the Russian operatic stage.

There was much in this opera by Stravinsky that must have appealed to Meyerhold: the grotesque gentlemen-in-waiting, the maids and cooks in the first act; the "bubbling" chorus of the female courtiers (imitating the nightingale's song by taking water into their mouths) in the second act; the chorus of ghosts and the Emperor's delirium in the third act.

Music critic B. Yarustovsky writes: "The conception is interesting in the concert duel between the forest and artificial [Japanese] nightingales... Excellent for its laconism is the alternation of the tonal "decorations' at the very end of the opera, when the funereal, somberly instrumented procession of the courtiers is replaced by the airy glissando of harps and the light, transparent chord of the woodwinds that lead into the quiet but joyful line of the healed Emperor: 'Greetings!'"[9]

Stravinsky's musical innovations in their essence coincided with their transformation by Meyerhold on the operatic stage. The staging of *The Nightingale* was an original sketch for new work in directing that would accent strongly the relativism of opera. For instance, Meyerhold placed a music stand with the score before each performer. As they moved from place to place the characters carried their music stands with them, placed them where necessary, commenced their solo at a sign from the conductor, sang while looking at the score and after completing their part would sit (or stand) with an absent facial expression.

This was Meyerhold's declaration of war against the dramatization of opera and attempts to induce the verisimilitude of drama into operatic art. Opera was seen as costumed *musical* action. Accordingly, on the right and left of the proscenium Meyerhold placed two totally immobile choir groups and limited to the extreme the movement of the leading characters. The soloists and choir were fated to remain static. Silent extras used pantomime to express the plot very dynamically. "The dead to the dead, the live to the living," Meyerhold said of the principle of this staging. The sole review we have today of this production, although permeated with undisguised hositility toward Stravinsky and Meyerhold, does indicate that the spectacle was most original.

The opera opens with a small orchestral introduction that flows directly into the first act. In V. E. Meyerhold's staging, the Fisherman is portrayed by a singer on the proscenium. The Fisherman sings of the Nightingale that has enchanted him—an invisible Nightingale. Meyerhold, however, has seated the female singer before the audience next to the Fisherman. Nightingale sings, as she is supposed to, of roses. Courtiers and the cook enter to hear the marvelous singing. Everyone listens carefully and expresses delight, first thinking that the lowing of a cow, then the croaking of a frog, etc., are the song of the nightingale, and finally, they invite Nightingale to the palace.

When the tulle curtains are lowered, the orchestra plays the interlude for the second act... To the brisk and lively music of this interlude there is bustle that represents the greeting of Nightingale. The interlude becomes a Chinese march. The tulle curtains rise slowly.

The audience sees the fantastic porcelain palace of the Chinese Emperor.

The third act, connected with the preceding by a brief interlude of a somber nature, represents the bedroom in the palace of the Chinese Emperor. At the bedside of the ill Great Khan stands Death, wearing the Emperor's crown on its head and holding his sword and banner in its hands. The voices of the Ghosts can be heard. The author's notes place the alto chorus behind the scenes. In Meyerhold's production, motionless ghosts are seated on the proscenium. Nightingale appears. Roulades in a very high tessitura (D flat) are sounded. Death is enchanted by Nightingale's song and asks that the singing, which has stopped, continue. Nightingale agrees on the condition that Death return to the Emperor his crown, sword and banner... Dawn comes. The Chinese Emperor appears in full Imperial dress in the blinding sunlight. The courtiers drop, astonished, fanning out with legs raised!

The reviewer objected to Meyerhold's staging techniques, saying that they smacked of "coarse clowning." He asked why "the foreign *Nightingale* was preferred to our native *Golden Rooster*," which, supposedly, was "nearer to the heart of the Russian." Probably the most reasonable comment was that "today we do not have the psychological basis suitable for the proper perception of *The Nightingale*."[10]

It is true that in the late spring of 1918 in Petrograd *The Nightingale* could be perceived as a "stage mirage," as this reviewer characterized the opera. It had no success, and it would be futile to seek its direct or even tangential connections with the "experienced moment" (as the newspapers wrote at the time). But there is no doubt of its connection to many later experiments in the renovation of operatic art.

Meyerhold's first two productions in 1918 were thematically and stylistically unconnected with the Revolution. The time was approaching, however, when he would express himself regarding the Revolution, directly addressing the issue and giving the Revolution revolutionary art. He was staging Mayakovsky's *Mystery-Bouffe*.

Meyerhold, whose perception of the Revolution at first was highly abstract and unstructured, was to express in theater the ideas of revolution with the clarity of direct political propaganda. This was the contradiction which was never completely resolved or resolvable. Hence the characteristic abruptness, directness and even coarseness with which Meyerhold began to solve his new problems.

In this sense Mayakovsky's evolution was especially similar to the evolution of Meyerhold. Until the tragic death of the poet they continued to live side by side, each sensing an ally in the other. Each strove to find a new structure for art which could express the truth of this new epoch in history.

Their efforts were difficult and complex. Their alliance was very limited. Like Mayakovsky, Meyerhold could have said of himself that in October 1917 he decided: "My Revolution. Went to Smolny." (Several days after the October Revolution the All-Russian Central Executive Committee [VTsIK], just elected at Soviet Congress II, undertook to establish contact with masters of literature and art. Petrograd writers, artists and actors were invited to the revolutionary headquarters at Smolny. Only five came: Blok, Meyerhold, Mayakovsky, N. Altman and R. Ivnev.)

In 1918 Meyerhold joined the Bolshevik Party and accepted the post of assistant director of the Petrograd artists society. All of Meyerhold's most active theatrical activity—both in the areas of organization and directing—during October and the Civil War was firmly in the field of political agitation. It was Meyerhold, as Lunacharsky observed, who was able to "adapt" Futurism "to the poster-rally period of our Revolution. Posters and rallies were necessary to the Revolution and, to some degree, made peace with the Futuristic approach. Futurism could produce the poster and could hold a cleverly staged rally."[11]

(It is necessary to note that in Lunacharsky's articles and speeches of the twenties the concept "Futurism" is used in a very broad sense. When speaking of the "Futurists," Lunacharsky has in mind all the "left" artists of the most varied sorts—beginning with the real Futurists, Cubists and Suprematists and ending with the Imaginists. Meyerhold is categorized by Lunacharsky as a "Futurist.")

When stating that Meyerhold adapted Futurism to Revolution, Lunacharsky meant, primarily, Meyerhold's alliance with the Futurist Mayakovsky. *Mystery-Bouffe*, staged twice by Meyerhold, was not a Futuristic production in the strict sense. Initially, when adapting it for propaganda, this play was to have avoided Futurist word distortions and excessively complex images. In *Mystery-Bouffe*, Mayakovsky's words have characteristically precise accentuation; with the impact of a poster the word breaks into the consciousness of the audience like an aphorism, and is remembered.

Osip Mandelstam, clearly with *Mystery-Bouffe* in mind, wrote:

Mayakovsky's service is in using the powerful resources of visual education to enlighten the masses. Like a schoolteacher, Mayakovsky carries a globe representing the Earth and other emblems of the visual method. He has replaced the repulsive newspaper of recent times, where no one could understand anything, with simple, healthy schooling. The great reformer of the newspaper, he has left his mark in poetic language, infinitely simplifying syntax and offering to the noun the honorable and leading spot in the sentence.

Mandelstam did, of course, observe that Mayakovsky turns his globe happily, that in his "simple and healthy school" education becomes propaganda, and that the agitation is enthusiastic and fiery, "ringing." The force and precision of his language, Mandelstam correctly indicated, brings Mayakovsky close "to the traditional carnival barker."[12]

The rhythms of the barker, the primitive precision of the ditty *(chastushka)* form in this period, also had penetrated Blok's poetry. The poem "The Twelve," published in 1918, astounded the fans of the bard of "The Unknown Lady" and "The Beautiful Lady" with its unexpected and unforeseen coarseness. B. Eikhenbaum was incredulous that Blok, the "quiet poet of the lyre," would write "the loud, screaming and hooting poem 'The Twelve', in which he learns from Mayakovsky."[13] Of course Blok did not "learn" from Mayakovsky, but the Revolution was remaking both Blok's poetry and the poetry of Mayakovsky. Several striking coincidences could be observed. The same bold blasphemy was expressed in Blok's poem and in Mayakovsky's play.

Mayakovsky, gibing and jeering, made fun of heaven and hell, intelligentsia and democracy, monarchy and republic. For Blok the entire image of the old world was like a "hungry dog." He praised "black rage" and "black rifle straps," the storm of hatred and destruction. But in the finale of the poem, illuminating its somber landscape and calming, concluding and even covering all its rough dynamism, appeared—"in a white halo of roses"—the image of Christ.

In the same way, Mayakovsky's humorous parody of the Biblical legend of the Flood, intentionally blasphemous, familiar, and coarse, was suddenly interrupted by the pathetic, exalted intonations of "Simply Man," by the promise of the Promised Land, by the "New Sermon on the Mount." The most striking, even puzzling coincidence is to be found in Blok's diary: pondering a play based on the life of Christ he writes: "Sermon on the Mount—rally."[14] In other words, Blok was feeling out themes that already were being implemented in a different way in *Mystery-Bouffe* by Mayakovsky.

Naturally, the rally and poster of *Mystery-Bouffe* were organically alloyed together with the carnival nature of the show. It was conceived of as a grandiose carnival of propaganda, as a "heroic, epic and satirical representation of our epoch." In this case, the roots all went back to the ancient traditions of street spectacle and, at the same time, everything was new.

Mystery-Bouffe was the *first* fully and thoroughly political play in the history of Russian theater. It was a play without love, without psychology, without plot in the previous, traditional sense. Its actual subject was contemporary political life. Therefore, the construction of the play presupposed and provided for the possibility of intrusion by new, living material, in accordance with the requirements of the "current moment" and actual problems of propaganda. In issuing the call: "those who perform, stage, read, print *Mystery-Bouffe*—change the content," Mayakovsky was not joking. When a new edition of his play was staged he proved that its body was capable of easily assimilating new pressing facts and events of the day.

In order to understand the problems created for the director by *Mystery-Bouffe*, we first should examine the structure of the play.

Looking closely at *Mystery-Bouffe*, one becomes convinced that five years before the publication of Sergei Eisenstein's famous article "A Montage of Attractions," Mayakovsky already had created such a montage.

All this predetermined a great deal in Meyerhold's subsequent stage compositions.

According to Eisenstein's theory, an attraction is "any aggressive element of theater." In other words, an attraction is the basic unit, the molecule of theatrical action. This may be a trick. ("A trick," indicated Eisenstein, "is but one form of attraction," but in his own *The Wise Man* there were a great number of tricks.) It may be a dramatic episode. It may be a monologue, a consciously planned rupture in the action, a song, a dance, a farcical scene. That is, in principle it may be anything at all: any whole, internally complete moment of theatrical action. There is but one essential condition: each attraction must be calculated for "specific emotional impact on the receiver," that then leads to "a final ideological conclusion." Eisenstein indicated further that in contrast to the trick, which is self-enclosed and intended for separate "sale" (tricks are "sold individually"), the attractions within the play's system are interconnected, assembled together.

The theory of attraction assembly did not refute but rather gathered together and gave new meaning to centuries of theatrical experience. For instance, it was possible to see as attractions episodes in Shakespearean tragedies and comedies, or even "phenomena" in, say, plays by Ostrovsky. Trying to divorce his theory from the past and to stress its fundamental newness, Eisenstein underscored the point that attractions are mounted and brought into the system not "in the plane of the unfolding of human problems." What was truly new in his theory was the perception of theatrical show as being, first of all, a special type of organized dynamic system.

The dynamic system was based on the ancient experience of the circus and on recent experiences in cinematography. Freed of the burden of psychology, aimed at the ideological organization of the viewer's reaction, the theory of "attraction assembly" foreshadowed some of the basic elements of Brecht's theory of theater.

The organic nature of Eisenstein's theory was proved in the first post-revolutionary years by the existence and performances of *Mystery-Bouffe*, a play which already in 1918 was constructed of attractions. Therefore, Eisenstein, who began the statement of his principles with the proud words: "First application. Requires clarification,"[15] was not entirely correct. His article ended with a list of attractions from the epilogue of *The Wise Man*. It is easy to compile an analogous list for *Mystery-Bouffe*. For instance, let us take the first act: 1. The clownlike entrance of the fisherman and the Eskimo who has plugged the hole in the globe with his finger. 2. The Frenchman's expository monologue. 3. Two paired clownlike entrances (the pair of Australians; the Italian and the German). 4. The fencing duel between the Italian and the German. 5. An acrobatic trick: the merchant falling onto the head of the Eskimo. 6. The parade of the clean and the unclean. 7. The rally scene. 8. Farce: commencement of the construction of the Ark.

All these attractions are in full accordance with Eisenstein's principle of "assembly" into a whole and are a unified dynamic construction. Naturally, the director may decide to increase their number. Even in the second author's edition of the play the number of attractions rose greatly. Probably, some of them had been dictated by Meyerhold's specific theatrical solutions.

Yet another point is interesting: the great number of attractions that are circus-like in nature. The "circusization of theater" in Eisenstein's *The Wise Man* without a doubt was suggested by Meyerhold's stagings of *The Magnanimous Cuckold* and *The Death of Tarelkin*, of which we shall speak further. The circusization of theater was first accomplished in *Mystery-Bouffe*. Theatrical actors had to become clowns and acrobats in order to realize the fantastically bold concept that united the parody and the mischievous juxtaposition of the Biblical legend (the past) with the reality of Revolution (the present) and the Utopian images of "the Promised Land" (the future).

There was only one director in the world whose experience could prove useful for the staging of such a production. This is where Meyerhold's previous experiments became useful—in the realm of Italian comedy of masques, his interest in farce, his work in numerous studios, primarily the Studio on Borodinskaya Street.

The intentionally over-familiar tone of *Mystery-Bouffe*, its saturation with the simplest and crudest tricks, and its gibing horrified the actors of the Alexandrinsky Theater, to whom Meyerhold first read the play in late September 1918. Meyerhold was delighted with *Mystery-Bouffe*.

For the staging of *Mystery-Bouffe* Mayakovsky and Meyerhold succeeded—with Lunacharsky's active support—in occupying for three days the hall in the Conservatory where the Music Drama Theater was working at the time. Actors were selected from among those answering an advertisement published in *Northern Commune (Severnaia kommuna)* and other Petersburg papers on October 12, 1918, less than a month before the premiere.

The premiere was on November 7, 1918, on the first anniversary of the October Revolution. The decorator for the staging was the Suprematist K. Malevich. The directors were Meyerhold and Mayakovsky.

The circumstance that the play was timed to coincide with the first anniversary of October had no formal meaning. All the artists who had accepted Soviet power and who were ready to praise the Revolution viewed this date as the most appropriate moment to give battle to conservative art, which had sealed its lips in proud and haughty silence. Tens of thousands of yards of canvas were being painted for street celebrations. N. Altman alone painted over 15,000 yards of cloth! Leftist art, wrote Ya. A. Tugendkhold, "not only 'decorated' the streets but carried out a revolutionary mission—covered up 'holy places,' palaces and monuments, destroying their usual appearance with new forms (as, for instance, Altman did to the Alexander column in the Palace Square); it *exploded* and *undermined* the old slave feelings. This was the destructive work required by the psychology of the moment...."[16]

Mayakovsky and Meyerhold felt themselves to be in the same fighting formation as Altman, Shterenberg, and other "leftists," and prepared their show with alacrity and enthusiasm.

In the Futuristic sketches for the first staging of *Mystery-Bouffe,* Meyerhold translated "poster and rally" into theatrical language: the exaltedly pathetic structure of Person's monologue and the entire group of "unclean" (proletariat) were intentionally contrasted with the clownlike representation of the "clean" (exploiters).

The "unclean" wore identical gray costumes. The artist K. S. Malevich consciously strove to represent them as a single *mass* of workers fighting for their rights, regardless of nationality or profession. This was the first experiment with actors' "overalls" *(prozodezhda)*, subsequently often used by Meyerhold. The intention to bring the struggling mass to the stage was most characteristic of the time.

The decorations were dominated by a cold steel coloring which Malevich also attempted to give to the ultramarine hemisphere that occupied the stage in the first scene, to the extremely relativistic forms of the Ark with bow facing the audience in the second scene, and the stalactite-like "Hell" in the third. The devils in "Hell" wore red and black costumes. "For 'Heaven,'" wrote the critic A. Fevralsky, using Malevich's words, "gray tones were selected. Clouds were represented by aniline-pink, light blue, crimson 'cakes' . . ." whose color combinations "made you gag."[17] The "Promised Land" was represented as a kingdom of mechanisms—steel, iron, a large mock-machine—this is how the future was seen.

A. Gvozdev and A. Pyotrovsky also noted that these "detached-mechanical traits" of Malevich's design contradicted (at least partially) the light carnival atmosphere of the show that had inspired Meyerhold and Mayakovsky. Mayakovsky was unhappy with Malevich's art and soon after the performance of *Mystery* he drew his own sketches for the costumes of the "clean" and "unclean." These sketches are lighthearted, very amusing, undoubtedly carnival-like for the "clean," and with a hint of a severe, fervid, poster-like quality for the "unclean."

"Meyerhold's direction," continued Gvozdev and Piotrovsky, "took the show along the line of propaganda, satire, uplifting pathos, and up-to-date politics, using farce and buffoonery to ridicule sharply the 'clean,' with particular effectiveness in the second act—on the ship."[18]

The characterization of the "clean" in the show was true to the principles of carnival, of Punch and Judy theater. One major aspect—that of class—comprised the entire content of the image. Priest is priest, merchant is merchant, "hustling" says it all, and no finer shadings were needed by anyone. These were masks again, returned to Meyerhold by the Revolution in their very first, most naive form, completely free of stylization. They no longer led away from modern confusion to the beautiful youth of popular theater, did not become a form for the ironic pushing aside of life, and did not pretend at all to represent its double meaning, masquerade-like quality or infernality. The masks were freed of the burden of symbolism, romanticism, retrospection and estheticism. They took on the tasks of lighthearted and specific political satire. Around them raged a storm of street mischief. The "clean" tied all of the "unclean" together with a single rope and, laughing and hooting, pushed them down into the hold—into the orchestra pit of the theater. In "Hell" red devils leaped onto the stage and cavorted, jumped and danced around like real acrobats.

Farce, which had attracted Russian artists and directors for so long, which had been their dream, a promise of unattainable joy and of the impossible brilliance of long-forgotten colors, became itself. In its disingenuous naturalness, it turned out to be coarser and more arrogant than the farce of ancient popular festivals Meyerhold, Sapunov and V. N. Solovyov had dreamed of. What is important is that Meyerhold, correctly sensing the moment, feared neither the arrogance, the coarseness, the vehemence, nor the blasphemous buffoonery of this farce.

Even before the first presentation of *Mystery-Bouffe* Lunacharsky published in the newspaper *Petrograd Truth (Petrogradskaia pravda)* a most positive review of Mayakovsky's play and predicted its success in advance. It is true that he feared, not without reason, "that the Futurist artists might make millions of errors in this staging" by supplying the play with "all sorts of extravagances," but he expressed his certainty that the "upbeat, sonorous flow of Mayakovsky's poetry will smash any junk that is too new. . . ." Lunacharsky insisted that the text of the play "is comprehensible to anyone, goes straight to the heart of the working man, the Red Army man, the representative of the poor peasantry. It speaks for itself."[19]

The first review of the show, angry and biting, indirectly supported this view. The critic Andrei Levinson, soon to emigrate, chided Mayakovsky for his desire "to please the new master." While accepting that *Mystery-Bouffe* had been conceived "in the ancient but unflagging spirit of Attic comedy," the critic was shocked by its "coarseness and vehemence," and asserted that the "derisive stateliness of the plot is undermined by internal inadequacies of execution." A. Levinson stated further that "our epoch does not desire to recognize itself in Mayakovsky's 'representation,' and the people celebrating its birthday did not think to glance at its reflection in this warped mirror."

This article contained some curious contradictions. The creators of the show were chided for an attempt to please the "new master," the revolutionary people, while at the same time stating that the people did not need the show. The author referred to "inadequate execution" and admitted in the same breath: "There was much that was interesting in this show—but only for us, the old frequenters of premieres in the Capital, carousers in artists' cafes, attenders of opening days." Levinson liked "the juicy coarseness of accidental puns, the cracks at yesterday's holy things. . . ." "Where," he wrote, "the author himself spoke his verse, its texture seemed more impressive, the rhythm conquered the ear. Each brief heavy line awakened a lengthy resonance, like a bullet hitting a wall. And as long as the melodic and powerful voice sounded, the acoustic enchantment remained." But Levinson remained convinced that all these aspects of the form were not accessible to the common people.

There was much that remained incomprehensible even for the most refined critic. Levinson fretted that "from the costumes it was impossible to tell a bricklayer from a chimney sweep," that it was "impossible to recognize a German or a Frenchman by intonation or bearing." He was irritated by the "choral reading," he "was depressed by the banality of the supposed innovation" of the actors' entrances through the auditorium. "Still," concluded Levinson, "some of the roles were memorable: Zhelkevich (the washer), Novgorodtsev (the merchant), and sometimes Shadursky (the laborer)... The decorations were drawn by Malevich; the arched 'Hell' is very picturesque, red and green. But his image of the 'Promised Land,' the cities of happy work, is uninspiring and dreary; in 'Heaven' the colorful cloud bubbles are gay."[20]

The contradictions of Levinson's article were explained in part by another review that was published somewhat later in the magazine *Red Corner (Krasnyi ugol)*. Here it was stated clearly that Mayakovsky's play "is not just a play, but the apotheosis of the Soviet commune," that it is intended "for extremely unrefined tastes," and that therefore "loud hurrahs, ovations and all the rest were guaranteed by the uncomplicated plot of the play."[21]

The play, consequently, ran with great success and its nonacceptance by some critics, such as A. Levinson, was political nonacceptance. Mayakovsky understood this at once. On November 21, 1918, he published in *Petrograd Truth* an open letter to Lunacharsky, objecting to the "dirty lies and insults to revolutionary feeling."[22] Artists understood this, too—among them A. T. Matveev, S. V. Chekhonin, and D. P. Shterenberg, who sent to the editor of *Life of Art* a group "Declaration Concerning *Mystery-Bouffe*." These artists wrote that, among other things, A. Levinson attempts to speak for the people and to force his "dead feelings" on the popular masses without foundation.[23] Lunacharsky responded to this declaration and to Levinson's article itself in a column "On the Polemic," in which he wrote that Levinson "allowed himself a totally unwarranted reading of hearts," and continued: "If we recall that an outstanding poet, which almost everyone agrees Mayakovsky is, has an opportunity to present a small sample of his art in a satisfactory environment for the first time—such an attack on *Mystery* from the realm of arguable ethics becomes all the more unattractive."[24]

Political passions became inflamed and very soon the theatrical polemic went even further in the direction of "arguable ethics," which surprised no one in particular. In the controversy surrounding the first presentations of *Mystery-Bouffe* one could hear already the severe, accusatory intonations characteristic of "Theatrical October."

"Theatrical October," with all its inevitable extremes, appeared in the unique circumstances of rapture over the victory of the Revolution and the dramatic intensity of the Civil War, which was already beginning. "Those were years," wrote Tugendkhold, "in which our art, just yesterday withdrawn and domestic, confronted the proud and bold dream of transforming the face of life itself, of leaping into the future, the kingdom of the Commune." This dream permeates *Mystery-Bouffe* and it is no accident that Meyerhold staged it twice. "Those were years," continued Tugendkhold, "when in the rapture, the high tide, of youthful energy it seemed that there would be nothing simpler than to burn all the ships of the old bourgeois culture behind us and to construct immediately a new, proletarian culture on the fragments of the past. Those were years when despite the blockade, poverty, and hunger, it seemed that art could at once begin to create a new milieu, a new environment for life, a new design for all daily life. Those were years when the revolutionary re-evaluation of all values was not stopped by any traditions."[25] This was true both for representational art and for theater.

Consequently, the prologue to *Mystery-Bouffe* poked fun at "theater wardrobes" ("sparkling operatic sequins and Mephistopheles's cape—everything in there!") and the "unclean" proclaimed:

> Today
> over the dust of theaters
> our motto shall light up:
> "Everything anew!"
> Stand and wonder!

In accordance with Mayakovsky's note, after speaking these words the "unclean" tore apart the curtain "painted with the relics of the old theater." Meyerhold decided on a simpler and more specific solution. In the prologue to *Mystery-Bouffe* the actors simply tore to shreds the posters from Petrograd theaters. In this way the enemy was named by name. This was no longer a general discussion of "old theater," but of quite specific, near, and well-known theaters.

War was declared on the carriers and conservers of tradition. If the "leftist" artists on the first anniversary of October covered the Petersburg palace complexes and monuments with their brightly painted canvases in order to "destroy," to "explode" their familiar forms and exteriors with new and hitherto unseen forms, then the director and the playwright of *Mystery-Bouffe* wished to destroy in the same way, "down to the foundations," the entire esthetic system of old theater.

A month later, in a speech on December 12, 1918, at a special session of the People's Commissariat for Education *(Narkompros)*, Meyerhold formulated his claims against old theater with sufficient clarity:

> Each theater has its own ideology... The State theaters proclaim their well-being, with reason. Perhaps they become blinded by their success when they present the audience figures—the number of people who have attended their theaters. It seems to me that at the same time they will never tell what they have fed these people... Does it not seem to them that this repertoire and the people who execute it are not presenting the transformed world? And I answer: yes, this is so. The Art Theater considers it normal to remain quiet and to continue to present to the audience, the new, modern viewer, what it presented ten years ago. Despite the fact that I respect its activity highly (no one is able to show the way the Art Theater shows), its silence nonetheless appears fateful to me. I would like to give a warning: tomorrow its silence may become death... All the indications that the theaters are flooded with people, that it is impossible to purchase tickets for the Art Theater, these do not mean that everything is well... The public, which is greedy for art, throws itself at doors that are open and into those theaters which still operate. This is not the end of the matter; it is necessary to analyze strictly what the public is fed as it breaks into these theaters...

"The silence of the Art Theater," continued Meyerhold, "is a symptom of being close to a real catastrophe."

In the same speech Meyerhold stated that he left the State Drama Theater (the former Alexandrinsky) "because they are losing the ideological plan." He said that the main task was to "freshen theater up...to attract specialists and make them serve the people's theater, which we are called upon to serve."

Meyerhold's position at this meeting, the first since October attended by nearly all the leading masters of Russian theater, differed substantially from the positions taken by Stanislavsky, Nemirovich-Danchenko, Yuzhin, Tairov, Komissarzhevsky, E. Karpov and others.

In establishing their relations with the newly-organized Theatrical Department (TEO) of the Commissariat for Education, the theater leaders for the most part defended themselves from the demands of the new Bolshevik government. E. Karpov was blunt: "The Theatrical Department for us, the workers in the new theater, is a bogeyman, an 'uncle' who can give us protection. We come to it to ask that we not be chased out of our apartments, that we be protected, that our possessions not be taken from us, that one theater or another not be closed, and that we not be presented with a repertoire and told to stage a play in three days."

Nemirovich-Danchenko formulated the question with far greater depth and breadth:

> It seems to me that if the present government ascribes such enormous significance to art for the people, if it thinks that theater is the greatest joy, which fills the whole life of the people, then theater will become for it a sort of religion that must fill everyday life with beauty...—if theater is to play such a colossal role, then all efforts must be directed toward making theater good... But there is one feature (which probably comes from the general direction of life) which is nonsense—this is what we have heard: "Not to lose the tempo of life." This is the greatest error... Art that is created in a rush, in one gulp, is always worse than it appears...

Stanislavsky supported Nemirovich-Danchenko: "I," he admitted, "am desperately apolitical and cannot judge who is correct—to the right, to the left or in the center. I confuse everything, I understand nothing in this matter." But he objected most firmly to rough modernization and the adaptation of his art for propaganda: "Theatrical art is very fine jewelry and must be handled delicately and finely."

Tairov expressed a fear "that now when all ideologies, views, and convictions have become mixed, at this time it is possible that the already long lost theatrical ideology, the ideology of art in general, will become lost utterly; not just ours, but theatrical human art in general."

A. I. Yuzhin's statement was the sharpest. Referring to the fact that in the past "everything that came from the center was of little significance, while everything that was created by theatrical ideologues came from below; all the foremost actors who created theater came from the people." Yuzhin objected to the principle of controlling theater from "above," to the very idea of State-controlled theaters.

> If in place of the old uniform we receive a new one, where is the difference?... I demand, if I may express myself in this way, I demand that the new government, which is providing generously for the beginnings of freedom and for the working individual, give that freedom to the actor's personality, without which there can be no creativity... I ask that the Russian actor, his working personality, be freed completely, just like blacksmiths, plowmen or anyone else; I ask that he be freed from all uniformed guardians, so that in no case would shiny buttons or these tasteless leather coats meddle in our affairs...

In objecting to Yuzhin, Lunacharsky insisted: "It is necessary to recognize the right to direct the theater" by the government if only because the state is financing these theaters. He further expressed the hope that the state theaters gradually "will begin to renovate the repertoire and seek artistic achievements that would occur before a huge popular audience." New directions, he assured, "will always find a heartfelt response in us and evoke a desire to help on the part of the Commissariat of Education."[26]

Thus, already in 1918 the basic trend was established for the argument which later was to become extremely acute. The directors of the old theaters, in one way or another, gently or quite definitely, expressed anxiety for the fate of their art and their lack of desire to adapt hastily to new political slogans. On the other side, Meyerhold was propounding the ideas of immediate renovation and the political activation of the repertoire. For him, the chief question was "what to feed" the public, how to express the ideas of October in art.

The Civil War interrupted Meyerhold's theatrical activity for a year and a half. He traveled to the Crimea for a cure, and was cut off from Soviet Russia unexpectedly by the Whites. With difficulty, he succeeded in reaching Novorossiisk where he was arrested by Denikin's forces and only in 1920, after the liberation of the Caucasus by the Red Army, did he return to Moscow. Lunacharsky at once appointed Meyerhold to head the Theatrical Department of the Commissariat for Education.

At this time the "leftists" were zealously and over-ferociously attacking the old theater, particularly those which were called academic, or "akas" for short. Subsequently, Lunacharsky wrote that "the resistance offered by the old theaters was exaggerated by the extreme leftists. The bitterness and radical animosity in their attitude toward old theater hindered its forward movement."[27]

Under such conditions the Soviet government's steadfast policy of protecting the old theatrical culture and of containing the "leftists" was correct and far-seeing. The "bitterness" of the leftists, their "radical animosity" toward the old theaters, thwarted administration, reorganization, and so on.

A characteristic document in this sense is the order by the People's Commissar for Education, Lunacharsky, published November 20, 1920. It reads: " . . . the policy of Soviet power in the area of theater is divided clearly into two tasks: 1) the revolutionary-creative formation of new theater, the raising of the level of theater for the masses and a revolutionary cleansing of theater that lacks artistic, cultural and political value, and 2) conservation of the best theaters of the past which undoubtedly deserve the attention of the State as conservers of artistic traditions."

In this document, "the entire direction of all theaters in Russia, naturally within the limits of the rights given to the center with respect to local jurisdictions," was given to the head of the Theatrical Department, i.e., to the newly appointed Meyerhold. However, there was a special list of exceptions—Meyerhold was not to control the "State Academic Theaters in Petrograd (the former Alexandrinsky, Mikhailovsky and Mariinsky theaters) and in Moscow—the Bolshoi, Maly and associated theaters: the Art Theater with its First and Second Studios, the Kamerny and, finally, the recently organized Children's theater." The named theaters remained "under the direct control of the People's Commissar for Education."[28]

Consequently, when assigning Meyerhold to run the Theatrical Department, Lunacharsky limited his power and did not transfer the academic theaters to the Department.

It was during this time, when he became head of the Theatrical Department, that Meyerhold proclaimed the program of "Theatrical October." The practical incarnation of the concept of "Theatrical October" took place on the stage of the new Theater RFSFR I, which Meyerhold organized at once. The mouthpiece for these ideas was the newspaper *Bulletin of the Theater (Vestnik teatra)* whose editor and inspiration was Meyerhold.

As soon as Meyerhold became head of the Theatrical Department, rumor spread that he would be leading the fight against professional theater generally. Meyerhold hastened to refute such rumors:

> I assert: I do not intend to carry on any struggle with the professional theaters. As for strengthening the position of proletarian theater, I feel it my duty to note that its position is so firm that it does not require my assistance. The Proletkult is a sufficiently powerful organization... The theatrical specialist ought to transmit carefully all his technical achievements into the hands of the new actor from the proletariat. Therefore, it is not in our interest to chase the specialists from the field of the theatrical arena.[29]

In this curious interview one can sense the clear uncertainty, even the bewilderment, of the new head of the Theatrical Department. Lenin's idea regarding the utilization of the experience and knowledge of specialists in the interests of the Revolution takes on, in Meyerhold's words, a fairly primitive form. "Specialists," i.e., professional directors and actors, must give their "technical achievements" to new "actors from the proletariat." Consequently, in the final analysis all hope is placed in these actors with proletarian backgrounds. The formulation of the matter is typical for the Proletkult. Equally characteristic is the statement about the supposedly very strong position of the Proletkult in general and of "proletarian" theater in particular.

In fact the theaters of the Proletkult were neither powerful nor proletarian. The truly popular and spontaneous theatrical movement that united thousands of theatrical circles and studios was extremely varied in composition. Many amateur workers and peasants did participate in the theatrical circles and studios. However, throughout the country, in the capitals and in the provinces, the circles were managed by actors. Professionals frequently performed in the circle and studio productions. The fact that they were attracted to amateur art is partly explained by the fact that during the Civil War amateur art had become a sort of political rostrum. Also, the Proletkult paid relatively better and it was profitable for any actor to combine work in the theater with work in one of the Proletkult's studios. And finally, the Proletkult's theaters took in a great number of unemployed actors. The colorful composition of participants, the eclectic repertoire, and the amateurish quality gave the Proletkult theater the imprint of overall ideological and artistic formlessness. This mass movement was chaotic. The theatrical theories of the Proletkult were extremely distant from the practice of its theaters and studios.

Great hopes, however, were centered on the Proletkult, and the organization as a whole was considered authoritative. In the beginning Meyerhold, apparently, expected to use it for support. Very soon, however, he rejected the illusions connected with the Proletkult.

On the pages of *Bulletin of the Theater* appeared the expression "theatrical front" and phrases about "Theatrical October." On January 4, 1921, the newspaper wrote: "On the facade of the TEO, finally, waves the banner of October." The same issue published Meyerhold's theses. Meyerhold now asserted that the "Proletkult is falling into bad professionalism and it contains little amateur art, given the generous influence of instructors from the Art Theater." He stated further that even "mass shows"—of which the Proletkult theoreticians were particularly proud and

Scene from the production of Leo Tolstoi's *Peter the Baker*, 1917

Stravinsky's *Nightingale*, N. Volevach
as the Nightingale

Stravinsky's *Nightingale*, G. Pozen-
kovsky as the Fisherman

Scene from Verhaeren's *The Dawn*

Finale of *The Dawn*

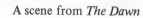
A scene from *The Dawn*

Bottom: Set design for Mayakovsky's *Mystery-Bouffe*. *Top left:* Ilinsky as the Menshevik in *Mystery-Bouffe*. *Top right:* Sketch of the Angel's costume for the same play.

which they considered the main and most promising form of theater—"must become suspect, since they contain too much drill and little of the living creativity of the masses themselves."[30]

The slogans of "Theatrical October" declared war against the apolitical nature of old stage art. The chief aim of theater was declared to be a rapprochement with the requests of the proletarian audience. It was considered that the "old" academic theaters would never be capable of attaining this end, and therefore their very existence was considered harmful or at best unnecessary.

The leader of "Theatrical October" then believed firmly that the social revolution must necessarily be followed by theatrical revolution. The drive for such an upheaval was expressed in his term "Theatrical October."

The future, thought the theoreticians of "Theatrical October" gathered around Meyerhold, necessarily would create a mass street theater of popular action, and they felt that Meyerhold was laying a path to such theater. "In the prognosis of the theater of the future we speak of monumental theater, of "mass action,"[31] wrote Em. Beskin "Mass action," insisted Alexei Gan, "is neither imagination nor fantasy, but a direct and organic necessity issuing from the very nature of Communism."[32]

Although Meyerhold, as we have seen, observed that in mass scenes there is "much drill and little living creativity of the masses themselves," and although he was extremely sour in his evaluation of the Proletkult in practice, he nonetheless supported these dreams in fairly vague terms. "Theater of the future will consist of elements of physical culture, joy, simplicity, sunniness, resolution and a striving toward overall brotherly unity throughout the world,"[33] declared Meyerhold. It was only the words about the elements of physical culture that gave this declaration any pertinent reality.

It was immeasurably easier to proclaim "Theatrical October" than to implement it, than to pit against the art of the old theaters art based on new revolutionary esthetic principles. Where were these principles to be taken from? The Proletkult's concept of speculative "conception" or "invention" of new, unknown forms of culture and art did not gain Meyerhold's sympathy for the simple reason that he, a practicing director, saw no reality behind the idea. The more philosophical the theoreticians of the Proletkult became, the further did their imaginations depart from reality. The theatrical forms that they envisaged were impossible to realize in practice—this alone was enough reason for Meyerhold to reject them. He could not inhabit the realms of verbal imaginings; he had to stage shows; he had to give to the Revolution and to bring out against the "old" theaters fully concrete artistic forms clothed in the flesh of living theater.

The propaganda plays popular in the Civil War years could not satisfy this director, nor could they suggest to him any direct routes to new art. The primitiveness, the linearity, and the elementary nature of the propaganda plays scared Meyerhold away, as they had Stanislavsky and Yuzhin. While fully sharing the combative pathos of the "agitki" he was faced with the extremely complex problem of creating new means of stage expression, esthetic forms which could contain and express the spirit of Revolution.

Such an attempt was made in the production of *The Dawn* in the Theater RSFSR I.

This new theater, created in the fall of 1920, was to demonstrate the capabilities of "Theatrical October." It was composed of the troupes of the New Theater, the Volny Theater and the "Gospokaz" Theater. Meyerhold believed, however, that the variegated troupe of actors would "cement itself together firmly," and he delivered fiery speeches before them. "The flame of the creative spirit must warm and inspire our theater. We shall call it the 'Theater of the Red Banner,' as the Spaniards once named their theater the theater of cape and sword. Let this banner become our emblem, the way the emblem of the *Sea Gull* in its day was the symbolic sign for the Art Theater."

"The psyche of the actor," warned Meyerhold, "must undergo some changes. No pauses, psychology or 'sufferings' on the stage or in the process of role development. Here is our rule. Much light, joy, grandeur and infectiousness, light creativity, engagement of the public in the action and the collective process of the creation of the show—this is our theatrical program."[34]

The Theater RSFSR I, in Meyerhold's plan, had to stage plays of two extreme genres: "revolutionary tragedy and revolutionary buffoonery."

As is known, the idea of staging Verhaeren's *The Dawn* also intrigued Vakhtangov. In the Symbolist play of the Belgian poet written back in 1898 there was much, as people said in those days, "in harmony" with the ideas of October. War became popular uprising, and a particularly strong motif was the coming together of soldiers and people on both warring sides in a revolutionary struggle against their rulers and warlords. The people of besieged Oppidomagne rise against the criminal rulers. The soldiers of the enemy army besieging the city turn their weapons against their officers and enter Oppidomagne as friends and brothers of the simple working people. It is true that in Verhaeren's play the populace is practically mute. The leaders (Hérénien, Hordain, Haineau, etc.) speak for the revolutionary masses, the city people and the soldiers, and the drama moves with their mutal struggle, their doubts, their hesitations, and their deeds.

In the post-October years such a view of the nature of revolution appeared both oversimplified and incorrect. But it should be noted that in the perception of revolution even by artists such as Meyerhold a certain abstract quality, a vague romanticizing, was inevitable. Therefore, *The Dawn* was quite appropriate for the times, and following the staging in the Theater RSFSR I the play was staged by many theaters throughout the country (for instance, in Ivanovo-Voznesensk, Ekaterinodar, Tambov, Tula, and other places).

The Theater RSFSR I obtained the building of the former Zon Theater on Sadovo-Triumfalnaya Street. The auditorium was cold, torn up, and dirty. In those years it was used mostly for political rallies. "The stage space is ragged," wrote Viktor Shklovsky. "The theater resembles a coat with the collar torn out. It is neither cheerful nor light."[35] But Meyerhold did not wish for it to be "cheerful or light," did not wish for the hall to have the coziness usual for a theater auditorium. The planned spectacle-rally fit organically into just such a hall. "The doors of this theater never knew a ticket collector... The railings had been torn from the boxes. The chairs and benches for the audience were poorly built and ruined the straightness of the rows. In the lounges you could chew nuts and smoke cheap tobacco... In this theater every person felt himself to be the master. The revolutionary street had broken into the theater."[36]

Along the walls of the auditorium there remained remnants of vulgar painted-over stucco moldings—relics of the half-theater, half-*café chantant* that had been there before. The curtain, however, was striking: black background with a red circle. A yellow area with the inscription "RSFSR" was cut into the circle.

Meyerhold threw out the old decorations of the Zon Theater, cleared off the stage and bared the brick walls of the building. The footlights were removed. The stage was connected to the auditorium by stage boards; the theater did everything possible to get closer to the "street." The walls of the corridors in the theater were covered with posters, slogans and cartoons.

The drive to find a common language with the mass of Red Army men and workers who filled the theater caused Meyerhold boldly to subordinate the literary basis of the show to the requirements of the "experienced moment." "If," Meyerhold told his company, "until 1917 we behaved with a certain caution and care for the literary work, then today we are no longer fetishists, we do not kneel down and call in prayer: 'Shakespeare, Verhaeren!...' Now we no longer defend the interests of the author, but those of the audience."[37]

"Meyerhold," wrote E. Kuznetsov, "modernized the play. Instead of Verhaeren's timelessness, in Meyerhold's staging they spoke of power to the Soviets and the Union of Action. The army was not presented as being any army, but that of the modern Imperialists. The hymn of the 'Great City' was replaced by the *Internationale.* Modernity was introduced into this play 'as raw material.' "[38]

The premiere of *The Dawn* was on November 7, 1920. The directors Meyerhold and V. Bebutov took the form for the spectacle from the "form" of a real revolutionary political rally. In this show the actors performed without makeup and without wigs and were, in essence, political orators. Their manner of speech, gestures, even their "hoarse voices, which evoked irony in experienced theatergoers, all this appeared "as at a rally." At times two orators would address the audience simultaneously. During the show the lights were left on in the hall.

The bond between the stage and the hall was strengthened by "actor-clappers" seated in the audience whose task was to react actively to stage events and serve as an example for the rest of the audience. One reviewer stated:

> No footlights. In the full sense of the word... *The Dawn* is staged on the principle of stage platform. The plane of the stage boards is used and nothing more. The lights are on full in the auditorium. The actors not only play in the area where the footlights used to be, but descend a wide staircase into the space that previously was occupied by the orchestra. The crowd speaking the author's lines is concealed below in a corner of the orchestra space and the impression is created that their lines are flying from the audience, to whom the heroes of Verhaeren's tragedy turn at such moments. This inflames, this excites. This sets up currents of living interaction expressed in the audience's applause to certain lines. From above comes the full sound of the concealed chorus, supporting the rumble of the crowd. The majestic and awesome tones of a funeral march sound over the casket of the murdered leader. I have seen how Red Army men in the audience instinctively remove their hats. In the theater you can feel the beating of a common pulse, a common rhythm. And when over the casket of the dead man the hands of workers use hammers to destroy the pillar of power of the old world, the entire audience and the actors unite to the sound of the "International"

in a vow to build a new world.[39]

Meyerhold and Bebutov in *The Dawn* used direct allegories, which were generally characteristic of propaganda and political rally theater during the Civil War. ("The hands of workers use hammers to destroy the pillar of power. . . .") Such allegorical scenes were accessible to everyone and their poster-like directness had the force of immediate effect.

Externally, however, the spectacle-rally was dressed up quite extravagantly. A student of K. Petrov-Vodkin, the artist Vladimir Dmitriev, erected silver-gray cubes, prisms and triangles on the barren stage against a background of one red and one gold plywood circle. The decorations were made of iron, wood, rope, wire: authenticity of materials became a principle. Over the geometric figures hung a piece of shining tin whose contour resembled a piano lid.

"Cubes, cylinders, curved surfaces done in local colors and intersected by the straight lines of wires were the representational material of the stage," wrote N. M. Tarabukin. "The stage platform, however, remained flat. The wings were retained. The relief forms of the props were immovable and performed essentially the function of decorations. But this 'Suprematist' form challenged flat and illusory decorations."[40] From Tarabukin's point of view this objectless formulation of *The Dawn* is still painting—not illusory but "spatial."

"The design for *The Dawn*," wrote S. Margolin, "led away from naturalism but not away from the decorative. The abstractness and objectlessness of this design created the impression of something amorphous and uncompleted."[41] Actors wearing silvery linen costumes declaimed from tall cubes or from below on the plane of the footlights. Below, in the orchestra pit, stood the "chorus" of the tragedy, several young men and women. This staging puzzled the audience somewhat. Lunacharsky, for instance, wrote that the workers, "embarrassed and practically sweating from the consciousness of their lack of culture, pointing fingers at one or another detail of the decorations," asked him "what this dream signifies."[42]

Verhaeren's text was equally bewildering. Mayakovsky commented with irritation: "The actor spoke for two hours about some sort of chimeras. This chimera does not participate in the current moment."[43]

The audience felt Verhaeren's text to be something of an obstacle. They argued only about the degree to which this obstacle was overcome.

The entire structure of the play was permeated with contradiction. This was felt expecially strongly in the performances of the leading roles. P. Kerzhentsev wrote that A. Zakushnyak "was out of place" as Hérénien. "There was in him too much of something gallant, of the salon; he was all pink and smooth..."[44] S. Yutkevich recollected that A. Mgebrov as the Prophet "pronounced his spells in a no less peculiar manner of pathetic declamation with an admixture of melodramatic wailing while standing on an enormous cube, but his eyes burned with a kind of real frenzy..."[45]

Em. Beskin, evidently quite justly, stated that in the show "there was a great deal of 'cultured' refinement which the new audience, stepping over the threshold of the theater en masse, was not yet able to assimilate."[46]

The most substantial innovation of the spectacle went unnoticed by the contemporary critics, probably because it was the most organic, and it naturally merged with the life of those times. This was the severity, the new strict asceticism, of the entire show, its military, surly, and proud bearing. The staging design for *The Dawn* was constructed in the spirit of a military march. Meyerhold arranged his silvery-gray extras in severe semicircles or in straight lines. They framed the show-rally, triumphantly and silently viewing its development. The "chorus" of the tragedy was interpreted as a formation of soldiers prepared for battle. The pathetic spirit of the Civil War appeared frozen in the monumental plastic of these thoroughly planned movements and reformations. Naturally, it was in contradiction to the melodramatic lines of the actor-orators. Naturally, it became an emotional barrier to the interaction between stage and auditorium that Meyerhold was striving to attain.

In a sense, *The Dawn* was the antithesis of *Mystery-Bouffe*: severe grandeur versus boisterous familiarity, dry asceticism and proud pathos versus personable simplicity.

The desired contact with the audience occurred at few performances. Evgeny Kuznetsov observed that at the show he attended the audience applause, which was supposed to interrupt Hérénien's speech three times, did not work out: " . . . the people were silent. The 'audience' in the orchestra applauds, the clappers applaud, which is unpleasant because it is obvious."[47] Yury Sobolev noted many errors and a certain laxness in the show: mistimed entrances, confusion in the lines, hurried gestures, the imprecise movement of the crowd. "The show staggers,"[48] he wrote—correctly.

Everything in *The Dawn* staggered, was flimsy. This was the instability of something new, something just born, out of the chaos of contradictions, and now uncertainly feeling out its form.

Therefore, the show had a mixed reception.

From N. K. Krupskaya's point of view, Meyerhold's experiment was decidedly a failure. "Someone," she wrote, "in an evil hour decided to adapt *The Dawn* to Russian reality... The Russian proletariat in the role of a Shakespearean crowd which any self-loving idiot leads where he pleases—this is an insult."[49] This well-known reaction was evidence, first of all, that Krupskaya was outraged by the politically imprecise, abstractly romantic rendition of revolution in the show. It is doubtful whether at this moment it could have been any different. In any case, the real history of the theater of those days has nothing to compare with *The Dawn* in this sense. One ought to recall, however, that Krupskaya was far from alone in her rejection of the show, while all those who saw the show as a victory of revolutionary theater also saw in it some serious inadequacies.

Arguments about *The Dawn* bothered neither Meyerhold nor his co-director Bebutov. Meyerhold was well accustomed to the fact that his premieres transpired in an atmosphere of polemics and discussions. He and Bebutov readily and heatedly answered their opponents, even those with the authority of Lunacharsky or Krupskaya. Valery Bebutov's answer to Krupskaya detailed, in the form of rhetorical questions, the grounds for nearly all the elements in the show and promised "to enter the path of even more radical alterations," instead of returning to Verhaeren.[50] Mayakovsky argued with Lunacharsky, O. Brik with the audience, S. Margolin with Brik, A. Mgebrov with Margolin—this was all in the course of things.

In the Theater RSFSR there were weekly "*Dawn* Mondays"—the dispute did not cease and it was supposed that the show-rally should continue in an atmosphere of debate and polemics.

Lunacharsky, however, speaking during the dispute over *The Dawn*, unexpectedly placed in doubt the idea of the show-rally itself. "Probably," he said, "there are few people in Russia who attend rallies as frequently as I, and I am considered a connoisseur and master in this area... And I will say: the rally has become so tiresome that there is no need to drag it onto the stage. The closer the stage approaches the rally the less effect it will have... Theater cannot be a rally, and must not be, for the reason that it is already obsolete."[51] Lunacharsky was readily supported on this point by A. Tairov: "It is high time to say," he jested, "that propaganda theater after the Revolution is the same as mustard after dinner."[52]

It became clear fairly soon that Lunacharsky was correct in principle. Russia no longer held political rallies and life after the Civil War gradually settled down. Nonetheless, he did like a great deal about the show:

> If you ask whether this show is successful or unsuccessful, I will say that it is a success... This truly is a real, true step forward. It is possible to disagree with everything in part, and with the overall structure of the show, but it must be said that a new bold revolutionary deed has been done; there has been real experimentation with the new and bright. And despite the reworking of Verhaeren's rhetoric and the pretentious Futuristic elements, there were frequent flashes of real mood, true feeling, in the staging. And there was the impression that life was being created, that this was the first and, possibly, colossal step, that this was an event of great importance... I cannot but congratulate all those who staged this show, for their names will be recorded as [the names] of the conquerors of a new area in the new proletarian Revolutionary theater.[53]

Mayakovsky asserted that theater had stepped onto "an extremely correct path," that the staging of *The Dawn* was "the first revolutionary tendency in theater."[54] According to P. Markov, this was one of those shows "that enter the history of theater not so much because of their long-term stage value, but as the progenitors of new stage directions. *The Dawn* was *The Sea Gull* of Meyerhold's theater... Dmitriev's cubes and buttresses, the tin and copper parts of the sets, the disjointed performance of the actors who met for the first time in this theater—this was all secondary to the sharpness and definition of the stage platform advanced by Meyerhold... The power of *The Dawn* lay in the fact that Meyerhold established the principles of a theater filled with a significant political idea, and a theater directed at the wide mass of viewers."[55]

On November 18, 1920, during the presentation of *The Dawn*, news of the taking of Perekop was announced. M. Zagorsky, who at the time was literary director at the Theater RSFSR I, described the improvisation:

> I had arranged contacts with the ROSTA, and news from the front was displayed at once in the corridors of the theater. The telegram about the decisive victory of our forces over Vrangel was handed to Meyerhold. And on the spot, in a flash of inspired genius, he decided to substitute it for Vestnik's lines announcing victory over the enemy.

It is difficult to describe what happened in the theater when this historic telegram was read. Such an explosion of shouts, exclamations, applause, such a universal, delighted, I would say furious, roar never was heard within the walls of a theater. The impression was strengthened because the news of the defeat of the enemy solidly and organically fit into the fabric of the entire show, as though supplementing it with a bright episode dictated by life itself. A greater merging of art with reality I have never seen in theater, either before or since.[56]

Subsequently, announcements from the ROSTA were no longer displayed in the halls but were read from the stage each time.

The success of the introduction of news into the text of *The Dawn* during the performance intrigued Meyerhold to the extent that he even planned a staging of *Hamlet* in which the gravediggers' scene would be a modern political overview. Mayakovsky was to rewrite the gravediggers' scene and all the other prosaic scenes of the tragedy and update them politically.

The idea of adapting *Hamlet* for purposes of political propaganda prompted cold irony from N. Efros. "I believe," he wrote in *Theatrical Culture (Kultura teatra)*, "that Mayakovsky collaborating with Shakespeare will not increase, but will necessarily decrease the revolutionary and agitational effect of Shakespeare's tragedy."[57] Marina Tsvetaeva, whom Meyerhold wanted to retranslate the verse of the tragedy, refused categorically to participate in this work.[58] During this period, the poetess was filled with vehement hatred for the Revolution, and saw the defeat of the Whites on the Don as a personal, painful tragedy. Clearly, Meyerhold's project did not appeal to her at all. For this and for other reasons the plan to rework *Hamlet* did not take place.

The director's specific interest in the gravediggers' scene, with their jesting and foolery, their cynical and blasphemous buffoonery, is symptomatic. By assigning Mayakovsky to rewrite this scene, Meyerhold not only expected to develop the possibilities that suddenly unfolded before him in *The Dawn* with the introduction of sensational "hot" information into the stage action, but he felt the need to return to the esthetic forms of *Mystery-Bouffe*. Following the triumphal pathetic quality of the show-rally with its dry and ascetic contours, he was again attracted toward farce and buffoonery. The Civil War ended, the difficult, nearly incredible victory had been achieved and its joy required expression. It was at this time that Mayakovsky brought to Meyerhold the second edition of *Mystery-Bouffe*.

An intense struggle preceded the new premiere of *Mystery*. A group of literary figures (among them A. Serafimovich, director of the LITO—Literary Department of the Commissariat for Education) wrote to the Bolshevik Party Central Committee that the play "is incomprehensible to the workers," that its staging would be "enormously expensive," and he protested against the intention of staging it.

In order to refute this opinion, Mayakovsky read the play at several workers' meetings with unbroken success. On January 30, an open public debate was held in the Theater RSFSR I: "Should *Mystery-Bouffe* be staged?" Meyerhold, however, was already directing rehearsals and on May 1, 1921, the first performance was held. The success was so great that *Mystery-Bouffe* subsequently was performed daily until July 7, the end of the season.

Meyerhold rejected the idea of a curtain and of futuristic, cubic design, and of design in general as a background to the actors' performance.

Decoration was replaced by a construction made by the artists V. P. Kiselev, A. M. Lavinsky and V. L. Khrakovsky: a system of staircases, bridges and scaffoldings surrounding a relatively small half-sphere—the upper half of a globe on which was written "Earth." This "Earth" lay to the right, and down at the very feet of the audience. The stage was united with the auditorium or, more precisely, the design spilled over into the hall.

M. F. Sukhanova, who acted in the show, recalled:

> The stage box was broken. The action was brought out into the auditorium, for which purpose several rows of seats were removed from the stalls. In front, in the foreground, a globe of the Earth was constructed or, rather, a portion of the globe. The wings were all removed. "Heaven" was piled up on the construction under the ceiling in the very back of the stage. Those of us in "Heaven" (I was an angel) stood with arms raised, and behind us with every movement trembled white wings made of thin wire covered with gauze. The devils had a place by the base of the globe. Objects and machines were placed in the loge boxes. "The Man of the Future" appeared in the right portal of the stage (looking from the auditorium) at the very top by the ceiling on a specially built platform.[59]

The action, consequently, was thrown out into the stalls and into the boxes, while on the stage it was performed in several planes located along the vertical (on several "floors"), beginning with the very bottom, where "Hell" was located, to the gridirons, where "Heaven" was located.

A large and fairly bulky wooden structure that occupied the stage did not represent the Ark, but nonetheless resembled the deck of a vessel, its ladders and catwalks. The performance on this construction was inventive and entertaining. The Eskimo sat on top of the half-sphere labeled "Earth." He was plugging a hole with his finger, saving the world from deluge. The Conciliator, in disgrace, fell off the meridian of this half-sphere and fell to the floor. When it was necessary to show Hell, the "Earth" turned and from an opening cut in it the devils jumped out and immediately began to cavort and hang from circus trapezes.

On the left, practically to the top of the stage, rose an azure tower reminiscent of a semaphore. Above and to the right were suspended planes, straight and curved. This "semaphore" and these mysterious planes seemed reminiscent of the Suprematism in *The Dawn*, which Meyerhold already had rejected. The design of *Mystery-Bouffe* was based on other principles.

M. Tarabukin wrote:

> The visual aspect of *Mystery-Bouffe* builds a bridge to Constructivism. The floor of the stage is "removed." The stage space has three horizontal floors, unfolds into the depth and runs upward along a parabola. The ladders, scaffolding and platforms create elements for putting the actors' performance into the highest relief. The stage design of *Mystery-Bouffe* may be considered Constructivist to a certain extent. Here we see elements of "arrangement." It also includes features of an architectural order. It may be considered the nucleus from which two basic trends in theater began to develop: Constructivism and an an architectural quality. Both trends are evident in *Mystery-Bouffe*, but each in embryonic,

undeveloped form. There was much here of the decorative, of props. Hence the indistinct form of the stage space, vague both in idea and expression. Nonetheless, this form "sounded boldly and quite harmoniously with other forms of art."[60]

While justly observing that *Mystery-Bouffe* was basic for the formation of the two essential lines of further development of design in Meyerhold's theater—Constructivism and "architecturality"—Tarabukin could have mentioned that it was simultaneously a sort of conclusion to Meyerhold's preceding works. It was as if all the previous experiments in connecting the stage with the audience were summarized here, the boundary between the stage and the audience was erased (at least to the extent that this was permitted by the specific conditions in the building of the former Zon Theater).

The interactions between actors and audience reached maximum freedom and looseness. The actors' performances reflected what we shall see as two of Meyerhold's fundamental ideas at the time: the sense of improvisation and sports-like training. The experiments from the times of the Studio on Borodinskaya Street were finally yielding perceptible results. What previously had been attempted, enthusiastically but uncertainly, boldly, and by guesswork—suddenly became matter of course, not just possible but essential.

The inspiring sense of clear goals, of direct relation to the concerns of the day, of the up-to-the-minute necessity of the created spectacle and (perhaps even more importantly) Meyerhold's sense of certainty that he was directing shows *for the people*, for the masses of soldiers and workers, evoked the master's joyous energy. The show was created in an atmosphere of emotional uplift. Everything merged here—the joy of victory which ended the Civil War, and the joy of the artist sensing his unity with the people.

Subsequently, recalling Mayakovsky, Meyerhold said: "Mayakovsky knew the nature of theater. He knew how to rule theater. He did not appeal only to the emotions and feelings. He was a true revolutionary. He did not speak to those who were attracted to music halls or stereotypes, he was a man saturated with what excites us all... I can say with certainty and speak quite responsibly: Mayakovsky was a true playwright who could not as yet be accepted because he had jumped several years ahead."

Meyerhold himself not only "accepted" Mayakovsky, but gave to the poet all his imagination, initiative and inventiveness. The writers of memoirs who report with a greater or lesser degree of outrage the unceremonious and blasphemously free way in which Meyerhold handled the plays by other playwrights, including the classics, all report the careful regard by Meyerhold for Mayakovsky's texts, his thorough implementation of all the—sometimes nearly impossible—notes by the poet. It seems odd, particularly now when one rereads Mayakovsky's plays—*Mystery-Bouffe* in particular—and becomes convinced of their practically improvisational casualness, how some episodes are barely outlined, while others are precisely and completely finished, how some roles are written while others are just devised, and not written at all, and how still other parts are not parts at all, but just appropriate outcries, etc.

Meyerhold himself gave the answer, when he casually observed that Mayakovsky "was brilliant in the area of composition..."[61]

Without a doubt, speaking of Mayakovsky's gifts for composition, Meyerhold had in mind primarily the poet's principle for the construction of drama which we have conditionally called "attraction assembly." We have noted already that this principle goes back to Shakespeare's theater. It is important to discover its essential relation to the nature of relativistic theater.

If the theater of experienced events imitates life and is interested in showing its continuous course, the "flow of life," including numerous details that are individually insignificant but which prove indirectly the validity of everything transpiring on stage, then relativistic theater rejects imitation and immediately, of course, makes it a principle to select the chief dynamic moments. It tears from reality the *substantial moment*, episode, fragment or "attraction," and offers it in the maximum concentrated form, paying attention to the connections of meaning and esthetics with the preceding or subsequent moment, but in no way attempting to create a sense of continuity of action. On the contrary, the disjointedness of action is one of the means of underscoring its relativistic nature. The disjointedness and selectivity practiced before the eyes of the audience are manifestations of the creative will of the artist. Its presence, its sensation, its constant and perceptible influence, transforming life and forming it according to the laws of art, these are the alpha and the omega of relativistic theater.

Specifically in the early 1920s, Mayakovsky offered Meyerhold the forms of relativistic theater that were nearest to the spiritual and emotional requirements of the times. In the second edition of *Mystery-Bouffe* the elements of the "circusization" of theater and of carnival are even more prominent than in the first edition. At the same time, there is a greater distinctness in the traits that draw together farce and the newly born form of political evaluation, a form with great prospects for development. All of these innovations by the poet were very dear to his director.

In other words, Mayakovsky's plays already contained principles of spatial, rhythmic and stylistic solutions that corresponded fully with Meyerhold's ideas on direction. Beginning in 1921 with the second edition of *Mystery-Bouffe*, Mayakovsky wrote for Meyerhold. In each episode of any of his plays there is contained the foreshadowing of Meyerhold's manifestation of the episode. He knew what Meyerhold needed, what was sufficient for him and what was excessive for him. When Meyerhold staged Mayakovsky, they were co-authors of the show in the full sense of the word.

Mayakovsky felt himself to be the master in Meyerhold's theater. Meyerhold said that he

showed himself in our joint work to be not only a wonderful playwright, but an excellent director. In all the years that I have been staging plays I never allowed myself the luxury of permitting an author to work with me on directing. While I was staging plays, I always tried to remove the author as far as possible from the theater since the playwright always interferes with the true director-artist... Mayakovsky I did not just allow in; I simply could not begin to work a play without him... I was unable to begin work until Mayakovsky himself began to cook it up... Mayakovsky was always present in my theater at all the initial rehearsals.[62]

Thus Mayakovsky determined the basic contours of the future show. But he readily and without complaint carried out any of Meyerhold's practical, technical, most prosaic requests, taking on the modest responsibilities of "assistant director." No one has recorded even insignificant disagreements between the director and the author. On the contrary, while taking turns or sitting together at the director's table they showed the fullest agreement and unity of intent in all matters.

If it can be said that Verhaeren's *The Dawn* was used by Meyerhold as an "excuse for a rally," that it was "filled with hints concerning modernity,"[63] then the second edition of *Mystery-Bouffe* was a ready text for an up-to-the-minute political review show that enlisted intense praise of the Revolution and the rough carnival satire of buffoon-like jeering at its enemies. The show began with a provocative joke. "One of the Unclean" opened the performance with the prologue:

> In a moment
> we shall show you...

threatened the audience with his fist and, after a brief pause, recollects A. Fevralsky, continued:

> the *Mystery-Bouffe*.

Acrobatic and circus approaches were introduced into the show: "An entire circus number was actually introduced: in the third act ('Hell') the popular circus artist Vitaly Lazarenko, invited especially for the purpose, descended a rope from above and, as one of the devils, performed various acrobatic tricks."[64]

In the second edition Mayakovsky added to the play an entire rewritten scene—the "Land of Fragments," in which the theme of combat with destruction dominated and where there was a role for Destruction—and this circumstance further increased the force of the piece. Many of the changes went in the same direction: for instance, the Red Army Man and the Engineer replaced the Chimney Sweep and Cobbler, the theme of electrification was brought forth in the "Promised Land," "Simply Man" became "Man of the Future," etc. In place of the Russian merchant of the first edition appeared a more up-to-date type—the speculator. Masks of Clemenceau, Lloyd George, Lev Tolstoi and Jean-Jacques Rousseau appeared. Mayakovsky and Meyerhold's farce poked fun both at the political enemies of the Revolution and at those thinkers whose ideas were considered hostile because they opposed the principle of revolutionary violence. The Student became the Intellectual, the Hysterical Lady became the Lady with the Cardboard Boxes (an emigrée) and, finally, the Conciliator appeared with "a pair of tearful cheeks—a little Menshevik," trying to "conciliate everything" and everyone and, therefore, like a redheaded clown in the circus, continuously being beaten up by both sides.

Several of the roles of the "clean" were performed with truly enthusiastic buffoonery and brilliance: the Intellectual was done by M. A. Tereshkovich; the American by V. F. Zaichikov; the Priest by P. P. Repnin; the Lady with the Cardboard Boxes by E. A. Khovanskaya.

The Conciliator was Igor Ilinsky's first major stage success. From this moment on people spoke of the birth of a new comic talent. Ilinsky performed in an unkempt red wig, a tangled red beard and, generally, was reminiscent of the Redhead of the circus. A small cape was on his shoulders, eyeglasses were stuck on his nose, while his hand clutched an umbrella. These eyeglasses and umbrella from that moment on and for a long time became in the theater and cinema the requisite attributes for the roles of various political renegades and capitulators... "The actor playing the Menshevik is magnificent," noted Lunacharsky, who at that time did not know Ilinsky's name.[65]

The "unclean" in the show, as compared to the "clean," were less distinctive. Their uniformity had been "assigned" by Mayakovsky. His satire sought the specific, if only the politically specific, and transformed each of the "clean" into an original, amusing figure, while his pathetic side demonstrated a tendency toward unification and the creation of an image of a uniform mass of victors.

Meyerhold transformed impersonality into a principle and a virtue, he turned it into the monolithic. He dressed all his "unclean" in identical costumes—blue shirts, coordinated gestures; together they were to blend into a single poster image of the victorious class.

Subsequently, the blue shirts of the "unclean" passed from this show onto the variety stage and became the uniform of numerous "Blue shirt" troupes in Russia and abroad.

Still, contemporary critics considered the monotony of the "unclean" as a substantial drawback, made even worse by the flowery declamation of V. Sysoev as "Man of the Future."

These drawbacks were noticed by few. The premiere of *Mystery-Bouffe* made an enormous impression. The form of the show was clear and energetic; it was easily comprehensible, with no troubles or misunderstandings.

In the theater the viewers were handed questionnaires in order to determine their reaction to *Mystery-Bouffe*. Most viewers answered briefly and happily—they liked the show. It was performed daily for over forty days in a row with unflagging success.

S. Margolin wrote:

> *Mystery-Bouffe* is a spectacle of maximum theatrical excess. Its power is unarguable, the show is forged of steel, its breadth is undoubted, the spectacle swallows people and throws them from its gigantic innards... Its frenzied movements captivate.
>
> I like the attempt to speak of the Cosmos from a single stage platform in *Mystery-Bouffe*, I like the scale of the action, the fragmented chiseled quality, the iron language, biting jests, the flame-throwing decisiveness, the self-reliance and the author's truly militant sincerity... In *Mystery-Bouffe* exaggeration is the essence of the theatrical presentation, an essence justified by the directors Meyerhold and Bebutov. The show is coarse, abrupt, material but powerful. The show could have been even more powerful, sharper and more frenzied. It should be no smoother or cleaner, this is not its style nor its element... Oh, this is no *Dawn*—the style of new theatrical writing has been found, the rhythm of a new shift in theater.[66]

Em. Beskin described the staging as follows:

There is no stage and auditorium. There is a monumental platform half moved out into the auditorium. One senses that it is cramped within these walls. It requires a city square, a street. These several hundred viewers which the theater houses are not enough for it. It requires the mass. It has broken away from all the machinery of the stage, has elbowed away the wings and gridirons, and has crowded up to the very roof of the building. It has torn down the suspended canvases of dead decorative art. It is all constructed, constructed lightly, conditionally, farcically, made up of wooden benches, sawhorses, boards and painted partitions and shields. It does not copy life with its fluttering curtains and idyllic crickets. It is all composed of reliefs, counter-relief and force lines, striking to the eye but extremely simple, fantastically interwoven. But every relief, every line, every step will play, will obtain meaning and movement when the actor's foot steps on it and the sound of his voice strikes it... Actors come and go on the platform-stage. The workers at once, before the eyes of the public, move, fold, dismantle, nail together, carry away and bring. The author and director are here. The performance is over and some of the actors, still in costumes, mix with the public. This is no "temple" with its great lie of the "mystery" of art, this is the new proletarian art...[67]

The review, written by a critic, a broadcaster of the idea of "Theatrical October," expresses clearly the polemical intent of Meyerhold's work. The spirit of debate permeated even .the programs, where it was explained that "it is possible to enter the auditorium during the performance. Expressions of approval (applause) and of protest (whistling) are permitted. Actors will respond to calls after each scene and during the performance." This amusing declaration decisively flouted the attitude of trepidation before art that had been formed in the Art Theater and its studios, rejected absolutely the very concept of the "theater-temple" and called for art that is born in free, brotherly, simple interaction with its audience.

D. Furmanov wrote in the Ivanovo-Voznesensk newspaper *Worker's Land (Rabochii krai)* that Mayakovsky's play "is fairly somber, raw and poorly finished," but that "the total innovation of the staging" by Meyerhold overcomes all these weaknesses of the script. "There is no finish, polish, external lacquer—on the contrary, here you are astonished by the extreme rawness and elementary simplicity bordering on coarseness, and coarseness bordering on vulgarity. However, there is much power here, strong power, heated faith and uncontrollable enthusiasm. You sense it in the voice, in the look, in the movement of the actor."[68]

In his diary, Furmanov also reacted unfavorably to Mayakovsky's play, and praised Meyerhold's work highly: "This is the conception," he wrote, "of a whole new area in theater. The new theater presses out into the audience with soul and body... The staging is marvelous, gives the impression of something vast, significant, powerful."[69]

Meyerhold was the only Soviet director who was able in the first years of the Revolution to transmit its heroic spirit. The particular type of political propaganda show that he created in those years was major-key, life-affirming. He became ever more joyous, loud, laughing victoriously at the enemies of revolution.

The overall meaning of Mayakovsky's and Meyerhold's efforts in the first years of the Revolution was that they strove to use the images of theater-rally and theater-farce to express the very essence of occurring events, to seize with thought and imagination the *entire* dynamics of revolutionary reality, revolutionary breakage.

This generalized, non-individual approach to reality permitted them to see the main thing in the vast picture of the Revolution.

In the atmosphere of heated debate that accompanied the premieres of *The Dawn* and *Mystery-Bouffe*, the attacks on the academic theaters became increasingly sharp and radical, speeches about "civil war in theater" were heard ever more frequently and insistently. Meanwhile, the Civil War in the country ended. The history of the brief but heroic period of war Communism was completed. The existence of propaganda art with all its inevitable extremes was no longer justified by necessity. Victory in the Civil War, that victory which *Mystery-Bouffe* praised so enthusiastically, signified that the art which had risen on the yeast of armed class struggle had lost the prospects of further development and now required change.

Almost no one in the camp of "Theatrical October" understood this as yet. Meyerhold himself probably was the first to understand or, in any case, to feel the inevitability of change, since he always very acutely and quickly sensed the movement of the times. But even he could not have expected the blows struck against "Theatrical October" by the sudden advent of NEP.

In February 1921 Meyerhold lost his position as director of the Theatrical Department of the Commissariat for Education, and shortly left the Theatrical Department altogether.

On September 6, 1921, performances of the Theater RSFSR I ceased.

The newspaper *Bulletin of the Theater*, the loudspeaker for the ideas of "Theatrical October," closed down in August 1921.

Each of these events had its own history, its own causes.

The building of the Theater RSFSR I was transferred to the "Mastkomdram," the Workshop of Communist Drama, a totally impotent organization despite its flowery name. It was supposed that the Mastkomdram would be able to turn the former Zon Theater into a profitable enterprise: the period of retrenchment began, the Revolution occupied itself with economics. However, the expectations of the profitability of the Mastkomdram were not fulfilled, and Meyerhold soon occupied the building again.

But the Theater RSFSR I no longer existed.

Subsequently explaining the circumstances that caused him to relieve Meyerhold of his duties as Theater Office Director, Lunacharsky wrote:

> The enthusiastic Vsevolod Emilevich immediately mounted a warhorse of the Futuristic type and led the followers of "Theatrical October" in a storming of the "counter-revolutionary" substance of academism. With all my love for Meyerhold I had to part with him, since such a one-sided policy was in distinct opposition not only to my own views but to the views of the Party. It ought just to be noted that the circumstances of that time permitted leftist artists in the field of the representational arts, for instance, to take into their hands a kind of semi-dictatorship, and that the Central Committee of the Party in a special resolution clarified the incompatibility between Futurist artistic forms and the real requirements of post-Revolutionary social life... In any event, I repeat, in full agreement with the staff of the Commissariat for Education and the directives of the Party, I was compelled to consider Meyerhold's extreme line unacceptable from the State-administrative point of view.[70]

Everything is correct in this story, and the justice in Lunacharsky's actions is evident. To clarify the situation further, it is necessary only to place the facts correctly in time, to understand the chronology of events. When Lunacharsky appointed Meyerhold to head the Theatrical Department, the leftists (or Futurists) were supporting Revolution and Soviet power with concrete creative acts. "Poster and rally were necessary for Revolution... Futurism could provide the poster and provide a cleverly staged rally." Therefore, not only the "circumstances of that time," but Lunacharsky himself, the People's Commissar for Education, gave the Futurists "some sort of semi-dictatorship." One of the forms of this "semi-dictatorship" was the installation of Meyerhold in the Theatrical Department. The equivocal nature of his dictatorship was, as noted above, provided for in advance: the academic theaters were not given to Meyerhold.

With the end of the Civil War those artists labeled "rightists" defined their positions. The period of vacillation, doubt, staggering, ended. The traditional "academic" forms, which had just been treated as foreign to revolution and to the proletariat, appeared not only ready but capable of answering the new requirements, the new spiritual interests of the people.

In late 1921, Lunacharsky was more than reserved in his reviews of Mayakovsky: "Mayakovsky is accepted (and it is good that he is accepted) by a portion of our youth and our proletariat. He is, of course, a very great phenomenon, but in no way a standard-bearer... The Party as such, the Communist Party, which is the chief blacksmith of the new life, is cold and even hostile toward not only Mayakovsky's former works, but also to those in which he appears as the trumpeter of Communism."[71]

There were reasons for this "coldness and even hostility." Futurism, wrote Lunacharsky, "could not provide a picture, could not provide drama." It continued to offer only posters and rallies, to propagandize, to yell at the top of its voice. "Meanwhile, the Revolution had grown stronger, been victorious and had moved on to construction. Then a general cry seemed to rise throughout the country: comrades, look around! Comrades, study your country, your enemies and friends and yourselves! Comrades, come closer to reality, to the matter at hand. And when the appropriate mood was finally formed, it turned out that Futurism contradicted this mood, that it created a strange dissonance in this respect."[72]

Lunacharsky, with maximum simplicity and precision, presents the objective causes for the crisis and end of "Theatrical October." The movement had exhausted itself.

Nonetheless, at the time when "Theatrical October" was a reality of revolutionary art, forms had been created that operated with social masks in the theater, a theater of wide generalities, uninterested in the soul and fate of individual man, but passionately interested in the fate and struggle of entire classes. These problems sparked the development of special means for stage expression that subsequently were included in the arsenals of Brecht, Piscator and other masters of political theater.

Yury Annenkov's portrait of Meyerhold

CONSTRUCTIVISM AND BIOMECHANICS

When the Theater RSFSR I was closed, Meyerhold appeared to halt in confusion.

After two years' rapid movement, a pause ensued. The slogans of "Theatrical October" had been sounding triumphantly. As early as 1922, however, Vladimir Blyum wrote: "In the society of revolutionary theater workers, upon mention of Theatrical October one frequently encountered on the face of an 'Octobrist' a dispirited, embarrassed smile. It seemed almost as if they had reached a silent agreement to forget about their 'October,' as if all this turbulent past was either an error or a shameful defeat... In fact, it is nothing like that." The critic was convinced: "There is nothing to repent of. We have made no error, and there can be no talk of any concessions."[1]

The voice of Meyerhold himself sounded less certain. "With the departure of the Theater RSFSR I from the theatrical front we do not see," wrote Meyerhold, "who in practice could continue from the monumental-heroic beginnings."[2] Five years later, Meyerhold would say that "very many interpreted the concept of 'Theatrical October' in a childlike way. It appeared to many that October in the theater means a vast red banner on the stage, means propaganda slogans and so forth. Today it can be admitted that these slogans were 'pale.' Then, all this was necessary only to end once and for all ideas about the theater's notorious apolitical stance... At one point people were saying 'away with tradition.' From our present perspective, continuing this thought, we must say distinctly: Do not throw out the baby with the bath water."[3]

In 1922, Meyerhold undoubtedly was already experiencing disillusionment with the ideas of the "Octobrists" and felt the need for new solutions. But he had no further program for action. The life surrounding the theater was changing literally before one's eyes and it was clear that the path that had begun with *The Dawn* had ended with *Mystery-Bouffe*. Yet another turn in a new direction was required. "For further movement forward it was necessary to enter the research laboratory and to analyze the accumulated experience," subsequently wrote A. Gvozdev.[4]

From this point of view the highly unpleasant fact of the closing of the Theater RSFSR I was a boon. In contrast to his own long-established principle of experimentation in the studio followed by presentation of the experimental results on a large stage, Meyerhold had just been compelled to test the durability of new theatrical ideas publicly before the mass audience of the Theater RSFSR I. Now that he had lost the large stage, fate returned him to the studio.

Classes in the State Higher Directors' Workshops became such a studio. Acronyms were epidemic in those days; the acronym for the workshops was GVYRM. Later, when the directors' workshops were renamed "theatrical," the new and no less ugly word GVYTM appeared. It was decided finally to change the workshops into an institute and a new, more mellifluous abbreviation was formed—GITIS (Gosudarstvennyi institut teatral'nogo iskusstva—State Institute of Theatrical Art). This name change occurred over a period of two or three years, and the reader must know that in essence it signified nothing. GVYRM, GVYTM, GEKTEMAS (Gosudarstvennye eksperimental'nye teatral'nye masterskie—State Experimental Theater Workshops), GITIS, were all just different signs. Under the cover of all these names Meyerhold worked with a single, fairly monolithic group of students and followers. Among them were young actors from the Theater RSFSR I: I. Ilinsky, V. Zaichikov, M. Babanova, then M. Zharov, D. Orlov, M. Lishin, N. Mologin, A. Temerin and the students S. Eisenstein, E. Garin, Z. Raikh, N. Ekk, S. Yutkevich, V. Fyodorov, V. Lyutse, M. Korenev, Kh. Lokshina, N. Loiter, M. Sukhanova. Many of these subsequently comprised the nucleus of Meyerhold's theater and walked with the Master (Meyerhold received this title as head of the Workshop in 1921 and retained it to the end of his days) for nearly all of his thorny path.

Meyerhold's theatrical guard consisted of youths who were still very green. Some of his pupils were seventeen or eighteen years old. The twenty-year-old men and women surrounding the Master were filled with enthusiasm and a readiness to rebuild the theater from top to bottom. Meyerhold, in Ilinsky's words, looked "younger than the young." His fighting spirit, fervor and limitless courage pleased the young students. They followed Meyerhold selflessly and without second thoughts. The Master, meanwhile, was charting his own course over the stormy seas of the theater of the early 1920s.

At the beginning of the Civil War, Meyerhold had a sort of monopoly—while the rest pondered, doubted and weighed the new circumstances, he acted. By 1920 the situation had changed drastically. Stanislavsky, Nemirovich-Danchenko, Vakhtangov and Tairov presented a number of highly interesting productions. On the theatrical horizon the star of Mikhail Chekhov began to shine brightly as he performed the parts of Khlestakov and Erik. These events in the life of the theater ought to be noted, particularly because the starting point of all the experiments, the source of all the theatrical rivers, remained in the Art Theater, which had rediscovered its power in studio presentations, first of all in Vakhtangov's shows. Again, as before, Meyerhold had to "clarify relations" with this art, with the method, theory and practice of the Moscow Art Theater.

In one of the articles signed by Meyerhold in 1921, the principles of the Art Theater were subjected to crushing criticism. Meyerhold ridiculed the method "brought up in the gyneceums of the Moscow Art Theater, born in the torments of psychological naturalism, in the hysteria of spiritual tension, with a bath-induced relaxation of the muscles... The notorious 'circle,' spiritual reticence, the cult of concealed heavenly beginnings—a form of fakirism is behind these staring eyes, the deliberateness and sanctity of its persona. The danger in this method is all the greater because its antitheatrical banality infects the associations of workers, peasants and Red Army soldiers. It is this danger that we point out."

Meyerhold offered another method in place of this one—"the method of true improvisation that pulls together, as in a magic trick, all the achievements and delights of true theatrical cultures of all times and peoples." He insistently attracted attention to "the physical culture of the theater." He asked: "What is needed?" And answered: "Culture of the body is needed, the culture of physical expression, perfecting this single tool of the actor's work" (i.e., his body). "A single gesture of the hands resolves the verisimilitude of the most difficult interjection 'akh,' which the 'leftovers' futilely force out of themselves, replacing it with impotent sighs."[5]

Thus the search for the internal truth of experience was sharply contrasted to the search for external, plastic, and verbal expressiveness.

It is interesting that at the same time, in April 1921, Meyerhold undertook an attempt to contrast the Art Theater to none other than its founder, K. S. Stanislavsky. Together with Bebutov, Meyerhold published in one of the last issues of *Bulletin of the Theater* their famous article "Stanislavsky's Solitude."

Bebutov and Meyerhold wrote:

Think what a tragedy! A man born for the theater of exaggerated parody and tragic concern, year after year under the pressure of the hostile forces of banality, was compelled to break and distort the essence of his Gallic nature, imprisoning himself in the tastes of people who go to the Hermitage, the Mauritania, the Ravine, and the Prague—all of these overdressed, stupidly self-satisfied shopkeepers from Kuznetsky Bridge, banking houses, offices, and coffee-houses...

It was necessary, since the office orders it, to work on an ideological base, to construct at whatever cost the notorious *system* for the armies of psychological leftovers, the performers of all these roles who walk, eat, drink, love, wear their jackets.

But fortunately an alchemist is preparing a reliable antivenom against the office: Vakhtangov, like a true armor-bearer, does not abandon his knight... Stanislavsky gives his lessons.

No suffering! Ringing voices! Theatrical walk! Suppleness! Expressive language of gestures! Dance! Bow! Battle with rapiers! Rhythm! Rhythm! Rhythm!—calls Stanislavsky... He and only he in his solitude is capable of restoring the lost rights of theatrical traditionalism with its *"relativistic improbability," "diverting action," "masks of exaggeration," "truth of passions," "verisimilitude of feelings under the proposed circumstances," "freedom of judgment by the street,"* and *"blunt openness of popular passions."*[6]

All of Pushkin's formulas underlined by Meyerhold and Bebutov point to the same ideal theater toward which Meyerhold himself was working and toward which he supposed Stanislavsky to be working and which, in any case, it was time to achieve.

Incidentally, in 1919-1920, during his enforced inactivity in Novorossiisk, Meyerhold studied most thoroughly Pushkin's thoughts on theater. His archives contain notebooks of extracts, comments, notes on the structure of Pushkin's plays, and ideas developing or supplementing Pushkin's brilliant formulas.

Finally, let us indicate the supportive attitude toward Vakhtangov expressed here by Meyerhold and Bebutov. Vakhtangov's central idea in the post-revolutionary years—to "return theater to theater"—was an old, pre-revolutionary idea of Meyerhold's. Following October, the circumstance that the principle of frank theatricality was proposed by Vakhtangov—a pupil of Stanislavsky, one of the leaders of the First Studio—must have inspired Meyerhold especially. The "psychology" so disliked by Meyerhold was being attacked from within, was being undermined within the very citadel of psychology and emotional experience. The tense situation within this citadel was, of course, well known to Meyerhold. He knew that the conflict between Stanislavksy and Nemirovich-Danchenko was intensifying, that Stanislavsky's "system" was not accepted by some and profaned by others.

He understood, too, that the complex processes which were taking place within the Moscow Art Theater in the context of a new social situation intensified all the conflicts within the theater. Thus, from the point of view of Meyerhold's argument against the "akas" and, primarily, against the Art Theater, the article "Stanislavksy's Solitude" was a crafty blow. Its purpose was to turn conflict into schism. It was permeated with the unconcealed desire to wrest from the Art Theater at least two of its strongest masters—Stanislavsky and Vakhtangov.*

In theatrical debate and combat Meyerhold demonstrated such craftiness more than once. The political coloring that the struggles on the "theatrical front" increasingly acquired often gave Meyerhold's speeches a demagogic and cynical character. He was one of the first to use a critical tone, to resort to political accusations and to coarse and cruel remarks in arguments over esthetics.

When reading the accounts of old theatrical disputes today, one becomes convinced of this with a feeling of disappointment that is particularly bitter because later Meyerhold himself became the victim of demagoguery and criticism, the target for political attacks and angry invective. Furthermore, he was attacked under altered social circumstances, where denouncements were no longer an empty disturbance of the air, but threatened the grimmest consequences. But this does not justify Meyerhold, since by no means everyone used such a tone.

The polemical techniques used by Mayakovsky, Meyerhold, and even Tairov were rejected with noble disdain by Stanislavsky, Nemirovich-Danchenko and the "old-timers" at the Moscow Art Theater. It is possible that Meyerhold's best excuse could be the uncalculated nature of his polemic, the almost childlike naivete of his craftiness. The relatively early article "Stanislavsky's Solitude" is one of the best examples of this. Obviously sensing its sensational nature, Meyerhold erred grossly in publishing the article. First, he erred in supposing that the "system" was something forced on Stanislavsky from the outside, something constructed on orders from the "office." The creation of the "system" was, of course, an intrinsically organic stage in the total creative development of Stanislavsky.

Second, he failed to understand that the resolution of any conflict was possible for Stanislavsky only on the basis of that cultural tradition whose highest expression was the art of the Moscow Art Theater. All the contradictions encountered by Stanislavsky, particularly his long-term conflict with Nemirovich-Danchenko, were contradictions within a single esthetic system of psychological realism and were the stimulus and form of its development, metamorphosis, and enrichment with new content. Third, notwithstanding all his sympathies for Vakhtangov, Meyerhold underestimated him. It was at this very time that Vakhtangov found ways to synthesize Stanislavsky's direction with Meyerhold's and achieve a real union of their most important theatrical ideas.

Vakhtangov literally followed upon the heels of the two great seekers, and the fact that he was slightly behind them helped him give a conclusiveness, cleanliness and precision of form to their astonishing guesses and visions.

---

*Stanislavsky left Bebutov and Meyerhold's article without an answer. Some theater specialists have tried to see an answer to Meyerhold in Stanislavsky's article "Concerning the Trade," which appeared in *Theatrical Culture*, also in 1921. The article was directed against routine and stereotypes and has no relation to Meyerhold's article. Evidently, it had been written a long time before it was published.

In a short period Vakhtangov showed Muscovites three masterpieces of direction—Chekhov's *The Wedding, The Miracle of St. Anthony* and *Princess Turandot*. The dependence of these works on preceding innovative experiments by Stanislavsky and Meyerhold is evident. Their stylistic unity was just as evident, while *Princess Turandot* was also emotionally innovative. Its theatricality was festive.

Meyerhold, like Vakhtangov, sensed in this moment the acute need for life-affirming theater in a major key. "Any theatrical essence" of the new theater, he asserted, must evoke in the audience *"delight in a new existence."* Making this idea more specific, Meyerhold called for "freedom from the hypnosis of illusion." The new audience, he felt, must "know that before them is a show and they must enter this show consciously."[7] In other words, Meyerhold propounded the principles of relativistic and joyful theater.

But the festive theatricality that celebrated victory, jubilant and happy in *Princess Turandot*, remained for Meyerhold a thing of the past. He had long ago forsaken the harlequinade and did not intend to become Doctor Dapertutto again. Vakhtangov, who had a fine sense for drawing conclusions, presented in *Princess Turandot* the quintessence of all the Russian variations on the themes of the Italian masked comedy. The clever and graceful production, perfect in form and exceptionally elegant, he connected easily and naturally with modern times, with the unsettled but hopeful life of the twenties. Meyerhold, meanwhile, set against the festive, opulent, and well-dressed theater a theater of ascetically simple contours. The period of "undressing the theater" had begun.

Comparing the art of Meyerhold in those years with that of Vakhtangov, A. P. Matskin wrote with full justification that "their positions were different, completely different." He continued:

> In those first post-revolutionary years Meyerhold was gripped by the tragic aspect of revolution, its great destructive problems, as well as its noble asceticism—caused by the conditions of War Communism. His esthetic ideal was totally polemical. He debated with the past, including his own past, contrasting the refinements and ornaments of Symbolist art with the contrived dryness and laconic poster-like coarseness of his post-revolutionary shows. Instead of the majestic colorful range of *Masquerade* we saw the bared brick walls and the blue canvas work clothing of *The Magnanimous Cuckold...* It appears to me that in this conscious simplification, in this underscored monotony, there was a logic of its own. Meyerhold understood the democracy of our socialist Revolution as an *equalizing process* and attempted to extract new poetic norms from it. This was a common prejudice in those times.[8]

There is much in this description that requires further clarification. The tragic side of the revolution had an impact on *The Dawn*, where strictness, asceticism and dryness were most obvious. His two stagings of *Mystery-Bouffe*, which were the most polemical with respect to past theatrical experience, were happy, variegated, and had the colorful amusement of farce, a joyful excitement. And although the revolutionary mass in all three shows did perform as a monolithic unit (underscored by the sameness of the overalls), this is not sufficient reason to say that Meyerhold viewed the Revolution as an "equalizing process." What should be stressed is his drive to use simplified means to create an image of the masses celebrating their victory. But in *The Magnanimous Cuckold* the overalls had a new and totally different function. *The Magnanimous Cuckold* expressed more powerfully than both editions of *Mystery-Bouffe* not the tragic, but the intoxicatingly happy acceptance of Revolution.

In a sense, *The Magnanimous Cuckold* was located at the intersection of the lines of *The Dawn* and *Mystery-Bouffe*. From *The Dawn* it received the ascetically dry form, but here the coldness of monumentality and the somberness were completely absent. From *Mystery-Bouffe* it obtained all the boisterousness and comedy which for the first time were organized into a sturdy body of rational, convenient and elegant stage form. But this show was not a capstone for previous achievements; this was a show of brilliant innovation that opened totally unexpected prospects before the art.

The first herald of the "undressing of the theater" was *A Doll's House*, staged by Meyerhold in a hurry—five days—and performed on April 20, 1922. Rehearsals with the actors took even less time: only three days. "I have met many people in my day," Eisenstein wrote many years later, then proceeded to list meetings with Chalyapin, Stanislavsky, Mayakovsky, Shaw, Pirandello, Douglas Fairbanks, Marlene Dietrich... After this cascade of famous names he concluded:

> But not one of these impressions will ever be capable of erasing from my memory those impressions that remain with me after these three days of rehearsing *A Doll's House* in the gym on Novinsky Boulevard.
> I remember constant trembling.
> This is not cold, it is excitement, it is nerves wound up to the limit...[9]

When Eisenstein wrote these lines Meyerhold's name was unutterable. Meyerhold's enormous archives, now accessible to all, carefully organized, numbered and microfilmed, were stored secretly in the dacha of Meyerhold's pupil, the director of *The Battleship Potemkin*.

There had been no time to prepare decorations for *A Doll's House*. On the day of the premiere five of Meyerhold's pupils—Eisenstein, A. Kelberer, V. Lyutse, V. Fyodorov, Z. Raikh—were sent to the stage

> on special assignment: to prepare a set for *A Doll's House* without spending a penny on materials, and guided by the arrangement of furniture suggested by the Master. By eight o'clock in the evening the setting was prepared, checked and approved. The setting used old decorations turned inside-out, parts of pavilions, gridiron guide bars, etc. Thus, the stage gave the impression that everything was collapsing, everything was going to the devil, down and out... Against this background the phrase of the self-satisfied bourgeois, Helmer: "It's nice here, Nora, cozy," could not but evoke a tempestuous reaction from the auditorium.[10]

Meyerhold's pupils had created chaos on stage. The reverse sides of the decorations had strange writing and numbers facing the audience: "Nezlobin No. 66," "side 538." The most different kinds of furniture were jumbled together. Tables, chests, chairs were placed so as to create playing positions for the actors. Still, this chaos was expressive in its way. The decoration (if it could be called such) represented the "disintegration of bourgeois life," the collapse of the milieu against which Nora was in rebellion. The former Nezlobin actress, B. Rutkovskaya, who played Nora, brought her heroine immediately into Meyerhold's bedlam, and Nora's fate was read against the background of his bedlam. Meanwhile, Meyerhold already was completing his work on a show where the stage design was to represent nothing and signify nothing.

There remains an interesting document written in a clear, youthful hand (undoubtedly the hand of one of Meyerhold's pupils) entitled "Theses for the Constructive Formation of *A Doll's House*." This is an attempt to present the esthetic reasoning after the fact. It says:

> The treatment of the text by V. Meyerhold has broken abruptly with the usual view of Nora. The treatment of the stage space has broken all connections with existing cabaret esthetic norms, has departed from any representation, thus taking from "the tragedy about Nora" all coloring of personal drama and abstracting it to a certain extent. The reversed decorations not only break with the esthetic standards of the past, but also establish new ones. *They demonstrate that the material of stage production as such,* shorn of any beauty and subjected to artistic processing, *gives the viewer, strange as it may seem, specific esthetic pleasure*, gives beauty... No external conditions shall thwart us...since we always come from the ground, from the material (no matter what it is like), through overcoming and organizing it.[11]

Although *A Doll's House* was a directorial impromptu, it is nonetheless evident from these theses that the thoughts that inspired Meyerhold were tested in his work with *A Doll's House*, which distracted him from Crommelynck's play *The Magnanimous Cuckold*.

Therefore, when V. Blyum wrote " . . . in the eyes of some spectators it was possible to read the mute question: is this Futurism? Constructivism?" and answered: "We can reassure you: neither one nor the other"—he was not totally correct. Characteristically for stage Constructivism, the dramatic situation was removed—however hastily and crudely—from the everyday environment in *A Doll's House*. "As for the so-called light decoration," continued the same critic, "it received short shrift, too. One shield was illuminated with a red reflector, the other —with a violet one. The result was a charming 'chantant,' a delight for the heart of a saleswoman from GUM." The article concluded with a rhetorical question: "What is this production—parody or...hoax?"[12]

This staging was neither parody nor hoax. It was only a hasty and bold experiment, quickly put on the stage in order to seize control of it. Meyerhold hurried to take over the building of the former Zon Theater, which had been taken from him and which was available again. Three days after the staging of *A Doll's House* he put on *The Magnanimous Cuckold* in this auditorium.

The conception of a Constructivist spectacle evidently had matured in Meyerhold's mind after he visited the exhibition of Moscow Constructivists, entitled "5 x 5 = 25" in the fall of 1921.*

The idea of Constructivism in theater meant primarily that the design of the

---

*Five artists participated in this exhibition (A. M. Rodchenko, L. S. Popova, the brothers V. and G. Stenberg, K. Medunetsky), each of whom displayed five pieces.

stage became free of problems of representation and meaning. The construction, in principle and ideal, was itself meaningless. It had one purpose only: to organize the stage space most conveniently for the actors, to create "working space" for the players.

Three days after *A Doll's House* (which astounded audiences and critics but was totally unsuccessful) and two months after the thunderous success of Vakhtangov's *Princess Turandot* on April 25, 1922, Meyerhold showed Muscovites his stagings of *The Magnanimous Cuckold*, by F. Crommelynck. This was the first and possibly only show in which the principles of stage Constructivism were applied thoroughly. For the first time, the decorations were replaced by a machine built by L. Popova. In this show Meyerhold wanted to reject completely not only the old principles of stage design, not only the painted or constructed realistic decorations, but also the latest Futuristic cubes, cones and planes—he rejected the resolution of all representational problems.

Popova's machine was placed on the stage of the former Zon Theater. The back brick wall was visible.

Popova united in a single construction several small ladders, platforms and wheels. According to A. Gvozdev, her machine was "a trampoline for the actor, which was justly compared with the contrivances and equipment of a circus acrobat. In the same way that an acrobat's trapeze has no intrinsic esthetic value, and it is indifferent to the circus performer whether it is beautiful or not—it need only be usefully designed for his work—so is the construction in *The Magnanimous Cuckold* designed wholly for the development of the actors' performance without any pretense of decorative significance."[13] I. Aksyonov observed that "this arrangement made it possible to perform as one does with a fan or hat."[14]

Although Constructivists repudiated the representational on principle and although Meyerhold rejected the need to solve representational matter, Popova's machine, however relativistic and crudely sketched, provided a sufficiently clear definition of a specific place of action. It is not that Popova portrayed a windmill. No. But the wings and wheels of her construction evoked an association with a windmill. The text of the play made this association more precise, clear, specific.

In Meyerhold's theater, Constructivism always included such associations. The construction always bore a relativistic image of the place of action. The "working place" of the actor simultaneously was the territory where the characters of the play dwelled.

Popova's "keyboard for the performers" also possessed an esthetic bond with the problems that the director set before himself in this case. Visually balanced, thoroughly harmonious, it gave an impression of impetuosity and bold dynamism. Impetuosity without nervousness, asceticism without severity, lightness, dryness, clarity in all respects—such was the form of this graceful construction which appeared self-enclosed, neutral with respect to the given stage space. The construction was not attached to the stage of the former Zon Theater. On the contrary, it was supposed that it could be transported to any other platform.

It is probably because in Popova's construction the windmill was easily recognized that N. M. Tarabukin saw here a certain element of compromise:

The traditions of painting, however subjectless, are reflected in L. S. Popova's work. The contrived frontality of *Cuckold* strikes the eye. The windmill's circles, white letters on a black background, red color together with yellow and black—these are all instances of painting and decoration. The "device" is dominated by planes and Suprematism. Its lightness and elegance are totally appropriate to the style of Crommelynck's farce. But from the point of view of utility the construction in some of its parts does not withstand strict criticism. We can point to the door on the second floor and to the platform behind it where the actors are compelled to go and where they fit with difficulty.[15]

Nonetheless, Meyerhold himself always ascribed exceptional significance to the staging of *The Magnanimous Cuckold* and believed that in this particular show it was "possible to carry through completely" the principle of Constructivism. Several years after the premiere, he wrote:

> The show was to have been the basis for a new technique of performance in new stage surroundings that broke with the idea of framing the place of action with wings and portal. In founding this new principle, it inevitably had to reveal every line of construction and to take this device to its furthest schematic limits.
>
> The fact that the extremity of style in this show, although it did scare a segment of the critics, was accepted with delight by the audience, demonstrated that the need for just such a style of theatrical work was urgently felt by the new audience which had obtained the theater among the other cultural conquests of the Revolution.[16]

It has been observed above that in turning to Constructivism Meyerhold first of all intended to solve the strictly utilitarian problem of creating the best conditions for the actor, and did not intend a strictly representational perception by the audience of the construction itself. He consciously bared the stage down to the brick wall of the theater building, striving to eliminate all illusion. At this moment, the painter was essentially banished from the theater. In his place came the "arranger" *(ustanovshchik)*, the engineer and the constructor. The costumer was chased out after the painter—the actors performed in identical blue overalls. It was as if all the externals of the show were being eliminated. Meyerhold was preparing to take theater out of the confines of the theater building into the open air and believed that the theater of the near future would retain decorations "only insofar as they recall elements of industry: the decorations will be ones that give the actor the impression of iron, stone, etc."

These little-known words of Meyerhold's—a director who was criticized constantly for ignoring the actor—are interesting for their complete readiness to subordinate everything in the theater to the actor. Meyerhold brought Constructivism to the theater for the actors. "The force of an actor with Revolutionary fervor," he said, "cannot tolerate daubed colors."[17] Characteristically, Meyerhold's espousal of Constructivism went hand in hand with his affirmation of "biomechanics," which will be discussed later.

I. Ilinsky, however, observed astutely that Meyerhold's urge to free the actor completely from theatricality, from "daubed colors" ("Here, on the bare platform-constructions, young actors without make-up, in canvas blue overalls, will show their skill, so to speak, in pure form, without the aid of theatrical illusions")—this attempt "unexpectedly, to some extent, for Meyerhold himself" suddenly obtained *"also another significance."*[18] What significance? Why did Constructivism capture the Soviet stage of the time so completely? Where was the explanation for the odd—from the modern viewpoint—involvement of directors with the hard, dry lines of stage machines, platforms, assemblies that were ever more complex, moving, shifting, illuminated one way and another? Why the fascination of the audience with all this machinery, which very soon ceased to obey the actor and became extremely difficult and inconvenient for him?

The manifestos of the Constructivists rejected art in general, on principle, as it were: "We, the Constructivists, reject art since it is not expedient. Art by nature is passive, it only reflects reality. Constructivism is active, it not only reflects reality but acts itself."[19] "We declare uncompromising war on art!" declared the "1st Working Group of Constructivists" in 1920. Such an interpretation of Constructivism was theoretically incompatible with modern theater. "Theater is amusing," wrote A. Gan, "when flashes of 'mass action' are the product of our days."[20]

Constructivists poeticized, almost deified the machine. "The machine resembles an animate organism much more than is commonly thought... Moreover, modern machines are alive to a far greater degree than the people that build them." Osip Brik admitted dreamily: "For us the factory and plant are the tools of collective creativity and we await wonders from them that are immeasurable compared to the tricks of individual handicrafters."[21] So it was—they awaited miracles.

I. B. Arbatov, one of the theoreticians of Constructivism, supposed with a sort of logic that theater must become "the factory of the qualified man," that the stage "inevitably will arrive at plotless theatrical art, thanks to which theater will have before itself the opportunity to experiment with the material elements of theater (dynamics of light, color, line, volume in general and in particular that of the human body). This will allow the results obtained in the stage laboratory to be transferred into life, creating anew our real everyday social life."[22]

In the theories and plans of the Constructivists, however, even such a theater of "new beginnings" was relegated to the very last place. The Constructivists were interested primarily in industrial structures, residential buildings and specific designs for everyday life.

From what has been said above, it is evident that John Gassner was greatly in error when he asserted in his well-known book *Form and Idea in Modern Theater* that "constructivism [of the stage—K. R.] was not the imitation of the architecture of industrial buildings and modern machines, but was a totally independent program of theater that strove for strictly esthetic ideas."[23] On the contrary, Constructivism overflowed into theater from industry and from other arts, primarily from architecture and painting.

It is, however, curious that in industry and in architecture in the early 1920s, Constructivism asserted itself primarily with declarations, projects, models, and with manifestos in poetry. In reality, Constructivism took root in this period in theater, right next to that "sorry modern character—action," which was ridiculed by the Russian theoreticians of Constructivism.

"Theater," wrote I. Aksyonov, "gave Constructivism its first opportunity to manifest itself in large forms and to come out into society with brilliance."[24] The young Republic was too poor to erect Constructivist towers, skyscrapers, glass palaces, clubs in the shape of screws, etc.—the days of new structures had not yet arrived. But in theater the ideas of the Constructivists were realized with the aid of ordinary boards and common (although in equally short supply) nails. Furthermore, the absence of real cement, concrete, iron and glass, and the very poverty of this Republic, which was racing forward into the future, stimulated with unusual energy the appearance of Constructivist stage machinery. Stage Constructivism was a sort of realization of the artists' dream of the future, of a technology which would bring the country from poverty into the mechanized, electrified, finely organized kingdom of socialism.

This is why Meyerhold's intention of turning the stage into the ideal "working place" for the actor immediately obtained an esthetic function. Meyerhold wanted for the stage to "represent nothing," for it to reject illusion totally. But the engineers and constructors, the "arrangers" who replaced the painter, immediately created first in Meyerhold's theater, then in other theaters, images of the future, images of the oncoming "Age of Machines," of mechanized life. Naturally, these had an emotionally exciting effect on the viewers.

In the Kamerny Theater, A. Ya. Tairov interpreted the ideas of Constructivism differently. His construction carefully concealed its connection with the world of machines and mechanisms, it was draped with colorful cloth, was painted bright and effective colors, was illuminated with colored projectors and was frankly representational. The most interesting construction by Tairov and his artists (the brothers V. and G. Stenberg and K. Medunetsky) was presented in 1924 in *The Storm*: the rough-hewn wooden unpainted parts of the setting "constructed" an image of a poor, wooden, but solidly nailed-together Russia. Tairov's estheticized Constructivism often demonstrated the capability of creating images of the past—in *Romeo and Juliet* (A. Ekster, artist), and later in W. Hasenklever's *Antigone*. Also, when the image of the show was permeated with the spirit of modern urbanism (O'Neill's *Emperor Jones*, Chesterton's *The Man Who Was Thursday*) Tairov's construction became refined and beautiful, luxuriously representational.

Meyerhold's theater consistently sought totally new imagery: it was counting on a feeling of the genuineness of the material, its texture (such as it was, it took on the function of color), the logic and dynamism of the structure of the construction.

Returning to *The Magnanimous Cuckold*, it should be noted that this first Constructivist show by Meyerhold, although experimental (and possibly *because* it was experimental), possessed greater unity and a more organic bond between the exterior form of the spectacle and the performances by the actors.

When the actors first stepped onto Popova's machine they found themselves in totally new and unfamiliar surroundings. These surroundings may be described in a single word: barren. The actor was no longer assisted by decorations and costumes. He appeared in a sterile-clean space, on the exposed and inclined planes and ladders of the machine, and on the bare floor of the stage. Each motion of the actor, regardless of his desires, obtained sculptural relief and significance. Now he was compelled to strive for the most exact expression of the plastic picture, he was obliged to move with the lightness of a dancer and with the grace of an acrobat. Acting became colored by the agility of sportsmen. The grace of the plastic picture inevitably caused a lightness of delivery of each line, with ringing and precise intonations.

All this taken together created a special system for the actors' performance, in the foreground of which was a joyful demonstration of professionalism, of confident and coordinated craftsmanship. With regard to Crommelynck's play this light, vital, and rhythmic craftsmanship yielded the unexpected effect of purifying the emotions which, undoubtedly, Meyerhold had expected. Only the dynamic diagram was extracted from an emotion: the moment of appearance, development (rises and falls), culmination, exhaustion. Here is the answer to the riddle of purity and health, freshness and youth that colored the risky tragi-farce on Meyerhold's stage.

The performances of Meyerhold's actors were grounded in the principles of biomechanics. In *The Magnanimous Cuckold*, biomechanics faced its first public test.

In the early twenties the principles of biomechanics were presented most solemnly and theoretically. In one article from the period, we find, for instance, the following panegyric to biomechanics:

> Based on data from the study of the human organism, biomechanics strives to create a man who has studied the mechanism of his construction, and is capable of mastering it in the ideal and of improving it.
> Modern man living under conditions of mechanization cannot but mechanize the motive elements of his organism.
> Biomechanics establishes the principles of precise analytical execution of each motion, establishes the differentiation of each motion for purposes of maximum precision, demonstrativeness—visual Taylorism of motion (Sign of refusal—the establishment of the start and end points of motion, a pause after each accomplished motion, the geometrization of movement in planes.) We must be able to show the modern actor on stage as a complete automaton. [25]

This is a clear attempt to establish direct bonds between biomechanics and the esthetic of Constructivism, the machinery that was poeticized and praised in the spirit of the times. Even more expressive is the idea of biomechanical perfection not only of the actor, but of man in general. The dream of man "organized" according to the principles of mechanics, of man ideally adapted to "mechanized life," connected biomechanics with one of the most popular ideas of the time—the idea of the rejection of art. It was supposed that the theater of the near future would be a sort of school giving the audience lessons in rational, laconic, expedient motion. Man was viewed as a machine that needed to learn how to control itself. The stage, accordingly, took upon itself the modest function of demonstrating the already well-adjusted human "mechanisms" as an example to all. This idea, like many similar ideas of the all-pervasive Americanization of life, remained a touching and unrealizable Utopia that appeared in the context of the poor and ill-organized life of the early 1920s.

In theater itself, however, biomechanics turned out to be an extremely useful school for actors' expression, plastic expression above all.

Meyerhold's biomechanics was based on the following main principles.

The actor's art is the creation of plastic forms in space. Therefore, the actor's art is the ability to utilize the expressive potential of his body correctly. This means that the route to image and feeling must begin not with experience, not with seeking to plumb the meaning of the role, not with an attempt to assimilate the psychological essence of the phenomenon, in sum, not "from within" but from without; it must begin with motion. This means the motion of an actor excellently trained, possessing musical rhythm and easy, reflectory excitability; an actor whose natural abilities have been developed by systematic training.

Biomechanics was called on to prepare technically the "comedian" of the new theater for any performance, including the most complex. Complexities were expected primarily in the realm of plastic and intonational expression. In order to overcome these it was necessary to have an actor who could "do everything"—an all-around actor. Biomechanics was to prepare such actors.

In 1935, Meyerhold, objecting to an article whose author stated that biomechanics "supposes the absence of feeling in the performing actor," wrote in the margin: "Does not suppose." Regarding the comment that biomechanics led to an undervaluation of the "psychic apparatus of the actor," Meyerhold expressed himself even more categorically: "Nonsense! We did not underestimate. In *The Magnanimous Cuckold* the psychic apparatus was in motion just like biomechanics."[26]

These objections by Meyerhold were based on his certainty that a precisely determined, polished and fixed external form "suggests" the required feeling, causes experience. Biomechanics, thought Meyerhold, gives the actor "motion of such a kind that all 'experiences' arise from its process just as easily and convincingly as a ball that has been tossed up falls to the ground."[27]

The actor's body must become an ideal musical instrument in the hands of the actor himself. The actor must perfect the culture of physical expression, must develop the sensation of his own body in space. As for "soul" and psychology, Meyerhold asserted that the route to them could be found only with the assistance of definite physical positions and states ("points of excitement"), whose rich score is the chief weapon of the actor. Biomechanics ascribed great importance to the rhythm and tempo of an actor's performance, required *musical organization of the plastic and verbal picture of the role*.

It is not correct to say that biomechanics in practice was confined to physical culture and acrobatics. "Physical culture, acrobatics, dance, rhythmics, boxing, and fencing are useful subjects," said Meyerhold, "but they can be useful only in the event that they are introduced as subordinates to the course of 'biomechanics,' the basic subject required of every actor."[28]

At the time when Meyerhold was proclaiming biomechanics, he contrasted it sharply with the Moscow Art Theater's system of actor training. The polemical sharpness of this contrast gradually became erased, but the general methodological "key" of biomechanics remained unchanged: from the external (which is easily caught, grasped and may be fixed)—to the internal (which even if understood to the end is not always grasped and in practice cannot be fixed for repetition). As it evolved and entered into new relations with changing reality, biomechanics became ever more elastic, ever more capacious.

As early as 1934, I. Ilinsky, describing the first stage of the development of biomechanics and referring to his personal experience as an actor, indicated ways in which it brings an actor to emotionally saturated performance and experience:

It is thought that biomechanics is something like acrobatics. At best they know that biomechanics is a series of stage techniques, the ability to slap a face, to jump onto the partner's shoulders, and so on and so forth. Few know that the biomechanical system of performance, which begins with a number of techniques consisting of the ability to direct one's body on the stage in the most successful and correct way, also extends to the most complex problems of acting technique, problems of coordination, of movements and speech, of the ability to direct one's emotions and one's acting excitability. The emotional saturation of an actor, temperament, excitability, the emotional sympathy of the artist-actor with the creative emotional experiences of his hero—this, too, is a fundamental element in the complex biomechanical system.[29]

Many are tempted to equate Meyerhold's biomechanics with Stanislavsky's "method for physical actions." Ilinsky writes directly that "there is a junction between Meyerhold's biomechanics and Stanislavsky's physical action."[30] A. Fevralsky states that the researcher who undertakes a comparative analysis of biomechanics and Stanislavsky's method "undoubtedly will find in them much that is in common."[31] Without entering into the special method of physical actions formulated by Stanislavsky in the last years of his life, we shall observe only that in accordance with Stanislavsky's teaching, the actor's work on himself is the first, initial stage of learning his "system." Then, upon the completion of the cycle of practice and etudes begins the new stage: the actor's work on the role.

This is where the "method of physical actions" comes to the aid of the actor. The third stage follows: the actor's work on the play. When expounding on his teaching, Stanislavsky stressed primarily the truth of emotional experience, the capability of an actor actually to begin to live the life of the character, to saturate his stage behavior with the absolute truth of emotional movements, intonations and true-to-life details and shadings of the action taken from real life. "The truth of the life of the human spirit" was seen as the fundamental basis for the actor's art.

In the beginning, biomechanics proudly billed itself as a system whose aim was to create "a man wielding his body...sturdy, strong and agile, useful not only for art, but at any moment ready to take a hammer and stand at the anvil."[32] In other words, biomechanics promised to transform not only the actor, but man in general (fully in tune with the LEF concepts of "life-construction" *(zhiznestroenie)*— which the new art necessarily was to pursue).

In 1922, Meyerhold's pupils outlined the basic laws of biomechanics:

Here they are: the body is a machine, the worker is a machine operator; discovery of center of gravity, equilibrium, stability, mandatory sign of refusal, coordination of bodily movements of the platform, orientation in space, surrounding by figures, the law of vocal reflexes, gesture as the result of the motion of the entire body, the laws of running and walking, the meaning of "parade" in exercises, Taylorization of movements, eye-reckoning, movements of the arms, legs, body as the producers of external word, and others.

From this list it can be seen that, basically, the discussion concerned the laws of movement on the stage platform. The Master's pupils believed, however, that *all work process in general* "will be transformed into that healthy work-art, work-joy toward which the workers of all countries are striving."[33] No more and no less!

L. Popova's collage of the set for Crommelynck's *The Magnanimous Cuckold*, 1922

Poster for *The Magnanimous Cuckold*

A scene from *The Magnanimous Cuckold*

Act III of *The Magnanimous Cuckold*

A scene from *The Magnanimous Cuckold*

Ilinsky as Bruno

Babanova as Stella

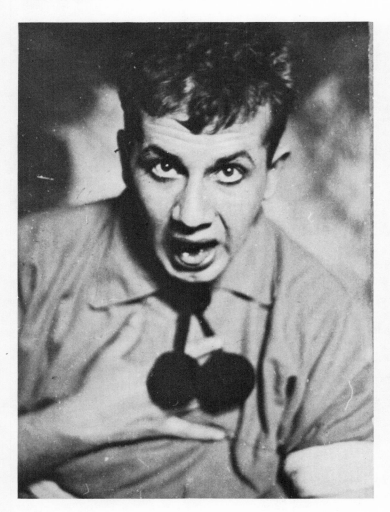

V. Stepanova's prop
design for Act I of
Sukhovo-Kobylin's
*The Death of Tarel-
kin*, 1922

Okhlopkov as Kachala,
Zharov as Brandakh-
lystova, Act III of
The Death of Tarelkin

Two scenes from *The Death of Tarelkin*

A scene from Sergei Tretyakov's *Earth Rampant*

Tretyakov's *Earth Rampant*

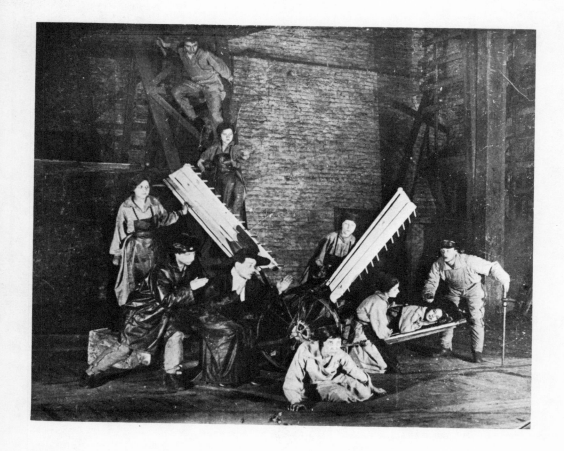

Earth Rampant

A scene from *D.E.*, 1924

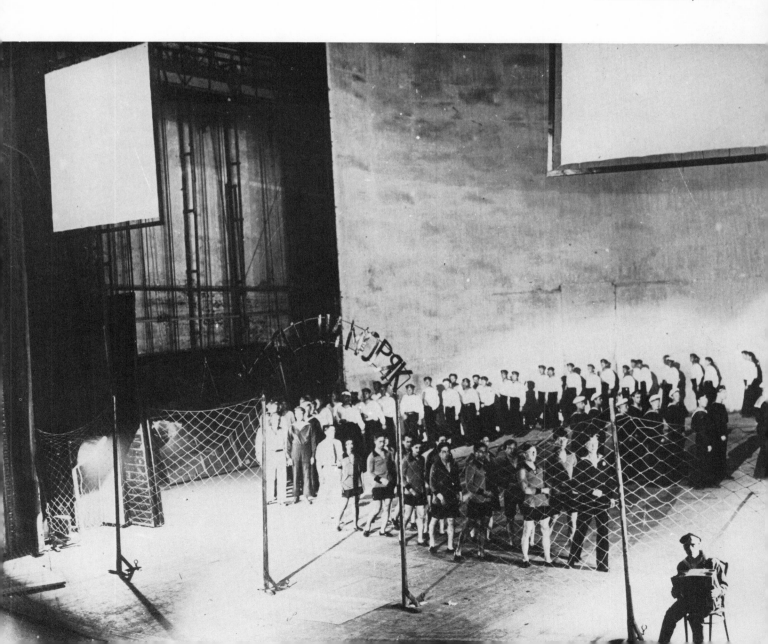

Later, after several years, when the slogans of "life-construction" ceased to elicit unquestioning trust, when B. Arbatov was compelled to observe "the ignoring of the idea of merging the theater with reality,"[34] one of the ideologues of LEF, S. Tretyakov, admitted that "theater has found its esthetic shores, constructions have become honest wooden decorations and biomechanics—a unique plastic,"[35] Meyerhold theories returned to intra-theatrical problems. In 1926 A. V. Lunacharsky certified biomechanics as a strictly technical means with whose aid the actor governs "the apparatus of his body and brings his physical training to perfection." Meyerhold objected only that "teaching of expressiveness enters into this, too."[36] Several years later Meyerhold went into greater detail: biomechanics must only "ease the actor's self-control and his entry onto the stage. In no way does biomechanics contradict the expression of the internal content of human emotional experience, etc."[37] Subsequently, this became reason to say that biomechanics, finally, did not pretend to the significance of a universal theory of actor's art, but remained completely within the limits of useful technique.

However, if biomechanics did concentrate the actor's efforts on his work "on himself" (and not on the role and not on the play; the independent labor of the actor could be discussed here only relativistically, since this labor was directed actively by a director), if biomechanics was in truth a training system then, it nonetheless taught and formed not just any actors—and certainly not actors of the "emotional experience school"—but actors whose bodily apparatus was precisely organized in accordance with the principles of musical rhythm. The primary issue was bodily expressiveness fully subordinated to the laws of musical organization of movement. According to the requirements of biomechanics, any motion was to be not true-to-life, not simply truthful (the truthfulness of accident, so common in life, was excluded definitely), but reasonable, compact, laconic and, particularly, *responsive* to the movement of the partner.

In other words, biomechanics trained and taught actors of a special type whose stage movements resembled those of ancient jongleurs, farce comedians—muscular, elastic, flexible, graceful, musical. These actors always were burdened by and uncomfortable in suit coats, frock coats, or morning coats, but, on the contrary, they felt fine in loose coveralls or tights. This is how they remained always, regardless of the costumes they wore, regardless of the plays they performed in—tragedy, comedy, vaudeville, drama—regardless of the content.

The main stress fell on movement: movement became a form for the development of the actor's action and its main structural element. One of Meyerhold's closest collaborators from as early as the days of the Studio on Borodinskaya Street, V. N. Solovyov, wrote on this subject:

One of the most characteristic aspects of actors' technique in Meyerhold's theater . . . is the plastic opening up and development of the image. Therefore, for Meyerhold's actor, the slightest movement on stage very often is as important as a lengthy monologue for an actor of the emotional school. Using motion, Meyerhold's actor transmits the external form of an image, its internal essence, and individual moments of his intense condition. Naturally, with the shift of the center of gravity into the realm of motion, a significant place in the actor's art is given to the stage pause. Very often the pause serves as the means for uncovering the most complex stage interrelationsips. Occasionally, only after a pause, does the meaning of the entire preceding scene become clear. In connection with the exceptional role of motion in Meyerhold's theater, the use of the word has new purpose. Verbal material undergoes special musical treatment, wherein the precision of the musical design and the utilization of tempos often cause the text to have a new sound.

Furthermore, Solovyov observed keenly that Meyerhold's biomechanics "to a certain degree trains each actor to be an inventor striving to discover ever newer means for theatrical performance. And very often, what appears to the viewer to be excellent work by the director is, in fact, the creative invention of the performer."[38]

The principles of biomechanics, based on the traditions of commedia dell'arte, farce and circus, entered forever into the flesh and blood of Meyerhold's performers and opened before them a great freedom of initiative and improvisation under what appeared to be strict conditions and limitations of directorial fiat. This technique was assimilated firmly and for a long time—it made itself felt in the mid-1930s when work with biomechanics ceased in the theater and the Master himself hardly brought it up any more.

It is true, however, that in this area Stanislavsky and Meyerhold pursued a common goal: they wished to rid the actor of uncontrolled muscular tension, to give him the freedom of stage presence, to teach him to control the "physical life of the role."

In the words of P. Markov, the production in which the capabilities of biomechanics were demonstrated for the first time—*The Magnanimous Cuckold*—"consolidated the actors' craft in a most categorical and pure form. Meyerhold freed the actor from the detailed weight of make-up and from the refinement of costumes, dressing the actors in coveralls common to all the characters and compelling them to perform almost without make-up, with faces free of daubed colors. He viewed motion not on the level of abstract esthetic beauty, but as the most reasonable and evident expression of the internal content of the given piece... But," stressed Markov, "these tendencies of Meyerhold's did not signify the destruction of the internal picture of the role... It was as though Meyerhold freed the substantial and clean lines of the development of the image."[39]

It is time to say a few words about the play by Fernand Crommelynck staged by Meyerhold, and the interrelations between the show and the times. *The Magnanimous Cuckold* was hammered together by the playwright with the happy roughness of farce. The theme of jealousy was brought to total absurdity. Bruno adored his faithful wife Stella, but according to the ridiculous logic of wild passion, while searching for the supposed cause of her infidelity, he forced Stella actually to betray him with everyone. "What I need," he yelled, "is to recognize among all those who come to her, the one who will not come." In the comically altered situation of Othello, Bruno played his own Iago. He inflamed his own suspicions, and worked up his own jealousy, holding forth furiously in front of the silent scribe Estrugot and his shocked, obedient, loving wife Stella. With no grounds for jealousy, Bruno, in his search for the unknown and hypothetical lover of his wife, himself gave her to all the men in the village. Finally, he lost Stella, who went to the crude and unlovable

Volopas, asking only an oath that Volopas would permit her to be...a faithful wife.

Meyerhold presented this entertaining and piquant paradox in a tragicomic key. He demanded that the actors become "tragicomedians." Each one's role was set forth exactly. Bruno—I. Ilinsky—"simpleton"; Stella—M. Babanova—"lover"; Estrugot—V. Zaichikov—"clown"; Volopas—N. Losev—"boastful knave";Count—M. Tereshkovich—"fop"; and so forth.[40] In the central role of Bruno, even though according to the role description he was a "simpleton," Meyerhold strongly and unexpectedly accented the theme of the self-excitement of the poet. He led Ilinsky to an image that was "poetic, childlike in its ingenuousness and mischief." This poetic quality given to Bruno as a leitmotif and the main motive force of the role changed the meaning of all the events in the play. Its situations, according to Ilinsky, were seen by the actors and by the audience "more as tragic than farcical or bawdy."[41] The poet and simpleton Bruno became in the production a tragicomic victim of his own grandiose, even monstrous imagination. His crazy behavior was ennobled by this childlike ability to entrust himself completely to his own fantasy. Every time Bruno brought himself to ecstasy, the wheels of Popova's construction would begin to revolve energetically, underscoring the significance of his words. "With increasing exaltation, Bruno describes the beauties of his wife's form," Meyerhold says in his directorial copy. "The white wheel begins [to revolve], then the red. At the words 'I am so excited by her beauty that it makes me catch my breath'—the black one."

One of the most effective scenes of the first act—when Bruno, describing the delights of Stella to her cousin Petri, made her undress, and then suddenly seeing the fire in the cousin's eyes, he slapped him—was constructed in such a way that the sound of the slap brought all the wheels into motion at once. In the finale of the first act, as soon as Bruno, in a heat, brought himself to the desperate conclusion that "I am a cuckold!" the three wheels again turned together.

The performance by the actors on the machine required a practically acrobatic agility. Meyerhold put together compositions like this one: "The burgomeister, saying his goodbyes, *strikes* with his rear the right half of the door, thus causing the left one to *strike* his nose. Then he *rounds* the door and *flies out* into the passage between the door and the left side of the gallery."[42]

All these blows, flights, falls, nudges, jumps, somersaults, etc., together with the complex score for the movement of the wheels and wings of the construction—clockwise and counterclockwise—gave the spectacle an image of sportslike clowning. The hint of bawdiness that is in the very situation of the farce was removed altogether. The fact that all the actors performed in blue coveralls decorated only occasionally with identifying details (red pompoms on Bruno's chest, gaiters on the Count, Stella's thin silk stockings), deepened the general feeling of freshness, health, and youth that Meyerhold strove to evoke.

P. Markov believed that Igor Ilinsky fulfilled Meyerhold's requirements best. He wrote:

Ilinsky is a realist. Among Meyerhold's constructions of iron and wood he appears just as concrete and material as the bared material of the construction. In him, despite all the softness of performance, despite all the charm of his craft, is the revelation of the physical and organic skeleton of a man. Ilinsky's art is fully organic, it seems to come from the "inside," at the same time Ilinsky is a representative of "biomechanics" who capably implements the director's concepts.[43]

In *The Magnanimous Cuckold*, three of Meyerhold's pupils celebrated a victory: Ilinsky, Babanova and Zaichikov. What they did was so new that people began to speak of a new formula of coordinated performance by this trio: "Il-ba-zai."

Explaining the content of the "Il-ba-zai" formula, A. Gvozdev wrote:

"Il-ba-zai" means, first of all, that Meyerhold's actor enters into a definite *system of characters*, subordinates himself to a hitherto unknown composition of groups. Retaining his individuality, the actor develops such an amazing *partner sense*, such an ability to coordinate all his movements with the partner's body, that in fact the former habits of critical evaluation of an actor's performance become inadequate and it becomes necessary to speak, abandoning the usual terminology, of "triple-bodied" characters.

Gvozdev even supposed (unfoundedly) that this new technique of collective performance by several actors in the future would develop gradually into the coordination of large groups, and that in this way a requisite actor's technique would develop for the incipient theater of mass action.

It is difficult to find more perfect harmony than the triad Ilinsky—Babanova—Zaichikov. The expressive means of the human body achieved in the mutual amplification and intertwining performance of these three wonderful actors make an impact of unforgettable force on the spectator. The *reasonableness of motion* creates a new, unified scale of pantomime speech.

The intensity and flexibility of Ilinsky finds its continuation in the special rhythmicality and musicality of Babanova, while Zaichikov creates for them a unique accompaniment with his precise tying together of all the gesticulation. Like the chorus in a Greek tragedy, he accompanies and clarifies in pantomime everything that possesses his partners in the turbulent exchange of passions.[44]

B. Alpers subsequently stated that *The Magnanimous Cuckold* marked the appearance of a new type of actor who "appeared to be the manifestation of the new man, free of the power of objects, of the power of stagnant, immobile society, who stands in a big spacious world filled with that life energy which permits an exceptionally exact calculation of each gesture or movement, newly rebuilding the house of the world."

The critic continued:

An actor in Meyerhold's theater built his house anew, created his art anew out of simple, logical and joyous movements of the human body. This art of his was dynamic, as was the entire rushing life of the Revolution.

The actor looked about himself.

Filled with *joie de vivre* and mobility, he ran up the steep steps of the construction in *The Magnanimous Cuckold*, rolled down its slide-boards, testing the strength of its forms and platforms. He measured the stage with great leaps, gesturing in the air with the victorious, powerful hands of a builder. He constantly played with the revolving door, the revolving wheels and the other simple parts of the machine...[45]

The premiere was an astounding success, unparalleled, as Ilinsky wrote, even in his professional biography—so rich with victories.

S. Tretyakov wrote:

> *Cuckold* satisfies. It is a rehearsal over which floats the aroma of work. Its coveralls do not distract one to psychology, everyday life and history. On the contrary, in the lines and tone of the clothing are presented the basic industrial-working associations of the present day. The human body as expressive material put into motion with a setting for action and not for emotional experience is utilized variously and widely.
>
> The gesticulative trash is discarded, the simplest, most economical, target-hitting gesture is sought—Taylorized gesture.
>
> But it does not fall into monotony, since the motivation of the plot dictates its application in the most various circumstances, while the Constructivist machine is the scaffolding for our housing under construction; it is our ladders and floors, bridges and overpasses that our muslces must overcome. And the wheels—these decorations themselves smile and jest along with the action.

Tretyakov's slender conception, however, was unable to encompass the entire show. Babanova resisted. "Stella's intonations," stated Tretyakov sadly, "often are impressive and psychological, which shifts the show in the direction of psychology and interrupts the sense of workshop." Any intrusion of psychology appeared to Tretyakov an unforgivable error. "Women," he complained, "even if just with their voices, will give psychology. They cannot hold back." Therefore, Tretyakov removed Babanova's name from the "Il-ba-zai" formula and proposed a two-syllable formula for the performing success of *Cuckold*: "Il-zai."[46]

However, another opinion was much more widespread and remained in force for a long time. "Babanova," asserted A. Gvozdev, "creates an unforgettable image with a most skillful shift from cloudless, happy sensation of the world to spiritual confusion and stress. Her movement achieves a rare animation thanks to the ability to govern her body, which is rarely observed in a dramatic actor."[47]

Five years after the premiere of *Cuckold*, M. Levidov, as though objecting specifically to Tretyakov, wrote: "In *Cuckold* Babanova was the most significant phenomenon of this significant production. Without Babanova and, partly, Ilinsky, the show would have been only a shining proof of a theorem, a wonderful experiment. Thanks to Babanova it became a *human* show, saturated with the compassion and emotional participation of the audience."[48]

The arguments concerning *The Magnanimous Cuckold* were verbose and furious. "When we are given a farce, circus acrobatics, and are told that it is leftist revolutionary art, we must protest, since the staging has absolutely no revolutionary content," said one orator during a dispute over *Cuckold*. Another asked, "Can it be that all the storms that have passed over the country and the theater in the past five years are reduced to biomechanics? All of Meyerhold's revolution is but the revolution of the anklebone!" Meyerhold, continued the orator, "wants to transform Russia into ancient Greece and make his actors participants in the Olympics.

This is a noble occupation, a valuable achievement, but has nothing in common with theater."[49]

Thus, passionately, the interrelations between the show and revolution, and between the show and art, were determined. Both these aspects of the dispute were possible and lawful, both problems were propounded and resolved anew by Meyerhold.

From a totally different position and with unexpected sharpness, A. V. Lunacharsky spoke against the production. He was outraged and shocked, first of all, by Crommelynck's play. He wrote:

> I consider this play an affront to man, woman, love and jealousy, a mockery, please excuse, miserably underscored by the theater. I left after the second act with a heavy feeling, as though someone had spit on my soul. It is not that the plot is indecent: it is possible to be more or less tolerant toward pornography, but it is a matter of the coarseness of form and monstrous tastelessness with which it was presented. One is sorry for the excellent actor Ilinsky, making faces and poorly imitating bad clowns, sorry for all these young actors, misguided by "searching." One is ashamed for the audience which howls with animal laughter at the slaps, falls and obscenities. One is ashamed that the audience laughs so...at a show staged by a Communist director.

The conclusion: "This is a decline for theatrical art, since this is a seizure of its territory by the clowns of the music hall."[50]

People's Commissar Semashko disagreed with Commissar Lunacharsky, was delighted with *Cuckold* and found no "pornography" in it at all. The majority of the reviews particularly underscored the healthy, clean, sports-like spirit of the production.

Meyerhold did not leave Lunacharsky's comments unanswered. "It appears to me," he stated ironically and bluntly, "that Mayakovsky was correct in stating that Anatoly Vasilevich speaks more with the voice of a playwright than with the voice of a People's Commissar and the voice of an art critic. Here is a taste that has grown up on Rostand, on little poems that absolutely require the accompaniment of a mandolin. Such a taste will never accept the healthy laughter, the healthy performance, the powerful and healthy engineering, nor the biomechanics that we present in the show *The Magnanimous Cuckold*."

He immediately attacked Lunacharsky's theatrical policy, placing on him personal responsibility for "the dirty life of our art, for all the plays and shows that call to the bad instincts of its bourgeois spectator." Meyerhold observed caustically that "against the background of NEP, theatrical enterprises sprout that, unfortunately, evoke no objections from Anatoly Vasilevich."[51]

Lunacharsky, who himself often utilized these same polemical techniques (in the review of *Cuckold* and, subsequently, in many other cases, for instance regarding *Days of the Turbins*, by Mikhail Bulgakov, whom he called a bourgeois, a "political gawker," a Philistine, etc.),[52] responded to Meyerhold's attack calmly and condescendingly. Excesses in debate, accusation, the personal, caustic, insulting tone at that time did not yet threaten anyone. The times were verbose, and if words sounded too sharp or too rough, then in any case they could be waved away. They caused only turbulence in the air. Furthermore, it is entirely possible that Lunacharsky understood that he had gone a bit too far. Subsequently, he admitted readily that in his evaluation of *Cuckold* he had "differed with the majority." Lunacharsky admitted that the show "perhaps did have a significance for Meyerhold's inner development, and in this respect was an essential 'moment,'" but still continued to recall with distaste its "extreme crudity."[53]

For many, the extremely sympathetic, if qualified, response by Nemirovich-Danchenko was an unexpected surprise. He said:

> The alive, flexible, trained, joyous human body is very good. The "package" itself is not new. But some kind of limits are needed. Acrobatics is an excellent thing, but it must not be taken as far as the circus, to the point where it leaves the plan of theater as such... In Meyerhold's *Cuckold* I saw an actor without make-up, an actor in uniform coveralls. Fine. I accept... But then, the wheels in *Cuckold* whose turning is to speed up the dynamics, the tempo of action, or to symbolize some peaks of this action—this is very much from the head. I feel no internal justification. I do not accept this as "new art," but just a new caprice of an artist. Does it excite me? No... Today, a ladder and a circle, and tomorrow there will be something else. This is not central.[54]

However, two years later, in 1924, Mayakovsky stated without reserve: "Meyerhold's highest achievement was *The Magnanimous Cuckold*."[55]

Developing the success of *The Magnanimous Cuckold*, Meyerhold applied the principles of Constructivism and biomechanics in his next work—another and totally new staging of *The Death of Tarelkin*, by Sukhovo-Kobylin. When undertaking *The Death of Tarelkin* once more, the director undoubtedly foresaw all the difficulties that the staging had in store for him. As we recall, he had gone through this play once before, but nonetheless he expected that he would be able to overcome the inevitable obstacles.

From the point of view of the goals that Meyerhold set himself, the selection of the play was practically paradoxical. The director wished to ridicule the newly defeated and rejected old world with raucous, farcical laughter. The play, however, was a scream of despair, a tragic farce. It should be remembered that the problems inherent in switching a play from one genre into another were always tempting to Meyerhold. He was intrigued by the visible allegory of the famous scene of "Rasplyuev mechanics" where incredible simplicity is used to show the entire system of head-cracking upon which Russian "justice" was based, as was the entire autocratic state. The play presented a great number of opportunities to take yet another step on the way to the theater of happy comedians, acrobats and circus performers. Naturally, a construction, a machine, a "place for performing," was created. But willy-nilly a more active form of "representation" and "illusoriness" was required in this case: the police station had to be shown so as to make clear that here people were tortured and questioned.

V. F. Stepanova's Constructivist "machine" represented something between a barred cage and a meatgrinder. Through this construction passed all the personages who were in the hands of the police. A table and chairs were necessary for the questioning. They appeared. These chairs cracked when sat upon and popped up when people arose. Each piece of furniture was conceived of as an "apparatus." There was, for instance, a tall box with a lid from which the head of an actor suddenly protruded.

The lid was closed, the head disappeared.

N. M. Tarabukin wrote:

> The prop designs for *The Death of Tarelkin*, made in 1922 by V. Stepanova, make a decisive break with decorativeness. They are limited to convertible furniture and several items that appear on stage only when needed. The white color that all the objects are painted underscores again that painting-decoration is gone. An object, be it a chair, table or something else, serves a utilitarian purpose: to be "the machine for the actor's performance."
>
> But if in *Cuckold* L. Popova created a stationary construction-machine on which the actor plays, demonstrating his plastic capabilities, then in *Tarelkin* there is a moveable machine-object that the actor plays around, demonstrating his pantomimic cleverness.[56]

Furthermore, in *The Death of Tarelkin* the construction was not single and unified: it was divided into separate units placed on the floor of a bare and empty stage.

The actors were all dressed in practically identical uniforms, and the prompter, wearing the same uniform, was seated in the first row of the hall. Meyerhold had his comedians fire pistols, beat their partners with clubs and inflated bull's bladders, pour water over each other, struggle with the whims of furniture that jumped, leaped and shot.

In one of the reviews, this strange sight, first performed on November 24, 1922, is described with sufficient detail:

> From the dirty, cold stage of the Zon Theater pressing in with its damp brick walls, everything has been removed, everything that made it a theater. Even the prompter is seated in the front row of seats and is dressed in coveralls. There are neither footlights nor costumes... Instead of decorations, there is some kind of surgical machinery. The white light of a projector pours from a reserved box... The projector is broken, it hisses, burbles and causes an extreme dejection in the spectator. The actors wear either hospital, or artists', or clowns' gowns and smack each other with paddles and sticks. The faces of the actors without make-up are, of course, impossible to distinguish... According to the play Tarelkin dresses as Kopylov, while in the theater the actor playing Tarelkin comes out as Kopylov, looking the same. The audience, of course, understands nothing.[57]

Further, the reviewer noted:

> Meyerhold's model is the carnival *à la* Devichii with all its particular movements, sticks, completely incomprehensible shooting (the auditorium stinks of gunpowder), and finally tricks like sniffing the rear end of the body and indicating with gestures how people stop in places where "stopping is strictly forbidden"... The male roles are played by women, the women's by men, a short-haired girl of seventeen plays the role of an old woman, and so on and so forth. One thing is certain: what is being shown under the name *The Death of Tarelkin* is neither art nor theater, and is not in harmony with our great Revolution.[58]

It would be easy to argue with this severe conclusion. "By directing his theatrical ship toward popular carnival and circus,"[59] Meyerhold not only was implementing his old ideas, but he ably tied them in with the play (where many of the indicated carnival crudities, such as the performance of Brandakhlystova's role by a man, were provided for) and the age.

A carnival atmosphere invaded the auditorium. Colored balls flew through the hall. During the intermissions enormous prop apples were lowered from the balcony and the spectators eagerly tried to grab them. Posters were tossed out: "Death to the Tarelkins—Make way for the Meyerholds," etc. This entire amusing scuffle (" 'Moscow's boss' Kamenev laughed gaily," mentioned one review[60]) happened only in the intermissions and was quiet during the performance. Meyerhold clearly was damaged by the poor and meager technology of the stage. The projector not only hissed and warbled, but would go off completely, leaving the stage in total darkness. The circus furniture was poorly built and worked badly. "All of Stepanova's furniture, which in theory was to be like mercury—in practice turned out to be helpless and miserable."[61] The costumes were bad, dirty yellow and, worst, baggy. Wearing these loose overalls, it was practically impossible to carry out the acrobatic tasks demanded by Meyerhold. This is why one reviewer wrote that the actors were "helpless in handling things with which they do not know how to play, and are no good at all in terms of tempo."[62]

Meyerhold's pupils insistently explained the true principles of the production to the spectators and critics. They objected to those who wrote with condescending indignation about the show: "Yes! *The Death of Tarelkin* is staged in the traditions of farce, carnival, and Petrushka. Meyerhold does not reject this, because the traditions of farce are the only healthy theatrical traditions needed for our time."[63]

Nonetheless, almost no one liked the production. Alexei Gan, one of the ideologues of Constructivism, asked in consternation: "Why was all this staged on the horizontal?... Can it be so that Tarelkin can: 1) pass through the screen, 2) climb into the box, 3) sit on the jumping chair, 4) stand on the chair-apparatus with the dropping seat, 5) lie on the armchair? For this one could quite successfully use everyday objects."[64]

In other words, Gan chided the theater for misusing the capabilities of Constructivist solutions. Stepanova herself also voiced the same criticism, but less audibly. All the objects on stage, she wrote, "were placed as apparatus, as armament for the given stage production, and not with a decorative purpose. This was not quite successful, since the work of the director and his actors became disconnected from the material environment and tore it away from the actor, because the theatrical tradition of playing with and through oneself is not yet dead. The objects appeared on their own...they became illusory and decorative."[65]

Meyerhold did not forgive Stepanova this stab in the back and she worked with him no more. His anger had its own justification: Stepanova knew better than others the meagerness and technical inadequacy of the theater, and vainly sought to find an esthetic conflict between the craft of the actors who, supposedly, were in the habit of "playing with and through themselves," and the principles of Constructivism.

The line of esthetic conflict did not pass through here. Meyerhold tried to give the production carnival mischievousness in many ways, and the critics wrote in a single voice of the nervous, worried course of this show, saying that the "sad picture of Russian reality jerked in convulsions of carnival-circus form."[66] This was an insurmountable contradiction. The efforts to transform *The Death of Tarelkin* into a "cloudless comedy of tricks" were useless, even though M. Tereshkovich strove to depict Tarelkin as a bold and jesting fellow, kidding Varravin himself. "Thirsty, tied hand and foot, Tarelkin, who has just clutched at a cup of water that has been presented to him," described S. Mokulsky, "suddenly rises up as though nothing was wrong, pulls a wine bottle from his side pocket and drinks, winking happily at the audience."[67] But the joyous mood did not work. A sense of "sickness, nightmare, some kind of internal disorder" arose.[68] "The audience," wrote B. Romashov, "is gripped by fear. It is not interested in tricks. It senses the most important: death mocking man."[69]

S. Margolin explained this failure another way. The point is, he believed, that "Tereshkovich does not know how to perform in a farce, he is humorless and therefore has nothing for the part of Tarelkin. His monologues perish like an echo in the desert. He is not infectious, and therefore destroys the show."[70] When V. Zaichikov replaced Tereshkovich in the role of Tarelkin, things did, in fact, become happier.

The duets by Zaichikov-Tarelkin and D. Orlov-Rasplyuev were the most interesting in the play. For Orlov, Meyerhold introduced a small episode into the score of the show, a separate "attraction": Rasplyuev's laughter. The laughter was satisfied, bawdy, and rolling. At this moment Dm. Orlov appeared to revel in the role of "victorious swine." With Zaichikov present, the others performed in a more positive way: M. Lishin-Varravin, M. Zharov-Brandakhlystova, N. Okhlopkov-Kachala. The production of *The Death of Tarelkin* had a fairly long stage run. However, Meyerhold's attempt to transfer the tragicomedy into the key of a carnival show failed.

There were, as yet, no Soviet plays that accorded with the director's worldview and stage principles as applied in *The Magnanimous Cuckold*. At this time Meyerhold's attention was attracted to *Night*, by M. Martinet, staged by A. Velizhev in the Theater of the Revolution. In 1922, Meyerhold undertook the direction of the Theater of the Revolution and examined the staging before the premiere. According to the recollection of Z. G. Daltsev, he "did not make a single comment. It became clear to me that there was nothing he could find fault with: everything was smooth. But was Meyerhold thinking of such a slicked-down production?"[71]

And, in fact, after approving Velizhev's "slick" production in the Theater of the Revolution, Meyerhold proceeded at once to stage *Night* in a version completely reworked by S. Tretyakov and retitled *Earth Rampant* on the stage of his own theater on Sadovo-Triumfalnaya Street.

In 1923, this theater was called the Vs. Meyerhold Theater *(Teatr imeni Vs. Meierkhol'da),* abbreviated TIM.

When taking the new Theater of the Revolution under his aegis, Meyerhold supposed that "at home" in the TIM he would experiment, search out new paths, while in the Theater of the Revolution the tested techniques of stage expression would be presented before a mass audience. In other words, the TIM was seen as a sort of large studio, while the Theater of the Revolution would be a theater for the masses. There was another substantial element introduced by the situation of the NEP: the Theater of the Revolution was intended as a profitable commercial business (even though Meyerhold did not intend to make allowances for the demands of the NEP-era public). On the contrary, Meyerhold intended to isolate the TIM, his laboratory, from the influence of the "cash box" altogether.

Meyerhold did not like Martinet's play at all. "This play is a dog," he once told Fevralsky gloomily. Nonetheless, in the Theater of the Revolution he gave his blessing to Velizhev's staging. For the TIM he asked Sergei Tretyakov to alter the play, to transform the melodrama into a sort of propaganda poster, to "stuff" it with the gunpowder of angry satire.

"The contents present clear propaganda against bourgeois militarism, the form shows military order as the most rational organization of human collectives; thus, the staging as a whole is an apotheosis of the Red Army... *Not the presentation* of war and revolution, but *military-revolutionary action*; not props, but real military hardware."[72] This is how the theater stated the basic principles of the show.

This "military-revolutionary action dedicated to the Red Army," first performed on March 4, 1923, consisted of episodes of pathos and satire: "Down with war!"; "At ease!"; "Truth of the trenches"; "The Black International"; "All power to the Soviets!"; "Knife in the back of the Revolution"; "Shearing the sheep"; "Night."

The staging was consistently Constructivist. N. M. Tarabukin wrote: "In *Earth Rampant* L. Popova is a completely orthodox Constructivist. Painted props have been chased from the stage. The artist has constructed something resembling a crane. There is one color here—red. The 'crane' lifts the actors and permits the molding of plastic scenes on its ribs. The unit is not connected with the portal. It stands on the platform of the stage just as it stood directly on the ground in the theater's shows in the area around Moscow."[73]

A. Gvozdev noted, however, that "this time it was not possible to create a successful, appropriate machine unit":[74] Meyerhold and Popova wanted a real crane in the show, but it turned out that it would be too heavy for the stage floor. A model of a crane was constructed. The model, however, did have its defect—it could not operate like a real crane and was not particularly useful. It was moved back to the rear of the stage.

In *Earth Rampant*, wrote P. Markov, in Meyerhold's staging, "through the auditorium onto the stage, roaring and popping, rolled motorcycles and automobiles."[75] This created a strong impression. Modern technology was for the first time brought on stage. It delighted people with its authenticity and its promise for the future.

The show, marveled Em. Beskin, "literally stands the theater on end. The proportions are living, engineered, technical... Next to the actor is a real thing. Motorcycle. Automobile. In the middle of the theater is a wide road with a sloping bridge leading to the stage. Bicycles roll on it, motorcycles fly up it, puffing, and even automobiles... This is already the destruction of theater. This is some sort of 'make room!' This is the rejection of any intimacy, any theatricality with its effects and effectlets, with its perfumery, with its chocolate-salon manners."[76]

For the first time in a staging a screen was used, located at the back of the stage. Propaganda posters and photographs flashed on it. Therefore, Popova's construction was proudly named "machine-photo-poster."

S. Mokulsky wrote:

Earth Rampant is an excellent propaganda show staged purely as a rally, with inflammatory speeches, with acute poster-like stage situations, with clear elements of theatrical satire... Political tendency permeates the entire staging: it organizes the speech, movement, and gesture of the actors, either in particularly grotesque clowning (Emperor, generals, priest, conciliators), or on the level of "inner" pathos, *high* realism, free of the elements of psychological theater (proletarian characters).

At the intersection of these two planes Meyerhold managed to avoid the contradictions usual in such cases. Highlighting the ideological contrast between the two groups of characters he at the same time stressed the unity of the stage whole achieved by way of *a single* method for the construction of the show—*Constructivism*.

"With all this," concluded the critic, "*Earth Rampant* still contains a number of compromises with old theater."[77]

The principle for the combination of high tragedy with carnival satire harkkened back to *The Dawn* and *Mystery-Bouffe*.

The compromise occurred simply because the heroic days of *The Dawn* were gone forever and the rally-performance could no longer take place. While attempting to retain his fidelity to his general principles, Meyerhold was compelled to apply the most striking means and the strongest effects. Only they worked. From the entire production of *Earth Rampant* the audience and the critics "selected" two episodes—the most farcical and the most tragic. All the rest was viewed with interest, but nothing more.

The farcical episode was done with cocky naturalism. The Emperor, dressed in uniform coat, helmet, and underpants, presided on a chamber pot to the delighted laughter and ovations of the audience. The orchestra thundered "God Save the Tsar." Then the Emperor's servant, holding his hand over his nose, carried the pot with a heraldic crown through the entire auditorium.

The tragic episode—the death of the hero—always created a powerful impression. Meyerhold composed the death scene excellently: the center of the composition was the body of the hero lying on a bench under the crane's girders, hand hanging down. To the left and right two frozen groups of war comrades. The breath of death wafts over the entire scene, which is unfurled like a bas-relief. It is stern and majestic like a headstone. But this is only the beginning of the director's development of the theme.

> Slowly, to the monotonous sound of a motor, a truck drives onto the stage. Pause. The close friends say farewell to the body of the dead man; the casket is loaded on the truck. The motor runs softly during the pause, its humble sound seeming to replace funeral music. The last farewell. The truck slowly begins to move, the motor's rhythm changes and the truck leaves the stage with a roar of the motor that in the distance continues to be heard from behind the stage. Those attending the casket freeze in place. This is the end of the episode, and this affective sound of the motor remains for a long time in the ears of the spectators caught up in the drama of the scene.[78]

These two episodes created the success of the show. P. Markov wrote: "In *Earth Rampant* it seems that Meyerhold anarchistically rejoices at the destructive force of civil war that destroys capitalism and brings great social upheavals in place of small and average feelings."[79] The problem, however, consisted of the fact that times had changed, that now both the small and the average feelings had become significant, that propaganda art which operated only through the collisions of entire classes essentially affirmed what had already been affirmed, and told the audience what it already knew. This is why Meyerhold was compelled to play the trumps of farce and tragedy in *Earth Rampant*.

The form of political revue created here by Meyerhold was clearly undergoing a crisis caused by the changes in social life. Nonetheless, a year later he returned to this form.

On June 15, 1924, came the premiere of the political survey *D. E. (Give Us Europe)*. The literary base for the show was a fairly grim montage by M. Podgaetsky based on Ilya Ehrenburg's novel *Trust D. E.* and the works of Pierre Hamp, Bernhard Kellermann and Upton Sinclair.

Ehrenburg objected strenuously to the use of his novel. "I request," he wrote, "one thing: give me the opportunity to make everything of my books that is possible to make of them." Meyerhold responded in a fearfully demagogic tone, referring to a conversation with Ehrenburg in Berlin, during which it supposedly came out "that even if you had undertaken a reworking of your novel...you would have made the play such that it could be shown in any city of the Entente, but in my theater, which serves and will continue to serve the work of the Revolution, tendentious plays are needed, plays that have but one aim in view: to serve the cause of the Revolution. Let me remind you: you decisively rejected the carrying through of Communist tendencies, indicating your lack of faith in social revolution and your natural pessimism."[80]

Describing this episode, Ehrenburg subsequently noted that "the answer was frightful—it reflected Meyerhold's frenzy."[81] If it were only frenzy... Curiously, Ehrenburg's supposed lack of faith did not keep M. Podgaetsky from extracting from his novel the key thought for the revue and the protagonist, Ens Boot. "Podgaetsky," observed the experienced critic K. Miklashevsky, "should not consider himself an author... Nearly everything good in the text comes from Ehrenburg; his all-destroying caustic humor sounds fine on stage. His text dovetails easily with the slogans of the day... We are indebted to Meyerhold and Ehrenburg for the creation of *Trust D. E.*"[82] The program for *D. E.* stated, however, that the theater had "achieved the transformation of I. Ehrenburg's antisocial (!) novel into a sharp tool of propaganda directed against the bourgeoisie."

It was supposed (and stated) that the political revue would present a "comparison between decomposing bourgeoisie and the ever-stronger proletariat." In other words, the naive plot design of the show—a fantastic struggle between an American trust striving to destroy Europe and...settle it with colonists from Africa on the one hand, and the international proletariat headed by the workers of the USSR on the other—was to be the grounds for a satirical assault on the bourgeois world and an emotional glorification of the coming world Revolution. The victory of world Revolution appeared in Podgaetsky's play as fairly amusing. While the predatory capitalists were conquering Europe (they managed to destroy Germany, Austria, Hungary, decimate France, bring the English to cannibalism, etc), the proletarians lost no time. They were digging a tunnel under the Atlantic Ocean to connect

Leningrad with New York. Then everything was simple. The American workers started a revolution, the "International Red Army" arrived through the tunnel and supported them, and Socialism was victorious throughout the world.

The depressing meagerness of the story was more than obvious. The play, said Mayakovsky, "is an absolute zero. The words in it, its stage material—miserable. To rework a literary piece into a play one must be above its authors, in this case Ehrenburg and Kellermann. Otherwise, the show is not and cannot be a weapon of the class struggle."[83]

Mayakovsky, however, missed the main theme of Meyerhold's show. This theme was unstated and even verbally unexpressed in the play, but it did exist and it attracted far greater interest to the production of D. E. than the loudly proclaimed idea of satirical exposure of capitalism and emotional glorification of the proletariat.

In order to understand the theme that became the true content of D. E., we should examine life in Moscow at the time. It had changed substantially because of NEP. One of the most characteristic facts of the time was the introduction of western art and fashion into the life of the Muscovites. In the evenings people danced the foxtrot and tango in restaurants. Moscow women studied Parisian fashion magazines, cut their hair short, wore round little hats pulled down to the eyebrows like Mary Pickford and short dresses above the knee. Theater marquees displayed the names of Max Linder, Conrad Veidt, Harry Pyle and Lia de Putti.

After a ten year break, the first foreign artists appeared on tour: conductors Bruno Walter and Oskar Fried, the pianist Egon Petri. They were met with ovations. A musical reviewer wrote that Egon Petri "strikes sparks from rocks of sound, hitting them with the steel hammer of his creative will."[84]

Nonetheless, everything western still was widely seen as being bourgeois. "Foxtrotting Europe" appeared to be the incarnation of evil and a threat to the world proletariat. He who danced a foxtrot had no right to be called a Young Communist. Something like a front line appeared in an innocent sphere. On one side of the line were young men in Russian blouses and shirts with turn-down collars, and girls in red scarves, on the other—young people wearing neckties and girls in hats... It was here, along this new line of fire, that the true struggles in the show D. E. developed.

Its true content was not at all the collision between world capital and international proletariat, but the contrasting of healthy sporting spirit, physical culture and military marches against the esthetic of the foxtrot, the slow and languorous rhythms of the tango and "decay" in general.

Biomechanics was very apropos here, while Constructivism became quite unnecessary and began to fall apart literally before one's eyes. During the show, Ens Boot demonstrated some mysterious and odd picture. "What is this?" he was asked. "Constructivism!" he responded importantly. Thus, theater admitted with a smile its treason to Constructivism. Sergei Gorodetsky wrote that Meyerhold's work went "under the sign of compromise between construction and painting," that in D. E. painting began to "eat away at architecture."[85] It would be more correct to say that here construction unexpectedly was put in the service of illusion.

The basic Constructivist element of the show was the moving walls. These were a source of pride for Meyerhold and of admiration in the critics. Meyerhold stated that instead of motionless construction, dynamic construction was first being offered in *D. E.* S. Mokulsky wrote: "The movement of these lacquered shields achieves an immediate change of place of action and, more importantly, moments are staged which hitherto were inaccessible to theater and were the sole property of motion pictures (flight and chase)."[86] With the use of moving walls, the stage was transformed instantly: what had just been a street became a hall of Parliament; here the mouth of a tunnel, here a stadium, there a set of rooms. But the main reason for making the construction moveable was to *represent*, to designate the place of action. This function of the moveable walls was in direct contradiction with the basic principle of stage Constructivism—to represent nothing. Secondly, strictly speaking, there was no discovery here.

Moveable screens were used in theater long before *D. E.*, by Meyerhold himself and by Mardzhanov, and by numerous other directors. "Screens again?" asked K. Miklashevsky. And he answered: "Yes, screens... But Meyerhold's screens are solidly built of lacquered railroad car wood and move on wheels. Their texture is a very good vicinity for the performance and touch of the actor. Particular craftsmanship is demonstrated in their construction and in their occasionally very complex and rapid movement."[87]

Railroad car wood—thin boards used to construct the walls of freight cars—was painted like railroad cars in a dark brick color. The red walls moved loudly but very rapidly. The chase scenes that delighted the public and caused the critics to say that Meyerhold was competing successfully with the cinema were done in this way. The actor ran from the proscenium into the back, while at the back of the stage two walls rolled toward each other from either side. The actor managed to slip between them before they closed. The result was an effect of instant disappearance. Nonetheless, Meyerhold noted skeptically: "The struggle with the cinema cannot achieve its goal."[88] Undoubtedly, he was correct. Still, Meyerhold intensified the effects of the movement of the walls with his ably organized light score: projectors shone spots of light onto the stage from the back of the auditorium, special reflectors illuminated the stage from the sides, sometimes the movement of the walls without an actor and the simultaneous movement of projector rays created the impression of tremendously dynamic action.

As we recall, there was a screen in *Earth Rampant*. In *D. E.* Meyerhold installed three screens: in the center and along the sides of the stage. Slides and signs were projected onto these. The side screens informed one of the actions of the two warring factions. The central screen gave the names of the episodes and this screen served also as the "means for expressing the relation of the director to what was transpiring on stage." The slogan "Hands off China!" was followed by a note to the spectators that now they would see a "Fossil from the White emigration," etc.

I. Shlepyanov's design for *D. E.* already contradicted functionalism and the strict asceticism of Constructivism, and took upon itself decorative tasks, but did not pretend as yet to unity of style.

This compromise of form was the inevitable consequence of the change of theme in the show, the transformation of political review into music and dance. In essence, the sole requirement dictated by this particular change was the requirement of dynamic mobility. This goal, of course, was achieved.

Meyerhold was transforming a pseudo-revolutionary play into a Soviet music-hall. In the show, the "decaying" west was represented first of all by jazz, which first sounded in the Soviet Union from the stage of *D. E.*

This jazz was directed by the poet Valentin Parnakh, who had just arrived from Paris. Evgeny Gavrilovich writes in his memoirs:

> I often read articles discussing who began to cultivate jazz in our country, but I vouch that it was begun by Parnakh... Parnakh was the first to bring a saxophone into the country and sets of mutes for trumpets and trombones, and was the first to give a jazz concert.
>
> The concert was held in the Press Building where, in those years, the most heated clashes regarding art and literature took place and the latest innovations were demonstrated in the area of the overthrow of old theatrical forms. The hall of the House, which had seen a lot in its day, was overflowing.
>
> Parnakh read a scientific lecture on the jazz band, then somehow (since no one in Moscow knew how to play the saxophone) jazz tunes were played. When Parnakh himself danced the strangest dance, the "Giraffeoid idol" *(zhirafovidnii istukan)*, the delight reached hurricane force. Among those who furiously clapped his hands and called for more was Vsevolod Emilevich Meyerhold.
>
> He immediately proposed that Parnakh organize a jazz band for the show that was then being rehearsed.[89]

This is how the jazz band in *D. E.* appeared. This was the main sensation of the show.

Moscow audiences heard the "confusion orchestra" perform well known and totally new foxtrots, tangos, and shimmies. The jerking, hoarse shouts, unexpected beatings of the gong, banging of drums—all this was startling. The spectators were surprised even more, probably, by the loose behavior of the musicians, who jumped up in time to the music, grimaced, hit the drum with a foot, the gong with a shoulder. So there would be no doubt that the "latest thing" in the dying west was being demonstrated, the programs read: the jazz band director Valentin Parnakh "invented a number of new dance movements which he demonstrated in (solo) performances in Paris, Rome, Seville, Berlin." The foxtrots and shimmy were staged by no one less than Kasyan Goleizovsky himself. Boris Romashov wrote in *The News (Izvestiia)* of the oppressive impression created by the "stifling-frenzied shimmy of a rotten civilization exhausted in lecherous dance."[90] This was spoken forcefully.

The more moderate A. Fevralsky asserted that the jazz-accompanied dances "with their aspect of perversity, are characteristic of the decaying bourgeois civilization in our days. However," he continued, "exercises in biomechanics and the acrobatic polka in the Soviet sportsground episode indicate the health and will to work of our Red youth."[91]

The acrobatic polka performed in one of the Soviet episodes by the "biomechanical group" of Meyerhold's pupils did indeed make a happy impression. Furthermore, soccer was played in the show. Biomechanics was demonstrated frankly: effective exercises were performed to a harmonica and military sailors marched calmly, also to a harmonica. Meyerhold simply called these sailors from their barracks—they were quite real. If the good old harmonica still could compete somehow with the new jazz, the real sailors moved much worse than Goleizovsky's dancers and Meyerhold's trained actors. "The entry of Red Army soldiers and sailors onto the stage is ridiculous," said Mayakovsky categorically. And he added bluntly: "This is some kind of institute for theatrical batmen." The entire show made a "dispiriting impression"[92] on him.

Mayakovsky did not even mention that in *D. E.* Meyerhold made wide use of the technique of actors' quick change. Meyerhold was very proud of this innovation and of the moving walls, and ascribed a fundamental importance to them. In *D. E.* there were no more and no less than 95 roles which were performed by 44 actors.

Garin, Ilinsky, Babanova, and Temerin performed in *D. E.* and transformed themselves in an instant into several roles each. Erast Garin succeeded in this most effectively. The steel king, Mister Jabs (played by Temerin) was visited by seven inventors in a row. Garin played all of them, demonstrating the art of quick change. In other roles, Ilinsky observed, the "transformation was less convincing, since the audience missed the transformation of many actors and was not certain whether these were new characters or old. Only with the help of the program could one know how many roles were played by an actor."[93]

As in *Earth Rampant*, the actors became lost in the dynamics of *D. E.* The reviewers approvingly mentioned Ilinsky as the meat king Twaift, Tereshkovich as Ens Boot, Zinaida Raikh as Sybil the American, M. Babanova as a dancer in a bar, B. Zakhava as Lord Haig, or M. Kirillov as the barber. But all these mentions were brief, like the appearances by the actors in the show. Mayakovsky was not the only one to look back into the past and recall *The Magnanimous Cuckold*. The dynamic revue devoured actors that the audience had begun to like, and the audience regretted this.

Furthermore, the basic emotional conclusion of the whole show remained in doubt. The public clearly liked the jazz, despite all the newspaper comments about "foxtrotting degeneration" and "lewd dances" of the west. As for healthy Soviet life, B. Romashov admitted that its images "appeared pale and unconvincing, sometimes stilted."[94] Although nearly all the reviews were good and the critics agreed that *D. E.* "is the most propagandistic show in the USSR," that Meyerhold "showed himself here not only as a genius director but a genius agitator,"[95] the "genius agitator" himself felt, evidently, that the time had come for new changes.

There was much guesswork as to the new direction that would be taken by the Master. 1923 was particularly rife with such guesswork when Meyerhold's double jubilee was celebrated—twenty years of directing and twenty-five years of acting. Em. Beskin exclaimed: "Toward the sun, onto the platform, to the masses comes Meyerhold. The theatrical *earth* must arise *rampant*. And will arise."[96] N. Semashko, on the other hand, supposed that time would bring changes "to Meyerhold's revolutionary destructiveness. Possibly," Semashko suggested carefully, "not everything that he throws aside must be swept away and not everything that he introduces ought to be introduced... Probably much will have to be 'corrected and filled out,' much will probably have to be softened."[97] N. Foregger unexpectedly and boldly compared Meyerhold to Picasso. "Meyerhold's eyes," he stated "are directed only at *tomorrow*. Meyerhold is to theater what Picasso is to painting. Their task is to search, to experiment, to chart new paths... Like Picasso, Meyerhold indicates possibilities. Without stopping at them, rushing to find strongholds that must be destroyed by the hand of the revolutionary warrior. It is funny to try to squeeze Meyerhold into the frame even of his own discarded stagings... Meyerhold must discover!"[98]

All these prognoses, hypotheses and predictions were on slippery ground. The basis for all judgments was Meyerhold's own previous practice. His contemporaries were unable to compare his movement with the events that were happening in the social life of the country, possibly because they simply did not grasp the changes in the social climate in time. Meyerhold himself, judging by his speeches, articles, and conversations of the time, was unable to define clearly his own interpretation of the new social situation or even his own intentions. His declarations remained practically unaltered, but his art was changing.

Sketch for a portrait of Meyerhold by P. P. Konchalovsky

BACK TO OSTROVSKY

Now
we shall turn the wheel of inspiration.
Vladimir Mayakovsky

When Meyerhold presented *A Profitable Post* in the Theater of the Revolution, the show passed almost without notice. Other premieres by Meyerhold were accompanied by fireworks of reviews and by debates, but this one, performed on May 15, 1923, remained in the shadows. The Master's cohorts from "Theatrical October," the critics, and the theoreticians of "leftist theater" lowered their eyes in shame. This production was seen as an example of a director's carelessness caused by purely practical rather than programmatical considerations. Since Meyerhold had taken on the direction of this clumsy and mediocre theater, which had dragged along somewhere to the rear of the "leftist front," he naturally would occasionally have to stage something there. Conceivably, *A Profitable Post* was selected for purely pedagogical reasons: the company in the Theater of the Revolution was varied and needed to learn at least the alphabet of biomechanics. Any play would have been suitable for this purpose. No one proposed to guess why Ostrovsky's play, specifically, had been selected. Possibly, the strange choice was dictated by commercial calculations. One way or another, from the "leftist" point of view, there was nothing fundamentally significant in this action by Meyerhold. Rather, there was an impression of a lack of principle here which no one cared to point out.

"Probably," wrote Sergei Auslender, "both the friends and the enemies of the leftist front will be somewhat disappointed by this staging. It contains no material for excessive applause or outrage. The staging is without gunpowder"...and, in fact, the critics did not pay much attention to this production.

Only V. Blyum was unable to restrain himself and wrote angrily in *Truth* of what was to him an incomprehensible "flash of piety for Ostrovsky, the apostle of mediocrity and middle-class values," saying that Meyerhold had betrayed himself and presented a play with shameful objectivity, "with the complete sincerity...of the Maly, the Art and sundry provincial theaters."[1]

As for the critics who were considered "rightists," they saw no reason to find in Meyerhold's staging of Ostrovsky's play any sign or hint of forthcoming substantial changes. Next to his other works of 1922-23, *A Profitable Post* did indeed appear to be a strange error. No one knew how to react. The show passed virtually unreviewed, and Meyerhold himself kept unusual silence and did not explain any new discoveries or innovations. Worse yet, in *A Profitable Post* there appeared none of those stage inventions with which Meyerhold usually was so generous. It appeared that the Master was working at half strength.

Two years later, when Meyerhold again staged Ostrovsky—this time in his own theater, the TIM—the critics could no longer remain silent. An explosion took place. But in this explosion *A Profitable Post* was not remembered.

Meanwhile, the production that had penetrated almost silently into the Moscow repertoire continued to play. It was performed in 1926 and in 1936, and its success continued to grow. Moscow theatrical life changed from year to year, brought ever new surprises to audiences and new names to the fore. But spectators continued to come to *A Profitable Post*.

"The longer the stage life of this staging by Meyerhold continued," wrote B. Alpers in 1937, "the more forceful and solid became the impression in theatrical society that the show was one of the deepest and most significant in the repertoire of Soviet theater."

Gradually it became evident that *A Profitable Post* was a masterpiece of direction by Meyerhold. It remained quite unclear, however, how it originated and how its apparently various and incompatible elements were placed in harmony. Even Alpers, already admitting the exceptional significance of the show, qualified himself: in Meyerhold's staging, "still, there was no unity."[2]

And truly, at first glance one could see contradictions in the artistic order of the show—for instance, in its exterior. The artist V. Shestakov presented a design that, oddly enough, was original in its compromise. It would seem that everything was in its place—walls, doors, rooms, tables, and chairs. Still, there was little resemblance to the usual decorations for a play by Ostrovsky. Where the audience expected to see wallpaper with some sort of bright bouquets, there was a solid plywood wall painted black. The staircases, straight and spiral, were in their bare simplicity reminiscent of ships' ladders. Pauline's room in the attic looked like a captain's bridge. In place of comfortable armchairs and stylish chairs were crudely nailed-together objects with right angles. Of course, these were chairs, armchairs, hewn benches, and stools. But furniture built from simple wooden slats and heavy boards in no way fit into Ostrovsky's world.

The artist appeared to say yes, I will leave everything untouched: the walls, the staircases and the furniture, but I will "translate" it all into the language of Constructivism, it will all be only utilitarian, will only serve its purpose. The wall limits the space. One can walk up the stairs. One can sit in the armchair. And that is all. I give no specific details of the time or the style of the age.It's all the same to me how Vishnevsky's living room or Pauline's room looked. I do not intend to transport you the audience into the last century. On the contrary, I wish to bring the play into our time, so here before you is a crude, uncozy set in which, if you wish, a completely different play could be performed.

The interior had an engineered look. The metal bridges with stiff railings, the staircases that wound in narrow spirals, permitted the director to carry on the action as Meyerhold liked to do, on several levels at once—on the stage floor, on the ladders, and on the bridges. From the point of view of Constructivism, however, this crude attempt to engineer the everyday or to subordinate the elements of Constructivist form to specifically representational problems did, of course, appear as a compromise.

Meyerhold and Shestakov together had taken yet another step back. In the costumes and wigs, they retained full historical verisimilitude. The uniforms, the frock-coats, the checkered trousers of the officials, the white shirts of the tavern waiters, the full dresses of the women—crinolines, hourglass waists—all these were strictly in the fashion of the mid-nineteenth century. The actresses wore wigs with ringlets and curls. Ladies' hair styles with ribbons, officials' sideburns and bald spots, the bowl cuts of the waiters—all were carefully reproduced. Furthermore, actual objects from Ostrovsky's time were introduced into the severe, ascetic setting of the play. A real brass orchestrion was in the tavern—a detail that even the Art Theater could envy. Brass candlesticks and crystal goblets suddenly glimmered on the rough tables. Yusov smoked an antique long-stemmed pipe...

All these museum pieces, in strange conjunction with the barracks-like roughness of the rest of the setting, unexpectedly obtained a somewhat ironic meaning. They became exotic, leaped to the eye. They brought with them the remembrance of a way of life destroyed, wiped off the face of the earth, now clearly inappropriate and already impossible.

The consciously discovered and strongly underscored contradiction between asceticism, the Constructivist aridity of the overall tone of the decorations, and the color and historical detail of the costumes and individual "museum-pieces" was the simple but precise form of the connection achieved in this staging between modern and past times. The contradictions in the artistic order of the show proved to be imaginary.

The external contradiction of the overall design also proved imaginary. There is no doubt that the enormous possibilities that opened up here—the combination of museum pieces and exotically-accurate costumes with the severe neutrality of the background—were not weighed thoroughly by Meyerhold. This time he passed by a discovery that later, in the 1950s and 60s, was utilized widely and variously by other directors. Meyerhold himself saw the solution that he and Shestakov found together as successful only for the given play. It was beneficial, since it allowed Meyerhold to "knock together" the old play with the auditorium of the early 1920s.

It turned out, however, that the selection of the play was far from accidental, that it evoked in the audience much more than modern associations. The NEP was in a time of "intoxication." The people who were called Soviet bourgeois or "Red merchants" or just plain Nepmen were organizing commercial affairs, founding new private enterprises, storming the walls of Soviet bureaucracy, always prepared to give the needed bribes. The concept of a "profitable post" again became quite real. Bribery, waste and theft became the order of the day, as was substantiated by the daily newspaper reports from the courts. In Moscow restaurants debauches were organized that made the amusements of Ostrovsky's officials seem like child's play.

"The profitable post without quotation marks," wrote Yu. Yuzovsky later, "is the simple key with which Meyerhold unlocked Ostrovsky again. Profitable post —this is the slogan, symbol, the law determining thoughts, feelings, truth, goodness, and beauty. In the most distant, fatherly-familial gesture of Yusov, in the most intimate, tender smile of the enamoured Belogubov, the profitable post peers out treacherously, insidiously, jeeringly and maliciously."[3]

The NEP situation, in contrast to the grand disinterestedness of the Revolution, brought forth monetary interest and the possibilities of quick profits. Any post could become profitable, every person ran the risk of yielding to temptation...

Meyerhold's directorial score accounted for all these new circumstances. Anxiety was the hidden theme of the show. It dictated the anxious rhythms, permeated the nervous design of the setting, and colored the relations among the characters.

The most successful roles in the show were Polinka and Yusov. Naturally, these two figures were brought to the fore thanks to the great talent of M. Babanova and D. Orlov. But this is not the entire reason. The images of Polinka and Yusov express most distinctly the idea that excited Meyerhold. In Yusov was the frightful and dangerous force of cynicism and corruption. Polinka concealed naive and pure spiritual health. Yusov was threat, Polinka—hope. Between these two poles stretched the electric force field of anxiety in the show.

Meyerhold outraged Ostrovsky experts because, for the first time in the stage history of *A Profitable Post*, he staged the entire play "without the usual deletions."[4] He made only one excision—he removed Vishnevskaya's monologue in the beginning of Act V. This time, every word of Ostrovsky's seemed necessary and inevitable to him. But to Ostrovsky's text—unhurried, substantial, comprehensible—he gave a new nervous and jumbled rhythm.

From this point of view, the most characteristic and most intense thing in the show was the great scene in the tavern. The blue light of a projector illuminated the tavern tables, moved out toward the proscenium. In the grim blue light the white tablecloths became a threatening swampy color. "The dead swamp of the bureaucrat," wrote Alpers, "looks at the spectator from the stage of the theater."[5] At the back of the stage the brass pipes of the orchestrion glimmered mysteriously. Zhadov (A. Torsky) sat alone at his table before a pale, burning candle. When the crowd of officials led by Yusov broke into the tavern room, the waiters brought in the candelabras and nervous lights flickered around the stage. An important and festive event was being celebrated: the birth of a new bribe-taker. Belogubov had decided, "had broken his fast," and was now entering society... The tables were moved together. They sat down—officials on the benches, Yusov, the boss, separately on a chair. The drunken "Russian conversation" began and quickly became somehow distorted. Very soon it turned to shouts, frenzy, and fury, but having brought the tension to the limit, Meyerhold suddenly, as though with a single motion, discharged it:

Akim Akimych, we invite you to dance!..

This drunken line brought the drunken Yusov from behind his table. Staggering, he stumbled out into the center of the stage, waved a red handkerchief, and softly and lightly began to dance the "Russkii." Of course this was not a spirited dance. It was the dance of an official, barely defined, self-important, worthy, but masterly in its own way and flawless in plastic form. It was as though Yusov were showing his underlings how one should dance without losing one's prestige... The officials clapped their hands in time to his dance, while the nonparticipating waiters, who had seen everything, framed this drunken group in a white semicircle, stared coldly at Yusov and calculated their tips. Then followed another, nearly hysterical, round of swaggering, bullying and honoring. Surrounded by the servile officials, Yusov, to show his contempt for the printed word, burned a newspaper on a tray.

This little *auto-da-fé* received a symbolic meaning in Meyerhold's score. The yellow flame danced in the semidarkness of the center stage, revealing the self-satisfied, lewd, arrogant and fawning faces of the bureaucrats.

When the officials finally left, Zhadov's lonely table remained in the sudden emptiness of the stage—Dosuzhev now sitting with him. A quiet, significant, serious, and hopeless conversation was carried on here, while behind the stage the drunken riot continued, to the mournful sounds of the "Luchinushka." Suddenly, out stepped a drunken official with a napkin stuffed under his collar. Grabbing at the black wall, with two fingers in his mouth, he made his way to the obvious place...

One had to have Meyerhold's boldness and Meyerhold's precision in order to give the audience such daring emotional blows, to construct the grim dance of the officials in the major key of the national dance, and to interrupt the sad, penetrating "Luchinushka" with the passage of this scabrous figure.

When Dosuzhev departed, the waiter removed the last candle from Zhadov's table. During the entire scene lights had dashed about the stage, paper had flamed... Now the stage was immersed in darkness. Zhadov wept, while the tragic "Luchinushka" accompanied him from behind the scenes.

The fourth act was concentrated on the small upper platform which symbolized Pauline and Zhadov's room. There, in the "birdhouse" and on the staircase leading up to it, Meyerhold constructed elegant and laconic duets between Pauline and Yulenka, Pauline and Kukushkina, Pauline and Zhadov. The finale of the act was worked out with special thoroughness, when Pauline would go away from Zhadov (down the stairs), then would return to him (up the stairs), then would vacillate (down-up-down-up), etc. Meyerhold calculated Pauline's caprice "by the step." Such a jesting solution was in full accord with the meaning of the scene and revealed Pauline's character. "The obstinacy of a mischievous girl, the urge to stand on her own, and the simultaneous consciousness of her wrong and the desire for reconciliation with her husband," wrote Alpers, "are all presented in this indecisive sliding along the steps and banisters of the stairs."[6]

Another scene organized by Meyerhold on a staircase had a completely different meaning. Belogubov—V. Zaichikov—ran quickly up a spiral staircase and at every turn—when he faced Yusov, who was sitting below—he bowed low to him. The busy flashing of Belogubov's epaulets created a quintessence of imagery, an active metaphor of subservience. A no less expressive and equally metaphoric scene was designed by Meyerhold for Yusov. Yusov's path to the door of Vishnevsky's office was charted along a long parabola on the stage floor. Following this parabola, Yusov gradually bent his knees, lowered his head, somehow shrank and became shorter. This staging subsequently became standard: nearly all the actors to play Yusov repeated or varied it for a long time afterward.

For all the acuity and the use of metaphor in Meyerhold's stagings, the overall composition of the show placed the actor in the forefront. The excellent male company trained by Meyerhold in the early 1920s consisted of happy comedians, rhythmic, exact, plastic, superbly trained, always prepared to carry out any acrobatic task, confident in body and voice. In many of Meyerhold's compositions they surrounded the single, incomparable heroine of this youthful theater—Maria Babanova. Babanova understood and learned all of Meyerhold's requirements with phenomenal ease. Rhythmical by nature, she took on and executed without hesitation the most difficult scenes, carried out the assigned design for the role with the most punctual precision. She "danced" each role flawlessly in accordance with the director's score and repeated each intonation as if from notes with her clear, ringing, and melodic voice. But this ideal "biomechanical actress" never did remain within the limits of just simply executing the director's assignments. Babanova's "trick," the secret of her successes, was the fact that each of her roles received a lyrical coloration.

"With Babanova," wrote Gvozdev, "movement is coordinated with word, makes it rhythmical, gives form to the emotional content and brings it to the spectator."[7]

As Stella in *The Magnanimous Cuckold*, Babanova carried through the entire action of the play the theme of an insulted woman's dignity, while in *A Profitable Post* the leitmotif of Pauline's role was childlike clarity of the soul.

Mischievous like a child, light and careless Pauline (Babanova) startled not only Zhadov (T. Solovyov) but herself and the audience when she automatically repeated the words of "wise people" like Yusov or her mother. With a self-important, lecturing tone which clearly was not her own, she told Zhadov: "It is known that Belogubov is better than you. He is respected by his superiors, loves his wife, is an excellent householder, has his own horses... And what of you?" But when her actual, true desire behind all these words became revealed, when with tears in her voice she proclaimed that she wanted a velvet dress and repeated several times in singsong, sweetly, "velvet...velvet," the auditorium responded with an explosion of happy sympathetic laughter. This childlike quality concealed hope for a power of goodness capable of defending Pauline (and the audience) from the onslaught of cynical monetary interest.

Oh, how well the young women in Moscow in 1923 understood Pauline's dreams of a new hat and velvet dress! The country, which had just escaped destruction by a miracle, which had broken away from the storm of destruction and hunger, was just beginning to dress itself. The hats and fashionable dresses of the Nepmen's wives caused bitter jealousy among the vast majority of wives who were forced to refuse themselves everything. Their husbands, uncompromising and hard idealists, were essentially Zhadovs. Meyerhold hinted elegantly and astutely at this similarity. In the fourth act, the scene of the quarrel and Pauline's explanation, his Zhadov wore a white shirt with a turned-down collar and severe, almost sports, trousers: just like a young man of the early 1920s with a young, open face. When the scene ended with Zhadov's capitulation, when he gave in to Pauline and agreed to go to his uncle and ask for a profitable post, he put on his official uniform and returned to the nineteenth century.

D. Orlov as Yusov also came forward with the most contemporary associations. The satiety, self-satisfaction, and even a certain Epicurean quality that shone in Orlov's Yusov, were extremely expressive. His very toadying before Vishnevsky was colored with bright joy, and pantomiming deep admiration, visibly abasing himself upon entering his superior's office, Orlov performed with his usual agility, with dash. It was evident that Yusov enjoyed self-denigration, that he was proud of his artistry, his craft. He backed out bowing from Vishnevsky's office, then turned to the audience and smiled with self-satisfaction: look what I can do!

The director A. Gripich observed that Orlov performed the entire part of Yusov "with happy slyness." Orlov was indeed a clever actor. It was as though he rounded off the strictness and sharpness of Meyerhold's plastic design. His movements were flowing, light and soft. Confidentiality sounded in his voice, it was as if the actor were inviting the spectators to be his cohorts, establishing close, almost familiar relations. His great charm was tinged with mischief. Somewhere in the heart of the image so thoroughly and exactly characterized hid—and peered out occasionally—the comedian.

He played Yusov almost without make-up, with a slightly thickened body, and with glasses which he used very cleverly: either glancing over them, looking haughtily at someone through them, "or his head would be stretched out forward with the pupils of his unblinking eyes staring at the superior, or his glasses would be on his forehead, eyes squinting and a buttery smile on his face... Yusov's walk," wrote A. Gripich, "was expressive. In front of his subordinates it was a majestic walk, springy, with a slight rocking of the body; before his superiors it was quick, fawning, with back bent; stately and sometimes overceremonious at Kukushkina's, where Yusov-Orlov permitted himself to stretch out in armchairs."[8]

This is where the long pipe, which Yusov smoked while lying back in the armchair, appeared, while Kukushkina, on her knees before him, obedient and delighted, lit the fire... "This seems like some sculpture," stated Yuzovsky.[9] Yes, this was another Meyerholdian staging: the plastic formulation of an idea.

In the finale, Yusov-Orlov retained his philosophical calm. He accepted Vishnevsky's catastrophe with epic lack of emotion. "Fate," he said in a sated and peaceful voice, "it is the same as fortune...as shown in a painting...a wheel with people on it..." He made a circle in the air with his finger and hung imaginary little people on it. A little later, he came up to Vishnevsky, who lay helpless on a sofa and carefully, in a businesslike manner, arranged his arms in a cross and straightened his legs, as for a dead man. These efforts of Yusov's "with Vishnevsky's body" also had a clear metaphoric meaning. After finishing his work and looking over the "corpse" with pleasure, Yusov-Orlov threw a quick, sly glance at the audience: of course we will all be there, but I will have time to bury more than one boss and remain whole!

This string of Meyerhold's staging metaphors inspired the actors, incited them to active and mischievous interaction with the audience.

Less than a year after the opening of *A Profitable Post*, Meyerhold staged another play by Ostrovsky—*The Forest*. The premiere was on January 19, 1924, and was impossible to ignore. First of all, it was presented in the TIM, i.e., in the very center of "leftist theater," and second, in contrast to *A Profitable Post*, the staging of *The Forest* was literally stuffed with the director's innovations and inventions. It shocked. One way or another everyone would have to react to it. And, in fact, reviews of *The Forest* poured out as from a cornucopia.

It was a highly characteristic response on the part of the leader of "leftist theater" to Lunacharsky's slogan "Back to Ostrovsky!" Lunacharsky himself soon observed that his slogan "was hopelessly misunderstood, they thought that I recommended writing 'like Ostrovsky' the way furniture is made 'like oak.' However, I intended that we, modern playwrights, must observe the life around us sensitively, like Ostrovsky, and unifying profound theatrical, I would even say, maximum effect, with precise, penetrating realism, we must present a constructive and explanatory mirror-image of our times."[10]

The "leftists," however, were frightened and shocked by the very name of Osstrovsky. "This is understandable," wrote Em. Beskin. "Ostrovsky still lives. Ostrovsky—this is the academic front, academic theater... Ostrovsky, on whose traditions the rightist-academic front intended to construct something, this Ostrovsky confused the cards. It was necessary to strike, and strike hard, at this camouflage-colored armor... It is no coincidence that under conditions of NEP Ostrovsky appeared so much on the advertising posts. There is no need to be particularly surprised by this. It is clear, logical. If anyone was dangerous, it was of course not Ryshkov or Artsybashev, but Ostrovsky."

Meyerhold's staging of *The Forest* created uniform consternation among the "leftist" critics who had long been grouped around Meyerhold and who tried with difficulty to follow his headlong movement. Meyerhold's work in the Theater of the Revolution, as has been mentioned, was received by them with relative equanimity—it was supposed that there Meyerhold was "paying tribute" to the cash box, while the TIM was the arena for innovations. And here, suddenly, *The Forest*. This so amazed the "leftist" critics that they accused Meyerhold of revisionism. "When Ostrovsky receives the attention of the recent leader of 'Theatrical October,' the source of inspiration, practically the banner for the entire 'leftist front,' this makes one pause," admitted Em. Beskin in the same article. "One must think here... After all the resistance to the slightest orientation toward Ostrovsky, after thundering 'down with'—is this not revisionism?.. A step down through stylized eccentricity to academic estheticism has been observed."[11]

Meanwhile, *A Profitable Post* demonstrated that Meyerhold's turning to Ostrovsky was historically logical. Meyerhold sensed the profound correspondence between the spiritual requirements of the Soviet audience of the mid-1920s and the lively emotion, clear tendentiousness and democratic nature of Ostrovsky's writing. In sensing the *appropriateness* of Ostrovsky, Meyerhold at this time agreed with Lunacharsky, who was insistently calling playwrights "into Ostrovsky's school." But Meyerhold, of course, had a different understanding of Ostrovsky's modernity and had other aims. In particular, he wished to take their banner—Ostrovsky—away from the academic theaters, to prove that Ostrovsky's democracy was related to the democracy of revolutionary theater.

Meyerhold was not satisfied with the "academic" Ostrovsky as he appeared in the Maly Theater. "The Sadovskys, Lensky, Rybakov are gone," said Meyerhold. "And in Ostrovsky's conversational theater—to use Apollon Grigoriev's expression—there sounded a note of peasant jargon. An inevitable falsehood reigned on the stage." Meyerhold felt that the academic theaters were incapable of dealing with Ostrovsky's plays "even to the degree to which the Moscow Art Theater mastered Chekhov."[12]

This time Meyerhold was able to win his competition with the "akas." Meyerhold's victory was in his bold "modernization" of Ostrovsky. Without fearing accusations of Philistinism, Meyerhold transformed Ostrovsky's comedy into a basis for a modern satirical show. Ostrovsky was usable for propaganda. We should recall that in 1924 Mayakovsky, addressing Pushkin, said: "I could entrust you even with propaganda shows *(agitki)*. I'd show you once: —like this, like that... You'd manage —you have good style."

The time of dashing assaults on the classics was withdrawing into the past, and revolutionary poets pledged their love for the classics ("I love you, but the living person, not the mummy..."). There was a happy, rough familiarity in their relation to the classics. There was not a trace of piety in their love.

Ostrovsky's *The Forest* must have put Meyerhold in an excellent humor. Of all Ostrovsky's plays, this one undoubtedly was the closest to the director. It sounded one of the director's beloved themes: the theme of the victory of comedy over life. The bad tragedian Neschastlivtsev was placed above the other characters of the play. This impoverished mountebank turned out to be smarter, cleaner, more noble and stronger than the masters of life.

Furthermore, the figures of Neschastlivtsev and his companion Arkashka Schastlivtsev, with all their social concreteness and lifelike definition, were inscribed into the system of images in the play with what for Ostrovsky was an uncharacteristic tendency to juxtapose two completely different, almost incompatible ways of life. These two "tumbleweeds" rolled into the stagnant "forest" life of the estate as though brought by the Devil. Those who wanted to could see in their very appearance the inevitable end of this seemingly solid way of life that slowly went from nastiness to nastiness, from deal to deal. Undoubtedly, Meyerhold was excited and inspired by just such an interpretation of the two figures. He interpreted the tragedian and the comedian as Satan and jester. The gay, threatening devilry was supposed to confuse all the cards in Gurmyzhskaya's long-range game. Furthermore, it was supposed to confound Ostrovsky's own game: as we shall see, the composition of the play broke up and changed.

As for Gurmyzhskaya and the other "masters of life," they were drawn in *The Forest* with a broad, acidly sarcastic brush. In this sense, *The Forest* stood out among the other plays by Ostrovsky that appealed to Meyerhold. He unabashedly entered comedy as if it were his own home, with a feeling of deep solidarity with the author. An attractive opportunity arose to "entrust Ostrovsky with an *agitka*," to apply the images of *The Forest* simultaneously to a sharp satirical attack on the "damned past" and to a glorification of the great, all-powerful, life-transforming force of theater. These intentions were to become expressed in new forms of spectacle, much more aggressive with regard to the literary source than, for instance, the forms of the show *A Profitable Post* had been.

On the one hand, in *The Forest* the usual calm narrative manner of Ostrovsky was somewhat disrupted. The bringing together of two levels of life which in reality were far removed from each other—the landlord's estate and theatrical comedy—caused a certain hiatus in style and rhythm. For all his attractiveness, Ostrovsky appeared phlegmatic. It seemed to Meyerhold that he was working the same ground for too long, was overstressing self-evident truths. Describing his plans for staging *The Forest*, Meyerhold insisted that the author of the play had written in obedience to the antiquated laws and customs of late nineteenth-century Russian theater, that Ostrovsky was bound by the underdeveloped technology of the stage and that that was the only reason for his division of *The Forest* into the traditional long acts, that in general Ostrovsky felt more kinship to the Shakespearean principles of composition that divided drama into short episodes.

These hypotheses were, of course, dubious and were expressed only in order to justify and provide grounds for Meyerhold's own urge for a multi-episodic structure for the play. This was suggested, too, by the atmosphere of the time in which the production was being put together and Meyerhold's consistent striving for dynamic action. Furthermore, as we have observed already, the multi-episodic structure of the show had for Meyerhold not only a technical but a fundamentally esthetic significance.

Fragmentation marked a new, fundamentally important esthetic approach by relativistic theater to the very structure of stage action. Psychological theater continued to view the continuous flow of action as one of the major guarantees of involving the spectator in the stage life, as the most reliable means for creating the illusion of the verisimilitude of this life. "Our decreasing *capacity for illusion*," wrote Strindberg back in 1888, "*suffers from intermissions* that allow the spectator to reflect and in this way to move away from the exciting effect of the author-magnetizer." In the same foreword to the play *Miss Julie*, he suggested that for the retention of the "magnetism" it was necessary to reject completely the division of the action. The masters of relativistic theater, Meyerhold in particular, did not strive to develop the capacity for illusion. On the contrary, they categorically denied its very necessity. Instead of the solid and continuous "flow of life," they wished to present only its dynamic clots to the public. The element of demonstrating creativity, the element selecting one conflict or another, was underscored strongly by breaking up the action into fragments, whatever they happened to be called—episodes, "attractions" or (as they were subsequently called by S. Tretyakov) "links."

Meyerhold broke the text of *The Forest* into thirty-three episodes. In doing this, he seemed to push the first and second acts of the comedy together, striving to quicken and sharpen its exposition. Ostrovsky waited until the beginning of the second act to present Schastlivtsev and Neschastlivtsev, while for Meyerhold it was important to begin the theme of the comedians, for him of paramount importance, as soon as possible. Therefore, he mixed the scenes of the first two acts and at once brought the wandering actors into the life of the Penki estate. By shuffling the episodes, Meyerhold, naturally, disrupted their connections of meaning and was compelled to reconnect them in new ways.

It cannot be said that these new connections were particularly firm or necessary to the plot. In any event, Meyerhold soon reduced the number of episodes to twenty-six, then to sixteen, but the show as a whole was retained.

The episodes were interconnected only by the broad band of the development of the main theme of the entire piece. They adjoined each other according to the principle of theatrical revue. Each episode could, theoretically, be shown separately, each was self-contained, was a distinct "number." One episode was separated from another by a brief darkening of the stage, at which time a sign was projected onto a screen: "Over the railroad ties," "Alexei—frivolous boy," "Society lady and street girl," "Cheats and prays, prays and cheats," "Moonlight sonata," etc.

One episode followed another rapidly in the show. The rapidity of the change obtained an emotional significance, since the audience was infected by the upbeat, hurried tempo of the agile and smooth work of the comedians, masters of their work, bold improvisers.

Meyerhold gave each of the thirty-three episodes a completed action: its own beginning, culmination and resolution. He consistently sought and found grounds for theatrical play. Every episode, in his words, had "a hook to catch the spectator," its own bait that the public swallowed greedily.

Favorsky engraving of Babanova as
Polinka in *A Profitable Post*

M. Pikov's engraving of Babanova

Favorsky engraving of Orlov as Yusov
in Ostrovsky's *A Profitable Post*

Drawing by V. Shestakov for *A Profitable Post*

A scene from A Profitable Post

A scene from *A Profitable Post*, 1923

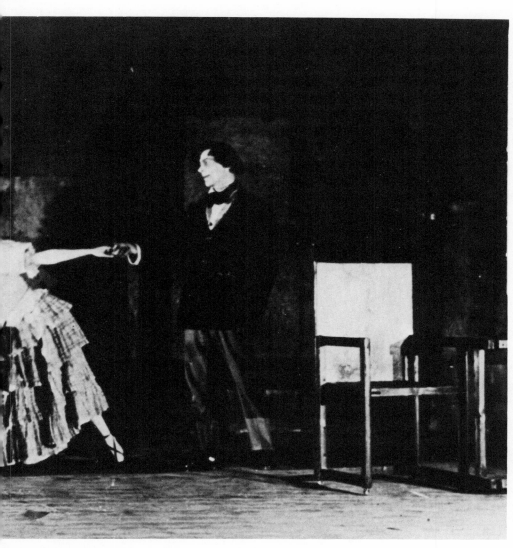

Scene from *A Profitable Post*

N. Ter-Osipian as Kukushkina, D. Orlov as Yusov in *A Profitable Post*

Babanova as Polinka, Solovyov as Zhadov

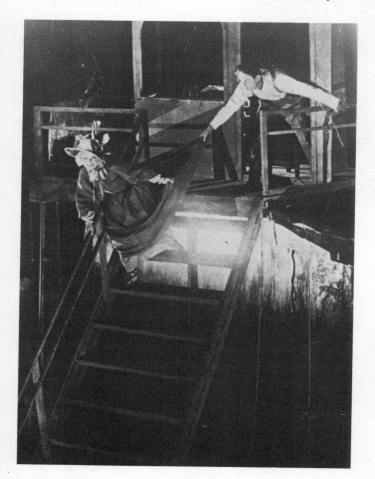

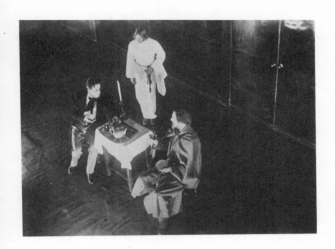

Scene from *A Profitable Post*

Orlov as Yusov in
A Profitable Post

Raikh as Aksyusha, Mukhin as Neschastlivtsev in Ostrovsky's *The Forest*

I. Ilinsky as Schastlivtsev, M. Mukhin as Neschastlivtsev, *The Forest*
Episode 14, *The Forest,* Raikh as Aksyusha, I. Kovalev as Samborsky

Above: The Forest. Below: The Forest, episode 16, I. Pyrev as Bulanov,
E. Tyapkina as Gurmyzhskaya, V. Remizova as Ulita

Above and below: The Forest, episode 18

Above: The Forest, episode 19. *Below: The Forest*, finale

Meyerhold's rape of the text of *The Forest* was not confined just to the break-up of the composition. Although the verbal material of the play was used completely in the show, the director's score frequently "consumed" one line or another, or would turn a casual phrase of Ostrovsky's into a significant one. In other words, Meyerhold insistently subordinated the text to his directorial tasks and, although apparently retaining its form, altered it in fact.

The interrelations between the characters in the course of these changes, noted Alpers, "shook apart." The characters became "much more free and independent of each other."[13]

This very astute comment indicates a point of principal importance. In the theater of direct correspondence to life the behavior of a person is developed as a series of actions and experiences directly or indirectly determined by the environment which this person inhabits. The thorough and true-to-life description of the environment, its characteristic moods and atmosphere, sharply enhances its significance. Connections between people are followed through with extreme detail and almost completely determine the image of each personage. He is characterized by others no less fully than by himself. In relativistic theater, where the task of so thorough a reproduction of the environment may not be staged at all, the personage becomes freed from such still determination.* *The Forest* is one of the clearest examples of such a destruction of the necessary bonds between an individual personage and the environment around him. With particular decisiveness and even with challenging directness, Meyerhold freed Aksyusha from such dependence. Her behavior in the show broke all the standards of social and historical verisimilitude: the servant berated her mistress, the poor girl brought in off the street continuously attacked her proprietress. Therefore, it would be more correct to say that the bonds between the characters in the play not only "shook apart," but that new forms of dependence were established and that the entire system of images in *The Forest* was reoriented in accordance with the intentions of the director.

A short time before the premiere, Meyerhold told of the way in which he systematized the personages in the play. It was all quite simple: "a) the decaying nobility—Gurmyzhskaya and company; b) the growing merchant class—Vosmibratov; c) protestors against the habitual way of life: Aksyusha, Peter; d) intermediate groups: the actors, the servants (*déclassé* element)."[14] The characters were classified in accordance with the elementary logic of popular, in this case even naive, sociology. Class attachment was viewed as basic and decisive. The rich and colorful, amusing and sad life of the heroes of *The Forest* underwent coarsening and simplification in accordance to this principle. One could believe (as people did believe) that another *agitka* was in preparation, that the dry, lifeless outline of "class existence" would be brought to the foreground of the show.

Asserting that this had been his aim, Meyerhold later stated:

We politically sharpened Ostrovsky's setting. He himself did not have the opportunity to sharpen it as we did, but he expected that the basic thought would reach the spectator

---

*However, the *problem* of the social determinism of human behavior may be viewed in relativistic theater and may be expressed by its specific means. This is proven convincingly in the works of Brecht and the "Berlin Ensemble."

from the stage. In the play there is the opposition of two camps. We underscored this opposition. In previous stagings, Gurmyzhskaya was interpreted wrongly: the exploiter was not
seen in her, she was considered simply to be a willful mistress with a streak of tyranny. We
show Gurmyzhskaya in such a way that all the colors of the class we wish to expose are
brought out. In Vosmibratov we exposed aspects of the *kulak* with which we are struggling.
Ostrovsky's Milonov speaks the most banal lines, which are clothing for reactionary thought.
He is a typical priest. Formerly, his priestly nature was not presented to the spectator with
sufficient clarity. Therefore, we presented him as Father Evgeny... Thanks to the reexamina-
tion of the characteristics of the roles in the comedy, the social theme sounds much more
strongly.[15]

Still, it was difficult to believe that Meyerhold would ignore completely the recent experience with *Earth Rampant* on the one hand, and *A Profitable Post* on the
other, and would arm himself again with the primitive club of the *agitka*. It would
be more plausible to suppose that the characters of the comedy, simplified in accordance with a strictly external class approach, would appear in a new and somehow special theatrical light.

So it was. The elementary nature of the class distinctions was translated by
Meyerhold into the language of grotesque comedy and clowning. Each role underwent decisive and bold exaggeration.

In the role of Gurmyzhskaya, for example (performed by E. Tyapkina), the
motif of lust and lewdness was strongly accented. Accordingly, Meyerhold gave her
a flaming red wig, a low, beckoning contralto, high polished boots, and a little riding
crop. Meyerhold, wrote Alpers, takes from Gurmyzhskaya "all the human traits,
turning her into an offspring of Hell with external strokes. She is repulsive to the
eye, dresses in coarse, tasteless costumes, speaks in a low hoarse voice, wears men's
boots and walks with a wide, heavy tread. Her lustfulness finds repulsive outlets.
Fat and mannish, she grabs the frail boy Bulanov with greedy hands. Thrilled with
passion, she sings sentimental romances with an intolerable off-key voice. Meyerhold
does everything to discredit her in the eyes of the spectator, to show her as a monster evoking distaste and revulsion."[16]

Gurmyzhskaya's helper and spy Ulita (V. Remizova), echoing her mistress,
developed and accented even more strongly the same theme of lust and falseness.
A clumsy, piled-up hair style, a passion for singing—off key, too, but in a high,
squealing voice—characterized this personage. She sang romances in the scene with
Arkasha Schastlivtsev—"Do Not Tempt Me Needlessly," for instance.

Milonov (S. Kozikov), as we have mentioned, was transformed by Meyerhold
into a sticky-sweet little priest, Father Evgeny. He wore a golden wig and golden
beard.

Bulanov, played by young Ivan Pyrev, wore a green wig and sporting clothes.
It was supposed that just such a "sporty Georgik" would appeal most to Gurmyzhskaya. Vosmibratov (B. Zakhava), all in black, with a red woolen beard, angular and
clumsy, looked like a perfect merchant. Bodaev (N. Karabanov) was also heavy and
grim. Everyone feared his handshake: he squeezed hands so hard that Gurmyzhskaya
squealed wildly and Bulanov grimaced with pain.

By the way, a couple of words regarding the wigs, which caused great consternation and puzzlement among the spectators at the first performances of *The Forest*.

Nemirovich-Danchenko, for instance, wrote: "These are the figures: Gurmyzhskaya —an actress of about 35, in a field jacket, short skirt, in high, polished boots and with a whip, wearing an enormous red wig. She is all *'yellow.'* Bodaev—a police officer with a large *green* beard. And Bulanov in a *green* wig and lawn tennis outfit. Aksyusha, naturally, is in a *red* dress. Vosmibratov—all in black (to be understood as the Black Hundred)."[17]

Among the list of his sins he was subsequently reminded most frequently of the multicolored wigs in *The Forest*. In response, he was inclined to say that these wigs had no fundamental significance, that this was a casual joke in the show. In fact, some of the particularly bright wigs, such as Bulanov's green one, Meyerhold eliminated fairly soon. "Here," wrote Igor Ilinsky recently, concerning the wigs, "was a tribute to pseudo-innovation and external sensation."[18] Still, it would appear that there was no real need for Meyerhold and Ilinsky to "disassociate" themselves in retrospect from the bright wigs. They fully accorded with the entire range of means of stage expression utilized in *The Forest* and with all the other, equally abrupt and excessive methods used to characterize the roles.

The comedians Schastlivtsev and Neschastlivtsev, and Aksyusha and Peter, who were contrasted by Meyerhold to Gurmyzhskaya and her circle, were characterized in another way. Neschastlivtsev (M. Mukhin) wore a wide-brimmed Spanish hat, a long black cape, a soft, loose shirt with an open collar, and wide trousers. The aureole of gray hair over the high forehead, the majestic, unhurried gestures—all these gave Neschastlivtsev a deliberately theatrical, romantic appearance. Schastlivtsev (I. Ilinsky) wore a small flat black hat, torn wide checkered trousers, torn shirt over which was a too-tight toreador's jacket. A narrow necktie hung from his neck. This was a clown, a real circus clown, suddenly entering the life of the manor. Both of the comedians broke into the exaggeratedly sleepy life, as though emissaries from a totally different, spectacular and dynamic other world. Somewhere on the boundary between these two worlds was Peter (I. Koval-Samborsky) in a long caftan and high boots, with a harmonica in his hands. Peter looked proud and victorious.

Aksyusha (Z. Raikh) was brought into the center of the play. In her role, Meyerhold accented "rebelliousness" strongly. Aksyusha, he said, "is not a bourgeois at all. She is in the same surroundings as Katerina in *The Storm*." Ten years later, before the jubilee performance of *The Forest*, he explained that "previously Aksyusha was portrayed as 'tearful,' sentimental, lyrically inclined. We showed an active person capable of struggle. Aksyusha may leave Gurmyzhskaya's service at any moment."[19]

It cannot be said that Aksyusha in Meyerhold's *The Forest* was particularly similar to Katerina in *The Storm*. She resembled more a Young Communist of the 1920s, and one of the workers in the audience said that Aksyusha "is a modern girl, strong and independent. When you look at her you think—a girl like this will not kill herself or drown herself."[20] The main conflict in the play, in Meyerhold's interpretation, was as follows: the energetic Young Communist Aksyusha against the Nepwoman Gurmyzhskaya at whose house she lived not as a poor relative but simply as a servant.

Such superficial allusions were grasped easily by the audience, but still they were less significant in the show. P. Markov noted another, more important meaning: "The aggregate of the episodes in *The Forest* presents the theme of prerevolutionary landowning Russia. Meyerhold . . . wishes to see from a bird's-eye view the life that flows on Gurmyzhskaya's estate. He looks at this long gone and dead life with the eyes of a pamphleteer, satirist and lyricist."[21]

Markov indicated the inner duality of the production. The reviewer in the *New Observer (Novyi zritel')* wrote essentially the same thing, but in different words: "The 'head-on,' direct political tendency in *The Forest* is shaped, colored, and enlivened by a depth of theatricality, directorial invention, and the inventiveness with which Meyerhold saturates his show."[22] Even more direct was the response by the outraged Kugel: "A book of ideas," he observed, "became also a circus poster."[23]

The stylistic duality of the show that everyone pointed to evidently was intended by the director and was clearly denoted in the very exterior of the production. "One part of the show is still 'theater rampant.' Half the stage is occupied by a bridge descending on steel cables from the gridirons... But here next to it, to the right of the spectator on the stage, there is something like a 'renaissance' of psychological-daily life theater, down to the hanging of real clothing on a line and such 'artistic' details as a yoke with buckets on Aksyusha's shoulders,"[24] wrote E. Beskin.

Thus, from one side was the "rampant" theatrical construction, on the other—the verisimilitude of life; on the one hand, head-on propaganda, on the other, totally apolitical circus-like methods; on the one hand, satire utilizing the most unrestrained grotesque exaggeration, on the other, a great stream of enlightened lyricism. Such were the open contradictions that joyfully proclaimed themselves. Their sincerity and their shameless and simple overtness were underscored even more strongly because very frequently episodes of different tonality followed one another. The rough farce of the "Moonlight Sonata" preceded, for instance, the romantically exalted episode "Between Life and Death." Nonetheless—or rather, therefore—the show possessed indubitable internal unity. This was achieved primarily by the militant and energetic intensity of the rhythm of the entire production. Secondly, by not concealing the principle of demonstrating various techniques of theatrical "work," one could "work" farce, could "work" a lyrical scene, could show tricks and ride enormous spheres, one could play a harmonica... All is permitted and all is possible, but everything must be lively, spirited, done with fire and excitement.

The design of the show by V. F. Fyodorov easily accepted this dynamic action and was adaptable to all its changes. On the left of the stage stood a construction: a wide spiral that descended in a flowing arc. Meyerhold himself conceived this structure. When the first version of the construction for *The Forest* was brought to him, Meyerhold took a clean sheet of paper and in its left corner sketched a laconic and light curved line. This was the origin of the main part of the construction—the road. Schastlivtsev and Neschastlivtsev walked along it into Gurmyzhskaya's estate, and "along the way" Arkashka was fishing, and catching butterflies. They prepared to sleep by the same road. Their famous dialogue was split into pieces and interrupted by episodes taking place below on the right part of the stage, where Gurmyzhskaya's estate was located. So the spectators would not be in doubt, to the right, over the entrance to the estate, was a sign: "Penki Estate of the Landowner

Gurmyzhskaya." In the center of the stage Fyodorov placed a giant stride. Commenting on the staging, N. M. Tarabukin wrote:

The design of *The Forest* is not Constructivist in the exact meaning of the term. Although elements of Constructivism are still significant here. The road going upward and to the back of the stage—this is far from "pure construction." To a significant extent this is an image, too. At some moments in the show its imagery and meaning become especially expressive. For instance, during the departure to the sound of Peter's harmonica. Objects gain the significance of landmarks which form the stage space. They become connected with a particular place on the stage or proscenium. Thus, for instance, the arch with the sign "Penki Estate of the Landowner Gurmyzhskaya" is an architectural conception that executes not only the utilitarian function of limiting space, but possesses a certain imagery. The laundry hanging from ropes, the giant stride, the green cage, the pigeons and a number of other objects obtain the significance of an image, i.e., possess meaningful expressiveness. *The Forest* is not so much material staging as *representational*, since the object becomes a representational sign signaling a particular meaning. A variety of colors again appears on stage. Objects, costumes, wigs are done in different colors. The monotony of the coloring and the standardization of the overalls in Constructivist staging is replaced by a variety of color.[25]

The tempo of the show corresponded emotionally to its external colorfulness. The rapid pace began in the prologue that parodied a procession and prayer for good harvest. The priest Milonov ran hurriedly onto the stage waving his censer and blessing anyone with his cross, followed quickly by the "masses" with gonfalons, dragging a huge ikon. Neschastlivtsev, walking from Kerch to Vologda, appeared above. And as soon as the procession of worshippers left the stage, Aksyusha came out, matter-of-fact, self-controlled, and began to hang the wash out on the line.

Zinaida Raikh, who played Aksyusha, succeeded in finely polishing the plastic aspects of the role. Her well-formed, agile and energetic gestures expressed spiritual health, happiness and cheer. Meyerhold took care that the "servant" Aksyusha was always busy. She hung and beat out the laundry in the beginning of the show and the beater rolled rapidly, firmly and strongly in her hands. From time to time, as though underscoring her own words, Aksyusha would slap the beater against the table in time to the conversation. She talked back boldly to her mistress, as many "conscious servants" did in those NEP years, and even thrust Gurmyzhskaya away with her shoulder when she interfered with Aksyusha's work.

A. Slonimsky commented:

Aksyusha's protest in the first dialogue with Gurmyzhskaya is expressed in the gradual increase in the force of the blows with the beater. The beater serves as a "dynamometer" for the dialogue. Aksyusha's final blow (to the words "what is the use of this comedy?") evokes an immediate "backfire" from Gurmyzhskaya: she grabs the roller and the beater and beats with all her strength on the table (with the words "how dare you?"). Gurmyzhskaya's loud double blow resolves the tension and forms the finale. This finale marks Gurmyzhskaya's temporary triumph ("This is my will!").

In the episode entitled "If It Were Near It Wouldn't Be Far, and If It's Far, That Means It Isn't Near," Aksyusha was setting the table. She banged the plates down roughly, threw the knives and forks. Aksyusha (Z. Raikh) expressed her contempt for the gentry with her entire demeanor.

The relations between Aksyusha and Peter (I. Koval-Samborsky), however, were presented in a key of enlightened lyricism, and the lovers carried on their dialogue while moving around on the giant stride. In this unusual way, Meyerhold expressed the victorious freshness of their young love. "The surge of hope is marked with Peter's three flights at the words: 'a day in Kazan, another in Samara, a third in Saratov.' With each circle he rises higher, after which for a transition to a narrative tone he jumps down from the strap. The scope of the flight renders the intonational movement precisely: the higher the tone the higher the flight."[26]

In the next scene with Aksyusha, Peter played the old waltz "Two Little Dogs" on the harmonica. Each of Aksyusha's dramatic lines was answered with a melancholy, lazy musical phrase that seemed to lessen the intensity of the situation. The "Number" was a tremendous success, and the song "Little Bricks" *(Kirpichiki)* was immediately composed to the tune of the old waltz in *The Forest* as performed by the virtuoso harmonica player Makarov. In the 1920s, this song conquered the country. "From Meyerhold's theater, 'Little Bricks' went merrily down the streets and through the villages. They found hospitable refuge in all the bars and taverns."[27] In 1925 the motion picture *Little Bricks* appeared.

In *The Forest* the prop design was of particular importance. The technique of performing with an object was used intensively and inventively. Alpers wrote:

> The stage was transformed into a moving system of things and objects the center of which was the actor himself. He ran around the stage performing short pantomime scenes, lively farces and sketches, and objects moved behind him in an unbroken flow, moving across the stage, endlessly taking each other's places... From behind the stage before the eyes of the spectators fruit, pumpkins, cans, pans, pitchers, tables, garden benches, pianos, mirrors, trellises, a giant stride and swings appeared and were taken away. All this moved, passed through the actor's hands, became light, turned into original objects for the juggler. Not only large objects played such a role. Small objects like a fishing rod, teapot, handkerchief, and a pistol were also included in this system of objects moving about the actor. It unfurled around him from the beginning to the end of the show like a magic ribbon in the hands of a Chinese conjurer.[28]

Thus the street-like carnival atmosphere of the entire production was strengthened.

Vladimir Blyum, one of the few "leftist" critics who approved of *The Forest*, wrote: "This is not a show but some kind of volcanic eruption of emotions—loud, frothing, thundering, piled one on top of the next, like a snowball..." He was delighted by the "sequence of the funny, the touching, the ironic, the angry, the sarcastic, the banal, the amusing, the bourgeois, the heroic, the passionate, the calculated, the primitive, the elegant, the coarse, the tender, the seductive, the repulsive," this whole gamut of emotions created by Meyerhold. "So this is Gurmyzhskaya: snub-nosed, evil, coarse, a fist in a skirt, a debauched old bat, singing cruel romances unbearably off key... The scene 'Take!.. Take!..' is one of genius, when Vosmibratov throws down before Neschastlivtsev's feet not only his wallet (as in Ostrovsky), but the contents of his pockets, his outer clothing, his boots and a caftan taken from his son."[29]

This act by Vosmibratov was preceded by a powerful artillery-like preparation. Preparing to amaze the merchant, Neschastlivtsev showed tricks to the inhabitants of Penki. When Vosmibratov arrived, Neschastlivtsev put his feet up on the armchair, majestically rolled himself up in a black cape and began haughtily to berate and shame him. At this moment Arkashka jumped out of his wide checkered pants and remained in black shaggy tights with a long tail. Then, he grabbed a pitchfork and thus uniformed as a devil he attacked the stubborn merchant. Finally, he accompanied Neschastlivtsev's monologue with fearful resounding blows made by hitting a stick against an iron sheet. All this noise and thunder suddenly inspired Vosmibratov, who began to yell, "Take!.. Take!.."

There were many such exaggerations in the show. Meyerhold would unfold a single line into an entire scene.

Neschastlivtsev behaved like a brash hoaxer; he played the buffoon and jeered at Gurmyzhskaya, and frightened her with a revolver. Gurmyzhskaya, holding her skirts up in fear, ran from him.

Arkashka (I. Ilinsky) took the leading role in the show, pushing aside the others —Aksyusha and Gurmyzhskaya—and became a living incarnation of the storm of humor that tore into Meyerhold's *The Forest*. Ilinsky said that Meyerhold saw in Arkashka "a happy-go-lucky jester and profligate." "In this treatment," he recalled, "Arkashka the man was forgotten." Ilinsky blamed himself too: "I, excited by the exterior comedy and tricks, missed the spiritual bitterness that Arkashka carries within himself."[30]

The bitterness truly had been "missed," and this Arkashka did not evoke even a shadow of regret. On the contrary, he reigned happily in the show. Here he was an evil, arrogant and resourceful clown. "Arkashka-Ilinsky does not remain calm for a single instant, he does not make a single gesture without constructing from it an entire comic episode or circus entree. He sings couplets, clowns around in different ways, plays with everything that comes into his hands. For him the world is a happy game in which living people, things and objects become balls that are thrown into the air and which execute various movements."[31]

With equal pleasure, gracefully and unselfconsciously, the gay and cruel jester caught fish (this was an entire etude for play with imagined objects: only the fishing rod was real, everything else—the line, the fish that dangled from it—was relativistically designated by the actor), sang romances, scared Ulita and swung with her on the see-saw...

This episode with the see-saw, the "Moonlight Sonata," was constructed with Aristophanean crudity. It began with Ulita's languid and squeaky roulades as she sang "Do Not Tempt Me Needlessly" and was accompanied by a series of unmistakable pantomimed gestures. "When Arkashka lowered his side of the board to the ground, the housekeeper, naturally, flew upward, squealing and gasping, jumping up after each of Arkashka's motions, her skirts fluttering," recalls V. Ardov. "The spectators were not confronted with a particularly decent scene..." The episode was concluded with equal unambiguity. Ulita froze in the air, pressing the thick beam of the see-saw between her legs. Below, Arkashka lit up a cigarette.

A. Gvozdev believed that the most valuable thing in the show was "the new

conception of the role of Arkashka Schastlivtsev on the level of popular clowning...
The incredibly impetuous buffoonery by the wonderful comic of our time—Ilinsky—
has brought new life to the original forms of popular comedy."[32] Even Nemirovich-
Danchenko, depressed by Meyerhold's *The Forest*, commented on Ilinsky's success.
Meyerhold himself, delighted with Ilinsky, explained his success this way:

> In Ostrovsky's plays, just as in Shakespeare's, there are no notes... This, like any real play,
> is just a score that must still be deciphered. People say: the Maly Theater and Ostrovsky!
> Hats off! But Ostrovsky is connected not with the present-day Maly Theater, but with the
> theater of Sadovsky, Rybakov and other great artists who are no more. I affirm that Ilinsky's
> performance in *The Forest* is in the tradition of M. P. Sadovsky—this is the source of this
> *gracioso* tone, this lightness, impetuosity, flippancy, and bravura. In turn, Sadovsky through
> Ostrovsky caught this line from the techniques of Spanish theater. And Ilinsky added an
> element of Chaplinism to all this. This is how the role matured.[33]

The circumstance that Meyerhold did not wish to observe Arkashka's misfor-
tunes, did not feel his "bitterness," his misery, did not wish to pity him, was a matter of high principle in *The Forest*. The wrenching theme of compassion for the
small people mistreated by fate—Aksyusha, Peter, Schastlivtsev and Neschastlivtsev—
that permeated Ostrovsky's comedy was rejected consistently and categorically by
Meyerhold. Sentimentality was totally foreign to him. The transposition of this
theme of pity into the key of aggressive attack was carried out without hesitation.
Since Gurmyzhskaya's song is almost over, there is no need to pity Aksyushka or
Arkashka. Therefore, Aksyusha is a cheerful, working, independent young woman,
while Arkashka is either a happy devil or a brash clown.

The director displaced the playwright and rethought the play in his own manner. "We," declared Meyerhold, "must take nothing from the theater of the nobility
and the bourgeoisie, but we must utilize the experience of popular theater of past
ages. Examples of such use—the introduction of the harmonica in *The Forest*, the
various carnival techniques of performance in *The Death of Tarelkin*. We require:
Red carnival (and not Red cabaret), ditties, clowns, of the Shakespearean and carnival types."[34] As for the play, he explained, it is *"the excuse for revealing its
theme,* in that plane in which its revelation *today* can prove to be alive."[35]

Meyerhold's *The Forest* unquestionably was alive. The success of the show was
great and lengthy, surpassing all expectations.

"If *The Magnanimous Cuckold* was accepted for the most part by intelligent
theatrical audiences and remained in many ways incomprehensible and foreign to
the masses of spectators," recalls Ilinsky, "then *The Forest* gained the acceptance of
the popular spectators, who came in flocks..."[36] *The Forest* was performed over
1700 times.

Theatergoers and critics were far from unanimous in their assessment of this
show. Its success shocked many. Before, Meyerhold had been under attack primarily
from the representatives of the academic theaters, but now the situation changed.
The very idea of staging *The Forest* was inimical to the leftists, contra-indicated for
them, while the character of this staging was unthinkable from the point of view of
the "akas." This is why both Nemirovich-Danchenko and Mayakovsky came out
against *The Forest*.

In a letter to O. S. Bokshanskaya, Nemirovich-Danchenko described the show in detail. "In the back of the stage," he observed disapprovingly, "people are walking around as if there were neither show nor audience... The scene between Peter and Aksyusha...takes place on a giant stride. First Aksyusha runs around and Peter watches, then he, then both. And while they are running, they carry on the dialogue." After commenting derisively on the costumes and wigs the director of the Moscow Art Theater concluded: "I watched only the first part. Could not take more. Was very bored... The actors, except for Arkashka (Ilinsky) are all bad."[37]

Mayakovsky's comments were blunt. "For me," he said, "Meyerhold's staging of *The Forest* is very repulsive..." And: "Ostrovsky's withered *Forest* on Revolutionary stage boards was a step back."[38]

A. Kugel called the show "spitting in the face of Russian culture" and was outraged that clowning—the lowest, coarsest kind of art—"is declared to be an achievement of the highest sort."[39] Viktor Shklovsky wrote that Meyerhold "passed through Ostrovsky like a blind man through a phantom."[40] During the performance, M. F. Andreeva "became so infuriated that I was afraid of cursing indecently."[41]

S. Radlov, too, was among Meyerhold's new opponents. He found eclecticism and "lack of system" in the actor's performance in *The Forest*. "All right together are Schastlivtsev—magnificent eccentricity, Neschastlivtsev—the darkest province, Aksyusha—home-grown lyricism, Vosmibratov—a grotesque not without psychological justification, Gurmyzhskaya—no concept as yet of what constitutes the actor's craft," he wrote. In Radlov's opinion, in *The Forest* Meyerhold "did not even feel his way to the necessary Constructivism, the movement of actors connected with the form of the stage design and the directorial composition... Everything has been sacrificed purely for the effect of plot significance. The foundations have been laid for theatrical neoperedvizhnikism."[42]

Consequently, after the premiere of *The Forest*, Meyerhold was attacked by a new combination: "leftists" and "rightists."

But at this time among the ranks of Soviet critics there was already a group of thoughtful, perceptive analysts independent of the passions of the "theatrical front." Among these, in addition to Lunacharsky, we should mention first of all P. Markov in Moscow and A. Gvozdev in Leningrad. Their reactions to *The Forest* were the most sober and exhaustive, and proposed two immediate theatrical problems: the problem of interpretation of the classics on the Soviet stage and the problem of the further development of Meyerhold's art.

Lunacharsky wrote:

> Beginning with *The Forest*, I sensed a positive break in Meyerhold's art. This sensitive man began to understand that innovations and tricks, the talented but mischievous breakage at any cost of old theater—all this may be good, but is far from what our audience needs like bread. In *The Forest* an attempt has already been made to stage an old problem in a new way—the distinction of social types, typical situations. The production, with all the riches of its discoveries, was, however, somehow unconvincing, one did not feel a single inner core. Meyerhold stood at the crossroads between "insolence" to the old theater and the actual creation of new realism.[43]

This brief but important remark by Lunacharsky on the "unconvincing" effect of the production led to a thought about the strictly temporary and rapidly changing nature of the relations between the classics and modernity established by Meyerhold in *The Forest*. In 1926, when Lunacharsky wrote the words cited, after Stanislavsky's *A Passionate Heart* and Meyerhold's *The Inspector General*, these relations already appeared too familiar. In two years Soviet theater had accomplished great strivings and discoveries, but this route had begun with *A Profitable Post* and *The Forest*. This is why A. Gvozdev saw Meyerhold's main achievement in the sharpness and irreconciliability of his social descriptions. "Landowner types, depicted in academic theaters in soft and careful tones, appeared here in hard images permeated with hatred for the serf-owning past, mercilessly stripping the mask of prettiness and coziness from descriptions of the landowning life traditional for the theater of the everyday."[44]

When listening to the polyphony of *The Forest*, "inspired and barbaric," in P. A. Markov's expression,[45] one catches in addition to this rough satirical tune the sound of other, more graceful melodies. The entire show was connected by an interrupted but audible theme, the devilish, light, brash and tricky theme of acting—the theme of Schastlivtsev and Neschastlivtsev. This was echoed by and occasionally blended with the simple, lyrical, harmonica-accompanied theme of the love between Peter and Aksyusha. Both these themes appeared to respond to the banging of the satirical drum; they appeared to offset the clumsy, dull, and wild force of upper-class swagger with the invulnerable and indestructible power of poetry.

The director's score for the show, as we know, required breaking up the text, restructuring and reaccenting its meaning. It is true that the paradoxically inclined Marietta Shaginyan stated unexpectedly that "only thanks to Meyerhold have we received, finally, the direct feeling of *Ostrovsky's text*," that Meyerhold "again compelled us to relive and feel the dramatic conflicts in *The Forest*, he revealed their undying theatrical effectiveness (outside the stereotyped theatrical effectiveness of their initial realization). In a word, he brought us into Ostrovsky's theater, bypassing our reading-book habits and premises."[46] More widespread, and closer to the truth, was the opinion that by removing the "reading-book gloss," Meyerhold destroyed the verbal fabric of the comedy. It was this impression of the "uselessness" of Ostrovsky's text, the impression of the play as an old *excuse* for a new directorial composition, that was the object of Markov's close scrutiny.

Markov believed that the director "missed the main significance of *The Forest*." It would appear that this circumstance could be viewed as decisive and predetermine a negative conclusion. However, speaking of the director's "single combat" with Ostrovsky, of the contradictions in the show "in the course of which the playwright's material avenged itself," Markov approached his conclusions more carefully and more dialectically.

Having felt Ostrovsky's popular element, Meyerhold purchased its freedom at the cost of the destruction of the remaining facets of Ostrovsky's artistic world view and art. A "rebirth of Ostrovsky" through his "transcendence" was not achieved. Neschastlivtsev's romanticism, the darkness of the inhabitants of *The Forest*, the severity and clever cragginess of Vosmibratov and, most importantly, Ostrovsky's word did not reach us. Another was heard: debauchery, expanse—everything that previously was felt in Ostrovsky was demonstrated for the first time with such force on stage by Meyerhold. The powerful attraction of this controversial show lay in the deeply-felt principle of carnival theater, of full-blooded popular melodrama, and not in individual techniques.

"In *The Forest*," Markov continued, "the cleverness and slyness of Meyerhold the artist showed through clearly. Simultaneously with the propagandistic intent of the show, Meyerhold brings in an element of bright and brave lyricism."[47]

In other words, while much was destroyed, there was much in Ostrovsky that Meyerhold was showing *for the first time*. The joy of these discoveries, the joy of the visual re-creation of the connections between Ostrovsky and popular theater was one of the greatest conquests of Meyerhold's *The Forest*. Another victory was the closeness between the comedy and the modern audience, obtained at the cost of undoubted coarsening and mischievous vulgarization.

Meyerhold's *The Forest*, despite his characteristic "childish disease of leftism," helped create a social-class approach to works from the past. In *The Forest*, this new approach was proclaimed by Meyerhold in a challenging, polemical way. Only two years passed, and Stanislavsky, who had not seen Meyerhold's *The Forest*, but who naturally was thoroughly informed of this philistine spectacle, staged Ostrovsky's *A Passionate Heart*. He staged it in the debate against all of Meyerhold's "alterations," but with an active interpretation and hyperbolic amplifications that the Art Theater could not have dreamed of earlier.

The tremendous success of *The Forest* evoked numerous direct imitations and variations, more or less talented copies. Most often these were unsuccessful, some because the principles applied by Meyerhold to *The Forest* were mechanically transferred to other classical plays (the splintering into episodes was particularly popular), others because they were created much later, under changed social and theatrical circumstances.

But if we examine Meyerhold's show independently of its various imitators, if we see this production in the context of its time, then it must be said that in *The Forest* the assimilation of the classical heritage was linked with the talented subordination of the classic to the "cause of the day."

Meyerhold's *The Forest* foreshadowed the appearance of new Soviet satirical comedy—a year later such comedy did appear on the stage of the Meyerhold theater.

MASKS AND IMAGES

Modernity in its most direct, unprocessed, newspaper- and poster-like aspect entered into political productions of Meyerhold's such as *Earth Rampant* and *D. E.* But, as we have observed, symptomatic changes were taking place, autonomously it seemed, in the forms of the political reviews. The genre of the political rally shows was dying out, merging with the contours of the music-hall type show, broken into separate "numbers." Meyerhold did not have a monopoly on these new forms. In Foregger's workshop propagandistic reviews were replaced by dance programs. Here the slogan of the "music-hallization" of theater was propounded. Meyerhold's pupil Eisenstein proclaimed another idea—the "circusization" of theater—and staged on the themes of Ostrovsky's play *Enough Simplicity in Every Wise Man* a real circus performance—a "montage of attractions" with tightrope walkers, jugglers, acrobats, and so forth.

All these more or less effective, more or less sensational experiments of the first half of the 1920s revealed one general all-pervasive law: the movement began with the *agitki* and ended with entertainment. From political declarations directed at audiences of workers and students, art moved with imperceptible but rapid speed to carefree dances, to jazz, the circus, to all kinds of attractions. The "leftist" studios, which had just been loudly proclaiming their revolutionary fervor, were turning into ordinary Nepmen's cabarets. Eisenstein avoided this fate and shortly left theater for the cinema. Foregger, however, at first a sincere and passionate supporter of Meyerhold, emptied the chalice. In the tiny Foregger's Workshop on Arbat Street opposite the Prague Restaurant where the "cream" of NEP Moscow gathered, "leftist" art smiled pleasantly at the cabaret frequenters and offered for their attention the extravagant dances of more or less naked "girls." This was something new, and the word "Foreggerism" *(foreggerovshchina)* was coined, referring to a piquant, slightly lewd variant of "leftism."

Meyerhold saw that the danger was real for him, too. It was necessary to chart a course through the highly complicated situation of NEP. In determining this course, it was necessary to note the clearly increased interest of the audience in the classics, particularly in his own renditions of Ostrovsky. All indications were that the art that operates with class conflict and not with the reality of human fates was exhausting itself. The public no longer was interested in the poster. Meyerhold was not content with the prospects of Foreggerism. His political temperament under these conditions could express itself fully only in contemporary drama.

Meyerhold's theater, reacting with sensitivity to all fluctuations in the political barometer and striving to be on the "firing line" in the political struggle, energetically sought contacts with young Soviet writers. Mayakovsky, Kamensky, Aseev, Tretyakov, Brik were close to the theater. For the time being, however, they were not writing plays. Meanwhile, Meyerhold was one of many people interested in the first translations of German Expressionist dramas which appeared at this time.

The great interest displayed toward plays by Ernst Toller, Georg Kaiser, Franz Werfel, Walter Hasenclever and other German Expressionist playwrights derived from the fact that these plays expressed temperamentally and tempestuously the protest against capitalist civilization, against the suppression of individuals' rights by the rigid organization of bourgeois society. In these plays, Soviet directors wished to hear the news of the oncoming world Revolution.

It is characteristic that the main themes of German Expressionist drama on Soviet stages were frequently turned inside-out. Fear before the rebelling crowd was followed by praise for the revolutionary masses. The theme of the tragic solitude of the leader misunderstood by his people was treated ironically, and the conflict between a people and an individual was resolved in favor of the people. Finally, the theme of hatred for the machine underwent the most radical metamorphosis: the Expressionists' plays were staged in Constructivist settings, and admiration of machinery and all-powerful technology became practically the chief content of these productions.

Such tendencies to alter the basis of Expressionist drama were felt as early as 1922 in the production of Toller's *The Machine Wreckers*, staged in the Theater of the Revolution by the young director P. Repnin, under Meyerhold's supervision. The artist V. Komardenkov designed the set in an urban spirit. The tragedy of the revolutionary without support from his people, in contradiction to Toller, was treated as the tragedy of a people lacking a consistent and steadfast leader.

Excited by the themes of Expressionist drama, the Theater of the Revolution under Meyerhold's direction rethought them in its own way, placing new ideological stress-marks. Particularly radical was the director's intervention in the artist structure of Toller's pathetic play-oratorio *Masses and Man*. This drama was staged by the director A. Velizhev with decorations by V. Shestakov in the Theater of the Revolution in 1923.

This production could have served as an example of a totally consistent rejection of Expressionist drama. The solitary hero is removed from his pedestal. The attitude toward him is ironic. The faceless crowd, on the contrary, is transformed into a heroic mass whose actions are thought out and aimed at a goal.

It was at this point, at the moment when Meyerhold was tiring of the Theater of the Revolution's thankless work with Expressionist dramas (which were not successful), that the young playwright Alexei Faiko appeared with his first play, *Lake Lyul*.

His play corresponded ideally with Meyerhold's intentions and desires of that time. Everything that the directors of the Theater of the Revolution under Meyerhold's supervision ascribed forcibly to Expressionist drama already existed in *Lake Lyul*. The single hero was uncrowned, the Revolution was glorified. The characteristic themes of Expressionist drama, its nervous, unquiet rhythm, its tendencies to urbanism, were in Faiko's plays adapted exactly in the manner in which they were reworked in the Soviet stagings of Toller's plays. And, naturally, in the end the lighthearted *Lake Lyul* had nothing in common with tragic Expressionist drama. There remained only a superficial similarity. (This led, subsequently, to many years of confusion among historians of theater and drama who stubbornly categorized this play in the Expressionist "department.")

Lake Lyul was tied to the Russian situation of the 1920s in the most direct way. This connection was already visible in the manner in which the author formulated his esthetic goals. "I believe," he said, "that modern revolutionary repertoire must be created not on the principle of poster-slogan—schematic shows whose propagandistic significance drowns in the naked cry and elicits no actual response from the spectator—but on the principle of schematically interesting action plays that are effective in the theatrical and stage sense, with a complex plot, intertwining intrigue and emotional saturation."

In other words, the main cure seen by Alexei Faiko for the casualness and approximation of form characteristic of propaganda theater was "entertainment," "plot," effective construction of the story line, and complexity of the story. The antithesis for theater of the "naked cry" was found in the theater of highly precise dynamic calculation.

"*Lake Lyul* is melodrama," said Faiko, "its element—tempo, passion and shock."

Tempo and shock became, indeed, the "element" of this play. Drawing "pictures of capitalist bacchanalia" which the playwright found in the atmosphere of "profits, competition, and crime" became the chief dramatic conflict for his cheerful melodrama. This is a conflict between two billionaires, Bulmering Sr. and Bulmering Jr. This is their battle for money, for power, and for the beautiful Ida Ormond.

Anton Prim's bold intervention into the struggle between the two billionaires and his equally rapid and ephemeral rise form the basic line of the plot in *Lake Lyul*.

"Roughly speaking," Faiko stated, "my assignment was to express the collapse of the individualistic world view."[1]

Roughly speaking, it did not work out.

The hero of the play, Anton Prim, entered the stage as the incarnation of the Nepman's dream of head-spinning, easy riches, of "pleasures" obtained through enterprise. Anton Prim was a seductive and, it must be admitted, a talented sketch of this ideal. The acute sense of the brevity of time allotted by life, the correct presentiment of doom that was the source of the so-called "NEP intoxication," all these compelled one to see in Anton Prim's simple program ("Your main goals?"— "Maximum pleasure") the sole meaning of earthly life.

What Alexei Faiko called, in all sincerity, Anton Prim's "individualism" was, in fact, a precise artistic rendition of the Nepmen's ideal: "If only an hour, it's mine!"

The attractive possibility indicated in *Lake Lyul* of cleverly and successfully cheating the Revolution, of walking the line dividing "Red" and "White," of balancing on this edge while picking "flowers of pleasure," these increased by a thousandfold the attractiveness of the figure of Anton Prim for the NEP-era audience. NEP simply could not have managed without such a hero, in whose image apostasy became cloaked in the romantic flair of adventure. Cynicism became transformed into nobility.

The luxurious, stunning Ida Ormond in her attire, her villas, her horses, her "marvelous legs" and other indescribable delights... The scene in which Ida, in Prim's presence, receives the seamstress, was the incarnation of the boldest aspirations of Nepmen's wives, mistresses, and daughters...

Faiko's dynamic, stinging, and rapid melodrama included the precise plot of detective literature, and experience from the already existing format of detective films. Faiko attempted to subordinate this "technology" to his purposes, but it beat him. It defeated him primarily because here Faiko was working with unknown, invented material, and the specifics of the actual time in which the play was written broke through into the writer's constructions independently of his will.

When Meyerhold staged *Lake Lyul* in the Theater of the Revolution, the danger of surrendering his art to the service of the Nepman audience was very real. In this opus, political theater became at least partially entertainment theater. Alexei Faiko wrote the following about the premiere, which took place on November 8, 1923:

> Undisguised melodrama was happening on stage, complete with arson, arrests, bankruptcies, treason and murder, while a festive mood reigned in the auditorium, replete with trusting good feeling and excited interest... The entire monumental back wall of the theater was exposed, metal fittings stuck out and cables and wires hung challengingly. The center stage was occupied by a three-story construction with corridors leading into the back, with cages, ladders, platforms, and elevators running not only vertically but horizontally. Slides with signs and advertisements were projected, silver screens shone from within. In contrast, against this background flickered the colored spots of rather unusual costumes: elegant women's attire, gleaming starched shirtfronts, sashes, epaulets, gold-embroidered liveries.[2]

The entire form of the show strove for effect. Viktor Shestakov's construction, the first on stage to have moving elevators (this was the largest "trump" of the staging), permitted the instantaneous transferral of the action (and the heroes) from one platform to another. Performing platforms were located on the three stories of the construction and were highlighted from time to time by the powerful light of a projector. Each setting represented a specific place of action—store, hotel, villa, railway bridge and so forth. The action developed with the brash coherence of a motion picture film. The tempo of the show was extremely fast and the critics wrote unanimously of Meyerhold's techniques of "cinema montage," of the cinema-like flickering of the individual "frames" of the show. The elegantly ornate costumes, the heady music—the Debussy Cake-Walk and other musical fragments written by N. Popov—furthered the attractiveness of the spectacle.

Yury Sobolev wrote with derisive irony:

> I watched *Lake Lyul* in the Theater of the Revolution and directly before my eyes appeared the image of some gentleman from a poster announcing a new detective film: hands thrust deep into the wide pockets of a most fashionable long overcoat with raglan sleeves and a well-ironed crease in the back; long shoes with narrow toes, top hat on the head, half-mask on the face... "Out from under the mysterious cold half-mask..." Without any explanation it is clear that a detective stands before us. Of course this is he, the immortal Pinkerton, fearless Nick Carter—the favorite of Soviet damsels thrilling with joy and freezing in terror during those cheerless Moscow evenings when like a sliding shadow, a pleasant phantom, he rushes past on the flickering screen in the stifling little movie theater Magic Dreams on Party Time *(Razgulai)* Street. Oh, the romance of the office typist, oh, the youthful delirium of the cigarette vendor, oh, the highest dreams of the lovers of the detective story, of the adventure novel, of American films... How much naive exaltation and delight you hide within yourselves!..
>
> "But why the Theater of the Revolution?" readers will ask. Quite right, I will answer them: why the theater of the Revolution?[3]

Still, some critics were able to answer this crafty question. Although Meyerhold did not alter a single word in *Lake Lyul* and although he amplified all the effects and seductions of the play, nonetheless the staging differed from the play in the exaggerated anxiety and nervousness of intonation. "The revolutionary theme of *Lake Lyul*, the rapid and dark decay of capitalist society, was presented by Meyerhold in tones of acute anxiety; anxiety generally was the basic note of the show," wrote P. Markov. Markov saw the rapid tempo of the production as "intermittent." He sensed a "dull hostility that connected the heroes of the play into a single whole."[4] B. Alpers received the same impression: "The anxious, leaping, broken rhythm of action transmits the flavor of doom, of disaster looming over the inhabitants of this imaginary center of capitalist culture..."

But the anxiety that permeated the director's score for the show was not conveyed to all the actors. B. Glagolin played Anton Prim, in the opinion of Alpers, "effectively, in melodramatic tones."[5] Yu. Sobolev continued: in Glagolin "the effect of the cinema poster (detective in the half-mask) is presented with wonderful ease... This is a triumph of the romanticism of Sherlock Holmesian tone and color."[6]

Seconding Glagolin was B. Rutkovskaya in the role of Ida Ormond. This actress long ago had assimilated the role of "cultivated, refined, infernal," very "luxurious" women, and the modeling of the heroine's dresses, sewn in the latest western styles, interested the audience no less than the adventurousness of the hero.

The leitmotif of anxiety and the nervous rhythm of the director's score were best captured by M. Babanova in the role of the song-girl Georgette Bienaimee, V. Zaichikov as the journalist Ignatz Vitkovsky and M. Tereshkovich as the banker Nathan Crown.

It was of substantial importance, however, that in *Lake Lyul*, as in *A Profitable Post*, Meyerhold's actors could not limit themselves to the "social mask" principle, which had been quite satisfactory in *Earth Rampant, D. E.* and in *The Forest*. Faiko's melodrama did offer characters, however sketchy or static. B. Alpers admitted (although this contradicted his overall concept) that in *Lake Lyul* "the design of the characters of the preceding repertoire of the theater is replaced by more detailed characterizations of the parts. These," he believed, "are still theatrical masks, but are modern masks that reveal their everyday life origins..."[7] It should be admitted that here the word "mask" is utterly inappropriate, since each character in the play possessed not only a social function but also personal concreteness.

Meyerhold's theater found itself balancing on this borderline between social masks and the image of the specific person in the mid-1920s.

There exists the opinion, best expressed in Alpers's book *The Theater of the Social Mask*, that Meyerhold's art always was the art of masks. "Meyerhold's entire ideological and artistic baggage, his entire contradictory artistic biography, may be reduced to one compressed formula: the creation and crystallization of type masks which with a small number of outlines or skeletons embrace the entire living variety of types from the past," Alpers asserted. He explained: "The theatrical mask, as a rule, usually expresses the ossification of a social type, the loss of individual traits that would make him still live; it expresses his extreme schematization and generality. It always resists *character* or its lowest step—the genre-figure."[8]

B. V. Alpers's book was written in the late 1920s and contained the first conceptualization of the development of Meyerhold's art. The book was a serious and penetrating theoretical analysis of the extremely varied stage practice of the director. In many of its positions, Alpers's work remains faultless even today. Today, however, the author's overall concept does appear too streamlined and inflexible. When studying the artistic structure of Meyerhold's productions one becomes convinced that the principle of "social masks" was not universal for the director. Even in the widest sense, this principle does not apply to the images in *The Magnanimous Cuckold* or *A Profitable Post*. It is applicable to the analysis of *Mystery-Bouffe, The Death of Tarelkin* and *The Forest* but, as we shall see shortly, it is not applicable to the analysis of *The Mandate, The Inspector General*, and *Woe to Wit* (although Alpers does define the images in these stagings as social masks).

The overall, leading tendency in Soviet stage art in the second half of the 1920s was against masks. The urge for the concrete, the individual, the urge to comprehend the character and psychology of the individual man, made an impact on Meyerhold's art as well. The first signs of this were the inevitable contradictions.

Meyerhold's art begins to examine the personality, the individual, to become interested in his inimitable concreteness and the contents of his soul.

This is the critical point. In perspective this is an invasion of the territory of the theater of direct correspondence to life, of psychological theater. Consequently, a question of cardinal importance arises: will the art of relativistic theater be capable of retaining its means of expression, the structure of its imagery, in this "foreign" area? Or will psychological theater work from within to seize the relativistic, to subordinate it?

This question also could be formulated thus: can new forms of realism possibly be based on relativistic theater?

Although in the staging of Faiko's play *Bubus the Teacher* (soon after *Lake Lyul*, on January 23, 1925), the art of the social mask did try to defend its right to exist, these attempts were very hesitant and, Meyerhold felt, required increased support. In this play Faiko intended to unfold the tragicomedy of conciliation, to ridicule the policy of timid inaction and the empty rhetoric of the false defenders of popular interests who, essentially, only hindered the workers' movement. The idea was clear and simple, and the story was quite appropriate. Bubus the teacher participated in a workers' demonstration. The demonstration was broken up, Bubus experienced "most genuine terror" and hid in the garden of the ruler, van Kamperdaf. A single quick movement of the plot and yesterday's rebel, the "representative of the popular masses" appears in the midst of today's rulers. Yet another twist of the plot and Bubus is nominated for the government, but it turns out that this windbag and coward can be of no use even to the ruling party. Again he "experiences terror" and he "vacillates." The Revolution takes place, but Bubus is not needed by the Revolution either, even though he himself wants to "meet the historic dawn of this historic morning together with the masses." The Revolution turns away from him.

If in *Lake Lyul* Faiko had added the dynamics of the detective film to the experience of melodrama, then in *Bubus the Teacher* vaudeville was aided by the crude techniques of an operetta libretto. Here, the "light genre" announced itself quite directly and smiled pleasantly at the Nepman audience.

—358—

The imported cheval-glass mirror of *Bubus the Teacher* reflected dimly the strictly Russian problem of the relations between the intelligentsia and the Revolution. The mirror, however, was dull and warped, it distorted proportions, caused confusion.

Why did Meyerhold decide to stage Faiko's play? It would be futile to seek an answer to this question in the special brochure published for the premiere or in Meyerhold's newspaper interviews preceding the dress rehearsal. The Master roughly outlined the plot and contented himself with generalizations. Faiko himself subsequently wrote that in his opinion Meyerhold already had devised a staging, had tasted its extravagant form mentally, and that *Bubus* simply was squeezed into the director's plan, quite independently of the play itself.

Faiko supposed that:

> Probably the bamboo that framed the entire stage and the piano in the music shell over the stage platform, and the frock-coated pianist at this piano, and the flashing zig-zags of the electric advertisements, and the *grenat*-colored rug covering the whole stage—all this accumulated long before, appeared in a dream, beckoned, matured, ripened, and, finally, required an outlet and a realization.
>
> Only a small detail was lacking—a play...
>
> The bamboo did not appear for *Bubus*, but *Bubus* adapted to the bamboo or, rather, the bamboo reigned on stage independently of the play and of anything else, like the Kantian "thing in itself."[9]

We shall discuss the bamboo and the rest of the set design by I. Shlepyanov later. Now we shall observe only that Faiko's hypothesis on the idea for the show, which supposedly arose prior to the reading of the play, appears unconvincing. It is entirely possible, however, that some details of this plan (at least the bamboo) had been in Meyerhold's mind for some time. Nonetheless, Faiko's lightweight comedy, strangely enough, was vitally important to Meyerhold at that moment, since it offered yet another opportunity to test the principle of the social mask. This purpose was served by the entire refined stage form of *Bubus the Teacher*, and it was created in the name of this goal.

The NEP situation hung a large question mark over the possibilities of a theater of rough social generalizations. Poster-like, directly propagandistic theater was rejected, there was no doubt of that. But when the social mask was presented in the form of an eccentric show, when it was accompanied by music and dance as, for instance, in *D. E.* and *The Forest*, when the director's score carefully and elegantly prepared for its appearance, then the mask still "went over," attracted live interest and had a precise and strong effect on the audience.

The operetta-like unpretentiousness and naivete of *Bubus the Teacher* were doubly an asset for Meyerhold. The play did not require (in contrast even to *Lake Lyul*) any precise individual characteristics. Its characters were easily attached to operetta roles and could be distinguished socially with equal ease: baron, capitalist, conciliator, liberal, etc. At the same time, the clear plot outline permitted the director to give the actor-masks all the assistance and capabilities of the theater.

This time, Meyerhold devoted particular attention to music. The production even received an unusual definition of genre: "comedy on music." Meyerhold warned:

"Here, music is a unique construction with the ability to ridicule sharply the masses of that class which is the target for the advancing proletariat." The generous introduction of fragments from Chopin and Liszt into the show (forty-six entire musical numbers!) and the intrusion of jazz saxophones playing foxtrots and the shimmy marked Meyerhold's totally unexpected return to a slow pace of action.

All of Meyerhold's post-Revolutionary productions had been accelerated and dynamic. The pulse of his art quickened, sometimes feverishly. In *Bubus* a melancholy calm descended onto the stage. Furthermore, for the first time in years Meyerhold did not need to conduct the action on various "floors" of a construction and did not wish to break the limitations of the traditional stage portal. The play descended to the stage floor and was enclosed in its frame. The stage floor was covered with a soft carpet so that the actors' movements would be silent and would not interfere with the music. The yellow bamboo, however, which hung from brass rings and surrounded the stage in a half-circle, would knock together significantly with every entrance and exit. The pianist Lev Arnshtam, together with the piano on which candles burned, was raised over the stage in a small open shell, which was gilded inside. The entire exterior of the show, severely and elegantly executed by I. Shlepyanov, was neutral with respect to the play. Although above, over the bamboo, the illuminated letters of advertisements would run past occasionally, it was still very difficult to take seriously the claim of the theater: "Here is a setting that is very like the decadent culture of dying Europe."[10]

This setting served an entirely different purpose. It was convenient for experiments in the area of "pre-performance," a new enthusiasm of Meyerhold's which he tested in *Bubus*. Briefly, the essence of the new idea was that Meyerhold required the actor to prepare plastically for each line and even, in essence, to replace the spoken word with the completion of the plastic design. We know that Meyerhold had done such experiments during his enthusiasm for pantomime. Now, pantomime forestalled the line and seemed to comment on it in advance, ascribing to it a definite meaning that was absent in the text. The puzzled author recalled later: "This pre-performance, as I understood it, was a sort of introduction to any stage action of the actor. Since not a single decisive line or key scene was managed without this pre-performance, this pantomime introduction so to speak, the entire play seemed to double, to be performed twice, which gave it a heavy, cumbersome and extremely slowed-down character. I saw how my light comedy became a drawn-out, pretentious and falsely significant production."[11]

Nonetheless, Meyerhold continued to assert to everyone that pre-performance was the weapon of the actor-tribune, a technique of propaganda theater! Using pre-performance, he wrote, the actor-tribune wishes to transmit to the spectator his attitude toward events on stage,

wishes to compel the spectator to perceive the action unfolding before him on stage in just such a manner and no other... The actor-tribune performs not the position itself, but what is concealed behind it, which he reveals for a specific reason (propaganda). This is why he, the "actor-tribune," not only speaks the "words given by the playwright," but reveals visibly the "roots that created these words." He continuously spins the thread of his distinct (again, propagandistic) intentions...[12]

Meyerhold's theoretical positions and declarations of the 1920s and 1930s were always more or less approximate. The need to pepper theory with political terminology confused the issue further. The essence of the technique used in *Bubus* was that pauses were utilized for the demonstration through pantomime and mime of the actor's relation to an image. Meyerhold's "pre-performance" opposed the Moscow Art Theater's concept of "subtext" with something like a "countertext." This was an attempt to enter psychology *from without*, to use pantomime and mime to *demonstrate* the spiritual movements of a character, to italicize them *before* the character speaks his line. Consequently, this was the first and, from the point of view of Meyerhold's further artistic evolution, an extremely symptomatic test of a totally new, external demonstration of "the life of the human spirit" (Stanislavsky's phrase). Psychology was revealed not by way of reincarnation, but by way of alienation from the role. The life of the body became demonstratively connected to the life of the spirit.

The principle of masks which Meyerhold wished to reestablish in *Bubus* still remained in doubt, however. Despite its mechanical nature, the pre-performance still provided each character with an abundance of individualized plastic means. This abundance became cumbersome and important.

The mask, born from mischief and political boldness of the carnival, was put on the face of the actor only after long musical and pantomimic preparation in *Bubus the Teacher*. Important significance led to simplicity. This technique, which by nature required lightness, jesting and straightforwardness, was "developed" before the audience painstakingly and with difficulty. "The actors," observed Faiko, "assimilated the concept of pre-performance with difficulty, mechanically executing the orders of the director."[13] Their performance of the show was hesitant and mediocre. This could be explained only in part by the fact that instead of I. Ilinsky, who had quarreled with Meyerhold during the rehearsals and had left, the role of Bubus was performed by B. Belsky, while the leading female role of Stefka, which the author had written for M. Babanova, fell into the hands of Zinaida Raikh, who did not possess Babanova's grace and ease. More significant was Meyerhold's elevation of weightiness into a principle. The pre-performance caused slowness.

Faiko's vaudeville was transposed into the genre of social melodrama, both monotonous and pompous. The action lurched from pause to pause and was suspended altogether while Arnshtam played Chopin and Liszt. "Chopin and Liszt were not brought into the show accidentally," announced the impressive theater program. "The bourgeoisie and the intelligentsia with their duality and decadence, with their refined pianism by Chopin and Liszt, this is what so fortunately has been constructed in this production..." Chopin and Liszt were called to assist in "the matter of discrediting the harmful overrefinement of the class that is perishing in its own decay."[14] These composers, asserted A. Fevralsky, rewording the positions of Meyerhold himself, "stress the decadent overrefinement of bourgeois civilization." Supposing that in the present case, too, Meyerhold "presents the *problem of form* as a problem of the method of maximum propaganda effect," A. Fevralsky insisted that even "intentional deceleration of the tempo of action" was desirable for purposes of propaganda.[15]

It is characteristic, however, that contemporary reviews as a rule ignored the theme, meaning, and content of the show. Only its external and formal aspect was discussed, either incredulously or supportively. Blyum wholeheartedly ridiculed Meyerhold's efforts:

The external design has "chic, sparkle, *immer* elegant"... Yes, for Meyerhold a totally unexpected strange recidivism into estheticism. There is not the slightest irony for this..."Igor Severyaninism *(igor-severianinshchina)*, everything is presented seriously and with complete rapture. This Baron alone—either a Chukhloma Wilde or a Kineshma Vertinsky!.. At times it even seemed as though you were sitting in some provincial affiliate of the Kamerny Theater. Oh, how dull![16]

B. Yakhontov played the Baron. Faiko reports that he "captivated Meyerhold with his enchanting voice and quite unique mastery of declamation."[17] The critics, however, were not charmed by Yakhontov, nor by Babanova in the small role of Thea, nor by Raikh in the large role of Stefka.

Only B. Alpers noted "the theme of perdition, of inevitable catastrophe, hanging over this stylish and elegant glass world" in the show.[18] The audience did not possess such refined perception, and the show was a flop.

From the point of view of the development of theater in those years, *Bubus* was an undoubted step backward for Meyerhold. *The Forest* was a human, happy and spiritually wealthy show. *Bubus* was spiritually meager, impotent, overestheticized. Its external glitter could not conceal the show's internal anemia.

However odd it may appear, it was under the impression of *Bubus the Teacher* that A. V. Lunacharsky counseled Meyerhold to replace biomechanics with "sociomechanics," to occupy himself with "those creases that cross our nature which are not a feature of a given man, but are social creases." He recommended that theater show "juicy social rears," even ones that were "caricatures, buffoonery," so long as these were "actual studies of our society."[19] That is, at this moment of clear crisis in the "theater of the social mask," Lunacharsky, preaching psychology (which inevitably destroyed the "social mask") essentially wished to return Meyerhold to the esthetic of *The Forest*, with its "caricature," but definitely "social," types. In *Bubus*, Lunacharsky asserted, "are the first indications of the creation of the social figure." But Meyerhold was never inclined to return to already traveled paths.

Less than a year later, Meyerhold himself admitted that his *Bubus* had not been a success. It is true that he did believe that his failure was "honorable," since purely experimental problems had dominated the show. Of particular significance to Meyerhold was the experience with actors performing against a musical background. Meyerhold came to the conclusion that the generous introduction of music into a dramatic production gives a director great possibilities in staging, independently of the text, occupying musical pauses. Such "stagings on music" were used later in the show *Woe to Wit*.

The Mandate, by Nikolai Erdman (the premiere took place on April 20, 1925), was one of Meyerhold's few productions that received general and unanimous acceptance. *The Mandate* was not debated, the show was the object of general delight. The director utilized with maximum effect all his past experience in this work. Meyerhold was able to implement brilliantly the experience of his satirical "polit-

reviews" and the capabilities of biomechanics. All the accumulation of seven years of leftist theater was applied in the area of contemporary Soviet comedy.

Erdman's play was rated very highly by Meyerhold. He believed that *The Mandate* was "a modern comedy of daily life written in the true traditions of Gogol and Sukhovo-Kobylin. The greatest artistic value of the comedy lies in its text. The characterization of the roles is welded closely to the style of the language."[20]

Critics also saw *The Mandate* as a development of the experience of *The Forest*. P. Markov wrote: "After an anatomical dissection of the corpse of *Bubus*, Meyerhold has returned to the happy ways of *The Forest*. This time the purpose of the show was not 'a satirical grin at the past,' as dictated by Ostrovsky's play, but very modern satire: Meyerhold has found support in Erdman's young comedy."

It is easy to understand why Meyerhold was so inspired by and attracted to Erdman's comedy, which to this day has not lost its charm. Erdman was the first to discover the comedy inherent in the situation of the communal apartment, already present in the NEP years and destined to continue for several decades. This was the situation of the enforced coexistence of families of different means, world views and ways of life. The country had received this unnatural way of urban life as its inheritance from the Civil War's destruction. Soon, people became used to such living and its paradoxes became the norm. When Erdman wrote *The Mandate*, the communal apartment was still an exotic innovation, although known to everyone. In this forced closeness among strangers, so favorable to comedy, Erdman concentrated the action of the play. The theme of revealing the bourgeois, traditional in Russian theater and close to Meyerhold's heart, was presented by Erdman in an unexpectedly powerful double illumination. The bourgeois appears in the light of the blinding projector of Revolution, of the new life to which he tries to adapt, overcoming fear and revulsion. Additional light on his behavior was cast by the altered and close quarters of daily life in which he found himself.

Under these conditions, the two amusing anecdotes, woven into one by Erdman, were unusually up to the minute. The story of quiet little Gulyachkin, who declared himself a Communist in order to marry off his old maid sister profitably, crossed the story of Nastya the cook, who through a strange combination of events was taken for the Grand Duchess Anastasia Nikolaevna and became the key figure in a comical plot by "former people."

Both anecdotes were unified esthetically by the general theme of the vagueness, the inauthenticity, the almost unreal quality of bourgeois life. Everyone is a fraud. Gulyachkin is no Communist, Nastya is not a duchess but a servant. The proletarian relatives are neither relatives nor proletarians. Only things are authentic, while people are doubtful and ghostly.

If we add that the play was written cleverly and stingingly, filled with slang that had just appeared in Muscovite life and immediately put to work by Erdman on stage, it will be clear how attractive *The Mandate* was in the theater. "The author," wrote Markov, "throws uncontrollable and smashing jokes and definitions at the audience, many of which will gain currency." These jokes, continued the critic,

grow from the in-depth exposure of life that is the essential axis of Erdman's comedy. Their bold exaggeration grows from concentrated and generalized images: we have the right to speak of the broad artistic typification of images, beginning with Gulyachkin and his mama and ending with the episodic lady "whose silver spoons were taken away in 1918." Erdman catches his bourgeois heroes at the most pathetic moments of their lives, when dreams of the rebirth of their former life arise and then disintegrate, catastrophically and hopelessly. Erdman sarcastically and satirically depicts people "whose old brains cannot stand the new regime."[21]

When designing *The Mandate*, Meyerhold used concentric discs (he called them "moving sidewalks"), whose opposing or unified movement was very effective. The entire stage platform was occupied by a huge disc whose first ring, the closest to the audience, was stationary. The next two rings, each a meter wide, moved either together, apart, or toward one another. The center stage remained stationary. Meyerhold was able to accomplish previously impossible stagings on the moving floor and therefore, as in *Bubus*, he was content to develop the action on a single level, without vertical compositions. Furthermore, *The Mandate* made use of moving walls, like those first used in *D. E.* "In the new construction for Erdman's comedy," said Meyerhold, "we present a combination of moving sidewalks and moving walls." The dynamic staging (done by I. Shlepyanov) showed his characteristic restraint, in contrast to previous Constructivist work by the theater.

The image of the bourgeois environment walled off from the outside world was paradoxically underscored by the very mobility of the walls. They moved apart only to come together again at once, to guard and protect the Gulyachkins from life. The "attachment" of these little people to things, to possessions, to "goods," was stubbornly and clearly depicted. They rode out onto the stage, delighted by the movement of the concentric circles, hanging on to their trunks, grabbing hold of their chairs, embracing their gramophones.

"We are presenting the characters," explained Meyerhold, "amidst the real objects which they have grown tightly together with."[22]

Their internal confusion and bustling in the first two acts contrasted with the majestically slow tempo of action. In the third act the tempo gained rapid and nervous speed. The grandiose bourgeois wedding, frothing and bubbling, reached a point of ecstasy, then suddenly and fearfully fell apart.

The poet Sergei Bobrov wrote:

> Moving objects became unmoving terrors. The modest gray trunk floating quietly across the stage therefore includes within itself all the sensations of the Neps that it is empty. All of these phantoms animated by Meyerhold become more significant than what transpires with the characters: things perform consistently and cleanly for Meyerhold, moving along the circumference, that is, at a constant distance from the center of action. The constancy of things is in grim contrast to the frenzied languor of the participants.
>
> The spectator grows tired of laughing. Finally, he is still. Meyerhold injects into Erdman's extremely harmless clowning a meaning that is utterly special and unforeseen by the author: and so the cruel and contemptuous comedy of an entire deck of living corpses is constructed; the bottom of the world, the cruel and self-interested passions of an awakened graveyard.[23]

Above and below: Lake Lyul, 1923

Set design for *The Teacher Bubus*

The Teacher Bubus, 1925, V. Yakhontov as Fuervari, Raikh as Stefka

Meyerhold, Nikolai Erdman, Mayakovsky, 1928 (?)

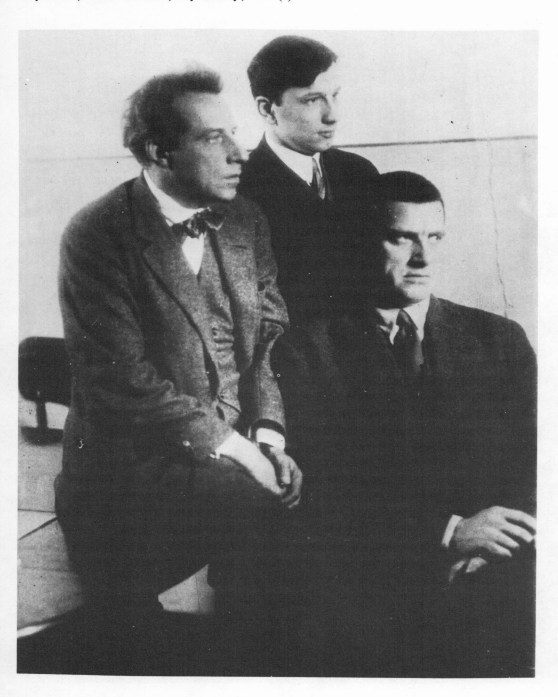

Caricature of Meyerhold, *The Mandate* and *D. E.* productions (drawn by the Kukryniksy, 1925)

E. P. Garin as Gulyachkin in *The Mandate*

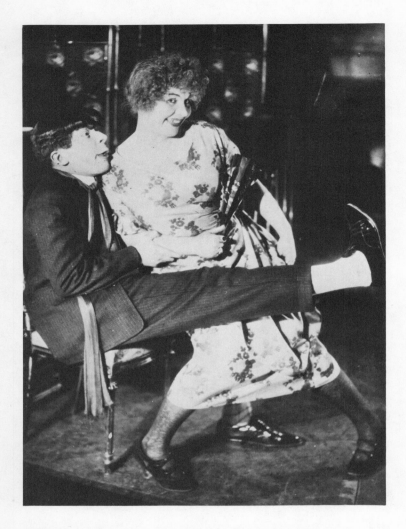

The Mandate, S. Martinson as Valerian, Raikh as Varvara

A scene from *The Mandate*

The Mandate

The Mandate

Performance of the acrobats in *Roar China*, 1926

Babanova as Boy in *Roar China*

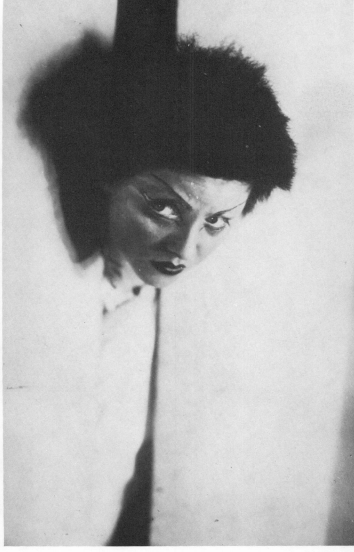

Scenes from *Roar China*

Scenes from *Roar China*

Meyerhold in 1927

Here we see clearly the main tendency of Meyerhold's work on *The Mandate*—the tendency toward grotesque anxiety, toward the extreme intensification of all the situations of Erdman's play, toward the creation of a staccato, nervous sketch for the staging and rhythm of the show. For this reason, the system of moving pantomime, so decisive for the artistic structure of the show, was carefully developed. "Bodily movement, for each person and for groups, unfurls here in a rich picture," wrote A. Gvozdev. "It is psychological in nature, since it depicts daily life. It is realistic because it stems from observation of real everyday gesture." The critics were particularly delighted by the craftsmanship with which Meyerhold ended individual scenes and acts—the finale was marked with the movement of a disc, carrying away frozen actors and objects.

Gvozdev praised such techniques of the director as, for instance, the entire development of the episode of the prayer by Gulyachkin's mother. Out from the depths of the darkened stage there slowly floated a table full of ikons with candles burning before them. A gramophone also stood on the table, a lighted candle burning in its loudspeaker. Gulyachkina was crossing herself and bowing while the machine played a deep priest's bass and drawn-out church music. Everything was ceremonious until the fool Nastya confused the records and instead of the church music put a fashionable operetta aria on the gramophone. "The table with the gramophone chapel," wrote Gvozdev, "rides away at the moment when the action has turned the 'religiousness' of the inhabitants of the honorable house inside-out and when the prayers have been replaced by the operetta aria and cursing."[24]

Most successful were the pantomime scenes in the third act, developed by Meyerhold with a genius of precision. "The comedy," wrote B. Alpers, "moves into a tragic plane. In the final scenes of the show, as catastrophe approaches, the conduct of the characters in *The Mandate* becomes colored with heart-rending dramatic tones. The revolt of the bourgeois takes on a sickly, frenzied pathos. The wedding ball is staged on a prewar scale. A brass band thunders, an army of waiters serves an endless number of luxurious dishes. Loud toasts are offered in honor of the 'reigning persons.' The maddened guests kiss the dress of the bride."

The downfall of the Russian "former people," continued the critic, "is asserted as final by Meyerhold's theater."[25]

A mournful tune was played on the harmonica and sounded particularly sorry and rickety after the chords of the brass band. All the characters stood frozen in the mute scene, and the revolving circles slowly carried them away into emptiness, into nonexistence... Markov wrote that Meyerhold's dynamic staging in this third act "achieves density, boldness and a Vakhtangov-like sharpness."[26]

For those days, this was the highest praise. Meyerhold, however, earned even higher praise.

According to P. Markov, K. S. Stanislavsky, after seeing *The Mandate* "returned from the show completely satisfied; he rated Meyerhold's production of the play highly, stressing particularly the brilliant directorial and decorative solution of the final act with the revolving stage circle and the moving walls. Furthermore, he stated quite categorically: 'Meyerhold has achieved in this act what I have dreamed of.'"[27]

M. V. Frunze wrote in the Meyerhold Theater's "Opinions Book," after seeing

The Mandate: "I did not expect to see and experience what I did in fact experience. There is life, there is good Revolutionary content. Something is lacking in the performance. It is as if there were too much exaggeration, but this is all minor. The main thing is the essence." Sen-Katayama stated: "*The Mandate* is the best work of Revolutionary art that I have ever seen."[28]

A. V. Lunacharsky was delighted with *The Mandate*, which he saw as an assertion of realism. "The culminating point of the realistic achievements of leftist theater," he wrote, "is *The Mandate*."[29] This was repeated by Lunacharsky more than once. "Erdman's *The Mandate* in Meyerhold's rendition stands above all the realistic plays of the past season," he wrote. Lunacharsky saw Meyerhold's direction as "the greatest theatrical phenomenon."[30] "If for the effective demonstration of a given social trait it becomes necessary to represent it as totally unlike its real manifestation, but in such a way that the distorted and caricatured image reveals what is concealed, shall we say, behind its superficially fine appearance and indifference, then this technique is, of course, very realistic." This is how Lunacharsky explains the hyperbole, the caricatures and deformation of *The Forest* and *The Mandate*, this is how he understands Meyerhold's proven ability "to show reality as more real than it appears in life."[31]

It is important to understand the routes Meyerhold took to this success and the specific new forms of realism that opened before the director in *The Mandate*. This show marks the first time that Meyerhold led his actors to a psychology that was occasionally quite refined. Although the Master made no statements on the matter, the clear interest in individual psychology in *The Mandate* nonetheless became the main reason for the show's unquestionable success.

In some sense this distinct shift in Meyerhold's art marked by the distance from *Bubus* to *The Mandate* was prepared by several of the best episodes of the shows *Earth Rampant*, *A Profitable Post*, and *The Forest*. On the other hand, this shift was dictated by Erdman's play.

First of all, social uniformity reigned. From the social point of view all the characters in this play were identical—all of them bourgeois, all of them "former people"—and the differences between them had to be found in any plane but the social. The "social mask" was inapplicable here if only because it equalized everyone, brought everyone to a common denominator. This did not signify, however, that Erdman offered the theater and the audience a gallery of full and varied bourgeois types. On the contrary, the typology here was simple and shades of a single type were varied. The force of the play lay in these variations. Erdman enthusiastically and with talent demonstrated the modern varieties of the bourgeois, offering new sketches from nature, new comic twists of his psychology.

Secondly, every person in the play was a small person. "This is human dust... the small lives of small people, but in a great era that shows light on them," wrote Lunacharsky. In *The Mandate*, "small people" were elevated to a principle. For Meyerhold, this was a new and totally unexpected task. Until now, he had always followed in practice the principle formulated by Mayakovsky: "theater is not a mirror, but a magnifying glass." It increased the scale of a Bulanov and a Milanov (to say nothing of an Aksyusha). Erdman's play completely rejected this possibility. Its power lay in the details of daily life and psychology—paltry but expressive, insignificant but full of meaning. Most importantly—specific in detail.

The director's "magnifying glass" was now directed differently by Meyerhold. Without enlarging the scale of Erdman's characters, he looked through the glass at their daily life and psychology. The enlargement was not of the character himself, but each of his actions was enlarged, exaggerated and examined as an event of extreme importance. Erdman's joking reprise was proclaimed as a slogan or motto. Small details of life were presented as major geologic shifts.

In this show, the daily life and psychology of small people obtained a grotesque and exaggerated significance. The fearful power of inertia contained in this lifestyle and psychology was also revealed in this way.

The play dictated the need for the actor to give foundation for the strange actions, the fantastic logic of behavior, the amusing accidents and the examination of an evident alogism of life knocked out of its rut. A living anachronism became the object of art. Art looked with alarm at walking paradox.

The movement of Meyerhold's art toward realism, compelled by the overall theatrical situation and by Erdman's play, turned sharply from traditional routes. Still rejecting the principle of psychological justification for the actions and words of a character, Meyerhold discovered a new, *eccentric* entry into daily life and psychology.

What is clowning (eccentricity) in twentieth-century acting? It is a jester's, a clown's, approach to the incredibly complex psychology of modern man. The actor-clown breaks into the refined spiritual world of the man of our time with habits accumulated since the days of Aristophanes. Insofar as the object of art is now a fragile and delicate matter, the actor's techniques correspondingly become refined and delicate. Only the basis itself for this actor's method remains unchanged: the demonstration of moments of the comic or tragicomic *incongruity of subjective actions and emotions with objective circumstances.* Inevitably, the stupid intermixes with the serious and the funny with the grim.

The development of clowning led to a most intensive enrichment of the actor's means of expression, opened the doors to the freshest truth of modern times and in this way laid the way to renewed forms of stage realism.

Markov and Lunacharsky understood this. This was not understood by critics contemporary with Meyerhold who were entranced by the term "social mask" and who saw the images of *The Mandate* as mask images. From this easily explained mistake on the part of these critics (Alpers among them) and from subsequent learned commentaries, the legend has come down to our day that the clowning school of the performing arts inevitably separated art from modern actuality, divorced theater from reality.

In fact, the school of performance, whose foundations were laid simultaneously by Meyerhold, Vakhtangov and Mikhail Chekhov, the school that based itself on the experience of biomechanics and which was represented in the TIM by a constellation of such excellent masters as Ilinsky, Garin, Zaichikov and Martinson, did not only actively bring Russian theater to modernity and a renewal of realism, but it also had enormous effect on the art of the most varied artists in Russia (from Khmelev to Glizer and from Mikhoels to Pevtsov) and abroad.

This is why the production of *The Mandate*, with its unity of method and style, when the eccentric school of performance first celebrated its victory, was a significant event in the history of the stage.

Alpers described the actors' performances in *The Mandate* with his usual impeccable precision. He noted that "the behavior of each character in *The Mandate* on the stage is constructed on an abrupt sequence of still and mute poses and mime sections followed by movement and the utterance of individual lines. There seems to take place a permanent mechanical resurrection of the character and then his return to 'nonexistence,' to immobility."

Alpers drew imprecise conclusions from this correct observation. He stated that the theater in *The Mandate* deals "only with socially harmless corpses," that "the grim comedy of these characters, these wound-up mechanical dolls, is constructed on the inconsistency between the frozen pose followed by movement and loud speech."[32] Later, G. Boyadzhiev, referring to Alpers, asserted that in *The Mandate* the actor "became a character from a wax museum. This exclusion of lifelike individuality of image led to a weakening of the creative will of the actor. Consequently, the image conceived as a sharp and generalized satirical type became strictly rational, 'manufactured,' stylized, lacking warlike satirical force and active propagandistic meaning." The subsequent, formally logical development of this position led Boyadzhiev to the conclusion that "the mask of Gulyachkin was the mask of 'the bourgeois in general,' the repulsive symbol of the bourgeois seemingly removed from the parentheses of modernity."[33]

So here we are, where students of theater have taken us, miles away from the living and breathing matter of the show whose central figure was Erast Garin, in the role of Gulyachkin.

Least of all could it be said of Gulyachkin that he appeared "removed from the parentheses of modernity." On the contrary, this used and worn bourgeois in his threadbare jacket and coarse cloth shirt from whose collar a long thin neck stuck out, this man with distraught face and muddled gaze was instantly recognizable. Such a person could be encountered in any Moscow side street. The condition of complete disorientation, of being thrown off track, was also quite typical for people of this circle. It was only stressed when such a figure entered the chaos of the ridiculous, almost fantastic events of the play.

Frequently, Garin-Gulyachkin would turn from this odd, phantasmagoric life under conditions he could not comprehend in a world hostile to his nature, his quiet habits and modest rituals, and with a whistling confidential whisper, would ask for support from the audience, for answers to tormenting questions.

Certainly, there were people just like him in the hall, confused, stunned by the Revolution? They, however, answered Gulyachkin with explosions of laughter. Meyerhold's theater counted three hundred instances of laughter during a performance of *The Mandate*.

Garin's performance was astonishing for the moments when a psychological condition was suddenly fixed, for moments of immobility, when movement suddenly stopped, when Gulyachkin's empty eyes stopped and stared at the auditorium in a lengthy pause of incomprehension, when his entire figure froze "in a frame," as though illuminated by a magnesium flash. Such "stops" caught the hero in instants of internal crisis. These pauses which fixed the crisis, the spiritual breakage and psychological catastrophe, carefully marked in the score for the role, were in fact the eccentric form of the actor's demonstration of the interior life of the hero. The dynamic was revealed by the static, by means of frozen poses, faces, glances.

Meyerhold selected such moments carefully and supported the actors' clowning with all the means of expression available to a director. When Gulyachkin-Garin, in some kind of Khlestakov-like delirium, suddenly surprised himself in the first act by saying majestically: "I am a Party man," this fatal phrase immediately terrified and froze him and those around him. The boarder Ivan Ivanovich, at whom the threat was directed, curled up in fear and crouched to the ground. Gulyachkin's mother and sister froze, mouths open. Gulyachkin himself, crazed his own heroism, stood petrified in an unnatural, simultaneously proud and frightened pose. At this instant this entire "sculpture group," this entire photograph of the explosion in bourgeois society, floated away to the back of the stage on the revolving floor.

"Eccentricity in the rendition of psychological failure is the best expression of realism, and the staging of *The Mandate* confirms this," one of the reviews said unexpectedly of Meyerhold's intentions.[34]

Meyerhold used the identical techniques to "accompany" Sergei Martinson's performance in the relatively small role of Valerian Smetanich. V. L. Yureneva gave an exact and expressive description of this virtuoso performance by the actor:

> The golden, thick hair with a curl in front leaves Martinson without a forehead. There is no neck, the head withdraws up to the ears into the shoulders. Elegant suit, scarf. When this frock-coated gorilla begins to speak, an impoverished squeaking note comes from his throat, without a sign of modulation. But the young man knows his worth. Everything that he does, *he* does, and everything comes down from above, demonstratively and with stress. Here he is alone with his bride. The conversation is becoming unstuck and he sits down at the piano with his back to the audience. With unbelievable flair, he hits the keys with chords of a heart-pinching Gypsy romance. His entire body plays. It is as though he is all hinged, first throwing himself back from the keyboard, then quickly throwing himself at it. His long apelike hands jump high into the air.
>
> Valerian's role was performed almost wholly with his back to the audience. His image stays in the memory of the spectator even independently of the play and the actors. For a long time one sees this golden-haired nothing, this human Torricelli vacuum with indecently chic manners, visiting cards and scarf.[35]

Meyerhold underscored the clowning in Martinson's performance, offering the actor scenes such as the one in which he was on the moving sidewalks, one leg going to the left, the other to the right. This was exactly the way in which the situation of the second act was staged—a careless line of Valerian's was interpreted by Varvara, Gulyachkin's sister, as an offer of hand and heart. He is frightened, does not know how to get out of the situation, and at this moment "the figure of the 'stuck' little lord is flattened out in movement: he lands on the moving sidewalks and, struggling against their movement, is involuntarily demonstrated in all his weakness. Bending far over, whirling around in search of equilibrium, he retains his learned 'elegance' of step and reveals to the end its ridiculousness in 'nonchalant' poses, steps and walk," wrote A. A. Gvozdev, who then concluded: "The actor works on a moving platform that manifests the absurdity of the psychology of a man whose vision is limited to the delighted appreciation of fashionable trousers and the shimmy."[36]

This principle of presenting the absurdity of bourgeois psychology, the presentation of its wild and unnatural twistings, was extended to the other performers in the show. V. Zaichikov played Ivan Ivanovich, "not a man but a boarder," basing the entire role on the sharp contrast been the "concluded softness of intonations" and the "animality of his deeds."[37]

The servant Nastka was rendered by E. Tyashkina as sleepy, dull, unexpectedly loud-voiced and clumsy, which made her transformation into the Grand Duchess and heir to the throne all the more effective and ridiculous. The plastic design for all the roles was unusually complete and clear. Uncertainty and disorganization of the plastic was perceived only in Mukhin, who played Father Smetanich, and in Zinaida Raikh as Varvara, Gulyachkin's sister.

At that time Zinaida Raikh was the "special problem" of Meyerhold's theater, a problem actively exaggerated in the lobbies and occasionally in the unceremonious press of those years. The Master idolized his wife and insistently tried to make her the leading actress in the theater. Raikh was beautiful, possessed a strong, expressive voice, but, as I. Ilinsky wrote later, "her helplessness on stage and physical unpreparedness and, simply speaking, her clumsiness, were too obvious..." This was sensed in *Bubus* and in *The Mandate*. A year after *The Mandate*, Meyerhold's intensive work with Raikh bore fruit in *The Inspector General*. "She managed to learn much from Vsevolod Emilevich and, in any event, became no worse an actress than many others," admitted the same Ilinsky.[38]

Still, giving the leading roles to Raikh inevitably led to a number of intra-theatrical conflicts. Although the superficial reasons for Babanova's leaving Meyerhold in 1927 were different, undoubtedly the main reason was the surrendering of the best roles to Raikh. Ilinsky's departure also was indirectly connected to the enthronement of Raikh. He left Meyerhold in 1925 but returned three years later.

This more or less private circumstance, the brief separation of director and actor, did have its esthetic equivalent. At the very moment when the actor appeared as the center of Meyerhold's compositions, this actor was not Ilinsky but Garin— the future Khlestakov and the future Chatsky. Major key, full of youthful energy, mischievous, charming Ilinsky left his post to the nervous, fragile, suddenly freezing, grotesquely anxious Garin. Energy was replaced with trance, the dynamic with the static, happy jesting humor with bitter and glum satire. The highly talented Garin expressed in relief the discord in the relations between Meyerhold's theater and the changing reality.

After *The Mandate*, satirical notes would long be dominant in Meyerhold's art. *The Inspector General* became their tragic apogee. It is curious that some perceptive critics saw a foreshadowing of *The Inspector General* as early as *The Mandate*. Adrian Pyotrovsky even entitled his article about *The Mandate* "On the Eve of *The Inspector General*," and during the course of Erdman's comedy he could not "leave the idea that before you are pieces of a future *Inspector General*." The critic felt this especially stongly in the finale of the production of *The Mandate*. The third act, which Meyerhold had intended as a grandiose picture of "the last judgment of the former people," was seen by Pyotrovsky as a "key unparalleled in Russian theater to the outcome of *The Inspector General* and the transposition, so painful to

Gogol, of his farcical comedy into a tragic, monumental spectacle."[39]

It is true that Meyerhold very soon proved that he had an altogether different solution to the outcome of *The Inspector General*. It is equally true that Meyerhold had long ago declared his intention to stage Gogol's comedy. But the critic predicted the tone of Meyerhold's staging of *The Inspector General* correctly, and before the actual production.

While Meyerhold was directing rehearsals for *The Inspector General*, his pupil V. Fyodorov independently began the preparation of Sergei Tretyakov's play *Roar, China!* This was the first and last time in the history of the Meyerhold Theater that a show signed by someone other than the Master appeared in its repertory. At first the posters stated, "Author of the production, V. F. Fyodorov." Very soon after the premiere, however, there was a scandal. Fyodorov stated in the press that he was leaving the TIM and renounced "responsibility for the artistic value of the show." Immediately, the magazine *The TIM Poster (Afisha TIM)* published a letter signed by the entire theater company which stated that Fyodorov had staged the show "as a student," that "many links" (i.e., the scenes—the play was called "An Event in Nine Links") "were completely restaged by Vs. Meyerhold," while others underwent substantial correction by the director. It was specially noted that the best role in the show, that of the Chinese boy played by M. Babanova, was entirely "staged and developed by Vs. Meyerhold."[40] Incidentally, this was later substantiated by Babanova herself, even after her rupture with Meyerhold.

I. Aksyonov testified that as soon as Meyerhold set to work "Fyodorov's stagings were forgotten."[41] As a result of the incident, changes were made in the show's billing. It now stated that *Roar, China!* was "the graduation work of a student of the State Experimental Theatrical Workshop *(GEKTEMAS)*—V. Fyodorov, who completed the full course in the directing department in the spring of 1926," and the addition "Direction corrected by Vs. Meyerhold."

The show, first presented on January 23, 1926, was a great success and had considerable social resonance.

It would appear that this was evidence in favor of "factual drama," "art without art," which was propounded by the LEF group (Leftist Front) and, in particular by one of its most insistent theoreticians, Sergei Tretyakov. The plot of the play was taken from a newspaper article about an English businessman who accidentally had perished in China. The captain of a British gunboat who was unable to find the culprits ordered the execution of the first Chinese he could find. "This is a fact. I hardly had to change anything," declared Tretyakov with his usual great pride in the foreword to the play.[42] But, in contrast to this declaration, it was precisely the alteration of the fact, its transformation into a dynamic subject base for a carefully developed drama, that comprised the emotional content and meaning of Tretyakov's work. Furthermore, the play presented not only the "fact," but the psychological motivations of the actions of all the characters, and an evaluation of these actions.

"A string of Chinese beggars magnificently sketched with rare ethnic precision," wrote A. Gvozdev, "passes before the audience. The masks of the individual actors become engraved in the memory. Exhausted faces, knotted hands, bent backs and hesitant, varied, fragile intonations destroyed forever the ornate and pretentious chinoiserie *(kitaishchina)* in theater and replaced it with a truthful penetration into the life of the working Chinese."[43] It must be added that such a concretely realistic development of mass scenes was a first on the stage of the TIM and clearly harkened back to the principles of the early Moscow Art Theater.

The scene in which the two coolies are executed, depicted in cruel and sharp realism, was in direct contrast to Meyerhold's recent convictions. The critic M. Zagorsky even stated that this scene evoked his "protest," "shown in all its repulsive details and constructed on techniques taken from theaters of the 'Guignol' type."[44]

But this almost naturalistic abruptness contained a true design: the director strove to evoke in the audience both pain and indignation against the colonialists and, in contrast to the dark color of the execution episode, he introduced the surprisingly poetic theme of the Chinese boy, played by M. Babanova, into the show.

Babanova's performance was the acting pinnacle of the show. The fragmented quality and brevity of the other roles in the play perceptibly limited the capabilities of the actors. P. Novitsky wrote later of Babanova's performance:

> The boy, before being hung from the mast, sings a sad little song in which courage and protest intermingle with the despair and fear of death. This is the most powerful episode in the show. It is experienced as a fearful and deep tragedy of a people. One remembers the little song for a lifetime. When you think of all the more powerful moments in the history of the Soviet theater, memory always yields the touching image of the boy in white cotton clothing, hands clasped prayerfully, with coarse black hair, pleading and angry eyes. He weeps with helpless childish tears and threatens a bloody and hard fate.[45]

Once again, in the heightened psychological dimension of this performance (Meyerhold rehearsed with Babanova, as we have noted), which demonstrated with extreme clarity the appearance of new expressive means in the esthetic system of leftist theater, Meyerhold sought for and found forms of realism that suited his temperament.

Of the images of "leftist theater," there remained the distinct division of the stage suggested by the artist S. Efimenko. In the back were the enemies, the British gunboat with its guns, officers, missionaries, etc., then the "boundary," a wide stretch of real water with boats and, finally, "our people" on the proscenium, where all the scenes with the Chinese coolies were performed. "This clear design," wrote A. Gvozdev, "made the show comprehensible and understandable."[46] S. Gorodetsky agreed, although he disliked the moments of "photographic naturalism," and although he objected to the movement "from disinterested Constructivism to the realistic." But Gorodetsky believed that "the best thing is the picture of the confrontation between the Chinese and Europeans in the finale" and that the most valuable moments of the show were the "moments of propaganda."[47]

The show *Roar, China!* became a field of expressive battle between propaganda theater and theater of life, between the theater of social masks and the theater of specific, living human images. The play's characters were distinctly and sharply divided into two groups. The list of characters indicated: "A) Europeans, B) Chinese." The white Europeans were exploiters, enemies; the yellow Chinese were exploited friends. Two principles of staging were applied to these two groups. S. Radlov testified:

The scenes of everyday Chinese life are staged with great craftsmanship, application and often with tenderness. This is the most powerful thing in the show. It is much worse in the European part... Staged in the spirit of the most elementary, intentional grotesque, it breaks the show into two completely unconnected stylistic halves. . . . When the horrible tourist couple enters the group of the "living," "lifelike" Chinese, there is a completely incomprehensible union of hack poster work with a good painting of the Repin school. When the Chinese are so human, so lacking in overblown and cardboard heroism, why then depict Europeans as so evil to small children?.. It is somehow uncomfortable to witness in Meyerhold's theater the use of techniques that have been worn out in all the amateur drama circles. The bourgeoisie, decaying in the inevitable foxtrot, evokes not anger but depression.[48]

This was the result: the psychologically complete images of the oppressed were contrasted with the rough poster-like masks of the oppressors. For Meyerhold in this period—between *The Mandate* and *The Inspector General*—this solution appears a strange and coarse anachronism and, evidently, it would be more correct to ascribe it to the "author of the staging," V. Fyodorov, despite the refutation of this authorship by the TIM cast. Meyerhold's "correction" gave the show its most refined and most effective episodes, transformed Babanova's brilliant performance as the boy into a masterpiece. But this correction not only did not remove, but placed in greater relief, the basic contradiction in the artistic structure of the show. The truth of the details of everyday life beat down the propaganda of the poster. The images of the very real, living Chinese, even minor ones like the boatman Chi (A. Temerin), excited audiences. The mask-images of the Europeans were viewed with cold indifference.

A year and a half after the premiere, the author of the play, S. Tretyakov, concluded sadly: "*Roar, China!*, constructed like an ethnographic sketch on the one hand and like a newspaper article on the other, was perceived by the majority as just an exotic and touching spectacle. The theater was unable to go out into the street and to dissolve its esthetic and emotional essence in action."[49]

This should have been expected. The *agitka* had long lost its popularity. It stalled and died, arousing no interest. But in the momentum of the first post-Revolutionary years, Meyerhold's theater was unable to rid itself of it, and continued to seek ever newer ways to use the beloved social masks by mobilizing the most various means to affect the public. In the production of *Roar, China!*, ethnography and the exact rendition of things Chinese were to be such an aid. It did not help, however. On the contrary, although planned as a background for the development of the propaganda art of political grotesque, it gained the foreground by virtue of its truthfulness.

P. Markov wrote:

It is interesting and curious to observe Chinese daily life such as it is shown in the Meyerhold Theater, without sweet decorations and exotic warping. To hear Chinese tunes, to watch the street scenes in a Chinese port—such is the ethnographic picture. But behind all this it is even more interesting and truly exciting to follow individual images and their conjunction. The Chinese "boy," who is played by Babanova, and the lyrical suicide scene which is staged with directorial perfection, explain more than the poster-like propaganda. In the fate of individual characters, in these fleeting figures, the tragedy of China showed through more clearly than in the fanciful construction. Thus transpired the long-awaited "opening of the parentheses," the unmasking of the propaganda outline, the movement of propaganda from the "poster" to the revelation of human fate.[50]

This opening of the parentheses signified a refutation of the poster-like simplicity of stage language, the realization in the show of the humanly specific images of the Chinese. The truth of genre, the truth of psychology, any concrete truth, was attractive. It was such truth that pushed away and muffled the social masks.

Their time was ending. It was time to hand them over to the theater museum. This is the central and, it must be said, long-maturing conclusion suggested by the production of *Roar, China!*.

New possibilities were opened for Meyerhold's art with *The Mandate*, and were powerfully demonstrated by *The Inspector General*.

Even after *The Inspector General*, however, the *agitka* recurred again, painfully. To celebrate the tenth anniversary of the Revolution, Meyerhold staged R. Akulshin's political review, *A Window on the Village* (premiere on November 8, 1927).

When preparing this production, Meyerhold discussed his plan as follows:

During the days of celebration of the tenth anniversary of October, the city must hear the voice of the village. The GTIM wishes for this voice to sound from the stage. The impression must be created that the village itself has broken onto the stage, that it is using the stage as a platform for the demonstration of its life, that it uses this show as a megaphone to sound that uplifting note which seizes the country, just like the city, on November 8, 1927. The task of the show is to bring cheer and joy to the auditorium. The show is constructed on the mechanical linking of a series of pictures permeated with unity of theme (the Soviet village) and unity of mood (the joy of building a new life).[51]

While comprehending, as did all his comrades in art, that the *agitka* was worn out, and rejecting it in words, Meyerhold in fact was creating a propaganda show, but one that was monumental, "vast," lacking plot (and therefore particularly dull), filled with fragments from newsreels which were shown during the performance and which served only to demonstrate all its unnaturalness, pompousness and unreality.

This was evidence not only of the exhaustion of the capabilities of the propagandistic theater. This defeat had another, more serious meaning: Meyerhold's theater was not finding direct contact with the altered reality and suffered a fiasco in its clumsy attempts to establish and glorify this reality.

REVIVED CLASSICS

Your truth, that is how to perform.

Boris Pasternak

In the mid-1920s, Meyerhold's rapid movement slowed abruptly. The period of rapidly changing stage forms ceased. *The Magnanimous Cuckold, A Profitable Post, The Forest*, and *The Mandate* all were staged in a period of three years, and in parallel with these works Meyerhold staged a number of other shows, too. But between the premieres of *The Mandate* and *The Inspector General* there was a distance of nearly two years—an unusual length of time for Meyerhold, particularly if we observe that he was diverted only once, to correct the direction of *Roar, China!* Gogol's *The Inspector General* was being prepared with incredible thoroughness. For Meyerhold, this work was simultaneously a conclusion and a beginning.

The time had come to gather the fruit, to collect together and to demonstrate the already tested, variously tried capabilities of the new theatrical system. But this was not enough. The time had come to demonstrate its new potential, hitherto unknown to anyone, including Meyerhold. This task was dictated not only by the development of Meyerhold's art, although both *The Forest* and *The Mandate* contained within themselves, within their imagery, the requirement for a more serious and in-depth approach to the problems that they proposed. In the pauses in these shows, in the musical interludes of *The Forest* and the strange palpitations of *The Mandate*, there was a kind of question. The auditorium and the stage were united in an interested and intense silence when, as though stepping outside the boundaries of the definite, happy, satirical theme, there was a sudden sound—seemingly quite out of place—of the harmonica in *The Forest*, or when Meyerhold's Gulyachkin froze, entranced, slightly mysterious, slightly horrified, but anything but amusing. The issue here was not the willful or accidental disruption of the comic genre. The problem was that the times were offering strange riddles that Meyerhold heard, repeated in his own way to the auditorium, but to which he himself was unable to reply.

He attempted to answer these riddles in *The Inspector General*. Getting ahead of ourselves, we shall state now that the first result of this brave intention was the transposition of Gogol's comedy into the genre of tragedy.

Another point must be remembered, too. At the moment when Meyerhold began work on *The Inspector General,* he no longer was the ruler of ideas in the theater. The brief moment of his autocracy in the theater was over. Meyerhold still was called the leader of leftist art, the one and incomparable revolutionary of the stage. His name was still uttered as a motto and slogan of theatrical innovation. But other names were already noted next to his. In the First Studio of the Moscow Art Theater the high-strung, sensitive and therefore especially attractive genius of Mikhail Chekhov was developing with alarming speed. Chekhov was rehearsing *Hamlet* while Meyerhold was preparing *The Inspector General*. It was difficult to predict what sort of Hamlet this would be, but already it was possible to see the threatening and significant combination of great actor and great role. After many years of silence in the Art Theater there was suddenly a joyous excitement. The young

—387—

students in the First Studio were preparing to stage Bulgakov's novel, *The White Guard*. This show also was being rehearsed at the same time as Meyerhold's *The Inspector General*. Furthermore, Stanislavsky himself was staging *A·Passionate Heart*.

All these were only promises, but Meyerhold understood their gravity. Even more impressive were the actual, undoubted successes of shows that had already been staged: *The Storm* in the hitherto completely unknown and ignored MGSPS Theater, *Virineya* in Vakhtangov's studio, *Lyubov Yarovaya* in the Maly, *The Flea* in the Art Theater's First Studio. Each of the above-named successes not only revealed new talent, but expressed the new demands of the times. It was quite difficult to find some single formula for these demands that would explain the simultaneous success of the rough village truth of *Virineya*, the farcical stylization of *The Flea*, the severe minutiae of *The Storm*, and the color of *Lyubov Yarovaya*.

Nonetheless, there was such a formula, and Meyerhold did sense and grasp it, if subconsciously. The general theme of the stage art of the mid-1920s was resistance to matter-of-fact prose, to sobriety, dryness, the gray tones of the everyday that made life colorless. This was the understandable yearning of people who had lived through a heroic era and who were adapting with difficulty to the banality of normal existence. Art objected to housekeeping. With identical tender emotion, it recalled the typhus-bearing louse in *The Storm* and Leskov's fairy-tale flea, marveled at Shvandi and Virineya. In Meyerhold's own productions it looked anxiously into a Gulyachkin, as though asking: why? This question inspired Bratishka's rushing about the stage in Bill-Belotserkovsky's play *The Calm*. This was the question with which Chekhov's Hamlet entered the stage. This was the question with which the Turbins dared face the audience. The answer was given in the productions of 1926.

There is a deep internal connection between Stanislavsky's *A Passionate Heart* and Meyerhold's *The Inspector General*. Primarily, this is one of theme. Both shows did not just carry out an unmerciful sentence on the social order that had been destroyed by the Revolution. This task was posed both by Meyerhold and by Stanislavsky. But each understood, of course, that this task was too limited and that in the ninth year of the Revolution it could hardly be of sufficient interest. Both Stanislavsky and Meyerhold planned their stage compositions on a larger, wider scale. They staged shows about Russia, her fate, the inevitability of destructive Revolution and about what survived the Revolutionary storm.

In connection with *The Mandate*, P. A. Markov had observed that Meyerhold "collects sharp observations about an empty and frightful, powerful and passionate life, in order to condense them into the form of new, concentrated realism. Meyerhold performs as the collector of Russian theater. He promises to replace his former fragmentedness with concentration."[1]

This promise of concentration became a reality in the work on *The Inspector General*. Meyerhold's collecting energy was manifested, first of all, in a new composition of the text. Meyerhold set for himself the goal of performing not *The Inspector General*, but Gogol as an artistic whole, Gogol as style and Gogol as a special world, Gogol as Russia. The problem of reproducing the author's style and more broadly the style of an age was made even greater here. Accordingly, the canonical text of the comedy was replaced by a text composed by Meyerhold and M.

Korenev from all six surviving author's editions. Lines that had been censored were included again, along with individual fragments, lines, and even episodic characters from *The Gamblers* and other small finished and unfinished works by Gogol. The extent to which such an approach coincided with the will and intent of the author could only be guessed, but this problem disturbed Meyerhold not at all. More important for him was the maximum enlargement of the limits and scale of the play. In essence, a new text for *The Inspector General* was being authored by Meyerhold.

The Inspector General was to be performed as if against the background of *Dead Souls*. The production was to be a stage poem of Russia. During the rehearsals and discussions about the production, Pushkin's famous phrase—uttered after he had read *Dead Souls*—"God, how sad is our Russia," was often repeated. It was this phrase that provided the emotional environment. Meyerhold told his actors: "It is necessary to avoid everything that is strictly comedy, everything that is buffoonery. Nothing must be taken from the commedia dell'arte and everything is to be presented as tragicomedy. *Hold course for tragedy...*"[2]

Gogol wished to "collect into a heap everything bad in Russia" and to demolish social ills with laughter. Meyerhold, setting to work on *The Inspector General* in 1926, seized Pushkin's theme of Russia's sorrow and switched the comedy into the plane of tragedy because the "ills" ridiculed by Gogol remained unaffected. Externally changed, these ills penetrated into the totally altered everyday life. Furthermore, they had a surprising ability to develop into hypertrophied forms on a new scale.

The impression of the aggressive power of the past probably was suggested also by Meyerhold's desire to wipe the dust from the play and to present *The Inspector General* on the scale of the capital. In the production, he showed not a dead and dismal province, but the gleaming capital of Empire; he lovingly reproduced the majesty of the Russian Empire, its porcelain, bronze and brocade, mahogany and Karelian birch furniture, its secretaries, bureaus, clavichords, its sparkling crystal... Each scene offered the audience elegant interiors and still-lifes of incredible beauty. This solution, it must be said, was far from arbitrary. Its basis was to be found in the canonical text of the comedy. Twenty years after the premiere of Meyerhold's *The Inspector General*, G. Gukovsky wrote that:

> although in *The Inspector General* there is the direct representation of some generalized, faraway city, throughout the production there is a sort of background or accompaniment, the theme and image of Petersburg, the capital. Petersburg, the center and source of evil, stands behind everything shown in *The Inspector General*... Petersburg is behind everything that happens in *The Inspector General*, and this gives birth to a particular element of the theatrical style of the comedy—fairly common instances, so to speak, lines reaching across the footlights, seemingly direct references in them to actual members of the capital's audience and—wider—of real Petersburg.[3]

In other words, in Gogol's *The Inspector General*, Petersburg was assumed to be the audience and the object of satire. Meyerhold needed Petersburg to be his magnifying glass. In the beginning, it is true, the director wanted the exterior of the production "to have the appearance of dirt, provincial dust, murk, grayness, as though fishes were swimming in a murky aquarium. Some are golden, elegant, while others make you want to spit—small catfish, salamanders, sediment that no one ever cleans. I asked the artist to find combinations of tones in a monotone greenish-brown scale."[4] Then he decisively rejected this swampy coloring and provincial dust and set another goal for himself: "to show 'swinishness' in the effective and beautiful, to discover 'brutishness' in the elegant form of a Bryullov model."[5]

"Brutishness in elegant form"—this was the esthetic formula for Meyerhold's *The Inspector General*. He did not represent the famous pigs' snouts, as though sensing that Stanislavsky would do it in *A Passionate Heart*.

In the usual pre-opening interview, Meyerhold stressed two circumstances: the play is modern, it is a "warning satire" and he is staging it "in the realistic plane." More precisely, "I would call, relativistically, the principle of the work on *The Inspector General* 'musical realism,' although this term of course requires deciphering."[6] Meyerhold took the course to realism firmly and consciously. He said:

> The conditions of continuity in theatrical techniques cause revolutionary theater, which strives to present the worker-audience a modern theatrical show, to make a practical study of the best examples of the theatrical culture of past ages. The success of *The Forest* and *The Mandate* proves that the true traditions of Russian realistic theater taken by the director and (in *The Mandate*) by a young playwright from the angle of the revolutionary era, evoke a warm response in today's audience and, primarily, in the worker-spectators.

Indicating further on that this time an "actors' show"[7] was being staged, Meyerhold observed:

> Thanks to the features of the material design of the show, we have, to use the cinema term, shot the main scenes of the show in close-up. This gives the figures an interesting precision and obliges the actors to perform somewhat differently than in the old theater. We have tried to take into account not only our previous experience and the achievements of the Shchepkin school, but have studied attentively the performing techniques of leading cinema actors and believe that to some extent we have achieved our aim.[8]

The mention of the close-up was a hint at the chief principle of the overall staging, which had the genius of simplicity.

While giving the production an epochal content, transposing the comedy into tragedy, rejecting the provincial setting and bringing the characters to the capital, Meyerhold at the same compressed, narrowed, and closed in the stage space.

The foreground of the stage was completely separated from the back by a solid arc composed of eleven doors, polished to look like mahogany. There were four more doors in the proscenium, two on the right and two on the left. All fifteen of these doors fenced in the semicircle of the stage. A solid mahogany wall was connected from above to the stage portal by a hanging of swampy, murky green. But this entire enclosed space was fully used only in four episodes of the show. In the main, the action took place on a small moveable platform (approximately three by four meters in size) which rode out into center stage. For this purpose, the three central doors would open like gates. Meyerhold had two such moveable platforms. While one was being used for the performance, the other was being prepared backstage for its "entrance." Nearly all the episodes of *The Inspector General* were performed on these platforms. The platforms were tilted slightly toward the auditorium.

The cinematic style "close-ups" that Meyerhold mentioned took place because the action, often with many participants, became squeezed into these small platforms that carried the actors out onto the proscenium. V. Shklovsky joked: "The actors were served up in portions on small platform-plates."[9] The need to construct practically the entire production of the grandiose spectacle "on plates" did not bother Meyerhold at all. On the contrary, this crowding inspired him and excited his imagination.

A. Gladkov recorded two of Meyerhold's statements on this subject.
Here is the first:

I arrived at the necessity for a small performing platform in *The Inspector General* because of my concern for being able to manage the voluminous text, saving the time spent on long transitions. But, having constructed such a platform, it became possible for me to comprehend the beauty of what I call "self-limitation." To varying degrees this principle lies in the nature of any art, and this apparent "unfreedom" is the source of advantages in the technique of expression: true craftsmanship is revealed in it.[10]

Here is the second statement: "Balzac said that the pinnacle of art is to construct a palace on the tip of a needle. In essence, both *A Magnanimous Cuckold* with its principle of external asceticism and *The Inspector General*, performed on a small platform, were infused with a similar goal."[11]

It ought to be mentioned that Meyerhold, dissatisfied with the sketches by V. Dmitriev and I. Shlepyanov, designed the construction himself. The artist V. Kiselev was assigned to do only the costumes, the make-up, the props and the selection of antique objects, of which there were many in the show. Meyerhold's moveable platforms, wrote N. M. Tarabukin, "permitted the localization of the stage space within narrow limits, thus transforming each episode from the representational side into a beautifully constructed, compositionally plastic, painted picture."[12] This unusual resemblance to a painting, the beauty of literally each moment, each "frame" of Meyerhold's *The Inspector General*, was unquestionable. Elegance and grace were the law of the show since, as we recall, the assignment was to demonstrate "brutishness in elegant form."

But the moveable platforms performed yet another function. Contradicting Shklovsky's clever remark, these "plates" offered up to the audience not actors but characters. A platform would roll slowly toward the proscenium in the dim light. Like a time machine, it brought to modernity an immobile picture of a past age—its objects, mahogany furniture, porcelain, bronze, silk, brocade—and the people of a bygone time. The strong beams of light from projectors lit up this picture immediately, flashing in the angles of crystal goblets, softly illuminating the delicate damask upholstery of the armchairs and ottomans, the dead, waxen faces. There was a lengthy pause over the picture, then everything suddenly went into motion.

The effect that this created is evident in this description by Sergei Radlov:

The crystal gleams, transparent and blue. The heavy silk shines and flows; the blindingly black hair and blindingly white breast of a slow-moving and important lady; a fop, drunk à la Hoffmann, romantically thin, brings a cigar with a somnambulistic motion to his tired mouth. Pieces of heavy and juicy melon are diced into a silver bowl. Enchanted objects, swaying slightly, float through the hands of hypnotized servants. Heavy, magnificent sofas, like mahogany elephants, sleep an opulent and majestic sleep.[13]

Connections between past and present were to break through this "sleep" in each episode. The characters of the show, which so straightforwardly restored the objects, life-style and external beauty of the bygone era, were obliged to prove their reality as if despite the setting in which they were brought to the stage. Therefore, the director's interpretation of the characters in the play became extremely important. The way Meyerhold saw and demonstrated the characters in *The Inspector General* revealed most clearly the principles of his "musical realism."

First of all, the classical system of creating stage characters was rejected with renewed vigor. Meyerhold refused to equate realism with psychology and, accordingly, did not consider it possible to examine a character as the sum of specific human qualities, as some psychological unity, however capable of development (within the framework of a given character). The principle of unity of character, which Chekhov had already placed in doubt, Meyerhold always rejected. It was not in the creation of "characters" that he saw the meaning and purpose of stage art in general and of the actor's art in particular. At one time in Meyerhold's theater, the principle of the social mask had been triumphant. The principle of social type replaced this principle. In Meyerhold's theater typical images possessed individual specificity. But this was not the specificity of a character. Rather, it was the specificity of a certain style, the specificity of the author, his manner. In the present case, it was the specificity of Gogol.

P. Markov noted at once that in this show Meyerhold "voluntarily rejects the active development of the internal seed of the image. With a glance, a step, a lowered hand, he shows more than the ordinary observer sees; shows (or wishes to show) the revelation of man's fate and, at the same time, a brilliant rhythmical theatrical effect... The actor performs the same condition for the duration of the entire episode, based on a most precise rhythmical picture, a gift from the director to the actor."[14] In other words, the individual was revealed in the rhythm, while the rhythm was that of the author. The director rhythmically and musically "read" the fate of each character in accordance with his feeling for Gogol's rhythm, Gogol's nerve.

The new principle was offered most powerfully and sharply in the figure of Khlestakov, played by Erast Garin. It was impossible to speak of unity and definiteness of character here. Gogol wrote that Khlestakov was a "phantasmagorical individual who, as a false, personified lie, dashes off in a troika, to God knows where."[15] It is this particular line that is the key to Meyerhold's Khlestakov. Garin played a chameleon—he was a different man in every episode. First, a wandering card-sharp, then a Petersburg bureaucratic official, then a brilliant Guardsman, a dreaming poet from the capital, a haughty, lucky careerist... But in all these transformations of Garin's Khlestakov there remained, unchanged, a note of cool, threatening arrogance. What was frightful in Khlestakov, as discovered five years before by Mikhail Chekhov, what would suddenly show through in Chekhov's twitching, sick little figure, in a saturnine smile and then would disappear again, was clearly delineated in Garin's interpretation. Slightly arrogant infernality became the basis for all the metamorphoses. Regardless of the form of Garin's Khlestakov, no matter what his clothing—plaid cape or rich Guardsman's coat or black jacket—the silent, enervated walk remained, the murky, indifferent stare, the oddly thoughtful intonations. "Before our eyes the frightened little fop becomes the phantasmagorical figure of an impostor," wrote A. Lunacharsky.[16] "Black little thing, fiction, mirage," wrote D. Talnikov.[17]

Mikhail Chekhov saw in this Khlestakov a man "driven mad by his own falsehood, one who has lost his sense of time, who would seemingly lie *forever*." Leonid Grossman wrote that Khlestakov-Garin was "a character from a tale by Hoffmann... seemingly immersed in the mirage of his tormenting visions."[18] B. Alpers observed: "From a past age this multi-faced phantom from the shores of the Neva looks out at the audience with cold colorless eyes, examining the world through the square lenses of his horn-rimmed glasses."[19] V. Volkenshtein was amazed by Khlestakov's "demonic confidence."[20]

Thus, the figure of Khlestakov was interpreted by all as infernal. This impression was heightened because Meyerhold's Khlestakov was pursued by a double. The "Visiting Officer," the almost silent traveler, always drunk, with furrowed brow, blue-pale, closely followed Khlestakov everywhere. A. Kelberer, who played the part of the Visiting Officer, gave him the stamp of fate. Every so often the Officer would stand leaning against a wall or column, hands crossed on his chest, with a mysterious and swaggering look and cynical smirk on his lips... There were other, equally mysterious visions in the production. The actor V. Maslatsov was given the almost wordless bit part of the Captain, but Mikhail Chekhov, for instance, was astounded by the way Meyerhold saw this "little officer, pale, insignificant, shabby, in a little light blue uniform; the little officer wanders silently about the stage, senselessly, purposelessly, vacant...and around him is emptiness—not one of the characters in the play notices him. So, what then is the little officer," asks Mikhail Chekhov. "An empty place in the show? Yes, of course, but not in the show, in the man. The 'idea' of the emptiness and purposelessness of life, imagined and incarnated by Meyerhold to a nightmarish degree of reality."

In the name of what goal did Meyerhold strive for this "nightmarish reality?" His ideal during the work on *The Inspector General* was, in his words, "calm sober clarity. Nothing more."[21]

His aim is easy to understand if we recall that the play was staged in a tragic key. Meyerhold wanted the sensation of inevitable catastrophe to hang over all this elegant and beautiful "brutishness."

This approaching crash, the complete collapse of all life, "the end of the world," shaped the conduct of the mayor as well. Even though in Meyerhold's production, the mayor was removed to the background and mixed with the crowd of officials, nonetheless in this crowd he remained the central figure. "The mayor and the bureaucrats," wrote Gvozdev with his usual precision, "are presented as choir leader and choir."[22] P. Starkovsky as the mayor appeared as "a striking, dandyish Guardsman with the noble intonations of Schiller's Marquis Posa," wrote M. Levidov.[23] And in fact, the mayor here was a relatively young, slightly Europeanized, plump man with a pleasing exterior. But the very beginning of the show found him already on the border of madness, in a totally frantic state. "Either they stand on the bell tower, or they want to hang you"—this is the phrase by Gogol that most exactly expresses his feelings. Naturally, the mayor had seen more than one Inspector General in his day and always had wound them around his finger. But this Inspector General, this werewolf, was too much for his mind. Confused, literally bewitched by falsehood, he stumbled through the show.

The mayor's wife, on the other hand, was given much attention and space in Meyerhold's production. This "Guards' tigress," this "provincial Cleopatra," "luxurious social lioness," "Russian Venus by Kustodiev," remained for the duration of the show in a state of playfulness and sensual arousal. For Anna Andreevna, satiated and luxuriant, overripe and greedy, the appearance of the inscrutable, inflamed and vacant Khlestakov was not a threat or disaster, but only the promise of some hitherto untried and consequently seductive delights...

Supposing, not without reason, that the role of Anna Andreevna was thus enlarged to serve Z. Raikh's actorial appetite, some critics were particularly acid in their comments about the mayor's wife. "The mayor's wife was on almost all the dishes offered to the audience," sniffed V. Shklovsky. "She mimes on all the plates. The others react to her with gestures and incomprehensible shouts... Changes of clothes, dances, singing, tears—the mayor's wife has them all. In a word, it is she who wrote *Yury Miloslavsky*. " Shklovsky's article was entitled "Fifteen Portions of Mayor's Wife."[24] This was not the angriest article dedicated to *The Inspector General*, but the most insulting to Meyerhold. Meyerhold reacted furiously and roughly. "Shklovsky is a Fascist," he stated.[25] Strong expressions of this sort were already in use, even though the impressions of Fascism were quite vague.

Meanwhile, if Meyerhold had not been blinded by fury and had been in a condition to argue issues, he could have objected to Shklovsky more convincingly. He could have said that the unusually expanded role of the mayor's wife had an extremely important function in his *Inspector General*: to tie the entire generalized concept to the specifics of the present day. But the situation in the theater was too heated, the matter of the artificial promotion of Raikh to the center of the show was too painful. Even Mayakovsky's defense of Meyerhold on this point was clumsy: "he does not give good roles to Zinaida Raikh because she is his wife, but he married her because she is an excellent actress."[26]

We shall return to the storm of debate around *The Inspector General*. Right now we shall attempt to recreate as exactly as possible the director's score for the show, since we are speaking of one of the most complete (if not the most complete) of Meyerhold's creations.

In absolute darkness in the center of the stage a gate opened silently and, as though from the misty darkness of the past, a small platform rolled out directly at the audience. It rolled up to the front edge of the stage and, suddenly, projector beams struck it from all sides, brightly illuminating the group of officials pressed around a round table. A long pause ensued... "It looks like a staging by the Moscow Art Theater," observed Gvozdev. "A piece of the real life of the 1830s."[27] Candle flames flickered. Long pipes smoldered. Hands lay on the polished surface of the table—some enervated, some tense. Hands, pipes, were presented in a close-up and everything was at once surrounded by clouds of tobacco smoke. Questioning, anxious expectation written on the officials' faces. The mayor, presiding in the center, wearing a bathrobe and clearly unwell, said, finally, very slowly and in a low note: "I invited you, gentlemen..." When this long sentence reached the words *Inspector General* all the officials suddenly jumped, fluttered as though stung, got up from the table and hid, some under the table, some behind the mayor's chair, some behind their neighbors, and then they froze again, awaiting developments. Several times in the course of this first episode ("Chmykhov's Letter") the same performance was repeated: confusion, excitement, a moment of flurried activity and a pause in trance, like a foreshadowing of the final, mute scene.

More and more officials appeared during the episode. One after another, they pushed their way through to the table and sofa, shoving and "reinforcing" each other. The impression of closeness was continually increased. The officials smoked their pipes, long and short, lit pieces of paper with the candles, and clouds of smoke floated before their pale faces. When the mayor demanded, "bring Lyapkin-Tyapkin," and any time he raised his voice, there would be a sudden dance of fear that started and then suddenly stopped in this smoky crowd. Heads were pulled down between shoulders, fingers trembled slightly. Meanwhile, Gibner, the doctor, massaged the sick mayor, slowly bandaged his hand, put drops in his eye and ear, saving him... At the same time the doctor managed to bandage the head of Korobkin, who had a toothache. This tightly bandaged head at the table looked sinister. Candles passed from hand to hand. Their unsteady light brought fear and stress to the stage. This was reflected most strongly in the nasal voice of Zemlyanika (V. Zaichikov). Only the appearance of the red-nosed postmaster (M. Mukhin) changed the rhythm. The mayor and the postmaster carried on their dialogue while clinking glasses hastily and automatically, as if marking the tempo of the dialogue with their clinking. Phrase—glass hits bottle. Half-phrase—another clink of the glass. Then the postmaster pulled a letter from the stack, threw it upward and someone caught it. Another letter flew through the air, the officials caught them in a lively way, tossed envelopes to each other, "unsealed them a little," read, giggled...

At this moment of general excitement two identical tiny figures—Bobchinsky and Dobchinsky—flew in screaming through the door, stopped in terror and crossed themselves three times. The entire "ensemble" of officials also crossed themselves thrice and froze. The officials, frozen in the strangest poses, stared at the mysterious messengers, Bobchinsky and Dobchinsky.

The second episode, "An Unexpected Matter," began with a tedious pause. In contrast to the tradition of many years, Bobchinsky and Dobchinsky's story was told in an exhaustingly slow tempo. Both Bobchinsky and Dobchinsky dug through their pockets long and carefully, and took a long time seating themselves hesitantly and unsurely at the table. Everyone stared at them silently. Meanwhile, Bobchinsky and Dobchinsky both were silent and simply laid their four hands down on the shining, polished surface of the table and moved their fingers slowly. These were serious, very concerned little men. Finally, they began to speak. Meyerhold gave their speech the inflection with which priests sing "eternal remembrance." As soon as one began his weak recital, the other would interrupt him weakly and significantly. A gaping pause, like a hole, appeared in the conversation. Bobchinsky would open his mouth, would notice that Dobchinsky had opened his, and both would close their mouths.

When one managed to squeeze out the words "by the booth..." the other would second it with his own "by the booth," like in a sad song. In time to this lifeless, continually failing speech, the short little hands would move. Every so often, in order to arouse interest, Bobchinsky and Dobchinsky would drum their fingers significantly on the table...

Naturally, the anxiety of the officials grew. Ever more frequently and angrily the ensemble of officials urged the tale-tellers on with a howl of general terror. But this only threw the two off track, and again over the table there hung a heavy silence in which the significant and careful speech began: "not bad-looking," murmured one voice, "...looking," echoed the other, stupidly. Nonetheless, the information needed by the mayor and the officials was squeezed out from this duet as from a tube. "My God, it is he. He, by God!" hurried Bobchinsky and Dobchinsky. The mayor froze in his chair with a groan. A general howl of despair drowned out the voices of the tale-bearers. Another heavy pause, and the officials began to offer the mayor their humble suggestions: "Send the leadership out ahead, the priests, the merchants..."

But the mayor's unexpectedly firm line: "No, let me take care of it myself!" suddenly exploded the episode. The action, so far weak and flaccid, suddenly set off at a gallop. Energetic farce began. Five servants suddenly ran to the mayor to help him dress and wash. The mayor combed his hair very quickly with a wet brush, then beat the water with the same brush, splashing those around him. The maid Avdotya sprayed him with cologne, the officials put their heads and handkerchiefs in the path of the spray... The mayor's commands grew louder, the policemen who ran in at his orders shouted, "I come. I stand," even louder. The district police officer rushed in. In each word, this district police officer would roll his "r," immediately infecting the mayor, who also began to growl his "r"s, like a drum. The choir of officials repeated and varied the mayor's every command three times, and he ran off in a state of furious agitation. Before, he had been barely alive. Now he was as active as an entire fire-fighting company. From this instant on, everything became possible, any impossibility could become a reality.

Therefore, the next episode, entitled "After Penza" by Meyerhold, began in a major key. The platform with Khlestakov's tavern scene rolled out. The scene took place under a staircase which framed the stove and the stove-bench where Osip, the sprightly country lad, presided on rumpled pillow and blanket. Osip's famous monologue was changed by Meyerhold into a dialogue with a girl scrubbing the floors. Monologues, said Meyerhold during rehearsals of *The Inspector General*, "sound bad." They "induce a lassitude that is intolerable in our theater... In our interpretation, in view of the fact that we are staging harsh realism, a monologue sounds 'theatrical.'"

Partly in order to assure that Khlestakov would have no monologues, Meyerhold gave him the Visiting Officer for a companion. "Then, since Khlestakov is one of a pair, we will work the text not as reflection, not as monologue, but as conversation," explained Meyerhold. For the same reason, Osip was given the charwoman as an audience. "The girl in the number is an element of the city. Dirty, worn," improvised the director. "She is urban, at the service of visitors. There is a dirty tint to her. It is necessary to create the atmosphere of bedraggled furnished rooms."[28]

Such an atmosphere was, in fact, created. But the girl was young, red-cheeked, and easily amused. When Osip told her about his master she laughed in peals with unexpectedly low, almost bass notes. Her strange laughter was always answered by the amazed laughter of the spectators. Then Osip would start singing a lusty country song.

The Visiting Officer, out of uniform, in a white shirt, leaned on the banisters and listened to this song with a grim, concentrated expression. There was something of Pechorin in him. His greatcoat with its rich beaver collar hung from a nail. Rumpled and torn pieces of paper lay on the floor, the opened valise seemed to yawn hungrily. The charwoman ran out, happily continuing Osip's song. Upstairs, Khlestakov appeared silently, submerged in thought, in a black top hat, rectangular tortoise-shell glasses, plaid across his shoulder and stick in hand. A doughnut-shaped roll hung on a string from his buttonhole. Garin descended the stairs. Thoughtful and elegant, he walked straight toward the audience, then stopped abruptly. There was a somber pause, then he turned in profile and again was still for an instant. He struck the table with his stick, stood motionless and silent for a time with his back to the audience. Then, with a regal gesture, as though presenting a medal, he handed the roll to Osip: "Here, take this!"

The true grandeur of this gesture was sensed when the theme of hunger, which was tormenting all three—Khlestakov, the Visiting Officer and Osip—became pronounced in all its clarity. The roll, Meyerhold's marvelous invention, immediately raised Khlestakov in the opinion of the audience. Himself famished, he had stolen the roll from somewhere, but did not eat it. Rather, he hung it from his coat and offered it to the servant!

Here, in this first episode with Khlestakov, began his "chameleon" theme. First, together with the Visiting Officer, he concentrated on "Adelaida Ivanovna," his favorite deck of marked cards. This deck and the whole theme of card-sharping, of the excitement of the game, were taken by Meyerhold from Gogol's *The Gamblers*. During rehearsals he would think out loud: "I want, somehow, to present Khlestakov as concrete. For instance, as a professional card-sharp. This will give a different motivation and another approach to the lines." At first, the director even interpreted Khlestakov as "one of the characters in *The Gamblers*." Accordingly, the Visiting Officer too, Khlestakov's double, was treated as "a specialist in card-sharping, proud of it and extremely serious about his work."[29] But all these ideas saturated only the very beginning of the "After Penza" episode. In the brief scene with "Adelaida Ivanovna" the theme of the game and card-sharping was quickly played out and soon removed altogether.

Prior to the arrival of the mayor, Khlestakov, without losing any of his composure, matter-of-factly and deftly bandaged his cheek in imitation of illness, put on his top hat again and crawled under a blanket. There, behind the stove on the stove-bench, he froze in a pose of slightly haughty expectation, staring straight ahead. The mayor slowly descended the stairs, head extended and down, wearing his beautiful coat, cap off, all courage lost. His first lines were soft and servile, while Khlestakov at once assumed a nervous, threatening tone. When the mayor muttered something clumsily about the non-commissioned officer's widow, Khlestakov quickly brought his stick from under the blanket: "You will not dare whip me!" The mayor looked unwaveringly at the stick, evidently certain that he himself would be whipped. This instant was decisive. Evaluating the situation, and understanding that he instilled fear, Khlestakov quickly slipped out from under the blanket. With one sure gesture, he put on the uniform of the Visiting Officer.

Garin's plastic altered immediately. Powerfully and firmly, marking every step and seeming to jingle his spurs, the new Guards officer paraded around the frozen mayor. Khlestakov's intonations became short and harsh, like military commands. He put on the greatcoat with the beaver collar and the cap...

"The tiny bureaucrat with no wardbrobe," wrote Lunacharsky on the subject, "cannot be almost unbelievable subsequently as Khlestakov. Meanwhile, this greatcoat with the fur collar, this tall shako, cannot but astound..."[30] Khlestakov's transformation clearly smelled of devilry. The mayor, looking at the Inspector General, crossed himself three times. His legs wobbled, he wanted to sit but was afraid to be seated in the presence of such a personage, he changed color and lost the power of speech. As though playing up to Khlestakov and wishing to finish off the mayor, Meyerhold staged a circus trick here. A door banged open above, and Bobchinsky, who had been eavesdropping, dropped from the "second floor" directly through a trap door in the stage. This, however, was not what frightened the mayor the most. What scared him more was how the unflappably majestic Khlestakov simply ignored Bobchinsky's fantastic flight. Khlestakov did not deign to notice him!

The episode resulted in the mayor's complete defeat. Now Khlestakov could wrap him around his little finger.

Then the action shifted to Anna Andreevna's boudoir. Having delineated the beginning of the main theme of the show—Khlestakov and the mayor—Meyerhold rushed to declare and emotionally initiate the second, no less important, theme— Khlestakov and the mayor's wife, Khlestakov and woman. If the dominant motif of the first episodes was the expectation of disaster, then the sultry, languid Anna Andreevna brought to the stage the theme of the expectation of sensual pleasure. The mobile platform with her boudoir appeared to back up against the enormous dresser that loomed up behind. Before the dresser stood a screen, behind which Z. Raikh was changing her clothes in preparation for her meeting with Khlestakov. More and more new outfits were pulled out of the dresser and, selecting the dresses, the mayor's wife strolled through the dresser.

Meyerhold had anticipated this possibility with pleasure even during the rehearsals. He asked:

What has the author written? Anna Andreevna "changes clothing six times in the course of the play." But I have never seen anyone change four times. This is not shown to the audience. That is, it is possible that the actress changes, but only behind the scenes and not before the audience so that the audience can, in fact, see that she has changed four times. But I will show that she changes not just four, but even more times. And I will show the dresser in which these dresses hang, and I will show all these dresses to the public, so it will see how many dresses she has.

Meyerhold was pleased the most, however, by the following circumstance: "The dressers of that time were designed in such a way that it was possible to enter them, to stand there and reach the dresses. Especially if the person is short, it is possible to enter and dig around in there for the dresses. The doors are open, they examine the dresses and talk with each other."[31]

As we shall see, Meyerhold used the facilities of the old dresser to the full.

Anna Andreevna's aggressive sensuality was expressed amusingly and straight-forwardly in her jealousy of her daughter. In order to keep her daughter from competing with her, Anna Andreevna dressed Maria Antonovna as a little girl. The ridiculous child's ribbon, the stick-like pigtails, the long lace pantaloons under the wide skirt—all these, in Anna Andreevna's plan, were to create the image of a ridiculous baby, practically an ugly duckling.

But the mayor's wife miscalculated. The combination of this clothing with Maria Antonovna's rough directness was quite piquant. M. Babanova played Maria Antonovna cheerfully and bravely. The daughter followed the mother, the wanton half-girl was drowning in the "sensual blizzard" that whirled around the mayor's wife, hitting even Dobchinsky. Dobchinsky came only in order to tell about Khlestakov, but even here, in Anna Andreevna's boudoir, he spoke with painful slowness, since here in the face of her fatal accessibility he immediately forgot everything that he wished to tell. He devoured the mayor's wife with his eyes, followed her every move, sifted words through his teeth. Nonetheless, the words were spoken and they pleased Anna Andreevna. The mayor's wife became excited; bold dreams arose in her head.

Anna Andreevna whirled before the mirror, adjusting her silk dress, revealing one shoulder, then the other. "The pose of the actress, the illumination, the color of the dress and furniture," observed B. Alpers, "all this transmits the style of Fedotov's paintings."[32] It appeared too that Fedotov's brush was used to draw Dobchinsky, all in a murky lust. When Anna Andreevna disappeared behind the dresser door to change her dress, Dobchinsky peered shamelessly, licking his lips. After finally saying goodbye to the mayor's wife, Dobchinsky, as though bewitched by Eros, walked off, not through the door but into the dresser. Pistol shots thundered immediately, and from the dresser, from under the couch, from all sides, came bold, handsome officers in shining uniforms. They surrounded the mayor's wife in a playful herd and whirled around her, filling the entire stage platform.

The officers were from beyond the edge of reality. They were interpreted as a sensual vision of the mayor's wife, dreaming of meeting Khlestakov.

They froze around Anna Andreevna in a graceful pantomime—elegant, young, without moustaches, they bowed before her, sang and played invisible guitars:

"It's all the same to me, it's all the same to me!.."

Mayakovsky was delighted by their serenade. "The scene between the mayor's wife and the soldiers who crawl from the cupboards is very correct. No mysticism at all. What is this? The realization of a metaphor, the realization of Gogol's small hint about the carnivorous essence of this lady—it is executed as a brilliant theatrical effect."[33]

"This serenade," applauded Lunacharsky, "is filled with magnificent *brio*, and the whole scene is noisily approved of by the audience. But where does all this take place?" he asked. "Is this reality? Something from Hoffmann? Hallucination?" And answered:

This is neither the first, the second nor the third. This a trick such as one a good illustrator may allow himself in a vignette. If, for instance, the author finishes a chapter with the words: "her head was ever filled with officers in bright uniforms, spewing compliments before her and ready to shoot themselves any minute for the sake of her eyes," then the illustrator could transform this expression into a vignette even in such a fantastic case where the above-mentioned officers are located directly within Anna Andreevna's skull. This is what Meyerhold does. He pretends to the identical rights that the cinema enjoys—dreams and various other characteristic internal experiences are staged as fantastic reality.[34]

Today, the explanations by Mayakovsky and Lunacharsky are interesting not for their content—for the modern viewer or reader there is neither mystery nor mysticism in Meyerhold's staging. The commentaries by the poet and critic do indicate, however, how unexpected the officers' serenade was for the audience of 1926 and they show the complications that attended the reception of Meyerhold's *The Inspector General* forty years ago. These comments help us understand the causes for the unbelievable scale of the debate that erupted following the premiere of the show.

The officers' serenade ended with an effective period. One of them pulled out a pistol, shot himself and fell to Anna Andreevna's feet. At the shot, another young officer jumped out of a hatbox and fell to his knees before the mayor's wife, proudly proffering her a bouquet of flowers.

Such was the extravagant first appearance on stage of the future director Valentin Pluchek.

The brief fifth episode, called "The Procession," opened the second act of the production. Along the stage, whose entire width was used for the first time in the performance, a low metal balustrade was erected in parallel with the orchestra line. A staggering, drunken Khlestakov appeared in front of this barrier. He walked majestically, like an emperor, pulling the slipping greatcoat continually over his shoulders, while behind the barrier the string of officials wound at his heels. The twisting, servile string of Gogol types appeared to have been copied from the bas-relief on Andreev's memorial. It crawled, weaving in the semidarkness, hopelessly trying to repeat every step, every wild and unnatural movement of its leader. All these creatures in uniform and civilian coats, caftans, overcoats, hats and caps, composed a single fantastic caterpillar on the stage. Khlestakov, losing his balance, grabbed at the balustrade—the only reality visible in the murk.

Suddenly he stopped, and all stopped. "What is this fish called?" asked Garin with painful longing. "Cod, sir," answered the ragged chorus. But Khlestakov's face continued to express a question. "Cod, sir! Cod, sir!" repeated the chorus over and over, while Khlestakov continued to seem to await something. Then Zemlyanika leaned out from the line and clearly, if nasally, pronounced "Cod, sir!" Khlestakov, finally, generously inclined his head and unexpectedly sang out in a piercingly high note: "Cod." The officials seconded him in a respectful chorus. Observing that the Inspector General was favorably inclined, the mayor pressed forward and dared to begin an impassioned speech about the "headaches of responsibility." The ray from a projector cut through the semidarkness and hit the face of the mayor, whose drunken pathos intensified. At the same moment, Khlestakov put his hand over his mouth and hurried backstage. The mayor continued to shout his pompous phrase about good works, before which everything is "dust and confusion." Here, Khlestakov returned with unsteady step and indicated with a gesture that he had vomited. Then he began to sing about how wonderful it is to pick the flowers of desire. His singing was interrupted by a loud belch, and he sent a large wad of spit unexpectedly into the corner of the stage. There, in the corner, motionless with hands crossed on his chest, stood the Visiting Officer.

"The Procession" conquered all. A. Kugel was delighted by the "dramatic expressiveness and dynamics" of the episode.[35] S. Radlov wrote that "The Procession" was "a masterpiece of development of a very complex scheme of movement parallel to the footlights."[36] Mayakovsky said: "I must definitely classify the scene with the cod among astounding things. This scene, which adds five per cent to Gogol, cannot but add to him, since this word is realized in action."[37]

Nonetheless, this scene, with all its exceptional virtuosity, was only a preface to the central episode of Khlestakov's lie, which was entitled "At the Fat-Belly's Bottle." The moveable platform for this episode was set very economically. To the left stood a gigantic, ornate sofa upholstered with thick, colored cloth. Khlestakov's sofa. To the right—a tiny couch for the mayor and his family. The rest can stand, decided the director. In the foreground he also placed a small round table. Among these few props Meyerhold constructed one dynamic staging after another, directing at Khlestakov currents of scared servility from the officials and, at the same time, the flirting of the mayor's wife and daughter. The tiny performing platform became a field of battle for Khlestakov. He was wined, dined, addressed with the servile whispers of the officials, the expressive cooing of Anna Andreevna and the giggling of Maria Antonovna. At first, no one dared sit on the huge sofa next to Khlestakov, no one except for the silent and seemingly invisible Captain in the blue uniform. The scene of meaningless society talk passed slowly, governed by Khlestakov, who really did look like an Inspector General here, one of the young and early careerists, indifferent, haughty.

All "flowers of pleasure" were offered to him. A pillow embroidered with flowers was placed under his feet. He smoked a cigar, drank wine. Anna Andreevna personally cut and handed him a juicy piece of melon. Khlestakov reveled, playfully touching the mayor's wife's little finger. He looked fearfully only at the bottle of "fat-belly"—some frightful green drink prepared for him by the mayor, which the servant continually brought up to him. Finally, Khlestakov grabbed a glass and emptied it into his mouth with a single gesture. Then, as if he had been burned, he stopped in the middle of a word, opened his mouth wide, stuck in a handkerchief, jerked convulsively and looked around angrily. Meanwhile, the servant went for the bottle again. Khlestakov waved the servant away angrily with the handkerchief and the servant backed away.

A pause ensued. Everyone awaited developments, the effect of the green drink. Khlestakov was seated, the rest were standing. "Sit!" he ordered contemptuously. Everyone obeyed immediately, even though there were not enough places for all. Many crouched down. Khlestakov's cold eyes slid over the frightened faces. Arrogantly, through his teeth, in a grim, deathly tone, he began to lie. The lie rolled condescendingly from his lips, slowly enchanting the officials. The mayor, Anna Andreevna, Zemlyanika, the judge, the postmaster, were all quiet. All were conquered by this hypnotic, show speech, during which Garin oddly and with threatening sibilance pronounced the letter "s": "minisster," "asssesssor."

Only the Visiting Officer at the round table in the foreground did not listen to Khlestakov. He was intently concentrated on getting drunk. Emptied bottles rolled at his feet.

The stifling atmosphere of this scene was broken by an unexpected shriek from Maria Antonovna, pinched unceremoniously by her mother for an untactful remark about Zagoskin. The shriek sounded like a signal. The lights dimmed, and in the semidarkness Khlestakov suddenly leaped up. It became obvious that he could barely stand. Nonetheless, some fantastic power of inspiration maintained him in a state of unsteady equilibrium. Khlestakov jumped, leaped about, fell on his side, was caught by servants, straightened up again. Throwing his legs out in different directions, blurting crazy words about a seven-hundred-ruble watermelon, about ministers and delegates, he flung himself to the left, to the right, jumped up onto armchairs and froze over the huddle of trembling officials, his outstretched hands raised. Then he suddenly grabbed a policeman's sword and began to wave it around. The blade flew over the officials' heads with a fearful whistle and dull flash. This was the apogee. Staring, Khlestakov fell into the arms of the mayor who, trembling, seated Khlestakov on the sofa next to Anna Andreevna. In this instant Khlestakov very calmly answered the line about Zagoskin—there is another Yury Miloslavsky and that one's mine.

From the semidarkness came the insistent repetition of Glinka's romance "The Fire of Desire Burns in My Blood..." Khlestakov, suddenly revived, grabbed hold of Anna Andreevna and began to waltz with her!

"His whole body," wrote Gvozdev, "strains downward, to the floor, to the soft sofa, to the arm of the chair, but he continues to struggle against this attraction to the ground, dances, finds unexpected support in his partner, leans on her, hangs on her, lays his head on her shoulders and dances with his remaining strength until, finally, he thumps down onto the desired sofa and falls asleep to the sounds of the same melancholy waltz."[38]

Dead silence ensued. All looked at Khlestakov. He suddenly removed his glasses, crossed his legs and quite suddenly opened his eyes again and—another metamorphosis!—with an odd dreaminess, pathetically and poetically spoke of his little fourth-floor room and the cook Mavrushka. Then his eyes closed again and in the deathly silence Khlestakov continued to mutter threateningly: "Nonsense!" "What is this!" Finally, the sleeper's lips uttered the magic word: "Co-o-o-od!"

The completely crazed officials responded with a burst of "va-va-va," "vu-vu-vu," bowed in a chorus while retreating backwards, sing-songed, "co-o-o-d, sir."

The director's score for the episode was built on the sudden, practically unfounded alteration of Khlestakov's rhythms. Khlestakovianism was revealed by the lack of motivation for the rhythmic shifts and was brought to a concentration of essentially tragic absurdity when the officials, trembling with terror, shook and stood helplessly before the snoring monster from Petersburg.

Khlestakov's dream continued into the next episode ("The Elephant Is Knocked Down"). The whole line of officials filed past his bed, marveling at the sleeper. Anna Andreevna and Maria Antonovna tiptoed into the room and looked at Khlestakov greedily. "In the dream," wrote Lunacharsky, "all these mugs dash past him in strange disarray. A string of flirtatious women passes before him. It seems to him that trembling hands give requests to him, that clouds of envelopes containing bribes fall on him..."[39]

In this episode, too, Meyerhold asked the audience to accept as reality something ephemeral—Khlestakov's dreams. The finale of the little scene was all the more acute: Khlestakov, awakening, lifted his legs, scratched, yawned, and said that he had "dozed well."

In the beginning of the "Bribe" episode, Khlestakov sat with his back to the audience. Next to him on the bench were Osip and the Visiting Officer. Only now was it shown that the solid red wall surrounding the stage was composed entirely of doors. The doors opened and in each doorway there was the figure of one of the officials. Each grasped a package in his hand, each package containing the promised three or four hundred rubles. The action of the episode developed across the entire stage platform. The efficient Zemlyanika-Zaichikov directed the officials, who resembled mannequins. Khlestakov, too, appeared mannequin-like, like a mechanical robot who identically repeated the same gesture: step, take envelope, stuff it into the coat, step, take envelope... Only once was this steady movement disrupted: Khlestakov found himself squeezed in between two of the opened doors. But in this situation, too, he behaved like a robot or automaton—he did not even try to free himself. His head stuck out from the crack like the head of a rag doll. His empty eyes stared, showed no emotion. He was set free and walked on: step, take envelope... "The bribery procedure," wrote B. Alpers, "is shown as a ritual, as a mechanical act."[40] Lunacharsky, however, interpreted this procedure otherwise, as the continuation of the preceding episode, as the "amusing stylization of a drunken dream."[41] Mayakovsky lamented the absence of augmentation in the scene, complained that it was monotonous. Kugel, on the contrary, asserted that the bribery scene was saturated "with such wonderful imagination and such comprehensive refinement of the director's talent that one forgives the altered text and the woodenness of the judge." Zemlyanika, wrote Kugel, here "is practically Satanic, within the limits of realism."[42]

In the episode "The Master of Finances," the theme of bribery was developed and reached Homeric proportions. A great long table crossed the stage diagonally. In front of the table were mass stagings of merchants and petitioners who were besieging Khlestakov, and policemen who were defending him. The petitioners came toward Khlestakov and tossed him more and more envelopes with cash. The episode began with the boisterous and noisy meeting between Khlestakov and the merchants. They crowded onto the stage, were contained by Derzhimorda and his police. Then, after this energetic entrance, there followed, wrote Gvozdev,

two little scenes (the non-commissioned officer's widow and the locksmith's wife) which had the sound of grotesque musical passages from Stravinsky's *Pulcinella*, in which the trombone carries on its comical conversation with the double bass. The sergeant's wife screams: "He whipped me, father, whipped me," and the chorus—this time a group of policemen—interferes with her lines and, as though cursing her furiously, shouts and mutters, accenting the doglike barking sounds:*"Vat', vat', vat'..."* This exchange is repeated like a musical reprise.[43]

The non-commissioned officer's widow (who disturbed Lunacharsky slightly at the moment when she clambered onto the table and was about to raise her skirts to show the "marks" to Khlestakov and the audience) and the locksmith's wife were both women of foreceful action. Without hesitation, the locksmith's wife beat the police about the face, assisted by the widow. After the noisy intrusions of these women Khlestakov remained along on the stage. With enervated melancholy step, he went along the long table, all in black, in top hat and with stick. He would sit at the table and, staring into the audience, whistle mournfully. "Solitary, strange, unearthly, he whistles into space mindlessly, emptily," observed D. Talnikov.[44]

Truly, Khlestakov was a bit scary at this moment. In the next episode, "Kiss Me," cold assuredness again entered his form. The episode began with a quadrille danced merrily by the agile quartet: Khlestakov, Anna Andreevna, the Visiting Officer, and Maria Antonovna. The figure of the quadrille in which the men exchange ladies was an epigraph of sorts for Khlestakov's further action with the mayor's wife and her daughter. In the heat of the dance Anna Andreevna suddenly stopped, listened to herself and...withdrew, clearly, "out of need." Khlestakov immediately stormed the daughter. He squeezed her familiarly and she struggled uncertainly, for form's sake only, since she first of all was triumphantly celebrating her victory over her mama and, secondly, she was burning up with impatience—what will happen, how will it end and, thirdly, she suddenly weakened in Khlestakov's arms. With rare precision, M. Babanova depicted this rapid sequence of emotion. The presence of the Captain in Blue at the piano and of the Visiting Officer who regarded the kissing pair with somber indifference gave the episode a particular aspect of the ridiculous. Then Anna Andreevna returned. "Ah, what a thing to happen!" she exclaimed. But Khlestakov shocked her with the sudden and forceful question: "Where were you?" While Anna Andreevna distractedly moved her lips, her daughter squealed and ran away.

Then followed a pantomime described by Gvozdev:

Khlestakov walks up to the Captain sitting at the piano on which he has just accompanied the singing of the romances. Khlestakov, in a black suit, stands with his back (to the spectators and Anna Andreevna) and looks at the music. A pause in the actors' performance permits the viewer to take note of Anna Andreevna's amazement and the desperate situation of Khlestakov, who has no way to justify himself. Words are useless—he is caught at the scene of the crime. In this moment, the spectator tensely awaits the resolution of the situation. Suddenly, Khlestakov bends down decisively and examines the music at close range, freezing in this bent-over position, in the pose of a person who is extremely interested in the music to the romance. This gesture unfailingly, in all four performances that I had the opportunity to witness, evoked a unanimous burst of laughter from the audience. This laughter was the release of the waiting, while Khlestakov's gesture was the final chord that resolved all the dissonances introduced by the preceding performance.

"We," summarized Gvozdev, "meet here a characteristic detail that is typical of the structure of *The Inspector General* as a whole. Before us is a pantomime scene constructed in the same way as a musical phrase in a musical composition. The theme is taken, dissonances are introduced, tension is created, and the final chord brings resolution."

Set drawing for
The Inspector General

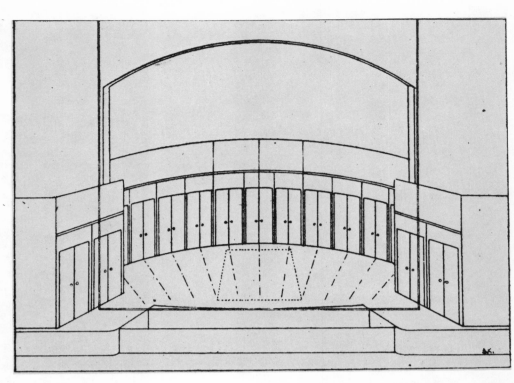

Announcement for the dress rehearsal of *The
Inspector General,* December 8, 1926

Caricature of Meyerhold, *The Inspector
General* in his hand

МОСКВА
1926

Среда, 8-го декабря

В

ГОСУДАРСТВЕННОМ ТЕАТРЕ

ИМЕНИ

Вс. МЕЙЕРХОЛЬДА

ГЕНЕРАЛЬНАЯ РЕПЕТИЦИЯ СПЕКТАКЛЯ

РЕВИЗОР

Начало в 8 час. вечера

The Inspector General, Babanova as Maria *(above)*, Garin as Khlestakov *(below)*

The Inspector General, Garin as Khlestakov *(above)*, Raikh as Anna Andreevna *(below)*

Khlestakov (Garin) descends stairs in the episode "After Penza"

"Carried Out with the Tenderest Love"*(above),* "The Procession" *(below)*

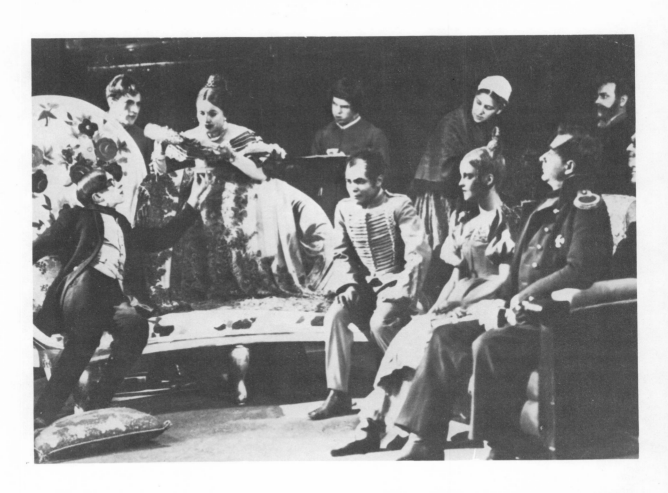

The Inspector General, the "For a Fat-Bellied Bottle" episode

Above: "For a Fat-Bellied Bottle"
Below: Raikh and Garin as Anna Andreevna and Khlestakov

"If they want a celebration, well, give them a celebration," *The Inspector General*

Above: "Mr. Finance," episode 10. *Below:* "Kiss Me," episode 11

The Inspector General, scenes from episode 15, "Incredible Confusion"

The finale of *The Inspector General*, the dumb scene, done with mannequins

At the end of the pantomime performance, Anna Andreevna is totally dispirited and defenseless before Khlestakov, who suddenly, easily, and elastically falls to his knees before her and states that he is dying of love. The scene between Khlestakov and the mayor's wife was constructed under the same conditions: the Visiting Officer regarded her with equal gloom and coldness, the blue Captain hammered out the romance "Kiss Me" just as automatically. But Z. Raikh performed differently. She spoke each line with such languor and embraced Khlestakov with such vigor that he tried to get away. The most powerful explosion of emotion came with the phrase: "If I am not in error, you are making a declaration about my daughter." At the words "my daughter," the mayor's wife literally dragged Khlestakov to her breast, clasped him tightly in her arms, choking him. His words, "My life hangs on a thread," suddenly obtained a real meaning. At this moment Maria Antonovna ran in and acidly sang out, "Ah, what a thing to happen!" Again, Meyerhold set up a little pantomime.

> The mother assumes the pose of insulted goodwill and begins emotionally to reprimand her daughter. Maria Antonovna listens to the threatening reproof. The Captain walks up to her, puts his hands in his trouser pockets and with an insolent look containing a reproach that accords with the mother's, stares at the embarrassed young lady. But in the moment when Anna Andreevna majestically chides her daughter: "You have other examples—your mother is before you," the Captain seizes his head with both hands and, bending his knees slightly, steps into the background, every movement of his body expressing the despair that has seized him at the thought of the mother's good deeds.[45]

A. V. Lunacharsky, commenting on this episode, called it "a comedy of love." He wrote: "Love—bourgeois love, in any event—is taken here into such a sharply critical bind, is burned through with such nitric acid, that the attentive spectator is gripped with emotion. Everything is here—sweet music, dancing, love and jealousy, the inconstancy of masculine love, feminine coquetry—those elements from which the continuously renewed fabric of love play is woven. And look at the horror that emanates from all this!"

Truly, this episode, with its farcical composition, was in the final analysis possibly the grimmest episode of the production, although it did evoke the laughter of the audience several times. Its secret and sacred theme was the revelation of the automatic nature of sensuality. The mannequin motif, quite basic to Meyerhold's *Inspector General*, entered spheres which both theatrical tradition and poetry kept as the arbitrary domain of emotions, limited in no way, designated for jesting or somber—but always free—play. Here, improvised eroticism, the storm of passion and the bright willfulness of lyricism could reign—anything at all, save for the uniform mechanics of shamelessness. It was into this sacred sphere of human joy that Meyerhold craftily introduced the automatic rhythm and the cynicism of mechanical repetition. "While watching this scene," admitted Lunacharsky, "I thought with some horror: is Meyerhold assaulting all love, all eroticism, here?"[46]

Meyerhold, of course, was assaulting neither love nor eroticism. But the profanation of love and the profanation of eroticism became the object of cruel study and the theme of grotesque images that sent distress signals decades into the future, to Fellini's images in *La Dolce Vita*.

In the third act, the pace of the action increased and approached the final catastrophe with ever greater velocity. The moveable platform for the "Benediction" episode rolled out two symmetrically placed—to the left and to the right—ikonostases. Behind hung two curtains through which the actors entered. The benediction itself was carried out by the mayor and his wife in a seeming trance. He was still terrified and could not yet assess the dimensions of his sudden good fortune. She was still distracted by Khlestakov's embraces and could not figure out whether she herself or her daughter was being married. Church singing came from behind the curtain. Khlestakov stood, hands loosely in his pockets, feet apart. The bride opened and closed her mouth repeatedly. Everything was as in a dream. Only Osip, relaxed and alert, understood what was happening and therefore urged his master to leave quickly.

Khlestakov's departure was the main event of the episode. "What, sir? It is your pleasure to depart?" asked the mayor. He was neither surprised nor frightened at this moment. He simply and finally comprehended nothing any longer, and had given up trying. But Khlestakov, wrote Talnikov, "thoughtfully scratched the corner of his mouth, his lip with his little finger—a relativistic, automatic gesture, and, after a pause, while all looked at him, dropped emptily: 'Yes, I'm going...for a moment...for a day...' with no content, empty words. He whistles...disappears."[47] Suddenly the coachmen's song and horses' hooves sounded, not from behind the stage, but somewhere from the other side of the auditorium, and then they were silent.

"The discoverers of realistic Americas," one newspaper reviewer stated drily, "have not yet thought of such a technique."[48]

"Dreams of Petersburg" was the title and content of the next brief episode. The mayor and his wife were finally thinking over the past events. They were happy, and their marital idyll was more than expressive. The mayor lay on the magnificent huge sofa, feet up. Next to him sat Anna Andreevna, with her sated and languid face. Each time the mayor slapped her back or pushed her with his foot she would smile beatifically. On the round table in front of the pair Meyerhold created a magnificent Flemish still-life. Sausages, hamhocks, fat sturgeon, geese, a rabbit, fowl, peaches and grapes in crystal vases, a sugarloaf, bags, packages... Some gifts did not fit on the table and lay on the floor. The mayor stood up, looked at all these presents and even, in his delight, began to dance the "Russkii." This was his moment of return to reality. Everything regained its place. The fact that he, the mayor, was still in power, and had even more power than before, was declared in the clearest, most familiar and natural language of the presents that he was examining lovingly. Furthermore, Khlestakov, who inevitably transformed tangible reality into slippery fantasy, had gone. And, having departed, having abstracted himself from the mayor, he became instantly comprehensible—no devil, simply a fine groom, an excellent match.

Here in this episode, Meyerhold sharply and precisely delineated the fateful limitation of a consciousness unable to assimilate changing reality but quite able to operate within habitual illusions, convenient patterns of the imagination, and to enjoy them.

The delighted duet turned into the mass scene of joy in the episode, "Celebration,

Real Celebration!" The small platform was framed by the splendid restless drawing of a gold triple mirror, filled to the limit by figures of officials, and their wives and soldiers. Uniforms shone, women's bare shoulders gleamed. Guests continued to arrive with a happy roar. There was nowhere to sit, chairs were being brought in, floated over heads, rocked, were put down. The Jewish orchestra behind the scenes played a march. "This piling together," wrote Kugel, "gives the impression of exceptional force, as though all passions, all faults, all phoniness, all envy, all hate, all stupidity, all cowardice and gloating were gathered into a single fist."[49] The mass of humanity, squeezed into these tiny limits by Meyerhold, was brightly lit by projector beams, wavered, shifted, babbled and pressed toward the mayor and Anna Andreevna, who were in the right corner of the platform. Then the postmaster appeared and made his way through the crowd, jumping up on chairs, falling down and disappearing from view. When he stopped, finally, clutching the fateful opened letter in his hand, the entire crowd immediately changed its orientation and pressed to the left corner, where the reading began.

Meyerhold laid precisely delineated lines of overall movement through the crowd: from backstage to the right, and forward then from backstage, left and forward. These main dynamic axes were interrupted periodically by episodic shifts. Thus, for instance, Zemlyanika, so people would not read about him, stuffed the letter into his trouser-leg. A small whirlwind of activity surrounded him, the letter was taken away from him, and all heads turned to the left again. The reader was like a choir leader, while the ensemble of officials rejoiced, howled, laughed, was silent and again began to cry out.

Babanova's tender and quiet solo broke into this babble. In a carefree and clear voice, standing on a chair in the crowd of officials, she sang with childlike naivete the romance "I Have Turned Sixteen," and like Ophelia she disappeared—drowned—in the thick colorful crowd of guests, unexpectedly leaving the show.

When the reading of the letter ended, Anna Andreevna uttered her desperate, melodramatic cry: "Antosha, this cannot be!" The unanimous jeering shout of the whole crowd answered her. The mayor's wife fell in a faint. The officers—the same ones who had serenaded her—caught her up, lifted her high and carried her behind the wings. On the emptied stage the mayor, completely out of his mind, began his monologue, as in a trance, and Gibner the doctor quickly dressed him in a strait-jacket.

At this moment the church bells began to ring and the police beat their drums. The mayor's command to "ring all the bells" was belatedly being obeyed. The fantastic mix of sounds, combining the ringing of the bells, the rattle of the drums, the squealing violins of the Jewish orchestra and the roar of the crowd, was heightened further by the piercing whistles of the policemen. The terrified officials ran from the stage at a wild gallop, shouting and yelling down the passages in the auditorium, and floundered in the stalls. Everything fell silent. A white curtain descended. On it was written: "The authorized Inspector General from Petersburg has arrived and requests the presence of all officials."

The curtain rose, and the spectators saw the characters of the show frozen in the poses indicated by Gogol. The sculptural group was immobile. Only after a long pause did the spectators guess that before them were not actors but dolls—that the "mute scene" was truly mute and dead.

"With a wave of the brilliant director's magic wand," wrote Lunacharsky, "Meyerhold suddenly shows the fearful automatic essence, the death-dealing horror of Gogol's depiction of the world that continues to live next to us... Having separated this world into peace and movement, Meyerhold said with the powerful voice of the clairvoyant artist: you are dead, and your movement is lifeless."[50]

Without a doubt Lunacharsky grasped Meyerhold's idea correctly. He estimated the structure of the work at its true worth, saw its deep and by no means obvious links to Gogol, and sensed acutely the modernity of Meyerhold's creation. There was much in this masterwork of Meyerhold's that was far in advance of contemporary stage practice and which was truly perceived by audiences only several years later, during subsequent seasons. In later times many elements of the total directorial form of the production were used in different ways by other directors of dramatic and musical theater, producers of music hall programs and films. Meyerhold's tremendous creative energy, which gave his grand Gogolian composition its harmony and dynamic unity, was the impetus this time too for the most varied and usually relatively moderate and diluted variations of Meyerhold's techniques. Other directors were led to the most extravagant, striking, and internally quite unfounded experiments. Immediately following the dress rehearsal and premiere of Meyerhold's *Inspector General*, only a few people accepted or understood it. Not everyone shared Lunacharsky's position—he had dedicated several delighted speeches and articles to the production.

Andrei Bely, describing the atmosphere of the first presentations of Meyerhold's show, recalled P. Annenkov's response to the premiere of *The Inspector General* in 1836: "Incredulity was written on the faces... There was almost no applause. At the end...incredulity...became outrage."[51] It is a fact that the first reviews of the premiere (December 9, 1926) were annoyed, distracted, and complained of boredom. "The show is not a success with the audience," telegraphed Leningrad's *Red Gazette (Krasnaia gazeta)*, following the dress rehearsal.[52] Demyan Bedny printed a "review-epigraph" in *The News*, entitled "The Murderer":

> You have crowned yourself with monstrous victory:
> Laughter, Gogol's laughter you have struck down![53]

Ten days later, however, the same *News* was stressing especially the difference "between the dress rehearsal of *The Inspector General* and the subsequent performances, which are much more easily appreciated."[54]

In part, this "difference" was explained by the several revisions that Meyerhold made in the show (such as combining the episodes "The Unicorn" and "Filled with the Tenderest Love" into one) and the elimination of several dragging passages. But the changes were individual and not changes of principle. Nonetheless, the success of the show grew from performance to performance. After the series of critical, poisonous, and jeering reviews, there were calmer responses, and others were quite delighted. The debate grew and expanded, gradually reaching a monstrous scale.

In the history of world theater there had been nothing like the discussion of *The Inspector General*. Dozens of tempestuous arguments, a countless number of contradictory reviews—praise, sharp criticism, epigrams, columns... It is sufficient to say that three special books are devoted to Meyerhold's *Inspector General*.* In addition to Lunacharsky, the defenders of the show included Mayakovsky, I. Glebov (Boris Asafev), A. Gvozdev, A. Slonimsky, A. Kugel, Bely, V. N. Solovyov, P. Markov, S. Tretyakov, N. V. Petrov. The opponents were Demyan Bedny, V. Shklovsky, V. Shershenevich, M. Levidov, L. Grossman, S. Radlov, M. Zagorsky, N. Semashko, Em. Beskin, V. Volkenshtein, O. Litovsky. Everything became confused—recent allies became opponents, while opponents on principle became, on the contrary, united in praising or abusing the show.

There was something very odd in the way the leftist critics Beskin and Zagorsky suddenly agreed with Demyan Bedny, who dedicated not only the epigram above to *The Inspector General*, but wrote an entire critical article in verse in a special feature for *The News*.† No less strange was the unexpected alliance between Mayakovsky and Andrei Bely.

It is possible to comprehend these unexpected things and to sort out the extremely varied judgments of Meyerhold's *Inspector General* only by keeping in mind a minimum of three very significant facts. First, the transposition of Gogol's comedy into tragedy was for many totally unthinkable.

Second, Meyerhold's rapid movement toward realism again puzzled and alienated his old leftist backers, while eliciting the sympathies of confirmed supporters of the realistic tradition such as Lunacharsky, Kugel, Markov, and I. Glebov (for all the differences in their positions). Third, the very forms of realism that Meyerhold felt out in this production (he spoke of "astringent," "concrete" and "musical" realism) were new, unusual, and bold. Realism which, in the inertia of the first post-Revolutionary years, was still considered modest and passive, in principle "declarative" and neutral with respect to content, suddenly developed aggressiveness, unexpectedly became capable of creating active stage forms.

"Against the politely uniform background of our theatrical life," wrote P. Markov, "Meyerhold's spectacle...loomed, a somber and magnificent mass, while the erstwhile intensity of the 'front-line' and now-liquidated struggle flamed around Meyerhold's latest directing work."[55]

All the fundamental innovations united by Meyerhold in this one show formed a spectacle that was extremely complex for the undeveloped perception.

Very diplomatically, using cumbersome and careful expressions, Lunacharsky wrote, nearly two years later: "The heated arguments raised about *The Inspector General* were one of the happy events in our society." But nonetheless, "the production of *The Inspector General* was somewhat overloaded with virtuosity and therefore could not yet be understood by the less artistically cultured portion of our politically advanced audience. For the most part, this was something new, and the new requires some thought and does not come in without effort."[56]

Truly, the show, as we observed earlier, was in many ways ahead of its time and promoted numerous theatrical concepts that subsequently were utilized in works by

---

*The collection *Gogol' i Meierkhol'd* (M, 1927); the collection *"Revizor" v teatre imeni Vs. Meierkhol'da* (L. 1927); D. Tal'nikov. *Novaia reviziia "Revizora"* (M. 1927).

†Dem'ian Bednyi. Meierkhol'dovskaia starina iz *Zolotogo runa*. *Izvestiia* (January 27, 1927).

other directors. Undoubtedly it fatigued some, surprised others, disappointed still others. Still, the most perceptive and refined critics praised it highly and understood the extent of its inevitable influence on the entire further development of the Soviet stage.

P. Markov wrote:

> Meyerhold requires artistic completeness on the part of the entire exterior side of the show, beginning with the setting and ending with the strictly rhythmical movements of the actors. He constructs the entire show on music, like a unique symphony. An enemy of pointless estheticism and photographic naturalism, Meyerhold selects the most typical objects of the period and, in a series of small pictures, gives the sensation of the times... Retaining the episodic principle, Meyerhold develops in each episode the fatedness and emptiness of man as the author of *The Inspector General* sensed it, thus stressing the social meaning of the play.[57]

The cardinal element in Meyerhold's production—the combination of specifically social motifs with the overall humanistic theme of the death of the human in man, the essentially Kafkaesque theme of the mannequin-like, automatic world stifling human feelings—was sensed by Andrei Bely, who defended the director's right to interpret *The Inspector General* as a tragedy. Meyerhold, he said "presented *The Inspector General* against the background of *Dead Souls* and 'Nevsky Prospect.' There was no real laughter in Gogol, except possibly in *Evenings on a Farm near Dikanka*. Behind his laughter looms a somber, black, enormous Russia."[58]

Igor Glebov (Boris Asafev), the well-known composer and music critic, devoted particular attention to the musical structure of Meyerhold's production. He wrote:

> It has been a long time since I have experienced in a dramatic theater such a bright and powerful *impression of musical order* as I found in the total concept of Meyerhold's *Inspector General*. The show is saturated with music: evident, concretely transmitted in song and in play, in the nuances of the intonations of speech, "concealed" from the spectator and auditor, but nonetheless always present... In *The Inspector General* one is amazed simultaneously by the scale, the mastery of form, and the perception in the use of music's ability to warn ("signal"), to call, beckon and hypnotize, to raise and lower the emotional current, to heighten mood and action, to change the funny into the sinister and fantastic, to color any everyday anecdote into a psychologically significant phenomenon. . . . Meyerhold's spectacle sounds like a score that is rhythmically harmonious, rich in imagination, technically perfect and full of emotional content. Here beats the pulse of life, no matter what angry defenders of Gogol or "theater-goers from the stove" may say.[59]

Nonetheless, both the "theater-goers from the stove" and the "leftists" who accused Meyerhold of creating a "decadent," "sinister," "heartrending show,"[60] a production that was "provincial,"[61] a "dreary, uncultured, unsuccessful show about which it is even boring to write,"[62] whose staging reminds one of "a chaotic nightmare woven of odd phantoms and phantom oddities,"[63] succeeded in knocking the director off balance, although it seemed that he would be accustomed to any abuse. In debates, Meyerhold called his critics impossible names. Mikhail Levidov, whom he insulted profoundly, even sued Meyerhold. The Association of Theater and Cinema Critics published a protest against "the unheard-of antisocial statement by Meyerhold...addressed to an entire category of workers in the Soviet press" and demanded that "Comrade Meyerhold be held responsible."[64] An atmosphere of tension and baiting ensued. Lunacharsky wrote that there began "extremely harmful judgments about the mysticism of Meyerhold's show, about Meyerhold's withdrawal from revolutionary theater. All this had a depressing effect on the high-strung and sensitive artist."[65]

Meyerhold was particularly stung by the coarse reviews of Zinaida Raikh's performance as the mayor's wife. At the end of the long debate, which lasted over a year, he probably came to the pessimistic conclusion that the production was comprehended fully only by the refined critics, and that the broad audience required clearer compositions.

This conclusion was not substantiated. *The Inspector General* continued to run until the closing down of the GOSTIM, and it enjoyed long-term success, even though, as the result of the replacement of a number of performers, this show—like so many of Meyerhold's old productions—lost its color and its rhythms wilted.

The striving for clarity and relative simplicity, and Meyerhold's unnatural concern for "profitability," caused some   flaws in the production of Griboedov's *Woe from Wit,* first performed on March 12, 1928. It cannot be said that the production of Griboedov's play was a conscious adaptation of the Gogol production. It was more likely the director's yearning for clarity that caused his long-windedness.

Meyerhold decided to oppose the imagery of *The Inspector General*, concentrated to the level of Symbolism, with a historically specific picture of a past age, its life and customs.

The painter N. Ulyanov, who was assigned the costumes, said before the premiere that he strove to show in the costumes "what a multicolored spectacle Moscow could present to any curious person. To everything that was supplied from Paris, to its styles and cuts of dress, there was added something local, something 'of oneself': inventions, spots that concentrated a foreign style accepted on faith... A Muscovite grimace already shows through in the ornamentation of faces and clothing, creating a most interesting artistic paradox."

It is true that on the same magazine page where Ulyanov's comments are printed, there was also the declaration of the artist V. Shestakov, who asserted that the design of the show was built "using the Constructivist method." That is, explained Shestakov, there is "a single machine organizing all the scenes in the show, mechanically changing and supplying individual scenes like the mounted frames of a show, carrying within their objective form the imprint of that era."[66]

In *Woe to Wit*, the construction rose above the stage (two ladders and two scaffolds on the sides, something like a captain's bridge in the back, center stage) proudly, majestically, more an accompaniment to the sumptuous and extravagant costuming than an objection to it. The construction was neither an apparatus nor a machine for the actor's performance: it performed the functions of a common decoration. The critics, who by this time had learned the principles of Constructivism well, trapped Meyerhold, observing that the side ladders and bridges were hardly played on, that they stood inactive.

"The Noah's Ark constructed by Shestakov," wrote Em. Beskin, "simply does not jibe with the director's treatment of individual scenes as miniatures. They drown in the optically unaccounted-for space..."[67]

"These Constructivist structures," concluded B. Alpers grimly, "are clear archaism, the remnants of an organ with atrophied functions."[68]

Meyerhold wished to show the audience all the rooms in Famusov's house. Accordingly, the episodes of the show were constructed not on the principles of meaning and dynamics, as in *The Inspector General*, but on the principle of finding new places of action. Thus they were named: "The Parlor," "The Dance Class," "The Portrait Hall," "The Sitting Room," "The Billiard Room and Library," "The White Room," "In the Doorway," "The Shooting Gallery," "The White Vestibule," "The Library and the Dancing Hall," "The Dining Room," "The Concert Hall," "The Den," "The Staircase." According to the director's plan, the spectators were to follow the actors around the entire house, or at least the public rooms, without looking into the kitchen or the servants' quarters.

As he had done in the case of *The Inspector General*, Meyerhold examined all existing author's versions of *Woe to Wit*, rejected the canonical text and created a new, "composite" variant of the text. Meyerhold actually did elicit from Griboedov's drafts all the motivations and possibilities for "unfolding" characteristic (more often, just colorful) episodes from everyday life. However, in this case the director's passion for demonstrating the various amusements and pastimes of the nobility was excessive.

Quoting from Apollon Grigoriev, Meyerhold said that "all comedy is comedy about boors." The boorish and ignorant world is contrasted with Chatsky, in whom Meyerhold wished to underscore the "traits that made him resemble the Decembrists." Meyerhold found support for this interpretation (subsequently the object of variation by numerous directors) in the historian V. Klyuchevsky, whose phrase he repeated in interviews: "The Decembrist served as the idea from which Chatsky was copied." Therefore, even the title for the show was not the canonical one, but one taken from Griboedov's rough draft—*Woe to Wit*. It was supposed that this title better expressed the conflict between the revolutionary Decembrist intellect and the stagnation and boorishness of the era.

This direct placement of Chatsky in opposition to his society was distinctly indicated in Griboedov, and was always shown on stage with maximum energy. Therefore, Meyerhold's depiction of Chatsky as a Decembrist had seemingly little chance of giving the play a "new interpretation closer to the true intent of the author, but also dictated by the requirements of the time."[69]

Still, Meyerhold did have grounds for such a claim. He planned a transposition of Chatsky's collision with Famusovism into a totally new key. This time he wished to avoid phantasmagoria and the intensity of the grotesque.

This time, he determined to depict the boorish world of the Famusovs and the Skalozubs, the Molchalins and Zagoretskys, as a well-organized society, healthy in its own way, powerful because of its nonspirituality and its lack of soul. Chatsky was confronted not with decay, dirt, and poverty, but with the opposite—satisfaction, satiation, consciousness of power, order—a well-regulated, fat, muscular, and strong existence.

Protazanov's film "The White Eagle," 1928.
Meyerhold as His Excellency, Kachalov as the General

Meyerhold, 1928, holding *Woe to Wit*

1928 caricature with A. Svidersky as The Teacher,
Meyerhold, Mikhail Chekhov, A. Granovsky, and
Nemirovich-Danchenko as Pupils

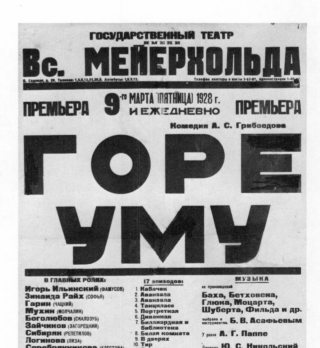

Poster for the premiere of *Woe to Wit*,
the number "9" in March 9, 1928
being pasted onto the already printed poster

Center: Chatsky (Garin). *Clockwise from top left:* Famusov (Ilinsky), Molchalin (Mukhin), Zagoretsky (Zaichikov), Skalozub (Bogolyubov)

Chatsky (Garin) and Molchalin (Mukhin)

Liza (Loginova), Sofia (Raikh), and Chatsky

Sofia (Raikh) and Molchalin (Mukhin)

The Dining Room episode of *Woe to Wit*

In this play, Meyerhold said, everything is light and clean, as if everyone had just gotten out of the bath.

The most important surmise by the director in the production of *Woe to Wit* was the sensation of physical health, energy and power in those opposed by Chatsky. Molchalin (M. Mukhin) was portrayed as brave, confident and handsome. In one review this Molchalin was called "pleasant and confident."[70] Famusov, performed by Ilinsky, was youthful, agile, a joker. Skalozub (N. Bogolyubov) appeared full of health and strength, a jolly and dashing commander. Sofia, bold and not at all shy, performed by Zinaida Raikh, had gone far in her romance with Molchalin and had no regrets. "Sofia," wrote Yury Sobolev, "is performed by a young lady refined in the science of passion, fiery and thoroughly permeated with sensuality."[71] V. Zaichikov played Zagoretsky, a lively roguish secret police agent.

All these characters were surprisingly amiable. "Don't touch us and we won't touch you." They became dangerous only when someone blocked their way, but otherwise were always ready to help, "to oblige a kinsman." They all lived for their own pleasure, all knew their way around in sensual pleasures, in eating, in playing. Everyone felt young and fresh. Even the old woman Khlestova (N. Serebryannikova) was well-proportioned and proud. Even Prince Tugoukhovsky (V. Maslatsov) looked happy. The ability to live life fully was underscored insistently by Meyerhold in his examination of Griboedov's art.

"Wild nobility" was portrayed as cheerful nobility in the show. A cohort of optimists stood before Chatsky. This is why it was more important to Meyerhold to show Famusov's *amours* with Liza instead of the "horrors of serf-owning."

Here, in this fundamental point, Meyerhold was completely misunderstood by the critics. V. Blyum observed that there were few "horrors": "For no particular reason Sofia...will strike the 'oppressed' Liza's skirts with a stick," or, behind the scenes "one can hear the sounds of a slap on the face... This is all the 'horror.'"[72]

It would be easiest to classify this concern with the "horrors" as vulgar sociology. But it was Meyerhold who caused all these objections and incomprehension. The magnificently divined theme of boorish optimism and bovine cheerfulness was presented in the show by a string of amusing absurdities. On stage there arose the contours of a world that was elaborate and exotic, not powerful or indestructible in its organization.

Meyerhold suddenly developed a taste for narration. He gave vent to his impulsive imagination and added entire scenes to Griboedov's comedy. These were not exactly impossible, but certainly unnecessary and barely convincing. The problem was not only that they were distant from Griboedov's intent and plan. The difficulty was that they retained full neutrality with respect to the plot of the "author of the production" (as he was called on the billboards)—Vs. Meyerhold.

The first episode was staged, unexpectedly, in a tavern. Meyerhold imagined that Sofia and Molchalin had driven away in the night "to the Gypsies" and sat silently at a table drinking, while in the back on a tiny stage two Gypsy women danced furiously. This episode had no text. It was executed by means of pantomime, since not a single line had been found in Griboedov's drafts.

However, the next episode (Chatsky's morning visit to Sofia) was based on Griboedov's text, actively interpreted. Since Chatsky arrived at Sofia's "at daybreak";

since he "had not stopped at home," Meyerhold assumed that the hero came to Famusov's house directly from the road, with all his packages, suitcases and baskets. The servants unhurriedly took off Chatsky's overcoat, scarf and hat—unwrapped him. The lackey brought the hero a cup of tea. Meanwhile, Sofia, just returned from the tavern, began to undress. Therefore, she could not come to meet Chatsky, and spoke to him through a partition.

The dialogue between Sofia and Liza was moved by the director into the dance class.

Famusov and Skalozub conversed while shooting pool.

The love scene between Chatsky and Sofia took place in the shooting gallery. With their backs to the audience, Sofia and Chatsky took turns firing at the targets and exchanged biting lines ("Dialogue—exchange of fire," explained Meyerhold).

All these amusements and pastimes of the nobility were more or less entertaining. But they "did not work for" the main assignment that Meyerhold had given himself: to show the physical energy, the greed, and the carnivorous aspect of Griboedov's characters. Spectators and critics were puzzled: why would Meyerhold give Famusov a whole large scene of love amusements with Liza? They criticized Meyerhold for the "eroticism" of this scene. They were angry, and asked to what end did Zinaida Raikh as Sofia change her costume ten times during the show, and why did she practice in dance class with long scarves, and why did she appear in the image of Flora, then Diana? Why did the theater, as if in response to Pushkin's observation that Griboedov "sketched Sofia unclearly: either a whore or a Moscow cousin," unhesitatingly reject the innocent "cousin" and prefer the shameless, impassioned easy woman? Liza evoked the fewest complaints. E. Loginova portrayed her as Sofia's keen-witted, efficient confidante, "plump and frisk," spontaneous and pliable. However, the appearance on stage of a real "bartender Petrushka," whom Liza was sighing over, was perceived as an inappropriate liberty by the director.

Meyerhold's idea did not come through actively enough in the show. It could be guessed at, but could be missed too. Even such a perceptive reviewer as B. Alpers believed that Meyerhold here "shows only the exterior dress of the era, the social ritual, daily etiquette..."[73]

The debate caused by the production occasionally entered completely unexpected spheres. D. Talnikov, for instance, wrote of the pool-room scene: "Skalozub and Famusov really play with all the techniques of regular players—they chalk their cues and spend time aiming, while Ilinsky amuses with various 'little things' and grimaces, and when he does shoot one into the pocket the audience applauds his success happily."[74] V. Blyum, who probably played pool better than Talnikov, had a different opinion on this score: "Here," he indicated, "the thing could have been done perfectly, so that a real, hardened player could have been satisfied. However, the sorry dilettantism as regards billiards on the part of unwilling actors and their mentor is too obvious to an eye that is unseduced by the art of this performance."[75]

Such arguments between the critics, consistent in their dislike of the show, testified to the fact that Meyerhold's idea of demonstrating healthy, powerful, playful, and energetic boorishness made a weak impression.

Meanwhile, the interpretation of Chatsky's role in Meyerhold's show depended completely on the boldly cheerful major-key interpretation of "Famusov's Moscow."

Chatsky, according to Meyerhold, passed through this self-satisfied, greedy, carnivorous, and brilliant world as a solitary and sad dreamer. B. Asafev, who selected and instrumentalized music from Bach, Beethoven, Gluck, Mozart, Schubert and other composers for the show, stressed the Beethoven theme in the image of Chatsky in commenting on the directorial and musical scores for *Woe to Wit*. He wrote:

> The penetration and depth of Chatsky's *feelings* becomes clear through the music: the power of his love and hate and fear of banality and satiated bourgeois existence. Who is Chatsky? A sensitive Russian man, artistically gifted, who visited the west at the time that Beethoven was offering humanity, with its tendency toward dull, Philistine living, priceless ethical demands in the sounds of his music. . . . Chatsky, for the duration of the play, is extremely tense emotionally. He takes his will power from music, which also unwinds his emotions. Chatsky lives, thinks and feels music, just as it was with Beethoven.[76]

The principle propounded by B. Asafev was realized in the show with monstrous consistency. Chatsky (E. Garin) kept sitting down at the piano. "In each room of Famusov's house a piano is at Chatsky's service. Three-quarters of his role is occupied with music. Some numbers are complete diversions," stated D. Talnikov. "On the placards for *Woe to Wit* they could have written below: 'Chatsky at the piano.' Truly, Chatsky never leaves the piano. He is all silent melancholy steps, silent Griboedovian whispered words, and extremely audible music."[77] Meyerhold's Chatsky, sneered V. Blyum, "as they do in movies, 'illustrates' his emotional experiences" with music—Beethoven, Schubert or Mozart.

A. Gvozdev reminded other reviewers that Griboedov himself was musical. "Griboedov the musician," he wrote, "merges with Chatsky the musician. Beethoven and Mozart nurture the revolutionary energy of the young musician-poet-Decembrist."[78]

It ought to be mentioned that the contrast between the spiritual Chatsky and the sensual, "fat" life of society was demonstrated by more than just this continuous music. From the very beginning of the show, after taking off his fur coat and remaining in his Russian shirt belted with a silken cord, Chatsky looks with disquiet and melancholy at active, forceful Moscow. "The mixture of young Werther and young Schiller,"[79] "some sort of neurasthenic pianist,"[80] joked the critics. Next to the monumental, dignified Molchalin, the cynical and sportive Famusov, and excited, pliable, bold Sofia, Chatsky appeared as a thoughtful, shy, pure boy. "The theme of Meyerhold's *Woe to Wit*," one of the reviewers guessed unexpectedly, "is the theme of solitude. Chatsky's story, as presented to us, is the story of an absolutely solitary soul who carries a dream through the world that surrounds him. Of what? No answer is given: it is no accident that Chatsky speaks not with words but with musical sounds... Chatsky passes through life as the only one living and the only one to be alone."[81]

We ought not to forget, however, that Meyerhold wished to represent Chatsky as a Decembrist. The dreamy, narrow-chested boy was occasionally surrounded in the show by silent, stern-faced young officers with decisive expressions who held banned books and leaflets (evidently proclamations) in their hands. When Famusov and Skalozub were shooting pool, Chatsky sat at the books in the back of the stage under a green lamp in the library, surrounded by these friends, reading poetry by Ryleev and Pushkin. Chatsky, wrote P. Kerzhentsev on the subject, lives "in his special world among his friends."[82] But the silent entourage of future Decembrists surrounding Chatsky was a phantom that only underscored his sad loneliness. "The play ends the way it began: with the note of Chatsky's total solitude, the loneliness of one who is alive thanks only to music,"[83] observed the most sympathetic review.

Only once in the show was there a collision between the two main themes—the theme of healthy boorishness and sad dreaminess withdrawn from life. This final collision had a powerful emotional impact. In the "Dining Room" episode Meyerhold, as he had done twenty years earlier in *The Puppet Show*, placed a huge white table along the proscenium and seated all the characters of the play at it, facing the audience. This front of energetically, carefully and thoughtfully chewing people was permeated with the consciousness of the ritual importance of the matter at hand. They are eating—what could be more important! They suck at the bones, look at their plates carefully before accurately and decisively aiming their forks and selecting the best pieces. The gossip about Chatsky's madness slowly moves from one end of the table to the other, nudged on in the pauses by the regular movements of jaws. "Meyerhold," wrote B. Alpers, "reproduces the worshipful ritual of destroying not only the food, but a living person. Famusov's guests at the long white table are chewing Chatsky himself with their stone jaws."[84]

Chatsky entered at the moment when the evil tale reached its apogee. Everyone at once fell silent and covered his face with a napkin. Frightened eyes looked out from behind the napkins at the madman. Chatsky walked along the edge of the stage next to the table, stopping in the center near Famusov and Khlestova. His words about "millions of torments" were heard in the deep silence of general fear. Music accompanied him while he slowly walked past the frozen diners toward the right wing.

Here, finally, Meyerhold's purpose in staging this play became evident. In addition to the theme of solitude the director was evidently excited by the theme of the collapse of idealism. He followed Chatsky with a glance of sorrow and compassion. Chatsky, so passionate, so inexperienced, reading revolutionary poetry with such inspiration and playing music with such abandon suddenly, here, found himself before a cohort of monumental diners... There was something to go mad from and, woe to wit!

All the threads of Meyerhold's plan stretched toward, but did not reach, this magnificent stage metaphor. It appeared suddenly and without preparation in all the glory of its stunning obviousness, a hard blow without advance warning. After this scene, the show again flowed in two independent, divergent streams. The opulent and dashing theme of the ball was developed in the background, flickered and rippled in the vestibule of Famusov's house, while in the foreground a disoriented Chatsky-Garin, going from corner to corner of the stage, pronounced his final monologue in a barely audible whisper.

Meyerhold planned a tragic finale. "Here," he said, "Chatsky's tragic awakening with respect to Sofia and Sofia's with respect to Molchalin."[85] But the tragedy did not work, if only because Chatsky as portrayed by Garin loved Sofia from the very beginning without any hope of reciprocity and even, quite Werther-like, became intoxicated with his sorrow. Sofia, meanwhile, was too inconstant for her "awakening" to sound tragic. She evoked no compassion, and it was clear that one like her would not perish.

A. V. Lunacharsky noted with reproach that *Woe to Wit* was long in preparation, "with a great waste of time," and concluded:"this production, which had great merit and shows that Meyerhold has the power to move forward along his selected path, is nonetheless unfinished and has turned out to be an artistic phenomenon lower, not higher, than *The Inspector General*."[86] Lunacharsky's opinion today appears to be the most reasonable.

The other critics met the premiere of *Woe to Wit* with a hailstorm of cruel articles. The general theme of nearly all the reviews at the time was the call: "Back to Griboedov!" Meyerhold was told that the canonical text of the comedy was superior to the combined text, that the title *Woe from Wit* was better than *Woe to Wit*, that it would have been better to perform the play in an "old, simple pavilion that did not distract the spectator's attention from the development of the play," and so forth.

An unexpected objection was expressed in an argument at GAKhN by the literary scholar N. K. Piksanov. He asserted that he found "the contrasting of serf-owning to Decembrism naive and insubstantial. The old legend about the Decembrists as knights without fear or blame is dead. Decembrism is a movement of average liberal nobility whose basis is serf-owning. Consequently, there is essentially no place for an antithesis."[87] This magnificent vulgarly sociological statement could have been continued: Chatsky and Famusov are both of the nobility. Consequently, there is no "antithesis" between them, and Griboedov's entire comedy is contrived...

There was another new note in response to *Woe to Wit*. V. Blyum dared to write that Meyerhold was finished, that his talent had expired. "It is time to say this: there is no more talent, since there is no craftsmanship, purposefulness or unity either in the content or in the form."[88]

Meyerhold, who had furiously answered his critics after the premiere of *The Inspector General*—even though at the time his allies and delighted admirers had been many—answered the unanimous attacks on his staging with stoic calm. He did not argue with his critics; only once did he respond, to curse N. Piksanov. As for the special debate dedicated to *Woe to Wit* in Leningrad, he simply "departed long before the end" and "did not answer the speeches of his opponents."[89]

Most plausibly, this could be explained by the fact that he himself was dissatisfied with the production.

The debate storming around Zinaida Raikh and her abilities as an actress (some praised them highly, others thought them worthless) became even more furious after her performance of the two important roles in Gogol's and Griboedov's plays. Some critics told Meyerhold crudely and directly that it was improper and unattractive to promote his wife in such a manner. I. Osinsky's review of *Woe to Wit* in *The News* concluded with the postscript: "Great restraint in the area of dress may be recommended not only to the wives of responsible officials but also to the wives of theatrical directors, and there is no need to change for every entrance in *The Inspector General* or *Woe to Wit*." The same article stated that "Zinaida Raikh is no good for the role of seventeen-year-old Sofia."[90] Yury Sobolev, usually a delicate and soft critic, sounded the same reproach: "You will not believe that her Sofia is seventeen."[91]

Meyerhold could have objected that Griboedov's Sofia never looked seventeen on stage, and that no one had ever said anything about it. But, as we mentioned earlier, he defended his staging of Griboedov weakly and without apparent conviction.

However, the new stage edition of *The Magnanimous Cuckold*, staged shortly before the premiere of *Woe to Wit* (January 26, 1928), was received—and not without reason—as Meyerhold's challenge in the argument over the art of Zinaida Raikh. Meyerhold gave Raikh the role of Stella, which Maria Babanova had played with phenomenal and unforgettable success. He seemed to be provoking the critics to make dangerous comparisons. Worse yet, in an interview with the reporter from *Evening Moscow*, the Master complained that in the first edition "the performer of the role of Stella [Babanova] was unable, due to her stage capabilities, to transfer her performance during the play from the plane of happy comedy into the plane of high tragedy" and, generally, "did not possess a clearly expressed characterization."[92]

The striking injustice of this statement was too obvious. The gauntlet thrown down by Meyerhold was immediately picked up by D. Talnikov. He wrote:

> Raikh moves heavily over the constructions and speaks her lines without animation. Her Stella has no fire, no spiritual infectiousness, no youth. This is an experienced woman who pretends to be naive and innocent. No matter how she rolls her eyes, no one will believe it... Raikh "switches" farce into serious (and very stupid) slowly crawling, limp drama. One unwillingly recalls the former, wonderful Stella—Babanova, rhythmic, light, young, using the rapid tempo of farce to portray the idyll of a naive, touching love with a mad crash into spiritual tragedy. Yes, Babanova and Ilinsky created a tragic farce on stage, while now on the stage there is a ridiculous, banal drama or a stupid vaudeville—something formless. Babanova is quite irreplaceable, a great loss for Meyerhold's theater.[93]

D. Talnikov was answered by Professor Vl. Sarabyanov. He began his response with the declaration: "I am not a theatrical specialist. I am an ordinary spectator." Consequently, it is he who has the right to judge, not subjectively but "objectively" whether the theater is carrying out the functions required by "our class, in this case the workers." From this "objective" point of view it turned out that Raikh "was able to make Stella's role accord with the assignment" by "eliminating the element of farce" from the spectacle and actively demonstrating against "husbands who humiliate their wives." This, supposedly, was very up-to-the-minute. "Just go and speak at a women's meeting in a workers' suburb," Sarabyanov invited.[94]

To these comical arguments by Sarabyanov, Meyerhold added his one angry and utterly unconvincing letter to the editor of the magazine *Contemporary Theater (Sovremennyi teatr)*. In the very first sentence he called Talnikov "a certain" compiler "well known to our theater." In the second sentence—an insincere and stupid critic. Then he wrote pathetically about Zinaida Raikh, "whose mind and talent helped me discover the tragic essence of this wonderful play by F. Crommelynck." Further, to prove that the theater had gotten along perfectly well before Babanova, he referred to shows in which she did not participate—*The Forest, The Mandate,*

Earth Rampant. He even asserted that in the 1922 *Cuckold* "form dominated content," while in the 1928 *Cuckold*, thanks to Raikh, "there took place the fortunate equilibirum between form and content."[95]

Alas, these passionate tirades exposed the uncertainty of the Master. With his ability to hear the audience, it was impossible for him not to sense that the *Cuckold* of 1928 received a worse reception than the old staging, that the old staging accorded with the times and the audience differently than before and with less success.

The atmosphere created around the GOSTIM changed rapidly. After the revival of *Cuckold* and the premiere of *Woe to Wit*, Meyerhold and his theater found themselves in a totally new situation when the majority of critical opinion turned hostile. Only part of the negative attitude of the press toward Meyerhold could be explained by his own intolerance and the briefly lessened creative intensity of the Master, which was generally sensed after *The Inspector General*. The altering social milieu, and the changing criteria for perception and evaluation of works of art, were creating more substantial circumstances of hostility, independent of Meyerhold. A. V. Lunacharsky wrote of the sudden manifestation "of a certain narrowness and one-sidedness in the objections leveled at theater," saying that "any theatrical production that deviates from the fairly narrow path of revolutionary-everyday life theater is perceived as socially suspicious." The Commissar for Education stated authoritatively that "neither the ruling organs of the Party nor the Government supports this point of view," and they do not back critics who voluntarily and with self-satisfaction proclaim themselves to be orthodox, "especially leftist." Nonetheless, he observed with unfeigned sadness, "a certain sharp and cold wind is felt all the time."[96]

The article was written in the fall of 1928 and was written about Meyerhold.

Several years later, Meyerhold again began to work on the comedy by Griboedov. "Virtually the entire staging has been reconstructed," he said in 1933. In the life of Griboedov's Moscow, he shaded "the traits of provinciality and Asiatic influence native to it... I strengthened the realistic aspects in the show."[97] The new edition was shown in 1935. M. Tsarev replaced E. Garin as Chatsky, P. Starkovsky replaced Ilinsky as Famusov. These changes only weakened the productions.

The only role that gained from the new edition was the role of Molchalin. He was now played not by Mukhin but by G. Michurin. The image of Molchalin was brought to the foreground partly because the other images had lost color, partly because the interpretation of the role was more active. Michurin played a "substantial and self-assured careerist knowing his own worth and in no way blinded by the magnificence of his patron... Molchalin," wrote D. Mirsky, "becomes the synthesized image of the entire Russian bureaucracy. . . . Meyerhold expands and raises Molchalin 'to certain levels' in order to demonstrate him again on these very levels in all his prehistoric baseness."[98] But a single role, however performed, could not make the difference.

The number of episodes was contracted from seventeen to thirteen. Meyerhold eliminated the introductory scenes in the tavern, rejected the dance class, managed without the pool room and forced the artist to simplify the decorations. All these operations not only lightened the show, but eliminated its previous conception. The director, however, proposed no new conception; the abridged show was very weak, and it dragged.

"The sensation among the theatrical audience," wrote V. Blyum in his relatively favorable review of the new edition of the show, "was caused by the fact that for *Woe to Wit* Meyerhold has hung a curtain." Such small sensations were, of course, symptomatic.

The 1930s posed new requirements. The same V. Blyum in the same long article expressed dissatisfaction that "instead of honest realistic walls" Meyerhold had transparent partitions through which "all the backstage is visible," which the spectator ought not see, and the curtain, too, "is too transparent..."

With the new viewpoint of the mid-1930s, Blyum also discovered a new "methodological error" on the part of the director: he forced, supposedly, Gogol's "pig snout" satire on Griboedov. Of course there was absolutely nothing of the "pigs' snouts" in Meyerhold's *Woe to Wit*. But the show that was quite declarative even when compared to *The Inspector General* now appeared too sharp and grotesque. "Our satire of Famusov's Moscow," wrote the critic on the subject, "still must stay within certain limits—it must not fall into the grotesque... Today we require that satire be extremely refined, involved, full, and it must resemble the criticized types. The grotesque, meanwhile, excluding verisimilitude and any outlining, unifying image, is triumphant in all the political satire contained in this staging of *Woe to Wit*."[99]

The conceptions of realism gradually reached a characteristic narrowness. It was clear already that the grotesque was undesirable and that certain limits ought not be crossed, even in satire. Already it was important to have a highly detailed characterization in everyday life of the criticized types. Under such circumstances the curtain appeared "too transparent" and Meyerhold's most restrained variation on the themes of the Russian classics became too radical.

Both editions of *Woe to Wit* were far from perfect. The second edition, performed by a less able cast, was also inappropriate for its time. It appeared at the time when Meyerhold's directorial art was perceived by numerous critics as a sort of opposition to the central esthetic criteria of Soviet theatrical art.

Caricature of Meyerhold, c. 1928

Dmitry Shostakovich and Meyerhold, 1928

THE MAGNIFYING GLASS

Despite all difficulties, Meyerhold's program for the "activation" of the classics in the productions of *The Inspector General* and *Woe to Wit* was carried through. The premiere of *Woe to Wit* took place in March of 1928, almost three full years after the opening of *The Mandate*. During this entire period, Meyerhold staged no modern plays. (As we have mentioned, *Roar, China!* was staged by V. Fyodorov and only edited by Meyerhold, and the unfortunate *A Window on the Village* had been directed by an entire "directorial collegium," i.e., by Meyerhold's students under his general supervision.) Meyerhold understood, of course, that full-blooded theatrical life was practically unthinkable without contemporary plays staged by himself utilizing his full capabilities.

This was supported by the depressing state of the box office receipts. In the late 1920s, Meyerhold's theater was no longer the most attractive for spectators. Audiences paid no attention to outraged critics and stood in incredibly long lines for tickets to *Days of the Turbins* at the Art Theater and to *Zoya's Apartment* at Vakhtangov's theater (until *Zoya* was prohibited). Audiences rushed to Meyerhold's old Theater of the Revolution to see his own production of *Lake Lyul*, and to the Moscow Art Theater II to any show with Mikhail Chekhov, or to *The Flea*, to the Kamerny Theater to see plays by O'Neill... And even though Meyerhold's theater remained at the center of attention for the press, and though everything that transpired or was planned in this theater immediately became a subject for critical discussions, Meyerhold still had to deal with the fact that his theater was operating at a loss.*

The GOSTIM (since 1926 the Meyerhold Theater had been called a State Theater), according to a quite competent Commissar of Education, evoked "irritation and disbelief on the part of state organs who observed a continuous deficit."[1]

There was only one way out of the unpleasant situation—a turn to the contemporary, to "up-to-the-minute" repertory, to new plays by Soviet writers.

Meyerhold had fairly comprehensive and very interesting plans in this direction. In 1927, he declared his intention to stage Andrei Bely's *Moscow* in the author's stage version, with decorations by V. Dmitriev. In 1928, rehearsals of the play *The Bloody Desert*, by the Armenian playwright S. Bagdasaryan, were begun. Meyerhold's theater awaited a new play by Nikolai Erdman. Finally, Meyerhold began to work energetically on a play by Sergei Tretyakov, *I Want a Child*.

It is worth saying several words about this play, particularly since Meyerhold defended it strongly and rehearsed it with inspiration. El Lissitsky was working with Meyerhold on the design for the show.

Today, one reads Tretyakov's play with a feeling of astonishment. The idea of the play is strikingly simple. The construction of the new world requires physically perfect and ideologically healthy cadres. Therefore, it is equally criminal to "waste

---

*"Profits from ticket sales are only 40-45%. Generally, the theater is 73% full. These figures indicate that the theater does not even find enough spectators to come for free," stated the head of *Glaviskusstvo*, A. Svidersky (*Sovremennyi teatr*, No. 42 [1928], p. 658).

sexual energy" and to bear children of men selected by the caprices of love. Healthy, strong, whole women of proletarian background must mate with healthy worker males. "The State," said one of the heroes of this play, the Disciplinarian, "encourages such selection" in consequence of which "a new breed of people" appears. He warned that "for all the sickly and the sexual wastrels" the "day of frightful fasting" was coming. Love, according to this program, was not totally eliminated, but was put off until better times. "When the human species is uplifted, you can love all you like, but for now, take it easy."

It was in accordance with this program that the heroine of the play, the young Latvian Communist woman Milda Grignau, organized her personal life. This strong, healthy lass invited a worker—Yakov the construction worker—to her room and asked him a number of form questions (such as whether there were any illnesses or, God forbid, foreign admixtures in his background). "Comrade, I want to have a child," Milda informed her selected one, "but I want a good child, I want his father to be a working man." After this, the heroine, not without difficulty, persuaded the astounded fellow to cohabit with her and then bore a child. Tretyakov particularly underscored this conflict. First, when Milda became pregnant she decisively refused any further services from her partner: the job was done, there was no point to any further waste of sexual energy. Secondly, Milda's "new morality" was equally opposed to the old bourgeois morality (bonds of love and marriage) and to amoral, dissolute and free relations between the sexes.

One blow was directed against "old-fashioned" lyricism that ignored the physical health and the social backgrounds of the ones in love. Another blow was aimed at "new-fashioned" love "without cherry blossoms," at women in silk stockings dancing the tango and foxtrot, carrying on their numerous affairs with no thought of the "breed" of people to come, even allowing themselves to undergo health-damaging abortions...

The play concluded on an idyllic note. The father selected by Milda turned out to be very good. At the newborn infants' contest, the son of Milda and Yakov, according to indications of "weight, feeding, chest dimensions, digestion, blood content, reflexes, temperament, conditions of conception, pregnancy, and birth" took first prize! Most importantly, Yakov proved to be good not just for Milda, but for siring the children of other women, too. It is true that some of them were jealous of Milda at first and even raised a fuss. But later, looking at the model offspring in the nursery school, they became extremely grateful to Milda. Even the neighbors, the miserable bourgeois inhabitants of the communal apartment who bore children without consideration for health, were compelled to admit that the path opened by Milda truly does lead to the renewal and happiness of all mankind.

The play propagandized eugenics with a single change: the racial criterion was replaced by the social criterion. In the magazine The New Left (Novyi Lef), which was steered by Mayakovsky, Aseev, Shklovsky and Tretyakov himself, it was said that the author "takes up the defense of rationalism and prudence if they are in the interests of a healthy, future generation. The author makes a general connection between the selective measures of the Soviet State and the obtaining of healthier progeny selected in a eugenically proper fashion."[2]

Before answering the question of why Meyerhold became involved in Tretyakov's theatrical Utopia, the basic reasons for this Utopia must be understood. In the play *I Want a Child*, it is easy to see the causes that impelled the author to suggest from the stage radical means for struggling with social maladies. The causes lay in the fact that in the late 1920s, the life of the general population remained unsettled. In the play, Tretyakov presented concentrated episodes from the dirty, dismal life of a workers' suburb laconically and sketchily, but with frightening verisimilitude. A crowd of hooligans raped a woman. People lived like roaches in the tight cages of communal apartments. An angry Asiatic bourgeois spirit dominated the barracks. Tretyakov dragged the screaming truth of cynical fact to the stage with intentional and cruel naturalism. He saw salvation from this misery only in science, in a rational and scientific solution to the problem.

Later, Meyerhold said: "Over a period of years, I—and not only I but Luna-charsky and other comrades occupying leading posts in Soviet theater—we all had the desire to see a so-called Utopian play on stage, a play that would state not only the problem of the present day, but which would look decades ahead."[3]

The artists of the late 1920s were convinced that the decade of new life had destroyed neither the bourgeois spirit nor the bourgeois man. L. Leonov, M. Zo-shchenko and A. Platonov wrote about this with concern. The immunity of the bourgeois, its stagnation and its swollenness, appeared as irreparable disaster. The bourgeois crept in through all the cracks and it seemed that the realm of the feelings belonged entirely to him. Olesha's play was even entitled *A Conspiracy of Feelings*. Feelings, primarily love, were viewed as the direct enemies of the new, rational, scientifically organized life. Beauty, lyricism, the spiritual—all were criticized and rejected. The positive program of Olesha and Tretyakov was Utopian. The Utopias of the time were prosaic ones. The most incredible fantasies were presented declaratively. Poets stepped on the throat of poetry and proposed prosaic, scientifically-based ideals. Olesha tried to praise cheap sausage, Tretyakov—eugenics. There is no fundamental difference.

When Meyerhold undertook to stage *I Want a Child* and debates about the play began in the Main Repertory Committee *(Glavrepertkom)*, no one dared to speak out against Tretyakov's "positive program." Eugenics was science, and who could argue with science? Only V. F. Pletnyov said shyly the play "perhaps appeared earlier than necessary." N. A. Ravich was shocked: "The text of the play," he said, "is filled with coarse expressions," and he requested "a number of abridgements." Other speakers were afraid that the play would evoke "undesirable responses" and said: "It is impossible to stage the play the way it is written. The expressions of the play are such that (a worker likes to go to the theater with his family) perhaps a sixteen-year-old girl should not hear them."

Although Meyerhold promised to stage the play "the way Soviet society, and not the author, requires" (and even said if he had staged *Days of the Turbins*, he would have done so "as needed by us"), and even though V. Blyum asserted that *I Want a Child* "is one of the best Soviet plays," and although P. Novitsky said that "presenting the matter is desirable from the point of view of social prophylaxis,"[4] the play was rejected after several meetings.

As far as we know, no one has yet observed the similarity between a number of themes central to the drama *I Want a Child* and the main themes of Mayakovsky's

The Bedbug. In each case a militant critique of the philistinism and dirt of modern life precedes a theatrically staged Utopia. Tretyakov's cruel drama attempts to bring Utopia directly into modern life, to organize and transform it by force, while Mayakovsky's satirical comedy moves Utopia half a century forward. But the very movement away from the actual unpleasantness of modern reality toward science fiction as the surest remedy is more than symptomatic. The dream that the power of science will rid the new society of "hereditary" social blemishes possessed the playwrights, even though their ideological and esthetic positions were quite different. This enthusiasm inflamed Meyerhold too, as he defended *I Want a Child* and later staged *The Bedbug*.

As early as May 4, 1928, Meyerhold telegraphed from Sverdlovsk to Mayakovsky in Moscow: "For the last time I appeal to your good sense. Theater is perishing. There are no plays. They compel one to reject the classics. I do not wish to lower the repertoire. I request a serious answer: can we expect to receive your play during the summer? Wire urgently...".[5] They were discussing *The Bedbug*, but Mayakovsky did not finish the play in the summer, and before the GOSTIM could receive it, events transpired that put Meyerhold under serious suspicion.

In the fall of 1928, Meyerhold went abroad. Mikhail Chekhov was in Germany at the same time, and the German press suddenly announced that he had signed a two-year contract with Max Reinhardt. In other words, Mikhail Chekhov was emigrating. The head of GOSET, A. Granovsky, who was also abroad, was working at obtaining permission for his theater to undertake a lengthy foreign tour. Granovsky's own intentions remained unclear for only a short time. It became known that he too would not return. At this same time two dispatches arrived from Meyerhold. In the first, Meyerhold announced that he was ill and that for reasons of health he intended to spend an entire year abroad. In the second, he stated that he had organized a European tour for the GOSTIM and requested permission to tour Germany and France.

A highly unpleasant picture developed. It seemed that the three leaders of Moscow's theaters intended to leave the Soviet Union at the same time. Chekhov and Granovsky had already left Russia. As for Meyerhold, his behavior looked fairly mysterious. Lunacharsky gave several interviews on the subject and published two extensive articles. He wrote that "the State values Meyerhold's talent highly," but then added, probably not without cause, that Meyerhold "is a very poor organizer," that "there were always disturbing events in his company," that his "best pupils" had left him, "the best actors." (Clearly, Babanova was being discussed here—she never did return to Meyerhold—and Ilinsky, who would return very soon.)

Then Lunacharsky expressed his conviction that the crisis in Meyerhold's theater was easily surmountable, and promised to permit the GOSTIM a lengthy tour "to demonstrate its achievements before a leading foreign audience" with the sole condition that the trip be financially practicable. "First of all, it is essential that Vsevolod Emilevich Meyerhold come here to Moscow to carry out these serious discussions. The *Narkompros* and *Glaviskusstvo* know that Meyerhold needs a rest and they are guaranteeing him that rest, even if it is abroad, but they insist categorically that the way out of the crisis be found by way of personal discussion."[6]

Neither then nor later did Meyerhold consider emigration. Two years later, in Berlin, Mikhail Chekhov tried to convince him to remain abroad, but according to Chekhov's own words this suggestion was rejected completely.

"I shall return to the Soviet Union," said Meyerhold. "To my question 'why?' he answered: 'because of integrity.'" Mikhail Chekhov added: "Meyerhold knew the theatrical Europe of the time. It was clear to him that nowhere but in Russia could he create in accordance with his genius." Naturally, the suspicion so clearly expressed in Lunacharsky's article insulted Meyerhold. Some people believed, however, that Lunacharsky was treating Meyerhold too delicately. In some newspapers, Meyerhold was labelled a "deserter." D. Zaslavsky wrote a stinging article in *Pravda* entitled "Give us Europe? No, We Won't." The writer there made fun of "the exaggerated softness of motion" and the "respectful whispers" with which Meyerhold was "being asked to return to the USSR and continue his work." He stated that Soviet theater could get along fine "without such leading figures to whom all is permitted for the sole reason that they are very talented." He asked, "is this compensation for a brilliant experiment in long-term disorganization of Soviet theatrical—and not just theatrical—culture?"[7]

Meyerhold responded calmly and practically to the uproar in the press. He stated that he was insulted by the newspapers' screams about "Meyerhold's escape" and the equation of his behavior with that of Mikhail Chekhov. He laughed at the assertion that he was undergoing a creative crisis. A State commission was formed which assigned thirty thousand rubles for the support of the GOSTIM but stated that "it leaves the matter of the theater's future open until the arrival of Vs. Meyerhold."[8] Meyerhold was quite agreeable to such a decision. On December 2, 1928, he returned to Moscow.

On December 25, 1928, Mayakovsky read his comedy *The Bedbug* in the Meyerhold Theater. The next day Meyerhold spoke with his company. "This play," he said with inspiration,

> is a new work by Mayakovsky not only in the area of dramaturgy. This work is amazing in its virtuoso treatment of the verbal material. It reminds you of the most wonderful pages of Gogol which make such a special impression when you read them. This is neither prose nor poetry, but some sort of new verbal formation. The verbal material is so uniquely constructed that entire chapters of research will have to be written. The play is also wonderful for the stage.

Meyerhold predicted that it "will occupy a special place not only in the repertoire of our theater, but in modern repertoire in general."[9]

This new meeting between Mayakovsky and Meyerhold was highly significant in many respects. It is reliably known that Mayakovsky experienced no great passion for the theater. "In all the years of our acquaintance," recalled N. Lunacharskaya-Rozenel, "I never met Mayakovsky at the Art Theater or at the Maly Theater, let alone at the Korsh Theater. Those close to the poet assert that he attended theater productions very rarely."[10] It is known with equal reliability, however, that Mayakovsky almost always attended Meyerhold's premieres. Undoubtedly, Mayakovsky and Meyerhold had a similar fundamental understanding of the tasks facing new stage art. Every time that the poet commented on Meyerhold's production—

The Forest, D. E., The Inspector General—he invariably criticized Meyerhold "from the left." For instance, Mayakovsky praised *The Inspector General*, but observed that on the whole *The Inspector General* "should not be staged," and so on. In all these and other statements there is one constant, highly important theme of Mayakovsky's: theater must serve the present day directly and actively. Meyerhold's return to the classics was seen by Mayakovsky as a retreat necessitated by the absence of new plays, while from his point of view the adaptations of classics to modernity were compromises—either futile *(The Forest)* or relatively acceptable *(The Inspector General)*.

Meyerhold's theater certainly did not always suit Mayakovsky. We should keep in mind particularly that over a period of many years in the poet's life there existed another unique theater that developed outside the framework of stage art in the precise sense of the word. We are speaking of Mayakovsky's own "theater," of his countless stage appearances, and the concerts the author gave in many cities across the country. This sphere of Mayakovsky's most active work has been studied from every angle save one—the theatrical. Meanwhile, there is no doubt that the poet and tribune, the polemicist and reciter, created the "one-actor theater" long before Yakhontov. In his theater he had his own well-planned "dramaturgy," a carefully constructed concert program with a specific combative beginning, striking culmination and, most often, an inspiredly optimistic summons as a finale. In this theater, the "action" was in extremely active and acute contact with the auditorium. The poet parried lines from the seats, answered notes, ridiculed his opponents, and so on. It was at such author's concerts that Mayakovsky first publicly tested the themes of *The Bedbug* and *The Bathhouse* and first sketched the approximate forms of these comedies. Look at the poster for Mayakovsky's show *Let's Make an Elegant Life*. (Mayakovsky performed with this program many times—in Rostov, in Novocherkassk, Tbilisi and other towns.) Nearly all the subject matter of *The Bedbug* is here. All of Mayakovsky's poems directed against the bourgeois are collected here into a single fist.

The fearful danger of the bourgeois was contrasted in the comedy *The Bedbug* with the "Utopia" so desired by Meyerhold—a rainbow-colored and jesting portrait of the year 1979.

Meyerhold set to work as soon as he received the play, and completed the production in six weeks. Meyerhold changed nothing in the text of the comedy. Mayakovsky, who participated in the rehearsals, requested only that several lines be added.

The first, the "modern," part of the show was designed by the artists named Kukryniksy. The second, "fantastic," part was designed by A. M. Rodchenko. The principles for the designs of the two parts were different. The Kukryniksy were assigned to provide maximum verisimilitude; their scenes (the first four episodes), according to Meyerhold's play, were to present the spectators with the banality that lived with them in their own rooms. "The department store, the objects carried from it to the customers, the dormitory corner, all this," said the Kukryniksy, "provides material for showing the horrifying tastelessness of the bourgeois. We include our work in the campaign . . . against the 'artistic' trash thrown out on the market to answer the needs of the inhabitants. The design for the show is one of objects.

Real things purchased in the State stores or in the market serve as examples of bad quality on stage. In the work on *The Bedbug* we have utilized our observations made in bourgeois apartments, in offices sullied with Oblomovism, in the streets, at parties, etc."

In the second half of the show, Rodchenko was to contrast the banality and poor taste of modern life with "simplicity, large forms, utilitarian objects . . . light, transparent construction." He said that in the second part of the show "there will be no solid walls" but "an imitation of glass," a "transformation of basic devices and objects. Poster-like costumes." The depiction of the life of 1979 was not taken seriously, however, and Rodchenko explained that these costumes, "rose and light blue—will demonstrate common notions of the future." Both the director and the artist sensed "the irony permeating Mayakovsky's descriptions of the future" and wished to transmit it.[11]

The music for the show was written by the young Dmitry Shostakovich. The leading roles were: Prisypkin—I. Ilinsky; Bayan—A. Temerin; Rozalia Pavlovna—N. Serebryannikova. The premiere was on February 13, 1929.

The first episode, "Sailored and Gone," took place in the street at the entrance to a department store. D. Talnikov immediately recognized Petrovka Street. "Here," he wrote, "is a piece of Petrovka with a department store, newsboys, a crowd, dealers in dolls and bras, trays with herring, a live policeman, seemingly transported from the street into the theater, the hawkers running from him into the crowd, the middle-class woman buying fish, outraged that the fish in the State store is shorter by a tail than the one being sold privately, car horns, noise, shouts..."[12]

Meyerhold brought curiously-dressed dealers in all sorts of items together in this crowd. Some with books, others with balloons, perfume. These dealers appeared from behind the wings, straight from the audience, from behind the department store windows, in the balcony boxes, and they ran away in all directions when the policeman appeared, and then again crawled out from everywhere. Among them there was, of course, a Chinese selling colored fans and noisemakers. This entire opulent picture preceded the majestic entrance by Prisypin, Rozalia Pavlovna and Bayan. Ilinsky, in his own words, played Prisypkin as a "monumental laggard and boor." The actor "stressed the broad stride, gave a dull, cretin-like expression to the monumental face, placed his feet a bit crookedly... Impressiveness became self-satisfaction, certainty—self-assured aplomb, opaque arrogance."[13] M. Zagorsky described Ilinsky's Prisypkin as follows: "His lower lip is thick and hangs down, his eyes are like slits, narrow and arrogant, a fat little belly, fat rear, highly unpleasant voice that squeaks and grunts."[14] In the debate caused by the premiere of *The Bedbug*, Ilinsky's success was admitted by everyone—even by D. Talnikov, who was not at all well disposed toward Mayakovsky.

Only S. Mokulsky was disturbed by the "soft, jesting manner" of Ilinsky's performance, and, moreover, by the circumstance that some critics compared Ilinsky "with S. Kuznetsov in the part of Sailor Shvandi in *Lyubov Yarovaya,* i.e., with a clearly positive character."[15] Ilinsky performed Prisypkin coarsely and roughly—there was no reason to speak of the softness of his performance. As for the comparisons with Shvandi, these were quite logical. Previously, Prisypkin had been a "brother." The dashing soldier of the Civil War defending his right to "hegemony" becomes a militant bourgeois—this is what Mayakovsky saw and why he connected the victorious boor Prisypkin with Rozalia Pavlovna and Bayan.

All three—Prisypkin, Bayan, and Rozalia—were dressed richly and bore themselves grandly. Meyerhold staged them in the first episode in such a way that Prisypkin and Rozalia Pavlovna moved almost not at all. They stood next to each other, a monumental pair: Prisypkin in a good brown coat and a traveling cap perched jauntily on his head, and Madame Renaissance in a little claret-colored hat with pearls, in a black silk overcoat with a gray fox collar. The hawkers came up to them with their wares, one after another. But Bayan, quick, flexible, in a short half-coat and checkered pants, dived into the crowd at once and thoughtfully maneuvered between the buyers and sellers. He was dynamism incarnate, obsequious dynamism serving the majestic stasis of Prisypkin and Rozalia. The dramatic scene with Zoya Beryozkina introduced into the lively color of the episode a sudden rhythmic disharmony so characteristic of Meyerhold's works. It sounded nervous, painful, a brief woman's cry immediately muffled by Prisypkin's arrogant voice.

The second episode, "Don't Move Your Lower Bust," was for Bayan-Temerin. The dancing lesson ("foxtrot teaching attraction") was performed as a quite crude farce. But Meyerhold was unable to assimilate the remainder of the Young Communist workers' text, which was weakly written by Mayakovsky.

Subsequently, when considering a new edition of *The Bedbug*, Meyerhold admitted that in the dormitory scene he "presented a sort of standard of behavior for the young... This, probably, is tradition, that when youth is on stage we must certainly jump, leap, laugh. This tradition probably leaked through to us... It is awful, like Kirshon or Shkvarkin."[16] And so it developed. Meyerhold's imagination limited itself to one happy trick: Locksmith (V. Egorychev) returning from work, undressed to the waist, washed, then suddenly turned to the audience—all soaped up. Then he daubed the foam on the other fellows.

But in the episode "Street Cars Gathered at the Marriage Registry," the episode of the "Red marriage," Meyerhold's imagination went wild. The director created a bourgeois bacchanal in which numerous mute characters participated—waiters, lackeys, barbers, guests—in addition to the ones mentioned by Mayakovsky. "Strive for the stilted," Meyerhold told his actors, "artificial primness, artificial nobility, artificial importance, artificial worldliness... It is necessary for the spectator leaving the show to offer resistance to all the old, the brutish, the retarded, and the bedbug-like in life."[17] Each line became cause for an entire pantomime scene—the slightly smelly ham of Rozalia Pavlovna, each toast, each exclamation of "bitter!" First one, then another character, received a solo part in the highly complicated director's score and took upon himself the entire attention of the auditorium.

A. Kostomolotsky performed an entire number as an old, bent-over and glum waiter who served ham to the guests. A. Kelberer as best man caused consternation in the over-all atmosphere of sated self-satisfaction with his scream, "Who said mother!" The sudden totally Satanic assault by the barber (M. Kirillov) with fork in hand on the seated mother increased the confusion. The collapse began.

But Bayan sat down at the piano, and music again gave the action a presentable form. Prisypkin in a black suit, white shirt with blue flowers, and a bright bow at his neck, danced majestically with his bride on the proscenium. His black hand moved steadily down along the snow-white dress. Prisypkin, smacking his lips with pleasure, pinched his bride. She began to beat his face with her fan. A fight began between Bayan and the best man, who was demanding that the former play on the white keys only. The best man beat Bayan over the head with a guitar, Prisypkin beat the accountant with a fish, the barber was invading the mother's tangled hair, someone turned over the stove, drunken voices began to sing. The fight expanded to the entire stage, at which point a tall tongue of flame came out from the piano. An instant later fire raged everywhere and cries of "Fire!" "We're burning!" resounded.

After a brief scene with the firemen, there was a stormy, grotesque musical interlude by Shostakovich. In it was the theme of the foxtrot that Bayan had just been playing, but this theme was devoured quickly by wild, unthinkable collisions between ever-stronger sounds.

The comical element in Shostakovich's rough and explosive music obtained the form of a stormy, gloomy cacaphony. Shostakovich's interlude bisected the show. The fantastic second part began.

In some works by scholars of theater it can be read that Meyerhold "did not find the correct approach to the interpretation" of the second part of the comedy, that the picture of the future was distorted by the stage design, in which "abstractions of a Constructivist-Futurist sort were partially reborn." This opinion finds support in Meyerhold's own words. Eight years later, he said that in his production "the contours of the future were not yet felt in all their concreteness..."[18] But many reviewers of the premiere believed that the second half of the show was better than the first.

Some solutions by Meyerhold in the second half of the show were undoubtedly successful. The triumphantly staged thawing out of Prisypkin was one such success. In the center of a silver stage on a sterile-white bed, surrounded by six doctors in white coats, the sleeping Prisypkin under the glass bell appeared as a lonely black smudge. Devices, dials, buttons, switches, glimmered behind him. The procedure was being directed by an impassive professor, also dressed in white. Upon his command, switches were thrown, bells rung, lights flashed. Prisypkin was dragged out, placed facing the audience, massaged and rubbed down. He was immobile. Finally, the first movement took place. Prisypkin suddenly raised his arm holding the guitar, stretched luxuriously, squinted, then opened his eyes and asked in a sleepy, normal voice, "Which precinct is this?"

Then Ilinsky had a magnificent number with a little bedbug that elicited the applause and laughter of the audience each time. There was the even more successful final scene in the cage. M. Zagorsky, commenting on this scene, wrote: "Ilinsky, while sitting in his cage, drinks vodka and smokes a cigarette, and immediately after the 'number,' makes an elegant circus gesture with his hand. In this desultory wave of the hand I sensed a tinge of contempt for the people who dared to put a— however retarded, bourgeois, but living, devil take it—man in a cage next to a bedbug for study and observation..."[19]

Zagorsky's astute observation was evidence that in the late 1920s the reception was not without complications for this stinging satire by Mayakovsky and Meyerhold—the two people least inclined to see the human in Prisypkin "living, devil take it." In many reviews of *The Bedbug* the poster-like directness of the play was criticized. The magazine *The New Spectator* complained that Mayakovsky "does not recognize psychology and other such things (!) that require a serious and in-depth approach to a work of art."[20] The more sober and substantial magazine *Theatrical Life (Zhizn' iskusstva)* ferociously called the comedy "clearly written in haste, a topical satire," "literary hack-work," and "a flat visual concoction," in an article by D. Talnikov.[21]

Totally different opinions were expressed, too. *The Bedbug* was the subject of arguments, perhaps not as heated as those about *The Inspector General*, say, but still sufficiently lively. V. Gorodinsky, who had come to Moscow from Leningrad to begin his work on the magazine *The Worker's Theater (Rabochii teatr)*, began his article with the words: "The first Muscovite theater-goer that met me, after the required questions about the cold in Leningrad, immediately asked: 'Have you seen *The Bedbug*?' Huge verbal battles are taking place because of *The Bedbug*. For *The Bedbug* or against *The Bedbug*? It is practically the question 'what is your religion?' "

V. M. Gorodinsky himself voted a decisive "for." He wrote: "Never yet has the image of a being who has completely lost all indications of social existence revealed such an unusual sharpness and such truly monstrous reality... Meyerhold's theater staged the entire scope of the problem of the infectiousness of the bourgeois spirit and signalled danger." Therefore, concluded the critic, "we are bold enough to state in conclusion that *The Bedbug* is one of the most brilliant productions in the current theater."[22]

The categorical tone of this review was the logical consequence of the "verbal battles" that raged around *The Bedbug*. Many things came together into a single, complex knot of problems. What came under question was the very possibility of, or rather the appropriateness of, poster-like, militant satire. Mayakovsky's satire did not accord with the RAPP* theory of the "living man," in accordance with which it was necessary to use the dialectic method to reveal the "conflict of contradictions" in each character. His desire to "say straight out who the rat is" was out of step. Meanwhile, RAPP had already seized key positions in literature, and the persecution of Mayakovsky had already begun. Furthermore, the very urge on the part of Meyerhold and Mayakovsky to criticize the petty-bourgeois spirit caused resistance, muffled, not overt, but very insistent. The bourgeois spirit was becoming more deeply ingrained and was reaching higher positions; already it was dictating its requirements to art. (Mayakovsky knew this, of course, when he depicted Bayan in *The Bedbug* and when he devoted *The Bathhouse* to this expansion of the petty-bourgeois into the sphere of art.) Therefore, the intention of protecting the bourgeois spirit from the blow became the common theme of all the articles whose authors were discomfited or annoyed by *The Bedbug*. Naturally, no one came to the direct defense of the bourgeois. However, the thought that Mayakovsky had depicted "the wrong" bourgeois, that he had directed his fire in "the wrong" direction, migrated through the articles.

Even before the premiere of *The Bedbug*, on the day that Mayakovsky read his play in the theater and the Artistic Soviet unanimously passed a resolution calling

*RAPP *(Rossiiskaia assotsiatsiia proletarskikh pistelei).* Founded in 1925 "to solidify the positions of proletarian writers." Mayakovsky joined in 1930–*(G. P.).*

the play a "highly significant work of Soviet dramaturgy," *Evening Moscow* stated that "in the lobby the need for discussion" had become obvious.

> In one of the upper rooms of the theater where some of those present at the reading had gathered, differences of opinion came up. Here there were differences of opinion about the play. B. Gusman, T. Kostrov, O. Litovsky and others indicated quite correctly a number of substantial deficiencies in the comedy. Mayakovsky has drawn a type of petty-bourgeois of, so to speak, "prewar quality"—the eternal bourgeois. This bourgeois should have been presented not only in everyday surroundings, but in his relationship to the collective, to political and social questions. It was necessary to show the particular features of the contemporary bourgeois.[23]

It was precisely this motif that subsequently was developed broadly in some reviews. The reviewer from *The New Spectator* asserted:

> The author's little ideas seem petty and insignificant in our day and, in any case, they are not those with which one must enter the theater to do battle with the bourgeois spirit. In the spreading growth of the bourgeois—a consequence of the zigzags in our political and economic situation, the result of increased class conflict in our Union—there are aspects and elements that are more in need of a blow than those that Mayakovsky attempts to attack. If only for this reason, the author's blast may turn out to be cannonfire at sparrows.[24]

S. Mokulsky continued the same basic line of thought. Mayakovsky, he wrote, "followed the line of least resistance... If the author wanted to take aim at the bourgeois [who is] dangerous to the work of building Socialism, then he ought to seek out another model."[25]

I. Turkeltaub agreed, commenting that "Mayakovsky's scope is correct," but "Prisypkin's existence is small change and not so terribly dangerous to the Revolution... *The Bedbug* clearly misses the target and becomes elementary even for a young Pioneer."[26]

Echoing the reviews in which the "harmless" Prisypkin was generously pushed back into the past, B. Alpers wrote that in *The Bedbug* "the contemporary bourgeois reveals certain traits that are timeless. A multiple *artificial enlargement* of the represented fact takes place. Instead of an everyday social phenomenon, defined according to class, typical only for a given, relatively brief segment of time, he becomes a fact of general human history that characterizes an indefinitely wide historical period."[27]

These words ought to be listened to. They appear to give in condensed form the main objections to Mayakovsky's satire. You say that "theater is not a mirror but a magnifying glass"? You must not *artificially magnify* the facts that are represented. Unpleasant phenomena of "everyday social life" are typical *only* for a "relatively short segment of time" and, accordingly, must be presented as the *specific*.

The very principle of satirical generalization and, moreover, satirical hyperbole, was rejected.

Satire was not appropriate to the time. For a brief but highly important period the esthetic platform of RAPP became dominant, "dialectically" combining the appearance of verisimilitude with an in-depth and concentrated criticism of individual, single carriers of imperfection. The famous RAPP bludgeon was militant in bringing order and peace to literature.

To the constant drumbeat of criticism, quiet, thoughtful pseudo-psychology held sway, which helped depict "the enemy" as an individual, psychologically imperfect and under the influence of bourgeois ideology—hence, an irrelevant sort, to be extracted by the roots.

Averbakh's and Ermilov's theory of "living man" essentially refused art the right to social generalization. War was declared on popular sociology, but this war was carried on not only against popular, but against all sociology, all attempts to think on the scale of the whole society.

It is clear that under such conditions, people did not wish to accept Prisypkin as a real danger. It is also comprehensible why the super-Red reviews that told Mayakovsky to find a "new model" struck very severe, metallic notes. The author of one of the reviews mentioned in passing that in Mayakovsky's comedy "the very representation of the people of the society of the future gives off a highly unpleasant, I am ready to say anti-soviet, air. These people all have one face, are dressed in identical costumes, are dry, impersonal, mechanized, automatic... Mayakovsky's socialism is the socialism of vegetarians and dried-up people." Furthermore, Mayakovsky's fantasy was equated with the works of "bourgeois authors writing nasty pamphlets about the Socialist order." It was stressed particularly that "in this case Mayakovsky is not joking, since the people of the future order are not the objects of his satire at all. Evidently *this* is precisely the way he imagines this system. But in this case his play becomes highly dubious from the Soviet point of view. This is the talented poet's usual *boutade*, which has brought him to a clear ideological breakdown."[28]

The critic was misled by his own lack of humor: when drawing the picture of the future, Mayakovsky undoubtedly was joking, and he even warned that "of course I am not showing a socialist society."[29] Meyerhold joked, too, merrily improvising on "the theme of the future." Later, when Mayakovsky was proclaimed "the best and most talented," and Meyerhold "alien to the people," the experienced hack critics easily reoriented themselves to the new situation and described the matter as follows: Mayakovsky created an inspired picture of a beautiful future, while Meyerhold distorted it, perverted it and infused it with that "anti-Soviet air" for which the poet had been blasted earlier.

All this, however, still was far ahead. In 1929-30 Mayakovsky and Meyerhold stood together firmly, met the attacks of the critics together, and answered together by staging *The Bathhouse*. Mayakovsky's new comedy delighted Meyerhold even more than the just-opened *Bedbug*. At a meeting in the theater on September 23, 1929, Meyerhold said:

the theatrical phantasmagoria which comes so easily to Mayakovsky makes him a playwright, not the composer of *agitki*, but a playwright of true popular comedy, and he speaks in an extremely accessible tongue. He provides jests that make the average spectator, any worker, smile. These jests of his will really be exciting and hit home... In the history of the theater only one playwright—Molière—had access to the lightness with which this play is written... If I were asked, what is this play? An event or not an event? I would say, with emphasis: this is the greatest event in the history of Russian theater, this is an event of the first magnitude, and we must, first of all, salute Mayakovsky the poet, who has managed to present us with a sample of prose crafted with the same mastery as his verse. To create, to heap up the verbal material as Mayakovsky has done! I listen to his prose, which touches our times—what language he uses!

Meyerhold went on to mention Pushkin and Gogol. Unlike many of his contemporaries, he was certain that when he was working with Mayakovsky, he was working with a genius.

After a series of productions of Russian classical plays, Meyerhold perceived Mayakovsky's comedies as the direct development of great literary and theatrical traditions. The capacity of the satirical images, the broad generalizations, the expressive coining of speech—all this in Meyerhold's eyes gave Mayakovsky's works the attributes of world significance. The director saw them as the direct continuation—using modern material—of those creative ideas that were tested in his *Inspector General* and *Woe to Wit*. Meyerhold angrily rejected any thoughts of making any corrections or putting any finishing touches on *The Bathhouse*. "To suggest to Comrade Mayakovsky that he alter this work is the equivalent of spitting into a well of good-smelling, wonderful liquid. I think with horror that I as director will have to touch this work... There is nothing to correct in this work... The play must go on the way it is written."[30]

Meyerhold's delight with *The Bathhouse* was inflamed further because this comedy presented an angry satirical rebuttal by himself and Mayakovsky against their common foes in art. In *The Bathhouse*, Mayakovsky took up the defense of Meyerhold's theatrical ideas during a very critical period for the director, and carried out this defense with a flourish that was unthinkable and unreachable for Meyerhold.

As a polemicist, Meyerhold bore no comparison with Mayakovsky. Too often, he gave in to personal dislikes for his opponents, readily tore the weapons of demagoguery from their hands, used the newspaper slogans of the day with alacrity, and was much more sure in protecting himself with a loud phrase than in defending his actual ideals, tastes and convictions. Therefore, the speeches and articles by Meyerhold that have come to us from his Soviet years speak more of the conditions under which they were enunciated than of his artistic efforts, discoveries and convictions. *The Bathhouse*, however, was a sort of esthetic manifesto signed by Meyerhold with a firm hand.

The significance of the fundamental joint declaration by Mayakovsky and Meyerhold lay, first of all, in the program scene in the theater (the third act of *The Bathhouse*). Here, satirically presented, consciously made stupid, set up for ridicule and derision, were those same claims with which Meyerhold had always been pestered: "unnatural, unlifelike, unlikely"; those demands with which he had been nagged: "This needs reworking, softening, poeticizing, rounding-off... You must caress my ear, not agitate it, your task is to caress the eye, not to agitate. Yes, yes, caress..."

In the world of art in the late 1920s, Mayakovsky, with the clarity of genius, saw the germination of those tastes that would flower a decade and a half later. "But of course," said Mezalyansova, "art must depict beautiful life, beautiful living people." Ivan Ivanovich echoed her: "Yes, yes! Make it beautiful for us! They always make it beautiful in the Bolshoi Theater. Did you see *The Red Poppy*? I saw *The Red Poppy*. Incredibly interesting! Various elves and...sylphs flutter around everywhere with flowers, they sing and dance." Along with the Bolshoi Theater, where things were "made beautiful," the Art Theater, too, was ridiculed. "Yes, yes, yes! Have you seen *Squaring the Cherry?*   And I was at *The Uncle of the Turbins*. Unusually interesting." Mayakovsky ironically equated *The Cherry Orchard* with *The Squaring of the Circle, Uncle Vanya* with *Days of the Turbins*. He wished to say in this manner that time was passing but the Art Theater was not changing; it was remaining a theater of Chekhovian intonations. On this point he was incorrect. It could more readily be said, and many said so loudly, that the forms of propaganda theater were lagging behind life and were already in contradiction to it.

But the large scene in the theater contained not only laughter at those theaters where things were "made beautiful." It also contained a parody of the *agitka*. The Director (a character in *The Bathhouse*): commanded: "Free male characters—to the stage! Stand on one knee and bend over, looking oppressed. Chop at invisible coal with an invisible pick. Faces, faces more gloomy... The dark forces are oppressing you savagely... Stand over here, Comrade Capital. Dance over everyone with a look of class supremacy."

This farce said directly and clearly that propaganda art had become speculative art, that in place of high-minded naivete and the rough revolutionary pathos of Civil War days, there was now cynical adaptability whose essence was also petty bourgeois and whose inspiration was the same slogan of "Make it beautiful for us." Mayakovsky retained no illusions on this score. His parody concluded thus: "Wave around imaginary garlands of workers of the universal great army of labor, symbolizing the flowers of happiness that bloom under Socialism. Good! If you please! Ready!"

"If you please!"—this lackey's expression summarized the entire esthetic program remaining in the *agitki* in the late 1920s.

A year before *The Bathhouse,* Bulgakov had written his parody *The Crimson Island,* which was produced by Tairov.

Bulgakov attacked the tasteless *agitka*, joked at the standard division of characters into "Whites" and "Reds," made fun of the cynicism and venality of theater operators.

Bulgakov's parody placed the eternal "magic" of true theater in contrast. Neither Mayakovsky nor Meyerhold could be inspired by this program, indifferent to politics and to radical social change. They both sought other answers. Mayakovsky wrote slogans for *The Bathhouse* in the spirit of the famous ROSTA windows. These slogans again blasted "drivelling psychology," art that depicted "apartment-cages," and again proposed to replace "MKhAT's" (Moscow Art Theaters) with "mass action." Mayakovsky anathematized the Art, the Bolshoi, and the Kamerny theaters, demanded "to shake individuals out of priests' robes." The thundering slogans were reminiscent of the terminology and emotion of the forever departed days of the Theatrical October.

Costume sketches for two street
vendors and Bayan (Kukryniksy).
Below: Meyerhold rehearsing *The
Bedbug* with Ilinsky, Bogolyubov,
and Remizova.

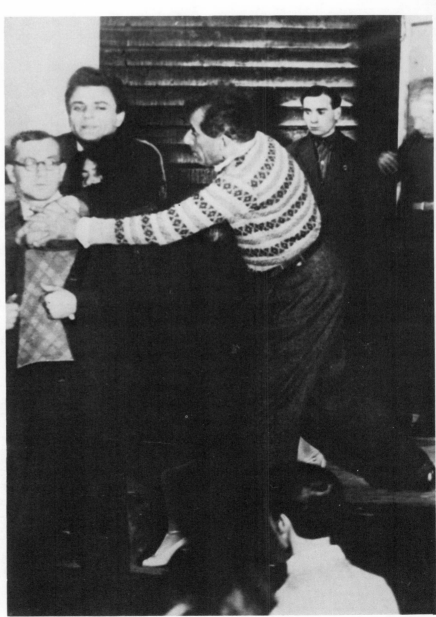

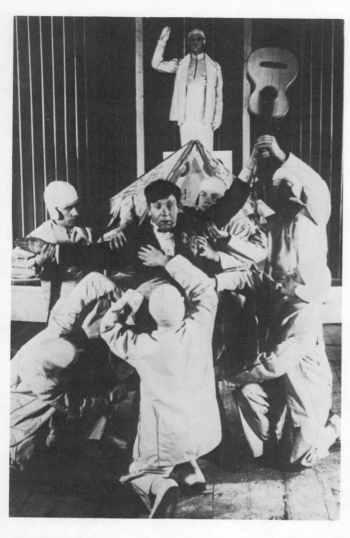

Scenes from *The Bedbug* with
Ilinsky as Prysypkin

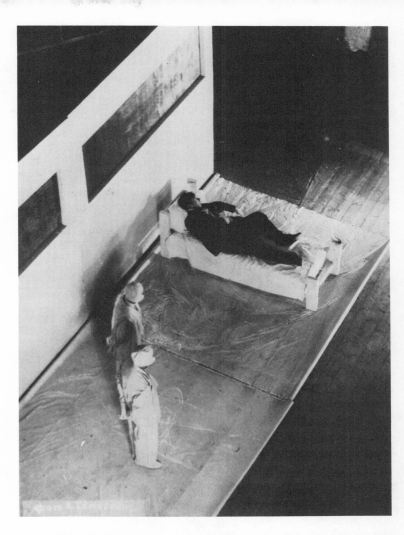

Scenes from *The Bedbug*, Ilinsky as Prisypkin

Ilinsky as Prisypkin

Ilinsky as Prysypkin in *The Bedbug*

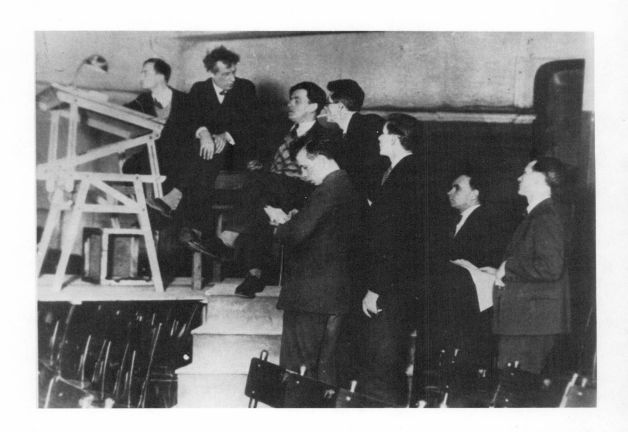

Rehearsal for *The Bathhouse*, Meyerhold talking to Mayakovsky
and the composer V. Ya. Shebalin

The Bathhouse, Act I, Velosipedkin and Chudakov (Chikul)

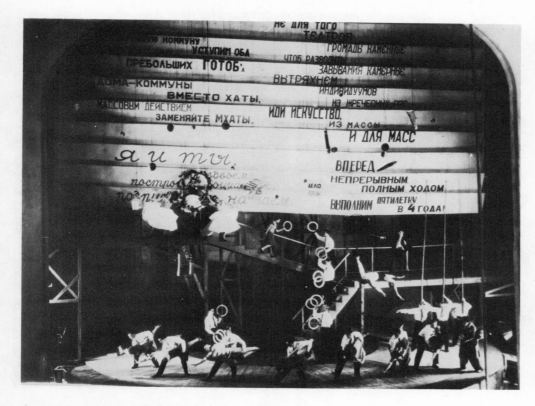

The Bathhouse, the moveable slat screens with changing slogans, such as:
"Communes instead of huts," "Forward, full speed ahead," "We'll do
the 5-year plan in 4 years," etc.

The Bathhouse, Shtraukh (seated) as Pobedonosikov

Pobedonosikov and the Phosphorescent Woman (Raikh)

Scene from *The Bathhouse*

Scenes with the Phosphorescent Woman (Zinaida Raikh)

The Bathhouse

El Lissitsky's set construction for the unfinished production of "I Want a Child" by Tretyakov. *Left to right:* A. Milman, Meyerhold, P. Tsetnerovich, I. Maltsiu

Scenes from Bezymensky's *The Shot*

"Everything is just as it was many years ago," a melancholy Alpers observed. "Meyerhold battles with the *akas*—in ballet and opera—and with the Art Theater, lowering from the gridirons in *The Bathhouse* enormous placards with poisoned but belated arrows of epigrams and angry slogans."[31]

This, however, was not the only problem. The question naturally arose: if the Art, The Bolshoi, the Kamerny and all theaters in general, where things were "made beautiful," were bad, if the "psychology" of individuals living in "apartment-cages" was unnecessary to anyone, while "mass action," praised in slogans and parodied in *The Bathhouse* itself, had degenerated to the ridiculous, then what direction was the theater of Meyerhold and Mayakovsky proposing?

The answer was given in a quatrain:

> Place the projectors,
>   so the footlights do not dim.
> Roll it,
>   so the action
>   rushes, and does not flow.
> Theater
>   is not a reflecting mirror,
> but—
>   a magnifying glass.

These lines have become standard reference and have become obscured by constant quoting. Nonetheless, it is easy to imagine Meyerhold's delight with this ringing formula, which appeared to condense wthin itself the many years of his directing experience. In those days, Mayakovsky said: "Theater has forgotten that it is spectacle. We do not know how to use this spectacle for our propaganda. The attempt to return spectacle to theater, the attempt to make the stageboards a platform—this is the essence of my theatrical work." He added: "Therefore, I gave *The Bathhouse* to the most effective, the most publicistic, Meyerhold."[32]

It is important, however, to grasp the main point: how, exactly, did Mayakovsky propose to reach his goals and to use theater again "for our agitation," to "make the stageboards a platform" again? What, specifically, did the principle of the "magnifying glass" mean?

By comparing *The Bedbug* and *The Bathhouse* even with *Mystery-Bouffe*, we easily discover in Mayakovsky's new comedies new means of expression. Agitation is understood in a different way, and other things are said from the "platform." In place of the social masks of *Mystery-Bouffe*, its allegories and relativistically depicted characters are monumental, large-scale social types—Prisypkin, Bayan, Pobedonosnikov, Optimistenko and others, thoroughly characterized, captured with all their specific lifelike qualities and, in the words of one of the poet's most ferocious enemies of the day, V. Ermilov, "giganticized." Satirical hyperbole in these new comedies by Mayakovsky dealt with the highly specific material of present-day reality. Figures familiar to all came under the "magnifying glass." The poet dragged them onto the stage together with their environment, ridiculed their attitudes and habits, their system of demagoguery and adaptability.

In other words, along with their rejection of the degenerated *agitki* of War

Communism days, Mayakovsky and Meyerhold sought and found new forms of contemporary political and propaganda theater. They rebuilt connections with the traditions of satires by Griboedov, Gogol, Shchedrin. In *The Bedbug* and *The Bathhouse*, they replaced the principle of social masks with the principle of substantial and multifaceted satirical attack on social types hostile to the moral standards and ideals of the new society. In "giganticizing" these hostile forces and using all the means of stage expression to indicate the social evil, they both were utterly unwilling to state that the danger they saw was easy to overcome. The fact that in *The Bedbug* and *The Bathhouse* the liberation from the Prisypkins and the Pobedonosnikovs was connected with the hope for the people of a distant future, with the theme of fantasy and social Utopia, is highly significant. The technique of shifting the action into the future allowed an assured removal of optimistic prognosis to "outside the parentheses" of modernity and permitted a relativistic elimination of contradictions, in place of their resolution in the dramatic struggle of the present day. Mayakovsky successfully used such a technique when writing *The Bedbug*, his comedy of the bourgeoisie. He repeated this technique in *The Bathhouse*, his comedy of the bureaucracy.

However, even before Meyerhold staged the production, *The Bathhouse* was subjected to furious criticism. On February 6, 1930, RAPP critics spoke out against Mayakovsky's comedy. "Mayakovsky," recalled one of the former directors of RAPP, Yu. Libedinsky, in the 1950s, "criticized us for 'psychology,' and we him for reducing the tasks of art to the *agitka* and poster." It was supposed that since the poet had joined RAPP he would have to subordinate his art to the principles of the then all-powerful organization. Meanwhile, the satire of *The Bathhouse* was in total discord with the RAPP theory of "living man" and the RAPP theatrical program in general.

Although the members of RAPP did not say so directly, satire did not fit into their theory at all. Therefore, articles immediately appeared, indicating that Mayakovsky again had selected the wrong target and was attacking an unreal danger. "It seemed to us then," admitted Libedinsky, "that Mayakovsky, stressing in the play *The Bedbug* 'the problem of the exposure of today's petty-bourgeoisie,' was exaggerating, that the bourgeoisie was finished. Today it is evident that we were wrong in this matter, that Mayakovsky was correct."[33]

The matter was the same in the case of the bureaucracy to which *The Bathhouse* was dedicated. One of the active members of RAPP, V. Druzin, wrote in 1929 about both of Mayakovsky's plays:

> The satirical representation of the bourgeois *(The Bedbug)* and the bureaucrat *(The Bathhouse)* must be recognized as petty. Such a stupid, cheap bourgeois and the equally overdrawn bureaucrat are unlikely and, probably, do not deserve combat. The real enemies of the new life are more subtle, more intelligent and more harmful. And the battle with them must utilize finer, more profound means—not sliding along the surface but cutting into the root. Mayakovsky's buffoonery, despite its unquestionable cleverness, misses the target.[34]

V. Ermilov stated that in *The Bathhouse* there sounded a false "leftist note," that in Pobedonosnikov Mayakovsky had presented the invented figure of a "degenerate Party man" and, worse yet, "giganticizes Pobedonosikovism to such an extent that it ceases to express anything concrete. . . . Pobedonosnikov's entire figure," he continued, "is intolerably off-key. Such a clean, smooth, completely 'faultless' bureaucrat, a cad, a complete scoundrel . . . is incredibly schematic and unlikely."[35]

All this sounded sufficiently threatening. Meyerhold rushed to defend the play. "Where did V. Ermilov get this, that Mayakovsky supposedly shows a Party degenerate in Pobedonosikov?" Meyerhold asked naively, but scarcely sincerely... "V. Mayakovsky masterfully shows in his play the tragic conflict between a worker-inventor and bureaucracy, red tape and narrow-mindedness."

But it was not so easy to stop Ermilov. He cited a string of extremely convincing quotes from the play "indicating that we are dealing precisely with Party degeneracy" and then spoke

> to the point, about the figure of Pobedonosikov. Judging by Comrade Meyerhold's comment, in the show he will not be portrayed as a specific carrier of that phenomenon that we call Party degeneracy. This is good and bad. Good, because in the way that he is presented in the printed fragment of the play, he is distinguished by an element of falsity that keeps him from becoming a fully convincing carrier of this phenomenon. Bad, because self-criticism "without respect of persons" requires great courage on the part of theater and only some theatrical officials, unfortunately, still sitting in our theatrical bureaus, managing and coordinating, could have objected to the need to subject this figure, too, to public ridicule. But theater must not be pointlessly "brave." It must be capable of demonstrating specific social phenomena, it must not go off tilting at windmills, must not exchange concrete social categories for abstract ones.[36]

A joyless situation ensued. It became clear that the RAPP critics stubbornly refused to take note of the new esthetic discoveries being offered by Mayakovsky, that it was precisely the generality, the capacity of the images in *The Bathhouse*, that was perceived as a flaw. Behind all of Ermilov's loud phrases there remained concealed one thought, highly characteristic of RAPP "devices": it is permitted to criticize and satirically expose only concrete and individual failings. Any generalization is an error (later called slander). While calling for bravery, Ermilov pushed toward cowardice.

However, his phrase about tilting at windmills signified that Ermilov knew whom he was dealing with. With true Quixotic abandon, both Mayakovsky and Meyerhold stubbornly ignored the specific circumstances of the day, including Ermilov's articles, and continued to prepare their show. Work on the play continued with many difficulties. Mayakovsky wanted Ilinsky to play Pobedonosikov, but Ilinsky did not like *The Bathhouse* and passed up the role, to his subsequent regret. The main role was given to M. Shtraukh. The decorators for the show, S. Vakhtangov and A. Deineka (who prepared the costumes and makeup), worked under the direct supervision of Meyerhold himself. His dream was that the construction would combine "static striving upward" and "kinetic force." This combination should be the result of "specially constructed scaffolding."[37]

The final staging was simple but not particularly expressive. The heavy bureaucratic comfort of Pobedonosikov's office, with its enormous leather chair and numerous telephones, was contrasted to a light staircase with three flights which the heroes ascended to the future; the very modern and very well-cut suits of the bureaucratic officials were contrasted to the overalls of the inventors, and the tights and aviator's helmet of the Phosphorescent Woman (Zinaida Raikh); the bureaucratic prose of the present was contrasted to the fantasy and poetry of the future. Meyerhold was unable to construct a "time machine." Effects were required which his impoverished theater was in no condition to demonstrate. (This is probably the reason why Mayakovsky indicated in his text that Chudakov, Dvoikin and Troikin bring in an "invisible machine"). The actors regretted this. M. Sukhanova, for instance, wrote: "The time machine was to have thrown out the bureaucrats, headed by the chief high leader Pobedonosikov, and that would have put a period on the finale. But this was not contained in the prop design. Everyone went upward somewhere on the construction, with suitcases and bags, and the spectator could not understand what was happening. This was a great omission."[38]

The idea of the design was similar to that of *The Bedbug*. The acting was less successful, although Mayakovsky expressed another opinion in a letter to Lily Brik. "With exception of details," he wrote, "I liked my first stage work. Shtraukh is excellent. The spectators are amusingly divided—one side says: we were never so bored; the others: we never had so much fun. There is no way to know what else they will say and write."[39] Later, however, according to the testimony of Sukhanova, Mayakovsky "said that the show was a flop. He was unsettled, gloomy, and those eyes which could look at a person as though they saw everything right through him no longer looked at anyone. Now he often would not even answer questions and would leave. It seemed to us that he was unhappy at the press response to *The Bathhouse*..."[40]

The press for *The Bathhouse*, first performed on March 16, 1930, really was bad, and poisoned the last days of the poet's life. Generally, the initial feeling of happiness that had begun to appear in Mayakovsky dissipated quickly. The show brought him many disappointments.

Among the slogans written by Mayakovsky for *The Bathhouse* was one in which it was stated that "bureaucrats are aided by the pens of critics like Ermilov..." Following the dress rehearsal, the directors of RAPP suggested that Mayakovsky remove this slogan. He obeyed. But in his last letter he recalled the incident: "Tell Ermilov that it's too bad I took down the slogan—I should have finished cursing."

There were various critical remarks concerning the play, but the reviews mostly echoed the RAPP theme that Mayakovsky's satire was missing the target, that the "plan of bureaucracy is taken outside class struggle and concrete mechanics of construction," etc.[41]

Another quite different system of objections was also developed on a wide scale. The reviewer for the magazine *Workers' Theater* (probably V. Blyum) did not believe that the satire in *The Bathhouse* was poorly aimed. On the contrary, he asserted: "The propaganda battering-ram of *The Bathhouse* is directed against bureaucracy in Soviet offices. The object of Mayakovsky's satire has been fixed in the language, the daily language of all these inky *glavnachpups* Pobedonosikovs and their secretaries, the Optimistenkos. Just by using the style of that language, Mayakovsky sticks his victims on pins, hangs them from nails and plays with them like rubber dolls."

The critic, however, believed the entire theatrical nature of the work to be archaic. He asserted:

> Mayakovsky's *Bathhouse* can only be perceived as a belated demonstration of the *agitka* that has missed "the passage of time." That blue-bloused design lies naked at the very basis of this slogan-ruffled attraction-style "drama with circus and fireworks." The production of *The Bathhouse* is designed in that jesting, farcical, clowning manner that always was the right hand of the *agitka*, invariably accompanying its enthusiasm for exposure. But the modern spectator receives such an *agitka-bouffe* coldly and inattentively. A fundamental lack of ideological nourishment has led to its drying up. The clowning has ceased to amuse, the *agitka*—to propagandize. Both, in their present thinness, offer to theater only their external "biomechanics": for this reason actors are sometimes replaced by dolls; *glavnachpups*-es, accenting the eccentric, are stretched like rubber, secretaries tootle on a broken-in pipe as if it were a brass fife, inventors in standardized costumes demonstrate their athletic, sometimes immodest feats, ordinary people prepare to ride a "time machine" to socialism with a live chicken "for supplies," phosphorescent women flash in music-hall costumes, and at necessary moments a revolving platform comes to the aid of all this commotion in order to move it from episode to episode, since the commotion itself has nowhere to go.[42]

The most unpleasant aspect for Mayakovsky and Meyerhold was, undoubtedly, the fact that the critics missed the esthetic innovation of the play and stubbornly pushed *The Bathhouse* into the past, to the times of the *agitki* and the blue blouse.

M. Zagorsky, writing in *Literary Gazette* combined into a sort of whole the two main criticisms of the show: our bureaucrats are not like this, and the esthetic system is obsolete. He inquired: "Who could recognize in this dressy, talkative Pobedonosikov our clever, self-effacing, working bureaucrat? However brilliantly he may be played by Shtraukh, an exceptional artist of the clown school of acting, he waves his arms at emptiness, at nothing, because no one in the auditorium believes in the possibility of this mask in our situation." He warned about "combining in a single show two totally different stage genres—the satirical and the Utopian-fantastic. The typical, everyday, earthly Optimistenko in *The Bathhouse* eats whole the contrived, squeezed-out 'phosphorescent' woman of the future..." He sighed about "how meager is the work of such an astonishing master as Meyerhold this time."[43]

"A tedious, confused show, which can be interesting only to a small group of literary epicures,"[44] concluded the review in *Workers' Gazette (Rabochaia gazeta)*, cruelly.

Although RAPP's attempts to place in doubt the appropriateness and the direction of Mayakovsky's satire appear today as, at the very least, comical, the question of the new interrelations between the theatrical art of Mayakovsky and Meyerhold and the time after the "year of the great break" is far from simple.

The new forms of political theater proposed by Mayakovsky and Meyerhold in *The Bedbug* and *The Bathhouse* were neither understood nor even noticed by the critics. The fear of wide generalizations, of hyperbole and of satire in general, became epidemic.

Satire evoked irritation—this comes through in practically all the reviews of the stagings of *The Bedbug* and *The Bathhouse*. Good reviews were given only to the fairly wretched satirical play *The Shot*, by A. Bezymensky, staged in the GOSTIM under Meyerhold's supervision by V. Zaichikov, S. Kozikov, A. Nesterov and F. Bondarenko (the premiere was on December 19, 1929).

The fate of Nikolai Erdman's *The Suicide* is characteristic—a talented satirical play that simultaneously interested Meyerhold and Stanislavsky. Both theaters energetically began rehearsals, and Meyerhold, unhappy that he was not the only one to have this comedy, even challenged the Art Theater to a Socialist competition. He said:

> Despite the fact that I have a contract here for this play, Markov* has done everything possible to obtain it. But, comrades, he's bitten off more than he can chew (laughter, applause). I am making a statement which I cannot make in print, since I hope that the theatrical departments that stubbornly hate me will not want to print my statement, so I am making it here. I challenge the Moscow Art Theater to a Socialist competition (applause) with respect to Erdman's play *The Suicide*. This competition will be formulated not on an artistic but on a political level. And I will not be afraid if Markov and all the other managers of the MKhAT try to put *The Suicide* together before us. I will not hurry, but will be thorough, and sooner or later will pin this theater to the floor. (Applause. Laughter.)[45]

Unfortunately, the fate of this play was not decided in the competition. The head of the Glavrepertkom at the time, O. Litovsky, felt that the play was "politically off-key and highly reactionary." This opinion triumphed on much higher levels, too. Nonetheless, Meyerhold began rehearsals and in 1932 he showed fragments of the comedy behind closed doors. The leading role of Posekalnikov was played by I. Ilinsky.

Meyerhold, explained O. Litovsky fairly recently, organized this viewing without permission from the Glavrepertkom. "I did not attend that show and know that Meyerhold was counseled not to stage it."[46]

We, said Meyerhold on October 2, 1932, showed the comedy to "our comrades, senior Party members who did not find it possible to permit it due to various awkwardnesses that are supposedly in it, and this play fell through."[47]

It is evident that Meyerhold was not convinced. Unwillingly, he submitted, and the play "fell through." The Art Theater did not stage it either.

This incident is significant because it demonstrates the unfavorable atmosphere for satire that appeared under the conditions of the RAPP dictatorship. Several years later, speaking of the death of Mayakovsky, Meyerhold, clearly exaggerating the specific role of Ermilov in this tale, asserted that the members of RAPP had dealt the poet a stab in the back. "This was a real knife in the back of the revolutionary Mayakovsky both by RAPP and by Ermilov who in his time, of course, played the role of D'Anthes in relation to Mayakovsky."[48]

Ermilov himself was not all that threatening. But with RAPP, a totally new type of people appeared in the realm of literature and art. They brought a new aspect into the atmosphere of stormy debate that accompanied the entire early development of Soviet art. Previously, too, arguments about phenomena or directions in art rapidly became political arguments. Previously, too, debaters at disputes and

---

*P. A. Markov was the literary director of the Moscow Art Theater at the time.

on the pages of the press often used demagogic techniques and rough arguments, resorted to threats and attached various labels to each other. But no one could deny that all these occasionally wild passions were real, that all these inflammatory and occasionally ridiculous speeches were sincere.

The members of RAPP brought an element of political intrigue into the complex panorama of ideological and esthetic struggle. A quote taken out of context became more important for them than any work. Their contribution to the esthetic experiments of the 1920s and their capstone to these experiments was the cynicial struggle for power in the spheres of literature and art. Using channels open only to them, they cleverly obtained official support for practically all of their specific recommendations, evaluations and characterizations.

Meyerhold understood the nature of RAPP perfectly. In 1931, one year before the dissolution of RAPP, he wrote to M. N. Pokrovsky: "The present management of RAPP leads a furious struggle against writers and other art workers (including Communists) who disagree with the creative method preached by comrades who are members of this management."[49] In this totally new atmosphere, Meyerhold's efforts to gain a place for bold political satire in theater were doomed to failure.

After the critics panned Mayakovsky's *The Bathhouse* and Erdman's play was not permitted, Meyerhold staged no more contemporary comedies.

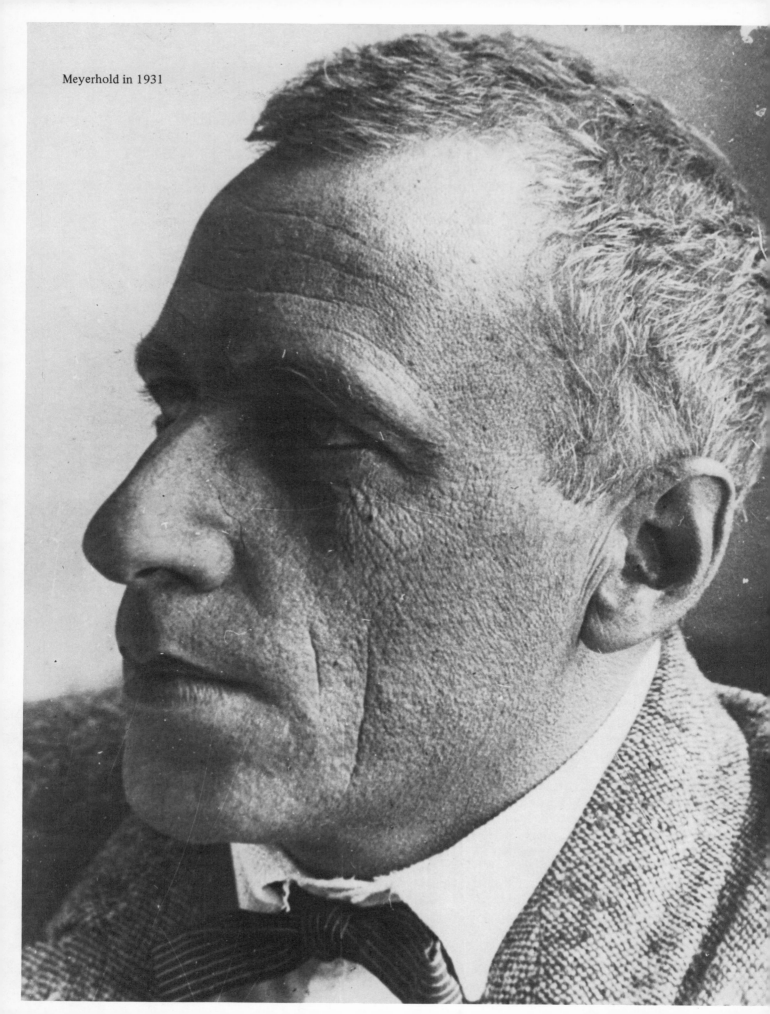

Meyerhold in 1931

SKETCHES FOR A TRAGEDY

In 1929-1933, Meyerhold made several attempts to stage contemporary tragedies. Strictly speaking, all of these—*The Commander of the Second Army*, by I. Selvinsky, *The Last Decisive Battle*, by Vs. Vishnevsky, *A List of Assets*, by Olesha, and *Prelude*, by Yu. German—were incomplete works. In each show Meyerhold succeeded in individual fragments, episodes or scenes. These were so successful that at that time, and later, they were (justifiably) spoken of as being among Meyerhold's greatest masterpieces. These episodes, created by Meyerhold with striking impact, became permanently engraved in the consciousness of the spectators; they created the impression of a theatrical miracle, of close contact with genius, and often they emotionally overlapped and even overwhelmed the perception of the overall show, which was much less intense, or occasionally weak and difficult.

The enormous explosive power of these directorial fragments by Meyerhold subsequently was comprehended by some historians as evidence of overall weakness, as a sign of his lacking the concept of artistic unity, or a deeply thought-out esthetic system.

In 1960, this point of view was expressed by A. P. Matskin. It is characteristic that his arguments were taken first of all from the above-named tragic shows. "What remains in the memory," wrote Matskin, "say from the staging of V. Vishnevsky's play *The Last Decisive Battle*, is young Bogolyubov in the last scene—a tremendous tragic flight (death of the hero sailor, defender of our borders); or from *Prelude* by German, young Sverdlin at the students' ball embracing the marble Goethe—realism brought to the level of symbol. Thus from show to show: poetry and grandeur in 'pieces,' astounding 'close-ups' and lack of clarity in the conception as a whole."

While offering these examples, the critic observed that in *The Forest* and then in *Krechinsky's Wedding,* Meyerhold "solved his problems *in portions,* that is, not along the entire front, but using operations of a local significance. He was inspired by details and in a fateful way he lost sight of the whole. A leading experimenter, he staged his experiments without controlling their final purpose. You will find this type of conformity in other productions by Meyerhold, including his best ones...constrained by the design he himself created, Meyerhold's talent goes into details, into the polishing of 'pieces,' into discoveries of a partial significance."[1]

It is easy to catch the contradiction here: if there exists a "design" created by the director for the play and for the show as a whole, then the unity (at least in the conception) does exist. The concept of the unity may be unconvincing, but in any event it is clear. A concept is unattractive, but clear. However, it is not this contradiction that causes us to dispute Matskin's conclusions, but considerations of a far more serious character. One can question the artistic unity of the production of *The Forest*. But such masterworks of Meyerhold's direction as *Masquerade, The Magnanimous Cuckold, A Profitable Post, The Mandate* and *The Inspector General* cannot possibly be examined as individual discoveries and successful "local operations," uncontrolled by a final goal.

As for the majestic and poetic fragments recalled by Matskin and all the other spectators at Meyerhold's tragedies produced in the late 1920s and early 1930s, the critic is undoubtedly correct. This fact requires special explanation.

The first comment we have on this matter is that in the entire history of Soviet theater only two works have been written that can with any certainty be called significant contemporary tragedies: Vs. Vishnevsky's *An Optimistic Tragedy* and L. Leonov's *The Invasion. The Invasion* appeared when Meyerhold was no longer living. Shortly, we shall explain why *An Optimistic Tragedy* passed him by. First, we shall establish one simple fact: all of Meyerhold's attempts to stage a modern tragedy were based on plays that were far from perfect.

Ilya Selvinsky's tragedy *The Commander of the Second Army* is a highly interesting episode in the struggle of ideas and esthetic principles that was so prevalent in the Soviet dramaturgy in the late 1920s. Immediately after the premiere, which took place on July 24, 1929, Selvinsky himself propounded the problem of the tragedy as follows:

> In my play, one can find the problem of the leader and the masses, the problem of the ideological pretender, the problem of technology and poetry; the collision between bourgeois revolution and proletarian revolution; the contrast between genius that has lost its way and mediocrity that knows what it is about; the growth of socialism into revolutionary practicality, and much more. However, all these problems are so intertwined, their appearance is so natural and inevitable in the present situation that the analysis of an individual question torn from the general fabric of the tragedy immediately distorts its timbre. But if we are to seek an overall form for the tragedy, its philosophical architecture, then I would say that it lies in the dialectic.

The author went on very briefly and concisely to express his unhappiness with Meyerhold's staging: "Unfortunately, this dialectical geometry of the poem was not realized in the theater and it was transposed to the level of propagandistic primitivism by the direction."[2]

Subsequently, in his memoirs of Meyerhold, Selvinsky laid out this "dialectic" more comprehensibly. He wrote that the main thing in his play was "the conflict between Commander Chub and the writer Okonny who, in the name of Revolution, entered into a plot against Chub, whom he considered incapable of resolving great matters of war." Selvinsky observed that in Meyerhold's treatment "the conflict became a struggle between a Red Chub and a White Okonny, although the author had intended both to be Reds dreaming of victory over the White Guards: this was a battle between two Revolutionary characters who interpreted the courses of the Revolution in different ways."[3]

Upon rereading Selvinsky's tragedy, however, one becomes convinced that the attractive simplicity of his latest explanations does not, unfortunately, coincide with the truth. Formally, Selvinsky is correct: Chub and Okonny are both Reds. Both are seen by the author as possible candidates for the leadership of the revolutionary masses. Chub already is performing this function, while Okonny aspires to it. It is this aspiration that becomes the subject of close scrutiny. Chub is "a worker from the peasantry and Tsarist labor camps." Okonny is an intellectual, has staff officer tendencies, is a dreamer, and a former accountant. Chub is laconic, direct, a man of few words. Okonny is verbose, expansive, and excited by revolutionary phraseology.

Chub thinks only of the victory, while Okonny thirsts for glory and great deeds. Chub is a man of action, Okonny—an office poet, a phrasemaker incapable of action.

Such a juxtaposition could have become the motive force for a tragedy. However, these characters, although constantly being compared by the author, fail to actually collide in the dramatic conflict. Secondly, and this is most important, the right to power, the central problem of the tragedy, is not tested by the truly high criteria of humanism and love of people. Both Chub and Okonny are certain that the ends justify any means, that the masses they both hope to rule require only a dictator, that these masses are blind and ignorant and will always remain so.

Both characters—Chub (who describes himself thus: "I was the leader of massed armies. / Immortal. Yours. Cherished. Dictator.") and Okonny—are equally cruel. The episode with the typhus victims is characteristic of the entire conception of the piece. There are three trains full of them. There is no one to treat them. Chub's decision is to "burn these trains" with artillery fire and place two machine guns "so that none of the ill individuals can escape." As if this were not enough, Chub orders a mounted detachment to "saber everyone" who tries to run away. Later, the same problem arises before Okonny, who has seized power. He does not like Chub's order. "We build the work, the joyous work of the Commune," he observes, "with the gloominess of a casket-maker." But Selvinsky wipes out all these humane thoughts about how "a single typhoid I" was dearer than future victories, since Okonny's humaneness in the play is explained by his self-love, his egotism. Very soon he sends the soldiers into a senseless battle and says: "Pawns are like nuts and must be cracked." It is not the Revolution that he defends, but only his own power, his own "dialectic," and he sends entire battalions to their deaths.

It turns out that both Chub and Okonny write off thousands of human lives with ease, the only difference being that Chub does so in the name of the victory of the Revolution, and Okonny for his own power. Since Okonny in the tragedy is connected to the entire complex of "obsolete" intellectual ideas, above all estheticism, the love of beauty, of Blok's poetry, the paintings of Gauguin and Levitan, then the criticism levied against Okonny is perceived as a judgment of "intellectualism" and Chub's victory as the victory of the proletarian class instinct. The critics were unanimous on this point in their analysis of Selvinsky's play, not Meyerhold's production of it.

An anti-intellectual "dialectic" of this sort could hardly have been of much interest to Meyerhold, who preferred to move the figure of Okonny into the position of an adventurer, if not exactly into the camp of the Whites (Selvinsky exaggerates). In the show, Okonny was simply extremely ambitious, an adventurer hungering for power, and a phrasemonger. "On stage Okonny is a babbler," wrote B. Alpers. "He is discredited before the audience at the very beginning of the show." As for Chub, Meyerhold made him a hero. Although Selvinsky "is somewhat bemused in his depiction of this iron dictator," in the show, observed the same critic, "Chub becomes an important positive figure growing out of the Red Army mass: the powerful and wise voice of the collective."

This is how matters stood between the two leading characters in the play and in the show. Meyerhold really did simplify them. But, in contrast to Selvinsky's assertion, he did not bring them to the level of "propagandistic primitivism." He had other tasks. He wished to penetrate deep into the period of the Civil War, to discover its epos.

In this show the Civil War was moved far into the past. It seemed as if not decades but centuries separated it from the audience. B. Alpers wrote:

> The heroic past appears on the stage of Meyerhold's theater like a legend. It becomes myth. This technique is particularly felt in the scene of the rally, in the choral interlude and in the scene where the Red Army man wearing a sheepskin coat sings the song about his brothers. Among these Red Army men and commanders in the rally scene, there is not one man who could have survived until our day. It is inconceivable to suppose that today one of them may be studying at the Academy or commanding a regiment, a division, an army. These were people who disappeared on the fields of battle in 1918-1919, legendary heroes from a legendary time. If we remove their sheepskins we will see smashed skulls, torn-out breasts, five-pointed stars carved into the body.
>
> This is why they stand so still with their long pikes. This is why their movements are so slow and majestic, and the stamp of strange thoughtfulness lies over them all.
>
> This transition from everyday life into legend in the stage characterization of the Civil War era is extremely interesting as a first experiment in modern theater. Moreover, it is realized by Meyerhold by using realistic techniques. The episode with the guard at the gates of the command post is resolved just as interestingly. His sad Scythian song colors the historical antiquity of all the action in *The Commander of the Second Army*. The heroic era withdraws into the distant past, takes on large, majestic outlines in contrast to the quick sketches of a dramatic chronicle of everyday life.[4]

This epic quality was achieved with the assistance of the artist K. Petrov-Vodkin, who finely stylized antique-like Red Army coats, helmets, pea jackets, sheepskin hats and short coats, gave long pikes to the cavalrymen and silver swords to the commanders.

The biographers of the painter have ignored Petrov-Vodkin's participation in this work by Meyerhold. However, although Petrov-Vodkin performed the modest functions of a costume consultant, his influence on the representational solution to the show was quite substantial. There is a visible connection between Petrov-Vodkin's well-known canvas *The Death of the Commissar* (1928) and the design of Meyerhold's show. Petrov-Vodkin's painting probably suggested to Meyerhold this epic interpretation of the Civil War as permeated by the breath of antiquity. In the tragic composition of Petrov-Vodkin, the images of recent battles are imperceptibly tied with the traditions of Russian ikonography. The ascetic faces of the dying Commissar and the Red Army man embracing him resemble the faces of saints. Inspiration shines through physical exhaustion. The entire cold color range of the work—from the brown-black leather coat of the Commissar to the bluish greenery on the hill—resembles the frescoes of Feofan Grek. The little figures of the unit's soldiers marching off to battle (in the background of the painting) step over the crest of the hill and appear to fall into eternity. The hill that they march over is the circumference of the earth's globe. They do not tread on earth and grass, but on the planet. Their naive, childlike, purposeful movement into the distance is painfully tragic. The heroic past sounds with the pain of farewells. This is a requiem, epic and bitter. The upper left-hand corner of the painting is occupied by a transparent, lilac haze. Time stands still and mute over the painting.

Undoubtedly, Meyerhold had seen it. Therefore, he invited Petrov-Vodkin to participate in the work on *The Commander of the Second Army*. For the Meyerhold of this time a look into the past was a look of farewell. The epic arose in the show as the result of a single desire: to say that the age of the Civil War was sacred in the memory of the artist, that its heroic asceticism, its pathos and its furious storm cut through the life of Russia like a magnificent and unforgettable boundary. Those people who today study at the Academies or command divisions are already cut off from their own legendary and fantastic past forever by a stripe of the "normal" which is incompatible with their former lives. The great deed remains behind in history. The battles of the Civil War are majestic and distant like the ancient battles with the Polovtsy and the Tatars...

This solution, which was directly and sharply polemical regarding numerous productions that, in Meyerhold's opinion, "were nth variations on *Lyubov Yarovaya*,"[5] a solution directed "against the joyless genre representation that rules in theatrical productions on the theme of the Civil War," was far from convincing. "The deathly motionlessness of historical 'landscapes,' their excessive removal from our days, inevitably meets with objections from the modern spectator," we read in the same article by B. Alpers. "The people shown in *The Commander of the Second Army* are simply too far removed from those participants in the Civil War among whom we live today."[6]

Adr. Pyotrovsky complained that *The Commander of the Second Army* gives "the impression of a 'presentation of recollections of the Civil War.'" And, furthermore: "In the Civil War itself the show underscores its archaic elements: the pikes in the soldiers' hands remind one of the nomadic days, the monumental decorations create an associative image of medieval castles. The spirit of the retrospective rules over the production."[7]

The critics were unanimous in their praise of N. Bogolyubov in the leading role. A. Gvozdev wrote: "Bogolyubov as Chub unexpectedly appeared before the audience as an actor-tragedian of substantial dimensions. He has broken decisively with the traditional actors' images of Bolsheviks on stage and has given that effort of will that neither the actors of the older generation (Sadovsky, Monakhov, Kuznetsov) nor the actors of everyday drama of MGSPS-type theaters were able to give."[8]

Alpers sensed precisely the connection between this figure and the overall stylistic solution for the show. "The excellent makeup, the intent, energetic face, the flashing eyes and rough, muffled voice of the artist magnificently transmit the image of the 'immortal, cherished dictator,' the iron commander. His entire image conveys the legendary quality of this military leader from the first Partisan years of the Revolution."[9]

The construction for the show, built by the architect S. Vakhtangov under Meyerhold's supervision, was designed to connect the stage to the auditorium. It was planned that a straight ribbon of road would begin in the auditorium and bisect the entire stage from left to right and from bottom to top. That is how one of the preliminary designs looked. But in the final version, this straight canvas was replaced by a wide semicircular staircase that began not in the auditorium, but on the lower left side of the stage floor and rose up and to the right. The construction, in contrast to the original plan, stood entirely on the stage floor and did not protrude into the audience. These changes were probably dictated by external, technical circumstances, but there was also an internal, esthetic significance. By consciously separating the sacred age of great deeds from the present, Meyerhold intended to lock the action within the limits of the stage, in contrast to his continuous passion for interacting with the audience. The epic separateness excluded on principle the feasibility of directly relating this time with the spectators. Furthermore, it required a rejection of excessive details from everyday life, generalizations, a laconic solution.

Meyerhold did in fact banish all verisimilitude of detail from the stage. It was replaced by several expressive major details, such as an enormous abacus the height of a man, with which Okonny appeared, the "close-ups" of the pulpit, and Vera's typewriter.

As we have mentioned, the costumes were stylized to epic antiquity and evoked unexpected associations with the poetry of *The Song of Igor's Campaign.*

Nonetheless, the production as a whole was not and could not have been a success. The pretentious, verbose and coquettish rhetoric of the text argued against the epic simplicity that Meyerhold attempted to give the tragedy. The role of Chub was successful, but Okonny was played by F. Korshunov with heartrending melancholy. Z. Raikh played Okonny's lover, Vera, quite satisfactorily, but the text of her part sounded contrived and rather trite.

Meyerhold, who even before the premiere feared that "the show will fail," since "the play is difficult and complex for the audience,"[10] was almost correct in his prognosis. True, the play did interest the critics. They wrote about it in detail and with enthusiasm. This is not surprising: whatever else one may say, this was the first attempt to create a Soviet tragedy. But even the critics commented: "The show is uneven" (A. Gvozdev); "The show is difficult" (O. Litovsky); "Meyerhold's attempts to construct a unified show proved futile" (B. Alpers). Spectators responded coolly to *The Commander of the Second Army* and attendance was poor. Meyerhold was quite successful in some episodes: in the large rally scene (Selvinsky's third act), in the magnificently staged "number" with the song of the sentry (fifth act) and in the great interlude in the middle of the fifth act.

The success of the show was predetermined in many ways by the fine organization of the mass scenes. Adr. Pyotrovsky wrote, it is true, that the stylistic solution for the mass scenes in *The Commander of the Second Army* reproduced characteristic traits of "Revolutionary productions of the Civil War period. The expressive means that Meyerhold uses here—choral reading, reading through megaphones, mass movements, military marches, passionate declamations, even the riding of horsemen onto the stage, all this is taken from the arsenal of Revolutionary productions. All this," added Pyotrovsky, "is brought to the level of perfection. The tempo of the mass movements in *The Commander of the Second Army*, the rhythm and timbre of the orchestration of the choral reading, all this is incomparable with its finish and shine to the rough technique of amateur productions.

"The scene 'Rally in the Steppe' must enter theatrical history as a classically finished example of high theatrical propaganda style."[11]

However, in this particular scene Meyerhold proposed a completely new system of relations between the masses and the orator-hero, the crowd and the leader, unknown to the propaganda theater of the Civil War years. During the "Rally in the Steppe," M. Kirillov as Boy, N. Bogolyubov as Chub, A. Loginov as Gubarev, and S. Fadeev as Deverin, entered into acute dramatic interrelations with the crowd, into intense struggle.

Each stepped onto the platform as onto a scaffold. Each word by an orator could be his last. A shot from the crowd could put an unexpected period in the middle of any sentence. Meyerhold ordered this intensity, constructing the entire scene on the principle of taming the rebellious storm. The crowd deposed the orators one after another until Chub subordinated it to his iron will.

The Sentry's song and the interlude in the last act were set to music by V. Shebalin. Meyerhold liked this music very much. In Shebalin, he wrote, "theater gains a composer of stature, capable of providing significant musical forms not just for a symphony orchestra but also for theater, for that 'musical theater' which we are currently occupied in creating."[12]

A. Gvozdev observed in his review that the introduction of music into the director's score was limited: "The powerful sounds ably evoked from the small orchestra by the composer (V. Shebalin) support the mass scenes that unfurl along the enormous staircase which horizontally cuts through lead panels that reach far upward. Simplicity and schematism characterize the entire staging, in which the mass declamation of rhythmically flexible and combative verse (the megaphone scene) infects the auditorium with a great, emotional, heroic intensity. The mass of Partisans is presented in a precise constructive bulk, as a single being infected with the will to win."[13]

The sensation of the unity of the collective will was expressed with special force in the concluding interlude. Meyerhold's solution was brilliantly simple: he arranged in a half-circle on the stage the male and female theater company, gave silver megaphones to all the members of this enormous chorus, and this chorus thundered as in a cathedral, rang with the pathos of self-sacrifice and sober readiness to die.

The interesting idea was realized only in such expressive and powerful fragments of the show.

The staging of Vs. Vishnevsky's play, *The Last Decisive Battle* (February 7, 1931) was even less likely to be accepted as an artistic whole. At least *The Commander of the Second Army*, with all its failings, had been written as a tragedy, but Vishnevsky's play had no signs of orientation in genre.

The play began with a long parodic prologue, a sort of student satire. This prologue poked fun at the Bolshoi Theater's *Red Poppy*. This was followed by the satirical adventures of two tipsy Red Fleet sailors on a boulevard in a port, Here Vishnevsky sharply contrasted cheap, anarchistic "romance of the sea" with discipline, organization, and the "magnificent vigilance" of the military marine. Only in the finale, much delayed, did there appear the main, tragic theme of the piece: Vishnevsky, looking into the near future, depicted an enemy attack on the Soviet Union, presented two quick episodes of the mobilization of the Red Navy and the concluding episode of the play, "Outpost No. 6," which became the hit of Meyerhold's production.

The "student satire" portion of the show was effectively presented. I. Kruti wrote:

The enormous stage of Meyerhold's theater is filled with people. When the bright light of the projector pours over this crowd standing, lying, sitting in "graceful" poses and the tasteless multitude of varicolored figures comes into motion, then the unpleasant "prettiness" of operatic baroque appears at once, bared to the limit. Powdered and rouged Soviet sailors languidly dance a "productivity" dance, a grimacing ballerina represents the Chinese Revolution, dainty youths "represent" our Red Army, and so on and so forth. The blow against the falseness of *The Red Poppy* is well-directed and smashing. . . . It is true that this prologue is somewhat overextended. Of course, the theater goes a little to excess in sucking the rotting bones of the operatic skeleton, and the spectator becomes slightly fatigued.[14]

P. Markov was more definite on this point. The parody in the beginning of the show appeared to him "unnecessary and excessive, exaggerated and not reaching its goal... While ridiculing the dances, couplets and arias, Meyerhold gradually becomes involved in the form of the construction of the parody, and this low, music-hall art form assumes a self-sufficient significance in the show." The most interesting and pointed comment made by Markov was *"The Red Poppy*, with its phoenixes, has not been surpassed—this ballet has more humor than the parody of it does, and the parody has more craftsmanship than the ballet."[15]

We should mention that S. Martinson performed the American's comic dance with particular brilliance. Delighted with his work, Meyerhold specially noted in the program: "His own dance composition."

V. L. Yureneva wrote:

Martinson appears for fourteen seconds. This is a parody of an American sailor. It is impossible to make this sketch more expressive. Here, as a drop of water reflects the entire sky, in this momentary dance, in this appearance and disappearance, there is contained the complete image of the dancer who in the ballet represents the American. Martinson wears a black pinstripe suit. Thin legs in bell-bottoms, stupid face, beret pulled down over the eyes, pipe. In addition to the dance—a spit to the side, a gesture with the thumb, and an eyelid pulled down—in a word, all the official attributes of the type mechanically dumped in one place. For a second, the auditorium freezes in attention, as though undergoing a slight artistic shock from the unexpectedness, boldness, and brightness of this theatrical moment.[16]

The satirical scenes on the boulevard in the port where I. Ilinsky played Anatole-Edouard, E. Garin—Jean Valjean, and Zinaida Raikh—the port prostitute Carmen-Pelagea, were staged by Meyerhold very colorfully, precisely and nervously. In the same article by Markov, we read:

The port and "Carmen" are presented in a complex intertwining of reminiscences of Odessa life and seaport debauchery. Dreary and irritating music written with great mastery by Shebalin accompanies these scenes. The past appears not as a mask, but in its contradictions still nesting in the psychology of modern man, who is not yet finally free of the inheritance of the past. Meyerhold is not afraid to introduce lyrical notes only to destroy them furiously the next moment... He constructs these scenes musically, introducing lyrical music of a parodic nature. A sensation of fatedness accompanies these scenes.[17]

Dress rehearsal of Selvinsky's *The Commander of the Second Army*, 1929.
Meyerhold is on the horse.

Two scenes from *The Commander of the Second Army*

The Last Decisive Battle, Vishnevsky.
Clockwise: American Sailor (Martinson),
Anatole-Eduard (Ilinsky),
Carmen (Tyapkina)

ГОСУДАРСТВЕННЫЙ ТЕАТР ИМЕНИ ВС. МЕЙЕРХОЛЬДА.

ВСЕВОЛОД ВИШНЕВСКИЙ
ВСЕВОЛОД МЕЙЕРХОЛЬД

ПОСЛЕДНИЙ РЕШИТЕЛЬНЫЙ

МОСКВА
7 ФЕВРАЛЯ
1931 Г

Facing page: scenes from "Outpost No 6" episode of *The Last Decisive Battle*

Above: poster for *The Last Decisive Battle.* "Vsevolod Meyerhold State Theater," Moscow, Feb. 7, 1931.
Below: "Outpost No. 6" episode

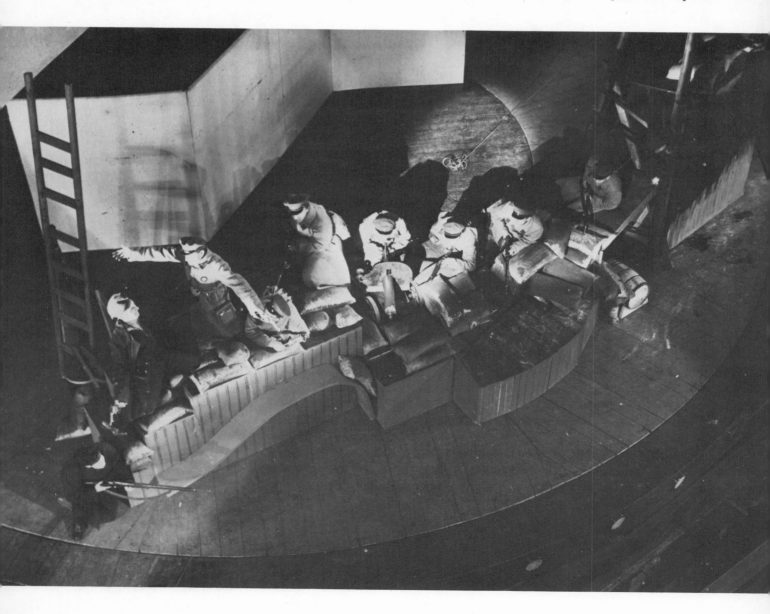

Last scenes of *The Last Decisive Battle*, Bogolyubov as Bushuev

Olesha's *A List of Assets*, 1931, main set.
Goncharova (Raikh) playing Hamlet.

A List of Assets, the "cabaret scene"

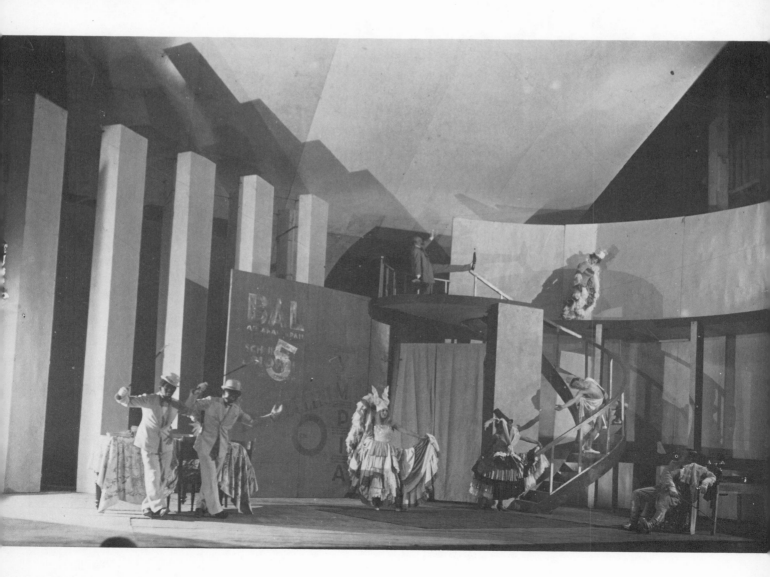

A List of Assets. The death of Goncharova (Raikh), held by the "Woman of the People," played by Serebryannikova

Prelude, 1933, by German. Episode 5, "Germany"

Prelude, episode 6. Professor Kelberg (Michurin), second from right below

Meyerhold, 1932

Meyerhold, 1932

However, the entire long and colorful ribbon of the show appeared to be cut and canceled by its tragic ending. "The red poppies and Carmen float away to the side," concluded Yu. Yuzovsky after seeing the performance. "Close-ups appear of rifle barrels, a machine gun, the beseiged outpost No. 6."[18]

In this concluding episode, Meyerhold and Vishnevsky show the death of all twenty-seven fighters, who took the first enemy blow upon themselves. This sudden vision of a future war appeared with frightening reality in the show. Here, Vishnevsky was attracted primarily by the representation of a mass deed. Meyerhold separated the sergeant Bushuev from the mass, gave this role to Bogolyubov, and moved the figure of the hero into the center of the episode.

In Meyerhold's concept, the border post battle took place in a schoolhouse. The entire score for the battle was executed with tremendous expression. The machine gun fired from the stage into the auditorium.

To the sounds of a radio, to the bouncy rhythms of a foxtrot and the grace-note warbling of Maurice Chevalier, the sailors died, one after another. Bushuev was the last to go. Mortally wounded, he raised himself up with difficulty and with a piece of chalk wrote on ordinary classroom blackboard:

$$
\begin{array}{rrr}
162 & 000 & 000 \\
- & & 27 \\
\hline
161 & 999 & 973 \\
\end{array}
$$

Then he dropped the chalk, fell smiling and looking at the audience with incomprehension, and died.

At this moment the leader would ask, with outrage: "Who is weeping?" Inevitably, there was weeping in the audience. Meyerhold unhesitatingly used a "plant." An actress sat in the stalls and would begin to cry at the appropriate moment, at which point all those around her would pull out their handkerchiefs. This plant angered some critics, but Meyerhold was certain that in theater "all means are good if they lead to the necessary result."[19]

This truly tragic scene was undercut because the idea and plot did not prepare for it. The play did not lead to it. Heroes fell who were not just nameless (except for Bushuev) but faceless as well. The spectators did not and could not know them. Only Meyerhold's stage score was capable of concentrating all the sympathies of the audience on these perishing men, each of whom had one, two, or at best three lines. Still, Meyerhold did create this miracle, and the final episode was staggeringly memorable.

It was the only episode to be mentioned. It was this episode that evoked the most furious attacks by RAPP. V. Kirshon jeered: "This arithmetical exercise has nothing in common with Bolshevism," he declared, since the 162 million (the population of the USSR at the time) includes kulaks, uncounted by Vishnevsky, "who will do everything possible to strike us from the rear on the first day of war," and "people who will be passive,"[20] and so on. Other critics used practically the same expressions to criticize the play. The show was criticized sharply by S. Dinamov, I. Grossman-Roshchin, Mate Zalka, V. Ermilov, A. Gurevich, and Yu. Yuzovsky.

Yuzovsky offered the strongest argument. Understanding that a tragic ending was planned, Yuzovsky asked: "Where is the *idea*, the great idea for which twenty-seven have died?.. There is no idea, no general philosophy to the show."[21]

Defenders of the production (among them were Lunacharsky, N. Semashko, Felix Kon, Nikolai Aseev) were unable to refute this argument. Markov agreed indirectly with Yuzovsky when, speaking of Meyerhold's victory, he declared the defeat of Vishnevsky and "the absence of a play."

Meyerhold, who had undergone many such experiences, defended Vishnevsky like a knight and protected him from the critics' fire. He believed in Vishnevsky's talent and immediately agreed with him to stage a new play, conditionally entitled *Germany*. The play was soon written and Meyerhold planned to stage it, even though, evidently, it did not particularly attract him. Vishnevsky offered Meyerhold a second version, which was also disappointing to the director. At this time the director was involved in Erdman's *The Suicide*. Vishnevsky criticized Erdman's comedy and opposed its staging at public debates and in print. The relationship between the director and the playwright deteriorated. *Germany* was given to the Theater of the Revolution, where it was staged under the title *A Battle in the West*. The loss was not great—Vishnevsky's play was not a hit. But, as a result of the conflict between Vishnevsky and Meyerhold, the *Optimistic Tragedy* went not to Meyerold but to Tairov, which Meyerhold greatly regretted.

In the year of the staging of *The Last Decisive Battle*, the State Academy of Art Studies (GAIS—an organization that existed only briefly) carried out a wide-ranging discussion: "On Meyerhold's Creative Method." The low theoretical level of the discussion was predetermined by the fact that the keynote speaker was V. A. Pavlov, the author of a sadly notorious book entitled *Theatrical Twilight*, in which the Moscow Art Theater was attacked from the most vulgar sociological perspective. He asserted that the "superficial assimilation of our Revolutionary reality" was characteristic of Meyerhold, that he was prone to "semi-Kantism" (!!), the "over-valuation of the significance of form," etc. Meyerhold responded delicately that he considered the paper "insufficiently grounded." He recalled firmly that "biomechanics in no way contradicts the expression of the internal content of human emotional experiences."[22] On the whole, this discussion, widely publicized in the press, was utterly scholastic. The speakers boisterously operated with scientific terms, philosophical and sociological categories, revealing, however, a total lack of comprehension of the nature of theater in general, and of Meyerhold's art in particular. It is necessary to mention this episode only in order to demonstrate the verbal trash that Meyerhold occasionally had to deal with while defending his positions.

Meanwhile, Meyerhold still continued to aspire to contemporary tragedy, and his next production—*A List of Assets* (June 4, 1931)—was perhaps in this sense the most expressive and the closest to the target. Yury Olesha's play was a new variation on his usual theme—the incompatibility of the emotional richness of an individual with a decisive reconstruction of the world, the inevitability of which this same individual comprehends mentally and even praises.

Olesha's play caught and amplified like a resonator those notes of doubt sounded by the intelligentsia. The "conspiracy of feelings," noted long before by Olesha, continued to exist. Feelings opposed what was accepted and approved by reason. This time, the specific implementation of the theme was undoubtedly suggested by the fates of those artists who had left the Soviet Union—beginning with the fate of Mikhail Chekhov, of paramount importance to both Olesha and Meyerhold. The heroine of the play, the actress Elena Goncharova, played Hamlet as Chekhov had, and traveled abroad in the same way. She does not yet know whether she will remain in Europe or will return to the Motherland (Chekhov also did not know this as he left for Berlin). She is torn. She has complex relations with the Soviet state and keeps two lists: one is of the Bolsheviks' good deeds, the other is of their evil deeds. Like Mikhail Chekhov, she is convinced that contemporary Soviet plays are "schematic, lying, lacking in imagination, linear" (Mikhail Chekhov wrote to Lunacharsky from Berlin that he would agree to return to the Soviet Union if he would be permitted to create a theater of classical repertory in which Soviet plays would not be staged at all).

The image of Mikhail Chekhov, abroad already for three years, peered through Olesha's play. Theatrical people guessed quickly what the subject matter was. N. Chushkin tells us that he asked Meyerhold directly whether these guesses were correct. Meyerhold acknowledged this and, "looking mysterious, stated that he had described 'something' of his talks in Berlin with Mikhail Chekhov to Yu. K. Olesha when the play was still in the planning stages, asking him to use this material, polemically sharpening some of the assumptions and situations." Therefore, the play was planned as a part of a polemic concerning Chekhov's action. Even the crude episode in which the director of the theater Marzheret suggests that Goncharova blow Hamlet's flute with her rear was an exaggerated rendition of an actual episode in the first months of Chekhov's life in Berlin. Chekhov wanted to play Hamlet in Berlin and unexpectedly encountered the question: "Do you dance? Why dance? We begin with a cabaret."[23]

Chekhov's dramatic fate tied the play together from afar. The tragedy in it was quite real. It depicted, with Olesha's usual talent and charm, the insoluble collision of a splitting personality. The personality was torn between the past and the future, between Europe and Russia, between feelings and intellect, between beauty and the practical, between the possible joy of the moment, this moment, and the distant idea of happiness for all. Unfortunately, however, this was only in the outline, since the play was begun with a purely geometrical grace, with a distinct desire to reduce the painful complexity of life to the simplicity of clear juxtaposition.

Hence, the two lists, "for" and "against" Soviet power, which in Goncharova's diary reduced to naive duality the entire "mystery of the Russian intelligentsia." Hence, too, the symmetrical construction of the Parisian scenes, where Goncharova finds herself between the White emigre Tatarov and the Soviet specialist Fedotov. "The two halves of Elena Goncharova," wrote A. Gurvich, "are presented by the author both in herself and in her diary as a document and, finally, they are materialized in the image of two separate figures: the White emigre Tatarov and the Communist Fedotov... Goncharova is drawn to both and hates both."[24]

Finding herself in the west, Goncharova is not rid of her duality. The geometry of the play inverts rapidly. In this world, too, there is no place for Goncharova. Here, too, she could keep a list "for" and "against," since she sees Paris with the eyes of a Soviet woman, a Soviet actress, since the new, which remains there behind the border, has already entered her and become a part of her soul. It is necessary to mention, however, that the faults of bourgeois society that confront Goncharova are drawn by Olesha with far less expression. There is a sense of the absence of personal impressions by the author, a repetitiveness of situations borrowed from other plays. But this is not the worst. The worst is that the play, which began with the immortal flute episode from *Hamlet*, is unable to break out of the strong grip of the author's design. Until the very end, Goncharova straddles two worlds (like Chaplin with one foot in Mexico and one in the USA). Even her death is a duality. Goncharova is killed *by a White Guard with a Soviet pistol.*"I demonstrate," explained Olesha at a dispute, "that both sides execute Goncharova." This is one of those rare cases in which one can say with certainty than any other solution would have been better. Any move away from the outline would have opened the gates for truth. Olesha's play began gracefully and ended roughly, began sharply and boldly but in the end tucked in its tail like a coward...

"Is Olesha's rebellion against the old world genuine?" asked A. Gurvich, and answered: "Yes, but with sadness. Is he stretching out his hands genuinely to the new? Yes, but also with insurmountable sadness or with the obedience of one without strength in an unequal contest."[25]

Falsity arose in the finale of *A List of Assets*, because this author's sadness, correctly identified by Gurvich, was not expressed. It was suppressed. It retreated to the protection of rationalistic indications of the duality of the very death of the heroine: the Soviet pistol in the White Guard's hand, the request of the dying Goncharova "to cover her body with the Red flag," and the contradiction of the last author's note: "Lyolya lies dead, uncovered."

There was nothing Meyerhold could do with this falseness. But he was extremely interested in the play and he worked on it with enthusiasm. *A List of Assets* appeared to conclude Meyerhold's movement toward the principles of architecturality in the design of the stage space, a direction first indicated in *The Inspector General*.

N. M. Tarabukin wrote:

Beginning with *The Commander of the Second Army* (1929), Meyerhold works with the architect Vakhtangov. Architecture in the TIM is in no way decorative in principle; it is based in Constructivism. In this case, too, Meyerhold marches in step with the new movements in modern architecture, rejecting props, the way he was in step with the painting of the "World of Art" during his Petersburg period of work.

The plan for *The Last Decisive Battle* is by Meyerhold and developed by Vakhtangov. Here, the ship is built by combining cubes and rhombuses painted white. This way the director avoided the illusionism and naturalism of *Roar, China!* In this production, the principles of Constructivism and architecturality are still struggling.

Finally, in *A List of Assets,* the principle of architecturality is triumphant. The colonnade forms the stage space. It is not only expressive in and of itself, but it is connected with the surrounding stage space. The line of columns repeats the edge line of the stage platform which this time is cut along a diagonal. This three-quarters "turn" of the stage with respect to the auditorium is a heroic effort by Meyerhold to "shift" the stage box: to disrupt the portal, to force the actor to present the three-quarters view to the audience and to alter the spectator's orientation by disrupting the frontality of the stage. Right before the general repair of the GOSTIM building Meyerhold was unable to resist, and turned the stage with a lever. He not only eliminated the floor, but broke the box, too.[26]

The role of Elena Goncharova was, of course, given to Zinaida Raikh. It was in this role that Meyerhold felt and expressed the tragic potential which had not been realized by the author. Three scenes with Goncharova—her first entrance in the costume of the Dane (black cape, boots, rapier in hand), her departure abroad, her leaving the director of the Paris theater who had insulted her—were brought together emotionally by Meyerhold and subordinated to a theme he found lyrical—the theme of the solitary and misunderstood artist. Here, he turned out to be more sharp and angry than Olesha.

The little scene from *Hamlet* (Act III, Scene 2) was performed sarcastically, acidly, by Raikh. "Why do you go about to recover the wind of me, as if you would drive me into a toil?" The question to Guildenstern sounded sharply challenging. Even more abrupt was the command to play the pipe. But the phrase: "'Tis as easy as lying" was pronounced calmly, with insidious goodwill. Then followed a real explosion of rage: "Why, look you now, how unworthy a thing you make of me. You would play upon me; you would seem to know my stops; you would pluck out the heart of my mystery; you would sound me from my lowest note to the top of my compass. . . . 'Sblood, do you think I am easier to be played on than a pipe?"

Meyerhold used Raikh's lips to answer many people. It was not without reason that he dreamed of staging *Hamlet* in those days.[27]

The episode of Goncharova's departure abroad was equally characteristic. In this episode, Olesha had a modest youth, a delegate from the workers, come to hand the actress a large bouquet of jasmine. He is quiet, polite and modest. In Meyerhold's version, describes one review, "the factory representative, a Young Communist, leaps onto the stage with a circus bound. He yells like a carnival Petrushka, repeats mechanically, with false feeling, the words of greeting that Goncharova asks him to transmit to the workers. Then he begins to behave like a cad, grabs the actress' diary from the table and begins to dig through it."

The Parisian scene with the theater director was performed as a natural and direct continuation of these two scenes. The director Marzheret was performed by M. Shtraukh. Meyerhold gave this role a clowning interpretation, transforming the substantial and cynical businessman into a sort of "animal tamer." D. Kalm wrote: "In red boots with spurs he tears about the stage and in the absence of tigers growls to himself, beating his boots with a stick. He carries on a filigree dialogue with numerous 'whys,' while constantly dancing around a canvas curtain prepared for this reason at the back of the stage."[28] S. Tsimbal saw in this figure the "living and convincing generalization of a fantastic dealer, an enthusiast for banality and a knight for tavern tastes."[29]

After the degrading conversation with Marzheret, who proposed that she "bare her rear and play minuets" on the flute, Raikh-Goncharova remained alone. I. Kruti said:

> She crosses the stage diagonally, bent over, slowly ascends a steep staircase and quietly crosses the upper platform. It is here in this mute scene that Meyerhold has gathered his

—493—

staging "fist," maximally concentrating and most fully expressing his directorial plan in this "point"... Now, it is either a slow extinguishing and the torment of final disillusion, or a complete rearmament in the name of the future. Hamlet-Goncharova has something to think about. Engrossed in these thoughts, bent under the lead of the errors of her entire life but already sensing the dawn of the new, with a ripening resolution, the actress Goncharova departs to die, after a series of new failures, in the ranks of demonstrating unemployed workers.

This scene is the most powerful in the play. The rest is not only of different value (the entire last scene can hardly be considered satisfactory—its daubed colors, doll-like capitalists and unnatural unemployed), but is debatable as well. The White writer Tatarov, for instance, appears as at least a Hoffmann hero.[30]

Here we shall interrupt the quote. The critics disturbed not only Hoffmann, but Dostoevsky, Leonid Andreev, Merezhkovsky and Rozanov in their attempts to fathom Olesha's fairly simple play. E. Beskin stated without hesitation that "Goncharova should have been exposed to the end and shown to be by nature (may Olesha forgive me) just as ordinary as the neighbor who accuses her of stealing apples."[31] D. Kalm, on the contrary, demanded that in the end Goncharova die to the sounds of the *Internationale*. The critic understood that he was proposing a stock solution. "Tens of hundreds of plays end in a mandatory *Internationale*," he admitted, "but in this particular play the hymn to Socialism must resound as a real ideological finish..."[32]

As we see, the schematic dualization of Goncharova continued in the minds of the critics, too. Some interpreted her one way, others—another. As for Meyerhold, he was not particularly interested in the outline suggested by Olesha and was continually distracted from it. Yuzovsky was correct in stating: "It may be said that this is a centrifugal show. It does not contain a central director's idea. The author of the show followed the playwright, retaining a sort of neutrality and noninvolvement in the philosophical matters of the play."[33]

But Meyerhold's centrifugal efforts had their own meaning and yielded their own results. The theme of solitude and the incomprehensibility of the artist delineated in the role of Goncharova was expressed most forcefully in the silent tragic scene of her leaving Marzheret. But in the role of the editor of a little White Guard newspaper, Tatarov, who was performed by one of Meyerhold's favorite actors—S. Martinson—there sounded a different theme pertaining not at all to Hoffmann, but very personal to Meyerhold and limited for Olesha—the theme of exposing envy of talent.

The tragedy of talent and the comedy of lack of talent—this became the most significant thing in Olesha's play for Meyerhold and became the theme of the best "pieces" by the director and the best performances in the show. Naturally, Meyerhold's direction of scenes that he found to his taste, such as the death of Goncharova—an effective massing with a large solo plastic part for Raikh—was thorough and brilliant.

Shot. Hit: Goncharova stretches to her full height, tense, still. Run: Goncharova runs up to the fountain, bends her head under the water for refreshment, comes out onto the proscenium. Shakes her wet head, staggers. The unemployed workers catch her up. She tenses again, straightens up, frees herself from their hands, staggers again. Almost falls. She is caught up again and carefully, quietly laid down on the floor. Raikh lay on her side, facing the audience. Then dropped her head back and onto the floor. Death.

But this flawlessly choreographed scene was less impressive than the simple, but absolutely saturated departure of Goncharova from Marzheret...

A List of Assets was the last show staged by Meyerhold in the theater building on Sadovaya-Triumfalnaya Street, where he had worked for ten years straight. This building, constructed long before the October Revolution, had become rickety long ago. "Over a period of several years, firefighters, sanitary and communal organizations had noted the gradual deterioration of the building." Finally, the Commissariat for Education assigned funds for capital repairs. But Meyerhold decided that there was no sense in repairing the old theater and suggested that it be demolished along with several old neighboring houses, that a new theater building be constructed. The Commissariat agreed.

A round sum of a million rubles was assigned at the beginning. The architects M. Barkhin and S. Vakhtangov, in close cooperation with Meyerhold, began developing a plan for a hitherto undreamed-of theater. Many of Meyerhold's fondest dreams were tied to this project. In the new building, he intended to stage Pushkin's *Boris Godunov*, Shakespeare's *Othello* and *Hamlet*, Mérimée's musical drama *Carmen*, in a new stage version by Isaac Babel and Nikolai Erdman, a new version of Mayakovsky's *Mystery-Bouffe* that was being worked on by Osip Brik, N. Aseev, and S. Kirsanov, and more. But all this was still in the distant future, although Meyerhold did not believe it to be so distant. "In the fall of 1932," the press reported, "the building is to be ready."[34]

Until that time, Meyerhold's theater wandered around clubs, performed for a time on Mamonov Lane, then obtained temporary space at 15 Tverskaya Street (where the Ermolova Theater is now). The Master began to work on the production of *Prelude*, based on the story of the same title by Yury German. Yu. German's story, Meyerhold told a reporter from *Evening Moscow*, "was praised highly by Maxim Gorky. The idea of turning this large tale into a play was suggested to the theater by the Commissar for Education, A. S. Bubnov."[35] The manner in which his story was turned into a play and the way the production, first shown on January 28, 1933, was put together is well described by Yury German himself.[36]

This time too the elements of the show did not form an artistic whole. First of all, this was because there was no play, but only a fairly ordinary adaptation, in which only three or four episodes permitted flashes of Meyerhold's talent. In this work, Meyerhold wished to "use techniques of Shakespearean theater," to treat in a Shakespearean manner the "complex collisions resulting from the conflict of contradictions";[37] he strove for tragedy. He succeeded only in isolated episodes of the staged narrative of the dismal fate of the German intelligentsia. I. Bachelis wrote that in the show there are "three or four episodes in which Meyerhold speaks with full voice, with the full measure of his amazing craftsmanship," that in those places where the director's creative gunpowder "is able to explode, it explodes with blinding force, blasting the spectator with the full heat of Meyerhold's genius, captivating him with all the force of his sudden and rapid movement."[38]

These episodes are memorable and well known. The high point of the show was the corporate dinner, the last scene of the second act, in which the scientist Kelberg, having returned from Shanghai to Berlin, meets his former schoolmates. The author had written an awkward, drawn-out scene: the guests entered the cafe one after another, presented themselves to those present, each one named himself... Meyerhold turned this stage clumsiness into an idiotic and rather eerie performance by the former students: theirs is a drunken play at a reception; everyone knows everyone else perfectly well and they have been drinking together for a long time, but each one leaves and appears again, grandly and stupidly naming himself. The rest laugh drunkenly; they roar and whinny...

"The cafe scene," wrote A. Matskin at the time, "is the height of the show from the point of view of direction. The glimmering candles, the shining top hats, the actors' slow movements, the hysterical note in the dialogue—all this creates a mood of condensed desperation, true tragedy."[39]

The soloist and emotional focus in this scene was L. Sverdlin in the role of Nunbach, once a talented engineer, a former builder of skyscrapers, and now a vendor of pornographic cards. Meyerhold, first of all, gave Nunbach a magnificent passage through the corporate crowd. In this way, observed Yuzovsky, the director

> tore the mask off with a single jerk and killed the European restaurant-foxtrot ideal of life that seems very attractive to many. Meyerhold achieves this in a single staging. This is the curved line that is followed by the tipsy Nunbach across the stage, half-foxtrotting to the music. These are not light, airy foxtrot steps that evoke a smile of pleasure instead of presupposed outrage. Each step by Nunbach is a step of despair, hatred, confusion, depression, anger—he tramples this banal little motif of petty-bourgeois well-being.

After the end of the party and the departure of all these deans and professors, the drunken Nunbach remained in the emptied cafe, alone with a marble bust of Goethe. The greatest of all Germans looked contemptuously down from his pedestal at this least of his descendants. Here, Nunbach-Sverdlin climbed up onto the table, embraced the marble Goethe, turned his face toward himself and asked: "Why do I not build houses?" Goethe, noted Yukovsky, is silent not only because he is marble, but because "he really has nothing to say." The incarnation of creative energy remained silent before the emasculated creator, the squashed, destroyed, effaced personality.

Analyzing the director's construction of the episode, the critic noted the merits of its musical score, carefully organized by Meyerhold and Shebalin. He wrote:

> This musical phrase is continuously cut through by rapid, nervous drumming. This is from the circus—before the "death-defying number," this is from the streets where the executions were accompanied by drums. This is very astute psychological motivation, preparation that has a resolution. Sverdlin, the actor, plays this role with great internal excitement, and Meyerhold does not move him into the background at all, as it may appear to some who accuse Meyerhold of undervaluing the actor. On the contrary, Sverdlin-Nunbach is in the foreground all the time, and the preparation, the drumming, is only the care of the director who supports the actor, helps him bring the idea to the audience.

The central figure of the show, however, was not Nunbach but Kelberg, played by G. Michurin. Kelberg's role developed slowly and drearily on an openly didactic plane. The scientist eventually came to the decision to leave Germany for the Soviet Union. Meyerhold could not change the elementary logic of the role. But he presented the moment of decision itself with maximum expressiveness and simplicity. "He gave us springtime, the window open wide, the fluttering curtains, the draft." This curtain reminded Yuzovsky of old Chekhov shows in the Art Theater. There, in Chekhov's plays, he wrote, curtains "moved, expressed the mood of an intimate, detailed experience, they closed the circuit," they "bespoke coziness."[40] Here, a huge curtain flew at the auditorium at almost a right angle. With this image of wind, light, and spring, Meyerhold expressed the powerful drive to happiness and indicated the possibility of leaving the tragedy behind.

In the reviews of *Prelude*, the critics observed with amazement the sharp psychology of Meyerhold's directing. "As never before," stated Matskin, "Meyerhold strives for psychological truth. He depicts the psychology of the protagonists with quick strokes."[41] I. Bachelis observed that:

> It is time to leave the legend of Meyerhold's anti-psychology. His last works make it absolutely necessary to speak of his mastery of the psychological study—a unique mastery, so bright and visible that it is impossible to ignore. In the system of a Meyerhold show some single psychological detail is brought to the foreground of the action. Meyerhold seeks a *tragic* sound for it, appears to place it under a magnifying glass, and the slight psychological movement obtains a tremendous Michelangelesque scale and proportion that borders on deformity, but is filled with tension and passion. Successfully or not, Meyerhold (in *The Last Decisive Battle*, in *A List of Assets*, and in *Prelude*) feels out his own approaches to *tragedy*. Of course he wants to stage *Hamlet*! And, perhaps, of all the modern masters of theater only Meyerhold could really cope with the problem of staging contemporary tragedy.[42]

The critic was correct and, subsequently, in the staging of *One Life* that the public never did get to see, Meyerhold proved most convincingly that he was capable of presenting not only fragments of tragedy, but a whole, powerful tragic show based on a single breath. In the early 1930s he had to content himself with episodes, individual tragic "pieces." Yuzovsky's article about *Prelude* was entitled "Author! Author..." because the critic awaited and called for "that unknown playwright whom Meyerhold awaits so impatiently." Again and again the critic, each time Meyerhold encountered a modern play, saw "a giant who is bedded down in a crib."[43]

This sort of tragicomic image inevitably appeared in the consciousness of the critics, since Meyerhold's directing talent was excessive for those plays that he staged with abstinence and inspiration. All the plays used by Meyerhold for his sketches of tragedy were almost never staged again. Neither *The Commander of the Second Army*, nor *The Last Decisive Battle*, nor *A List of Assets*, nor *Prelude*, had any real stage history outside of Meyerhold's theater. Meyerhold's relations with contemporary playwrights deteriorated. Vishnevsky and Selvinsky were in conflict with him. Erdman, depressed by the fate of *The Suicide*, wrote no more. After *A List of Assets* Olesha was silent for a long time too. The plays by Afinogenov and Kirshon, the most performed playwrights of the day, could not be of interest to Meyerhold. It could be supposed that if Meyerhold had staged Pogodin (who sent him his comedy *The Snow*), Leonov, or Kulish at that time, the results would have been significant and interesting. But such speculations are fruitless. Equally fruitless, however, were plans to stage new plays by V. Volkenshtein, A. Bezymensky, and P. Zheleznov, about which the Meyerhold Theater informed the public. The matter went no further than newspaper interviews.

Meyerhold turned once again to the classics.

AGAIN THE CLASSICS

The small group of classical plays staged by Meyerhold between 1933 and 1935 (*Krechinsky's Wedding, Camille, The Queen of Spades* and *33 Fainting Fits*) is interesting first of all for two basic themes that emerged in the director's works of these years: the striving for unity in the production and the harmonization of all its aspects, first of all, and secondly, the extremely intensive psychology. Both these themes appeared in Meyerhold's directing work with a certain biographical regularity.

He fully realized that only fragments had been successful in the shows of the previous cycle. He understood, too, that the main cause of the fragmented nature was the sketchiness or the schematic nature of the plays he worked on. Now, by selecting works possessing unblemished theatrical reputation, he undoubtedly wished to demonstrate brilliant mastery in the staging of the play, not the scene, not the episode, but the entire production. That he was not uniformly successful is another question, as we shall see.

Further, in the same natural fashion, Meyerhold's art demonstrated an ever-increasing interest in psychology, in the uncovering of the inner motivations for the protagonist's actions, the tragic or the comic traits in his soul. Meyerhold with his usual sensitivity to the audience, to the reactions of the auditorium, sensed the intense attention that brought particular success to the most striking episodes of his tragedies. The audiences of the early 1930s clearly preferred those fragments of Meyerhold's directorial score in which the dynamism and expressiveness of his stage solutions "served" the figure of the hero and brought the actor emotionally to the foreground. The episode with Bogolyubov in the finale of *The Last Decisive Battle*, Raikh's silent passage in *A List of Assets*, Nunbach's scene with the bust of Goethe in *Prelude*, all took on the character of superbly staged "solo numbers" by actors against a background of relative neutrality. This was explained not only by the refinement and power of these solutions by Meyerhold (some mass scenes in these productions were masterful, too), but also by a characteristic selectivity on the part of the audience, which required human specifics in the development of any thought, the concentration of any theme into the deed of a given hero.

This mood in the audience was clearly contradictory to one of the fundamental principles that had been developed gradually in Meyerhold's art—the principle of panoramic representation of the world in its crises. In Meyerhold's shows there appeared living concentrations of the epic contradictions and conflicts evoked by the greatest changes of the century. It was difficult to change the point of view. And although the 1930s dictated evident changes in Meyerhold's art, it changed painfully and with difficulty.

In his productions of the classics in the first half of the 1930s, the interpretation of an individual role becomes more substantial in principle than the interpretation of the milieu, the social picture of life, and more significant than a new interpretation of the style and world-view of the author. In the shows of his new (and, as it turned out, his last) cycle, the central figures of the classical plays step into the foreground.

If we schematize the director's evolution somewhat, we can say that if previously Meyerhold needed human figures as points of support for the composition and presented them only insofar as was necessary for the development of the episode, to reveal its direct or metaphorical meaning, now he constructed the entire episode so as to present a concrete figure with maximum freedom of movement and to give a more distinct expression of its essence. Previously, the "unit of measure" had been the director's episode that pretended to arbitrariness, to a specific esthetic interpretation of reality. Now this task was given to the protagonists of the show. The director's scores served them, presented them. Interest in the general processes of history, in styles and philosophical ideas, was replaced by interest in the interior world of man.

Meyerhold manifests an unusual, early passion for the stage portrait, for the detailed and acute characterization of a character, for his movement through the show. By concerning himself with the personal, the individual, and the characteristic in these years, Meyerhold closely approaches a psychology of special, intense and nervous contours as never before. It is symptomatic that in this particular time he recalls his favorite actors with particular tenderness—from Lensky and Komissarzhevskaya to Moskvin and Mikhail Chekhov. The notes made by A. K. Gladkov in the 1930s eloquently testify to this.

When beginning the rehearsals of *Krechinsky's Wedding*, Meyerhold suddenly reminds his company of Mikhail Chekhov's "incredible performances" in *The Affair*, and immediately produces a fantastic plan for the immediate return of Chekhov to Moscow, to no place other than the GOSTIM cast. Chekhov, he said, has now "moved closer to our borders. He now lives in Lithuania, in Kovno, where he is the director of a theater studio and leads some kind of class; he has grown a little beard..." Therefore he, Meyerhold, is ready to "turn to the appropriate places" and together with his friend the Lithuanian Ambassador Yu. Baltrushaitis, to fly to Kovno to get Chekhov. "He won't have time to gasp when the bear sits on him." If the collective permits, continues Meyerhold, "I will ask that he take the part of an actor with us, since I believe that he will not damage our 'structure.' "[1] Most likely, Mikhail Chekhov never even learned that the bear was planning "to sit on him." This incident, however, is expressive in that it shows what kinds of actors Meyerhold was dreaming of in the early 1930s and the actors' solutions he was striving towards.

The dream of an actor of Chekhov's type and makeup (if Chekhov's own genius was inaccessible) was in full accord with that extreme activity with which Meyerhold turned at this time to plays that were not only standard repertory, but which could be said to be overplayed, dirtied by the stage. He re-examined the traditional routine techniques for performing them. *Krechinsky's Wedding*, Chekhov's vaudevilles, *Camille*, by Dumas *fils,* had been over a period of many years the mainstays both of serious stage in the capitals and of non-serious provincial and amateur theater. Tradition had given all the roles in these plays a particular interpretation, and routine had burdened them with entire collections of cliches, devices repeated hundreds of times and effects that were unfailingly striking.

Verdi's opera *La Traviata*, written on the subject of *Camille*, was performed in virtually every operatic theater in the country. The same was true for Tchaikovsky's

The Queen of Spades.

The fact that in these years Meyerhold stages well-worn works is in itself an indication of the aggressiveness of his intentions. He wishes to wipe off the banal makeup of routine—both dramatic and operatic—from these most popular works. This direction of his efforts under the conditions of the temporary stage space at 15 Tverskaya Street is no doubt connected with the parallel, highly intensive preparation of the shows which Meyerhold hoped to present on the new stage in the new building of his theater—first of all, the productions of *Boris Godunov* and *Hamlet*.

The elimination of routine and of the yoke of established stage traditions in the treatment of the most popular roles becomes a means for a completely new reading of the classics, a method for the discovery of new connections between its images and contemporary life. The realism of new outlines must be preceded by the removal from the classical texts of the sediment that dirtied its past—this is the starting point for all of Meyerhold's work of this time, in particular his work on *Krechinsky's Wedding*.

When Meyerhold had staged *Krechinsky's Wedding* for the first time in 1917, on the Alexandrinsky stage with V. Davydov as Rasplyuev and Yu. Yurev as Krechinsky, he had not tried to oppose the long-established interpretations and variations that had encrusted each part. These incrustations were so great that the play was practically no longer felt beneath them. According to M. Levidov's clever comment, the play "became a sort of piano for the exercise of mighty virtuosos."[2] The two best roles—Krechinsky and Rasplyuev—were, naturally, the most standardized. These were the ones that now attracted Meyerhold's special attention.

Before the opening, which took place on April 14, 1933, Meyerhold said that in his understanding "Krechinsky is a type of willful and frightful swindler, called to act in the world as an agent of great Capital." He compared Krechinsky to characters from Balzac and Mirbeau. He believed that the entire play "is a tragedy of people with money, because of money, in the name of money."[3] Hence, from such an interpretation of the main theme of the play appeared the desire to enlarge extremely, to present Krechinsky's figure on a grand scale. This intention suggested the selection of the performer, too. Yu. Yurev—Meyerhold's old Don Juan and his Arbenin—was invited to play Krechinsky. The fact that Yurev had played Krechinsky for many years before that on the Alexandrinsky stage, including Meyerhold's 1917 production, in no way demonstrated Meyerhold's readiness to continue the old, traditional interpretation of the role but rather showed his desire to reinterpret it in a new manner. Yurev attracted Meyerhold because of his ability to attribute to his stage images a cold demonic quality, an arrogant significance. This is precisely what was required. In Meyerhold's 1933 production Krechinsky was a monumental, willful, powerful and cynical adventurer.

In his direction Meyerhold stressed particularly the infernal quality and the horrifying mystery of Krechinsky. Meyerhold's Krechinsky, wrote Yuzovsky, "cannot humble himself. He is important. He is filled with dignity. Meyerhold appears to bring Krechinsky out supported under the arms. He ascribes significance to each of his words and gestures. He does not show him all at once. First, he only presents a hand (from behind a screen). Krechinsky is as majestic as fate, as destiny, before which all is powerless."[4]

Accenting this fateful majesty, Meyerhold constructed all the stagings in the first act in such a way that the spectators could not see Krechinsky's face—only his back or his hand "performed." This man hides his face. Furthermore, in Meyerhold's idea he is not a solitary swindler but the head of a whole gang, a band called Krechinsky & Co. In the second act this gang was brought out on stage in Krechinsky's apartment. Characters added by the director, members of Krechinsky's "guard," flickered and circled before him in his semi-dark lair and then, in the last act, they were present as members of an orchestra invited by Krechinsky. When Rasplyuev became entangled in his lies, they drowned out his words with horn music. When Nelkin broke in with his revelations, they dragged him away. But, of course, their main task was to underscore Krechinsky's power and force.

Such an active enlargement of the scale of the leading role and such a representational, demonically-majestic interpretation of the part by Yurev entered into an uneasy and even slightly comical contradiction with the relatively modest and simple plot of the play. The tragedy that Meyerhold wished to present here was subverted by the plot. A. Gvozdev wrote that it "inevitably drops and changes into melodrama."[5] Yu. Yuzovsky also stated: "Meyerhold's gigantic Krechinsky requires corresponding actions, thoughts, deeds. But these actions, thoughts, and deeds needed by Meyerhold's plan were absent in *Krechinsky's Wedding*." In consequence, continued the critic, "this whole tragedy is false. Krechinsky's image, unsupported by the play, hangs like a heavy weight in the show."

Quite unexpectedly, the interpretation of the role of Nelkin, performed by M. Chikul, was very convincing. Meyerhold suddenly presented the fairly helpless *raisonneur* of Sukhovo-Kobylin as a romantic hero. He gave Nelkin Pechorin's uniform, a Caucasian wool hat and the angry, easily inflamed nature of Chatsky. "He is a dreamer and a rebel," wrote Yuzovsky about this Nelkin. "He is not just in love with Lidochka, his love for her is the incarnation of a romantic ideal of happiness... Here, Meyerhold presents a fine flashback from *Woe to Wit*. There the audience sympathizes with Chatsky, here, with Nelkin."

In the same article, Yuzovsky observed that Meyerhold "bypassed" the role of Muromsky, that he "inked over" Muromsky in the play, "did not remove him from the play, but at the same time appeared to remove him."[6] The director actually did move Muromsky to the background. This figure did not interest him, and in his conception of the play Muromsky was given a passive, suffering role. The theme of Rasplyuev, however, was developed with extreme thoroughness.

Meyerhold sensed the theme of Rasplyuevism, the theme of the loss of human dignity, the shamelessness of evil, the delight in one's own baseness, as the theme of Fascism, in 1933. He said: "From the stage of our theater Rasplyuev will shine with material which modern Fascist Caliphs may find useful as material for the formation of a model soldier in the Crusade against the new world that is being created by the new humanity."[7]

I. Ilinsky, who played Rasplyuev, wrote subsequently that in this show there was much

good and healthy imagination by Meyerhold. When in the second act Krechinsky fought with Rasplyuev and shook him on the sofa, playing cards fell from the most varied and unexpected parts of Rasplyuev. The card-sharp Rasplyuev, in Meyerhold's humorous conception, had a mass of decks and marked cards which he had stuffed everywhere possible. The collecting of the buttons ripped off after the fight was very well handled.

Rasplyuev's first appearance was also done in a new way. Rasplyuev entered the stage unexpectedly, backside first, quickly rushing through the door, then he fell stock still, listening to what was going on behind the door, to see whether he was being chased. On the back of his coat there was chalked the enormous handprint of one of his pursuers, evidently that of Semipyadov himself. Having made sure that he had managed to avoid pursuit, he slowly turned to the audience with a ten of spades in his hand and plaintively, "mystically," said: "What is this? Money...cards...fate...happiness...an evil, frightful delirium! Life... Everything has been used. Impoverished and wretched!" This was the beginning of Rasplyuev's role. There were many humorous details.[8]

It is characteristic, however, that Ilinsky recalled mainly just the purely comical discoveries he and Meyerhold had made, and the "humorous details," but he wrote almost nothing at all concerning those moments in the show where his Rasplyuev was "frightful" and echoed the Rasplyuev from *The Death of Tarelkin*. Meanwhile there were undoubted efforts made in the show to overcome the humor and to take the empathy of the audience away from Rasplyuev. For instance, Rasplyuev's famous monologue about "little birds, little children," who "will die from hunger and cold," was performed by Ilinsky with intentional indifference and with a clear tint of falseness. The director and the actor did not wish for the spectators to believe Rasplyuev at this time or to feel sorry for him. Many precise acting strokes in the characterization of Rasplyuev were designed to evoke distaste for him. Ilinsky, wrote A. Matskin, "is most interesting in the tragic episodes. He plays fright, hatred, fear—more graphically and expressively than satiety, satisfaction and happiness."[9] Gvozdev observed that "great expressive force is used to mark the scene in which he, on his knees, kisses the banknotes brought in by Krechinsky. In Rasplyuev are depicted the traits of the future Derzhimorda-type police chiefs."[10]

Still, these were not the dominant traits. The critics came to the conclusion that Ilinsky "is funny, very funny, touching in places."[11]

Externally, Meyerhold's directing activity with regard to the play was relatively minor. He did indicate that "Sukhovo-Kobylin's text is repaired, altered in places. There are a number of pieces that I have recomposed ('bridges' where there are cuts, the so-called 'director's modulations,' and new scenes that are richer than those that the author brought forth under the conditions of ancient theatrical technique)."[12]

As we have mentioned, he introduced into the play seven confederates of Krechinsky and several other "characters by the author of the show"—the barber Joseph, Bek's wife and daughter, two Tatars, the janitor, coachman, three police "musketeers." He moved the last act from Krechinsky's apartment to the kitchens hired by Krechinsky, purely for advantage. But all these additions and corrections, as compared to Meyerhold's work on the texts of *The Inspector General* and *Woe to Wit*, were careful, fairly modest and indirect.

The design by V. Shestakov was also distinguished by restraint and modesty. The white planes of the walls were broken up by a few expressive details—two candlesticks, a vase with flowers, a painted portrait... This design did not pretend to emotional or stylistic significance, but rather was satisfied with a purely serviceable role. It designated the place of action and gave the action an essentially neutral background. Neither the projector that projected signs onto the curtain, "information about events," nor the music by M. Starokadomsky went outside the limits of the usual subsidiary functions.

All the director's energy was thrown into the interpretation and the re-evaluation of the roles in the play, toward the creation of several figures. This is where it turned out that Meyerhold's basic intentions remained unexecuted. The tradition against which he warred so boldly conquered the roles anyway. Yurev gradually returned, according to Ilinsky, to "his former picture of the role."[13] Ilinsky himself quietly slipped back into the "classical Rasplyuev." Levidov wrote of him: "You can say: ah, here's Davydov, here's Kuznetsov."[14]

This sort of reverse movement was predetermined—however strangely this may sound—by the passivity of Meyerhold's plan. Despite his radical re-evaluation of the roles of Krechinsky and Rasplyuev, he did not attempt this time to explore the relations between his characters and the modern life that surrounded the theater. Mentally, he moved Sukhovo-Kobylin's heroes far to the west. Krechinsky, he said, "must be perceived as the image of lying bourgeois reality, as the life that still exists in capitalist society." Rasplyuev, he asserted, "is again called to life in the west."[15] The images of the old Russian play became separated from the new Russian way of life. The real problem, however, was that the powerful and infernal Krechinsky as seen by Meyerhold really did evoke no close associations. Furthermore, the theme of money that rang with such spirit through the show was fairly relativistic for the audience of 1933. The ration cards for food and household goods and the closed shops of that day made money a pure fiction. No one asked "How much does it cost?" The question was: "Where do they have it?" Under such circumstances, Krechinsky's "full million" meant nothing, and the chase for a million appeared ridiculous. It was already the subject for the amusement of the readers of *The Twelve Chairs*, the novel by Ilf and Petrov. A year later, in 1934, *The Golden Calf* was published. The hero of this novel, a direct descendant of Krechinsky, did obtain the longed-for million. It turned out that there was nothing to do with this million and nowhere to go. The spectators at *Krechinsky's Wedding* knew this very well.

This is why the old actors' tradition gradually smoothed over and rounded off the breaks made in the role of Krechinsky by the hand of the director. This massive figure, neutral with respect to the new life, was returned to the waxworks of the types of a "former period." The spectators' interest was concentrated around Ilinsky-Rasplyuev. The tragicomedy of this scum, performed with clowning and cynical straightforwardness, became the final, true content of the production.

Ilinsky wrote in his memoirs that *Krechinsky's Wedding* was an unquestionable success, but added that the show "did not have the sound, did not thunder like shows by Meyerhold thundered in their time."[16]

Still, one supposes that it was not a success. A sensation of depression, lassitude, and despondency spread through the auditorium. Only Ilinsky broke through the gloom of the slow-moving and somber spectacle with his bold "entrees" that overcame the gap between stage and audience. Something was wrong in Meyerhold's theater. With this show, Meyerhold shocked no one, outraged no one, did not irritate or surprise.

Krechinsky's Wedding, for all its interesting moments, was permeated with the spirit of waning and diluted talent. No one wrote about this. On the contrary, many articles thoroughly analyzed and commented on Meyerhold's staging. But the attitude of these articles was compassionate. People began to pity Meyerhold. Now he was written about respectfully and carefully, like an old, accepted virtuoso.

It is likely that this new compassionate tone did not make Meyerhold happy. The substantial, serious articles by Yu. Yuzovsky and A. Matskin were more than filled with good will; they methodically indicated all of Meyerhold's successes, but just as methodically noted all the injustices to the unity of the show, all the disruptions to the sequence and logic of development. By this time the popular sociological conceptions had already been rejected. New criteria for realism were advanced, the demand for truth of feeling was ever greater. Drama, the conflict of passions, a new beauty and new harmony were expected of theater. This was presented in several shows from the early 1930s: in Tairov's *An Optimistic Tragedy*, in *Egor Bulychov* in Vakhtangov's theater. Meyerhold, accustomed to be in advance of any theatrical movement, now had to do the catching up.

With an irritation   comprehensible to the historian he could speak of *Dead Souls* in the Art Theater, could believe that he had lost *An Optimistic Tragedy* through an accidental combination of unfortunate circumstances, could interpret variously the successes of Vakhtangov's company and those of the Theater of the Revolution, where Alexei Popov brilliantly staged Pogodin's *My Friend*. But all these circumstances of theatrical life taken together pointed to the fact that outside the Meyerhold Theater there was something new, that his stage system was weak in some link and, therefore, now less attractive to audiences. Yuzovsky wrote concerning *Krechinsky's Wedding*: "This is not a unified show, not an ensemble connected together by a single plot—this is a gallery of heroes who, independently of each other for the most part, pass across the stage... The interconnection is torn, since the common ground on which the heroes come together is destroyed."[17]

This rebuke could be applied to more than just *Krechinsky's Wedding*. The attention to *individual* figures that Meyerhold was now exhibiting harmed the unity of the show in the same way that the active interpretation of *individual* pieces, fragments of the director's score, had recently destroyed the unity. The time, however, demanded harmony, longed for it one might say, and clearly preferred all forms of balance, well-proportioned parts, and artistic unity. Structurally disharmonic art and art that saw the world as crisis were rejected. The time illuminated everything with a happy smile: Vishnevsky's tragedy was optimistic, Shchukin's Egor Bulychov danced at his own funeral, while Pogodin's enthusiasts, who worked until they dropped, spoke of themselves as "the nervously ill people of today," and joked as they rebuilt the world. Humor became universal, the major key was triumphant. When Alexei Popov staged *Romeo and Juliet* he cleansed Shakespeare's tragedy of the "black colors" of tragedy and praised young, victorious love. This production was dedicated to the Young Communists.

Another important theme appeared. Just recently there had been arguments about whether classics were necessary at all, and when the classics were defended in principle, they were broken on the wheel of popular sociology. In 1928, in *A Conspiracy of Feelings* by Olesha, the "new man" Andrei Babichev wanted to name a new type of sausage Ophelia. But already by 1932 Akimov's *Hamlet* elicited a unanimous outcry of outrage. Previously, calumny had been the lot of those who staged the classics. Now the outrage was directed at those who distorted its noble and unfaded beauty. The idea of access to the magnificent and great heritage of the art of previous years became one of the central ideas of the time.

Meyerhold guessed and understood these new requirements. His response— both sudden and decisive—was *Camille*.

The selection of this play aroused a wave of objections. Was it worth staging the over-performed melodrama by Dumas *fils*? He is not a classic, his place is not on the Soviet stage—these were the approximate arguments of many critics. "There is nothing to be said about this typically petty-bourgeois play in terms of any social significance," glumly stated D. Talnikov. The fact that Marguerite Gautier had been performed by Sarah Bernhardt and Eleonora Duse was not justification for Meyerhold in the eyes of the majority of his critics. On the contrary, they rebuked the director for supporting the disproportionate actorial pretensions of Zinaida Raikh, for his barely concealed desire to make her an important actress. D. Talnikov cited Dumas *fils* on the subject of a director of the Parisian Vaudeville Theater who at first did not wish to stage the play, but "found a role there for his wife and accepted it."[18]

Meyerhold was becoming ever more tolerant. He did not respond to this attack. He ignored all the critical objections to *Camille*. Primarily, this was probably because the show enjoyed a tremendous success, was continuously sold out (something the GOSTIM had not seen for some time), and the voices of the critics did not sound very convincing against this background.

There were two causes this time for Meyerhold's incredible and sensational success.

First of all, in contrast to his usual practice, he oriented all his work on *Camille* specifically toward the mass Moscow audience. He did not argue with the public, did not cross it or get ahead of it, did not force unassimilated criteria on it, but moved simply and directly to meet its tastes. By exaggerating the situation somewhat (but only slightly!), it may be said that in *Camille* Meyerhold seriously worked to satisfy the requirement that Mayakovsky had ridiculed in *The Bathhouse*: "make it beautiful for us."

Secondly, in order to carry out this task, Meyerhold mobilized and simultaneously stabilized all the tested capabilities of his craftsmanship. In this production, possibly for the only time in his entire artistic life, he performed not as an experimenter, but as a master.

It is known that in the theater he was always called the Master. "The Master said, the Master decided..." This is how it had been, and Meyerhold liked it. But in the full sense—in the self-limitation of the artist and the reining-in of the experimenter—he became a master only in his work on *Camille*.

The declarations that preceded the show, first performed on March 19, 1934, presented, as usual, the political justification for the director's intentions. They had never sounded as relativistic or as formal as they did this time. Meyerhold stated that he was striving to expose "a bourgeois who corrupts a young girl of the people," quoted Babel and, finally, he said weakly that the "heavy battle for existence compels women under these conditions to act in ways that they probably would not follow under better conditions." All this, however, had no real connection with the actual content of the play.

Its true sense was the defense of eternal womanhood, a defense that was particularly notable in that it was carried out as a melodrama of the life of a *demimondaine*, a strictly private life. Furthermore, this very individual, hero-less life, totally alien to social interests and social inspiration, this petty and narrow life, became the subject of consistent and tender beautification. The theme of femininity was connected directly with the theme of beauty, which was presented in this production of Meyerhold's in a most concrete sense. The director forced the spectators to marvel at the beauty of the setting, the costumes, the staging compositions and the colors throughout the show. In *Camille*, admiration became law and the sole possible form for its perception. Even opponents of the production succumbed to the magic of its beauty.

"Unarguably, *Camille* is a very beautiful show," wrote Yuzovsky. "Meyerhold puts a real antique vase on the table. And the whole stage is reflected in and admires itself in this vase, strives to resemble it and to compose a finished grouping with it."[19] Talnikov, who called *Camille* a "grandmothers' show," also could not help observing the graceful craftsmanship "in the stagings, in the overall composition... in the overall impression which delights with its whiteness, clarity, and freshness... Marguerite," he wrote, obviously admiring Meyerhold's composition, "in a black dress against a background of white spaciousness and flashing lights..."[20]

Meyerhold gave beauty, external beauty, to the entire show, and in this sense *Camille* appeared to cancel out his previous post-Revolutionary experience. A. Gvozdev explained:

> Meyerhold has wisely taken into account the correction that our mass audience brings to the perception of a show. Meyerhold has taken into account that our mass audience has grown up culturally, that in the Second Five Year Plan he, the spectator, will be able to place an entire range of social accents in the play and be content with the hints that the director provides for him. Therefore, Meyerhold speaks to the mass audience in a different theatrical language than the one he used in *The Forest* ten years ago. Then, a sharp, poster-like accentuation was needed—green and red wigs, screens with the sign "prays and cheats, cheats and prays." Today, such acute accenting of social masks, such a blow at the forehead, such exposés suggested to the spectator, yield to other methods of influence that are far more refined.[21]

Thus, Gvozdev answered the question of why Meyerhold did not alter the text of Dumas *fils*' melodrama, why he did not use at least the technique of active directorial re-interpretation of its leading roles—after all, he had just used this method in *Krechinsky's Wedding*. Still, Gvozdev's explanations were not particularly convincing, since the "refinement of social nuance" that he referred to had disappeared from the production.

A. Afinogenov wrote in his diary: "*Camille*... Fine poison of decay...this was the attraction of the old world, brilliance, velvet, silk, shining objects...and the story that a prostitute is also a woman...take pity on her, poor spectators, give her a hundred thousand francs so she can straighten out her fate with Armand... And the spectators applaud with delight and cry out bravo!... Not a spectacle but gratification, not mysticism but decay, bustle...nonsense, and rot!"

This comment is in expressive contrast to Afinogenov's intention "to write a play with songs and sadness," to his discussions of how "people wished to live better, more beautifully,.." to his remarks that "artists tore themselves apart trying to carry out orders for decorating apartments,..." that "the painting of walls, paintings, porcelain, hygiene...everything penetrated into life and made it wonderful." After seeing the film *Little Mama* with Francesca Gaal, Afinogenov was enraptured. "She played a young girl who found an abandoned child, and she herself was declared to be the mother. This is how the role of the mother was portrayed, while the young man, who did not even love her in the beginning, was declared the father. And their happiness was made by the child that did not belong to them..." After telling this sugary tale, the writer concluded: "The performance and particularly the scenario are excellent" and he was angry that some of his colleagues thought the whole plot to be bourgeois: "What a great slice of life they give up to capitalism!"[22]

It is tempting to continue endlessly with excerpts from Afinogenov's diary: with delightful sincerity they present the climate of the time, clearly show the social and the moral situation in which *Camille* was staged. However outraged Afinogenov may have been by this show, Meyerhold was expressing his, Afinogenov's, esthetic ideal and realizing his dream and, naturally, doing it better, more gracefully, and more finely than Francesca Gaal.

Vishnevsky, who at the time was Afinogenov's direct antipode and argued with him at length, speaking out against the chamber drama, also criticized *Camille*, not in his diary but in *Literary Gazette*. He accused Meyerhold of diffidence: "This play by a bourgeois moralist remains untouched in its main lines." He asserted that "the show is asocial" and that its theme should be quite different. Further, Vishnevsky listed, without a ghost of humor, the items omitted by Meyerhold: Parisian Communards, Garibaldi's men, Thiers, Hugo, the inauguration of the First International, the Marseillaise, "the black-skinned sons of France awaiting freedom..." When reading this crackling list one cannot but be amazed. Vishnevsky complained: "The concept of satire, the grotesque, the pamphlet, the concept of hate has disappeared somewhere." He asked: "can it be that 'Theatrical October' is not October at all?" But even Vishnevsky admitted unwillingly that the show was "beautifully, masterfully engraved."[23]

What was this beauty and what kind of beauty was this? When working on this play by Dumas, Meyerhold tried to see it with the eyes of Edouard Manet and Renoir. The painter I. Leistikov reproduced the style of "transparent and fresh Impressionism, those light and tender lilac blue and rose tones, of Renoir or Manet that pour with a fine light through the entire atmosphere of this show."[24] The music by V. Shebalin varied the themes of Lecocq and Offenbach. The artistic and musical atmosphere of the show, consequently, was borrowed from the epoch in which the play had been written by Dumas *fils* and was to transpose it into the key of true art of that time. The melodrama was beautified by marvelous creations that had appeared at about the same time as the play. While retaining externally a calm neutrality with regard to Dumas's text, Meyerhold insistently tore away the rust of sentimentality. No one less than Nemirovich noted this. To M. M. Yanshin's question of whether Meyerhold's staging of *Camille* contains sentimentalism, Vladimir Ivanovich replies: "Dumas's play is permeated with sentimentalism: society rejects the courtesan Marguerite, but in the end all these people turn out to be very good, and everything that happened is explained as a misunderstanding. ·Meyerhold has staged *Camille* bravely, since sentimentalism is not the same as sentimentality..."[25]

Meyerhold wished to present this melodrama as a tragedy—drily and with restraint, dynamically and intensely. Nearly all the stagings were unfolded diagonally. Meyerhold avoided frontal compositions, since the harmony of the whole, in his idea, had to appear in the finale as a sum of disharmonious, unbalanced, and nervous director's pieces, as the conclusion to a rapid and thought-out alternation of rhythm. The show was constructed according to the laws of a musical work. Following a piece staged in *andante* rhythm was a *capriccioso* piece, then a *grave* piece, and so on. The stagings were in each case astonishing in their graceful and laconic nature.

The beginning of the first act. The static, cool scene of the chatter between Varville (P. Starkovsky) and Nanine (N. Serebryannikova) preceded Marguerite's entrance (Zinaida Raikh). Varville was playing the piano, Nanine, at the other end of the stage, was knitting. They tossed lines back and forth weakly. Suddenly, the stage was crossed by a fantastic cavalcade: two youths in frock-coats, top hats raised high over their heads, leaped around, representing horses. Behind them, with whip and reins, ran Marguerite. Following her, her friend Adele ran, with a warm scarf in her hand—the only indication of Marguerite's illness. In general, Meyerhold rejected the traditional image here of a consumptive, frail Marguerite, and began her theme as victorious, carefree and happy.

As for Marguerite's doom, there was a metaphorical reminder of this in the finale of the act, in the little costume ball scene where Meyerhold again created for an instant his beloved masquerade. He brought out a crowd of coquettes and "golden youths" in ridiculous large masks, opulent wigs, long noses, glued-on beards—an unpleasant frolicking crowd of grotesques and cretins. In this crowd there was also a mask of Death—as though direct from *The Puppet Show*—with a grinning skull face and a scythe in hand. But this mask did not pretend to symbolic significance. It appeared briefly, like a hint and a threat, then rapidly disappeared in the laughter of the short masquerade. It was only a detail, a fragment of the director's stage painting. For Meyerhold, the main task was to make the exposition of the play vivid, to do it in an artistic major key.

This tendency closely accompanied the entire development of the dramatic situation. The scene of the parting between Marguerite and Armand (M. Tsarev) was carried out entirely in a light blue color. The main color spot was Marguerite's blue jacket. Meyerhold, however, was not satisfied with this and illuminated the scene with a soft blue color. Then Marguerite took a blue cornflower from Armand's lapel—for remembrance.

The idyllic scene in Bougival: the veranda, large window, lavender curtains, a grapevine climbing up the wall, the sunny, live ("Mkhatian"—in Talnikov's acid phrase) illumination, a real parrot in a cage on the table, the gardener who brought in potted flowers, the country breakfast—milk, buns—all this was stage painting.

But these paintings, even such idyllic ones, were penetrated by anxiety that was expressed first of all in the stagings, in their nervous and trembling, rhythmically sharp movement. Furthermore, Meyerhold insistently introduced the theme of spiritual emptiness, of the cynicism and cheap effect of the *demimonde* into the show. Not everyone understood him in this. The same Talnikov was angry: "Marguerite's entire entourage, all of it, is pitiful and miserable. The morose little songs sound off-key and without temperament in the supposedly captivating mouths of these 'divas' of Meyerhold's theater; the cheap can-can lacks any sparkle or fire..."[26]

It was strange to suppose that Meyerhold would be unable to stage a can-can with "sparkle" and with "fire" or to carry out the elegant number with the singers. This, of course, was not his intention. The bravery of the staging consisted in the beautiful depiction of a life that was unbeautiful, "miserable," nonspiritual and without temperament. Under the conditions of such cheap petty-bourgeois lack of beauty Meyerhold built his spectacle like some build a fortress, in order to defend the sole real value of this world—Marguerite's feminine beauty.

This is precisely why things became the objects of beautification in this production. This plan of Meyerhold's was guessed by none of the critics. Talnikov fumed that "dead things" performed "as the replacement for the living force of the actor. In place of the actor," he asserted, "under the light of the projectors here 'perform' magnificently the marvelous goblets, recalling the play of Venetian glass, the fine real furniture of the age, real tables instead of props, chairs and sofas with wonderful pillows, vases of various kinds and colors, candelabras that create little corners pleasing to the eye in these interiors of living and dining rooms."[27] Yuzovsky believed that all these elegant fabrics, colors, dresses, vases, and glasses serve "to demonstrate the hypocritical plot by Dumas... Beauty asks the spectator to be tolerant toward a life that he wishes to see in a completely different light. Beauty attempts to provoke the spectator to 'lower his class vigilance.'[28]

In fact, Meyerhold's idea was very simple. Things are beautiful, the people that live among these things are miserable, banal, cruel and cynical. This simple contrast was quite pithy and found its development literally in all the staging constructions.

In the fourth act, in the scene of the decisive conversation between Marguerite and Armand, Meyerhold seated Raikh in a chair on the stage floor and compelled Tsarev to begin his monologue at the top of the stairs. A narrow, aimed beam of light grabbed the actor's face from the dark. Armand spoke, and after every sentence made a step forward, gradually approaching and descending toward Margherita diagonally, from the back right part of the stage, down to the lower left corner of the stage, right by the footlights.

The movement was constructed against a fresh white background among flickering lights. Marguerite, all in black, sat motionless. Then, in desperation, she jumped up, ran upward to that landing of the stairs that Yuzovsky called the "place of execution," and fell. At this moment Meyerhold doused the lights. Long shadows stretched along the walls cast by the candelabras that stood on the table, on the white tablecloth near two large vases with fruit.

The emotional conclusion was very clear. The man turned out to be pitiful, cowardly, insubstantial and ugly, while the woman was brought down and degraded, and the still life that concluded the scene was mournful and sad in its beauty that was independent of man and useful to no one...

The finale of the show—Marguerite's death—was resolved by Meyerhold in a staging of life triumphant. According to the play, Marguerite, dying, says: "You see, I am smiling, I am strong...life goes on! It is life that shakes me." In Meyerhold's show Marguerite spoke these words, rose suddenly from the chair and, grabbing the shade with both hands, opened the window. A bright ray of sunlight illuminated the room. Without letting the shade go from her right hand, Marguerite sank back into the chair, her back to the audience. After a long pause her left arm dropped from the chair's arm and hung down loosely. This is how Meyerhold established the instant of death.

Meyerhold, according to A. Gladkov, said: "When I staged *Camille* I hoped that a pilot who attended our show would fly better afterward."[29] This dream came true. *Camille* transmitted to the audience a sensation of the joy of confident mastery, the enjoyment of art, the freedom and lack of constraint of the director's gift for composition. Many masters of the theater believed (and continue to believe) this production to be Meyerhold's best. It would be fairly difficult to agree with such an evaluation—the problems resolved here by the Master were modest in comparison to those that he dealt with even in *Don Juan, Masquerade* or *The Inspector General*. One thing is without doubt—the production of *Camille* was beautiful, graceful, and harmonious.

But Meyerhold's very next work brought him again into the sphere of more complex esthetic problems. We are speaking of *The Queen of Spades*. After a long interval, Meyerhold again undertook to stage an opera, and a classical opera at that, one of the most popular on the Russian stage. This production was staged in Leningrad, in the Maly Opera Theater, where the idea of the need to renovate operatic art had already brought about a number of interesting experiments. The invitation tendered to Meyerhold was already evidence of the theater's reformist intentions. In his turn, Meyerhold was impressed by the activity of the young collective. Setting to work on Tchaikovsky's opera, he at once offered a number of radical suggestions that were to eliminate any "reader-book gloss" from *The Queen of Spades* and to make for a completely new interpretation of the work.

As we recall, he had already staged an opera with a story by Pushkin—Dargomyzhky's *The Stone Guest* in 1917. At that time he had sensed no contradiction between the music and the text for the simple reason that Dargomyzhsky had retained Pushkin's text in full. In *The Queen of Spades* the literary basis for the opera was the libretto by Modest Tchaikovsky which, first of all, moved Pushkin's story from the nineteenth to the eighteenth century and, secondly, moved the theme of the love between German and Liza to the foreground. Meyerhold was dissatisfied with the overworked libretto by Modest Tchaikovsky, and he assigned V. I. Stenich to write a new text containing as much verse by Pushkin as possible and returning the action to Pushkin's days, to the 1830s, bringing back both the plot and the spirit of Pushkin's story to the opera. Accordingly, the "staging plan" of the opera changed. Throughout the show Meyerhold strove to establish new and direct connections between Tchaikovsky's music and Pushkin's story, bypassing the situations of the old libretto wherever possible.

This approach was vulnerable in one critical point. Tchaikovsky had written the music following the libretto by his brother. Therefore, a real danger arose that some of the musical fragments would be in contradiction, in emotion or content, with the new staging plan.

The problem that Meyerhold set for himself was formulated as follows: to extract from Tchaikovsky's music "Pushkin's ideological equivalent," to express in the show "Pushkin's complex conception of *The Queen of Spades*, in particular of its central image, German...to deepen the theme of German, the theme of fateful, maniacal passion for money." At the same time he wished to "have no empty spots in the opera"; he wished that "all the communicating scenes sound Pushkin-like," and promised "to change completely the connections between phenomena throughout the opera."[30]

Ideally, Meyerhold would have liked "to saturate the atmosphere of the wonderful music by P. I. Tchaikovsky in his *Queen of Spades* with the ozone of the even more wonderful story by A. S. Pushkin." In complete solidarity with the director on this point were the conductor S. A. Samosud, the artist L. T. Chupyatov and the young soloists N. N. Kovalsky (German), A. I. Sokolova (Liza), N. L. Velter (the Countess), V. P. Grokholsky (Tomsky), A. P. Atlantov (Surin), O. N. Golovina (Polina) and others. The premiere of *The Queen of Spades* took place January 25, 1935.

Meyerhold had yet another extremely important idea for the direction. He constructed the plastic and dynamic picture of the spectacle not in accordance with the principle of synchronous following of the movement of the music, but strove this time for "*contrapuntal* merging of the fabrics—the musical and the stage."

The stagings were not controlled by the musical development of a theme, but occasionally seemed to argue with it, sometimes being constructed as though "crossing" the music; or they were unfolded in a pause, at the intersection of two musical pieces. Striving to overcome the "metrical chopping," Meyerhold also wished to clear Pushkin's show of that operatic routine which he called "*Vampuka* of a new quality, but still *Vampuka*."[31]

Despite all the assertions that the libretto by Modest Tchaikovsky would be retained "as a foundation," Meyerhold and Stenich unhesitatingly threw out at once the carefully worked out theme in this libretto of the love triangle between German, Liza and Eletsky. The canonical libretto began with a scene in the Summer Garden, but Meyerhold, following Pushkin, replaced it with the card game scene at the Horse Guardsman Narumov's. It is true, however, that he did present a "piece of landscape" prior to this scene.

"The overture where Tchaikovsky gave all the characteristic traits of opera," said Meyerhold, "brings the viewer to such a pleasant state that we should give him a *little piece of landscape* after this overture. We shall show him transparent iron gates with an incredible filigree design, of the kind that are plentiful in Leningrad. Then, we shall show a solitary standing German—his back still to the audience. He regards the magnificent view, the marvelous gate."

This is precisely how Meyerhold did stage the beginning of the opera. The "piece" of Petersburg landscape that glanced through the gate was somber and autumnal. German's solitary figure wrapped in a black cape underscored the lowering and melancholy mood of this "illumination" for the show. However, as soon as

Krechinsky's Wedding, above: Rasplyuev
(Ilinsky). *Below:* Act I, Lidochka
(Sukhanova) and Atueva (Tyapkina)

Scenes from Dumas' *Camille*. Marguerite (Raikh) and Armand (Tsarev)

Raikh as Marguerite

Program for the production of *Camille* ("The Lady with Camillias")

Raikh as Marguerite, Tsarev as Armand

Chupyatov's set for *The Queen of Spades*

Pushkin's *The Queen of Spades*, 1935
production. Velter as the Countess

The death of the Countess

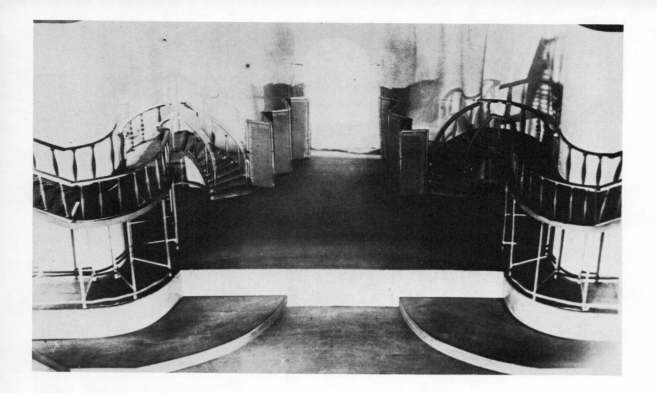

Shestakov's set for *33 Fainting Fits* (Chekhov), 1935.
Sketches of Popova (Raikh) and Smirnov (Bogolyubov) in *The Bear*

Scene from "The Jubilee" section of *33 Fainting Fits* and (below) a
scene from "The Proposal" section with Ilinsky and Loginova

the door opened to Narumov's room the stage was·seized by the carefree gaiety of a bachelors' party. To the accompaniment of childrens' drums and pipes, Meyerhold's "Asenkova," a jaunty girl in a Hussar's uniform, jumped onto a table and sang a warlike march. Then the card play began. Gold gleamed on the table; the theme of excitement, risk, the greedy pursuit of fortune, sounded powerfully. The figure of German, who closely, silently, and excitedly followed the game, was consistently brought out to the foreground and attracted attention.

Then, Meyerhold made a "clean change": the street by Narumov's house, a bleak white night, the players depart. Their capes are blown by the wind, in the low light one sees hands in white gloves, gleaming swords. Some are being congratulated on their winnings. Others, the losers, silently disappear into the darkness, while German continues to stand to one side. Here, according to Meyerhold's score and Stenich's libretto, two events take place: a brief duet with one of the card players on the luck of the game, and the meeting with Liza. Liza passes by arm in arm with the Countess, notices German and says in passing: "He is here again..."

At the illuminated approach to Narumov's house, Tomsky sings his famous ballad about the Countess. The players receive this as a banal society anecdote, laugh and joke. But in this moment the projector's beam rips German's face, distorted by fearful emotion, out from the billowing darkness.

The scene in which German visits Liza was illuminated by Meyerhold with the pale and unsteady flickering of many candles. The expressiveness of the scene was increased and stressed by Meyerhold in the complex score for Liza's behavior. As soon as German appeared in the vestibule and knocked on the door she tore around the room, put out the candles with trepidation and finally opened the door. Pale little flames wavered, long shadows moved around the room... In this scene, in Meyerhold's version, German had not yet met the Countess, had only heard her voice from behind the scenes.

The first meeting between German and the Countess took place at the ball.

The scene was constructed "without luxury." Meyerhold wished only to give a somber and even dull mood and regularly, by lowering little curtains, he broke up the space of the dance hall, as though carving out intimate corners and at the same time fixing the spectator's attention on the figure of German.

In Meyerhold's production the Countess was not at all like the monstrously feeble old women that we usually see in stagings of *The Queen of Spades*. She was old, but slender, bore herself upright and haughtily. Nonetheless, she was afraid of German. The sight of the military engineer in his green uniform, somber, possessed by something, made her afraid. In his extremely skillful score of the ball, the Countess continually, seemingly accidentally, collided with German. Every so often they appeared face to face among the dancing couples and looked intensely at each other. Once, the Countess, in a pale yellow dress stitched with silver, with black lace trim and black belt, even fell for a moment into German's embrace, then broke away from him in fright. German looked at her anxiously. Chekalinsky and Surin teased him: "There's your lover! Look, there's your Queen of Spades!"

In the next scene German penetrated into the Countess' bedroom. The light semicircle of the white staircase, placed diagonally to the footlights, appeared to embrace the alcove under the white canopy and organized the space with a broken and nervous movement. The bed was concealed behind red screens. To the left, over the fireplace, a dim oval mirror reflected the candle flames. A gallery of portraits wearing powdered wigs trailed upward along the stairs.

After entering, German stood for a long time in indecision on the proscenium. He ascended the stairs with uneven tread and stopped at the very top, by the portrait of the Countess, which showed her as the young "Venus of Moscow." Then he descended and disappeared somewhere in the wings.

The Countess appeared. Meyerhold, again in contrast to operatic tradition, did not allow her to be followed onto the stage by the crowd of servants—only the chambermaid followed her mistress and, bowing low, left. The Countess remained alone. She stopped by the fireplace before the mirror in the same pose in which she had been painted many years before. With an easy motion she took the earring from her ear, sat down in a chair and began to sing quietly a song from Grétry's opera *Richard the Lion-Hearted*. While she sang, German slid past the screens into the alcove. Meanwhile, the old woman fell asleep in the chair. The decisive moment for German had come.

German's hand appeared from the darkness and slid along the staircase railing. He came out from behind the screens, creeping quietly, carefully came up to the Countess and said tenderly: "Do not be afraid, please God do not be afraid!" Meyerhold constructed the scene in strict accordance with the logic of life. The psychological picture was unimpeachably correct. "The entire scene with the Countess," Meyerhold explained, "German conducts very carefully, very softly, fearing to frighten her even more, scared as she is." Here, in the image of German there was nothing fatal. Humble and degraded, he mastered his passions, and undemandingly and with flattery tried to break through to the old woman's compassion. But all his attempts to elicit her commiseration proved futile.

Then German, said Meyerhold, "steps up to the fireplace, takes the pose of a duelist... The Countess raises her fan as if wishing to protect her face from the pistol that does not yet exist, and this fan falls from her hand when German says "you are old." She drops the fan and moves toward the door. German, continuing his monologue, does not see the Countess. He is delirious." The Countess runs to the door, the door does not open. She walks toward the footlights, stumbles over a chair, sits down, weak. But she utters not a word.

Here, continues Meyerhold,

> German determines to use his pistol, pulls it out, stands like a duelist and aims at the Countess. The Countess cries out, but does not fall and remains in the chair. German comes up to her. "Enough childishness! Do you want to tell me the three cards or not?" Silence.
>
> It is as if a chorale suddenly begins and then ends. The Countess sinks to her knees. We try to make her fall coincide with the chord, so she falls silently. The fall, then the chord...[32]

In the fifth scene, in the barracks, the Countess' ghost comes to German. Meyerhold insisted that the ghost be presented simply, naively, without any special lighting effects. He even mentioned his idea for the appearance of the phantom in *Hamlet*, which subsequently was implemented literally, but with a pomposity completely foreign to Meyerhold's idea, by N. Okhlopkov in his staging of *Hamlet*. The Countess simply appeared before German from behind the stove! I. Sollertinsky believed that the scene in the barracks was one of Meyerhold's most powerful: "after the truly un-proplike frightful appearance of the Countess from behind the stage there follows a realistic motivation for the hallucination—the orderly enters with a candle. Then follows the second appearance of the phantom and the revelation of the fateful secret of the three cards."[33]

The sixth scene, at the Winter Canal, was a sort of lyrical, sad intermezzo that preceded the turbulent drama of the following scene.

The seventh scene, the Gaming House, is one of Meyerhold's marvels of direction. The right half of the scene was occupied by a gigantic ottoman. On and around this ottoman, on pillows thrown around the floor, on bearskins, in chairs and at tables moved up to the ottoman, Meyerhold organized a mass scene of absolutely fantastic beauty. This entire space was filled with well-dressed men and women who lay back on the ottoman, on the floor, in armchairs, on the skins, with glasses, bouquets, colored scarves, bottles, lorgnettes in hand, casually, embracing, lying side by side, and so on. Guards' and Hussars' uniforms—red, green, blue, black, golden epaulettes, gleaming medals and shining buttons, black frock coats, the white spots of starched shirts, the satin, brocade, and velvet dresses—delicate blue, ash, rose, pale-yellow, opened fans, furs, the burning stones of pendants, diamonds, bared shoulders and breasts—these fairy-tale riches of color were presented in motion, in an excited Bacchic state of animation. All this was reflected and doubled in the huge mirror that Meyerhold hung over the ottoman, which he also surrounded with garlands of burning candles. Nowhere and never in the history of theater had there been such a mind-reeling picture.

The idea that he once realized in *The Inspector General* on a cramped, small platform, the director now spread across the entire breadth of the operatic stage. It was as if human bodies had been used to knot a huge carpet of all colors. In the center of the stage, as though controlling its movement, a drunken Hussar danced furiously to the sound of Tomsky's jaunty song.

To the left stood a gaming table. German presided over this table in feverish excitement. Twice he won. "German," said Meyerhold,

bets such huge sums that they cannot be taken from his pocket. He chalks the sum that he bets on the table. People are afraid to play with him. Many hang back, and he remains almost alone. He challenges: who will play with him?

A character appears who was not previously in the play. I call him "The Unknown." He enters and says: "I will play..." He comes up to the table and begins to play. During the time that he walked up to the card table and everyone's attention was directed at the meeting between German and The Unknown, the Countess in her yellow dress appears unnoticed at the table. She sits with her back to the audience and follows the game between German and The Unknown.

German says: "My ace!.." A long pause. And, in the dry air free of music, the words "No, your Queen is beaten" are pronounced not by The Unknown but by the old woman.

German screams: "What Queen?" Again a pause. The old woman continues: "The one in your hand, the Queen of Spades."

Showing the card, the phantom Countess falls back slightly as though preparing to fall.

German sees the Countess in the same dress she had been wearing in the bedroom, and falling in the way that she had fallen in the bedroom after he pointed the pistol at her.

The lights go out. Immediately, a new set: the room in the Obukhovsky Hospital, the bed cuts into the footlights. German sits in a robe. The same music heard in the barracks before the appearance of the ghost of the Countess begins.

German pronounces what the Countess' phantom had said there, as if speaking for her.

"Thus," says Meyerhold, "ends *The Queen of Spades* by P. I. Tchaikovsky. Thus ends *The Queen of Spades* by A. S. Pushkin."[34]

The tremendous, one may certainly say revolutionary, significance for operatic art in Meyerhold's staging of *The Queen of Spades* was grasped immediately. Musical critics justly observed that much in the work was debatable. I. Sollertinsky, for instance, pointed out the contradictions that appeared between the libretto by Stenich and Tchaikovsky's music. Still, he called Meyerhold's *The Queen of Spades* "a magnificent, staggering spectacle which is overflowing with creative energy."[35] V. Gorodinsky, analyzing the musical fabric of the show, cited the words of the conductor S. A. Samosud: "The single powerful flow of musical thought pervading *The Queen of Spades* washed away the islands of individual selected numbers and favorite little sections of the opera..." "This observation," wrote V. Gorodinsky, "appears to me to be very important. This is the platform on which the conductor and the director are unified. This is the platform of ideological and artistic unity in Tchaikovsky's work of genius. From these positions, Samosud and Meyerhold lead the battle against the traditions of 'costumed concert,' and under the aegis of Pushkinization gained a victory which perhaps is fated to be one of the major events in the history of Soviet operatic theater."[36]

B. Asafev and D. Shostakovich were even more emphatic in their comments. B. Asafev, who had written the unsurpassed and perceptive analysis of the music to *The Queen of Spades*, supported in principle all the basic decisions taken by Meyerhold. D. Shostakovich said: "I believe that this is the first disclosure of *The Queen of Spades*, the first disclosure of Tchaikovsky's score, the first disclosure of this tragedy..."

Meyerhold worked with great and completely understandable inspiration on *The Queen of Spades*. Equally comprehensible is the lack of energy that showed through in his last staging in the GOSTIM—that of Chekhov's *33 Fainting Fits* (March 25, 1935). Relations between the Soviet theater and Chekhov were very cold at this time. "The Chekhov of *The Cherry Orchard* and *Three Sisters*," stated Meyerhold when beginning his work on Chekhov's play, "is not at all close to us today." As we shall see, Meyerhold placed no particularly great or exciting tasks before himself when setting to work on the "other" Chekhov, Chekhov the vaudevillian. All his dearest and most cherished plans were being shelved until the construction of the new theater building. Meyerhold began rehearsals of *Boris Godunov*, planned *Hamlet*, devoted much time and inspiration to meetings with the architects Barkhin and Vakhtangov, considering down to the smallest details the project whose basis was his own new ideas.

Among all these cares that Meyerhold immersed himself in, the staging of Chekhov's show was the least essential. Although Meyerhold did invest some of his soul into this work and used much inventiveness in it, his attitude toward the show remained fairly cool. There had been numerous failures in Meyerhold's life. But never before had he admitted them to be failures so quickly and readily as this time. Although a great deal was written about the production, and even though some reviews praised it, Meyerhold spoke of it sourly and pointed out its weaknesses more categorically than the critics.

The plan was the desire to present a Chekhov who was not the Chekhov of *Three Sisters* or *The Cherry Orchard*, but a different Chekhov—the satirist and unmasker. When unifying three of Chekhov's vaudevilles into this single show—*The Jubilee, The Bear* and *The Proposal*—Meyerhold said that Chekhov interested him as "the incomparable portraitist of paltry little people, the portrayer of their tiny little passions and details from their lives, our firm ally in the battle against the remnants of disgusting petty-bourgeois life in all its variety." The title *33 Fainting Fits* was given to the show because in the three above-named vaudevilles Meyerhold counted exactly thirty-three times when the characters fainted. He said:

> In *The Jubilee* there are fourteen fainting fits, nineteen in *The Bear* and *The Proposal*; thus, *33 Fainting Fits* is not hyperbole.
> The fainting fits in Chekhov's vaudevilles are a string for the director and the actor, on which it is important to play all three plays in a single tone.[37]

I. Ilinsky subsequently recalled:

> All these fainting fits were extremely varied and had the most various tints and characters... Each fainting fit was accompanied by music that corresponded to the character of the fainting fit: lyrical character, sharp, nervous shock, or fall. The fainting fit passed, the music quieted down and disappeared, the action continued. Of course it was interesting! Still the formally posed problem of framing the action of such fainting fits with all their variety did weigh the show down somewhat.

Fainting fits by men were accompanied by the percussion, wind and brass instruments of the orchestra; those of the women by strings. The music that accompanied every fainting fit was selected with an eye to the comic effect. At one rehearsal of *The Proposal*, Meyerhold said that Chubukov's fainting fit must be accompanied by "stupid chords, so as to make his woodenness felt." A "very dull, ridiculous, bass" sound was necessary, he suggested. Borodin's funeral march was selected in accordance with these requirements.[38]

According to the testimony of the same Ilinsky, Meyerhold "magnificently sensed Chekhov's vaudeville style. He demanded that everything be very simple, humorous, and light in the show, and it seems to me that the performers avoided the intensity and clowning that are in no way part of Chekhov's humor. They were life-like, but still a little heavy."[39]

Still, one must suppose that the bulkiness, the significance, and the slow movement appeared in this show not just because the actors were "a little heavy." The clumsiness was hidden in the director's score, which was too loaded down and complicated, and in the overly elaborate and occasionally heavy staging pictures. After counting up the number of fainting fits and deciding that each must be a striking moment in the show, Meyerhold unexpectedly concluded that this cascade "of fainting fits, nervous fits, hysteria, dizziness, etc." was nothing other than "the manifestation of the neurasthenia that was highly prevalent in Chekhov's period... Neurasthenia is a bright indicator of the weakness of will and the passivity that is characteristic of Chekhov's characters."[40]

Meyerhold spoke insistently, and spoke a great deal, of this neurasthenia. Chekhov, he asserted, selected the fainting fit from the entire arsenal of "jokes characteristic of the theater." And Chekhov led his characters to the condition of "faintingness," according to Meyerhold, because the 1880s and 1890s were the age of neurasthenia. "In the course of studying this age and milieu represented by Chekhov we collected a substantial number of materials that were evidence of the unusual incidence of neurasthenia in the intelligentsia of the 80s and 90s, a sort of epidemic (in theater there even appeared a special role: 'the neurasthenic'). We know perfectly well what the social basis for this phenomenon is."[41]

Zaslavsky immediately caught up and developed this idea of a "social basis." He wrote:

> Everyone passed by the fainting fits in Chekhov's vaudevilles. They thought that this was just a comic detail. Meyerhold penetrated into the secret of the author's plan, which was carefully concealed from Chekhov's critics and friends. It turned out that the fainting fits were the essence. They unite the three vaudevilles, written at different times, with different characters and different subjects. All these characters, all these plots—are secondary. The central thing is the fainting fit. Fainting fits bespeak the neurasthenia of the ruling class and, consequently, the vaudevilles expose the doom, degeneracy, and impotence of the landlords and bourgeoisie.

But following this loud approval in his article of Meyerhold's idea, D. Zaslavsky expressed amazement that "the actors continuously grimace, jerk exaggeratedly, and try to convince the spectator in every way that the bourgeoisie was oh so frightfully neurasthenic."[42]

This strange and contrived theme of neurasthenia was, undoubtedly, one of the main causes for Meyerhold's failure in this case. Neurasthenia is not characteristic of the heroes of Chekhov's vaudevilles. Their nerves are in order. Even Lomov in *The Proposal* only pretends to have weak nerves, and if he does lose consciousness from time to time, this is not from neurasthenia but from an excess of passion for litigation. Chekhov does not show people with nervous ailments but rather people who are completely well but who lose their human form because of their total immersion in stupid, ridiculous passions as they try to appear different from what they really are: completely wrapped up in petty-bourgeois banality.

Em. Beskin wrote with amazement on the subject of Ilinsky in the role of Lomov: "Ilinsky's performance in the role of Lomov is debatable. What is the point of this collapse of a man who is almost ill with nerves? Why this clinical picture of disintegration? Where did it come from and why? Chekhov's note says: 'healthy, well-fed, but very anxious landowner.' From here to the hospital is a great distance. Such a Lomov makes the joke meaningless, gives it unnecessary and completely incorrect tones."[43]

Meyerhold himself admitted very soon that *The Proposal* (in which this neurasthenia was expressed with special force) was not a success. "We were too clever," he said to A. K. Gladkov, "and consequently lost the humor. Truth must be faced squarely. Any amateur production of *The Proposal* gets more laughter than there was in our theater, even though the performer was Ilinsky and the staging was by Meyerhold. Chekhov's transparent and light humor did not withstand the load of our cogitations, and we suffered a failure."[44]

A. Fevralsky asserted that Meyerhold, ridiculing the characters in Chekhov's vaudevilles, "attacks them from the position of life-affirming optimism." But the theme of neurasthenia that threaded through the show was brought to nothing by this optimism in nearly every case, with the sole exception of *The Bear*.

The overall staging of the show by Meyerhold and the artist V. Shestakov is succinctly described in Fevralsky's article. "Here," the critic wrote, "is a combination of three different methods of prop design developed by the Meyerhold State Theater: staircases from 'pure' Constructivism; a panel with door (in *The Jubilee* and *The Proposal*) and a new type of pavilion (in *The Bear*) from the panel system; curtains as a background—a method first used in *Camille*. Light texture, light colors and soft lines characterize this design. Its emotional direction is answered by an even, white light that continuously pours onto the stage."

Meyerhold, continued Fevralsky, "constructs a series of moments based on the materialization of the text and of the situation in the play with objects. An object with no connection to the text gains the significance of a 'symbol' and that at the same time expresses an emotional state. The napkin that Lomov and Natalya Stepanovna tear away from each other, or the tray that they shift around, 'symbolizes' the subject of their fierce argument—Ox Meadows."[45]

Fevralsky's indications of the repetitiveness of an entire series of staging techniques and director's motifs, a repetitiveness unnatural for Meyerhold on principle, and in the present case far from useful, are highly significant here.

For instance, the theme of "playing with an object" was too coarse and linear for Chekhov's comedies. Because the "debated" Ox Meadows "were represented" as napkins or trays that the characters tore from each other's hands, the relations between the heroes became simplified and a joke precisely at the point where they are serious and substantial. For Chekhov's characters, completely gripped by litigiousness and plotting, the Ox Meadows are more important than anything else on earth. The entire vaudeville is constructed on the issue that because of the Ox Meadows and the dogs the characters miss their own happiness. To give this situation a toylike lightness means to break the mainspring of the vaudeville.

Much more successful were several other, less linear techniques by Meyerhold. Toward the end of *The Jubilee* one of the members of the bank turned with a congratulatory speech to a stuffed bear, thinking that he was addressing Shipuchin. Meyerhold, believing that the finale in Chekhov's vaudeville "is insufficiently built up," explained: "I wished to expose even more strongly the insignificance, the biological quality, of Shipuchin, and so I wanted to make such a *quid pro quo* in the end..."[46] A little later, he said even that this staging "is the most significant find in my work and I am proud of this discovery, since it gives the work the necessary social direction."[47]

After the speech addressed to the bear there was a small mute scene that concluded the vaudeville: the ladies fell in a collective fainting fit into the arms of the men and Shipuchin appeared from the cupboard, head bandaged. He, too, was dragging his wife, who had fainted, and dumped her on the floor like a sack.

This was Meyerhold's idea for the conclusion of the *Proposal* vaudeville. Natalya Stepanovna strikes Lomov with a bouquet. This is a hint: "She is a wife who will later beat him." Then, said Meyerhold, "begins the conjugal happiness. They all drink champagne as one—slowly, because conjugal happiness is a long and boring story. This is so the audience will understand: well, it's really beginning. To give the impression that these quarrels will continue for some seventy-five years... As though this were quinine dissolved in alcohol."[48]

Throughout *The Bear* a bouquet of red roses lay on a white piano. The bouquet seemed to suggest that the deep mourning of the widow Popova is dubious, that her endless sorrow is a sham. At the rehearsals Meyerhold called Popova "Tartuffe in a skirt," "practically a Donna Anna," who in the finale becomes Laura the courtesan. He indirectly characterized Popova and the large portrait of her husband, a Hussar with a flourishing moustache; this dead husband was the spitting image of Smirnov, the same kind of coarse person, a rake. With the words: "No, what a woman!" Meyerhold's Smirnov jumped onto the piano as though mounting a horse. "Like a horseback rider in a circus, who constantly slides back to the rump of the horse," Meyerhold insisted, "he must speak this monologue under the complete illusion that he is on a horse. There must be the total illusion of horseback riding here."[49]

Most interesting of all is that Meyerhold put Smirnov's lines into verse form, rewriting Chekhov's text in purposely bad verse. For instance, Smirnov's line "I love you! Love as I have never loved! I have left twelve women, nine have left me, but I loved none of them the way I love you," in Meyerhold's version was:

> I love you!
> I love you,
> As I have never loved...
> Forever mine! Forever for me!
> Twelve women did I leave
> And nine left me,
> But not one of them did I love
> As I love thee![50]

In the finale of *The Bear*, as the melting widow (Zinaida Raikh) hung herself around Smirnov's (N. Bogolyubov's) neck, he pressed her to him with one hand and with the other picked up the bouquet of red roses from the piano.

The fine and jesting use of music in the show should also be mentioned. Thus, for instance, in *The Jubilee* the scene of Khirin's despair was set to a sad *andante*. The Procession of Shipuchin's subordinates with the gifts was accompanied by triumphant drumming. The love scene in *The Bear* was accompanied by fanfares, etc.

"There was a continuous urge to "'whip up' the show," wrote Yuzovsky. "Tempo, tempo! What a weak pace, a slowed pace! After all, this is vaudeville. Vaudeville's happy blood rages here! Where did these oddities come from?" The critic, quite justifiably, found the cause for this lassitude in several excesses contained in Meyerhold's directing score. He continued: "Meyerhold wished to intensify the coursing of the vaudeville blood. To this end he placed obstacles before it that intensified the circulation of the action, when they were overcome. These obstacles—the play with objects, and the theatrical convention of the actor's using any excuse to unfurl additional action, the so-called 'theater jokes.'"[51]

33 Fainting Fits, a relatively unsuccessful and weak show that was really funny and talented only in one part—*The Bear* vaudeville—became by the will of fate the last of Meyerhold's creations to be shown to the public. Meyerhold himself, who felt that many of his works were unfit even to be listed and preferred to forget many of his first stagings during the provincial seasons altogether, marked Chekhov's vaudevilles as number 111. *The Queen of Spades* was "Opus 110."

An old newspaper clipping informs us that Meyerhold intended to show *33 Fainting Fits* to K. S. Stanislavsky. This was published in *Komsomol Truth (Komsomolskaia pravda)*:

> In the next few days Vs. Meyerhold's State Theater will perform in the apartment of the people's artist K. S. Stanislavsky its new premiere, *33 Fainting Fits*.
>
> In a conversation with our reporter, people's artist V. E. Meyerhold stated the following:
>
> "The art of A. P. Chekhov is very close to K. S. Stanislavsky. The most eloquent testimony to this is the great number of Chekhov's works realized under his management in the Art Theater. Therefore, we are very desirous of showing the eminent master of Soviet theater three farces by Chekhov: *The Jubilee, The Bear* and *The Proposal*, in a new interpretation.
>
> "K. S. Stanislavsky, because of his illness, cannot leave his home, and our show can be presented easily in the studio that is located in his apartment."[52]

It is difficult to say why this was not done. Either because Meyerhold soon became disenchanted with his own work and guessed that Stanislavsky would not like it, or because Stanislavsky did not approve of the idea of such a show.

In any event, another meeting took place between Stanislavsky and Meyerhold two years later, under different and far less happy circumstances.

Meyerhold in 1933, in front of a picture of his wife, Zinaida Raikh

Zinaida Raikh in 1933

Pasternak and Meyerhold, 1934

Meyerhold in 1935

Meyerhold in 1934

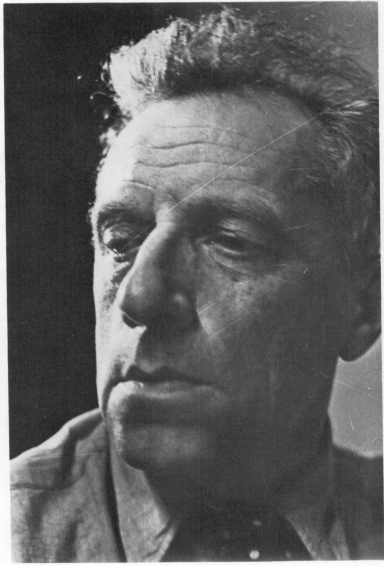

Meyerhold in 1937, below at the
construction site of his new theater

Meyerhold in 1937, at the construction site of his theater

EPILOGUE

On Triumfalnaya Square, where the banner of "Red October" was first raised, the construction of the new theater continued. True, the work was progressing much more slowly than Meyerhold wished. The schedules were being continually extended. Meanwhile, Meyerhold, together with the architects M. Barkhin and S. Vakhtangov, kept introducing new details into the plan. It was not a simple reconstruction of a building that was being planned. No. A theater of a completely unusual, unprecedented type was being planned. Meyerhold's theatrical ideas were to find their materialization in its architecture and in the new principles of the design of the stage.

In 1931, it was reported that:

> In the center of the new building there will be an enormous auditorium constructed as an amphitheater. The total number of seats has not been determined. The floor of the auditorium and the stage is on ground level, permitting the entrance of processions, automobiles and motorcycles from the street. The stage box is totally destroyed. What replaces the stage is a platform that cuts into the hall, somewhat like a stadium. In back, this platform is bounded by a semicircular corridor into which the doors of the actors' dressing rooms open. This corridor and doors are not concealed from the public at all, and in this way the entire process of the show will be open on all sides. The location of these doors with respect to the stage will recall the construction of *The Inspector General*. The orchestra will be located over the stage, similar to the way that it was in *Woe to Wit*. The actors' dressing rooms are oriented with respect to the stage not as they are ordinarily—vertically—but horizontally, in two stories. Each dressing room will have a special window through which the actor in the dressing room can hear the entire show. This eliminates the complex system of using assistant directors to call them out to the stage. In the upper gallery is a mobile, revolving projection booth that allows a screen to be set up anywhere on the stage or in the auditorium.[1]

Such was the first outline of the future theater. Subsequently, however, radical changes were introduced into the plan. The chief of these was that on the performing platform, surrounded on three sides by spectators, two revolving discs were built —one large, one small, located along a longitudinal axis. In this way the oval stage platform could undergo radical metamorphoses before the eyes of the audience. When necessary, both discs were lowered into the hold, where they could be "loaded" with the required decorations for the show. Over the stage, along the ceiling, trailed a complex curved monorail which could be used to hang, lower, and raise to any height additional playing platforms.

The basic principles of the new theater were formulated as follows:

—Unity of auditorium and stage.

—The construction of stage action in such a way that it could unfold freely in all directions, horizontally or vertically, and be perceived from everywhere, from all sides.

—The capability of illuminating the auditorium with daylight through a glass ceiling.

In accordance with these principles, Meyerhold's theater erased all the boundaries between auditorium and stage. The curtain, footlights and orchestra pit were eliminated. In the intermissions the spectators would exit onto the stage platform, not into a foyer.

It was supposed that the theater would be the largest in Moscow, with a capacity for three thousand spectators. Then the architects were told to develop a "more realistic" plan and to cut down on expenses when possible. A fairly modest variant with a capacity for sixteen hundred was prepared, which did retain, however, all the fundamental features. Meyerhold saw the materialization of his idea in reinforced concrete and brick. However slowly, the building was under construction. By 1937, its frame had been erected.

Meyerhold wanted to enter the building with new productions.

With youthful fervor, he worked on *Boris Godunov*. Here, many things came together auspiciously and well. During almost his entire life, Meyerhold had been occupied with and inspired by Pushkin's thoughts on theater. In the 1930s, while striving quite consciously toward a theatrical realism of new, simultaneously monumental and laconic outlines, Meyerhold seeks the theoretical foundations for this realism in Pushkin's formulas, and the specific means of stage expression, in the resolution of Pushkin's play. The remaining notes on the rehearsals of *Boris Godunov* have brought down to our day the atmosphere of bold directorial improvisations, of frequently unusual interpretations of the text, and of the intense energy which was being put into the composition of the tragedy. What is significant here is not only Meyerhold's desire "to stage the classics with no alterations" (but still to "show them anew"), nor the notable fact that when rehearsing *Boris* the director continually recalled the early years of the Art Theater and his work with Stanislavsky. More important is the heightened sense of the connections between the theater of Pushkin and that of Shakespeare, the intention to express the truth of history and simultaneously Pushkin's perception of it, and attitude toward it.

From the point of view of the search for the theatrical form of tragedy, there is Meyerhold's significant definition of Pushkin's lightness: "In Pushkin," said the director, "one feels a sort of air between the words, while these same words are somehow compressed by this air. These words are light."

Meyerhold strove for equally light and compressed forms of stage expression. His new tragedy appeared as the logical development and conclusion of previous productions of the classics. All the best that had been found over the course of many years of quest was to have crowned this thoroughly planned and inspired structure. *Boris Godunov* was seen not as a retreat from previously tested principles, but as their powerful and carefully based assertion at a new stage in the artist's life. The show was to demonstrate the maturity of the method.

Simultaneously, Meyerhold considered productions of *Othello* and *Hamlet** and planned a new production of Mayakovsky's *The Bedbug*. This plan was permeated with optimism. "If in 1928," said Meyerhold, talking about the new reading of *The Bedbug*, "the contours of the future were not yet felt in all their concreteness, then now, after the completion of two Five Year Plans, when life has sped ahead of

---

*Regarding these rehearsals and plans by Meyerhold, see: Aleksandr Gladkov, "Iz vospominanii o Meierkhol'de." *Moskva teatral'naia* (M. 1960); A. V. Fevral'skii, "Meierkhol'd i Shekspir." *Vil'iam Shekspir. Materialy i issledovaniia* (M: AN SSSR, 1964); the collection *Vstrechi s Meierkhol'dom* (M: VTO, 1967).

boldest dreams, the theater is getting all the capabilities for maximum stage realization of that 'future' setting that throws into relief even more the insignificance of the Prisypkins, the 'bedbugs.' Theater is setting itself the task of demonstrating the fantastic future today, of saturating the stages of the future with a demonstration of the achievements of the USSR, first of all by showing the new people."[2]

For this, he wished to use the principle, once used in *The Dawn*, of breaking the action in order to bring to the stage the famed heroes of the Five Year Plans, those whose names thundered throughout the land. "For instance, the action stops, Stakhanov is called for and Stakhanov steps forward with a small speech. We will show real, living people."[3]

This idea was expressed by Meyerhold at a gathering of the GOSTIM company on January 19, 1936, and the actors responded with delighted applause. They were happy with the Master's effective discovery, which so simply and clearly expressed the theater's readiness to greet the new heroes of the age. Furthermore, they were naturally delighted that the legendary Stakhanov would appear on the stage of their theater, possibly to be followed by Busygin, Maria Demchenko and other famous sons and daughters of the people...

The fact that in December 1935, Stalin had stated that "Mayakovsky was and remains the best, the most talented poet of our Soviet era" was naturally a source of great inspiration for Meyerhold. He heard a promise of support in these words for that art whose principles Mayakovsky and Meyerhold had defended together. Mayakovsky's memory was sacred to Meyerhold. Shortly after the death of the poet, Meyerhold said in his theater: "We would like for the new building to have a memorial spot for Vl. Mayakovsky. We are considering ways to devise a stage that would include a memorial." Furthermore, he proposed to include a permanent Mayakovsky museum in the new GOSTIM building. "The circumstances are such," he said, "that the theater is considered to be connected with the name of Mayakovsky."[4]

After Mayakovsky was called "the best and most talented," came the idea for crowning the GOSTIM building with a statue of the poet. But the hopes of Meyerhold and of Mayakovsky's friends that the names of the director and the poet would be thus joined forever did not come true.

From the beginning of 1936, the press, including *Pravda,* began to publish more and more often sharp criticism directed against Meyerhold's art. The term "Meyerholdism" gained currency, denoting formalism in theater. This term was used widely and by many. Some articles and speeches demanded that Meyerhold be relieved of his duties as director of the theater.

Meyerhold attempted to ward off the blow, appearing in Leningrad with a speech entitled "Meyerhold against Meyerholdism." In this speech he spoke a great deal, but weakly and unconvincingly, about his errors. A newspaper report observed:

> Meyerhold was insufficiently self-critical here, less consistent, and not as sharp as in the characterization of the overall state of our theater. He mentions several formalistic misinterpretations that he himself permitted in his time: the green wig in *The Forest*, the slowed pace in *Bubus*, the absence of makeup and the overalls in *Cuckold*, and so on. In each work, says Meyerhold, many deficiencies can be found. Some of the errors were uncritically used by

many directors in their own productions. Naturally, it is easiest for those who collect tricks from everywhere and senselessly transfer them into their own work to get their own work done.

The main enthusiasm in the speech was the exposure (often equally unfounded and unjust) of other directors who mechanically borrowed Meyerhold's formal discoveries and applied them thoughtlessly and inappropriately. This Meyerholdism is formalism. In any case, as for himself Meyerhold's path was consistent, logical, and inevitable, from the point of view of overall development.

Furthermore, Meyerhold said that when exposing formalism the discussion frequently is of form only, isolating and divorcing this concept from the meaning and content of the staged work. "This," he prognosticated, "may cause an artist's 'formophobia.' The artist may lose the form, and this is disastrous for him."[5]

As though intending to substantiate the justice of these words with his own example, Meyerold, in a condition of "formophobia," staged *Natasha* by L. Seifullina, a drama of everyday life which was unsuccessful and completely foreign to his style. This time he tried to depict the full, rich taste of country abundance. In the foyer of the theater cabbages and apple tree branches were carefully reproduced. The play was brought to dress rehearsal. A. K. Gladkov recalled later "the weight on the soul" brought on by watching it. "We were too uncomfortable to look each other in the eye, so tragically helpless was the uninspired Meyerhold, the Meyerhold subsisting on his 'waste'... The poison of artistic falsehood spread through the entire spectacle from the weak, inert, it is terrible to say, 'stamped out' episodes..."[6]

Meyerhold admitted his failure. The production was not shown and his opponents gained yet another argument: the GOSTIM cancelled the staging of a modern Soviet play. Meyerhold's statements against Meyerholdism had no effect. His self-criticism was perceived as inadequate, a half measure.

The GOSTIM collective, however, placed great hopes in Meyerhold's preparation of the show *One Life* (a staging of N. Ostrovsky's novel *How the Steel Was Tempered*).

The production was being prepared for the twentieth anniversary of the October Revolution and was planned as a high tragedy. Meyerhold carried on rehearsals with great energy. The attempts at compromise that he had sought in staging Seifullina's *Natasha* were rejected. This time, Meyerhold was firmly determined not to betray himself. Undoubtedly, he was inspired by the thought that he was incarnating the images from the book that at the time was exciting every reader and which was perceived as the greatest event in Soviet literature.

The roles were distributed as follows: Pavel Korchagin—E. Samoilov; Zhukhrai—N. Bogolyubov; Sema—L. Sverdlin; Man with the Beard—V. Zaichikov; Commander —V. Mukhin; and others. V. Stenberg designed the props, the music was first ordered from D. Shostakovich, then (after Shostakovich refused) from the composer Gavril Popov, the author of the music for the film *Chapaev*. The author of the stage version, E. Gabrilovich, spoke later of the rehearsals for *One Life*:

This was the real birth of a new revolutionary spectacle, far from the former clowning but still retaining its distant echoes in its depths. This was a sharp, stormy, romantic, furious show—such a Nikolai Ostrovsky I have never seen since, neither on stage nor on the screen.

I distinctly recall one episode, when during the construction of the railroad Pavka Korchagin roused his comrades to work. All were mortally tired, hungry, hopeless, angry. None wished to go to the site in the rain and cold. And here, after exhausting his entire vocabulary, referring to the international situation, joking and calling, Pavka suddenly, slowly, and uncertainly began to dance. He danced completely alone in the dimness of the damp barracks. His comrades, first with amusement, then with surprise, looked at him from their bunks. He continued to dance, ever more quickly, more happily, circling, crouching, with no music, even without humming to himself. Then someone hit his palm against a bunk in time to his dance, then another, and a third—a soft accompaniment of tapping began. Another lad jumped into the middle of the barracks and began to dance next to Pavka. Others jumped up. The tapping of the accompaniment became stronger and stronger—the lads were pounding their fists now. And now not only Pavka, but ten, fifteen, twenty lads were dancing to this noise. The noise grew into thunder, the orchestra drums joined in. The rays of the projectors, slowly at first, then more rapidly, began to jump across the stage, as though dancing. And now everything appeared to be dancing—the lads, the lights, the drums, the very walls of the barracks. Still no music, just the rhythmic pounding of the hands, fists and drums. Suddenly, in this storm and thunder, very quietly, somewhere, seemingly in the depths, in the heart of the barracks there began the sound of an old Revolutionary song. It grew, gained strength, expanded, and the dance and the banging died down. The lads, sweaty, hot from the dance, in torn clothing, in ragged shoes, sang this wonderful song that had been composed by their brothers and fathers in prisons and in exile. And to the sound of this song and in the light of the calmed projectors, they went to work in the rain and cold.

There was an astonishing scene in which the blinded Korchagin, doomed by the doctors to immobility, rose from his bed and dressed himself in order to go to a rally and resist the opposition. Meyerhold had this scene performed numerous times at the rehearsals. Dozens of times he would run up onto the stage boards and we were staggered and astounded when there appeared before us a blind man slowly arising from the bed, the hands of a blind man, seeking, fumbling in the air, the fingers of a blind man feeling things in search for the clothing. This was a life of hands and fingers that was so full of intensity, sensitivity, and drama that one caught one's breath. The blind man dressed himself slowly, again fumbling at what we do mechanically every day. And, dressed, he walked toward the door—at first in a direction quite different from where the door actually was, then a bit to the side, and finally in the right direction. There was such force of will, I would say passion of will, in his every movement, in his hands and his fingers, with all the unevenness, constraint, and unsureness of these movements that this small, completely wordless episode gave a unique sense of inexorability, of Bolshevik steadfastness—the sensation that we so often and with such futility strive to achieve in numerous modern productions by means of long dialogues and personal statements by the characters.[7]

The commission of the Committee on Art did not accept the show. The tragic theme was perceived as a pessimistic theme—Meyerhold had not found a major-key solution for the drama. *One Life* never was shown to the general public. This work was declared to be a complete ideological and creative fiasco of the part of the director.

On January 7, 1938 the Committee on the Arts, after a series of sharply critical articles that appeared in the central newspapers, resolved to liquidate the Meyerhold State Theater. The motivation for this was that "the Meyerhold Theater over the entire period of its existence had been unable to free itself from thoroughly bourgeois formalistic positions alien to Soviet art."[8]

It is known that after the closing of the GOSTIM, Stanislavsky himself offered Meyerhold the hand of friendship. Needless to say, Meyerhold's spirits rose, new plans developed in his mind...

The circumstances of this last creative meeting between Stanislavsky and Meyerhold have been told many times.[9] However, sometimes it is given the significance of an esthetic capitulation on the part of Meyerhold, and is examined as a return by Meyerhold to the principles of realism of the Art Theater. When explaining why Stanislavsky called Meyerhold to him, G. Kristi, for instance, writes: "Where he saw a retreat from the artistic principles of realism, there Stanislavsky became irreconcilable, occasionally even cruel. Stanislavsky perceived Meyerhold as an artist who, sooner or later, after many wanderings, must return to the path of great art, and was prepared to greet him with open arms, like the prodigal son."

The touching picture of the prodigal son's return, as painted by G. Kristi and several other authors, is easily refuted by the facts that they themselves provide. Kristi's article mentions, among other things, that as early as the season of 1935-36, Stanislavsky answered the question of whom he considered to be the best Soviet director: "The only director I know is Meyerhold."[10] Specific information about Meyerhold's work in Stanislavsky's operatic theater gives no reason to believe that Meyerhold, when brought into proximity with Stanislavsky, changed, became transformed, or ceased to be himself. Even if he had wished for such a thing, he would have achieved no success. Meyerhold already had discovered the perniciousness of the idea of compromise during his bitter experiment with Seifullina's *Natasha*. In addition to all else, a new compromise, any possible compromise, still would not be able to cross out the four decades during which he had followed his own path.

In 1969, Kristi discovered in Stanislavsky's archives an unpublished record that probably dates from the late 1920s or early 1930s. Stanislavsky wrote:

> Now we are involved in the development of new plans, points of view, and possibilities in stage and theater. The question arises—in general, and not specifically for a given play or production. All the colors and lines and forms of painters have been known and outlived. They have disappointed. Truest of all is Meyerhold's path. He starts with general possibilities and principles of stage and direction. He resolves them boldly and simply (the same cannot be said of his work with actors; he is weak in that respect). Thus, for instance, one must most of all struggle with the theatrical frame, the portal. Its enormous space crushes the small space occupied by the decoration and the person of the actor. How to remove this great crushing space of the portal, the curtain, cloth arches, etc.? Meyerhold abolished them, too. He reveals the entire behind-the-scenes part of the stage. It is well whitewashed and clean. This is the building itself, an extension of the auditorium. He does not conceal it in this large hall either (which is seemingly joined to the auditorium), he shows the small screens, the furniture that he requires, etc. Along with this he devises various tricks. Either he rolls the furniture up, or it appears together with the wall (the furniture is attached to the wall), or comes up from under the floor, etc.

Meyerhold remained Meyerhold, that director of whom Charles Dullin said beautifully:

Meyerhold is the creator of forms, a poet of the stage. He has his own theatrical language, a language of gestures and rhythms that he invents for the expression of his intention, and which says as much to the eye as the text does to the ear. He creates his means for expression on the basis of the inner meaning of the work; he removes the skin from the fruit, eliminates everything that is extra, goes straight to the core... His art is closely tied to the Revolution. Inevitably, it had to suit the spirit of a people that is greedily striving to build after having destroyed.[11]

Eisenstein had an interesting comment on the relations between the theatrical systems of Stanislavsky and Meyerhold. He insisted that both schools were "not in a 'metaphysical' " but in a "natural opposition at different stages." He stated:

> The entire secret is in the fact that the highly gifted representatives of both schools, systems, and directions *are not* one-sided.
> When propagandizing for their system and basing themselves in their own method (particularly theoretically) they include the sum of the experience of the other direction into their practice.[12]

Eisenstein's thoughts lead us straight to the idea that the tempting idea of directly contrasting Meyerhold with Stanislavsky, an idea that had seduced Vakhtangov in his day and which remains intriguing to many, essentially and inevitably simplifies and schematizes the complex processes of the renewal and development of realism in Russian and Soviet theater, and leads to a superficial and deceptive antonym of "innovator" Meyerhold and "traditionalist" Stanislavsky.

Meyerhold himself rejected such comparisons. "It is necessary," he said in his GOSTIM, "to finish with this nonsense, with this foolishness that Konstantin Sergeevich and I are antipodes. This is not true. We are two systems, each of which completes the other." Meyerhold was convinced that Stanislavsky's system also had taken in the experience of Meyerhold's searching: "the system is not only what he thought through himself, but includes a lot of what was done by other comrades in art—Vladimir Ivanovich Nemirovich-Danchenko, and Vakhtangov, and me, sinner that I am."[13]

And in fact, Meyerhold's art, so similar to the style of the art of Mayakovsky and Eisenstein, is perceived in the overall panorama of the development of twentieth century theater as the direct consequence of the great revolution created by Stanislavsky. This most talented of Stanislavsky's pupils passed through a complex and difficult route of independent theatrical innovation. A discoverer of new things and an experimenter, a bold creator of unprecedented stage forms, Meyerhold came into contact with an extremely wide range of artistic phenomena from the past. For all of his surprising changeability, for all the suddenness with which he moved from show to show, decisively rejecting what he had just found and asserted, Meyerhold was consistent in his own way. The dynamism of his art, first of all, possessed a concealed personal inner logic of development (a connection that we have tried to follow through the movement of time and the alteration of the social climate) and, secondly, it retained permanent contact with the cultural heritage, with tradition, with what Stanislavsky calls the eternal in theater. The effectiveness of Meyerhold's innovation and his sensitivity to the "news of the day" were theatrical in the fullest, ancient meaning of the word. He was a man of the theater and changed much in the theater.

Meyerhold reached over the head of the traditions of the late nineteenth century, which he rejected polemically, back to the older traditions of French classicism, Japanese Kabuki theater, Russian buffoonery and the Italian comedy of masks. This permitted Meyerhold to establish direct contact with the element of popular theater, with farce and street shows, and to give modern theater a truly democratic and free popular spirit.

Meyerhold was always intrigued by play on the border between stage and auditorium, on the proscenium, on its very edge. Meyerhold's actor stepped across the footlights, walked through the so-called fourth wall without deigning to admit its existence. He strove to activate the audience, to involve it in the action, to enter into direct relations with it.

The relativistic nature of the theatrical performance and its basis in play were stressed in the name of creation in conjunction with the audience. This close contact with the spectators furthered the ideological saturation of Meyerhold's art. It developed like an art thirsting for wide philosophical and poetic generalizations, capable of expressing not only the experience of the individual man, not only the meaning of his fate and drama, but the experience of history, of the age, of society. This art tended toward metaphor expressed directly in the stagings, toward a musical polyphony in the director's scores. It was able to operate with the elementary means of the stage poster and slogan, the sketchiness of the social mask, and the highly complex associative moves, significant symbols, and the methods of "making strange" *(ostranenie)* and with the actor's virtuoso performance with his own character or with the world of things around him. Meyerhold's art turned simultaneously to the emotions and the intellect of the spectator, caused him to investigate and assimilate anew the too well known and habitual world. It judged a man according to the highest laws of beauty, attacked the everyday life of the petty-bourgeois, and strove to draw the audience out of its state of inertia.

Meyerhold's theater is a significant phenomenon in the spiritual culture of the prerevolutionary and the postrevolutionary periods, incorporating and expressing many essential traits of a turbulent and dramatic period in history. Time has left its mark on this art and has infused its humanism with a new, unusual character. Meyerhold's art was foreign to compassion, avoided the traditional theme of the little man, rejected the spiritual tepidness of psychological realism and traditionally intimate forms of relating to the spectator. Nonetheless, in the unsteady symbols, the rough social masks, in the great richness of the metaphorical images of this art, true humanity was expressed. Meyerhold's art turned to man with faith in his power, in his ability to rise above daily life and the routine of social connections. It carried with it the idea of the might of poetry, and the will to transform reality according to the laws of reason and beauty.

NOTES

Poster for an exhibit honoring the 100th birthday of Meyerhold

ABBREVIATIONS USED IN THE FOOTNOTES

TsGALI—Tsentral'nyi gosudarstvennyi arkhiv literatury i iskusstva.

TsGTM—Tsentral'nyi gosudarstvennyi teatral'nyi muzei im. A. A. Bakhrushina.

BMM—Gosudarstvennaia biblioteka-muzei V. V. Maiakovskogo.

GBL—Gosudarstvennaia biblioteka SSSR im. Lenina.

V. E. Meierkhol'd, *Dvukhtomnik*—V. E. Meierkhol'd, *Stat'i, pis'ma, rechi, besedy* (Moskva: Iskusstvo, 1968).

NOTES TO PART I

Chapter One

1. Vl. I. Nemirovich-Danchenko, *Iz proshlogo* (M: Academia, 1936), 126

2. Cited from Nikolai Volkov, *Meierkhol'd*, v. 1 (M: Academia, 1929), 47.

3. Ibid., 57. The originals of Meyerhold's letters to Olga M. Munt, which Nikolai Volkov had at his disposal, have since been lost. The letters are quoted hereafter according to Volkov.

4. K. S. Stanislavskii, *Sobranie sochinenii*, v. 1 (M. 1954), 186.

5. Nemirovich-Danchenko, *Iz proshlogo*, 72

6. O. Knipper-Chekhova, *Zhelannaia vstrecha* (February 5, 1934).

7. O. L. Knipper-Chekhova, Iz vospominanii, "Ezhegodnik MKhAT 1949-50" (M. 1952), 283.

8. Nemirovich-Danchenko, *Iz proshlogo*, 115.

9. Volkov, *Meierkhol'd*, 88, 89.

10. K. S. Stanislavskii, *Sobranie sochinenii*, v. 7 (M. 1960), 129.

11. Vl. I. Nemirovich-Danchenko, *Izbrannie pis'ma* (M. 1954), 118.

12. Stanislavskii, *Sobr. soch.*, v. 7, 137.

13. Ibid., 133.

14. TsGALI, fond 998, ed. khr. 626, 1. 96 (ob).

15. Stanislavskii, *Sobr. soch.*, v. 7, 669.

16. Ibid., 142.

17. Vs. Meierkhol'd, "Teatr (K istorii i tekhnike)," in *Teatr. Kniga o novom teatre*, sborniki statei (St. P. 1908), 149.

18. Vs. Meierkhol'd, "Chekhov i naturalizm na stsene," in *V mire iskusstv*, No. 11-12 (1907), 24.

19. Nemirovich-Danchenko, *Izbrannie pis'ma*, 141, 147.

20. Quoted from the article: E. A. Polotskaia, "Chekhov i Meierkhol'd," *Literaturnoe nasledstvo*, v. 68, 420.

21. S. Glagol', " 'Chaika' v 4-kh deistviiakh Antona Chekhova," *Kur'er* (Dec. 19, 1898).

22. A. Urusev, "Vtoroe predstavlenie 'Chaiki,' " *Kur'er* (Jan. 3, 1899).

23. N. E. Efros, *Moskovskii Khudozhestvennyi teatr 1898-1923* (M.-Pd. 1924), 224.

24. N. E. Efros, "Chekhov i Khudozhestvennyi teatr," *Solntse Rossii*, No. 7 (1914), 10.

25. Stanislavskii, *Sobr. soch.*, v. 7, 201.

26. Ibid., 204.

27. Aleksandr Gladkov, "Meierkhol'd govorit," *Neva*, No. 2 (1966), 205.

28. Nemirovich-Danchenko, *Izbrannie pis'ma*, 207.

29. Letter from A. L. Vishnevskii to A. P. Chekhov (Jan. 12, 1901), Manuscript division, Lenin Library, Moscow.

30. M. F. Andreeva, *Perepiska. Vospominaniia. Stat'i. Dokumenty. Vospominaniia o M. F. Andreeve* (M. 1961), 33, 334.

31. Pis'ma Meierkhol'da k Chekhovu, *Literaturnoe nasledstvo*, v. 68, 227.

32. Ibid., 436.

33. Muzei MKhAT, Arkhiv KS, No. 45, director's copy of *Lonely Lives*, 91, 100, 103.

34. N. R-skii [N. Rossovskii], *Peterburgskii listok*, Feb. 21, 1901.

35. *Perepiska A. P. Chekhova i O. L. Knipper*, v. 1 (M. 1934), 111.

36. Muzei MKhat, arkhiv Nemirovich-Danchenko, No. 1587.

37. TsGALI, f. 998, ed. khr. 625, 1. 2, 3.

38. Pis'ma Meierkhol'da k Chekhovu, *Literaturnoe nasledstvo*, v. 68, 438.

39. TsGali, f. 998, ed. khr. 625, 1. 9 (ob.).

40. Ibid., 1. 21.

41. Ibid., l. 43.

42. Muzei MKhAT, arkhiv Stanislavskii, no. 627, materials for *A Director's Notes*, [sheet] 17, 34.

43. Pis'ma Meierkhol'da k Çhekhovu, *Literaturnoe nasledstvo*, v. 68, 439, 440.

44. Aleksandr Gladkov, "Meierkhol'd govorit," *Novyi mir*, No. 8 (1961), 224.

45. Aleksandr Gladkov, "Vospominaniia, zametki, zapisi o V. E. Meierkhol'de," *Tarusskie stranitsy* (Kaluga, 1961), 302.

46. Pis'ma Meierkhol'da k Chekhovu, *Literaturnoe nasledstvo*, v. 68, 442, 443.

47. TsGALI, f. 998, ed. khr. 625, 1. 38, 39.

48. K. S. Stanislavskii, *Sobr. soch.*, v. 1, 250, 251.

49. TsGALI, f. 998, ed. khr. 625, 1. 31, 32.

50. Vl. I. Nemirovich-Danchenko, *Izbrannie pis'ma*, 225.

51. K. S. Stanislavskii, *Sobr. soch.*, v. 7, 217.

52. V. E. Meierkhol'd, *Stat'i*, v. 1, 73.

53. *Perepiska A. P. Chekhova i O. L. Knipper*, v. 2 (M. 1936), 173.

54. Pis'ma Meierkhol'da k Chekhovu, *Literaturnoe nasledstvo*, v. 68, 444.

55. *Perepiska A. P. Chekhova i O. L. Knipper*, v. 2, 318.

56. Ibid., 322.

57. *Kur'er* (February 22, 1912).

58. Ibid. (February 24, 1902).

59. *Perepiska A. P. Chekhova i O. L. Knipper*, v. 2, 105, 118.

60. Ibid., 128.

61. Muzei MKhAT, Arkhiv Nemirovich-Danchenko, No. 1595.

62. K. S. Stanislavskii, *Sobr. soch.* v. 7, 228.

63. Ibid., v. 1, 249-50.

64. Tat'iana Bachelis, "Rezhisser Stanislavskii," *Novyi mir*, No. 1 (1963), 203.

65. V. Veresaev, *Vospominaniia* (M. 1946), 247.

66. M. Gor'kii, *Sobr. soch.*, v. 30 tt., v. 28, 113.

67. Ibid., 277.

Chapter Two

1. Aleksandr Gladkov, "Vospominaniia, zametki, zapisi o Vs. E. Meierkhol'de," *Tarusskie stranitsy* (1961), 302.

2. *Perepiska A. P. Chekhova i O. L. Knipper*, v. 2, 371.

3. Gladkov.

4. I. N. Pevtsov, "Beseda ob aktere," *Illarion Nikolaevich Pevtsov (1879-1943)* (L. 1935), 36.

5. *Teatr i iskusstvo*, No. 41 (St. P. 1902), 750.

6. *Iug*, 28/IX (Kherson, 1902).

7. Letters to Chekhov from B. A. Lazarevskii, 13 & 17/IV 1903, Ms. Division, Lenin Library, Moscow.

8. I. N. Pevtsov, 39.

9. *Teatr i iskusstvo*, No. 6 (St. P. 1903), 158.

10. Franz von Schönthan, *The Acrobats*, tr. from German [into Russian] by N. A. Butkevich & Vs. E. Meierkhol'd, M. Sokolov's Theater Library (M. 1903).

11. Ibid., 73, 74.

12. TsGALI, f. 998, ed. khr. 179, 1. 1-2.

13. V. Lenskii, "Po povodu," *Iug* (Feb. 17, 1903).

14. D. Merezhkovskii, "O prichinakh upadka i o novykh techeniiakh sovremennoi russkoi literatury (St. P. 1893), 42-43.

15. K. Bal'mont, *Gornie vershiny*, Bk. 1 (M. 1904), 75, 96.

16. A. Remizov, Teatr-studiia, *Nasha zhizn'*, 22/IX 1905.

17. *Iug* 17/IX 1904.

18. Meyerhold's letters to Chekhov, *Literaturnoe nasledstvo*, v. 68, 446.

19. *Teatr i iskusstvo*, No. 8 (1904), 178.

20. Ibid.

21. De Lin', "Siluety," *Iug*, 14/XI 1903.

22. *Teatr i iskusstvo*, No. 46 (St. P. 1904), 860.

23. Aleksei Remizov, "Tovarishchestvo novoi dramy, Pis'mo iz Khersona,"*Vesy*, No. 4 (1904), 36, 37.

24. *Literaturnoe nasledstvo*, v. 68, 446.

25. Remizov, 38, 39.

26. *Teatr i iskusstvo*.

27. Ibid., No. 49 (1903), 945.

28. Ibid., No. 8 (1904), 178.

29. Pevtsov, 35.

30. *Literaturnoe nasledstvo*, v. 68, 488.

31. Pevtsov, 35.

32. TsGALI, f. 998, ed. khr. 625, 1. 5-6.

33. Quoted from Nikolai Volkov, *Meierkhol'd*, v. 1, 185.

34. *Teatr i iskusstvo*, No. 41 (St. P. 1904), 734.

35. *Teatral'naia Rossiia*, No. 1 (1904) [trial number], 30.

36. *Tiflisskii listok*, 11/XII 1904.

37. *Teatr i iskusstvo*, No. 51, 923.

38. *Kavkaz* (Tiflis 1904, 13/X 1904.

39. *Tiflisskii listok*, 8/II 1905.

40. *Teatr i iskusstvo*, No. 42, 720.

41. *Studiia*, No. 1 (M. 1911), 21.

42. Gladkov, 297.

43. *Teatr i iskusstvo*, No. 49, 879.

44. *Teatral'naia Rossiia*, No. 11 (1905), 180.

Chapter Three

1. K. S. Stanislavskii, *Sobr. soch.*, v. 1, 278, 280.

2. Muzei MKhAT, arkhiv N.-D., No. 1614.

3. Ibid., 1613.

4. Ibid., 1595.

5. Stanislavskii,v. t. 1, 261, 262.

6. Muzei MKhAT, arkhiv N.-D., No. 1595.

7. Ibid., 1614.

8. N. Berdiaev. *Sub specie aeternitatis.* Opyty filosofskie, sotsial'nye i literaturnye (1900-6 gg.) (St. P. 1907), 3.

9. V. Briusov. "Vchera, segodnia i zavtra russkoi poezii." *Pechat' i revoliutsiia*, kn. 7 (1922), 40.

10. Stanislavskii, v. 7, 300.

11. Ibid., 304.

12. Muzei MKhAT, arkhiv N.-D., No. 1605.

13. Stanislavskii, vol. 7, 308.

14. Muzei MKhAT, arkhiv N.-D., No. 1614.

15. Stanislavskii, v. 1, 281.

16. Ibid., v. 5, 207.

17. Muzei MKhAT, arkhiv Studii.

18. Muzei MKhAT, arkhiv N.-D., Nos. 1614, 1615.

19. Muzei MKhAT, arkhiv K. S., No. 5182.

20. Stanislavskii, v. 1, 281.

21. K. S. Stanislavskii, *Stat'i, besedy, rechi, pis'ma* (M. 1953), 175.

22. See Stanislavskii, *Sobr. soch.*, v. 1, 475.

23. Ibid., 283, 284.

24. See Anna Satz. "Muzykal'naia sushchnost' Il'i Satsa." V sb. *Il'ia Sats* (M-L. 1923), 18, 19.

25. TsGALI, f. 998, ed. khr. 187, 1. 40.

26. Ibid., 42.

27. Vs. Meierkhol'd, *Teatr (K istorii i tekhnike)*, 135.

28. TsGALI, f. 998, ed. khr. 186, 1. 130.

29. Muzei MKhAT, arkhiv Studii.

30. TsGALI, f. 998, ed. khr. 188, 1. 39.

31. Ibid., 20.

32. Meierkhol'd, 129.

33. Aleksandr Gladkov, "Meierkhol'd govorit," *Novyi mir*, No. 8 (1961), 228.

34. N. P. Ul'ianov, *Moi vstrechi* (M. 1952), 133.

35. Meierkhol'd, 137.

36. M. V. Alpatov, E. A. Gunst. *Nikolai Nikolaevich Sapunov* (M. 1965), 20.

37. Meierkhol'd, 129, 130.

38. TsGALI, f. 998, ed..khr. 186, 1. 8.

39. Ibid., 16-19, 22, 26, 50, 54.

40. Sb. *O Stanislavskom*, (M: VTO, 1948), 358.

41. Stanislavskii, *Sobr. soch.*, v. 1, 285.

42. Sb. *O Stanislavskom*, 359.

43. Stanislavskii. *Sobr. soch.*, v. 7, 325.

44. Ibid., 324, 325.

45. Sb. *O Stanislavskom*, 360.

46. Ibid., 345.

47. Ul'ianov, 135, 136.

48. Meierkhol'd, 168.

49. Ibid., 157.

50. Ibid., 131.

51. Sb. *O Stanislavskom*, 359, 360.

52. Ul'ianov, 136.

53. Avrelii [V. Briusov], "Iskaniia novoi stseny," *Vesy*, No. 1 (1906), 72-74.

54. Stanislavskii, *Sobr. soch.*, v. 1, 285.

55. T. I. Bachelis, "Stanislavskii i Meierkhol'd," ms., 18-20.

56. Meierkhol'd, 138.

57. Gladkov, 227.

58. Bozhena Vitvitskaia, "Revoliutsiia, iskusstvo, voina," *Teatr i iskusstvo*, No. 18 (1917), 296, 297.

59. TsGALI, f. 998, ed. khr. 626, 1. 254-255.

60. Stanislavskii, *Sobr. soch.*, v. 5, 412, 638.

61. Ibid., v. 1, 285, 286.

62. Ibid., v. 5, 385, 412.

63. Meierkhol'd, Sulerzhitskii, *Birzhevye vedomosti*, morning ed. (Dec. 20, 1916).

64. TsGALI, f. 998, ed. khr. 626, 1. 256.

Chapter Four

1. Aleksandr Gladkov, "Meierkhol'd govorit," *Novyi mir*, No. 8 (1961), 226.

2. TsGALI, f. 998, 1, 198, 1-8.

3. Georgii Chulkov, *Gody stranitsvii* (M: Federatsiia, 1930), 214-216.

4. V. Podgornyi, *Tvorcheskii put'*. Sb. *Tvorchestvo v teatre* (Kharkov, 1937), 26.

5. V. Meierkhol'd, *O teatre* (St. P. 1913), 192.

6. Ibid.

7. Ibid.

8. TsGALI, f. 998, ed. khr. 626, 1. 286.

9. From a conversation with V. F. Komissarzhevskaya, "Novosti sezona" (Sept. 2, 1908), 8.

10, Ibid.

11. N. Turkin, *Komissarzhevskaia v zhizni i na stsene* (M. 1910), 137.

12. Gladkov, 232.

13. *Tarusskie stranitsy*, 304, 305.

14. Andrei Belyi, *Simvolizm. Kniga statei* (M. 1910), 223.

15. Ibid., 285.

16. Viacheslav Ivanov, *Borozdy i mezhi. Opyty esticheskie i kriticheskie* (M. 1916), 264, 265.

17. Ibid., 285.

18. *Vesy*, v. 1 (1904), 6, 7.

19. Nikolai Berdiaev, *Sub specie aeternitatis.* Opyty filosofskie, sotsial'nye i literaturnye 1900-06 gg. (St. P. 1907), 31, 32.

20. F. F. Komissarzhevskii. "Sapunov-dekorator," *Apollon*, No. 4 (1914), 16.

21. Yu. Beliaev, "O Komissarzhevskoi," *Novoe vremia* (Nov. 29, 1906).

22. A. Kugel', *Profili teatra* (M: Teakinopechat', 1929), 84, 85.

23. V. Azov, "Otkrytie teatra," *Rech'*, No. 215 (1906).

24. N. Iordanskii. "Individualizm na stsene,"

Sovremennyi mir, No. 1, Sec. II (1909), 61.

25. *O Komissarzhevskoi. Zabytoe i novoe* (M: VTO, 1965), 79.
26. Aleksandr Blok, *Sobr. soch.*, v. 5, 97.
27. TsGALI, f. 998, ed. khr. 626, 1. 300.
28. Meierkhol'd, 189.
29. Tal'nikov, *Komissarzhevskaia* (M-L. 1939), 312.
30. N. Evreinov, "Khudozhniki v teatre V. F. Komissarzhevskoi," v. 1, *Alkonost* (1911), 129, 130.
31. A. Lunacharskii, "Eshche ob iskusstve i revoliutsii," *Obrazovanie*, No. 12, Section 11 (1906), 187.
32. Quoted according to the article by Vl. Orlov, "Na rubezhe dvukh epokh," *Voprosy literatury*, No. 10 (1966), 120.
33. V. Verigina, *Teatr na Ofitserskoi ulitse.* Sb. *Komissarzhevskaia* (L-M. 1964), 268, 269.
34. A. A. Mgebrov, *Zhizn v teatre*, vol. 1 (M-L. 1929), 373.
35. Meierkhol'd, 196.
36. TsGALI, f. 998, ed. khr. 196, 1. 1-3.
37. Ibid., 5 (back).
38. Meierkhol'd, 196.
39. Blok, v. 5, 98.
40. Verigina, 270.
41. Meierkhol'd, 194, 195.
42. Liubov' Burevich, "Na putiakh obnovleniia teatra," *Alkonost*, v. 1 (1911), 186.
43. Blok, v. 5, 237.
44. Meierkhol'd, 197.
45. T. I. Bachelis, *Rezhisserskie iskaniia Meierkhol'da.* Ms., 31.
46. Meierkhol'd, iv.
47. Blok, v. 7, 13.
48. Ibid., 301.
49. *Pis'ma A. Bloka k E. Ivanovu* (M-L. 1936), 125.
50. Blok, v. 7, 169, 170.
51. Meierkhol'd, 198.
52. Ibid., 172.
53. Ibid., 198.
54. Sergei Auslender, "Moi portrety. Meierkhol'd," *Teatr i muzyka*, No. 1-2 (1923), 427.
55. *Pereval*, No. 4 (1907), 59.
56. *Vesy*, No. 6 (1907), 67.
57. *Literaturnoe nasledstvo*, No. 27-8 (1937), 391.
58. *Vesy*, No. 5 (1908), 65.
59. A. Zonov, "Letopis' teatra na Ofitserskoi," *Alkonost*, v. 1 (1911), 66, 67.
60. *Blokovskii sbornik* (Tartu, 1966), 415.
61. Georgii Chulkov, *Gody stranstvii* (M: Federatsiia, 1930), 221.
62. Auslender, 427, 428.
63. *O Komissarzhevskoi. Zabytoe i novoe*, 87.
64. A. Kugel', "Teatral'nye zametki, *Teatr i iskusstvo*, No. 1 (1907), 18.
65. *Blokovskii sbornik*, 430.
66. TsGTM, No. 281709/1405.
67. Meierkhol'd, 145.
68. Eizenshtein, v. 3, 338.
69. O. Mandel'shtam, "Revoliutsioner v teatre," *Teatr i muzyka*, No. 1-2 (1923), 425.
70. Blok, v. 5, 189-191.
71. V. P. Verigina, "Vospominaniia ob Aleksandre Bloke," *Uchenye zapiski Tartusskogo Gos. Universiteta*, Issue 104 (Tartu, 1961), 335.
72. Muzei MKhAT, arkhiv N.-D., No. 11303.
73. K. Chukovskii, "Peterburgskie teatry," *Zolotoe Runo*, No. 3 (1907), 75.
74. Meierkhol'd, 199.
75. Ibid.
76. Ibid., 178.
77. Blok, v. 5, 190; v. 6, 132.
78. N. Negorev (A. Kugel'), "Maska doloi!" *Teatr i iskusstvo*, No. 2 (1907), 35, 36.
79. *Teatr i iskusstvo*, No. 7 (1907), 115.
80. Sb. *Komissarzhevskaia* (L-M. 1964), 164-65.

81. *Novosti sezona* (Sept. 2, 1908), 7.
82. A. Kugel', v *Teatr i iskusstvo* 7 (1907), 115.
83. K. S. Stanislavskii, *Sobr. soch.*, v. 7, 420.
84. A. Kugel', "Teatral'nie zametki," *Teatr i iskusstvo*, No. 9 (1907), 160.
85. Sb. *Komissarzhevskaia*, 168.
86. Tal'nikov. *Komissarzhevskaia*, 335.
87. Sb. *Komissarzhevskaia*, 163, 165.
88. N. Manykin-Nevstruev, "Beatrisa (po povodu gastrolei Komissarzhevskoi)," *Russkii artist*, No. 1 (1907), 10.
89. N. Efros, "Moskovskie vpechatleniia," *Teatr i iskusstvo*, No. 39 (1907), 634.
90. K. Smurskii, "Novye formy. Beseda s K. S. Stanislavskim, *Stolichnoe utro* (Oct. 6, 1907).
91. Iu. Kalashnikov, *Traditsii realizma na stsene. Uslovnyi teatr v otsenke K. S. Stanislavskogo* (M: VTO, 1964), 65.
92. *Teatr*, No. 38 (Sept. 9, 1907), 9, 10.
93. Blok, v. 5, 194, 195.
94. *Teatr*, No. 47 (Sept. 20, 1907), 10.
95. *Teatr*, No. 46 (Sept. 19, 1907), 8.
96. N. Tamarin, "Dramaticheskii teatr," *Teatr i iskusstvo*, No. 38 (1907), 613.
97. K. S. Stanislavskii, *Sobr. soch.*, v. 7, 355.
98. Vl. I. Nemirovich-Danchenko, *Izbrannye pis'ma*, 273.
99. A. Rostislavov, "Ne to," *Teatr i iskusstvo*, No. 43 (1907), 701.
100. "O chem govoriat i pishut," *Teatr*, No. 71-72 October 14-15, 1907), 22, 23.
101. Ibid.
102. N. Tamarin, "Dramaticheskii teatr V. F. Komissarzhevskoi, *Teatr i iskusstvo*, No. 41 (1907), 661, 662.
103. *Golos Moskvy* (Oct. 13, 1907).
104. Blok, v. 5, 200-202.
105. Ibid., v. 8, 216.
106. N. Volkov, *Meierkhol'd*, v. 1, 353, 354.
107. D. Tal'nikov, *Komissarzhevskaia*, 336.
108. N. Tamarin, "Dramaticheskii teatr," *Teatr i iskusstvo*, No. 45 (1907), 735.
109. Meierkhol'd, 200.
110. Sb. *Komissarzhevskaia*, 167.
111. Ibid., 168.
112. V. Verigina, *O Vere Fedorovne Komissarzhevskoi.* Ms., VTO Archive, 30, 31.
113. TsGALI, f. 998, ed. khr. 626, 1. 322.
114. Verigina, 31.
115. Nik. Eremeev, "Peterburgskie pis'ma, *Russkii artist*, No. 7 (1907), 103.
116. "Final 'Meierkhol'dovshchiny,' " *Obozreniie teatrov* (Nov. 11-12, 1907), 17.
117. Zigrid (E. Stark), "Na chto on byl nuzhen?" *Obozrenie teatrov* (November 15, 1907), 14.
118. S. Ia., "A. P. Lenskii o Malom teatre," *Teatr*, No. 126 (1907).
119. Quoted according to N. Volkov, *Meierkhol'd*, v. 1, 350.
120. Ibid., 354.
121. Teatral. "U V. E. Meierkhol'da," *Peterburgskaia gazeta* (October 1, 1908).
122. N. Volkov, *Meierkhol'd*, v. 1, 354.
123. N. Turkin, *Komissarzhevskaia v zhizni i na stene*, 140.
124. "Iz besedy s V. F. Komissarzhevskoi," *Novost' sezona* (Oct. 2, 1908), 8.
125. N. Iordanskii, "Individualizm na stsene," *Sovremennyi mir*, No. 1, Pt. II (1909), 63, 64.
126. E. Znosko-Borovskii, *Russkii teatr nachala XX veka* (Prague: Plamia, 1924), 228.
127. See A. Lunacharskii, "Kniga o novom teatre," *Obrazovanie*, No. 4 (1908); Iu Steklov, "Teatr ili kukol'naia komediia?" in sb. *Krizis teatra* (M. 1908).
128. Kugel', 827-29.

—547—

Chapter Five

1. TsGTM, No. 226023, 46.
2. TsGALI, f. 998, ed. khr. 626, 323.
3. TsGTM, No. 225640, 186.
4. *Obozrenie teatrov*, No. 260 (Nov. 27, 1907).
5. "O priglashenii V. E. Meierkhol'da na impera-torskuiu stsenu," *Obozrenie teatrov*, No. 349 (March 4, 1908).
6. TsGALI, f. 998, ed. khr. 626, 325.
7. "Teatral," U V. E. Meierkhol'da, *Peterburg-skaia gazeta* (Oct. 1, 1908).
8. "Teatr i muzyka," *Slovo* (Oct. 10, 1908).
9. "Lektsiia Meierkhol'da Aleksandrinskoi trup-pe," *Peterburgskaia gazeta* (Sept. 7, 1908).
10. *Teatral'noe nasledstvo* (M: Iskusstvo, 1956), 448, 452, 522.
11. TsGTM, No. 225646, No. 17, 19.
12. "Teatral."
13. TsGTM, No. 225646, 53.
14. N. Khodotov, *Blizkoe-dalekoe* (M-L. 1932), 323.
15. TsGTM, No. 225646, 43-44.
16. Omega (F. V. Trozinev), "U tsarskikh vrat," *Pe-terburgskaia gazeta* (Oct. 1, 1908).
17. Yu. Beliaev, "U tsarskikh vrat," *Novoe vremia* (Oct. 3, 1908).
18. L. Gurevich, "Aleksandrinskii teatr," *Slovo* (Oct. 2, 1908).
19. L. Gurevich, "U tsarskikh vrat," *Slovo* (Oct. 4, 1908).
20. TsGTM, No. 224646, No. 68, 60-rev.
21. Vs. Meierkhol'd, *O teatre*, 67, 68, 71, 72.
22. Vs. Meierkhol'd, "K postanovke *Tristana i Izol'dy* na Mariinskom teatre 30 oktiabria 1909 goda," *Ezhegodnik imperatorskikh teatrov*, v. V (1910); see also V. Meierkhol'd, *O teatre*, 56-80.
23. Meierkhol'd, *O teatre*, 57, 58.
24. I. Sollertinskii, "V. E. Meierkhol'd i russkii opernyi impressionizm," *Istoriia sovetskogo teatra*, v. 1 (L. 1933), 311.
25. TsGTM, No. 225743, 43, 56, 68.
26. Sollertinskii, 310.
27. TsGTM, No. 225781, No. 51.
28. Omega (F. V. Troziner), "Aleksandrinskii teatr," *Peterburgskaia gazeta* (March 10, 1910).
29. N. Rossovskii, "Aleksandrinskii teatr," *Peter-burgskii listok* (March 10, 1910).
30. E. Znosko-Borovskii, *Russkii teatr nachala XX veka* (Prague: Plamia, 1924), 304, 305.
31. V. Piast, *Vstrechi* (M: Federatsiia, 1929), 169-176).
32. Znosko-Borovskii, 302, 303.
33. Ibid., 311, 312.
34. M. Fokin, *Protiv techeniia* (L-M. 1962), 219, 220.89. Ts
35. Meierkhol'd, O teatre, 121.
36. Meierkhol'd, "Don Zhuan. K obstanovke," *Aleksandr Iakovlevich Golovin. Vstrechi i upechat-leniia. Pis'ma. Vospominaniia o Golovine* (L-M: Iskus-stvo, 1960), 159-161.
37. Ibid., 178.
38. Meierkhol'd. *O teatre*. 122.
39. Ibid, 124, 125.
40. *Aleksandr Iakovlevich Golovin*, 111.
41. Ia. Maliutin, *Aktery moego pokoleniia* (L-M: Iskusstvo, 1959), 84, 85.
42. Time, *Dorogi iskusstva* (M-L: VTO, 1962), 163.
43. Maliutin, 112.
44. Time, 163, 164.
45. Iu. Iur'ev, *Zapiski* (L-M: Iskusstvo, 1948), 524.
46. Ibid., 525.
47. Ibid.
48. A. Golovin, "Iur'ev i *Don Zhuan*," *Iu. M. Iu-r'ev. 1892-1827. Sbornik* (L: Priboi, 1927), 57.
49. TsGTM, No. 225837, 118, 118-rev.

50. TsGTM, No. 225837, No. 123.
51. "L. Vas-ii" (Vasilevskii), "Aleksandrinskii teatr. *Don Zhuan*," *Rech* (Nov. 11, 1910).
52. Iu. Beliaev, "O chem rasskazyval gobelen (Don Zhuan)," *Novoe vremia* (Nov. 11, 1910).
53. Golovin, 55, 56.
54. Meierkhol'd, *O teatre*, 127.
55. N. Rossovskii, "Aleksandrinskii teatr," *Peterburgskii listok* (Oct. 10, 1910).
56. Beliaev.
57. *Novoe vremia* (Nov. 14, 1910).
58. TsGTM, No. 225866, 5.
59. A. Kugel', "Teatral'nie zametki," *Teatr i iskusstvo*, No. 47 (1910), 901-904.
60. Aleksandr Benua, "Khudozhestvennye pis'ma. Balet v Aleksandrinke," *Rech'* (Nov. 19, 1910).
61. A. Kugel', *Profili teatra* (M. 1929), 40.
62. Meierkhol'd, *O teatre*, 161, 162.
63. TsGTM, No. 225866, 48.
64. TsGALI, f. 998, ed. khr. 721, 4.
65. *Kuda my idem? Sbornik statei i otvetov* (M: Zaria, 1910), 104, 105.
66. Znosko-Borovskii, 302, 303, 317.
67. *Birzhevye vedomosti* (Jan. 4, 1911).
68. Aleksandr Benua, "Vozobnovlenie *Borisa*," *Rech'* (Jan. 9, 1911).
69. TsGTM. ed. khr. 225903, 107.
70. *Rampa i zhizn'*, No. 36 (1911), 7.
71. "Novye puti (beseda s Vs. E. Meierkhol'-dom)," *Rampa i zhizn'*, No. 34 (1911), 2, 3.
72. N. Rossov, "Ne dlia polemiki," *Rampa i zhizn'*, No. 36 (1911), 5.
73. V. I. Nemirovich-Danchenko, *Iz proshlogo* (M. 1936), 371.
74. "Pokoi," "Za materialom dlia *Zhivogo tru-pa*," *Russkie vedomosti* (Aug. 2, 1911).
75. TsGTM, ed. khr. 225903, 91, 91-rev.
76. TsGTM, ed. khr. 225903, 100-rev, 102.
77. Kugel', "Teatral'nye zametki," *Teatr i iskuss-tvo*, No. 40 (1911), 746.
78. L. Gurevich, "*Zhivoi trup* v Aleksandrinskom teatre," *Russkie vedomosti* (Oct. 1, 1911).
79. Kugel', "Teatral'nie zametki," 746.
80. Meierkhol'd, *O teatre*, 204.
81. TsGALI, f. 998, ed. khr. 240, 2.
82. Ibid.
83. M. Fokin, *Protiv techeniia* (L-M. 1962), 500, 501.
84. Meierkhol'd, *O teatre*, 204.
85. *Aleksandr Iakovlevich Golovin*, 116.
86. Fokin, 349.
87. Meierkhol'd, *O teatre*, 205.
88. See, for instance: "O postanovke *Orfeia* (be-seda s M. M. Fokinym), *Obozrenie teatrov* (Dec. 14, 1911).
89. TsGTM, ed. khr. 225935, 19.
90. TsGTM, ed. khr. 225993, 60.
91. *Rampa i zhizn'*, No. 51 (1911), 8.
92. Vas. Bazilevskii, "Peterburgskie etiudy," *Rampa i zhizn'*, No. 1 (1912), 13.
93. Benua, "Khudozhestvennye pis'ma. Postanov-ka *Orfeia*," *Rech'* (Dec. 30, 1911).
94. M. Kuz'min, *Uslovnosti* (Prague, 1923), 58.
95. Meierkhol'd, *O teatre*, 201.
96. Ibid.
97. Ibid.
98. A. Mgebrov, *Zhizn' v teatre*, v. II, 193, 194.
99. Mikhail Babenchikov, "Teriokskii teatr to-varishchestva akterov, muzykantov, pisatelei i zhivo-pistsev," *Novaia studiia*, No. 7 (1912), 8.
100. Meierkhol'd, *O teatre*, 203.
101. A. Mgebrov, *Zhizn' v teatre*, v. II, 200.
102. Aleksandr Blok, *Sobranie sochinenii*, v. 7, 138.
103. V. P. Verigina, *Vospominaniia ob Aleksandre Bloke*, 353.

104. Blok, v. 7, 155.
105. Meierkhol'd, *O teatre*, 202.
106. Blok, *Zapisnye knizhki* (M-L. 1965), 214.
107. Verigina, 352.
108. Ibid., 354, 355.
109. Mgebrov, *Zhizn' v teatre*, v. II, 219.
110. Babenchikov, 8.
111. Verigina, 356.
112. Blok, *Sobr. soch.*, v. 8, 398, 399.
113. Mgebrov, *Zhizn' v teatre*, v. II, 222.
114. "Binokl'" (Bozhena Vitvitskaia), " 'Predislo-vie' k segodniashnei prem'ere *Zalozhnikov zhizni* (be-seda s rezhisserom V. E. Meierkhol'dom)," *Peterburg-skaia gazeta* (Nov. 6, 1912).
115. TsGTM, ed. khr. 225993, 99, 101.
116. K. Arabazhin, "*Zalozhniki zhizni*. Aleksan-drinskii teatr," *Vechernee vremia* (Nov. 7, 1912).
117. "Omega" (F. Troziner), "Aleksandrinskii teatr," *Peterburgskaia gazeta* (Nov. 7, 1912).
118. Iu. Beliaev, "Krasivyi vecher," *Novoe vremia* (Nov. 8, 1912).
119. Benua, "Khudozhestvennye pis'ma. O posta-novke *Zalozhnikov zhizni*," *Rech'* (Dec. 6, 1912).
120. D. Merezhkovskii, "Osel i rozy," *Rech'* (Nov. 10, 1912).
121. A. Chebotarevskaia, "Koliuchie rozy. Otvet D. S. Merezhkovskomu," *Rech'* (Nov. 18, 1912).
122. Blok, *Sobr. soch.*, v. 7, 176.
123. K. A. Koval'skii, "*Zalozhniki zhizni* (Dia-log po povodu p'esy F. Sologuba)," *Novaia studiia*, No. 11 (1912), 1, 2.
124. "Homo novus" (A. Kugel'), "Zametki," *Teatr i iskusstvo*, No. 46 (1912), 902.
125. D. Filosofov, "*Zalozhniki zhizni*," *Rech'* (Nov. 8, 1912).
126. Beliaev, "Krasivyi vecher."
127. P. Iartsev, "Aleksandrinskii teatr. O predstav-lenii *Zalozhnikov zhizni*," *Rech'* (Nov. 8, 1912).
128. TsGTM, ed. khr. 226023, 97, 100.
129. *Aleksandr Iakovlevich Golovin*, 127.
130. Aleksandr Gladkov, "Meierkhol'd govorit," *Neva*, No. 2 (1966), 204.
131. Sollertinskii, 318.
132. Meierkhol'd, *Dvukhtomnik*, v. 1, 314.
133. K. S. Stanislavskii, *Sobr. soch.*, v. 1, 444.
134. Fokin, *Protiv techeniia* (L-M: Iskusstvo, 1962), 221.
135. Stanislavskii, v. 1, 444, 445.
136. Timé, *Dorogi iskusstva* (M-L: VTO, 1962), 64.
137. A. Levinson, "*Pisanella, ili dushistaia smert'*. Pis'mo iz Parizha," *Rech* (July 8, 1913).
138. A. Lunacharskii, "*Pizanella i Magdalina*," *Teatr i iskusstvo*, No. 25 (1913), 517, 518.
139. "*Pisanella* v Parizhe," *Russkoe slovo* (May 12, 1913).
140. "Homo novus" (A. R. Kugel'), "Zolotaia mukha," *Teatr i iskusstvo*, No. 25 (1913), 517, 518.
141. Blok, *Sobr. soch.*, v. 7, 239.
142. Ibid., 186, 187.
143. Ibid., 187, 188.
144. Ibid., v. 8, 415.
145. Ibid., 417.
146. Ibid., v. 7, 248.
147. Blok. *Zapisnye knizhki* (M. 1965), 209.
148. Blok, *Sobr. soch.*, v. 7, 248, 249.
149. Ibid., 246.
150. TsGALI, f. 998, ed. khr. 734.
151. Published in the notes to v. 7 of Stanslavskii's collected works (M. 1960), 753.
152. Stanislavksii, *Sobr. soch.*, v. 7, 539.
153. T. Bachelis, "Rezhisser Stanislavskii," *Novyi mir*, No. 1 (1963), 207.
154. T. I. Bachelis, *Stanislavskii i Meierkhol'd*, Ms. 41.
155. N. M. "V. E. Meierkhol'd o sovremennom teatre," *Teatr* (Oct. 24, 1913).
156. TsGALI, f. 998, ed. khr. 625, 101-116.
157. Ibid., 102.
158. TsGALI, f. 998, ed. khr. 626, 491.
159. "Homo novus" (A. R. Kugel'), "Zametki," *Teatr i iskusstvo*, No. 5 (1914), 113-115.
160. Znosko-Borovskii, *Russkii teatr nachala XX veka*, 304.
161. Blok, *Zapisnye knizhki*, 200.
162. Verigina, "Vospominaniia ob Aleksandre Bloke," *Uchenye zapiski Tartuskogo gos. universiteta*, issue 104 (Tartu, 1961), 361.
163. Blok, *Sobr. soch.*, v. 7, 187.
164. A. V. Bobrishchev-Pushkin, "Apel'siny i videniia," *Teatr i isskusstvo*, No. 15 (1914), 347.
165. TIM Museum. Catalogue to "Piat' let" exhi-bition, 1926, 5.
166. Mgebrov, *Zhizn' v teatre*, v. II, 249.
167. Znosko-Borovskii, "Spektakli, posviashchen-nye Aleksandru Bloku," *Sovremennik*, v. 11 (1914), 120-121.
168. Bobrishchev-Pushkin, 347.
169. Verigina, 361-364.
170. Ibid., 363.
171. "Neskol'ko slov po povodu postanovki liri-cheskikh dram Aleksandra Bloka *Neznakomka i Ba-laganchik...*" *Liubov' k trem apel'sinam*, No. 4-5 (1914), 89.
172. N. D. Volkov, *Meierkhol'd*, v. II, 322.
173. Verigina, 364.
174. Meierkhol'd, "Voina i teatr," *Birzhevie no-vosti*, evening edition (Sept. 11, 1914).
175. "Teatr A. S. Suvorina," *Teatr i iskusstvo*, No. 33 (1914), 678.
176. Bureevich, "Lermontovskii spektakl'," *Rech* (Dec. 12, 1915).
177. "Homo Novus" (A. Kugel'), "Aleksandrinskii teatr," *Den'* (Sept. 2, 1916).
178. Z. Gippius, "Zelenoe-beloe-aloe," in her *Ze-lenoe kol'tso* (Petrograd: Ogni, 1916), 141, 142.
179. TsGTM, ed. khr. 226179, 99.
180. N. Tamarin (N. N. Akulov), "Aleksandrinskii teatr, " *Teatr i iskusstvo*, No. 8 (1915), 127-128.
181. Gurevich, "Aleksandrinskii teatr. *Zelenoe kol'tso*," *Rech'* (Feb. 18, 1915).
182. Blok, *Sobr. soch.*, v. 8, 441.
183. V. N. Solov'ev, "A. Ia. Golovin kak teatral'-nyi master," *Apollon*, v. 1 (1917), 25.
184. "Viktor" (V. M. Zhirmunskii), "*Stoikii prints* Kal'derona na stsene Aleksandrinskogo teatra," *Liubov' k trem apel'sinam* (1916), v. 2-3, 138.
185. Ibid., 136-138.
186. "Miron Makiel' Zhirmunskii" (V. M. Zhir-munskii), "*Stoikii prints* na stsene Aleksandrinskogo teatra," *Liubov' k trem apel'sinam* (1916), v. 1, p. 74.
187. Ibid., 76.
188. "Zigfrid" (E. Stark), "Aleksandrinskii teatr," *Peterburgskii kur'er* (Apr. 26, 1915).
189. Gurevich, "Proshchal'nyi spektakl' Ozarov-skogo," *Rech'* (Apr. 25, 1915).
190. "Homo novus" (A. Kugel'), "Zametki," *Teatr i iskusstvo*, No. 40 (1915), 736-737.
191. Gurevich, "Mikhailovskii teatr. *Pigmalion* Bernarda Shoy," *Rech* (Apr. 28, 1915).
192. Meierkhol'd, "K vosstanovleniiu *Grozy* A. N. Ostrovskogo na stsene Aleksandrinskogo teatra," *Liubov' k trem apel'sinam*, v. 2-3 (1916), 107-116.
193. "V. Meierkhol'd o postanovke *Grozy*." *Bir-zhevye vedomosti* (Jan. 4, 1916).
194. *Aleksandr Iakovlevich Golovin*, 129.
195. V. N. Solov'ev, "A. Ia. Golovin kak teatral'-nyi master," *Apollon*, No. 1 (1917), 29.
196. "Omega" (F. Troziner), "*Groza* v Aleksan-drinskom teatre 9-go ianvaria," *Petrogradskaia gazeta* (Jan. 11, 1916).

197. Solov'ev, 30.

198. Liutsii, *"Groza," Novoe vremia* (Jan. 10, 1916).

199. R. M. *"Groza v Malom teatre," Rannee utro* (Oct. 1, 1911).

200. A. Kairanskii, *"Groza (Malyi teatr)," Utro Rossii* (Sept. 1, 1911).

201. Iu. Iur'ev, *Zapiski*, 536.

202. "Homo novus" (A. Kugel'), "Zametki," *Teatr i iskusstvo*, No. 3 (1916), 60, 62.

203. Benua, *"Groza v Aleksandrinke," Rech'* (Sept. 30, 1916).

204. TsGTM, ed. khr. 226219, 143-144.

205. TsGTM, ed. khr. 226219, 145-rev.

206. Vl. Botsianovskii, "U rampy," *Birzhevye vedomosti* (Jan. 10, 1916).

207. N. Khodotov, *Blizkoe-dalękoe*, 339.

208. Iur'ev, *Zapiski*, 536.

209. "Omega" (F. Troziner).

210. Liutsii, *"Groza," Novoe vremia* (Jan. 10, 1916).

211. "Omega" (F. Troziner).

212. B. Alpers, *Teatr sotsial'noi maski* (M-L: GIKhL, 1931).

213. Bozhena Vitvitskaia, "Prival komediantov," *Teatr i iskusstvo*, No. 17 (1916), 342.

214. Solov'ev, "Sudeikin," *Apollon*, No. 8-10 (1917).

215. R. A., "V. E. Meierkhol'd," *Teatr* (Mar. 1, 1916).

216. Gurevich, "Aleksandrinskii teatr. *Romantiki Merezhkovskogo," Rech'* (Oct. 23, 1916).

217. TsGTM, ed. khr. 226251, 78.

218. -skii, "Vs. E. Meierkhol'd o postanovke *Kamennogo gostia," Birzhevye vedomosti* (Jan. 25, 1917).

219. A. Chesnokov, *"Kamennyi gost'* na stsene Mariinskogo teatra" (Clipping, VTO Archives).

220. Al-yy, "Mariinskii teatr," *Teatr i iskusstvo*, No. 6 (1917), 111.

221. Benua, "Khudozhestvennye pis'ma. Postanovka *Kamennogo gosti* na kazennoi stsene," *Rech'* (Feb. 3, 1917).

222. Stanislavskii, *Sobr. soch.*, v. 1, 366-370.

223. Fedor Sologub, "Zabytoe iskusstvo," *Birzhevye vedomosti* (May 3, 1915).

224. TsGTM, ed. khr. 226224, 38-rev.

225. Ibid., 39-rev.-41-rev.

226. "Homo novus" (A. Kugel'), "Zametki," *Teatr i iskusstvo*, No. 10-11 (1917), 192-194.

227. A. P. Kugel', *Profili teatra* (M. 1929), 51.

228. Timé, *Dorogi iskusstva* (M-L: VTO, 1962), 204.

229. Ia. Maliutin, *Aktery moego pokoleniia* (L-M: Iskusstvo, 1951), 91-92.

230. TsGTM, ed. khr. 226224, 42-43.

231. A. Golovin, "Kak ia stavil *Maskarad," Krasnaia panorama*, No. 17 (1926), 12, 13.

232. Nikolai Petrov, *50 i 500* (M: VTO, 1960), 129.

233. Meierkhol'd, *O teatre*, 11.

234. TsGALI, f. 998, ed. khr. 268. Published in Iur'ev, *Zapiski*, v. II, 360-362.

235. Maliutin, *Aktery moego pokoleniia*, 99, 100.

236. Timé, *Dorogi iskusstva*, 204.

237. Solov'ev, "Maskarad v Aleksandrinskom teatre," *Apollon*, No. 2-3 (1917), 73.

238. B. A. Al'medingen, "Iz vospominanii o rabote Golovina v teatre," *Aleksandr Iakovlevich Golovin*, 270.

239. See: *Maskarad M. Iu. Lermontova v teatral'nykh eskizakh A. Ia. Golovina* (M-L: VTO, 1941).

240. Al'medingen, 274-276.

241. TsGTM, ed. khr. 226224, 39-rev.

242. TsGALI, f. 998, ed. khr. 626, 744.

243. TsGALI, f. 998, ed. khr. 268, ??.

244. Iu. Iur'ev, *Zapiski*, 640, 650.

245. Ibid., 535.

246. Maliutin, *Aktery moego pokoleniia*, 94.

247. G. Stebnitskii, "Ob osnovnykh techeniiakh v dekoratsionnom iskusstve," *Teatral'no-dekorativnoe iskusstvo v SSSR 1917-1927* (L. 1927), 63.

248. K. Kerzhavin, *Epokhi Aleksandrinskoi stseny* (L. 1932), 184.

249. M. Rabinovich, "Aleksandrinskii teatr." *Rech'* (Jan. 27, 1917).

250. Bozhena Vitvitskaia, "Otkrytie dramaticheskogo gosudarstvennogo teatra," *Teatr i iskusstvo*, No. 36 (1917), 616.

251. Maliutin, *Aktery moego pokoleniia*, 241, 242.

252. Vl. S. (V. N. Solov'ev), "Petrogradskie teatry," *Apollon*, No. 8-10 (1917), 96.

253. Nekto, "Toska po gorodovomu," *Obozrenie teatrov* (Nov. 21-22, 1917), 9.

254. "Homo novus" (A. Kugel'), "Zametki, *Teatr i iskusstvo*, No. 44-46 (1917), 708.

255. Maliutin, *Aktery moego pokoleniia*, 346, 350.

256. Kuz'min, *Uslovnosti* (Petrograd, 1923), 40.

257. Meierkhol'd, *Duukhtomnik*, v. 1, 313.

258. Pasternak. *Okhrannaia gramota* (L. 1931), 91-2.

NOTES TO PART II

Chapter Six

1. A. Lunacharskii, "Teatr Meierkhol'da," *Izvestiia* (April 25, 1926).

2. *Liubov' k trem apel'sinam*, No. 1-2-3 (1914), 140.

3. *Nashi vedomosti* (Jan. 12, 1918).

4. *Petrogradskoe ekho* (Jan. 13, 1918).

5. *Istoriia sovetskogo teatra* (L. 1933), v. I, 147.

6. A. Ia. Al'tshuller, "K istorii akademicheskogo teatra dramy im. A. S. Pushkina v pervye gody Sovetskoi vlasti" "*Uchenye zapiski" Gos. NII teatra i muzyki* (L. 1958), v 1, 32.

7. Bozhena Vitvitskaia, "Legenda L. N. Tolstogo na Aleksandrinskom teatre," *Teatr i iskusstvo*, No. 12-13 (1918), 131.

8. A. Ia. Golovin, *Vstrechi i vpechatleniia*, 186.

9. B. Iarustovskii, *Igor' Stravinskii* (M. 1963), 86, 87.

10. N. Malkov, "*Solovei* Igoria Stravinskogo," *Teatr i iskusstvo*, No. 20-21 (1918), 213, 214.

11. *A. V. Lunacharskii o teatre i dramaturgii* v. I, *382, 383*.

12. O. Mandel'shtam, "Buria i natisk," *Russkoe iskusstvo*, No. 1 (1923), 11.

13. *Knizhnyi ugol*, No. 1 (1918), 3.

14. Aleksandr Blok, *Sobr. soch.* (M-L. 1963), v. 7, 17.

15. Sergei Eizenshtein, *Izbrannye proizvedeniia* (M. 1964), v. II, 270-272.

16. Ia. Tugenkhol'd, *Iskusstvo oktiabr'skoi epokhi* (L. 1930), 18.

17. A. Fevralskii, "Misteriia-buff," *Maiakovskii. Materialy i issledovaniia* (M. 1940), 196.

18. *Istoriia sovetskogo teatra*, v. 1, 220.

19. *A. V. Lunacharskii o teatre i dramaturgii*, v. I, 150, 151.

20. Andrei Levinson, "Misteriia-buff Maiakovskogo," *Zhizn' iskusstva* (Nov. 11, 1918.

21. *Knizhnyi ugol*, No. 5 (1918), 2-5.

22. Vl. Maiakovskii, *Poln. sobr. soch.*, v. 12, 15.

23. "Zaiavlenie po povodu *Misterii-buff." Zhizn'*

iskusstva (Nov. 21, 1918).

24. Lunacharskii, "O polemike," *Zhizn' iskusstva* (Nov. 21, 1918).

25. Tugenkhol'd, 16.

26. TsGAOR, f. 2306, op. 24, d. 33, 1. 1-69.

27. Lunacharskii, "Klassovaia bor'ba v iskusstve," *Iskusstvo*, No. 1-2 (1929), 11.

28. "Ot narodnogo komissara po prosveshcheniiu," *Vestnik teatra*, No. 74 (1920), 16.

29. "Beseda s V. E. Meierkhol'dom," *Vestnik teatra*, No. 74 (1920), 16.

30. "Ob uiazvimykh mestakh teatral'nogo fronta," *Vestnik teatra*, No. 78-79 (1921), 15.

31. *O teatre* (Tver', 1922), 9.

32. Ibid., 73.

33. *Vestnik teatra*, No. 78-79 (1921), 15.

34. Ibid., No. 72-73 (1920), 19, 20.

35. Viktor Shklovskii, "Papa—eto budil'nik!" *Zhizn' iskusstva* (Dec. 10-12, 1920).

36. B. Alpers, *Teatr sotsial'noi maski* (M. 1931), 23.

37. *Vestnik teatra*, No. 72-73 (1920), 8.

38. Evg. Kuznetsov, "Chemu smeetes'?" *Arena* (1924), 88.

39. K. Famarin (Em. Beskin), "Drama v Moskve," *Vestnik rabotnikov iskusstv*, No. 2-3 (1920), 62.

40. Nikolai Tarabukin, *Zritel'noe oformlenie v GOSTIMe*. Ms. TsGALI, f. 963, ed. khr. 139.

41. Samuil Margolin, *Khudozhnik teatra za 15 let* (M. 1933), 17.

42. Lunacharskii, *Teatr i revoliutsiia* (M. 1924), 106, 107.

43. Maiakovskii, v. 12, 246.

44. P. M. Kerzhentsev, *"Zori,"* *Vestnik teatra*, No. 74 (1920), 4.

45. *Vstrechi s Meierkhol'dom* (M: VTO, 1967), 208.

46. *Vestnik rabotnikov iskusstv*, No. 7-9 (1921), 31.

47. *Arena* (1924), 88-89.

48. Yurii Sobolev, "Iz moskovskikh nabliudenii," *Vestnik teatra*, No. 80-81 (1921), 19.

49. *N. K. Krupskaia ob iskusstve i literature* (L-M. 1963), 141.

50. Valerii Bebutov, "Chto vse eto znachit?" *Vestnik teatra*, No. 74 (1920), 6.

51. "Beseda o Zoriakh. V. Teatre RSFSR," *Vestnik teatra*, No. 75 (1920), 13.

52. "Ob uiazvimykh mestakh teatral'nogo fronta (disput na ponedel'nike Zor')," 16.

53. "Beseda o Zoriakh. V Teatre RSFSR," 14.

54. Maiakovskii, v. 12, 246.

55. P. Markov, "Pis'mo o Meierkhol'de," *Teatr i dramaturgiia*, No. 2 (1932), 20.

56. M. Zagorskii, O *"Teatral'nom Oktiabre,"* Ms. VTO archive.

57. *Kul'tura teatra*, No. 4 (1921), 9.

58. *Vestnik teatra*, No. 83-84 (1921), 15.

59. M. F. Sukhanova, "Tri p'esy V. V. Maiakovskogo," *Maiakovskii v vospominaniiakh sovremennikov* (M: GIKhL, 1963), 308.

60. Tarabukin, N. TsGALI, f. 963, ed. kh. 139.

61. V. E. Meierkhol'd, "Slovo o Maiakovskom," *Maiakovskii v vospominaniiakh sovremennikov*, 284, 285.

62. Ibid., 285.

63. P. Markov, *Noveishie teatral'nye techeniia* (M. 1924), 42.

64. *Maiakovskii. Materialy i issledovaniia* (M. 1940), 214.

65. *A. V. Lunacharskii o teatre i dramaturgii* v. 1, 778.

66. Margolin, "Vesna teatral'noi chrezmernosti," *Vestnik rabotnikov iskusstv*, No. 10-11 (1921), 122.

67. Em. Beskin, "Revoliutsiia i teatr," *Vestnik rabotnikov iskusstv*, No. 7-9 (1921), 31.

68. D. Furmanov, "Moskovskie pis'ma," *Rabochii krai* (Ivanovo-Vosnesensk [June 16, 1921]).

69. Furmanov, *Sobr. soch.* (M: GIKhL, 1961), v. IV, 254.

70. Lunacharskii, *Teatr segodnia* (M-L. 1928), 106.

71. *Pechat' i revoliutsiia* (1921), v. II, 226.

72. Lunacharskii, *Teatr segodnia*, 101-102.

Chapter Seven

1. V. Blium, "Na perevale," in *O teatre* (Tver', 1922), 2, 3.

2. *Pechat' i revoliutsiia* (1922), v. 1, 307.

3. "Vs. Meierkhol'd o teatre (speech in the Leningrad Hall of Unions), *Novyi zritel'*, No. 40 (1927), 10.

4. A. A. Gvozdev, *Teatr imeni Vs. Meierkhol'da (1920-1926)* (L. 1927), 27.

5. Vs. Meierkhol'd, V. Bebutov, K. Derzhavin, "O dramaturgii i kul'ture teatra," *Vestnik teatra*, No. 87-88 (1923), 3.

6. V. Bebutov, Vs. Meierkhol'd, "Odinochestvo Stanislavskogo," *Vestnik teatra*, No. 89-90 (1921), 3.

7. *Pechat' i revoliutsiia*, v. 1 (1922), 307-309. Underlined by Meierkhol'd.

8. A. Matskin, "Vakhtangov, staraia i novaia Turandot," *Teatr*, No. 12 (1963), 5-6.

9. S. Eizenshtein, *Izbr. proizv. v shesti tomakh* (M: Iskusstvo, 1964), v. 1, 309, 310.

10. "Nakanune Rogonostsa," *Afisha TIM*, No. 1 (1926), 3.

11. Tezisy k konstruktivnomu postroeniiu *Nory*. Ms. Archive of VTO.

12. Sadko (V. Blium), *"Nora v Teatre Aktera,"* *Izvestiia* (April 20, 1922).

13. A. A. Gvozdev, *Teatr imeni Vs. Meierkhol'da* (L. 1927), 28.

14. I. Aksenov, "Prostranstvennyi konstruktivizm na stsene," *Teatral'nyi Oktiabr'* (L-M. 1926), 34.

15. Nikolai Tarabukin, *Zritel'noe oformlenie v GOSTIMe*. Ms. TsGALI, f. 963. ed. khr. 139.

16. Vs. Meierkhol'd, "Kak byl postavlen *Velikodushnyi rogonosets*," *Novyi zritel'*, No. 39 (1926), 6.

17. Vas. Sakhnovskii, *Meierkhol'd. Vremennik RTO*, v. 1 (1925), 231.

18. I. Il'inskii, *Sam o sebe* (M. 1961), 148.

19. *Literaturnye manifesty. Ot simvolizma do "Oktiabria"* (M. 1924), 257-258.

20. Aleksei Gen, *Konstruktivizm* (Tver', 1922), 3.

21. Coll. *Iskusstvo trudiashchimsia*, Issue 1 (1921), 8, 31.

22. B. Arvatov, *Iskusstvo i klassy* (M-Pg. 1923), 85.

23. Dzhon Gassner, *Forma i ideia v sovremennom teatre* (M. 1959), 220.

24. I. Aksenov, "Prostranstvennyi konstruktivizm na stsene," in *Teatral'nyi Oktiabr'*, 34.

25. Stinf, "Biomekhanika (Iz besedy s laborantami Vs. Meierkhol'da)," *Zrelishcha*, No. 10 (1922), 14.

26. Aleksandr Gladkov, "Iz vospominanii o Meierkhol'de," *Moskva teatral'naia* (1960), 358.

27. Vs. Meierkhol'd, V. Bebutov, K. Derzhavin, "O dramaturgii i kul'ture teatra," *Vestnik teatra*, No. 87-88 (1921), 3.

28. "Akter budushchego. Doklad Vs. Meierkhol'da," *Ermitazh*, No. 6 (1922), 10-11.

29. Igor' Il'inskii, "Molozhe molodykh," *Vecherniaia Moskva* (Feb. 9, 1934).

30. Il'inskii, *Sam o sebe*, 155.

31. *Tartusskie stranitsy* (Kaluga, 1961), 291.

32. V. Fedorov, "Meierkhol'd v Politekhnicheskom," *Zrelishcha*, No. 9 (1922).

33. "Nas—vosem'desiat. Pis'mo uchenikov," *Ermitazh*, No. 7 (1922).

34. B. Arvatov, "Novogodnie Pokhorony," *Zhizn' Iskusstva*, No. 46 (1927), 7.

35. S. Tret'iakov, "Dramaturgovye zametki," *Zhizn' iskusstva*, No. 46 (1927), 7.

36. A. Lunacharskii, *V mire muzyki* (M. 1958), 201.

37. "O tvorcheskom metode teatra im. Vs. Meierkhol'da," *Rabis*, No. 5 (1931), 14-15.

38. Vl. Solov'ev, "Aktery teatra im. Meierkhol'da," *Zhizn' iskusstva*, No. 42 (1927), 6.

39. P. Markov, "Akter epokhi revoliutsii," *Sovetskii teatr*, No. 10-11 (1932), 11.

40. TsGALI, f. 963, ed. khr. 298, 1. 5-6.

41. Il'inskii, *Sam o sebe*, 152, 149.

42. TsGALI, f. 963, ed. khr. 300, 1. 9, 10.

43. P. Markov, "Sovremennye aktery," *Vremennik VTO*, v. 1 (1925), 259.

44. A. Gvozdev, "Il'-ba-zai," *Zhizn' iskusstva*, No. 27 (1924), 8, 9.

45. B. Alpers, *Teatr sotsial'noi maski*.

46. Sergei Tret'iakov, "Velikodushnyi rogonosets," *Zrelishcha*, No. 8 (1922), 12-13.

47. A. Gvozdev, "Etika novogo teatra," *Zhizn' iskusstva*, No. 22 (1924), 9.

48. Mikh. Levidov, "Teatral'nye siluety," *Sovremennyi teatr*, No. 9 (1927), 140.

49. "Tartiufy kommunizma i rogonostsy morali," *Teatr i muzyka*, No. 1-7 (1922), 24.

50. "Narkom po prosveshcheniiu Lunacharskii. Zametka po povodu *Rogonostsa*," *Izvestiia* (May 14, 1922).

51. TsGALI, f. 963, ed. khr.

52. A. Lunacharskii, *Teatr segodnia* (M-L. 1928), 77, 78.

53. *A. V. Lunacharskii o teatre i dramaturgii*, v. 1 (M. 1958), 393.

54. *Izvestiia* (Dec. 5, 1922).

55. V. Maiakovskii, *Poln. sobr. soch.*, v. 12 (M. 1959), 472.

56. Nikolai Tarabukin, *Zritel'noe oformlenie v GOSTIMe*. Ms. TsGALI, f. 963, ed. khr. 139.

57. Z. M., *Teatr Vs. Meierkhol'da ("Smert' Tarelkina" Sukhovo-Kobylina)*. Clipping, VTO Archive.

58. Ibid.

59. A. Gvozdev, *Teatr imeni Vs. Meierkhol'da*, 33.

60. "*Smert' Tarelkina*. Zritel'nom zale," *Zrelishcha*, No. 15 (1922), 18.

61. Arkadii Pozdnev, "Smert' Kandida Tarelkina i traktat o nei Alekseia Gana," *Zrelishcha*, No. 17 (1922), 9.

62. V. Tikhonovich, "P'esa, Rezhisser, Akter," *Zrelishcha*, No. 15 (1922), 8.

63. Vas. Fedorov, "Retsenziia na retsenzii," *Zrelishcha*, No. 16 (1922), 9.

64. Aleksei Gan, "Smertel'noe iavlenie v dome umershogo Tarelkina," *Zrelishcha*, No. 16 (1922), 11.

65. "Beseda s V. F. Stepanovoi," *Zrelishcha*, No. 16 (1922), 11.

66. V. Sakhnovskii, "Meierkhol'd," *Vremennik RTO* (1925), 239.

67. S. Mokul'skii, "Pereotsenka traditsii," in *Teatral'nyi Oktiabr'* (L-M. 1926), 28.

68. Sakhnovskii, 238.

69. B. Romashov, "Veselie poprishchinskie dni," *Teatr i muzyka*, No. 11 (1922), 234.

70. Samuil Margolin, "Balagannoe predstavlenie," *Teatr i muzyka*, No. 11 (1922), 232.

71. *U istokov*. Collection of articles (M: VTO, 1960), 214.

72. *V. E. Meierkhol'd* (Tver', 1923), 13, 14.

73. Nikolai Tarabukin, *Zritel'noe oformlenie v GOSTIMe*. Ms. TsGALI, f. 963, ed. khr. 139.

74. A. Gvozdev, *Teatr imeni Vs. Meierkhol'da*, 35.

75. P. Markov, *Noveishie teatral'nye techeniia*, 46.

76. E. Beskin, "Teatral'nyi LEF," *Sovetskoe iskusstvo*, No. 6 (1925), 53.

77. S. Mokul'skii, "Gastroli Teatra Meierkhol'da,"

Zhizn' iskusstva, No. 23 (1924), 12, 13.

78. Il'inskii, *Sam o sebe*, 182.

79. P. Markov, "Pis'mo o Meierkhol'de," *Teatr i dramaturgiia*, No. 8 (1932), 25.

80. "*D. E.* v Teatre im. Meierkhol'da," *Novyi zritel'*, No. 18 (1924), 16, 17.

81. Il'ia Erenburg, *Sobr. soch.*, v. 8 (1966), 337.

82. Konstantin Miklashevskii, "Malen'kii fel'eton (po povodu postanovki D. E.)," *Zhizn' iskusstva*, No. 26 (1924), 7.

83. Maiakovskii, v. 12, 472.

84. V. Karatygin, "Egon Petri," *Zhizn' iskusstva*, No. 1 (1924), 35.

85. Sergei Gorodetskii, "Konstruktivizm i poslednie prem'ery," *Iskusstvo trudiashchimsia*, No. 54 (1925), 6-7.

86. S. Mokul'skii, "Novaia postanovka Meierkhol'da," *Zhizn' iskusstva*, No. 27 (1924), 11.

87. Miklashevskii, 8.

88. Maiakovskii, v. 12, 472.

89. Evg. Gabrilovich, "Rasskazy o tom, chto proshlo," *Iskusstvo kino*, No. 4 (1964), 61.

90. *Izvestiia* (June 16, 1924).

91. A. Fevral'skii, "Teatr imeni Vsevoloda Meierkhol'da," *Sovetskoe iskusstvo*, No. 1 (1925), 62.

92. Maiakovskii, v. 12, 472.

93. Il'inskii, *Sam o sebe*, 196.

94. *Izvestiia* (June 18, 1924).

95. Mokul'skii, 11.

96. *V. E. Meierkhol'd*, 5, 6.

97. Ibid., 28.

98. Nikolai Foregger, "Iubilei eto..." *Zrelishcha*, No. 30 (1923), 15, 16.

Chapter Eight

1. Sadko (V. Blium), "*Dokhodnoe mesto* v Teatre Revoliutsii," *Pravda* (May 23, 1923).

2. B. Alpers, "Ostrovskii v postanovkakh Meierkhol'da," *Teatr*, No. 1 (1937), 44, 45.

3. Iu. Iuzovskii, *Spektakli i p'esy* (M. 1935), 245.

4. B. Alpers, *Teatr Revoliutsii* (M. 1928), 52.

5. Ibid., 52.

6. Ibid., 54.

7. *Zhizn' iskusstva*, No. 15 (1925), 6, 7.

8. A. Gripich, "Nachalo bol'shogo puti," *Dmitrii Nikolaevich Orlov. Kniga o tvorchestve* (M: VTO, 1962), 201-203.

9. Iuzovskii, 250.

10. Lunacharskii, *O teatre. Sb. statei* (L. 1926), 5.

11. Em. Beskin, "Teatral'nyi LEF," *Sovetskoe iskusstvo*, No. 6 (1925), 57, 58.

12. "Ostrovskii—Meierkhol'd," *Zrelishcha*, No. 67 (1923), 9.

13. B. Alpers, "Ostrovskii v postanovkakh Meierkhol'da," 35.

14. "Ostrovskii—Meierkhol'd," 9.

15. V. E. Meierkhol'd, *Dvukhtomnik*, v. II, 56-57.

16. B. Alpers, 38.

17. MKhAT Museum, N.-D. Archive, No. 349.

18. Igor' Il'inskii, *Sam o sebe* (M: VTO, 1961), 191.

19. Meierkhol'd, v. II, 57.

20. "Rabkory o novom teatre," *Pravda* (Feb. 19, 1924).

21. P. Markov, "Pis'mo o Meierkhol'de," *Teatr i dramaturgiia*, No. 2 (1934), 22.

22. V. T., "Zhivaia voda," *Novyi zritel'*, No. 8 (1924), 13.

23. A. Kugel', "Po povodu postanovki *Lesa*," *Rampa*, No. 15 (1924), 9.

24. Beskin, 58.

25. Tarabukin, 9.

26. A. Slonimskii, "*Les* (opyt analiza spektaklia)," Sb. *Teatral'nyi Oktiabr'* (L-M. 1926), 68, 69.

27. A. Gladkov, "Po povodu odnoi melochi,"

Zhizn' iskusstva, No. 1 (1926), 17.

28. B. Alpers, *Teatr sotsial'noi maski*, 29.

29. Vlad. Blium, "Ostrovskii i Meierkhol'd," *Novyi zritel'*, No. 4 (1924), 6.

30. Il'inskii, 189, 190.

31. Alpers, *Ostrovskii v postanovkakh Meierkhol'da*, 37.

32. A. Gvozdev, "*Les* v plane narodnogo teatra," *Zrelishcha*, No. 74 (1924), 5.

33. "Disput o *Lese* v Akademii," *Zrelishcha*, No. 75 (1924), 9.

34. "Doklad tov. Meierkhol'da dlia klubnykh rabotnikov Krasnoi Armii," *Pravda* (Jan. 19, 1924).

35. "Meierkhol'd o svoem *Lese*," *Novyi zritel'*, No. 7 (1924), 6.

36. Il'inskii, 193.

37. MKhAT Museum, N.-D. Archive, No. 349.

38. Vladimir Maiakovskii, *Poln. sobr. soch.*, v. 12, 265, 472.

39. A. Kugel', 9.

40. Viktor Shklovskii, "Osoboe mnenie o *Lese*," *Zhizn' iskusstva*, No. 26 (1924), 11.

41. Sb. *Maria Fedorovna Andreeva* (M. 1961), 335.

42. Sergei Radlov, "Uteriannyi levyi front," *Zhizn' iskusstva*, No. 15 (1924), 7.

43. *A. V. Lunacharskii o teatre i dramaturgii*, v. 1, 393.

44. A. Gvozdev, *Teatr imeni Vs. Meierkhol'da*, 37, 38.

45. "A vashe mnenie o *Lese*?" *Zrelishcha*, No. 72 (1924), 6.

46. Marietta Shaginian, "*Les* Meierkhol'da," *Zhizn' iskusstva*, No. 15 (1924), 7.

47. P. Markov, *Pravda teatra* (M. 1965), 348-351.

Chapter Nine

1. "*Ozero Liul'*. Beseda s A. Faiko," *Zrelishcha*, No. 60 (1923), 1.

2. Aleksei Faiko, "Tri vstrechi," *Teatr*, No. 10 (1962), 117.

3. Iurii Sobolev, "Kommentarii k moskovskim spektakliam," *Khronika teatra*, No. 4 (1923).

4. P. Markov, *Pravda teatra*, 349.

5. B. Alpers, *Teatr Revoliutsii*, 59, 60.

6. Sobolev.

7. Alpers, 21, 22.

8. Alpers, *Teatr sotsial'noi maski*, 58.

9. Faiko, 119, 120.

10. "*Uchitel' Bubus*. Tri akta Alekseia Faiko." Program from the Vs. Meierkhol'd Theater (M. 1925), 7, 11.

11. Faiko, 121, 122.

12. "*Uchitel' Bubus*," 7, 11.

13. Faiko, 122.

14. "*Uchitel' Bubus*," 7, 11.

15. A. Fevral'skii, "Teatr imeni Vsevoloda Meierkhol'da," *Sovetskoe iskusstvo*, No. 1 (1925), 62.

16. Sadko (V. Blium), "*Bubus* (Teatr im. Vs. Meierkhol'da)," *Vecherniaia Moskva* (Feb. 2, 1925).

17. Faiko, 121.

18. Alpers, *Teatr sotsial'noi maski*, 48.

19. A. V. Lunacharskii, *V mire muzyki* (1958), 201-202.

20. "K postanovke *Mandata* (Beseda s Vsevolodom Meierkhol'dom)," *Vecherniaia Moskva* (Apr. 6, 1925).

21. P. Markov, "*Mandat* (Teatr im. Vs. Meierkhol'da)," *Pravda* (Apr. 24, 1925).

22. "K postanovke *Mandata* (Beseda s Vsevolodom Meierkhol'dom).

23. S. Bobrov, "*Mandat* Meierkhol'da," *Zhizn' iskusstva*, No. 19 (1925), 7.

24. A. Gvozdev, "Kontsovki i pantomima (*Mandat* Meierkhol'da-Erdmana)," *Zhizn' iskusstva*, No. 35 (1925), 10.

25. B. Alpers, *Teatr sotsial'noi maski*, 64, 65.

26. P. Markov, "*Mandat*," *Pravda* (Apr. 24, 1925).

27. P. Markov, *Pravda teatra*, 43.

28. *Zritel' o Teatre imeni Vs. Meierkhol'da* (M. 1926), 11-14.

29. A. Lunacharskii, "O politike Narkomprosa v teatral'nom dele," *Sovetskoe iskusstvo*, No. 3 (1925), 5.

30. A. Lunacharskii, *O teatre* (L. 1926), 8, 9.

31. A. Lunacharskii, "Teatr Meierkhol'da," *Izvestiia* (Apr. 25, 1926).

32. Alpers, *Teatr sotsial'noi maski*, 55, 65, 66.

33. A. Anastas'ev, G. Boiadzhiev, A. Obraztsova, K. Rudnitskii, *Novatorstvo sovetskogo teatra* (M. 1963), 235, 236.

34. G. Gauzner, E. Gabrilovich, "*Mandat* u Meierkhol'da," *Zhizn' iskusstva*, No. 19 (1925), 6.

35. V. Iureneva, "Sergei Martinson," *Sovetskii teatr*, No. 7-8 (1932), 39.

36. Gvozdev, 10.

37. Vl. Solov'ev, "Aktery teatra im. Meierkhol'da," *Zhizn' iskusstva*, No. 42 (1927), 6.

38. Igor' Il'inskii, *Sam o sebe*, 200.

39. Adr. Piotrovskii, "Nakanune *Revizora*," *Zhizn' iskusstva*, No. 35 (1925), 5.

40. "Pis'mo v redaktsiu," Afisha *TIM*, No. 2 (1926), 26, 27.

41. *Teatr i dramaturgiia*, No. 8 (1933), 45.

42. S. Tretiakov, *Rychi, Kitai! Sobytie v 9 zven'iakh* (M-L. 1930), 5.

43. A. Gvozdev, *Teatr imeni Vs. Meierkhol'da (1920-1926)* (L. 1927), 47.

44. M. Zagorskii, "*Rychi, Kitai!*" *Zhizn' iskusstva*, No. 6 (1926), 12.

45. P. Novitskii, *Obrazy akterov* (M. 1941), 280.

46. Gvozdev, *Teatr imeni Vs. Meierkhol'da (1920-1926)*, 47.

47. S. Gorodetskii, "Teatr im. Meierkhol'da. *Rychi, Kitai!*," *Iskusstvo trudiashchimsia*, No. 5 (1926), 9-11.

48. Sergei Radlov, *Desiat' let v teatre* (L. 1929), 144-146.

49. S. Tret'iakov, *Dramaturgovye zametki*, No. 46 (1927), 7.

50. P. Markov, *Pravda teatra*, 404.

51. "Teatry—k desiatiletiu Oktiabria. *Okno v derevniu* (Beseda s Vs. Meierkhol'dom," *Pravda* (Oct. 25, 1927).

Chapter Ten

1. P. Markov, "Tretii front (Posle *Mandata*)," *Pechat' i revoliutsiia*, v. 5-6 (1925), 291.

2. TsGALI, f. 998, ed. khr. 76, 1. 26.

3. G. A. Kukovskii, *Realizm Gogolia* (M-L. 1959), 468, 469.

4. TsGALI, f. 998, ed. khr. 76, 1. 28.

5. Vsevolod Meierkhol'd, "Neskol'ko zamechanii..." Sb. *Gogol' i Meierkhol'd* (M: Nikitinskie subbotniki, 1927), 79.

6. "Pochemu i kak stavitsia *Revizor* (Beseda s. Vs. Em. Meierkhol'dom," *Vecherniaia Moskva* (Nov. 27, 1926).

7. A. F. (Fevral'skii), "*Revizor* u Meierkhol'da (Beseda s V. E. Meierkhol'dom)," *Pravda* (Oct. 25, 1925).

8. "Pochemu i kak stavitsia *Revizor*," *Vecherniaia Moskva* (Nov. 27, 1926).

9. Viktor Shklovskii, "Piatnadtsat' portsii gorodnichikhi," *Krasnaia gazeta* (Dec. 22, 1926).

10. Aleksandr Gladkov, "Meierkhol'd govorit (Zapisi 1934-1939 godov)," *Neva*, No. 2 (1966), 206.

11. *Tarusskie stranitsy*, 302.

12. N. M. Tarabukin, TsGALI, f. 963, ed. kh. 139.

13. Sergei Radlov, "*Revizor* u Meierkhol'da,"

Krasnaia gazeta (Dec. 14, (1926).

14. P. Markov, "Novosti teatra. *Revizor* Meier-khol'da," *Krasnaia niva*, No. 5 (1927).

15. N. V. Gogol', *Sobr. soch.*, v. 6, 259.

16. *A. V. Lunacharskii o teatre i dramaturgii*, v. 1, 402.

17. D. Tal'nikov, *Novaia reviziia* Revizora (M-L. 1927), 50.

18. Leonid Grossman, "Tragediia-buff," Sb. *Gogol' i Meierkhol'd*, 42.

19. B. Alpers, *Teatr sotsial'noi maski*, 67.

20. V. Vol'kenshtein, "*Revizor* Meierkhol'da," *Izvestiia* (Dec. 22, 1927).

21. TsGALI, f. 998, ed. khr. 76, 1. 26.

22. A. A. Gvozdev, "Teatr imeni Vs. Meierkhol'-da," 52.

23. Mikh. Levidov, "Propala verevochka! (*Revizor* Meierkhol'da)," *Vecherniaia Moskva* (Dec. 13, 1926).

24. V. Shklovskii, *Krasnaia gazeta*, Dec. 22, 1926.

25. *Odesskie vechernie novosti* (Jan. 9, 1927).

26. Ibid.

27. Sb. *"Revizor" v Teatre imeni Vs. Meierkhol'-da* (L. 1927), 33.

28. TsGALI, f. 998, ed. khr. 76, 1. 24-25-rev.

29. TsGALI, f. 998, ed. khr. 76, 1. 24, 27, 25.

30. *A. V. Lunacharskii o teatre i dramaturgii*, v. 1, 402.

31. V. E. Meierkhol'd, *Dvukhtomnik*, v. II, 114, 115.

32. B. Alpers, *Teatr sotsial'noi maski*, 56.

33. Maiakovskii, *Poln. sobr. soch.*, v. 12, 310.

34. *A. V. Lunacharskii o teatre i dramaturgii*, v. 1, 402, 403.

35. A. Kugel', "V zashchitu," *Zhizn' iskusstva*, No. 3 (1927), 5, 6.

36. Radlov.

37. Maiakovskii, v. 12, 309.

38. A. G. (Gvozdev). "Muzykal'naia pantomima v *Revizore*," *Zhizn' iskusstva*, No. 1 (1927), 10.

39. *A. V. Lunacharskii o teatre i dramaturgii*, v. 1, 404.

40. B. Alpers, 71.

41. *A. V. Lunacharskii o teatre i dramaturgii*, v. 1, 404.

42. Kugel', 5, 6.

43. Sb. *"Revizor" v Teatre imeni Vs. Meierkhol'da*, 37.

44. Tal'nikov, 63.

45. A. G. (Gvozdev), "Muzykal'naia pantomima v *Revizore*," 9.

46. *A. V. Lunacharskii o teatre i dramaturgii*, v. 1, 404, 405.

47. Tal'nikov, 50.

48. Zritel', "Piatnadtsat' episodov (montirovoch-naia repetitsiia "Revizora" v Teatre im. Meierkhol'da), *Vecherniaia Moskva* (Dec. 7, 1926).

49. Kugel', 5, 6.

50. *A. V. Lunacharskii o teatre i dramaturgii*, v. 1, 406.

51. Andrei Belyi, "Gogol' i Meierkhol'd," Sb. *Gogol' i Meierkhol'd*, 10.

52. "*Revizor* v Teatre Meierkhol'da. Na general'noi repetitsii," *Krasnaia gazeta* (Dec. 10, 1926).

53. Dem'ian Bednyi, "Ubiitsa. Epigramma-retsen-ziia na meierkhol'dovskuiu postnovku *Revizora*," *Izvestiia* (Dec. 10, 1926).

54. *Izvestiia* (Dec. 22, 1926).

55. P. Markov, "Novosti teatra. *Revizor* Meier-khol'da."

56. A. Lunacharskii. "O teatral'nykh trevogakh," *Krasnaia gazeta* Nov. 13, 1928).

57. P. Markov, "Teatr," *Pechat' i revoliutsiia*, v. 7 (1927), 152, 153.

58. "Disput o *Revizore*," *Odesskie vechernie novosti* (Jan. 9, 1927).

59. Igor' Glebov, "Muzyka v drame (O *Revizore* V. E. Meierkhol'da)," *Krasnaia gazeta* (Jan. 30, 1927).

60. E. Beskin, "*Revizor* Meierkhol'da," *Vecherniaia Moskva* (Dec. 11, 1926).

61. V. Shklovskii, *Krasnaia gazeta*, Dec. 22, 1926.

62. Viktor Shklovskii, "Revizor," *Kino* (Dec. 21, 1926).

63. M. Levidov, *Vecherniaia Voskva*, XII, 13, 1926.

64. "Disputy," *Novyi zritel'*, No. 2 (1927).

65. Lunacharskii.

66. "Kak delalos' *Gore umu*," *Sovremennyi teatr*, No. 11 (1928), 222.

67. Em. Beskin, "Gore umu," *Novyi zritel'*, No. 16 (1928), 8.

68. Alpers, 58.

69. "*Gore umu* (Beseda s Vs. Meierkhol'dom)," *Pravda* (Mar. 2, 1928).

70. N. Osinskii, "*Gore umu* ili Meierkhol'dovye prichudy," *Izvestiia* (Mar. 15, 1928).

71. Iur. Sobolev, "*Gore umu* v Teatre V. Meier-khol'da," *Vecherniaia Moskva* (Mar. 16, 1928).

72. V. Blium, "Gore...komu?" *Novyi zritel'*, No. 29-30 (1928), 7.

73. Alpers, 71.

74. D. Tal'nikov, "Gore umu," *Sovremennyi teatr*, No. 13 (1928), 268.

75. Blium, "7.

76. B. Asaf'ev (Igor' Glebov), "O muzyke v *Gore umu*," *Sovremennyi teatr*, No. 11 (1928), 223.

77. Tal'nikov, "Gore umu," 269.

78. A. Gvozdev, "Gore umu," *Zhizn' iskusstva*, No. 12 (1928), 6.

79. Blium, 7.

80. N. Osinskii, *Izvestiia*, March 15, 1928.

81. S. Mstislavskii, "Odinokii (K diskussii o *Gore umu*)," *Zhizn' iskusstva*, No. 16 (1928), 7.

82. P. K-tsev (Kerzhentsev), "Gore umu," *Pravda* (Mar. 17, 1928).

83. Mstislavskii.

84. Alpers, 71.

85. "Kak delalos' *Gore umu*," *Sovremennyi teatr*, No. 11 (1928), 222.

86. A. Lunacharskii, "O teatre Meierkhol'da," *Komsomol'skaia pravda* (Sept. 14, 1928).

87. "Na dispute o *Gore umu*," *Vecherniaia Moskva* (Mar. 20, 1928).

88. Blium, 8.

89. "Disput o *Gore umu* v Akdrame," *Zhizn' is-kusstva*, No. 17 (1928), 14.

90. N. Osinskii, *Izvestiia*, Nov. 13, 1938.

91. Iu. Sobolev, "*Gore umu* v teatre V. Meier-khol'da," *Vecherniaia Moskva* (Mar. 16, 1928).

92. "Teatr Meierkhol'da vozobnovliaet *Velikodush-nogo rogonosta*," *Vecherniaia Moskva* (Jan. 20, 1928).

93. D. Tal'nikov, "Velikodushnyi rogonosets," *Sovremennyi teatr*, No. 9 (1928), 184.

94. Vl. Sarav'ianov, "S pristrastiem?" 184-185.

95. "V. E. Meierkhol'd o *Velikodushnom rogo-nostse*." Letter to the editor. *Sovremennyi teatr*, No. 10 (1928), 203.

96. A. V. Lunacharskii, "O teatre Meierkhol'da," *Komsomol'skaia pravda* (Sept. 17, 1928).

97. "*Gore umu*. Beseda s Vs. Meierkhol'dom," *Izvestiia* (Nov. 13, 1938).

98. D. Mirskii, "Gore umu," *Literaturnaia gazeta* (Nov. 24, 1935).

99. V. Blium, "*Gore umu*—spektakl' Vs. Meier-khol'da," *Teatr i dramaturgiia*, No. 2 (1936), 73, 75.

Chapter Eleven

1. A. Lunacharskii, "O teatre Meierkhol'da," *Komsomol'skaia pravda* (Sept. 14, 1928).

2. "Tekushchie dela," *Novyi Lef*, No. 2 (1927), 47.

3. V. E. Meierkhol'd, "Slovo o Maiakovskom," *Maiakovskii v vospominaniiakh sovremennikov* (M: GIKhL, 1963), 286.

4. "Vokrug p'esy *Khochu rebenka*," *Sovremennyi teatr*, No. 51 (1928), 827.

5. A. Fevral'skii, "Kak sozdavalsia *Klop*," *Literaturnaia gazeta* (Dec. 9, 1935).

6. A. V. Lunacharskii, "O teatral'nykh trevogakh," *Krasnaia gazeta* (Sept. 13, 1928).

7. D. Zaslavskii, "Daesh Evropu?—Net, ne daem," *Pravda* (Sept. 16, 1928).

8. A. Orlinskii, "Sud'ba Teatra Meierkhol'da v ego rukakh," *Sovremennyi teatr*, No. 41 (1928), 638.

9. TsGALI, f. 963, ed. khr. 46, 1. 19-20.

10. N. Lunacharskaia-Rozenel', *Pamiat' serdtsa* (M. 1962), 40.

11. "*Klop* Maiakovskogo v GOSTIMe. Chto govoriat khudozhniki," *Sovremennyi teatr*, No. 7 (1929), 111.

12. D. Tal'nikov, "Novye postanovki," *Zhizn' iskusstva*, No. 11 (1929), 10.

13. I. Il'inskii, *Sam o sebe*, 226.

14. M. Zagorskii, "Tol'ko ob akterakh," *Sovremennyi teatr*, No. 14 (1929).

15. S. Mokul'skii, "Eshche o *Klope*," *Zhizn' iskusstva*, No. 13 (1929).

16. N. Basilov, *Meierkhol'd repetiruet*. Ms., BMM.

17. G. Krasnoshchekov, *O Maiakovskom*. Ms. BMM.

18. *Literaturnaia gazeta* (May 30, 1936).

19. M. Zagorskii, *Sovremennyi teatr*, No. 14, 1929.

20. Bor. Novskii, "*Klop* v Teatre im. Vs. Meierkhol'da," *Novyi zritel'*, No. 10 (1929).

21. Tal'nikov, 10.

22. V. Gorodinskii, "*Klop* v Teatre im. Meierkhol'da," *Rabochii i teatr*, No. 10 (1929).

23. "*Klop*. Novaia p'esa Vl. Maiakovskogo," *Vecherniaia Moskva* (Jan. 2, 1929).

24. B. Novskii, *Novyi zritel'*, No. 19 (1929).

25. Mokul'skii, 10.

26. I. Turkel'taub, "*Klop* v Teatre im. Meierkhol'da," No. 12 (1929), 7.

27. B. Alpers, *Teatr sotsial'noi maski*, 63.

28. Mokul'skii.

29. A. Fevral'skii, "Kak sozdavalsia *Klop*," *Literaturnaia gazeta* (Dec. 9, 1935).

30. TsGALI, f. 963, ed. khr. 46, 1. 24-26.

31. B. Alpers, *Teatr sotsial'noi maski*, 96.

32. Vladimir Maiakovskii, *Poln. sobr. soch.*, v. 12, 199, 200.

33. Iu. Lebedinskii, *Sovremenniki* (M. 1958), 172.

34. V. Druzin, "Vmesto LEFa-REF," *Zhizn' iskusstva*, No. 42 (1929), 12.

35. V. Ermilov, "O nastroeniiakh melkoburzhuaznoi 'levizny' v khudozhestvennoi literature," *Pravda* (March 9, 1930).

36. V. Ermilov, "O trekh oshibkakh tov. Meierkhol'da," *Vecherniaia Moskva* (Mar. 17, 1930).

37. *Vecherniaia Moskva* (Mar. 13, 1930).

38. M. F. Sukhanova, "Tri p'esy V. V. Maiakovskogo," *Maiakovskii v vospominaniiakh sovremennikov* (M. 1963), 313.

39. Maiakovskii, v. 13, 136-137.

40. Sukhanova, 314.

41. T. Kostrov, "*Bania* v Teatre Meierkhol'da," *Rabochii i iskusstvo*, No. 6 (1930).

42. V. B. (Blium?), "*Bania* v Teatre Meierkhol'da," *Rabochii i teatr*, No. 18 (1930).

43. M. Zagorskii, "Dialog o *Banie*," *Literaturnaia gazeta* (Mar. 31, 1930).

44. N. Goncharova, "*Bania* V. Maiakovskogo," *Rabochaia gazeta* (Mar. 21, 1930).

45. TsGALI, f. 963, ed. khr. 55, 1. 16-17.

46. O. Litovskii, "Tak i bylo!"(M. 1958), 129, 130.

47. TsGALI, f. 963, ed. khr. 55, 1. 40, 41.

48. TSGALI, f. 963, ed. khr. 55, 1. 73.

49. TsGALI, f. 998, ed. khr. 109, 1. 2.

Chapter Twelve

1. A. Matskin, "Igor' Il'inskii i ego kniga," *Novyi mir*, No. 1 (1960), 265.

2. I. Sel'vinskii, "*Komandarm 2*. O p'ese," *Literaturnaia gazeta* (Sept. 30, 1929).

3. *Vstrechi s Meierkhol'daom*, 388.

4. B. Alpers, "*Komandarm 2*. Teatr im. Meierkhol'da," *Novyi zritel'*, No. 40 (1929).

5. Aleksandr Gladkov, "Meierkhol'd govorit," *Neva*, No. 2 (1966), 208.

6. B. Alpers, *Novyi zritel'*, No. 40 (1929).

7. Adr. Piotrovskii, "Kuda idet TIM?" *Zhizn' iskusstva*, No. 43 (1929), 7.

8. A. Gvozdev, "*Komandarm 2*. Gosud. teatr im. Meierkhol'da,"*Zhizn' Iskusstva*, No. 42 (1929), 5.

9. B. Alpers, *Novyi zritel'*, No. 40 (1929).

10. Semen Gets. "*Komandarm 2* v Teatre im. Meierkhol'da," *Zhizn' iskusstva*, No. 31 (1929), 10.

11. Piotrovskii, 7.

12. Vs. Meierkhol'd, "*Komandarm 2*. Neskol'ko slov o postanovke," *Literaturnaia gazeta* (Sept. 30, 1929).

13. Gvozdev, p. 5

14. I. Kruti, "Poslednii, reshitel'nyi Teatr im. Vs. Meierkhol'da," *Sovetskii teatr*, No. 4 (1931), 12.

15. P. Markov, "Porazhenie Vishnevskogo i pobeda Meierkhol'da," *Sovetskii teatr*, No. 4 (1931), 12.

16. Vera Iureneva, "Sergei Martinson," *Sovetskii teatr*, No. 7-8 (1932), 40.

17. Markov, 12.

18. "V sporakh o *Poslednem, reshitel'nom*," *Vecherniaia Moskva* (Feb. 17, 1931).

19. *Tarusskie stranitsy*, 307.

20. V. Kirshon, "Metod, chuzhdyi proletarskoi literature," *Sovetskii teatr*, No. 4 (1931), 14.

21. "V sporakh o *Poslednem, reshitel'nom*."

22. "O tvorcheskom metode Teatra imeni Vs. Meierkhol'da. Diskussiia v Gos. akademii iskusstvoznaniia," *Rabis*, No. 5, 14, 15.

23. N. Chushkin, *Gamlet—Kachalov* (M. 1966), 257-259.

24. L. Gurevich, *Tri dramaturga. Pogodin, Olesha, Kirshon* (M. 1936), 163.

25. Ibid., 174.

26. N. M. Tarabukin, *Zritel'noe oformlenie v GOSTIMe*. Ms. TsGALI, f. 963. ed. khr. 139.

27. Ref: A. V. Fevral'skii, "Meierkhol'd i Shekspir." In Sb. *Vil'iam Shekspir. K chetyrekhsotletiiu so dnia rozhdeniia* (M: Nauka, 1964).

28. D. Kal'm, "Perechen' 'zlodeianii' Vs. Meierkhol'da nad *Spiskom blagodeianii* Iur. Oleshi," *Literaturnaia gazeta* (June 29, 1931).

29. S. Tsimbal, v *Smena* (Oct. 17, 1931).

30. I. Kruti, v *Sovetskoe iskusstvo* (June 8, 1931).

31. E. Beskin, v *Sovetskoe iskusstvo* (July 8, 1931).

32. Kal'm.

33. Iu. Iuzovskii, v *Literaturnaia gazeta* (6/15/31).

34. *Sovetskoe iskusstvo* (Oct. 9, 1931).

35. "Vs. Meierkhol'd o predstoiashchem sezone v GOSTIMe," *Vecherniaia Moskva* (Sept. 18, 1932).

36. Iurii German, "O Meierkhol'de," in his *Operatsiia "S novym godom"* (M. 1964), 395-421.

37. TsGALI, f. 963, ed. khr. 757.

38. I. Bachelis, "Vstuplenie v Teatre im. Meierkhol'da," *Komsomol'skaia pravda* (Mar. 11, 1933).

39. Matskin, v *Izvestiia* (March 27, 1933).

40. Iu. Iuzovskii, "Avtora, avtora...," *Rabis*, No. 3 (1933), 33.

41. Matskin. 42. Bachelis. 43. Iuzovskii.

Chapter Thirteen

1. TsGALI. F. 963, ed. khr. 55, 1. 22-23.

2. M. Levidov, "Master mysli. *Svad'ba Krechin-*

skogo v Teatre Meierkhol'da," *Vecherniaia Moskva* (May 12, 1933).

3. V. E. Meierkhol'd, *"Svad'ba Krechinskogo,"* *Krasnaia gazeta* (Apr. 14, 1933).

4. Iu. Iuzovskii, "Meierkhol'd-dramaturg," *Literaturnyi kritik*, No. 3 (1933), 81-82.

5. A. Gvozdev, "Svad'ba Krechinskogo. Na prem'ere v Teatre im. Meierkhol'da," *Krasnaia gazeta*, morning edition, (Apr. 17, 1933).

6. Iu. Iuzovskii, "Meierkhol'd-dramaturg," *Literaturnyi kritik*, No. 3 (1933), 83, 84, 78, 79, 75.

7. "Meierkhol'd o Svad'be Krechinskogo," *Vecherniaia Moskva* (May 6, 1933).

8. Igor' Il'inskii, *Sam o sebe*, 242, 243.

9. A. Matskin, *"Svad'ba Krechinskogo,"* *Izvestiia* (June 2, 1933).

10. A. Gvozdev, *Krasnaia gazeta*, IV, 17, 1933.

11. M. Levidov, *Vecherniaia Moskva*, XII, 13, 1926

12. "Meierkhol'd o *Svad'be Krechinskogo*.

13. Il'inskii, 243.

14. M. Levidov, *Vecherniaia Moskva*, XII, 13, 1926.

15. "Meierkhol'd o *Svad'be Krechinskogo*."

16. Il'inskii, 244.

17. Iu. Iuzovskii, *Voprosy sotsialisticheskoi dramaturgii* (M. 1934), 1.

18. D. Tal'nikov, "Spektakl' rasseiavshikhsia mirazhei. *Dama s kameliiami* v Teatre im. Meierkhol'da," *Teatr i dramaturgiia*, No. 5 (1934), 27.

19. Iu. Iuzovskii, *Zachem liudi khodiat v teatr...* (M. 1964), 42.

20. Tal'nikov, 29, 30.

21. A. Gvozdev, "V sporakh o novoi rabote Meierkhol'da. *Dama s kameliiami*," *Rabochii i teatr*, No. 13 (1934), 14.

22. A. Afinogenov, *Dnevniki i zapisnye knizhki*. (M. 1960), 154, 155, 180, 186, 267.

23. Vs. Vishnevskii, "Posle spektaklia," *Literaturnaia gazeta* (April 6, 1934).

24. Tal'nikov, 29.

25. L. M. Freidkina, *Dni i gody Vl. I. Nemirovicha-Danchenko* (M. 1962), 462.

26. Tal'nikov, 30.

27. Ibid., 31.

28. Iuzovskii, *Zachem liudi khodiat v teatr*, 42, 43.

29. *Tarusskie stranitsy*, 303.

30. "Pushkin i Chaikovskii. Doklad V. E. Meierkhol'da v klube masterov iskusstva," *Literaturnaia gazeta* (Nov. 20, 1934).

31. Vs. Meierkhol'd, *Pushkin i Chaikovskii—"Pikovaia dama,"* Sb. *statei i materialov* (L. 1935), 9.

32. Ibid., 10, 11.

33. I. Sollertinskii, "Chaikovskii i Meierkhol'd," *Rabochii i teatr*, No. 3 (1935), 4, 5.

34. Meierkhol'd, 11.

35. Sollertinskii, 5.

36. V. Gorodinskii, "Pikovaia dama v postanovke Vs. Meierkhol'da i S. Samosuda," *Literaturnaia gazeta* (Jan. 26, 1936).

37. "33 obmoroka. Beseda s narodnym artistom respubliki Vs. Meierkhol'dom," *Pravda* (March 25, 1935).

38. TsGALI, f. 968, ed. khr. 1083, 1. 15.

39. Il'inskii, 248.

40. A. Fevral'skii, "33 obmoroka," *Sovetskii teatr*, No. 2-3 (1935), 9.

41. "33 obmoroka. Beseda s narodnym artistom respubliki Vs. Meierkhol'dom."

42. D. Zaslavskii, "Shutka na stsene," *Teatr i dramaturgiia*, No. 8 (1935), 39.

43. Em. Beskin, "33 obmoroka," *Rabochaia Moskva* (April 3, 1935).

44. A. Gladkov, "Meierkhol'd govorit," *Novyi mir*, No. 8 (1961), 228.

45. Fevral'skii, 9.

46. TsGALI, f. 998, ed. khr. 451, 1. 4.

47. TsGALI, f. 998, ed. khr. 450, 1. 17.

48. TsGALI, f. 998, ed. khr. 445, 1. 17-18.

49. TsGALI, f. 998, ed. khr. 446, 1. 13.

50. TsGALI, f. 963, ed. khr. 1074, 1. 48-49.

51. Iu. Iuzovskii, *Razgovor zatianulsia za polnoch* (M. 1966), 255, 256.

52. "Teatr Meierkhol'da na kvartire K. S. Stanislavskogo," *Komsomol'skaia pravda* (April 3, 1935).

Epilogue

1. "Steklobetonnyi neboskreb. Novoe zdanie Teatra im. Vs. Meierkhol'da," *Sovetskoe iskusstvo* (Oct. 9, 1931).

2. "Maiakovskii-dramaturg. Doklad Vs. Meierkhol'da v Leningrade," *Literaturnaia gazeta* (May 30, 1936).

3. TsGALI, f. 963, ed. khr. 55, 1. 85.

4. TsGALI, f. 963, ed. khr. 55, 1. 23.

5. "Meierkhol'd protiv meierkhol'dovshchiny. Doklad v Leningradskom lektorii," *Sovetskoe iskusstvo* (March 17, 1936).

6. *Tarusskie stranitsy*, 296.

7. Evg. Gabrilovich, "Rasskazy o tom, chto proshlo," *Iskusstvo kino*, No. 4 (1964), 68-69.

8. "Postanovlenie o likvidatsii Teatra im. Meierkhol'da," *Teatr*, No. 1 (1938), 1.

9. See G. Kristi, "Stanislavskii i Meierkhol'd," *Oktiabr'*, No. 3 (1963), memoirs of Iu. Bakhrushin and P. Rumiantsev in sb. *Vstrechi s Meierkhol'dom* (M. VTO, 1967).

10. Kristi, 183.

11. Sharl' Diullen, *Vospominaniia i zametki aktera* (M. 1958), 71-72.

12. S. Eizenshtein, *Izbrannye proizvedeniia v shesti tomakh* (M. 1966), v. 4, 433.

13. V. E. Meierkhol'd, *Dvukhtomnik*, v. 2, 469.

INDEX

Compiled by Francey Oscherwitz

ABOUT THE AUTHOR

The eminent theater historian and critic Konstantin Lazarevich Rudnitsky was born in 1920. He attended the State Institute for Theater Arts (GITIS) in Moscow. After graduation in 1943 he served in the Army and was decorated for valor during World War II.

He has a long list of publications to his credit, including articles on current productions and the history of the Russian theater, as well as essays on such individual classics as Chekhov and Bulgakov. His major books include *Alexander Sukhovo-Kobylin* (1957), a study of the 19th-century playwright; *Portraits of Playwrights* (1961), essays on dramatists from the 1920s to the 1950s; *Productions of Various Years* (1974), studies of the Soviet theater scene of the sixties and seventies; and the present work, *Meyerhold the Director* (1969), which brought him great acclaim.

Currently he lives in Moscow with his wife, the film historian Tatyana Bachelis.